American Foreign Policy in a New Era

DONALD M. SNOW

University of Alabama

PATRICK J. HANEY

Miami University

PEARSON

Boston Columbus Indianapolis New York San Francisco Upper Saddle River
Amsterdam Cape Town Dubai London Madrid Milan Munich Paris Montreal Toronto
Delhi Mexico City São Paulo Sydney Hong Kong Seoul Singapore Taipei Tokyo

To Eugene Brown and John Lovell

Senior Acquisitions Editor: Vikram Mukhija
Editorial Assistants: Beverly Fong, Isabel Schwab
Marketing Managers: Wendy Gordon, Lindsey Prudhomme
Production Manager: Fran Russello
Project Coordination and Text Design: Franklin Mathews/Integra Software Services Pvt. Ltd.
Cover Illustration/Photo: Niklas Meltio/Corbis
Printer and Binder: Courier Companies, Inc.

For permission to use copyrighted material, grateful acknowledgment is made to the copyright holders on p. xviii, which are hereby made part of this copyright page.

Library of Congress Cataloging-in-Publication Data
Snow, Donald M.
American foreign policy in a new era / Donald M. Snow, Patrick J. Haney.—1st ed.
p. cm.
ISBN-13: 978-0-205-21024-4 (alk. paper)
ISBN-10: 0-205-21024-4 (alk. paper)
1. United States—Foreign relations—Textbooks. 2. United States—Foreign relations—21st century—Textbooks. I. Haney, Patrick Jude. II. Title.
JZ1480.S545 2013
327.73—dc23 2011040927

10 9 8 7 6 5 4 3 2 1—CRW—15 14 13 12

ISBN-10: 0-205-21024-4
ISBN-13: 978-0-205-21024-4

BRIEF CONTENTS

CONTENTS

PART I Foreign Policy Processes 67

PREFACE

On May 2, 2011, American Navy SEAL Team 6, an elite unit of the Sea, Air and Land Special Operations Group, attacked a compound in Abbottabad, Pakistan, where the United States public enemy number one, terrorist and founder of Al Qaeda Usama bin Laden, was hiding in virtually "plain sight" in the Pakistani town that houses the Pakistani military academy and is the residence of many retired Pakistani military officers. In the process of the raid, bin Laden was killed, and his body was whisked upon a waiting U.S. military helicopter and transported to an American carrier sitting offshore in the Arabian Sea. After full preparation of the body according to Islamic standards, bin Laden's remains were interred in deep waters.

The killing of bin Laden was an important accomplishment for the United States and event for American foreign policy. It occurred nine years and eight months after bin Laden masterminded the September 11, 2001, terrorist attacks against targets in New York and Washington that had traumatized the country and dominated its foreign policy for a decade. Whether the removal of the Saudi leader from the scene will provide the beginning of closure from the terrorism theme that has overshadowed American foreign policy since 2001 remains to be seen, but it certainly provides a milepost in the evolution of America's contemporary dealings with the world.

The title of this book suggests that we are in the midst of a "new era" of foreign policy. That statement represents both a description of how the authors see the contemporary environment and a justification for a new text premised on and reflecting the differences in the contemporary environment that are highlighted in the pages that follow. It is our view that the world of American foreign policy has experienced sufficient change to constitute a new era that justifies both a fresh look and way of looking at the field. At a more or less mundane level, the fact that an American assassination of a foreign leader would be so transfixing and nationally important certainly represents a change in how Americans view international interactions: The United States has certainly tried to "rub out" foreign leaders in the past, failing in some cases (Fidel Castro, for instance) and succeeding in others (Chile's Salvador Allende), but the event has rarely been so widely applauded or seen as so consequential in the past (news of the death of Adolf Hitler is an exception). The operation was not undertaken against the head of a constituted sovereign government, but against a "nonstate actor," the head of a worldwide terrorist organization that has or claims no exclusive national territorial base or identity. Such nonstate-based actors are an increasing part of the web of foreign policy.

The bin Laden incident illustrates other dynamics that are part of the central core of the text and form the basis for asserting this is a new and different period in American foreign policy. One difference is the higher visibility of foreign events in American life than was previously the case. The killing of bin

Laden, of course, was a major event that would have received wide publicity at any time, but its announcement, telling, and retelling was a major political event in itself, and one that engaged the political spectrum both at home and abroad. The "good news" of bin Laden's demise (accompanied by the vivid images of the Obama team watching the operation unfold from the White House Situation Room) provided a welcome oasis in a desert of economic bad news and provided Obama with a welcome boost in opinion polls about his presidency. Internationally, it was acclaimed almost everywhere except in Pakistan where it occurred and where the incursion was more widely greeted as an unauthorized violation of Pakistani sovereignty, since it was carried out on Pakistani soil without a prior notification of the government of Pakistan.

Two of the most central themes of the book are also illustrated by the example. One of these themes is the idea of the *intermestic nature* of contemporary foreign policy—the idea that events are rarely ever entirely *inter*national or do*mestic* but contain interactive elements of both and are thus, as the hybrid word suggests, intermestic. In a world of intermestic politics, most decisions are effectively two-level games where decision makers must weigh both the domestic and international consequences of what they do. In the bin Laden case, the Obama administration had to weigh with particular care the possibility that the raid would fail and might have disastrous consequences for the president's reelection bid, as the failed mission to rescue the kidnapped inhabitants of the American embassy in Tehran (Desert One) did to President Carter in 1980. Internationally, the United States knew its action would raise the wrath of ally Pakistan, but felt the risk worth the possible benefit. Clearly, these were not the only considerations that the Obama decision team had to confront, but they do illustrate the intermestic content of those concerns.

The other major theme raised in these pages is the impact of domestic political *hyperpartisanship* as an influence on all policy, including foreign policy. For most of the history of the Republic, the guiding political principle surrounding the disposition of foreign policy was captured in the saying, "politics ends at the water's edge." The gist, of course, was that while political disagreement is a normal part of the conduct of domestic politics, the United States suspends such disagreements in dealing with the outside world, so as to provide a united front toward foreigners (the "water's edge" is a symbol of the boundary of the United States). The consensus around that principle has been eroding since the early post–World War II period and especially since the end of the Cold War, when the United States lost a commonly agreed momentous opponent against whom a unified front was necessary.

At the same time, American internal politics have become increasingly partisan and polarized. The genesis of this trend is not important for this purpose, but its consequences are. Gradually, the American political process has become dominated by ideologically distinct groups within the two major parties, so that by 2011, it is not unfair to say that the moderate middle of the spectrum that used to be dominant in both parties has eroded to the point of ineffectiveness. Instead, the political "left" and "right" dominate political dialogue and decision-making positions, and the art of compromise has been replaced by the politics of confrontation and bitter disagreement along partisan lines. The outcomes of this trend include the gridlock (the inability to achieve consensus) so evident in current economic interactions and the tendency toward a virtual "knee-jerk" opposition to the views of others on all matters of concern.

These two trends have combined to define the gradual extension of hyperpartisanship to the foreign policy realm. Some of that extension reflects the dynamics of the world discussed here. One reason, for instance, that the water's edge analogy could be sustained in the past was because the substance and consequences of foreign policy were largely discrete. In an intermestic world, virtually every domestic event or dynamic has some foreign policy implications, and most foreign policy actions have some kind of impact on domestic issues on which partisans disagree. If nothing else, a foreign policy triumph (or defeat) for the president has likely consequences for the next election cycle, a prospect that brings out the partisan instinct on both sides. When the political parties and their spokespeople disagree fundamentally on virtually everything, that disagreement overrides any previously existing barriers between domestic and foreign policy.

Hyperpartisanship was not so evident in the bin Laden case, because his demise was widely viewed as a national triumph, but it was not entirely absent either. One of the controversies that immediately surrounded the event was whether the administration should have provided more concrete proof that bin Laden was indeed dead. Because he was interred quickly at sea, no one who was not an immediate part of the operation ever saw the corpse, and the Obama administration's decision not to release photographs of his remains (fearing an adverse reaction in the Islamic world) further provided a wedge for the obsessively partisan. Clearly, the intent was to diminish the aura of resolute and correct decision making by Obama; it largely failed, but it does demonstrate that even the most positive foreign policy event cannot elude the partisan web altogether.

Understanding, interpreting, and applying these kinds of trends are what help define the new era and lend a unique value to this text. It contains traditional elements and organization: sections on American political institutions and decision making within them and the broad contours of the major substantive areas of foreign policy that are covered in most texts. It views some of these elements in more and some in less detail than other texts, but it has the additional element of weaving contemporary trends into the discussion as well. What it offers is, as much as anything else, a *fresh* look at American foreign policy that the reader will hopefully find valuable and enjoyable.

FEATURES

There are numerous survey textbooks available in the area of American foreign policy that provide a broad and comprehensive compendium of foreign policy processes and policy areas. Most of these books are longer than the present text, having grown from design or happenstance into broad, encyclopedic sources of information and interpretation in the field. While the resulting products have value, the authors believe that there is a place in the literature for a more compact, interpretive approach to the subject that covers the fundamental subject matter that a course in foreign policy must cover, but does so in a different and more appealing manner. The differences between what this book does and what others accomplish is the basic answer to the question, "Why this book?"

The authors believe that this text differs from other texts in three ways. First, it is shorter than most. Its length was purposeful and has two basic rationales: It allows a less costly product, and it facilitates the assignment of a supplementary text or texts to augment its coverage and thus "customize" the course to the individual instructor's needs. Second, it covers conventional topics for a text in the field, but in ways and with emphases that are different from those found in other texts. The section of the book that examines policy institutions and decision making, for instance, has extensive coverage of the various executive branch agencies that contribute to the foreign policy process (the "interagency process") at a level and depth not provided in most other texts, and it has a more extensive coverage of more informal parts of the process such as think tanks than is found in other texts. Third, the book is organized and infused with those dynamics of the foreign policy environment that constitute the new era of policy that is a central emphasis of the book. The result, it is hoped, is a text that both covers the important topics and also tells the story of a dynamic foreign policy in an engaging and readable manner.

The table of contents reflects these concerns. The first two of the thirteen chapters provide the setting for the contemporary examination of American foreign policy. Chapter One, "A New Foreign Policy Era," lays out the case that the context for making policy is changing and the major trends that constitute the changed environment (for example, intermestic and hyperpartisan politics), and allow the reader an opportunity to assess his or her own values about foreign policy. Chapter Two, "Paradigm Lost: The Cold War to the Present," provides an interpretive historical overview of the post–World War II period, emphasizing the comparative orderliness of the Cold War and the paradigm of containment in contrast to the greater conceptual uncertainty that has surrounded organizing foreign policy since the Cold War imploded in 1991, rendering the Cold War analogy inappropriate but providing no obvious replacement worldview.

The remainder of the text is organized into two major parts that reflect the major concerns of scholarship in the field: an emphasis on the political processes by which policy is made, and a survey of the major substantive areas of that policy. Part One, "Foreign Policy Processes" consists of six chapters. It begins with an overview of different approaches to understanding the dynamics of foreign policy decision making from a variety of disciplinary perspectives. As such Chapter Three, "Decision Making and U.S. Foreign Policy," is intended to provide useful analytical tools for organizing an understanding of the other chapters in Part One.

The rest of Part One is devoted to individual chapters discussing different formal and informal institutions in the foreign policy process. Chapters Four through Six concentrate on the major constitutionally prescribed political institutions. Chapter Four, "The President," looks at the formal and informal powers and constraints on the chief executive and provides a framework for looking at the performance of different presidents and their administrations based on personal attributes of the incumbent. Chapter Five, "The Role of Executive Agencies," examines the variety of executive branch agencies that assist the president in the making and implementing of policy, including core actors such as the State and Defense departments, the intelligence community, and new additions such as the Department of Homeland Security and the various economic agencies with foreign policy responsibility. Chapter Six, "Congress and Foreign Policy," mirrors the discussion of formal and informal powers of the federal legislature, and adds sections on the sources and manifestations of Congressional activism in the foreign policy area, including an examination of the War Powers Act. The remaining two chapters in Part One move to informal influences on the process from institutions and individuals outside the formal structure of government. Chapter Seven, "Interest Groups and Think Tanks," analyzes sequentially the major organized institutional players seeking to influence government, with an emphasis on those with major foreign policy interests and expertise. Chapter Eight, "The Public and the Media," looks at how the public's view of foreign policy matters is articulated, including major sources of limitation on its effectiveness and the sometimes controversial role of increasingly ubiquitous media coverage (especially by the burgeoning and multifaceted electronic media) on the process.

Part Two, "Foreign Policy Outcomes," looks at the three most prominent functional areas of substantive foreign policy, including two chapters each on national security and economic issues and a single chapter on trans-state (sometimes called transnational) issues. Chapter Nine, "Traditional Issues in National Security," looks at the two major areas of defense concern that are legacies of the Cold War, so-called "conventional" and strategic nuclear forces, and suggests how these may be changing as issue areas and national priorities in a world where major threats are not expressed in traditional military ways. Chapter Ten, "Contemporary National Security Problems in an Asymmetrical World," follows on to this discussion, applying it to the conditions in the current national security environment where most of the threats are nontraditional (that is, asymmetrical), where traditional solutions may not be appropriate, and where additional dynamics such as nation building come into play.

Chapter Eleven, "Economics and Foreign Policy," introduces the economic dimension of foreign policy, beginning with and concentrating on the reorganization of the post-1945 international system around the principle of free trade and the various critiques and variations of arguments about international economic interaction that have developed from and continue to influence economic discussions in the current stressed environment. Chapter Twelve, "Economic and Political Instruments of Foreign Policy," looks more specifically at questions about how the so-called "economic instrument of power" can be invoked to achieve foreign policy goals and the opportunities and limitations that attach to different mechanisms and approaches. Chapter Thirteen, "Trans-State Issues and American Foreign Policy," concludes the book with an examination of the concepts of trans-state problems (for example, international problems insoluble by the actions of individual states acting alone) and applications of that concept to two major recurring substantive issues: human rights and the environment.

The goal of the authors is to take both a fresh look and a fresh way of looking at foreign policy; and to facilitate the transmission of this approach and material, the authors have invoked a number of pedagogical devices the purpose of which is to facilitate reader comprehension and the organization of the material within each chapter. To this end, each chapter has a common series of features:

- Each chapter begins with two "guideposts" to help explain to the reader what is to follow. The first of these is a short "Preview" that summarizes the principal organization and flow of the chapter. The second is a list of key terms and concepts in the pages that follow. The concepts are listed in the order they appear in the text, and each concept is highlighted in the text itself as a way to guide readers to the most critical ideas in the chapter.
- An illustrative case study of a contemporary or historical foreign policy event introduces each chapter. The purposes of this introduction are both to engage the reader with an interesting vignette and to provide an introduction to the kinds of concerns raised in the chapter, which the examples are intended to illustrate.
- Two *Intersections* boxes are found in each chapter. The purpose of these boxes is to provide additional information and perspective on materials in the chapter and to carry out a major recurring theme of the book: the intermestic nature of foreign policy, hyperpartisanship, or examples of a changing environment, for instance.
- The end of each chapter contains a series of elements designed to reinforce comprehension of the materials in the chapter through active internalization of materials, to promote review of those elements of the chapter of greatest importance, and to provide resources for further exploration. These are contained in the three parts of the "Where Do We Go from Here?" ending of each chapter. The "Applications" section provides ways in which the reader may apply the contents to personal experience or broadening of experience. The "Study/Discussion Questions" provide questions that guide the reader through the most important points in the chapter. Finally, the "Further Readings" section is divided into two parts: an annotated list of core resources in the area, and a suggested list of further materials that are either cited in the text or may provide useful resources for further inquiry.

SUPPLEMENTS

Pearson is pleased to offer several resources to qualified adopters of *American Foreign Policy in a New Era* and their students that will make teaching and learning from this book even more effective and enjoyable. Several of the supplements for this book are available at the Instructor Resource Center (IRC), an online hub that allows instructors to quickly download book-specific supplements. Please visit the IRC welcome page at **www.pearsonhighered.com/irc** to register for access.

MySearchLab

For over 10 years, instructors and students have reported achieving better results and better grades when a Pearson MyLab has been integrated into the course. MySearchLab provides engaging experiences that personalize learning, and comes from a trusted partner with educational expertise and a deep commitment to helping students and instructors achieve their goals. A wide range of writing, grammar and research tools and access to a variety of academic journals, census data, Associated Press newsfeeds, and discipline-specific readings help you hone your writing and research skills. To order MySearchLab with this text, use ISBN 0-205-85364-1.

Passport

Choose the resources you want from MyPoliSciLab and put links to them into your course management system. If there is assessment associated with those resources, it also can be uploaded, allowing the results to feed directly into your course management system's gradebook. With MyPoliSciLab assets such as videos, mapping exercises, *Financial Times* newsfeeds, current events quizzes, politics blog, and much more, Passport is available for any Pearson political science book. To order Passport with this book, use ISBN 0-205-24932-9.

Pearson MyTest

This powerful assessment generation program includes multiple-choice questions, true/false questions, and essay questions for each chapter. Questions and tests can be easily created, customized, saved online, and then printed, allowing flexibility to manage assessments anytime and anywhere. Available exclusively on the IRC.

Longman Atlas of World Issues (0-205-78020-2)

From population and political systems to energy use and women's rights, the *Longman Atlas of World Issues* features full-color thematic maps that examine the forces shaping the world. Featuring maps from the latest edition of *The Penguin State of the World Atlas*, this excerpt includes critical thinking exercises to promote a deeper understanding of how geography affects many global issues.

Goode's World Atlas (0-321-65200-2)

First published by Rand McNally in 1923, *Goode's World Atlas* has set the standard for college reference atlases. It features hundreds of physical, political, and thematic maps as well as graphs, tables, and a pronouncing index.

The Penguin Dictionary of International Relations (0-140-51397-3)

This indispensable reference by Graham Evans and Jeffrey Newnham includes hundreds of cross-referenced entries on the enduring and emerging theories, concepts, and events that are shaping the academic discipline of international relations and today's world politics.

Research and Writing in International Relations (0-205-06065-X)

With current and detailed coverage on how to start research in the discipline's major subfields, this brief and affordable guide offers the step-by-step guidance and the essential resources needed to compose political science papers that go beyond description and into systematic and sophisticated inquiry. This text focuses on areas where students often need help—finding a topic, developing a question, reviewing the literature, designing research, and last, writing the paper.

ACKNOWLEDGMENTS

Some readers may recognize the outlines of some of the materials in the book, and in particular the organization and content of Chapters Four through Eight. Versions of these materials go back to the collaboration of the late Eugene Brown and one of the authors (Snow) at the U.S. Army War College from 1989 to 1991. That collaboration resulted in the earlier iterations of this material in books such as *Puzzle Palaces and Foggy Bottom* and *Beyond the Water's Edge,* among other places. Much of the inspiration for this work came from Gene Brown, which is why he is one of the people to whom this volume is dedicated. The other person in the dedication is the late Professor John Lovell of Indiana University, where both of the authors (separated in time) pursued doctoral degrees in which John was a mentor, colleague, and inspiration. Hopefully, he would also approve of this work.

We would also like to thank the reviewers, whose insightful and thoughtful comments helped shaped the book, including John Creed, College of Charleston; William DeMars, Wofford College; Al Eastham, Hendrix College; Ewan Harrison, Washington University–St Louis; David Rezvani, Harvard University; Catherine Scott, Agnes Scott College; Amy Skonieczny, San Francisco State University; and Min Ye, College of Coastal Georgia.American Foreign Policy in a New Era

CHAPTER 1

A New Foreign Policy Era

When President Obama and Israeli Prime Minister Benjamin Netanyahu met in Washington in May 2011, one of the principal issues dividing them was the question of Israeli settlements on the occupied West Bank depicted in this photograph.

PREVIEW

American foreign policy is changing in multiple ways that collectively constitute a new era for understanding and thinking about the subject. The international setting in which foreign policy is played out with other countries and entities has been subject to multiple alterations that have broadened the context and range of new actors in an increasingly public foreign policy environment. Domestic American politics has been increasingly partisan and contentious, and these domestic and international environments collide at the "intermestic intersection" between international and domestic concerns. This nature of contemporary foreign policy affects how one analyzes and views foreign policy and one's individual orientation toward foreign policy generally and on particular issues. Tensions in relations between the United States and Israel illustrate these principles.

KEY CONCEPTS

Israeli-Palestinian peace process
two-state solution
Israeli settlements
public diplomacy
intermestic policy
hyperpartisanship
sovereignty
state
state centrism
globalization
nonstate actors
national security state
realism
idealism
liberalism
conservatism
neoconservatism

During the third week and a half of May 2011, a foreign policy disagreement between Israel and the United States flared into public view and dominated media venues for several days. The public brouhaha surrounded the visit of Israeli Prime Minister Benjamin Netanyahu to Washington on a state visit for consultation with the Obama administration and to give speeches to the U.S. Congress meeting in joint session and the American-Israeli Public Affairs Committee (AIPAC), a powerful pro-Israeli lobby. On the surface, very little of this itinerary was unusual, but the visit was controversial because of the underlying disagreement about U.S.-Israeli policies manifested in contrasting views about the **Israeli-Palestinian peace process** between Obama and Netanyahu, which became very public as the visit proceeded.

The heart of the disagreement between the two closely associated states has centered on the best way to create a durable peace between Israel and its neighboring Arab states. The major focus in that process has been the creation of a separate state of Palestine carved from part or all of the territories occupied by Israel after the 1967 Six-Day War with its neighboring states—Egypt, Syria, Jordan, and Iraq, an initiative known as the **two-state solution.** The major stumbling block in defining a Palestinian state has been the existence and, more important, the continued construction of **Israeli settlements** (housing areas) in parts of the occupied territories, mostly on the West Bank of the Jordan River that presumably would form the new Palestinian state and the suburbs of East Jerusalem.

Since entering office in 2009, the Obama administration has been a vocal champion of the "two states for two peoples" outcome and has sought to reinvigorate talks between the major antagonists suspended in 2010. The initiatives have not been fruitful, as the Israelis and the Palestinians blame each other for subverting the process through their insincerity and obstacle-raising actions. The result has been an impasse in which continuing Israeli building in the occupied territories leads many to believe that a two-state solution is decreasingly possible, due to increased Israeli habitation of areas generally thought of as forming parts of the Palestinian state.

As in all real situations of foreign policy disagreement, there are two sides to the argument, and in this instance, both sides have adherents in both countries. The position of the Obama administration, generally considered to be "liberal" in both countries, is that stability is the ultimate goal in the region, stability can only be achieved by a negotiated settlement of the Israeli-Palestinian dispute, the best basis for such a settlement is one which creates two independent states (Israel and Palestine), and such an outcome will require considerable concessions on both sides. The clearest outcome is a new Palestinian state encompassing Gaza and nearly all of the occupied West Bank. This approach and outcome is favored by the opposition to the Netanyahu government in Israel's parliament (the Knesset) headed by Kadima Party leader and former foreign minister Tzipi Livni. Within the United States, this approach is also favored by generally liberal American Jews and their supporting organizations, such as the so-called "J Street" lobby described later in this book.

The opposing view, generally considered "conservative," is associated with the government of Prime Minister Netanyahu. It does not reject the two-state solution out of hand (although its critics, including Obama, believe its policies are making that outcome increasingly impossible to achieve), but rather attaches greater stipulations on such an outcome that make it far more difficult to negotiate. Specifically, Netanyahu rejects the idea that talks should begin with the pre-1967 borders of Israel (before Israel gained the occupied territories as part of the war in that year) as a starting point for negotiations, because an agreement based on such a presumption would leave Israel unacceptably militarily vulnerable. Moreover, he and his supporters believe that Israel is only acceptably secure if an eventual settlement leaves Palestine essentially unarmed and possibly with a permanent Israeli military presence on its soil. This position is supported by conservative Jewish elements in the United States (as represented by AIPAC) and conservative American admirers of Israel generally prominent in the Republican Party.

The positions were thus drawn before Netanyahu's arrival in Washington: the Obama administration focusing on the necessity of a revived peace process, Netanyahu more clearly focused on Israeli security. Such a disagreement is not unusual among states and is the traditional "stuff" of foreign policy. What is notable, and the reason for raising the incident here, is the way it has been handled, evidence of a new foreign policy era.

This diplomatic episode illustrates important characteristics of the new foreign policy era that is the major theme of this book. The entire incident was played out in full public view, and it is not clear that influencing U.S. public opinion as a way to pressure the Obama administration was not Netanyahu's major objective. The use of the U.S. Congress essentially as a background prop for delivering Netanyahu's message was clearly distinctive, and the interplay of domestic and international concerns is also symptomatic of the new foreign policy environment.

Three notable points thus emerge about the way the situation unfolded. The first and most striking aspect of the interchange was its extraordinarily public nature. **Public diplomacy**, the idea that foreign policy interactions should be open and transparent rather than conducted behind closed doors and reaching secret agreements, is not a new idea; indeed, its most public advocate goes back, in the sense of the term being used here, to the American President Woodrow Wilson in the early twentieth century. (Another meaning of the term, elaborated on elsewhere in the book, uses the term to connote direct public involvement in the foreign policy process.) In this case, however, the whole process was a very public event, where the intent seemed as much to influence public opinion in the United States as it was to conduct serious diplomacy.

Apparently intent on preempting what he saw as an impending Israeli initiative to dampen the prospects of a revived set of peace negotiations based on its preferred formula, the Obama administration struck first. On May 19, 2011, the President addressed employees of the U.S. Department of State on national television, laying out publicly his position that the current impasse was "unsustainable" and calling for talks to resume, using the pre-1967 Israeli boundaries adjusted by mutually agreed "land swaps" as the basis for physically forming the new Palestinian state. Before leaving Israel, Netanyahu responded that the 1967 boundary idea was "indefensible" from an Israeli viewpoint, a notion he reiterated, also on national television, in his speeches to AIPAC on May 23 and before the U.S. Congress on May 24, emphasizing the dictates of Israeli security. These very public, opposite views became the reference points for inconclusive private talks between the two leaders later.

The second major point was the clearly partisan content of the messages on both sides. The traditional view of foreign policy is that diplomacy proceeds when both sides take initial positions from which they can retreat because the public does not know the initial (and usually inflated) demands and thus is not disappointed when they are not achieved in whole. By making their positions public before discussions, both sides removed this ability to retreat and compromise, leaving the conclusion that the positions were not negotiating stances at all, but rather partisan policy preferences intended to rally the support of adherents rather than either to convert opponents or to create positions from which compromise would be possible.

This leads to the third and related point: the visit as a domestic political event for the United States. In particular, the GOP and other members of the political right seized on the Netanyahu visit as a partisan political matter, evidence of the shortcomings of the Democratic Party leadership of Obama. Congressional Republicans (who had been instrumental in issuing the invitation to Netanyahu to speak to them) cheered repeatedly as Netanyahu took positions in direct contravention to those of the sitting American administration (a spectacle that would have been inconceivable a half century ago), and GOP presidential contender Mitt Romney went so far as to accuse the president of "throwing Israel under the bus" by suggesting the pre-1967 borders as the basis of negotiations. The traditional convention that the United States should rally behind the commander-in-chief and show a united front toward the world was clearly not in evidence in Washington during the week of May 23, 2011.

This incident also demonstrates the dynamics of four relatively new influences on the foreign policy process, all of which are highlighted in the pages that follow. The first is the high visibility of foreign policy in the national political debate. Beyond the purely ceremonial aspects of foreign visits, foreign policy has traditionally occupied a much less prominent, visible, and thus controversial place on the public agenda than it does now. There are numerous reasons for this increasing visibility, including the impact of electronic mediation of events, and these influences will be explored in subsequent chapters. What they mean, however, is that foreign policy is no longer an exotic, abstract policy area, but one to which citizens have regular access and about which they increasingly have formed opinions. Indeed, one way to view the Netanyahu visit was as a media event the purpose of which was to influence American foreign policy opinion and thus to put pressure on the U.S. government to support those views.

A second and related dynamic is the changing audience and context within which foreign policy is conducted. Despite constitutional imperatives that empower the executive branch (with some limits) to conduct foreign affairs, it is clear that multiple new actors and influences exist within the system. The media is clearly one of these, and it is, for instance, not at all coincidental that Netanyahu concluded his visit by granting person-to-person interviews with reporters from essentially all the leading television networks and cable outlets. The Congress got to play an unconventional role by hosting a foreign dignitary whose views were in direct contradiction, even defiance, of a sitting American chief executive and applauding his basic disagreements with their own government. At the same time, the power and influence of interest groups, in this case AIPAC, was on full display, as first Netanyahu presented his views to a sympathetic gathering of AIPAC members and Obama followed in an effort to clarify his May 19 remarks to the same group.

Third, the interplay between domestic and international aspects (what some have called **"intermestic" politics**) is the third theme illustrated by this incident. The term itself is a hybrid formed from the **international and domestic** content of modern political situations. Part of the historic consensus on foreign policy derived from the separation of the two realms: Foreign policy did not affect domestic politics, and vice versa. That is no longer true in most instances, and the Netanyahu visit is an example—not so much of the direct consequences of those relations but how those relations can be used for domestic political purposes. It is probably not unfair to say that the purpose of the Netanyahu visit was as much to influence the outcome of the 2012 U.S. presidential election as it was about U.S.-Israeli relations.

The fourth major theme is **hyperpartisanship,** one of the major and continuing influences on contemporary American politics. There are basic divisions in the United States about the role and proper policies of government that have arguably produced a dysfunctional, polarized political system in which political advantage is more important than political outcomes and in which political compromise is virtually a forgotten, discredited idea. As it unfolded, the Netanyahu-Obama interchange in Washington had some of that flavor: The purpose on both sides was not so much to convert or find common ground on which to resolve differences as it was to publicize and to gather further support for established positions.

FOREIGN POLICY SETTINGS

During most of the history of the American republic—and certainly in the early days when the American Constitution was formulated as the basic context within which politics would take place—foreign policy was not considered either particularly important or controversial. The Constitution's provisions, discussed in more detail in subsequent chapters, are fairly sparse in dealing with foreign relations, mostly because the founding fathers did not expect these to be either very extensive or very important most of the time. The first century and a half or so of American history reinforced this judgment: The United States was a developing country outside the heart of a European-dominated international system, and the international system did not need to involve the United States intimately in its affairs, an attitude that was compatible with American primary concern with internal development and the settlement of internal difficulties (namely, the Civil War). It was not truly until the twentieth century, and especially World War II, that the United States was drawn into the vortex of heavy involvement in international affairs, a condition that broadened and intensified and has continued to today.

In these earlier days (see Chapter Two), there was an unwritten principle that guided the conduct of foreign policy: "Politics ends at the **water's edge.**" It is a simple but elegant description about the parameters of political activity in the foreign policy realm. The underlying idea is that there is a fundamental difference between domestic and international politics in the American political system: While domestic politics may be filled with conflict and the subject of considerable public (including partisan) disagreement, this disagreement should end when the United States faces—at the "water's edge" that is the boundary between the United States and the rest of the world save Canada and Mexico—the outside world. In foreign affairs, the country should unite against foreign powers and present a common front that cannot be misunderstood or exploited by America's opponents. The underlying, and critical, assumption was that the domestic and foreign policy political environments were mutually exclusive and separate, thus allowing conflict and animosity in one and allowing cooperation and unity in the other.

This principle had both strong domestic and international ramifications. Domestically, it meant that whenever the United States faced foreign powers, especially in times of crisis or confrontation, Americans of all political stripes were expected to rally behind U.S. policy. Disagreement with policy was tolerated, even encouraged, before policy decisions were made, but once determinations were reached, even those who disagreed with the outcomes were expected to suppress their reservations in the name of national unity. Foreign policy, in other words, was bipartisan and above the common political fray.

Internationally, the water's edge also symbolized the American attitude toward the intrusion of the outside world on the United States. A major part of the American political culture from the beginning of the foundation of the republic (discussed in Snow, *National Security for a New Era*) had been a negative reaction to European power politics, which Americans viewed as cynical and tainted, and the United States had largely been populated by immigrants fleeing the political horrors of other places, first in Europe, later in Asia, and more recently Latin America.

The concept of the water's edge seems oddly quaint in a world where virtually everything appears to be politicized, where partisanship is rampant and extends to almost all aspects of publicly affected life, and where there is little distinction between domestic and foreign affairs. There are some good, and some not-so-good, reasons for this transformation of the foreign policy environment, some of which can be explored by examining each of the two environments, foreign and domestic, and their conjunction separately.

Each of the four influences introduced in the opening case is highlighted within the threefold distinction. The high visibility of foreign policy events is largely the result of greater awareness because of media coverage than used to be the case. It is difficult to imagine, for instance, a major "flap" over Pakistan arresting and interrogating Pakistanis who cooperated with the U.S. effort to take down Osama bin Laden in June 2011 a decade or so earlier, because Americans would simply not have been aware of the action. New actors and influences are a characteristic of both the international and domestic environments and help create and define the intermestic phenomenon. Hyperpartisanship is primarily a domestic phenomenon, and its extension to the international and intermestic arenas is one of the telling characteristics of contemporary foreign policy.

The International (Foreign) Environment

There are two basic characteristics of the international system that make it fundamentally different from domestic politics. The first is that the underlying, bedrock principle of international relations is **sovereignty**, which is defined as "supreme authority." Within any political entity, the possessor of sovereignty is supreme, meaning there is and can be no superior authority above whatever individual or institution possesses sovereignty. The other characteristic is that sovereignty in international relations is possessed by **states**. *State* is a legal and political term referring to recognized jurisdiction over a piece of territory and recognition of that jurisdiction by other similar entities (other states).

Put together, these two principles define the international environment as a **state-centric** political system, in which the member units possess sovereignty over their realms and in which no other states can legitimately claim influence or sway. The result is to create the legitimate authority of states to regulate relations within their boundaries, but it also means that the relationship between them is one between legal equals in which none can simply dictate the outcomes of their interactions. The international system is, in more precise terms, a system of **anarchy** (the absence of government).

The stark application of these principles can easily be overstated and distorted. An entirely state-centric international system based on sovereignty suggests that states do not and should not interfere in the internal workings of the other countries with which they deal, and that has never been the case. Through methods as diverse as lobbying, influence peddling, espionage, and other forms of interference, governments and their representatives have always interfered with one another to try to influence the outcomes of their foreign policy interactions in their favor. The Netanyahu visit to Washington is vivid evidence of how the principles are relaxed in application.

In practice, foreign policy interactions between states are regulated by a set of rules, but state sovereignty limits the ability to monitor and enforce those rules. Occasionally, states break the rules: An embassy official from one country tries to bribe a counterpart in the country to which he or she is accredited, or a government may mount a propaganda drive to influence an election outcome in favor of a candidate who supports a position they favor, for instance. Both of these kinds of acts constitute interference in the domestic politics of another country and are impermissible under the concept of sovereignty. That such practices occur anyway is simply evidence that the rules are not sacrosanct.

Organizing and playing in a pickup game of basketball or football offers an analogy. If one plays in such a game, you know there are rules to be followed and penalties for breaking them. In a basketball game, for instance, hacking an opponent is a foul and means the fouled team either gets the ball out of bounds or gets a free throw, depending on conditions. In a regular game, there is a referee, who effectively acts as the sovereign regarding rule enforcement, to call fouls. What distinguishes a pickup game, however, is that there is no referee. The players, in effect, are all sovereign, and if there is an alleged infraction on which the two sides disagree, there is no clear, definitive way to resolve the resulting disagreement. There are still rules, and in principle they are enforceable, but only the players themselves can enforce them. For many purposes, international relations are much the same.

If state sovereignty has always been a partial myth in practice, the modern dynamics of international politics are further eroding the purity of state centrism that is at the heart of the environment in which foreign policy is made. Both the idea of an inviolable and absolute state sovereignty and the exclusivity of the state as the sole actor in the international realm have been affected by change. While it is possible to overstate the degree to which change has occurred, alterations in the way international politics are conducted have contributed to changes in the way the system operates and to the blurring of distinctions between foreign and domestic politics. Two examples, the phenomenon of economic globalization and the rise of nonstate actors (discussed in more detail in Chapters Two, Nine, and Ten), will help illustrate both the impact and limitations of change on foreign policy.

The most dramatic contemporary instances of the internationalization of world affairs come through the process of economic **globalization**, the spreading of economic activity across national borders by private companies and corporations resulting in a high level of economic interdependence among and between countries. The effect is to create, in the economic sector, a great deal of activity such as movement of capital, products, ideas, and people across state boundaries beyond the effective control of governments. A primary example is the pressure of governments to reduce or eliminate trade barriers (namely, tariffs, quotas) toward other countries, a practice by which countries historically have controlled the penetration of their border economically and by which they have protected indigenous industries from outside competition.

States have lost much of their ability to control economic activity as a result. To some, this is philosophically desirable, since it has meant the effective transfer of economic power from the public to the private sector, a movement they find advantageous. Since one of the dictates of successful globalization is the free movement of people, goods, services, and capital across international boundaries; one of the other consequences has been to make it more difficult to control the boundaries between states, since effective control slows the pace of economic intercourse across boundaries.

One can, of course, make too much of these effects. One of the arguments champions of globalization sometimes make is that the global economy is becoming so intertwined and interdependent that truly independent national economies are disappearing, replaced by the international composition of goods and services. At its extreme, proponents argue that the result of globalization is to make it extremely difficult, even impossible, for countries to go to war with one another, because they are too dependent on one another for the wherewithal to mount independent war efforts. Unfortunately, the same arguments were made about the effects of an earlier spate of globalization on the eve of World War I.

There has also been a dramatic rise in the frequency and impact of so-called **nonstate actors**: politically active groups operating across state borders that are not the formal representatives of governments. There are, and always have been, multiple examples of this kind of actor. The most obvious group are nongovernmental organizations (NGOs), groups with international memberships that perform different kinds of services but are not affiliated with nor are representatives of governments. The International Red Cross and Amnesty International (AI) are examples. NGOs number in the tens of thousands in the international system and, in some cases, seek to influence the foreign policies of states. AI, for instance, has sought to influence American foreign policy by publicizing alleged American violations of the human rights of Americans and foreign citizens at places such as the detention facilities at Guantanamo Bay, Cuba.

The more problematical examples of nonstate actors are informal groups that act outside the normal channels of international interaction, often for nefarious and destructive purposes. The most obvious examples of this kind of group are international terrorist organizations, with Al Qaeda as the most notorious case in point. These organizations operate across (usually ignoring) state boundaries and engage in illegal, often violent activities against states and their citizens. Since a prime (some would argue *the* prime) purpose of the state is the physical protection of its citizens from harm, terrorist and other criminal groups (for example, foreign drug cartels) pose a particular threat to countries outside the normal channels of international discourse.

Foreign policy is the process and tool by which the state tries to accommodate and shape influences from outside its borders to maximize the country's interests and to minimize danger and damage to those interests. Every state has a foreign policy mechanism to deal with this problem, and the interaction between the foreign policy mechanisms of states is the major, and historically most prominent, means by which foreign policy is conducted. State-to-state interaction via diplomacy and the other instruments available to states is the natural way in which foreign policy occurs in a state-centric system guided conceptually by the principle of sovereignty, and the emphasis of people who analyze foreign policy from an international viewpoint has historically been on the outcomes of these interactions. Modern foreign policy is not as simple as the interaction of diplomats, as the examples just cited have suggested, making contemporary foreign policy more complicated and often contentious and thus more of a problem for domestic politics, where the processes by which decisions are reached are more of a central concern of analysts.

The Domestic Environment

In historical terms, domestic politics are not supposed to play a major part in the making or execution of American foreign policy. The U.S. Constitution provides the framework within which foreign policy is considered and delineates who has the authority to oversee and limit foreign policy actions via the separation of powers that is at the heart of the U.S. constitutional system. The Constitution itself is fairly spare in its description of the foreign policy roles of the branches of government it created. As in all matters, the branches are generally considered coequal, although in the foreign policy realm the judicial branch has generally adopted a lesser role, mainly confined to adjudicating jurisdictional disputes between the executive and legislative branches. The executive and legislature are given roughly equal and countervailing powers, creating what has been called an "invitation to struggle" both on jurisdictional and substantive lines.

Within that framework, the executive branch is given the more public and initiating role, largely because of the nature of international relations. The diplomatic system that evolved in the European-dominated international system of the seventeenth and eighteenth centuries was based on the notion that the relations among countries were to be conducted by the heads of government and their representatives (known as plenipotentiaries) to provide order within those relations—so that the government of one state could know what entities in other states could conduct business on behalf of their states.

Since the president is a single individual, whereas the Congress is two aggregations of diverse and independent officials, it logically followed that it made more sense to designate the president, who is the head of government, to be the representative with whom other states would interact. Because the president is the designated "contact point" between the United States and other governments, the presidency has often been elevated in the general mind to a position of superiority in the foreign policy realm, although that reputation is not constitutionally based.

The Congress has constitutional prerogatives and powers that countervail the powers of the president. For one thing, the president's chief foreign policy advisors, from the Secretary of State and his or her principal assistants to ambassadors to foreign countries, must be confirmed by the Senate, providing a limit on the kinds of people (and views) that represent U.S. foreign policy with other countries. The Constitution anticipated that significant U.S. business with other countries would be concluded as internationally recognized treaties, and it gave the Senate the power to "advise and consent" or to reject treaties, thereby accepting or rejecting them as binding on the country. There are, of course, other examples, some of which will be raised in Chapters Four and Six.

This formal balance of powers has been altered in the contemporary pattern of foreign policy in two basic and interrelated ways. One of these has been the emergence of a much greater concern with American national security than has been the case historically, and the other, which derives at least in part from the higher and more visible foreign policy stakes created by the national security state, has been the rise in partisanship and acrimony in the general political process. Each is sufficiently important to warrant at least some concern in these introductory remarks.

The Rise of the National Security State The elevation of a concern with the physical security of the American state as a primary foreign policy problem is largely an artifact of the post–World War II international environment (a concern raised more systematically in Chapter Two). The protection of the citizens and territory of the state from physical harm is, of course, the most basic purpose of government in a world organized around sovereign states, but before World War II, it was largely an abstract concern for most Americans most of the time. The United States had no basic, longtime enemy bent on its enslavement or destruction, and even if it had, the country could only be attacked by enemies who would have had to sail across the Atlantic or Pacific Ocean to launch an invasion, a feat beyond the military capabilities of virtually all states. The land borders of the United States, at the same time, were shared with comparatively weak and benign neighbors (Canada and Mexico). In this atmosphere, the concept of national security was far less of a national concern than it has subsequently become.

The end of World War II and the subsequent emergence of the Cold War changed that situation dramatically. The Soviet Union and the United States emerged during the 1940s as the world's two most powerful and opposed powers. The basis of their antagonism was ideological—the confrontation between Soviet communism and American capitalist democracy—and it had a significant, even overriding, military content. The Soviets and the Americans came to view themselves as deadly enemies, and with the invention and perfection of missile-delivered thermonuclear arsenals against which neither could possibly defend itself, the question of national security and survival became inextricably intertwined. Foreign policy was no longer simply about diplomacy; it was about national life and death.

This transformation had two basic effects on the domestic political environment. The first was to raise the visibility and importance of foreign policy in a much more prominent and inevitably contentious area, and one on which virtually every political actor or entity would have an opinion and want to play a part. The "Communist threat" to the United States became a ubiquitous part of national existence and dialogue, and maintaining the integrity of the United States against the "red menace" became the highest order of national business. Politicians and other leaders clamored to establish that they were not "soft on communism" and that they were more vigilant in the face of the threat than their political opponents. The result was a level of enthusiasm that sometimes raised serious questions about the levels of personal sacrifice people should endure in areas as diverse as civil liberties and levels of taxation to support the Cold War effort. Inevitably, questions of patriotism entered the mix as well, further dividing an increasingly acrimonious and partisan debate. While the substance of the Cold War division dissipated with the end of operational communism in the Soviet Union over twenty years ago, much of the same tone and even arguments extended to debates about international religious terrorism.

The other effect was structural. An increasing obsession with national security subtly brought with it the rise of something that became known as the **national security state**. The idea underlying this construct was that the problem of national security was so overwhelming that the political system had to adapt itself to this reality in the process. This transformation became evident as early as 1947, when the United States enacted the National Security Act, which created basic structures such as the National Security Council (discussed more fully in Chapter Five), made foreign and national security policy synonymous for some purposes, and created the Department of Defense and Central Intelligence Agency as independent executive agencies.

U.S.-Soviet competition gave rise to the creation of a national security state in the United States, but the structures and mind-sets that were adopted for the specific Cold War problem did not disappear with the end of that confrontation. After an essentially awkward decade of the 1990s when the structure of the threat facing the United States became increasingly opaque and debatable, the terrorist attacks of September 11 facilitated the identification of a new object of concern, international religious terrorism, which has become the focus of a new level and quality of operation of the national security state. This transformation is discussed in Chapter Two.

Partisanship and Hyperpartisanship The appropriate level of concern, exertion, and importance of national security became an important element in the partisan political debate within the United States as well. Over the past two decades, American domestic politics has descended into one of its periodic cycles of extreme **partisanship**, in this case largely defined along party lines that reinforce and are reinforced by political ideology. While the degree of partisanship—which some have labeled "hyperpartisanship" to emphasize what they view as its extreme quality—currently being displayed in American politics certainly has historical precedents, the degree to which it has spread to foreign policy is abnormal and is the legitimate source of concern in understanding American foreign policy.

Unraveling the detailed nature and dynamics of the current spate of partisanship goes beyond present purposes. The rise of the contemporary partisanship that threatens to stalemate current governance has its most obvious origins in the post–Cold War 1990s. This period witnessed two important and parallel dynamics that helped define the current partisan morass. One influence was an ideological divide among Americans that increasingly defined the Democratic and Republican parties. The other influence was the end of the Cold War and the consequent need to develop a new foreign and national security paradigm to replace the Cold War framework.

The current case of ideological purification of American domestic politics goes back to the 1970s and even before with the emergence and rise of the modern conservative movement. Associated most clearly with the presidency of Ronald Reagan and the so-called "Reagan revolution," conservatism sought to draw sharp philosophical differences between its adherents and so-called liberals (who now mostly refer to themselves as progressives) and even moderates. Increasingly, the conservatives concentrated their efforts on transforming a Republican Party in which they had shared control and influence with moderates into a conservative-dominated party. In at least partial reaction, the Democratic Party increasingly defined itself in terms of its liberal base, although moderates maintained some influence in Democratic politics. The redefinition around distinctly liberal and conservative political parties helped set in motion the dynamics of contemporary partisan gridlock.

The conservative-liberal division is as old as the United States itself. Conservatives have generally begun from a philosophical preference for limited government and a consequent minimal role for government, expressed as opposition to government "intrusion" on private life. Contemporary conservatives share this position, largely couched in opposition to current or expanded levels of taxation. In current politics, these *fiscal* conservatives are joined by so-called *social* conservatives, who favor traditional social and family values such as opposition to abortion. Liberals/progressives, on the other hand, have a much more positive view of the role of government in promoting social values, and especially questions of social equity. These philosophical positions are sometimes reversed when moving from domestic to foreign policy areas, as will be discussed in building profiles of foreign policy beliefs.

The hyperpartisan effects of this process have been especially obvious in the early twenty-first century. It is not an unfair caricature of contemporary politics to typify it as consisting of a liberal Democratic party and a conservative Republican party in which moderates are not revered by either party and in which philosophical oddballs in either party are not tolerated and are subject to purging. In this situation, political action is determined by ideological loyalty manifested along party lines, and the result is extreme, rigid partisanship across the spectrum of political issues. One can argue whether such sharp distinctions are meritorious on domestic issues; applied to foreign policy, the result has clearly been to undermine the consensus and unity of outlook and appearance toward the outside world that previously distinguished American policy, as the May 2011 Netanyahu example demonstrates.

Much of this political change has occurred during a period when the basic American way of organizing its view of the international environment was also undergoing fundamental change. The Cold War period from the latter 1940s until the early 1990s had produced a well-defined and durable consensus on foreign policy that had great support across the political spectrum and thus was not, except at the margins and details of policy, a matter of partisan political disagreement. The foundation of this consensus was agreement on a concrete adversary in the form of Soviet communism, opposition to which galvanized a broad foreign policy consensus.

The end of the Cold War shattered that consensus. The consensual formula lost a recognized opponent around which opinion and action could congeal. The Soviet threat was not replaced by a menacing alternative during the 1990s, and thus there was decreased common ground around which to shape a new policy. This void allowed a debate to emerge over the nature and extent of the threat in the environment. This debate became political and ideological, with conservatives generally arguing that a more ominous and threatening environment required a more robust posture to oppose than liberals, who tended to believe a less threatening environment permitted greater attention to domestic priorities. The absence of any major crises during the 1990s suppressed the rhetorical heat of this emerging ideological division, but it did create the bases for the extension of political disagreement to the foreign policy realm.

The threat, of course, returned with the terrorist attacks of September 11, 2001, and with it a consensual, concrete enemy to be opposed and a general agreement on the need to oppose that threat. Development of a coherent, consensual policy, however, had to be attempted in the context of a growing ideologically based partisanship and questionable and potentially divisive foreign policy acts such as the Iraq War. While a general consensus emerged and has been sustained that international religious terrorism remains a durable opponent, there has been a growing, and largely partisan, disagreement about both grand strategy and specific policies for dealing with that enemy. Disagreement about the ongoing prosecution of the War in Afghanistan is an example of this disagreement.

The Intermestic Intersection

The historical barrier between foreign and domestic policies as fair game for public partisan disagreement has clearly been breached: politics clearly no longer ends at the water's edge. The roots of that breakdown are partially based in changing domestic and international political environments that have eroded earlier inhibitions about publically admitting differences to the world. But that is not all.

Part of the water's edge analogy was also based in the assumption and perception that foreign policy actions did not have direct domestic effects on individuals or groups of Americans. If different foreign policies do not have varying impacts on different Americans, there is less reason to debate and disagree about them than if these decisions do affect different American differently. However, if a foreign policy decision produces advantages for some Americans and disadvantages for others, then it bridges the gap between foreign and domestic policy and arguably becomes a legitimate part of the partisan political debate.

This is the essence of what makes an issue part international and part domestic—and hence intermestic. When foreign policy decisions by the United States have domestic consequences for some or all Americans, or when domestic decisions have foreign policy consequences, the line between the two environments is blurred, as are the distinctions and boundaries about how they are treated politically. Increasingly, many, if not most, foreign policy decisions have a domestic impact, and many domestic decisions have foreign policy consequences as well. This phenomenon has implications for the content of foreign policy and its impact on people and for how foreign policy is studied.

The Impact of Intermestic Politics The dynamics of the intersection of domestic and international politics work in both directions: Foreign policy actions can have domestic political consequences, and domestically motivated actions can have foreign policy implications. An example of each direction may clarify the dynamics of intermestic politics.

During the early Clinton administration, there was a concern about balance-of-payments imbalances between the United States and Japan (the value of American goods exported to Japan was far less than the value of Japanese goods imported into the United States). One of the most glaring areas where this disparity occurred was in automobiles: Americans bought a large number of Japanese cars, whereas the Japanese bought very few American automobiles. The issue was contentious. The Japanese argued that their people did not buy U.S.-made cars because they were unattractive: poorly made and producing low gas mileage. Americans countered that the reason for the imbalance was that the Japanese erected high economic barriers to the importation of American autos (for instance, very detailed inspection procedures that added considerable cost to American cars) that made U.S. vehicles artificially uncompetitive in Japan.

The Clinton administration suggested a solution with both foreign and domestic policy implications. To redress the trade balance, President Clinton suggested that the Japanese voluntarily agree to buy and install more American parts on their cars for export (tires, batteries, and the like), thereby increasing American exports to Japan. The Japanese balked at this suggestion, because it would have had an adverse impact on Japanese producers of the same components. When they did so, the President announced that the United States would impose an import tariff on selected Japanese cars. The domestic impact was purposely partisan: The administration announced it would tax Japanese *luxury* cars (which presumably would affect wealthier and thus more likely Republican consumers), but not the small, inexpensive imports presumably preferred by Democratic voters.

The announcement triggered a political firestorm in both countries. Republicans fumed at the domestic impact of the tariff, and the Japanese argued that it was a violation of antitariff obligations the United States had agreed to as part of its accession to the World Trade Organization (WTO). When the Japanese threatened to sue the U.S. government in the WTO, the administration backed away from the tariff, and the crisis passed. While the issue had little long-term impact on U.S.-Japanese relations or the buying habits of American car buyers, it did illustrate how domestic and foreign policy matters can become intertwined.

The situation works in the other direction as well. At about the same time the Japanese automobile brouhaha was going on, the U.S. government, along with its counterparts in Mexico and Canada, was completing work on the North American Free Trade Agreement (NAFTA). The negotiation was complicated in many respects, and in order to gain enough domestic support to get the legislation through the U.S. Congress, a number of compromises were necessary. One such agreement largely overlooked at the time was a domestic issue with what has proven to have great foreign policy cogency: the question of corn subsidies to American agribusiness.

Agricultural subsidies (payments to farmers for growing or, in some cases, not growing crops or livestock) are a venerable domestic political issue. Originally enacted to try to protect small farmers from the vicissitudes of agricultural economics (changing prices for commodities, the effects of weather, and the like), the primary beneficiaries are now large corporate farming holdings known as agribusinesses, which have powerful lobbies to ensure they receive these taxpayer-financed incentives. In the United States, one of the crops that have historically been subsidized most heavily is corn, and the major corn producers were determined to maintain their advantageous subsidies when NAFTA was negotiated. These subsidies flew in the face of the more general intent of the trade agreement, a major part of which was to remove government protections and thus to allow the principle of comparative advantage to operate across the borders of the free trading area.

Corn subsidies became an exception to this rule. Within the NAFTA region, the principal competitors to American producers were small Mexican producers, largely peasant farmers working small pieces of land. The impact of U.S. farm subsidies within the NAFTA framework was to lower the cost of

American corn in Mexico below what Mexican producers could offer, which put many Mexican corn farmers out of business. Many of these farmers, in turn, were further buffeted by economic turmoil in the Mexican financial industry in the 1990s that resulted in the foreclosure of mortgages on many of these farms. As a consequence, many Mexican farmers were thrown off their land and became destitute and homeless. This plight turned into a foreign policy question for the United States because many of them became a core source of Mexican economic immigration to the United States that has fueled the controversy over illegal immigration both within American domestic politics and in relations between the United States and Mexico.

Intermestic Political Science The professional study of American foreign policy also reflects the intermestic distinction. That study has two primary focal points: the international environment that forms the context and set of circumstances in the world to which American foreign policy must react, and the American political system that provides the predispositions and processes by which the United States arrives at political decisions, including those with foreign elements. Within the discipline of political science as it is practiced in the United States, the international environment is the realm of a subdiscipline of international relations (IR), whereas domestic policy processes are within the domain of American politics. The study of American foreign policy falls at the boundary of these two distinct areas of study and concern, with an interest in both but not entirely grounded in either.

Most of the people who study American foreign policy have their primary grounding in one of these areas or the other, and their approaches to the subject reflect their subdisciplinary concentration. Thus, American foreign policy students whose interests are primarily grounded in IR generally emphasize the international dynamics of foreign policy: the nature and structure of international politics as the environment of foreign policy and specific international interactions and outcomes between the United States and foreign countries in particular situations, for instance. Students of foreign policy with grounding in American politics, however, are more likely to focus on American political processes, such as the impact, structure, and dynamics of the American political system on how the United States organizes to deal with the world.

The new era of foreign policy affects students of both American and international politics. Students of IR have historically viewed domestic politics as a sort of "black box" that did not greatly affect the affairs of state; as the Netanyahu-Obama introduction shows, that situation is no longer the case. The intrusion of foreign policy concerns into domestic contexts also provides a new avenue for American politics, since foreign policy concerns affect and activate elements of the American policy community previously not included (all Congressmen must at least pretend to understand world affairs, for instance), and because foreign policy concerns are different from traditional domestic policy areas and thus offer new avenues of inquiry.

The intermestic nature of foreign policy study is primarily interesting to those seeking to carve out a position among those who seek to investigate and report on foreign policy. Both approaches are relevant, and it is difficult or impossible to understand American foreign policy without a grounding in and appreciation of each. Without an understanding of the international environment, the student or practitioner lacks the context within which to analyze and respond to stimuli that come from beyond the water's edge, and without an understanding of the American domestic political system, it is equally impossible to know how and to what extent those domestic responses are likely to take.

THINKING ABOUT FOREIGN POLICY

The purpose of this volume is to help introduce students to an understanding of foreign policy and how that policy affects them. To help move in that direction, the rest of this chapter will deal sequentially with two further areas of concern: the specific way that Americans view foreign policy matters (the American political culture) and a framework within which the reader can organize his or her own particular views and those of others about foreign policy (personal inventory). Each contributes to the context for further analyzing and understanding this subject area.

Foreign Policy Culture

No two countries have had identical histories or have evolved in identical ways, and the differences among and between them have consequences regarding how they view and deal with the world. The result is that all countries have their own distinct worldviews that are the composite of influences that one can describe as a **foreign policy culture**, a set of influences that contributes both to the style and substance of different states' views of foreign policy. Citizens of a country like Poland, for instance, which has a long history of invasion and counterinvasion, brutal wars, and even periodic dismemberment as an independent entity, have a far different view of the importance of national security and military force than a country like the United States, which has experienced essentially none of the misfortunes that have befallen the Polish people. Different experiences predispose different people in varying ways.

The American foreign policy culture has been conditioned by a number of factors, two of which can be highlighted here for exemplary purposes. The first is the accident of geography, a physical circumstance that has provided the United States with physical protection from foreign predators and, for most of its history, a level of resource abundance that has minimized its needs for exogenous sources of materials necessary for its prosperity. The second is the Anglo-Saxon heritage, the grounding in its beginnings as an outgrowth of the English experience that includes a measured level of suspicion toward military force and a high level of commitment to constitutional rule.

An entire historical approach to the study of international relations focusing on the impact of geography on states flourished in the early twentieth century. Known as *geopolitics* (a term that has since acquired a broader meaning to be nearly synonymous with power politics), it examined how things such as size, geographical position, climate, and other factors influenced how countries developed and how they interacted with the rest of the world. Applying the geopolitical perspective to the American experience, two factors stand out as particularly important in how the country developed and how it views the world.

The first geographical impact is *location*. The contiguous forty-eight states of the United States are effectively an island protected from the rest of the world by broad oceans, the Atlantic and the Pacific, that make it virtually impossible for foreign enemies to contemplate menacing or, in the extreme, invading the American homeland. Combined with benign, less powerful geographically contiguous neighbors, the result has been that the United States has had to expend very little of its history overly concerned about its physical survival, a luxury not available to most European and Asian powers. The last time American soil was meaningfully attacked was during the War of 1812, and until the then–Soviet Union made operational nuclear-tipped intercontinental ballistic missiles (ICBMs) capable of reaching and devastating American territory in the late 1950s, the United States was effectively an impregnable fortress. In that circumstance, the United States never developed the same sense of urgency about matters of self-defense and survival as most other states.

INTERSECTIONS

Is America Still an Island?

If taken literally, the question raised in this title is nonsensical, since the only major parts of the United States that are not parts of the North American land mass are Hawaii and the Florida Keys. The idea of the analogy, of course, is figurative, suggesting that, like a large island, the United States is effectively protected from hostile outside intrusion by its geographical location.

Has that comfortable position changed? In recent years, there has been growing pressure on the southern border of the United States in the form of illegal immigration and narcotics trafficking northward. In one sense, this phenomenon is a part of the global trend of population movement from the less to the more developed countries, but it has become an acute intermestic issue in the United States, with a strong domestic element as well as implications for Mexican-American relations.

There is no easy solution to this assault on the impregnability of the American borders. Domestic American politics militates toward tighter border control possibly to the point of sealing the boundary. Such an action would, however, have negative foreign policy effects, including interrupting the legal flow of authorized people and goods and services between the two countries that is part of the North American Free Trade Agreement (NAFTA) that includes Mexico and the United States.

The second geographic effect is *natural resources.* The North American continent is blessed with natural resources that have made it essentially resource independent for most of American history. That abundance has included mineral and energy resources that were easily and economically available and abundant, as well as rich soils and climate to support agriculture capable of feeding the population without outside sources. The result was that the United States never had to plumb world availability of the things it needed to survive and prosper in the way that such relatively resource-poor countries as Japan and England did. That independence has, of course, partially evaporated. Indigenous, easily (cheaply) available energy resources such as petroleum have largely been exhausted, the need for exotic minerals like titanium that are not found here must be sought elsewhere, and the American appetite for exotic foodstuffs requires importation. Resource abundance has sometimes been a curse as well as a blessing in some places (the Nile River delta has been not only a coveted granary but also a magnet for foreign invaders), but in the U.S. case, its secure location has guarded the country from such disadvantages.

The other conditioning factor arises from the United States' beginning as an essentially Anglo-Saxon country. Although the United States has become an ethnic and national melting pot wherein Caucasians of European lineage are projected to lose majority status in the next half-century, the country began as an offshoot of Great Britain, with most of the seventeenth- and eighteenth-century settlers sharing a British background. That influence was certainly evident at least through the revolutionary period, with two major impacts worth noting.

One of these influences is an aversion to the military, at least to the possession and retention of military forces during peacetime. In large measure, this aversion is a reflection of the English experience during the Cromwellian period during the seventeenth century, when Oliver Cromwell used British forces to suppress English subjects, a practice ended after the Glorious Revolution of 1688 restored the monarchy and restricted the permanent stationing of British forces on English soil. When the British in effect rescinded this policy in the American colonies after the French and Indian Wars in 1763 (to protect the Americans from the Indians and the French, protections the colonists believed they did not need), this intrusion helped set in motion forces that would lead to the American Revolution a decade later. In the wake of American independence, the United States began a long tradition of maintaining a very minimal standing Army during peacetime, a tradition that was not interrupted until the wake of the Korean War in the 1950s.

The other prominent Anglo-Saxon legacy is a tradition of limited, constitutional government, including a strict adherence to individual political rights. Much of this sentiment was originally directed at the creation of a political system for the new republic in which it would be impossible for an autocratic leader to arise and seize power in a way similar to the perceived tyranny of the English crown that had been the object of the revolution in the first place. This thread is occasionally tested in times of national security crisis, and can be seen in the current debate over dealing with terrorists and rights they may or may not possess under the law (a problem considered in Chapter Ten).

The elements of foreign policy culture generally have an indirect and implicit impact. While enthusiasts of gun ownership may be able to trace their advocacy back to the influence of views toward limited government and suspicion of governmental authority, specific attitudes are more closely related to individual political belief systems. To help the reader more closely define how he or she feels about foreign policy, it is thus useful to examine the individual bases for such attitudes.

Individual Inventory

There is no immutably correct or "American" view of foreign policy. The foreign policy culture creates parameters within which the debate over proper foreign policy proceeds, but those boundaries are sufficiently spacious to accommodate a variety of contrasting views. Thus, a lively debate and level of disagreement are normal, healthy elements of the discussion of foreign policy. This ongoing debate varies depending on the issues and events to which policy must react, but there are an identifiable series of concerns around which one can organize the debate over any particular issue and which differentiate the general views of different individuals about foreign policy. For present purposes, four admittedly condensed dimensions will be identified, including the basic categories of positions on each dimension. (The categories are adapted from the discussion in Snow, *National Security in a New Era.*)

Basic Worldview In the most general terms, worldview asks how people look at the dynamics of the world around them and how they assess that environment. Basic points of differentiation include the acceptability of the world the way it is, the immutability of ongoing conditions, and how or whether changing those conditions is possible or worth the effort. It really consists of two basic judgments about the world: How acceptable is it? What, if anything, can be done to change things about the world that one does not like?

Two basic positions have dominated American debates about worldview. The first, and at least historically more dominant, has been *realism*. The heart of the realist position is that world politics is a geopolitical (in the broad sense of that term) struggle between sovereign states in an international system of anarchy (the absence of government). The central dynamic of the system is the interplay of states seeking to maximize their individual national interests. Realists accept this situation as normal, and believe that the role of policy makers is to manipulate the system to their state's maximum advantage. For many adherents and critics alike, the realist position includes a pessimistic view of the human condition and a suspicion of the prospects of change. The term "realism" itself arises from the assertion that its adherents are indeed realistic, seeking to describe and manipulate the world the way it is, rather than how they might like it to be.

The other basic position is *idealism*. Idealists see the world differently than do realists. Although most idealists accept the realist description of the world as accurate, they contest whether it is either natural or immutable. Idealists accept the world as imperfect, but believe change is both possible and can be effective in improving the human condition. In terms of the operation of the international system, idealists tend to see the condition of international anarchy as a prime structural imperfection that results in the violence (war) that they see as a particular fault in need of reforming.

Both ideas are present in the American foreign policy culture. Partly because it purports to be based in "reality" (as opposed to unreality), realism has generally been the dominant philosophy among policy makers. At the same time, elements in the American tradition suggest an imperfect world in need of change and even an American mandate as part of the U.S. self-image as a world role model. In some cases, the two instincts even intermingle. The George W. Bush administration, for instance, believed that its response to the terrorist attacks of September 11, 2001, was a realist reaction to a provocative world, but that response contained the decidedly idealistic assumption that the promotion of political democracy (the American ideal) would be the best way to promote that change.

Political Orientation This dimension refers largely to the role that one believes that government should play in public life, which effectively translates into the question of governmental activism and the degree to which government as opposed to private solutions to problems is preferred. As such, it is a distinction most often applied to domestic politics and the hyperpartisanship of contemporary politics, but it applies to foreign policy questions as well.

Political orientation has become iconic and highly controversial in modern political discourse and is the real basis of the sharp bipartisan clash that has nearly paralyzed the American political system. The basic division is generally made between *liberalism* and *conservatism*, but these terms have become little more than pejorative labels without much substantive meaning. By slightly expanding the continuum beyond its liberal-conservative core to five categories across the spectrum, one can at least begin to make some sense about what it means to be of one political orientation or another.

It is arbitrary but necessary to start at one end of the spectrum or the other. The extremities are generally grouped as "left" or "right," terms which originally described seating in the French Assembly during the revolutionary period, when what are now called liberals (or leftists) sat to the left looking out from the speaker's rostrum and conservatives (or rightists) sat to the right.

The far left of the spectrum is radicalism. Radicals normally support major (radical), even fundamental political change. The change they prefer is normally associated with an increase in the role of government, and they are distinguished by a willingness to employ drastic, even violent (once again, radical) means to bring about change. True, operational communists can be thought of as radicals, as can contemporary religious *jihadists* (whose view of government involvement is decidedly theocratic). Almost all violent revolutions have a radical component.

Next to the radicals are the liberals. Classic liberalism starts from two basic premises. First, it emphasizes tolerance of the views and opinions of others; one synonym for the adjectival use of the term liberal is tolerant, and the opposite of liberal is illiberal or intolerant, generally pejorative terms. The other sense of liberal is change-orientation. Liberals generally have a positive view of social and political change—especially toward a more egalitarian, or in their view democratic, end, and they share a positive image of the role of government in promoting these ends. This sense of the term liberal is associated with both idealism and progressivism. In foreign policy, liberals generally support cooperative efforts in multilateral settings to global problems.

In the middle of the spectrum is pragmatism. Pragmatists begin from a generally neutral position on the role of government and social change, but believe that each case should stand on its own individual merits and should be assessed outside the bounds of any previous predilections. Historically, the synonyms for pragmatist have been moderate or centrist and have been considered virtuous. As the American political system has become more polarized, moderation has become equated with political blandness, indecisiveness, and even weakness. As indicated, it has been the so-called "moderate" wings of both political parties (but especially the GOP) that have suffered the most; many people who consider themselves moderate also classify themselves politically as independent.

To the immediate right of center are the conservatives. In its literal sense, the heart of conservatism is the preservation of the status quo: conservatives seek to "conserve" existing relationships among people and between people and the government. In operational terms, this translates into a preference for limited government and a lesser intrusion of government on the lives of individual Americans. This latter distinction varies in practice between the so-called "fiscal" and "social" conservatives. Fiscal conservatives more consistently oppose governmental activism because it intrudes on private commerce, whereas social conservatives are often quite active in the role they seek for government in matters about which they have particular concerns. Most conservatives do not extend their opposition to governmental intrusion to matters of national security and quite readily embrace the idea that governmental power should be used to intrude on the lives of those accused of opposition to the United States (for example, accused terrorists). While this position is certainly defensible, it is hardly conservative. While most conservatives favor limited government, they tend to support a strong national security stance.

Finally, reactionism stands at the far right end of the spectrum. Reactionaries not only want to hold onto the status quo, but also want to work actively to revert the existing order to some earlier set of relationships between government and citizens. They are "reactionary" in the sense that they react negatively to change and desire to effectively "roll back" ongoing governmental efforts. Like the radicals at the other end of the spectrum, some reactionaries favor violence (namely, anarchists) as a way to achieve their ends, but that is not universally true. Within the contemporary political debate, the clearest example of reactionism is libertarianism.

Two comments should be made about these distinctions. First, the boundaries are broad categories and are not rigid, nor is it always possible to adequately brand all individuals or groups into one or another category. By the definitions provided, for instance, the core constituency of the modern Republican Party is conservative and/or reactionary in philosophy, but which individuals or groups are one or the other? For the most part, it has become a positive attribute to be referred to as a conservative, but is it accurate to describe all Republicans as conservatives (for example, Kentucky's Rand Paul)? Similarly, one can make an argument that radical *jihadists* are either radicals (they favor change) or reactionaries (the change they favor is toward a past status quo). Second, people are not necessarily politically consistent across the range of political issues. George W. Bush, for instance, consistently thought of himself as a conservative on domestic issues, but elements of his foreign policy were decidedly liberal and activist (for instance, the promotion of democracy in Iraq).

Approaches to World Involvement The third distinction centers on the question of how active Americans should be in the world. Historically, there have been two major positions on American level of involvement in world affairs: internationalism and isolationism. Internationalists, as the name may suggest, view American involvement more positively, believing it is an inevitable and necessary duty of the United States to participate actively in world affairs. The reasons for this belief vary from a sense of obligation arising from America's unique position and moral place in the world to a simple observation that a country as large, powerful, and influential in the world as the United States, and thus possessing important interests globally, has little alternative to activism in the world. Isolationists, however, start from the same premise of exceptionalism as do the internationalists but reach the opposite conclusion. They believe that American uniqueness and prosperity are best served by concentrating on domestic issues and avoiding, to the greatest extent possible, interaction and involvement with outside influences.

These two positions have been more or less dominant at different times in American history, with the prominence of the United States in the world system a prime indicator of which approach predominates. The isolationist approach, minimizing foreign contacts and especially obligations, clearly dominated at the birth of the republic and is reflected in George Washington's Farewell Address, where he called for friendly relations with all states but "permanent alliances with none," and in Thomas Jefferson's first inaugural address, in which he warned against "entangling alliances." Some degree of isolationism remained throughout the nineteenth century, as the United States spread across the continent and confronted its great internal contradictions (the Civil War) and benefited from a minimal foreign policy. After being drawn reluctantly into World War I, the country returned to its last serious embrace of the isolationist philosophy during the interwar years.

Pearl Harbor and the subsequent German declaration of war on the United States effectively discredited isolationism, and when the United States and the Soviet Union emerged from the war as the two major standing powers in the world, internationalism replaced it as the dominant American approach. The successor to the isolationist preference, so-called "neoisolationism," preaches a much more diluted form of avoidance of international commitment, seeking to minimize but not to avoid U.S. involvement with the world altogether. Within the internationalist consensus, however, disagreement still

INTERSECTIONS

Neoconservatism

Paul D. Wolfowitz, seen with U.S. troops in this photograph, was deputy secretary of defense from 2001 to 2005 and is widely described as the principal architect of the U.S. War in Iraq. Wolfowitz was a leading neoconservative advocate and advisor to President George W. Bush.

A group of foreign policy advocates began to emerge in the 1980s and come to the fore during the Bush administration who have added to the partisan contentiousness of the foreign policy environment. The core of this group were disaffected Democrats who banded together as "Reagan Democrats" during the 1980s and are known as the neoconservatives (or "neocons"). Their position is distinctive and can be understood in terms of distinctions drawn in the text.

If one combines the concepts of approaches to involvement and participation preference in matrix form, the result is a rough approximation of the foreign orientations of different prominent groups in the United States. The matrix is represented in Figure 1.1.

The traditionally dominant schools of thought are located on the diagonals in Cells 1 and 4. During the Cold War, for instance, the dominant belief was that American involvement in and leadership of the Cold War was both necessary and correct (internationalism) and that the task could only be accomplished through cooperation with friends and allies (multilateralism), the positions represented by Cell 1. By contrast, the early period of American history was dominated by a strong

(Continued)

(Continued)

		Participation Preference	
		Multilateralism	Unilateralism
Approaches to	Internationalism	Cell 1	Cell 2
Involvement	Neoisolationism	Cell 3	Cell 4

FIGURE 1.1
Involvement and Participation Preference

belief in American aloofness from the world (isolationism, now neoisolationism) and that the United States should involve commitments to other countries (unilateralism), represented by Cell 4.

Neoconservatism is represented by Cell 2 of the matrix. The neoconservatives are specifically and explicitly internationalist in their orientation; during the Cold War, for instance, their lineal predecessors were highly militant anticommunists who believed in aggressively confronting communist expansionism. Since the end of the Cold War, they have switched their emphasis to the Middle East, where they are pro-Israeli and antiterrorist, with a particular emphasis on the promotion of the democratization of the Islamic Middle East as a way to achieve stability in the region by undercutting the terrorist appeal and thus reinforcing the security of Israel (their pro-democracy advocacy makes them idealists in realist-idealist terms, a categorization most of them reject). They are, however, also openly unilateralist in orientation, quick to assert that the United States should relegate to secondary importance multilateral considerations when those conflict with what they perceive to be American interests. This unilateralist penchant, it might be added, contributed to the international unease with Bush foreign policy, and the professed intention of the Obama administration to move the United States back toward a Cell 1 orientation was a large factor in international enthusiasm for the Obama candidacy.

exists on how that interaction should occur and using which instruments of policy, which form the last two dimensions of the personal inventory.

Participation Preference This dimension refers to preferences about the quality and nature of American interaction with the world, and it is a distinction that applies regardless of the approach to involvement one espouses. The two basic preferences are multilateralism and unilateralism, and both titles are descriptive. On the one hand, multilateralists prefer a cooperative approach wherein American policy and actions should, generally and wherever possible, be developed and coordinated with the policies of others, especially American friends and allies. The underlying assumptions of this approach are that American interests include keeping friends (which cooperation nurtures) and that the wisest and most durable policy solutions result from obtaining as broad an international consensus as possible. Unilateralists, on the other hand, believe that the United States should place its primary emphasis on its own national interests and should act on that basis, quite apart from what other countries may feel on a subject. Unilateralists are thus more willing to defy international opinion when that opinion is at cross-purposes with what are perceived as American interests, and it denies that cooperation is, in and of itself, an interest.

During the George W. Bush presidency, when the unilateralists had significant influence on foreign policy decisions, these two positions were portrayed as being more fundamentally at odds than they in fact are. Multilateralists, for instance, prefer solutions with maximum international support, but they will support unilateral decisions when international consensus is impossible. They will, however, ask if the fact that everyone else opposes a policy might be a warning sign about the virtue of that policy. Unilateralists prefer broadly agreed-upon solutions, but they are more willing to accept individual national responses to policy. The difference thus boils down to a more subtle distinction about preferences than it does to a basic division.

CONCLUSIONS

This chapter was introduced with a foreign policy event—the reaction of the Obama administration to a visit to Washington by Israeli Prime Minister Benjamin Netanyahu in 2011—that was intended to highlight emphases in the chapter. The thrust of the example was on the interchange as both a domestic and an international event. The domestic reaction centered on the way the administration dealt with the unofficial visit of a foreign leader with a very close relationship to the United States who was in the country soliciting support among supporters of Israel for particular policies opposed by the American government. The international dimension centered on the Israeli policy and disagreements between and among Americans and Israelis on how best to deal with the problem. The policy dispute crossed the intermestic intersection because of the domestic importance of support for Israel in the United States and partisan attempts to portray the Obama administration favorably or unfavorably for domestic political advantage by both the Israeli and American opponents of Obama.

The disagreement between the two countries also reflects the way the United States approaches foreign policy, the idea of a foreign policy culture. While the United States has been critical of the Israeli settlement policy, its opposition has been tempered by a level of sympathy for the Israelis that is not present in all countries, notably not in Europe, who have close relations with the Middle East. In turn, how individual Americans view this issue is a reflection on the individual collection of values that individuals have about foreign policy—the personal inventory.

Within the themes such as intermestic politics and hyperpartisanship introduced in this chapter, two major points of emphasis emerge that are reflected in the way that analysts approach and analyze American foreign policy, and each is a major vantage point from which the rest of the text proceeds. These two major vantage points are foreign policy processes and foreign policy issues. Following Chapter Two, which sets the historical context within which each of the vantage points must be viewed, the text is divided into two parts, one devoted to each vantage point and reflecting the themes already introduced.

Part One (Chapters Three through Eight) deals with foreign policy processes, as its title advertises. Chapter Three introduces the idea of policy process as an analytical tool for studying foreign policy and offers a sample of ways analysts have devised to conduct those studies. This chapter helps create a framework for studying the various formal institutional (the President and executive agencies assisting him and the Congress) and informal (interest groups and think tanks, the public and the media) actors in the other chapters of the process part. In Part Two, the emphasis shifts to different foreign policy issue areas. Two chapters each are devoted to the most prominent substantive aspects of policy: national security and economic issues. The final chapter addresses a number of important nontraditional policy matters, sometimes called trans-state issues.

WHERE DO WE GO FROM HERE?

This chapter represents the beginning of the path of examination of study of American foreign policy. As will be the case in subsequent chapters, this final section consists of three elements: an application of the principles discussed in the chapter, some study questions to help organize an understanding of the chapter, and some selected bibliographical references.

APPLICATION: YOUR PERSONAL INVENTORY AND THE OBAMA-NETANYAHU EXAMPLE

Using the following questions as a guide, rate yourself on the four dimensions of the personal inventory on foreign policy attitudes:

1. Basic worldview: Should the basic orientation of policy makers be to adapt to and make the best of the world situation as it is (realism), or should they primarily try to change world conditions (idealism)?
2. Political orientation: Should government seek to change policy greatly through any method (radicalism); promote change toward social justice through moderate, tolerant reform action (liberalism); view situations and the desirability of change solely on the individual merits in situations (pragmatism); seek to preserve existing relationships within a limited role for government (conservatism); or seek to remove or roll back existing conditions (reactionism)?
3. Approaches to World Involvement: Should the United States play a basically activist leadership role in the world (internationalism), or should it seek to avoid international involvement wherever possible (neoisolationism)?
4. Participation Preference: Should the United States generally try to build international consensus before acting (multilateralism), or should it look at its own interests first with less regard for international preferences (unilateralism)?

After assembling your own personal inventory, apply the inventory to the principals in the Israeli-U.S. example, Barack Obama and Benjamin Netanyahu, on the question of the two-state solution. The Obama position is essentially that resistance to creating a Palestinian state is "unsustainable," a deal breaker, in trying to achieve an internationally acceptable Israeli-Palestinian peace settlement. The Netanyahu position is that a settlement based on the pre-1967 borders is "indefensible," because it would jeopardize Israeli national security. Build your inventory as best you can given the limited amount of information you have about the actors. Compare the two profiles. Compare the profiles to your own. Whose comes closer to yours? How do you feel about the issue? Does this analysis help clarify your thought processes?

STUDY/DISCUSSION QUESTIONS

1. Discuss the dispute between Israel and the United States that came to the fore in March 2010. On what issue does the dispute rest? Given the nature of the dispute and the reasons for Netanyahu's visit to Washington, what was the U.S. government response, and was it appropriate?
2. What are the various environments in which American foreign policy is made? How have they changed over time? Include in your answer the changing concept of the "water's edge"?
3. Discuss the changing nature of the international environment for foreign policy, including sovereignty, state centrism, and the rise of nonstate actors.
4. How has the domestic environment changed since the end of the Cold War? Specifically, what have been the causes and consequences of the rise in extreme partisanship?
5. Discuss how changes in the domestic and international environments have affected the "intermestic intersection" where much foreign policy is made?
6. How are the environmental distinctions important in understanding how foreign policy is studied? Elaborate.
7. Describe and discuss the dimensions of the personal inventory for determining orientations toward foreign policy.

CORE SUGGESTED READINGS

Carr, E. H. *The Twenty-Years Crisis: 1919–1939*. London: Macmillan, 1939. This is the classic critique of the idealism that predominated during the period between the world wars on international relations, emphasizing how the world drifted toward World War II. Its critique and its advocacy of what became realism still have considerable relevance to understanding contemporary politics.

Fromkin, David. *The Independence of Nations*. New York: Praeger Special Studies, 1981. This slender volume written by a leading international lawyer is one of the clearest expositions about the nature of a state-centered international system grounded in the principle of sovereignty.

Kagan, Robert, and William Kristol (eds.). *Present Dangers: Crises and Opportunities in American Foreign and Defense Policy*. San Francisco: Encounter Books, 2000. At the time of its publication, this book was considered the "bible" of neoconservatism. While its authors' analyses of particular problems are somewhat dated, its underlying themes remain central to the neoconservative value system.

Nye, Joseph S. Jr. *The Paradox of American Power: Why the World's Only Superpower Can't Go It Alone.* New York: Oxford University Press, 2003. Nye's exposition is a classic representation of the traditional internationalist/multilateralist position and a direct attempt to refute the neoconservative argument, including an exposition and defense of the idea of "soft power" (the power of American ideals).

Singer, Max, and the Estate of the Late Aaron Wildavsky. *The Real World Order: Zones of Peace, Zones of Turmoil* (Rev. ed.). Chatham, NJ: Chatham House, 1996. This is one of the most original yet compelling analyses of the contemporary world environment. The categories and discussions remain relevant and intriguing a decade-and-a-half after they were originally published.

ADDITIONAL READINGS AND REFERENCES

Brooks, Stephen G., and William C. Wohlforth. "Reshaping the World Order." *Foreign Affairs* 88, 2 (March/April 2009), 49–63.

Brzezinski, Zbigniew. "From Hope to Audacity." *Foreign Affairs* 89, 1 (January/February 2010), 16–29.

Carafano, James J., and Paul Rosenzweig. *Winning the Long War: Lessons from the Cold War and Defeating Terrorism and Preserving Freedom.* Washington, DC: Heritage Books, 2005.

Ferguson, Niall. "The Axis of Upheaval." *Foreign Policy*, March/April 2009, 55–60.

________. "Complexity and Change." *Foreign Affairs* 89, 2 (March/April 2010), 18–32.

Gates, Robert. "A Balanced Strategy." *Foreign Affairs* 88, 1 (January/February 2009), 28–39.

Gelb, Leslie. "Necessity, Choice, and Common Sense." *Foreign Affairs* 88, 3 (May/June 2009), 56–72.

Joffe, Josef. "The Default Power." *Foreign Affairs* 88, 5 (September/October 2009), 21–35.

Kissinger, Henry. *A World Restored.* Boston: Houghton Mifflin, 1973.

Machiavelli, Niccolo. *The Prince.* Irving, TX: University of Dallas Press, 1984 (Original work published in 1513).

Miller, Steven E. "The End of Unilateralism or Unilateralism Redux." *Washington Quarterly* 25, 1 (Winter 2001/2002), 15–30.

Newhouse, John. "Diplomacy, Inc." *Foreign Affairs* 88, 3 (May/June 2009), 73–92.

Nye, Joseph S. Jr. *Bound to Lead: The Changing Nature of American Power.* New York: Basic Books, 1990.

Snow, Donald M. *Cases in International Relations* (5th ed.). New York: Pearson Longman, 2012.

_______. *National Security for a New Era* (4th ed.). New York: Pearson Longman, 2011.

_______, and Dennis M. Drew. *From Lexington to Baghdad and Beyond* (3rd ed.). Armonk, NY: M E Sharpe, 2010.

Thucydides. *The History of the Peloponnesian Wars.* New York: Penguin, 1994.

Tucker, Robert W., and David C. Hendrickson. "The Sources of American Legitimacy." *Foreign Affairs* 83, 6 (November/December 2004), 18–32.

Walt, Stephen M. "Taming American Power." *Foreign Affairs* 84, 5 (September/October 2005), 105–120.

Watanabe, Akio. "A Continuum of Change." *Washington Quarterly* 27, 4 (Autumn 2004), 137–146.

CHAPTER 2

Paradigm Lost: The Cold War to the Present

The most famous Russian spy exchanged by the United States at the July 2010 "swap" was Anna Chapman, a Russian-born agent who had been living in New York since 2008 and pleaded guilty to conspiracy to act as the agent of a foreign power without registering with the U.S. government as a term of her exchange back to the Russian Federation.

PREVIEW

Modern American foreign policy has been through two distinct periods since the United States emerged as a major international power at the end of World War II. The first period was the Cold War, which developed during the second half of the 1940s and ended with the demise of the Soviet Union in 1991. The United States developed its first broad, overarching foreign policy paradigm, containment, to deal with that period. The collapse of Soviet communism represented the first of two "fault lines" that ended the Cold War and changed the nature of the international system and thus the environment in which foreign policy operates. The second fault line was September 11, 2001. These two events have left the policy of containment questionably applicable to the contemporary world, necessitating the search for a new paradigm to help organize policy toward a changed world.

KEY CONCEPTS

isolationism
collective security
Cold War
containment
bipolarity
Cuban Missile Crisis
superpowers
arms control
neutralism
deterrence
Truman Doctrine
Marshall Plan
North Atlantic Treaty Organization
fault lines
globalization
terrorism

In late June 2010, Americans were surprised by the revelation that ten Russian "sleeper agents" had been arrested in the United States as the culmination of a long investigation and surveillance by the Federal Bureau of Investigation. While it was not clear at the time exactly what espionage or intelligence function these agents were supposed to be performing, it nonetheless came as an unpleasant surprise to see that the United States' former Cold War adversary was apparently up to the same old tricks as those in which it engaged when it was the Soviet Union. It was also a reminder that the current clandestine competition with international religious terrorism is not something unique in purpose or in methods: Efforts to find and expose Al Qaeda and other terrorist spies or espionage agents have their parallels in the Cold War.

The idea of sleeper agents, persons who have, in the words of the Internet encyclopedia *Wikipedia*, "infiltrated into the target and 'gone to sleep,' sometimes for many years" is certainly nothing new, in fact and within the imagination of writers and moviemakers. Possibly the most infamous sleeper agent was Soviet spy Kim Philby, who penetrated deeply into the British security and intelligence system in the 1950s before fleeing to the Soviet Union. Before him, Soviet spies penetrated the inner workings of Nazi Germany, and these "illegals," as the Russians named them, became prominent heroes of the post-Soviet External Intelligence Service (SVR), praised by leaders no less prominent than Russian former president and current Prime Minister Vladimir Putin. Indeed, the 2010 scandal appeared to have been orchestrated by SVR, a successor of the old Soviet-era KGB's Directorate S. The crisis even ended in a way familiar from Cold War days: The Russian sleepers were convicted in a U.S. court, then whisked onto a jet airliner and transported to Vienna, Austria (itself a Cold War espionage hot spot), where the ten spies were exchanged for four Russians who allegedly had spied for the United States and who were discreetly transferred from a Russian plane to the waiting American airplane. Although the exchange occurred in the sunlight of a clear day in Vienna, one could not help but compare it to the closing scene of the 1942 movie classic "Casablanca."

The common theme of phenomena like sleeper agents is to remind Americans of the threat posed by hostile powers who act in various ways to weaken the position of the United States in the world through overt and covert action. The perpetrators during the twentieth century were the Nazis and Soviet communists, but they, by and large, have died off or dissipated in strength and numbers. They have, however, been replaced by the rise of international religious terrorists, Islamic *jihadi,* either having infiltrated into the United States (or Europe) or having been recruited from vulnerable communities in Western countries to carry out clandestine acts of violence. According to Bakier (writing in a 2008 publication of the Jamestown Foundation), "the security and intelligence echelons of the United States have been preoccupied with the possibility of domestic Al-Qaeda sleeper cells being activated to perpetrate additional terrorist attacks." The worst nightmares surround so-called "lone wolves," what Bakier calls "highly trained loners" whose isolation makes them especially difficult to detect and defeat.

What the 2010 incident demonstrates more clearly than anything else is the continuity of foreign policy. In the frenetic atmosphere of the post-9/11 environment, there has been a temptation to believe that the world had changed so fundamentally that it is impossible to compare it with previous periods. That the onslaught of terrorist violence has changed much of the context and even some of the direction of policy is unquestionable, but whether what has happened is the simple substitution of one adversary for another is a proposition not to be dismissed out of hand. Terrorists do what the Soviets and Nazis and others before them have done for reasons that are not necessarily all that different from the motives underlying the actions of current adversaries. While what worked in the past may not work perfectly in the present or future, it may provide useful ways to view and organize thinking about and dealing with the present. Until proven otherwise, the past is not irrelevant.

The title of this chapter is "Paradigm Lost." It is, of course, a play on words, but it reflects a more substantial consideration. For most of the second half of the twentieth century, the United States was engaged in a serious competition with the Soviet Union, and this country adopted an effective framework for dealing with the challenge posed by Soviet (and Chinese) communism: the Cold War paradigm of containment. With the collapse of the Soviet Union and the withering of operational communism (adherence to the general political and economic dictates of Marxism), that paradigm became irrelevant to understanding the world, an historic oddity that simply did not fit current and evolving threats. To organize dealing with the post–Cold War effort, for twenty years the United States has needed to develop a new framework, a paradigm for the one that has been lost. The effort is ongoing.

The spy scandal is a reminder of the truth that while things change, they also remain the same. The quest for a new organizational paradigm for the contemporary world requires looking at the recent past to see how that past affects the present and what may be learned from it to help better organize understanding the future—hopefully leading to a new paradigm found.

THE COLD WAR

The modern era of American foreign policy, which provides the context for dealing with the present and future of America's dealings with the world, begins at the end of World War II. The reason for selecting that event as the break point for the evolution of U.S. foreign policy is not arbitrary: World War II is the event that propelled the United States into the absolute center of international politics as one of the world's leading powers, a position that it had not occupied previously and which it had been reluctant to assume before the second great conflagration of the twentieth century.

The Postwar World

Prior to World War II, the United States had occupied a growing but peripheral role in the international scheme of things. In the early days of the American republic, it had been a relatively underpopulated territory far from the European center of world affairs, the involvement of which in the major affairs of states was neither necessary nor particularly solicited. The importance of the United States grew in the last third of the nineteenth century, as a post–Civil War United States earnestly engaged in completing its Manifest Destiny within the contiguous forty-eight states and evolved as a major industrial power, the productivity of which challenged that of the great states of the European balance of power by the early twentieth century. When the European balance collapsed into the bloody disarray of World War I, the power of the adolescent United States was ultimately called upon to help restore order, but after the war's conclusion, the United States returned to the cocoon of international noninvolvement for one last period of "splendid **isolationism,**" wherein the United States retreated (isolated itself) from engagement in politico-military but not economic foreign affairs.

The limited role of the United States in the world during the first century and a half or so of American existence was both a matter of choice and circumstance. For much of this period, the United States was, in the terms used now to discuss such matters, a developing country, and one that needed and preferred to devote most of its energy to transforming its part of the

North American continent. That transformation required waves of immigrant populations to settle the great spaces of the continental United States and the influx of large amounts of capital, mostly from Europe, to provide the financing for the transformation. In the middle of this period, the country turned fratricidal to determine what the character of the emerging country would be like, a further drain on resources and incentive to turn inward, not outward. In these circumstances, the best foreign policy was the least foreign policy.

Circumstances conspired to reinforce and allow this emphasis. The French Revolution, which began less than a decade after the American Revolution concluded, introduced new political and social forces into Europe with which Europeans would have to grapple for most of the nineteenth century, including political democratization and the Industrial Revolution. Such outward looking as the Europeans engaged in was directed at colonizing those parts of the African and Asian world that had not previously been the "beneficiaries" of European domination. Major conflicts occurred at either end of what amounted to a century of adjustment: the Napoleonic Wars that ended in 1815 and World War I. Symptomatically, the United States became involved in both: The War of 1812 was a very peripheral theater of the Napoleonic Wars (happily for the Americans, because it meant a halfhearted British effort against them), and the United States became a pivotal source of fresh strength to help bring about the end of the Great War in 1918.

The seeds of the changes that would transpire in 1945 had their origins in the period between the world wars. World War I did not settle the fundamental divisions between the European powers that centered on French-German rivalry so much as it offered a third installment (the first two being the Napoleonic Wars and the Franco-Prussian War of 1871) in what would be a four-round slugfest that left both countries prostrate. At the end of World War I, President Woodrow Wilson played a major role in trying to restructure international politics, but due to a number of factors that included domestic partisan politics, the United States did not sign the peace settlement or join the League of Nations that was supposed to organize an enduring peace in Europe. Instead, the United States retreated for one last nostalgic period of isolation from the politics of the world.

World War II completed the transformation of the international system and the American place in it. At the international level, the old European balance of power lay shattered, with the traditional powers such as Great Britain, France, Germany, and Italy either defeated and occupied or triumphant, but so materially and physically exhausted by the effort that they could no longer assert their leadership roles in the world. Only two countries retained significant power in the world—the United States and the Union of Soviet Socialist Republics (USSR or Soviet Union)—and they would have to step forward and reorganize international politics with themselves as the principal anchors of the world order.

The emergence of these two powers was in many ways enigmatic. Both countries came to the center stage of world politics as relative amateurs. The United States had little experience in managing world affairs as a matter of self-preference, and considerable domestic opposition remained after the war to an activist foreign policy that would thrust the country into the center of world affairs. The Soviets were much more enthusiastic about the chance to become an international power, as it gave them the opportunity to spread the communist gospel, but they were equally inexperienced, having been consciously shunned as members of the European community after the Bolshevik Revolution of 1918 (especially after it failed to collapse).

The two countries came out of the war with very different circumstances. American casualties in the war were comparatively light (a little over 405,000), the United States was never directly attacked and physically ravaged, and turning the Great Depression-ravaged American economy into the "arsenal of democracy" helped pull the United States back toward economic prosperity. In balance, the United States was the only major country in the world that was actually strengthened by the war. By contrast, the Soviet Union had been invaded by Germany in 1941 and had incurred enormous destruction to its infrastructure (industry and population centers) and had lost nearly twelve million people, mostly military personnel. The United States stood at the pinnacle of economic capability and military power—being the sole possessor of nuclear weapons, whereas the major and virtually only claim of the Soviets to a position of importance was the retention of a huge standing armed force in occupation of much of Central and Eastern Europe after the war.

Their emergence as the antagonistic pillars of a new international order was curious and enigmatic, however. Prior to the end of the Cold War, the Americans and Russians had no sustained history of animosity between them after the Russian foray down the American West Coast during the nineteenth century was stopped and reversed in California and concluded with the sale of Alaska to the United States ("Seward's Folly"). At the same time, the countries possessed different, contrasting, and ultimately incompatible worldviews, and each possessed an evangelical belief that their vision of the world should be shared and spread—and since they were so diametrically opposed, support of one became opposition to the other.

The grail for the United States was capitalist democracy, a commitment to the economic free enterprise system and political democracy. The contrasting view was communism, based in Marxism tempered by its autocratic application to the Soviet Union. From Marxism, the Soviets inherited an adherence to socialist economics. Theoretical Marxism is also highly democratic: the ultimate form of communism is supposed to be anarchy, in which everyone makes all decisions for themselves—thus total democracy. Apart from the practicality of this vision, its adoption by the Soviet communists had added authoritarian political rule as a pretended way to facilitate the transition to the communist "utopia." In reality and practice, it meant that a socialist, authoritarian Soviet Union faced a capitalist, democratic United States. It was a face-off in which there were few if any common points of reference. One of the victims of this situation was the practicality of a minimal foreign policy: least was no longer best.

In the early evolution of the war's aftermath, the question that increasingly arose was what the character of the Soviet–American relationship would be. Clearly, that relationship would be the linchpin of the new international order; the poles of possibility were a continuation of the wartime collaboration and cooperation, or the emergence of an ideologically based competition. To those who would formulate the international system after World War II, the consensus was that cooperation would likely be the victim of the competition. Events would reinforce this belief.

The planners of the postwar peace hedged their bets institutionally on this question. The United Nations succeeded the League of Nations as the primary international body to try to organize and sustain the peace. It did so by assigning matters of world security to the Security Council, composed of the major victorious Allies (the United States, Britain, France, the Soviet Union, and China) as permanent members and a rotating cast of other states as nonpermanent members. Under the original conceptualization (which was never implemented), the physical task of enforcing the peace was to fall on the armed forces of the permanent members aided by others as required, and each of the permanent members was given a veto over any proposed action. Beyond constabulary forces, the rest of the world was to be substantially disarmed, leaving the permanent members with an overwhelming preponderance of world force to ensure that potential violators of the peace could and would be frustrated in their efforts.

For this scheme to work, the wartime Allies had to be in substantial agreement about the kind of peace they would enforce and when, if at all, force was to be tolerated to bring about change. This requirement followed from the assignment of hegemonic force to them acting in concert, whereas such a monopoly of force would not obtain if they acted individually. What the framers created was a mechanism for the peace to be maintained if the member states could make that system work; the linchpin of utility, however, was cooperation, principally among the two major powers (the United States and the Soviet Union), who maintained the majority of military power at the time.

The system came with a disabler in the form of the veto, which shut down the **collective security system** that underlay the plan. The idea of collective security, briefly put, is that if all powerful members of a system agree to enforce the peace, they will have sufficient forces available to deter any potential violator of the peace, who will know in advance his attempt would be defeated. This was done purposefully by the framers of the UN Charter, who were mindful of the prospect of U.S.-Soviet discord rather than cooperation. As Inis Claude put it eloquently a half century ago, "Cooperation (between the major powers) was not necessarily certain, but it was certainly necessary" for this system to work. In the event that world peace could not be organized around the UN ideal (which most analysts suspected would be the case), the UN Charter provided for a conventional organization of the system among competing blocs (Article 51 of the Charter, the so-called "collective defense" article). Thus, the UN Charter hedged its bets by producing the parameters for the emergence of two fundamentally different ways of organizing the peace.

What unhinged the development of a system of world peace organized around the United Nations was the very real gulf between the United States and the Soviet Union on the political shape of the world they would oversee. Any collective security system is status quo (the situation as it is) loaded, in the sense that it poses a barrier to change, in this case by violence. In order to be willing to shed blood to maintain a status quo, one must agree on the world one is saving. In the case of the Soviet Union, their preference was for a system increasingly composed of communist states, whereas the United States had an equally heartfelt preference for a system of market democracies. Since the two systems could not coexist (and one might well succeed at the violent hand of the other), there was no world on which the two could agree. In that circumstance, a world peace centered on the Security Council was simply disabled, effectively put in mothballs until circumstances might arise, as they at least partly did in the 1990s, wherein the major powers could agree on a world order they could mutually support.

Events in the late 1940s reinforced these divisions. The Soviets gradually tightened their stranglehold over the occupied states of Eastern Europe over Western objections, and the democracies of Western Europe came together in the North Atlantic Treaty Organization (NATO), among other forms of cooperation. In 1947, Winston Churchill declared at Fulton, Missouri, that an "iron curtain" had descended on Europe, dividing the communist and noncommunist halves with a steel fence. At the same time, the competition between the United States and the Soviet Union was extending to other parts of the world. These kinds of events were effectively answering negatively the question of whether collaboration and cooperation between the two was possible. For any who may have had lingering doubts, the definitive answer came when North Korean communist forces, presumably aided and abetted by the Soviets, streamed across the border into South Korea in June 1950. All doubts that a Cold War would ensue were removed by that act and the Korean War that followed.

The Cold War Concept

The Cold War was the overarching structure and dynamic of international politics during the second half of the twentieth century. Since it was "cold" (it involved no physical, "hot" war) throughout, it was not so much a war as it was a competition that its practitioners feared might somehow be transformed into an actual war at any time—one with apocalyptic consequences for the participants and possibly humankind as a whole. The dynamics of the Cold War grew gradually during the second half of the 1940s, and the designation of any starting point is nebulous and arbitrary, as actions and counteractions by both sides gradually led to deteriorating relations and increased enmity. Certainly the basic dynamics were in place by the time of the Korean War.

The end of the Cold War is easier to describe. Since the principal dynamic of the Cold War was Soviet-American competition, the Cold War ended with the surprising demise of the Soviet Union at the last click of the clock in December 1991 in Moscow (when the Soviet Union was formally dissolved). A number of events in the 1980s helped lead to that fateful and largely unanticipated event, but the climactic event was the end of the Soviet Union and the dramatic decline of communism as an active force in the world.

The Cold War was not a static event, but rather a dynamic set of circumstances and relationships that evolved, and it is with that evolution that the discussion begins. From the evolutionary nature of the competition, a number of characteristics of the competition emerged that form the basis of some comparison with the current system. As part of those changing dynamics, the United States developed a major paradigm for organizing and dealing with the Cold War in the form of the policy of **containment**, the paradigm that has been lost with the end of the Cold War. The ways in which the Cold War deadlocked and ended in turn have effects on how Americans and others continue to look at the post–Cold War world.

Cold War Evolution

The Cold War was not immutable and unchanging. Rather, the set of very complex relationships between the two sides changed and evolved across the forty-plus years of the competition. It was probably most intense and the expectations about it most pessimistic during its early years (the 1950s and early 1960s), and although competition, distrust, and mutual fear continued until the end, the intensity and pervasiveness of the relationship slowly and gradually relaxed as the two sides came to understand the necessity of avoiding overt conflict (war) between them.

The core of the international system of the Cold War was **bipolarity**, the idea that there were two major powers (or poles) in the world system, and other states tended to congregate around those major powers, attracted by similarities of ideas and ideals, bound by force, or some combination of the two. The principal source of attraction for those countries attracted to the American "orbit" (as the association around the poles was sometimes described) was American economic prowess and political ideals; the Soviets tended to keep their orbit together more through the imposition of military force upon their "allies."

The nature of bipolarity, like the nature of the Cold War itself, evolved across time. In the early years of the competition (through the latter 1950s, and arguably somewhat afterward), the relationship was described as one of "tight" bipolarity, meaning the two major powers could maintain strict—or tight—control over their satellite states. This form of bipolarity gradually evolved into what was called "loose" bipolarity, a condition wherein client and affiliated states could still be controlled for some purposes, but in which those states could exercise increasing levels of independence of action in selected areas. The bipolar control of the two major powers was also loosened by the gradual trend toward decolonization in the Afro-Asian world, wherein the former colonies of the European states achieved independence. These countries, by and large, were not interested in being involved as partisans in the Cold War competition and thus could not easily be controlled by the major powers. Bipolarity gradually receded from descriptions of the two sides, and by the time the Cold War unraveled, it was hardly ever used to describe the system's dynamics.

Parallel to the evolution of bipolarity was a gradual change in the intensity and inevitability of the relationship. When the Cold War was first engaged, there was the widespread belief that it was pervasive and intractable, a sentiment accompanied by morbidly fatalistic predictions about its outcomes. The underlying basis and assumption of this dire outlook about the present and future was the shared perception that the two competitors were totally and absolutely opposed to one another on all matters and at all depths, that there was no common ground between them on which they could base a mutual future, and that the result was that the competition could only end in some fiery Armageddon, from which both would perish. For many, the question was not whether this would happen, but *when.*

This set of beliefs was particularly strong in the 1950s. In some ways, it was politically hysterical in the United States, featuring a whole series of anticommunist "witch hunts" to root out supposed communists and their insidious influence from American institutions. The hysteria was particularly associated with the fiery junior senator from Wisconsin, Joseph ("Tail Gunner Joe") McCarthy, whose communist hunting finally crashed on the shore of attempting to purge the U.S. Army of supposed subversive influences. In the process, the era spawned a bizarre, even ghoulish popular culture. Americans seriously debated the question of "better red than dead" or "better dead than red," a way to distinguish whether it was preferable to die in the irradiated flames of nuclear war or to surrender to "godless communism" (a reference to the atheistic basis of Marxism). Movie box offices were enriched by apocalyptic films such as *On the Beach* (where the world is destroyed by the lethal aftermath of a nuclear war) and *Dr. Strangelove* (where the world ends in some part because of plans to avoid its destruction). What fueled acceptance of these projected outcomes of the Cold War was the intensity born of the belief that a violent conclusion in the form of a nuclear World War III was not only the likely, but the inevitable, outcome of the competition and that it likely could not be avoided, only its avoidance prolonged.

The event that transformed the Cold War and which, in retrospect, served as its watershed was the **Cuban Missile Crisis** of 1962. The missile crisis was, in the view of most observers at the time, the closest that the two Cold War contenders had ever come—or subsequently came—to making the Cold War go hot. The phenomenon that made the Cuban crisis as significant as it was came from the development and deployment of large and growing arsenals of nuclear weapons by both sides that had added qualitatively to the deadliness of a hot war between them. In the end, it was the recognition that the outcomes of such a conflict were totally unacceptable to both sides that caused them to understand that they indeed had a common interest in not destroying the world, a realization that served as the wedge for improving relations between them, thereby serving as a watershed in the competition.

A positive outcome was certainly not apparent when the crisis began. The heart of the crisis was a Soviet attempt to place nuclear-tipped missiles (intermediate range ballistic missiles or IRBMs) clandestinely on the Cuban island, aimed at the United States. The reasons appear, in retrospect, to have been threefold. First and most important, they were intended to narrow a large gap in nuclear capability between the two countries; at the time, the U.S. advantage in deliverable warheads (nuclear bombs that could reach targets in the Soviet Union) was about five to one, and the Cuban missiles would narrow that gap. Second, Nikita Khrushchev, the Soviet leader, perceived U.S. President John F. Kennedy to be too weak and indecisive to react to the deployment; the Soviets thought they could get away with it. Third, Khrushchev was under pressure from his own military to act more forcefully toward the U.S., and deploying missiles to Cuba seemed a way to flex Soviet muscle.

American U-2 reconnaissance flights over Cuba, however, revealed the construction of sites to accommodate the missiles, and the United States reacted with strong objections and demands that the sites be dismantled and the project abandoned. After tense deliberations within the U.S. government (Allison's account is the most definitive, Robert Kennedy's the most intimate), the Kennedy administration announced a naval "quarantine" of the island (effectively a blockade) to keep Soviet ships bearing missiles from reaching the island. For several days, the ships continued to sail toward the blockade line, and there was growing fear that the Cold War was about to go hot. Only at the last moment, after intense negotiations, did the Soviets back away from the delivery of the missiles and agree to destroy the missile sites on the island.

The missile crisis was an enormously traumatic and cathartic event. It was the first time that both countries seriously confronted the very real prospect of a nuclear holocaust that would destroy them both, and the prospect frightened them. Humankind peered into the abyss and did not like what it saw, and from that revelation, there gradually emerged what was at the time a revelatory realization that the two nuclear giants did share at least one value: their own survival. While that recognition may seem narrow in scope, it did provide the wedge for the beginnings of some cooperation between them, a "necessary peace," as one of the authors described it in a 1987 book, which could gradually expand.

The Cuban Missile Crisis thus traumatized the **superpowers**. In the Cold War world, the term *superpower* had been devised to describe the most powerful countries in the world, and the defining characteristic of power was the possession of nuclear weapons in large numbers. The lesson of the missile crisis, however, was that there was a very real difference between *possessing* these weapons and actually *using* them that included the notion that nuclear weapons possession might have utility for keeping an opponent from using its nuclear weapons against you, but that their utility might end at that point: When the nuclear bombs started dropping, everyone began to lose. This fundamental realization may still have considerable relevance, an idea explored later in the book.

The major manifestation of the recognition of a shared survival interest grounded in fear was the beginning of nuclear **arms control** negotiations between the superpowers. These negotiations had two major emphases at that time and since: the limitation of the size and nature of the nuclear arsenals of nuclear weapons–possessing states, and the limitation of the number of states that gain nuclear weapons (nuclear proliferation). The two superpowers, along with Great Britain, signed the first such agreement a year after the Cuban crisis in 1963—the Limited Test Ban Treaty—and the first agreement on limiting the spread of nuclear weapons to states that do not already possess them in 1968 with the signing of the Nuclear Non-Proliferation Treaty (NPT). These efforts remained vital elements in Soviet–American relations throughout the remainder of the Cold War, providing the basis for détente between the two countries that saw the nuclear arms control common ground expand to other areas of discovered mutual interest. Both of these arms control thrusts remain active security emphases in the contemporary environment.

Many of these beneficial dynamics were not immediately evident at the end of the missile crisis, and in some ways, the competition between the two superpowers only expanded and worsened in the years after the Cuban adventure ended. In particular, the nuclear arsenals of the two sides expanded greatly, from the roughly two thousand weapons available to each combatant in the early 1960s to strategic arsenals (weapons capable of being launched against the other's homeland) of well over ten to twelve thousand at the height of the competition. Much of this expansion was due to technological innovation, notably the advent and deployment of so-called multiple independently targetable reentry vehicles (MIRVs), devices that allowed several nuclear weapons to be delivered by a single rocket. Despite this expansion, the underlying dynamic of the relationship was subtly changing, a realization of which was not truly achieved until the 1980s, when the Cold War began to unravel.

This change can be described in terms of the relationship between the *deadliness* and *dangerousness* of the nuclear relationship. As arsenals grew in size, the potential deadliness of a nuclear exchange in terms of the devastation it would create grew exponentially and, arguably, to a physical capability that overwhelmed any possible use to which it might be directed (what could be accomplished by launching twelve thousand nuclear weapons on either side?). Nuclear arsenals gradually reached and surpassed the level of mutual assured destruction (MAD), whereby both sides would be destroyed utterly if "the balloon went up," the euphemistic description of starting a nuclear war.

The recognition of deadliness affected the dangerousness of the relationship: the likelihood that matters would be allowed to deteriorate to the point that nuclear war might occur. The relationship was inverse and enigmatic: The more deadly the weapons balance became, the less dangerous it became. The driving motive was not, of course, any altruistic feeling on either side about the other, but a cold calculation that nuclear war was "inadmissible," as the Soviets liked to describe it. The two sides would probably have come to this realization had they not peered into the abyss in the missile crisis, but having done so certainly helped lead to the enigma of a more deadly but less dangerous world.

The Cuban Missile Crisis was thus truly a watershed event. Prior to the missile crisis, the relationship between the two Cold War combatants was marked with numerous crisis events (for example, the series of clashes over Berlin, including the Berlin airlift and the construction of the Berlin Wall) with escalatory potential that the two sides did not act rapidly to defuse. After 1962, however, those kinds of traumatic events essentially disappeared, as both sides progressively avoided direct confrontations that could devolve to face-to-face encounters that might somehow get out of hand and lead into an unwanted maelstrom of nuclear war. Although recognition of it was slow to occur, the aftermath of Cuba also began to point to the futility of the entire enterprise of a Cold War that could have no climactic outcome. The Cold War could not be allowed to become hot, and over time, the meaningfulness of a competition with neither end nor victor became increasingly anomalous.

This 180-degree turn in the underlying dynamics of the Cold War was not at all obvious to the participants at the time. The mere fact that the Soviets had tried to place nuclear missiles in America's "backyard" infuriated Americans and intensified anticommunist furor in the United States. Anticommunism was reinforced by the other dynamics of the Cold War relationship, some of which are encapsulated in the characteristics of that relationship.

Cold War Characteristics

Two decades after the end of the Cold War, it is difficult to appreciate just how overarching and dominating a phenomenon it was. The Cold War was the most important international reality for two generations of Americans and most of the rest of the world, and it was a not-so-tender embrace from which neither side saw any end—until it was over. The Cold War was both the premier foreign policy fact of life for over forty years and an enduring reality with no apparent end point. The characteristics of the Cold War helped to reinforce the images that its participants held and made the end of the Cold War all the more traumatic and incomprehensible.

For the present purposes, three overlapping and reinforcing characteristics can be identified and briefly described. First, the Cold War was *the dominant politico-military reality of the international environment.* The two superpowers and their adversarial relations represented the premier reality with which others in the world, as well as the participants, had to deal. The international system throughout the period was bipolar, a depiction that both described the number of dominant players in the system and how they interacted with one another and the rest of the world. Particularly in the first decade-and-a-half or so before the emergence of newly independent countries in Africa and Asia, international actions were largely measured in terms of their compatibility with and impact on the Soviet–American relationship. Clearly, the major focus of this concern was on the nuclear balance between the two and the perception that the relationship was fragile, such that anything that might upset it would sever the Damoclean thread that served to prevent nuclear war.

This pervasiveness and global reach gradually deteriorated. A major factor was the effect of the independence of the formerly colonized states of Africa and Asia. Their impact was double-edged, however. Most of these new states came to conclude that their best interests were not served by partisan dedication to one or the other Cold War side. The result was the rise of **neutralism**, or noninvolvement, in Cold War considerations beyond playing one side off against the other for developmental assistance that they hoped would narrow the material gap between themselves and the most developed countries.

The developing world also became the major ground for Cold War competition aimed at converting the uncommitted to one evangelical philosophy or the other. Many of the new countries were politically unstable, providing a base from which opposition movements, often violent, would emerge, and these conflicts provided surrogates for the superpowers to pursue their competition. Since most of these new states were politically, economically, and geographically peripheral to the central competition, however, the outcomes of these surrogate competitions were generally not so important that either side could not avoid defeat, thereby minimizing the incentives to escalate situations to the point that the two major powers might come toe-to-toe. For most purposes, involvement in Third World conflicts was a "safe" form of Cold War competition in escalatory terms; that it could prove damaging for the individual sponsors, however, is given testimony by the American adventure in Vietnam during the 1960s and 1970s and the Soviet imbroglio in Afghanistan during the 1980s.

Second, the Cold War was conceptualized as a *protracted conflict*, a term introduced by Yugoslav dissident Milovan Djilas in 1957 in a book titled *The New Class*. The concept described the Cold War and how the communist bureaucrats (who formed the new class) managed it as a long-term competition for which only great patience would suffice and the management of which required great vigilance. The bases of the Cold War division were pervasive and intractable, making it a kind of zero-sum game (one side wins what the other side loses), and the positions and existence of both sides was considered durable. Given the consequences of trying to conclude the competition decisively in one direction or the other, the competition seemed extremely important to maintain as such; the perceived alternative to the Cold War was much worse than its continuation.

Protraction served both as a predictor and as a prime value. The basis of these assessments was the durability of both the major powers, an assumption that is, in retrospect, ironic, particularly as it applies to a Soviet state which did, after all, collapse. The implosion of the Soviet system was almost entirely unpredicted, largely because protraction was believed to be so enduring and durable.

The enigma of Soviet durability is more apparent now than it clearly was at the time. The perceived base of Soviet strength was the totalitarian nature of Soviet rule. The argument maintained that Soviet communism could not fail because the regime had so much coercive power that any opposition would be crushed mercilessly and efficiently. This ability to destroy any opposition that might try to emerge substituted for the lack of broad popular support for the regime.

Given Western, and more specifically American, values and beliefs, this was always a curious proposition. Democratic theory argues that the basis of political stability is the popular support of the political system; in other words, legitimacy forms the basis of stable rule and is the source of strength for democratic political systems. The coercive base of the Soviet system asserted just the opposite: The reason that the Soviet system required great coercive power was because it lacked the legitimacy of popularly supported rule. That the Soviets needed this coercive strength was an admission that their system lacked a solid base among the people, and as such, was an admission of the weakness, rather than the strength, of Soviet rule. Despite this anomaly, the argument of Soviet durability showed that in the Soviet case, coercion effectively trumped legitimacy.

That this anomaly should dominate the debate about the ongoing nature of the Cold War speaks to the paranoia and even irrationality that were masked as orthodox reality during the period. The myth of Soviet invincibility rested on a fundamental contradiction: that their system was simultaneously fundamentally flawed and overwhelmingly irresistible and undefeatable. Soviet savagery toward its own people (the purges of the 1930s that resulted in the deaths of millions of Soviet citizens, reportedly a million or more in 1937 and 1938 alone being the most extreme example) was viewed as evidence of regime strength, when the major reason for bloody repression was to suppress basic opposition to the regime. Similarly, when the Soviets engaged in highly illegal and bloody ways in conducting the clandestine side of their foreign policy (namely, espionage), these atrocities were viewed as evidence of Soviet virility and produced wide calls for American duplication as a response. At the same time, merely suggesting the possibility that the Soviet façade was in fact a false front masking a rotten core brought cascades of vilification (that is, being "soft" on communism) that effectively squelched any debate.

This belief in the protracted nature of the relationship led to the third characteristic, the *improbability of an acceptable end to the Cold War*. If one began with the dubious proposition that the Soviet threat was interminable, it clouded the analysis of how, or if, that relationship might change and thus what measures should be taken either to maintain or seek to alter it.

Trapped in the reality of the Cold War, there were always three possible visions of the future. The first was an indefinite continuation of the competition—keeping the Cold War cold. Certainly there had been and would continue to be alterations in the details of the relationship, but the basic incompatibility of the two philosophies that underlay the Cold War seemed intractable enough that this status quo seemed likely. The second possibility was that the relationship would deteriorate and that through some purposeful or, more likely, accidental occurrence that the two sides would go to war—the Cold War turning hot. Given the nuclear capabilities of the two sides, such a possibility would likely be apocalyptical, at worst a fiery Armageddon in which humankind effectively destroyed itself. Since both sides understood that this was a possible outcome of any conflict in which they both became actively involved on either side, this was the outcome both sought to avoid. The third possibility was that one side or the other would weaken or collapse—the Cold War would fizzle out like a wet firecracker—and the side that did not disintegrate would be the winner. This prospect was considered the least likely of the three and was a vision espoused publicly by only a few, such as George Kennan, the father of the U.S. policy of containment and New York Senator Daniel Patrick Moynihan.

Perceptions of the probabilities of these possible futures changed across time. In the early years before the Cuban crisis, the second outcome (the Cold War turning hot) seemed the fatalistically most probable. After the crisis in Cuba, however, the idea of **deterrence**, the avoidance of war, became the primary value in order to avoid the abyss that the Cuban crisis revealed. Avoiding a hot war meant elevating the maintenance of the status quo (the first possibility, keeping the Cold War cold) not only to a prognosis but to a value to be pursued as well. What made this emphasis particularly appealing was the underlying belief that the third possibility, a peaceful end in which the Cold War ended with a whimper rather than a bang, was so far-fetched and utopian as not to be taken seriously. This dismissal by virtually all observers made the actual collapse of the Cold War all the more incomprehensible and helps explain why the "victors" were unprepared to accept and exploit it.

The Containment Paradigm

Containment, the first coherent and comprehensive U.S. foreign policy in American history, was a product of the downward spiral of U.S.–Soviet relations during the 1940s that negatively answered the question of whether the wartime collaboration between the two could be extended into the postwar world. From an American perspective, the period between 1945 and 1950 was one of growing animosity accentuated by a series of what the United States viewed as Soviet provocations. Between 1945 and 1948, Soviet armies of occupation installed communist governments in the Eastern European countries they occupied in what the United States argued was a clear violation of wartime agreements calling for self-determination in occupied territories. Crises in the Iranian province of Azerbaijan and the Greek Civil War provided evidence of Soviet intransigence in 1946, and in 1948, the Soviet occupiers brutally overthrew the elected government of Czechoslovakia and imposed the Berlin Blockade on the former German capital. In 1949, Mao Zedong's communists were triumphant in China. The North Korean invasion of South Korea in June 1950 provided an exclamation point to this trend.

Policy makers in the United States were appalled but not entirely surprised by this chain of events, and they responded with the policy of containment. As already noted, the basic concept for this policy was developed by George F. Kennan, a career American diplomat and Soviet expert who was stationed in Moscow as the second in command (*charge d'affaires*) of the U.S. Embassy after the war. In 1946, Kennan sent an analysis of the developing conflict to the State Department, which became known as the "long telegram" and was subsequently published in 1947 in the journal *Foreign Affairs* as "The Sources of Soviet Conduct" under the authorship of "X" to protect Kennan's identity in the embassy.

Kennan accepted Soviet animosity and expansionist intentions, but he maintained that these could be countered. He believed the communist regime to be hostile but also fragile, a distinction often underemphasized during the Cold War but of crucial importance to the policy. The regime's fragility meant that it had to be treated carefully. In particular, Kennan maintained that it would be unwise to back the communists into a corner that might threaten their control, in which case they would be forced to lash out violently like a cornered animal, an undesirable prospect given Soviet military capabilities. At the same time, Kennan argued that regime fragility was the result of a basically flawed system that likely could eventually collapse on its own. As he put it in the "X" article, "the possibility remains (and in the opinion of this writer is a strong one) that Soviet power...bears within it the seeds of its own demise" and that "the future of Soviet power may not be by any means as secure as Russian capacity for self-delusion would make it appear." This latter observation, which proved prophetic, was largely lost as the Cold War progressed. Kennan also observed that the communist ideology on which the regime rested confidently predicted the inevitable dialectic triumph of communism over capitalism, meaning the Soviet regime could accept tactical setbacks that did not threaten their existence, since their long-term success was in the cosmic cards.

The basic philosophy of containment flowed from those premises. What Kennan proposed, in essence, was that the United States and its allies adopt a "long term, patient but firm, and vigilant containment of Russian expansionist tendencies." This involved drawing a figurative line on the political map of 1947, which became known as the containment line, and informing the Soviets and their allies that they would not be allowed to extend communism beyond those places where it already existed. The policy thus sought to "contain" the Soviet threat while the internal flaws of the Soviet system gradually undermined the communist experiment. Containment was a nonprovocative policy because it did not seek forcefully to reduce the Soviet domain and activate a Soviet perception of being cornered. When he proposed it, Kennan intended the policy strictly to contain Soviet expansionism in Europe. To Kennan's chagrin, the containment line was expanded all along the Chinese-Soviet (Sino-Soviet) periphery after Korea, an action he opposed on the grounds that it overburdened U.S. capabilities.

The containment philosophy was implemented through a series of concrete policy actions by the United States that both paralleled Soviet provocations and provided precedents for the rest of the Cold War period. Three of these occurred in 1947. The first was the **Truman Doctrine**, by which the United States agreed to replace Great Britain as the principal provider of economic and military assistance to the government of Greece in its civil war against communist insurgents. The Truman Doctrine became the precedent for providing assistance to governments besieged by communist insurgencies elsewhere in the world throughout the Cold War period. The second was the

Marshall Plan, by which the United States provided a large pool of funds to the governments of European countries devastated by World War II to aid in their recovery and, not coincidentally, to make them more resistant to the appeal of indigenous communists. The Marshall Plan provided the basis for extending developmental assistance to anticommunist governments worldwide during the Cold War. Also in 1947, the United States passed the National Security Act, which reorganized the government and placed it on a more national security footing (the act and its consequences are discussed more fully in Chapter Five). Finally, in 1949 the United States signed the **North Atlantic Treaty**, which created the North Atlantic Treaty Organization (NATO) as the first peacetime military alliance in U.S. history. The clear (if unstated) object of NATO was the Soviet expansionist threat, and the treaty provided the precedent for the United States to develop a whole series of military security arrangements globally to dissuade the Soviets from trying to breach the containment line by crossing over into and challenging noncommunist regimes.

These actions formed the underpinning of the containment paradigm that organized the Western side of the Cold War. The idea was to build a ring around the Sino-Soviet periphery that represented the outer boundaries of communist expansion, and success came to be defined as keeping that line intact without provoking a hot war with the Soviets. While it largely succeeded, Kennan's premonition was lost regarding how the strategy could not only contain the Soviet menace but also lead to the third possible future, a peaceful implosion of the Soviet side. In the view of its formulator, containment was more than a strategy to restrain and manage the Soviet threat, it was a way to defeat it (or more precisely, to allow it to unravel and defeat itself). In the end, Kennan was proven correct.

Deadlock and the Collapse of the Cold War

In retrospect, the Soviet Union was, fittingly, the ultimate Potemkin village. The analogy comes from Russian history in the nineteenth century, when the Russian Czarina Katherine the Great visited the Crimea. One of her ministers, Count Potemkin, sought to deceive the Czarina by building a series of false fronts in the villages through which she travelled that made the area seem more prosperous than it was, and false façades have forever since been known as Potemkin villages.

The Soviet state was, in the end, a false façade, the beguiling illusion of which was created by Soviet military power. In fact, Soviet military might (and its manifestation in authoritarian coercive rule) masked the deep kind of societal rot that Kennan had predicted. The internal failure of the Soviet experiment began to become evident in the economic sector in the 1970s (a deterioration Kennan had predicted in the 1940s), and as a failing economy became increasingly incapable of supporting the mammoth military structure, it too began to feel strain. Stress in the two dimensions of economic and military performance became evident to the Soviet leadership in the 1980s under Mikhail Gorbachev, leading to the traumatic but necessary conclusion that the Cold War had to be terminated, because the Soviets were losing.

The Economic Dimension The first cracks in the façade began to emerge in the 1970s, what later Soviet analysts would call the "era of stagnation." In the early 1970s, economic growth ground to a halt in the country and, if one removed vodka production (the one growth industry in the Soviet Union), it actually declined. The government did not acknowledge this phenomenon, and due to the arcane metrics by which the government measured its own performance, it is not clear that the top leadership, the so-called *nomenklatura*, even recognized what was going on, since they were personally insulated from the privation being suffered by virtually everyone else. The Potemkin village shielded the state of the Soviet economy from outsiders and its own leadership alike.

Soviet economists outside the government recognized the economic malaise and communicated it among themselves in academic economic journals that presumably were sufficiently obtuse that the censors did not realize the sedition in what they were reading. These economists understood the ramifications of a declining economy but had no authoritative voice to express their revelations. They eventually found an ally in Mikhail Gorbachev, a rising figure in the Communist Party of the Soviet Union (CPSU), whose wife Raisa was also a faculty member at Moscow State University. When Gorbachev rose to power in 1985, this cadre of economists was available to analyze and prescribe for the ailments of the Soviet economy.

A failing economy had several serious consequences for the Soviets. First, a flat, even declining, growth rate meant the system was decreasingly able to meet even the basic needs of its own citizens. While privation had always been a part of life in the Soviet "worker's paradise," outsiders who visited the country noted a gradual deterioration in the quality of existence that was unsustainable in the long run. Second, a declining economy was increasingly less able to satisfy the voracious needs of a military establishment that demanded an estimated one-third of Soviet resources, and those demands in turn helped contribute to the malaise the economy was experiencing. Third, the disparity between the economic performance of the communist and noncommunist economies was becoming increasingly apparent. This was particularly true in the Eastern European countries, which had access to Western television, but it also became apparent to the Soviets as well.

Fourth, and most important, there seemed little prospect that these trends could be reversed without some basic changes in policy. An example may help illustrate the dilemma in which the Soviet leadership found itself in the mid-1980s. There was no greater source of disparity between the economic performances of the Soviet system and the Western world than in the area of electronics, and particularly computers. Increasingly, economic change and growth and computer proficiency were becoming synonymous, and the Soviets (because of decisions reached by the Soviet Academy of Sciences in the 1960s) lagged progressively behind the West in the technology both to develop and exploit computers. Because one generation of computers is the developmental platform for the next, more powerful and capable generation, falling behind is cumulative. By the mid-1980s, the Soviets were at least a generation behind and falling further in arrears.

There was no good solution to the problem. The Soviet scientific base had been stripped away from computer development (to military technology), so the Soviets could not catch up by dint of their own efforts. The Soviets had tried stealing existing state-of-the-art Western designs, tearing them apart, and rebuilding them (so-called "reverse engineering"), but that process actually took longer than it took for the West to produce a new generation. They could not buy computers from the West, because computers are "dual use" (they can be used for civilian and military applications), and the West thus had banned sales to their Soviet adversaries. As long as the international status quo existed, the Soviets were in an increasingly apparent position of economic loss.

The Military Dimension The illusion of Soviet competitiveness and strength was always largely built around the image of the Soviet military, and by the 1980s, there were strains at that level as well. The sources of this strain were not immediately apparent in the West, but their roots were parallel to those affecting the economic dimension, with the added factors of Ronald Reagan's first-term military buildup and the Soviet Afghanistan adventure as further sources of strain. All of these factors were occurring within a growing realization that war between the two countries had to be avoided at all costs, thus making the military competition an exercise in avoiding, not preparing for, war.

Military competitiveness, particularly in the area of strategic nuclear weapons, had been the chief source of Soviet challenge to the United States and the symbol to security-oriented Americans of the Soviet threat for most of the Cold War period. Although Soviet forces were generally not as technologically sophisticated as their American counterparts (their missiles, for instance, were generally less accurate), they compensated with larger numbers and destructiveness (larger explosive power) of weapons, and the Soviets continued to maintain a large nonnuclear, conventional (and largely conscript) force under arms, menacing Western Europe across the Iron Curtain.

All of this was terribly expensive, especially as a drain on a Soviet economy estimated to be one-third to one-half the size of the American economy. This cost became an increasing concern as fissures in the economy's ability to support Soviet military might became more evident, and as the Soviet technological base was progressively taxed trying to match the lethal inventiveness of the much more robust American technological sector.

Two major events accentuated this problem during the 1980s. The first was the election of Ronald W. Reagan as president of the United States in the 1980 election and his subsequent massive investment in military spending. Reagan had deplored the lack of emphasis on U.S. military spending in the years after the American withdrawal from Vietnam and campaigned in 1980 to reverse what he called the American "unilateral disarmament" of the 1970s. Once in office, he initiated a massive increase in defense spending during his first term (which tapered off due to a lack of public support after 1983) to contain and match Soviet power. It is part of the conservative mythology that Reagan "spent the Soviets into the ground" with defense expansion and his actions during the first (but *not* the second) term, although that may have been a byproduct rather than a reason for the spending.

The Soviets were further bled dry by their adventure in Afghanistan. During the Christmas period of 1979, the Soviets invaded the mountainous country to support the communist regime there by overthrowing one communist leader and replacing him with another. In typical Afghan style, the Soviet occupation spawned a resistance aided by the West that bogged down the Soviets in a long, expensive, bloody, and ultimately unsuccessful endeavor from which they finally extricated themselves in 1989, having achieved none of their goals, but having further impoverished themselves and undermined the morale of the Soviet military.

The context of these gyrations was a growing recognition of what has previously been called the necessary peace. Leaders on both sides as far back as Nikita Khrushchev and Dwight D. Eisenhower had declared publicly what the Soviets referred to as the "inadmissibility" of nuclear war between the two countries, and gradually after the Cuban crisis, the philosophy of both sides had shifted to a primary emphasis on deterrence—the avoidance of a nuclear war that could destroy both. Despite this recognition, military preparedness and spending continued at rarefied levels that increased the deadliness of a potential World War III. President Reagan and Gorbachev reiterated the determination that nuclear war must be avoided at all costs in 1985, and their declaration became a basic foundation of their close collaborative relationship. The problem was that these preparations were increasingly hollow and ritualistic, since both sides were quite genuinely committed to the avoidance of war (although many in the West, and presumably many in the East, questioned the sincerity of the other in that conviction). Nevertheless, both sides continued to spend and prepare at dizzying levels for a conflict that both were committed to avoid.

The final factor in this equation was the gradual recognition that the dynamics of necessary peace applied not only to the nuclear balance between the two superpowers, but also to any military interactions. Not only could a direct nuclear confrontation lead to the destruction of both sides, but so could a nonnuclear military confrontation that might somehow escalate to a nuclear confrontation. The two sides had implicitly recognized this dynamic since the Cuban crisis by avoiding involvement in situations that might militarily bring them face-to-face, but they had implicitly denied the broader reality that any military confrontation between them, whether it began as a conventional or a nuclear conflict, *could* escalate to Armageddon. Moreover, since such a confrontation had never occurred, neither had any realistic idea of how it might happen and how or whether it might be manageable. The reality that the only way to avoid being destroyed in a nuclear war was to avoid fighting one (deterrence) expanded to the realization that this entreaty extended to *any* military clash between them.

The logical extension of this insight was that the entire military structure and effort of the Cold War was being directed not, in conventional thinking, to preparing for war, but exclusively to preparing to *avoid* war. This meant that hundreds of billions of dollars and rubles that might be put to other, presumably more productive, uses were instead being devoted to the negative goal of avoiding their use. In flush economic times, such a paradoxical (arguably nonsensical) use of resources might have been (and had been) tolerable. For a Soviet Union on the verge of a collapse that was partially economic in origin, the paradox became unbearably real. The Cold War military competition had become not only an albatross, but an unaffordable one, and that made the prospect of the other solution to war avoidance—unraveling the competition that gave rise to it—seem all the more attractive.

Convergence and the Decision to End the Cold War By the time Mikhail Gorbachev rose from the Soviet succession crisis of the early 1980s to assume control of a teetering Soviet state, these influences converged. The Soviet economy was in tatters, with no obvious solutions to righting it and making it competitive. The military competition with the West was an albatross around the Soviet neck, sucking relentlessly at the meager Soviet resource base and helping to assure the penury of the economy. Gorbachev instituted a series of internal reforms that he outlined in his 1986 book, *Perestroika.* Internally, he suggested basic reforms of the communist system; internationally, he suggested a normalization of relations with the rest of the world by recasting the Soviet Union as a more orthodox, normal member of the international community. Both thrusts arose from the increasing realization that the Soviet Union desperately needed outside help to surmount its crisis and that such help required a recasting of the Soviet state and its place in the world.

At the foreign policy level, the heart of the Gorbachev reforms was in redefining the Soviet Union as a normal state. The reasoning was straightforward. The Soviets could not attract the kinds of assistance they needed to revive the technological and financial sectors without help from the West, and that help would not be forthcoming as long as the Soviet Union remained the enemy. A Soviet policy of global expansionism was also terribly expensive, propping up corrupt, inefficient, and unpopular regimes in places such as Cuba, and jettisoning that burden made economic sense, as well as decreasing the Western perception of the Soviet Union as a hostile, revisionist state.

The military competition was also part of the problem. The Soviets could, and did, publicly declare their belief in reducing military tensions, and Gorbachev and Reagan personalized this effort in Reykjavik, established a close working relationship, and even engaged in efforts to reduce the likelihood of nuclear war, a prospect about which they shared a particular mutual dread.

Gorbachev was increasingly impaled on the horns of dilemma. The internal reforms that he proposed were initially framed within a Marxist framework, and they were generally ineffective and certainly did not narrow the gap with the West. Despite his efforts to normalize relations with the West, there was great international skepticism about his sincerity or his ability to end animosity.

Gorbachev was thus left with a devil's choice. He could try to maintain the status quo of a powerful, vibrant communist Soviet Union, but the Potemkin façade of such an effort was becoming increasingly obvious. Thus, he could maintain communism but run the risk of losing the Soviet stature as a competing superpower. His other alternative was to shuck the communist system and try to join the general Western prosperity. Thus, he could attempt to remain a superpower but one that was no longer communist. Because Gorbachev was personally a believing Marxist, he wanted to do both—to be both communist and at the helm of a superpower—but that was increasingly impossible, and hanging onto the illusion ran the risk of accomplishing neither. Ultimately, Gorbachev decided the only course he could follow was to join the rest of the international community. The Cold War had to be ended.

In a series of steps between 1989 and 1991, that is exactly what he did. In early 1989, Gorbachev and his foreign minister, Eduard Shevardnadze (later the president of Georgia) travelled to the communist states with a simple message: Make peace with your people, including change. If you do not, you are on your own, as the Soviet Union will no longer come to your aid. This bold move encouraged the blossoming of previously covert anticommunist political movements in the Eastern European countries that became the basis for overthrowing communist regimes during the remainder of 1989. This process began physically on August 19, 1989, when the Polish people elected Tadeusz Mazowiecki, a member of the *Solidarity* reform movement, as Poland's first noncommunist prime minister since 1945, and culminated symbolically on November 9, when the Berlin Wall fell. By year's end, communism in Eastern Europe was effectively ended.

The same process began in the Soviet Union in 1989 as well. On August 23, 1989, upward of one million citizens of Latvia, Estonia, and Lithuania (the Baltic republics forcefully annexed to the Soviet Union in 1939), rallied to protest fifty years of Soviet occupation without violent repression by the government, signaling the unraveling of the Soviet Union itself. The last vestiges of international communist domain in Europe imploded in 1991. The Warsaw Treaty Organization (WTO), the military alliance that faced NATO across the Iron Curtain, voted itself out of existence. During the year, the constituent republics of the Soviet Union began to break away from the Soviet Union. On December 8, Russian, Ukrainian, and Byelorussian leaders declared that the Soviet Union had ceased to exist, and on December 17, Gorbachev announced that all central Soviet governmental institutions would cease operations at the end of the year. On December 31, the Soviet hammer-and-sickle flag flew over the Kremlin for the last time. On January 1, 1992, it was replaced by the Russian tricolor. The Cold War confrontation had ended, not with the nuclear bang that most had feared if it ended at all, but with hardly a whimper.

AFTER THE COLD WAR

The end of the Cold War was almost as traumatic as its existence had been. While the Cold War was potentially a very deadly place, its dangerousness had become more tolerable as it evolved and both sides came to understand its dynamics and how to manage them. The Cold War paradigm of containment served the United States for over forty years, and it was an intellectual construct that translated into a series of implementing policies that had become familiar and, in a sense, comfortable. The Cold War was not necessarily a condition that was relished, but it was one that had produced a level of predictability and order that was comfortable to those who managed it.

The end of the Cold War shattered that comfort level. Soviet analyst Georgi Arbatov commented to the Americans as the disintegration was ongoing, "We have done a terrible thing to you. We have deprived you of an enemy." His lament was quite literal and discomforting, because it raised into question the entire rationale of containment and the various structures and policies that had been erected in its name. As the process of decommunizing the world proceeded during the 1990s, Westerners, and especially Americans, worried greatly about the destabilization of the successor states of the Soviet Union itself and the fledgling democratic regimes in most Eastern European states, but none of the worst of these fears truly came to fruition. Rather, most of the peoples who had been under communist rule shucked the communist system and its leaders with glee and rushed to join the greater prosperity of the West. By the end of the 1990s, the only communist regimes that still existed in the world were in China, Vietnam, North Korea, and Cuba, and of those, the only remaining acolytes of Marxist economics were in North Korea and Cuba, two of the poorest and most forlorn states in the world.

If the communist half of the Cold War physically ceased to exist, so did the intellectual basis of the American response to that challenge, the paradigm of containment. The United States was simply unprepared for what happened between 1989 and 1991, for the simple reason that hardly anyone had thought seriously about the possibility and thus analyzed what to do should it occur. The part of Kennan's writings that had pointed to communist implosion had been conveniently forgotten in the more "manly" pursuit of containing (especially with military force) the communist threat, and the few dissenters from the orthodoxy of communist robustness and invincibility like Moynihan were viewed as little more than idle dreamers out of touch with the "reality" of an endless, protracted competition.

Because so few had foreseen the demise of operational communism, there was also no alternative paradigm for dealing with a very changed world. Rather, policy makers and analysts alike rued the process and its outcomes. The George H.W. Bush administration, for instance, scrambled throughout the period leading to the dissolution to find ways to keep the Soviet Union intact, for fear of a worse—certainly more unpredictable—alternative if it came to an end. University of Chicago political scientist John J. Mearsheimer captured the intellectual response in the title of a 1990 *Atlantic Monthly* article, "Why We Shall Miss the Cold War." Losing the Cold War was not quite like losing an old friend so much as it was like losing a cranky but predictable next-door neighbor: Would the successor be worse?

The search for a new paradigm has been ongoing ever since, and it is difficult to maintain that it has entirely succeeded. What is clear is that the old, Cold War paradigm does not apply in any straightforward way. Containment assumed a concrete, expansionist, state-based adversary whose clear desire was to expand territorially, thus providing the needs for resistance and opposition. This led to a politico-diplomatic and economic strategy of posing a superior alternative force in contested areas and a military posture capable of resisting expansion and, because of that ability, deterring expansionism. The recognition that neither side could take the chance of direct military confrontation contributed to the dynamics by which the Cold War ended. All of these policies flowed in a reasonably neat deductive manner from the containment paradigm.

The great accomplishment of the peaceful end of the Cold War was that it avoided the horror scenario of a nuclear war that had fueled the morbid fascinations of the generation that lived in the "shadow of the mushroom-shaped cloud" (to borrow from the title of an early monograph by one of the authors). That accomplishment, however, must probably be tempered. By avoiding nuclear war the superpowers did indeed avoid destroying the world, but the decision to have done so would, without doubt, have been the single stupidest (and possibly last) decision in the history of humankind. Instead, humankind proved itself at least not to be entirely suicidal.

INTERSECTIONS

"Horror Scenarios"?

While there is no current national security threat that even approximates the potential horror of an all-out nuclear war between the Cold War superpowers, that does not mean there are no longer any situations where American interests are under threat or where the worst possible turn of events could have serious consequences for the United States. The new horror scenarios may not be as apocalyptic as a nuclear Armageddon, but they nonetheless exist.

A prominent example is Pakistan. With the world's sixth largest population, possession of a stock of nuclear weapons generally thought to number less than one hundred, and with a strategic location between India and Afghanistan, the Pakistani situation is difficult to ignore under any circumstances, but there are other causes of concern as well. Domestically, Pakistan is politically unstable, with an uneasy relationship between the military and civilians, between Islamists and more secular population elements, and among major ethnic groups. Most of the country is desperately poor, and Pakistan has long been a haven for terrorists and extremists operating in Afghanistan and in the hotly disputed Indian state of Kashmir. Its relations with the United States, its major benefactor, are strained by Pakistani objections to American violations of its sovereign territory in pursuit of terrorism—the bin Laden operation, for instance—and by American questions about Pakistani diligence in the war on terror.

Most observers see Pakistan as a potential failed state. State failure, in the worst horror scenario, would mean the collapse of central government and, in the absolutely worst outcome, the capture of Pakistani nuclear weapons by extremists—possibly for use against the United States. The U.S. policy question is whether anything can be done to avoid this horror. (For a more detailed discussion of the problem, see Snow, *Cases in American Foreign Policy*, Chapter Six.)

The paradigm and its resulting strategies and policies do not so obviously apply to the post–Cold War world. At the most apparent level, there is, and has been, no equivalent of the Soviet threat to contain, and there is little likelihood that an opponent formidable enough to need containing in the way Soviet communism had to be contained will emerge. Thus, understanding the contemporary environment must begin with the absence of any agreed framework within which to organize foreign policy.

The rest of the chapter will be devoted to introducing the causes of change and the major emphases of policy that have emerged, which are examined in subsequent chapters. It begins by introducing the idea of **fault lines**, traumatic events in the international system that result in basic changes in how the international system operates. It then moves to the dominant new features that have emerged from these fault lines and which continue to dominate the environment in which policy is made, if not to the same degree or extent to which the Cold War dominated the latter part of the last century.

Fault Lines

The basis of the fault line analogy is geological: the idea that there are natural formations in the earth that occasionally shift (Allison and Blackwill, in a 1990 article, referred to them as "tectonic shifts") resulting in sizable changes in the subsequent landscape. Another way to think of these occurrences is as traumatic events that challenge how things are done and the rationale for doing them.

The Cold War itself was the result of the action of a tectonic shift in terms of the outcome of World War II. The increasingly fragile structure of the European balance that had dominated world politics for nearly three hundred years before the second global conflagration of the twentieth century shifted measurably, and the wreckage it produced left a landscape in which the United States and the Soviet Union were the only visibly standing structures. In the aftermath of the earthquake that erupted along the fault lines, the Cold War evolved as the principal way for understanding world politics and the organizational rationale (or paradigm) around which such management would be ordered.

In the past quarter-century, the international system has revealed two new basic fault lines. The first of these was the end of the Cold War itself, the effects of and accommodations to which dominated the balance of the 1990s. The second was the terrorist attacks of September 11, 2001, which revealed the basic fissure represented by international religious terrorism. The balance of the 2000s has been largely devoted to responding to that trauma, a process that is ongoing. The common characteristic of the reactions to both fault-line eruptions is that neither has spawned a new organizational paradigm with the central organizing power of containment. The first fault line undermined the containment paradigm, but it has not been replaced by a comprehensive new central tenet. The second fault line produced a new central problem with which to grapple that the period between the fault lines lacked, but it has not been a sufficiently well-defined threat to dictate a paradigm around which a response can be fashioned in the way the Cold War did.

In systemic terms, the first fault line was by far the more consequential in the sense that it undermined an international order that had emerged and solidified over a forty-year period. Despite changes in the details of relationships between the superpowers and the superpowers and the rest of the world, the international system was fundamentally bipolar, and the most important international problems revolved around the relations about the poles and in the interactions between the poles. The rise of a developing world for which the central feature of communism versus democracy was not of paramount relevance eroded some of the universality of bipolarity, but it did not erase it.

The trauma of the end of the Cold War was to leave the world with a single major power, the United States. Throughout the decade of the 1990s, the major systemic debates developed about what this phenomenon meant. Would the disappearance of one pole produce a power vacuum that would make the new system unstable in ways the Cold War was not? This concern certainly dominated thinking in the West, and especially in the United States, in the early days after 1991, but fortunately, it turned out that the feared destabilization did not, by and large, emerge. There was also the question of the role of the United States. Would the United States enjoy, as neoconservative columnist Charles Krauthammer put it in a *Foreign Affairs* article title, a "unipolar moment"? Given that the United States was now the sole remaining superpower, just how powerful was it? Was its power so politically dominant as to represent hegemonic power, or was it something less? The United States may have become, as Secretary of State Madeleine Albright put it in 1996, the "indispensable nation," but what exactly did that mean? This question about the new balance of power has reverberated since the end of the Cold War.

Fortunately for those seeking to make the adjustment to a post–Cold War world, the environment during the balance of the 1990s was a relatively tranquil time. With the major source of power conflict resolved by one power quitting the field, there was essentially no basis for the kinds of systemic threats that had animated the Cold War. Rather, the concentration of world affairs was on adjusting to an environment lacking the Cold War in a more relaxed, less confrontational mode of interaction. The fact that the underlying paradigm of containment no longer fit the situation or provided direct policy guidance that required a replacement philosophy was less important than it would have been during the Cold War.

This tranquility, in turn, was reinforced by a general global economic prosperity that began shortly after the fall of communism and extended throughout most of the 1990s. The prosperity was especially pronounced in an economically resurgent United States that had suffered from economic decline during the 1970s and 1980s, but it extended to much of the rest of the world as well. The process of so-called globalization was generally credited for this prosperity and the general optimism that accompanied it.

Although generally unnoticed outside the expert community, the seeds of the second fault line were also at work below the surface in the inter–fault-line period. Al Qaeda was born in 1988 (by most accounts) and established its initial training camps in Sudan in 1989. Its first attacks were in Yemen in 1992 against a hotel housing American troops headed for Somalia. The frequency and deadliness of these attacks increased through the 1990s (as discussed in Chapter Ten).

The attacks of September 11, 2001, of course, provided the second fault line, and it is the trauma with which the international system and American foreign policy is still grappling a decade later. In some ways, the terrorist threat and the ensuing "war on terror" represent a return to the dynamics of the Cold War, but the fit is not exact, and thus the old paradigm of containment is no more applicable than it was to the more tranquil environment of the 1990s.

The most obvious point of positive comparison between the Cold War and the post-9/11 environments is their high national security content. Both the Soviets and the terrorists of which Al Qaeda is the most visible symbol represent real threats to the physical safety and well-being of Americans, and there has been a natural tendency to treat them in the same sorts of ways. The war analogy regarding terrorism is the most obvious manifestation of this perception, as have been emphases on larger military spending and even activism. Antiterrorist sentiment even has some of the character and intensity that were attached to anticommunism a generation ago.

The threat is not, however, the same in important ways, and that fact makes the transfer of the containment paradigm to the present a poor fit. The Soviet threat emanated from a concrete, identifiable sovereign state, which provided a focus for containment that the more nebulous, nonstate-based threat of terrorism totally lacks. The United States, for instance, knew how many weapons systems of different categories the Soviets and their allies possessed and generally how they might be used in war, and this permitted the United States and its allies to develop military capabilities to counter the Soviets and thus to deter their use. Moreover, the dynamics of the central nuclear balance rested on the deterrent threat that should the Soviets attack the physical territory of the United States, their territory would be devastated in return, thereby giving them pause.

Such calculations clearly do not apply to the much more amorphous terrorist threat. Al Qaeda (and other terrorist organizations) does not represent a physical sovereign state, although they are provided sanctuary in states (more or less enthusiastically by their hosts). Generally speaking, their numbers and physical characteristics are only known in general terms, and there is little sense that countervailing capabilities can be developed to negate terrorist threats. There are no specific "antiterrorist" weapons one can stockpile to counteract any particular terrorist capability in the same way that tanks can be countered with antitank weapons. Moreover, when terrorists threaten or physically attack American targets, it is unclear against whom or what to retaliate (as in nuclear retaliation against the Soviet Union). In addition, the value of martyrdom held by some of their members raises questions about whether deterrence is even possible under any circumstances.

The magnitude of the problem is different as well. The Cold War produced a threat of incredible deadliness (the consequences of nuclear war) but of decreasing dangerousness (because of the realization of those consequences), but the dynamics are reversed in the post-9/11 environment. This environment is very dangerous, because there is apparently very little sense of fear of the consequences of their acts by terrorists. At the same time, the threats that terrorists can carry out are less deadly than the system-threatening consequences of a general nuclear war. This calculation could, of course, change if terrorists were to gain control of nuclear weapons.

In terms of American foreign policy, the major impact of the fault lines, as should be apparent, has been to discredit the utility of the containment paradigm, but not to suggest a compelling replacement for that policy. In the 1990s, there was very little of importance to contain, but the resulting irrelevance of the paradigm was tolerable in a generally benign climate. The second fault line produced a threat worthy of containment, but it is a threat that does not neatly fit the implications and actions that flowed from Cold War containment. The military difficulties the United States has encountered in places such as Iraq and Afghanistan illustrate the practical, applied difficulties of the post–Cold War experience and the arguable inadequacy of Cold War–style preparations to deal with these changes.

Major Dynamic Changes

The periods that followed the traumas of exposing the fault lines also produced dominant new influences that accelerated or complemented the impact of the fault lines themselves. The fall of communism was followed rapidly by the flowering of economic globalization, a concept introduced in Chapter One and the source of much of the general optimism during the 1990s. The second fault line revealed, as the prominent outcropping of its fissure, the face of international religious terrorism as an ongoing, negative, and conflict-producing force. Both of these influences continue to have an impact on contemporary foreign policy and the search for a new paradigm. While each is covered in more detail in later pages, their introduction here helps provide a bridge from the past to the present.

The roots of the current phenomenon of globalization go back into the 1970s and 1980s. The core idea of globalization is increasing economic activity across international boundaries, which stimulates economic growth and prosperity within and among all the places that participate in it. As such, it is not a particularly new idea: A similar growth in international commerce occurred at the turn of the twentieth century, as noted in Chapter One. The globalization dynamic of the contemporary period owes much of its special character to trends of the 1970s and 1980s.

The first of these trends was the revolution in high technology, principally in computing and telecommunications. Both of these related technological areas revolutionized the way products are produced and services provided and allowed the ever-expanding communications of information around the world—all crucial to the emergence of an increasingly integrated and mutually interdependent world economy. The other phenomenon was the wave of deregulation and privatization of economic activity in the 1980s associated with the neoliberal philosophies of Ronald Reagan and British Prime Minister Margaret Thatcher. The result was a stimulation of entrepreneurial activity and economic growth to provide the basis for an expanding and globally integrating economy.

The impact of globalization was to create a positive-sum economic climate where economic prosperity was tied to international cooperation in supporting and expanding the globalizing economy. Previously, economic integration had been largely confined to the evolving European Union, but globalization made it increasingly worldwide, as associations appeared in the Western hemisphere (the North American Free Trade Area, for instance) and Asia (the Asia-Pacific Economic Cooperation, as an example) and even globally (as in the World Trade Organization). The major underlying dynamics of this expansion were the promotion of free trade and the idea of comparative economic advantage transferred to the global stage.

Globalization became a bedrock part of American foreign policy in the 1990s. Because it both encouraged and produced cooperation among countries, it was a major element in the peaceful transformation of the international political order through mechanisms such as integrating the formerly communist states of Eastern Europe into the emerging capitalist-based economy. Moreover, the basis of globalization was firmly anchored by the dual ideas of capitalist economics and political democracy, the two basic Western premises in the Cold War competition with socialist authoritarianism emanating from the communist world. The promotion of globalization became part of President Bill Clinton's foreign policy of expanding the "circle of market democracies," a way to consolidate the triumph of Western ideals in the Cold War.

Globalization became a prominent international phenomenon at about the same time that the Cold War was winding down, thereby creating a linkage between the increasing rise of this source of intermestic politics and the rise of partisanship in politics that blossomed during the Clinton administration and has continued—even intensified—since. Neither of these concerns was an important consideration during the Cold War. The possible connections are explored in the *Intersections* box that follows.

The euphoria that surrounded globalization had begun to dissipate by the end of the decade. In some cases, economic expansion had been too rapid and too uncontrolled, resulting in many of the kinds of economic excess overseas that had plagued the United States in the first decade of the 2000s. At the same time, although the bulk of the 1990s was a period of economic expansion, by the end of the 1990s growth had slowed, and a mild global recession had begun to take hold. As the millennium approached, the post–Cold War world was headed toward a darker future.

International religious terrorism is the horror scenario and major threat of the new century to date. Terrorism per se is certainly nothing new: Most scholars of the subject date the phenomenon—if not necessarily the name—back two thousand years to Jewish resistance to the Roman occupation of Palestine. Terrorism has been around ever since, if in different guises and conducted for different political ends.

The employment of terrorism by Middle Eastern–based, religiously motivated terrorists is the current face of the most important systemic threat that American foreign policy has had to face since the Cold War. It has been approached in a variety of ways, most of which are either directly military

INTERSECTIONS

The End of the Cold War, Intermestic Politics, and Partisanship?

One of the great symbols of the end of the Cold War and the process of improving relations between the United States and the Soviet Union/Russia was the fall of the Berlin Wall in 1989.

While there were certainly partisan divisions within the American political system during the Cold War, they tended not to overflow into a foreign policy environment dominated by the confrontation between communism and anticommunism on patriotic grounds. The end of the Cold War greatly decreased the apparent need for political solidarity and thus loosened inhibitions to criticizing the positions of different groups on foreign policy issues where the consequences no longer seemed so dire. At the same time, the end of the Cold War more or less coincided with the overt rise of globalization, which became the dominant international phenomenon of the 1990s and, in the process, greatly increased the intermestic content of many political actions, thereby lowering the barrier between the partisan fight over domestic political impacts and foreign policy.

The question is whether these two occurrences—the end of the Cold War and the rise of globalization—are spuriously or causally related to the extension of partisanship into the foreign policy realm. This is a complex and probably unanswerable question in any deterministic way, but it is an interesting source of consideration and speculation nonetheless. Part of the complexity is the relationship between the Cold War's end and globalization itself: Would an international

(Continued)

(Continued)

system still fixated with that confrontation have been able to shift its emphasis to a positive concern with capitalist-based international economic activity, or would the Soviets and their allies have sought to disrupt the flowering of globalization? At the same time, would the flowering of globalization, which helped pave the way for the transition away from communist rule as the former communist states clamored to join the globalization system, have helped stimulate the end of the Cold War, or would it have become the source of even greater division between the two camps? Would the increased level and extent of partisanship have been as intense if only one of these two influences had been present: partisanship in a globalization-influenced Cold War, or an environment without the Cold War or globalization? One can only speculate.

(for example, the military occupation and attempt to eradicate Al Qaeda in Afghanistan) or semimilitary (for instance, the antiterrorist methods associated with domestic homeland security). These efforts are discussed later in the text and do not need to be detailed fully here.

What is important for current purposes is the impact of the second fault line's manifestation on American foreign policy. The terrorist threat has been encompassing and engaging enough to call for the development of a paradigm that will provide as powerful a tool for negating its impact on the United States and the rest of the developed world as containment did for communism. Much of the language of policy reflects the continuing conceptual hold of containment—the depiction of the competition as a form of war, for instance. The war analogy does not exactly fit the problem. Normal conceptions of war more closely are associated with military campaigns against other countries or overt movements within states, a depiction that does not hold in the case of international religious terrorism. There is a clear enemy involved, of course, and this makes the robust rhetoric of the Cold War seem appropriate, but the object of that rhetoric, while as evil (or more so) than the Soviet adversary, is much more nebulous.

With over a decade of dealing with terrorism as the central focus of foreign policy, no worthy successor paradigm to containment has arisen to ground foreign responses to environmental stimuli, and there is no clear indication that such a formulation will appear in the near future. Whether that situation is tolerable or not depends to some degree on the durability of the terrorist threat. Had the Cold War lasted less than a decade, for instance, there would have been less reason or need for a strong framework to direct long-term foreign policy, but the Cold War was, in the term used by former Secretary of Defense Donald Rumsfeld to describe U.S. military efforts in Iraq, a "long slog" that required a durable policy plan.

The presumption that American foreign policy needs a new paradigm implicitly asserts that the contest with international religious terrorists will be a similarly long competition, one that, like the Cold War, is intractable and seemingly endless. Such a conclusion may be entirely correct and appropriate, and indeed, most Americans would agree with that assessment. At the same time, Americans of the 1970s routinely described the Cold War in these indefinite terms that allowed only for apocalyptic exits, and those assessments were wrong. Could the same thing be true about the current threat? What impact, for instance, does the death of Osama bin Laden in May 2011 have on the continuing nature of the terrorist threat?

CONCLUSIONS

This chapter was introduced with the June 2010 "sleeper cell" Russian spy case. It did not represent an important crisis in international relations or U.S.–Russian relations, as both sides moved very rapidly to resolve it by exchanging the Russian spies for Russians who had allegedly been working in Russia for American intelligence agencies, and it was very clear that both sides simply wanted to get the episode behind them as quickly and thoroughly as possible. What the incident did demonstrate, however, is that old habits and ways of doing things do persist—that the past has some relevance to the present and the future.

The past from which the incident arose was the Cold War, which is also the backdrop against which current American foreign policy is being forged and applied in a world where the Cold War adversary is now basically a friend and other adversaries have arisen to take its place. From the Cold War, the United States inherited a policy framework, the paradigm of containment, around which to organize its view of the world. Since the Cold War no longer exists, is there any reason to retain the premises and outlooks of that period for organizing and conducting foreign policy in a very different environment?

Answering that question began by looking at the underlying dynamics of the Cold War. Clearly, the problems the United States (and the rest of the world) faced in the late 1940s are different from those faced in the second decade of the twenty-first century, but how different are they? There have, after all, been two seismic international events (or fault lines revealed) in the past twenty-five years: the end of the Cold War and the terrorist attacks of September 11, 2001. These events have certainly altered the international landscape in ways analogous to the effects of two large earthquakes. The question raised in this chapter is whether there is a need for a new paradigm for dealing with these tectonic shifts and their effects.

WHERE DO WE GO FROM HERE?

To readers who were not alive or were in their infancy when the Soviet flag last flew from atop the Kremlin in Moscow, the discussions in this chapter may seem abstract, yet the context and framework that arose from the historical experience of the Cold War is, in some important ways, still a dominating part of the contemporary scene. What is particularly striking, as has been argued in the chapter, is that there is currently no accepted successor to the foreign policy of containment.

APPLICATION: APPLYING THE COLD WAR EXPERIENCE TO TERRORISM

The policy of a "long term, patient but firm and vigilant containment" (Kennan's terms) provided the basis by which the United States organized its opposition to Soviet communism, and the application of those principles eventually led to the triumph of the United States and the peaceful demise of Soviet power, an outcome few other than Kennan envisaged as possible. The major question is whether the continuation of something like containment will work in the face of international religious terrorism. Recognizing that the reader may feel uncomfortable reaching definitive conclusions due to a shortage of information, this problem can be approached by asking several questions associated with the Kennan analysis of the earlier foe.

1. Would a strategy of containment work against terrorism? Is the opponent containable in the same way that a territorially based Soviet state was capable of being deterred from hostile activity and thus contained? Can you draw a meaningful terrorist territorial containment line like that drawn around the Sino-Soviet periphery?
2. Is it possible that a strategy of containing terrorism would reveal the kinds of "seeds of its own decay" that Kennan saw in communism? If so, how might these "seeds" be exploited to make these negative influences accelerate? If not, is it possible to contain the problem of terrorism?
3. For a long time, it was assumed that the Cold War was a protracted, essentially never-ending competition. Is such a depiction of the competition with terrorism valid? If it is, are the possible outcomes the same as what people thought about the Cold War? What are the implications of those outcomes for conducting the competition?
4. Given these kinds of factors, does containment offer a model for fashioning a new paradigm, or does it suggest the need for an entirely new approach?
5. Can you visualize an end to the competition with terrorism and what the world would look like in that event?

These are not necessarily all the questions that might be asked about whether containment provides a reasonable framework for a post–Cold War paradigm for organizing foreign policy, but it is a start on which the reader can build. It would clearly be a matter of great relief to envision a time in the future when the analog to the Russian sleeper spy case could occur with radical Islamic terrorists in a similar exchange in an atmosphere where both sides were relieved to see the end of an embarrassing artifact of a past problem.

STUDY/DISCUSSION QUESTIONS

1. What is a sleeper agent? Compare and contrast the application of the concept as it applies to the Cold War and now. What is its significance in trying to understand American foreign policy?
2. Discuss the evolution of U.S. foreign policy before World War II. How well did this experience prepare the United States for the post–World War II world? Summarize the debate over whether U.S.-Soviet cooperation was possible after the war.
3. Discuss the beginning and evolution of the Cold War. Include the idea of bipolarity in the discussion. What was the Cuban Missile Crisis, and why was it so important in this evolution?
4. What is necessary peace? Why is it important in understanding the way the Cold War evolved? Apply this analysis to the deadliness and dangerousness of the Cold War.

5. Summarize the major characteristics of the Cold War. How did these characteristics help give rise to the policy of containment. Describe the containment paradigm.
6. How did the Cold War end? Include the concept of a Potemkin village in your answer and how it applies to the collapse of the Soviet Union.
7. What are fault lines? What have the two fault lines of the past quarter-century been, and how have they changed the environment of foreign policy?
8. What two major trends have emerged from the fault lines? How do they affect the contemporary problem of American foreign policy and the viability of the containment paradigm?

CORE SUGGESTED READINGS

Allison, Graham. *Essence of Decision: Explaining the Cuban Missile Crisis.* Boston: Little Brown, 1971. This book is considered the classic, definitive case study of the Cuban Missile Crisis, and its analysis remains as relevant as it was at the time in understanding decision making in crisis situations.

Djilas, Milovan. *The New Class: An Analysis of the Communist System.* San Diego: Harcourt Brace Jovanovich, 1957. This classic examination of how communist systems operated in the Soviet Union and Eastern Europe was written by a leading Yugoslav dissident and offers insights into both how communism operated and the foibles and weaknesses of the system well before the vulnerability of communist regimes was suspected or recognized.

Gaddis, John Lewis. *Strategies of Containment: A Critical Appraisal of Postwar American National Security Policy During the Cold War* (Rev. and exp. ed.). New York: Oxford University Press, 2005. The original edition of this acclaimed history and critique of the Cold War was written in the early 1980s, when the Cold War was ongoing. The revised edition updates and interprets both the dynamics and chronology with the advantage of hindsight.

Gorbachev, Mikhail. *Perestroika: New Thinking for Our Country and the World.* New York: Harper & Row, 1987. At the time of its release, Gorbachev's pronouncements, particularly regarding the Soviet Union's intention to become a more normal state, were greeted with great skepticism. A fascinating aspect of reading this book is to see how many of his promises came true.

Kennan, George F. "The Sources of Soviet Conduct." *Foreign Affairs* 25, 4 (July 1947), 566–582. Based on the Long Telegram of 1946, this is the text of the definitive underpinning of the American strategy of containment during the Cold War, including Kennan's assessments of the weaknesses and vulnerabilities of the communist system, insights long overlooked or ignored in the West.

ADDITIONAL READINGS AND REFERENCES

Allison, Graham, and Robert Blackwill. "America's Stake in the Soviet Future." *Foreign Affairs* 70, 3 (Summer 1991), 77–97.

Bakier, Abdul Hameed. "The 'Lone Wolf' and Al-Qaeda Sleeper Cells in the United States." *Terrorism Focus* (online) 5, 2 (January 15, 2008).

Beinhart, Peter. "Think Again: Reagan." *Foreign Policy* July/August 2010, 28–33.

Bialer, Seweryn, and Michael Mandelbaum (eds.). *Gorbachev's Russia and American Foreign Policy.* Boulder, CO: Westview Press, 1988.

Brzezinski, Zbigniew. "The Cold War and Its Aftermath." *Foreign Affairs* 71, 4 (Fall 1992), 31–48.

Claude, Inis. *The Changing United Nations*. New York: Random House, 1967.

Freedman, Lawrence D. "Frostbitten." *Foreign Affairs* 89, 2 (March/April 2010), 136–144.

Gaddis, John Lewis. *The United States and the End of the Cold War: Implications, Reconsiderations, Provocations*. New York: Oxford University Press, 1992.

Gorbachev, Mikhail. *The Coming Century of Peace*. New York: Richardson and Stierman, 1986.

Heymann, Philip B., and Juliette Kayyem. *Protecting Liberty in an Age of Terrorism*. Cambridge, MA: MIT Press, 2005.

Kagan, Robert. "The September 12 Paradigm." *Foreign Affairs* 87, 5 (September/October 2008), 25–39.

Kennan, George F. *American Diplomacy, 1900–1950*. New York: New American Library, 1951.

________. *Memoirs*. Boston, MA: Little Brown, 1976.

Kennedy, Robert F. *The Thirteen Days: A Memoir of the Cuban Missile Crisis*. New York: W. W. Norton, 1999 (originally published in 1963).

King, Charles, and Rajan Menon. "Prisoners of the Caucasus." *Foreign Affairs* 89, 4 (July/August 2010), 20–34.

Krauthammer, Charles. "The Unipolar Moment." *Foreign Affairs* 70, 1 (Winter 2000/2001), 23–33.

Legvold, Robert. "The Russia File." *Foreign Affairs* 88, 4 (July/August 2009), 79–93.

Mearsheimer, John J. "Why We Shall Miss the Cold War." *Atlantic Monthly* 266, 2 (August 1990), 35–50.

Nye, Joseph S. Jr. *The Paradox of American Power: Why the World's Superpower Can't Go It Alone*. New York: Oxford University Press, 2003.

Rose, Richard, William Mishler, and Neil Munro. *Russia Transformed: Developing Popular Support for a New Regime*. New York: Cambridge University Press, 2006.

Sestanovich, Stephen. "What Has Moscow Done?" *Foreign Affairs* 87, 6 (November/December 2008), 12–28.

Shevtsova, Lilia. "Russia's Ersatz Democracy." *Current History* 105, 693 (October 2006), 307–314.

Simes, Dmitri. "The Return of Russian History." *Foreign Affairs* 73, 1 (January/February 1992), 67–82.

Snow, Donald M. *The Necessary Peace: Nuclear Weapons and Superpower Relations*. Lexington, MA: Lexington Books, 1987.

_______. *The Shadow of the Mushroom-Shaped Cloud*. Columbus, OH: Consortium for International Studies Education, 1978.

Trenin, Dmitri. "Russia Reborn." *Foreign Affairs* 88, 6 (November/December 2009), 64–78.

Tucker, Robert W., and Donald C. Hendrickson. "The Sources of American Legitimacy." *Foreign Affairs* 83, 6 (November/December 2004), 18–32.

Zelikow, Philip D. "The Suicide of the East." *Foreign Affairs* 88, 6 (November/December 2009), 130–140.

PART I

Foreign Policy Processes

CHAPTER 3

Decision Making and U.S. Foreign Policy

Nixon (left) and Kissinger were a close foreign policy team, but sometimes they differed on policy, as was the case with Cienfuegos.

PREVIEW

The purpose of this chapter is to provide an overview of a range of theories and concepts that have been developed to explain the foreign policy decision-making process. Political scientists and others have made a consistent effort to try to explain why and how particular policy decisions are reached. The effort cuts across several types of explanation and is multidisciplinary in many ways, with concepts borrowed from political psychology, social psychology, management studies, organizational behavior, economics, and history—to name just a few. This chapter provides a brief overview of some of the key ways that students of the American foreign policy process approach the task of explaining the work of foreign policy decision making.

KEY CONCEPTS

perception
cognition
political belief systems
operational code
historical analogies
cognitive consistency
personality
groupthink
vigilant decision making
Bureaucratic Politics paradigm
standard operating procedures (SOPs)
policy types
crisis
constructivism

After a meeting of President Richard M. Nixon's key foreign policy advisors in September 1970, the Director of Central Intelligence, Richard Helms, stayed behind to show some satellite reconnaissance photographs taken by a U-2 spy plane to Henry Kissinger, Nixon's National Security Advisor. The photographs showed a relatively large naval facility under construction at Cienfuegos, Cuba; the pictures also showed that a soccer field was being prepared. A CIA analyst apparently noted that Cubans played little soccer, so the field was probably meant more for Soviet naval crews than for Cubans—suggesting that the Soviet Union was on the verge of a significant increase in its naval presence (including the presence of nuclear armed submarines) very close to the U.S. coast.

Kissinger then took the photographs to the president, showing them to Nixon's Chief of Staff, H.R. "Bob" Haldeman, before briefing Nixon on the developments. Haldeman, recalling the incident in his memoirs (*The Ends of Power*), apparently did not grasp the gravity of the soccer field. Kissinger boiled it down for him: "those soccer fields could mean war." With Haldeman still not understanding the connection, Kissinger explained further: "Cubans play *baseball*, Russians play *soccer*."

Leaving aside the fact that Cubans did, in fact, play soccer, Kissinger was right that there was construction under way for some kind of Soviet naval base at Cienfuegos in 1970. It could not have come at a worse time. The war in Vietnam was raging, there was a crisis in Chile and another one in Jordan, *and* Nixon's popularity was dropping (dipping below 50 percent for the first time in his presidency). These were the kinds of times of which Kissinger would regularly quip, "We can't have a crisis this week, my schedule is full."

You have probably never heard of this episode, one some feared could blossom into a second Cuban Missile Crisis, in part because President Nixon decided not to let this situation mushroom into a full-blown crisis. Calls were made and agreements were reached, and while the incident did break briefly into the news, mostly it was handled quietly.

The very fact, however, that an incident like this presents such a wide degree of choice to top policy makers in the United States (with Kissinger thinking the episode was critical and Nixon wanting it handled quietly) underscores how difficult the task is of understanding the foreign policy-making process. What happens when the president of the United States and the group of advisors the president assembles actually make decisions? What theories or concepts are available to help one understand this process, to "see" the decision-making process and make sense of it (even though it often happens in secret)?

This case highlights the many different and complex dynamics that are a part of the policy-making process. Who the individuals are that are in positions of power makes a difference; after all, different people come into their jobs with different beliefs, experiences, and policy preferences. The dynamics that are set in motion when individuals operate in small groups are also important; sometimes groups fight among themselves, sometimes they work well together, and sometimes they become a mutually reinforcing clique that fails to do their work vigilantly. The role of bureaucratic settings also may exert influence on the process; how the bureaucracy is structured, peoples' place in the bureaucracy, the influence of standard operating procedures (SOPs), and the games that bureaucrats play when policy equals power and information is the currency that is used—all these too play a role.

The case also underscores that the meaning of all events does not come clearly defined. Individuals imbue events with meaning, constructing the significance, or lack thereof, regarding events in world politics. Certainly policy makers try to be "rational," but there are inherent limits to rationality. How are we to understand foreign policy decision making?

This chapter discusses some of the main theories and concepts that foreign policy analysts use to try to understand the way American foreign policy is made. Some of these factors are discussed in more detail later in the book (see, for instance, Chapter Five); here explanations that focus on individual, small group, and bureaucratic factors receive special scrutiny. The chapter also examines some of the ways that political scientists have tried to explain foreign policy making across these different decision-making settings.

Sometimes it seems there are as many academic approaches to the study of the foreign policy process as there are scholars writing about the process. Even though the approach to understanding foreign policy decision making in general, and American foreign policy making in particular, is laced with work from many disciplines outside political science, there are some central theoretical families that have common reference points. Many of these tend to cluster around three different decision-making settings; that is, they operate by exploring the decision-making dynamics from the perspectives of individuals, small groups of individuals, or large-scale organizations and bureaucracies. A particular analyst normally tries to build explanations at one of these levels because he or she is persuaded that it is the setting most important for understanding how decisions get made.

Some other approaches try to get at the dynamics of decision making in other ways. The latter part of the chapter, therefore, will focus on some of main ways that such an analysis proceeds, including the **policy types** approach and an approach often called **constructivism** or "social constructivism." There is some overlap across all of these theories, but analysts tend to be rooted in one or another of these approaches to explaining American foreign policy decision making.

The purpose of this chapter is to introduce students to some of the key scholarly approaches to the study of foreign policy making. At the outset, it is useful to recall that the domestic context within which U.S. foreign policy is crafted today and into the future, as noted in Chapter One, is one that is increasingly intermestic, hyperpartisan, and fractured—making the job of crafting foreign policy perhaps harder than ever before. At the same time, the global context that U.S. policy makers work within is increasingly globalized, interconnected, and interdependent—making foreign policy problems perhaps more complex than ever before, and making it extremely difficult to craft global solutions. One of the real "tests" for these approaches to the study of the foreign policy process is therefore the extent to which they can capture and explain these dynamics.

WHO MAKES DECISIONS AND HOW?

One of the things that distinguishes the study of foreign policy (often called "foreign policy analysis") as a subfield is that academics in this area are dedicated to building explanations of foreign policy behavior that mirror as much as possible the actual dynamics of decision making. Much of the study of international relations assumes away these complexities, arguing instead that states act "as if" they were rational actors, and therefore bypass these complicated (and sometimes contradictory) dynamics. While explanations that emerge from foreign policy analysis are perhaps less parsimonious, they are nonetheless sometimes far richer and more realistic.

The interest in building explanations of foreign policy behavior—and for the purposes of this book, U.S. foreign policy behavior—comes from more than just a preference for complex constructs as opposed to simpler ones; it is inspired by the sense that to understand foreign policy decisions and behaviors the analyst must be able to see situations as the policy makers themselves saw them. In other words, the study of foreign policy decision making begins with the assumption that policy is made by individual decision makers working in groups. Policies, decisions, and behaviors are, in that sense, linked to the nature of the process that is used to reach policy decisions (or to decide *not* to make a decision). Process *is* policy; change the people, change the process, and the result may be a different policy. Scholars working in this area often think of the "decision" as the unit of analysis in a study, and thus focus on how decision makers define the situations they face.

Beyond this starting point, however, there are many roads. Some scholars have focused their efforts on understanding the psychology and beliefs of individuals as the key to understanding decision making. Others have focused on the dynamics (and often the malfunctions) that emerge when individuals work in small groups. Still others have focused on the role of bureaucracy and bargaining among decision makers as the "essence" of decision. The chapter will briefly review the concepts and dynamics that have been developed at each of these theoretical clusters: individual, small group, and bureaucratic politics.

Individual Explanations

One reason to focus on individuals as the key to understanding the policy-making process arises from the fundamental assumption that individuals matter, individuals make a difference, and individuals are different. Policy decisions depend in some nontrivial way on how the individual sees the world. Different people in the same situation can make different choices. When a person is in a position to actually decide, or to influence the one who does make the decisions, it makes sense to study those people, their role in the process, and how they came to the policy preferences that they hold. Of central importance to those who study the individual decision maker are the concepts of **perception** and "**cognition**"—how do leaders see the world and think about it. From this perspective, it is perhaps less important how you as a student of foreign policy see a situation; what matters is how the policy makers see the situation and how they perceive the world.

Much of the work with this type of analysis has focused on ways to try to study the **political belief systems** of important leaders. A political belief system is a coherently integrated set of images about politics and the political world. Not everyone has a fully developed political belief system, but the presumption is that political leaders are likely to have one. Belief systems are formed by a combination of memories, values, and historical precedents. The belief system is a way of making sense of a complex world. It is a political anchor, as it were, that screens out what is not important and highlights what is important. These screens, meant to be helpful, shape a leader's view of new situations and can perhaps drive policy preferences.

One interesting way that scholars have tried to understand and study belief systems has been to study a leader's **operational code**. A leader's operational code is a set of beliefs about the nature of the political world and about the effective strategies for dealing with that world. By examining a leader's speeches, books, articles, memoirs, and even letters, one can develop an outline of that person's operational code, even "at a distance" (as opposed to having direct access to that person so as to ask questions of him or her). Then one can try to find links between the leader's beliefs and the policy choices that the person made.

One classic example of this type of analysis was a study of Eisenhower's Secretary of State, John Foster Dulles. Dulles was one of the most important players in Ike's foreign policy process during the 1950s. Dulles's operational code about the Soviet Union was so rigid that when the Soviets acted contrary to Dulles's mind-set about them, the information would be discarded rather than updating the operational code. When the Soviets behaved "better" than his operational code believed possible, that information would be rejected. Negative behavior would only underscore the validity of the belief system. Such a closed, rigid mind-set can easily contribute to misperception and policy error.

How one sees or perceives the world is influenced by a variety of factors. One of the primary screens through which information of the world must pass inside individuals is the memories that policy makers have of the past. Some memories are of things that they experienced; others are lessons they've learned from history. How policy makers see the world is thus conditioned to some extent by what they have seen in the past (or learned from it). New information and new experiences get put into place inside this memory, given meaning in that context.

The way that policy makers use history, and in particular utilize **historical analogies**, has received close scrutiny from students of the decision-making process. Analogies are a form of cognitive shortcut, a quick way to make meaning out of something new by referring to something from the past. To say that Situation X is *like* Situation Y from the past is to employ an historical analogy. Just as students can get these wrong on the SAT or ACT test, however, it turns out policy makers are often not very good at applying historical precedents. Maybe a lesson to learn from Munich in 1938 (when Great Britain's Neville Chamberlain worked out what he thought was a deal with Hitler, only to find that Hitler would go on to take more of Europe, leading to World War II) is that "appeasement" can be a dangerous strategy; but is it always *wrong*? Or in another case, just because Korea and Vietnam were both countries divided by an artificially imposed line separating the communist north from the U.S.-allied south, did that mean that the same dynamics were playing out in Vietnam as had played out in Korea, requiring the same kind of policy response? Historical analogies can be great mental shortcuts, but they can also quickly lead one down a path to disaster when the analogy provides to be false or misleading.

In his 1992 book *Analogies at War*, Yuen Foong Khong scrutinizes how American policy makers use analogical reasoning in the decision-making process. Khong argues that analogies are devices that policy makers use to help them make decisions, especially in novel situations. Unfortunately, policy makers have a tendency to select analogies that do not quite fit the new situation, which often leads policy astray. The Munich analogy, and also Korea, Khong argues, likely predisposed leaders to view events in Vietnam in a particular way with a particular policy prescription (aggression that required a military response).

One thing that the studies of leaders and political psychology have general agreement about is that human beings are cognitive misers, meaning that they try to find mental shortcuts to reach a decision, and that the techniques used to be miserly can have a profound impact on how one sees the world and responds to it. Several decision-making "pathologies," or failures to be particularly rigorous about decision making, appear to be linked to these shortcuts. One is the way that the effort to attain **cognitive consistency** can harm the decision-making process. *Cognitive consistency* refers to the tendency to process information so as to keep one's views of reality consistent with one's underlying conceptions of reality. Individuals thus often filter out information that does not fit their underlying political belief systems. To the extent that George W. Bush saw the world as divided between "good" and "evil," these categories were also shortcuts that could be used to more quickly respond to the behavior of other states.

The effort to achieve cognitive consistency can be healthy and adaptive. However, when individuals persistently filter out relevant information that does not fit their underlying set of beliefs about politics, the effort has veered off into the area of what is sometimes called "irrational" consistency seeking. This can take one of several forms. One is premature cognitive closure, which means that a decision maker shuts down the process of decision making early, before a rigorous examination of information and preferences is carried out. With such a quick decision, the concern is that it can often lead into disaster. President Eisenhower used to say to his advisors, "Let's not make our mistakes in a hurry," as a rejoinder against this tendency.

Foreign policy is an inherently complex issue area, laden with tough choices and difficult trade-offs. The lack of perception of trade-offs is another example of irrational consistency seeking. Here a decision maker fails to take into account trade-offs that are invariably a part of political decision making. To see a world without trade-offs is perhaps a sign that a rigorous decision-making process has broken down. U.S.-Cuba policy exemplifies this phenomenon. Decision makers have been so wedded to absolute outcomes (the fall of Castro and communism or its retention in pure form) that intermediary solutions that involve trade-offs have perhaps not been given full consideration in trying to fashion that policy.

Bolstering, or postdecisional rationalization, is another sign of irrational consistency seeking. The idea here is that after the fact a decision maker creates all the reasons why a decision was made and why it was the right decision to make. Unfortunately, this only happens after a decision is made, not as part of the decision-making process. Thus it is called "bolstering," because the presumption is a person is trying to bolster his or her sense of having made a good decision (even when the person perhaps did not). A leader might thus delude him- or herself into thinking the policy process was rigorous. The postinvasion rationalizations of the wisdom of invading Iraq may be a good example of bolstering by the Bush administration.

The previous dynamics all dealt with shutting down a thorough decision-making process. Hypervigilance, however, is quite the reverse. Here, time pressure and stress might drive a leader—who wants to make a good and careful decision—to become too open to information, and thus lose the ability to sift it and reach decisions based on it. The capacity for critical reasoning is lost, and a leader might be either frozen in indecision or extremely susceptible to the influence of others. Some have argued that President Carter found himself in this position during the 444-day crisis with Iran, during which Americans from the U.S. Embassy were held hostage.

One thing that is important to note is that the presence of stress is likely to heighten the dangers of these dynamics. Governing is inherently stressful, and foreign policy crises are by definition very stressful events. Crises threaten the country, offer limited time to develop a response, and often emerge by surprise. These situations often include options to use force associated with them as well, and so are literally matters of life and death. Stress, like all the other damaging impacts on purely rational decision making, can result in less-than-optimal outcomes.

If people matter, and people make decisions, then it would follow that different people might behave differently even in the same situations. Following this line of thinking, a great deal of research attention has been paid to **personality** differences among leaders, especially among U.S. presidents. There are a variety of ways that scholars have tried to define and measure "personality" and how it has an impact on decision making. Chapter Four discusses one way that presidential personality and advisory group structures interact, for example. Here it is worth pondering how leaders' personality characteristics shape the decisions they make.

Foreign policy scholars often focus on an individual's need for control, cognitive complexity, and degree of policy experience as central to framing a leader's political personality. As Preston's research shows, for example, Bill Clinton had low needs for control and a high level of cognitive complexity, along with foreign policy inexperience. His preference for less formal decision-making processes and high reliance on expert advisors meant that Clinton often had a more "decisive" style than other presidents. This was evident in the 1993–1994 crisis over North Korea's nuclear program, where Clinton deferred greatly to expert advisors, heavily sought information, and was constantly open to new information and new policy options for dealing with North Korea, in contrast with the style employed in the George W. Bush administration. This contrast is discussed in the *Intersections* box that follows.

Small-Group Explanations

Very often when the president is faced with a difficult decision, a small team is assembled to help sift through information, generate alternatives, and make suggestions about what policy the president should select. Keeping in mind that the individuals who are members of this small group may well be experiencing some of the personal dynamics mentioned above, when a group of individuals is constructed to help make a decision, many would argue that special small-group dynamics can emerge that impinge on the decision-making process. In those cases where a small group is the "ultimate decision unit," then it makes sense to study the group as the locus of decision.

INTERSECTIONS

"Beliefs and Policy Toward North Korea"

U.S. policy makers disagree about how to deal with North Korea, home of the world's fourth largest military and a small nuclear arsenal.

In the early years of the Clinton administration there was grave concern that North Korea, also called the Democratic People's Republic of Korea (DPRK), was trying to develop nuclear weapons. At that time, 1993–1994, the North Korean weapons program was driven by taking "spent fuel" from nuclear reactors to a "breeder plant" at Yongbyon where it was processed into weapons grade plutonium. Absent good military options for eliminating the North Korean weapons program and believing that diplomacy was the only possible way to prevent North Korea from becoming a nuclear weapons state, the Clinton administration entered into negotiations with North Korea. While there were a number of contacts between the governments of the United States and North Korea, the most public (but to some extent "unofficial") contact was when former President Jimmy Carter went to North Korea to personally negotiate a deal.

Ultimately an Agreed Framework was reached in October 1994. Under the Framework, North Korea promised to halt its reprocessing activities and allow inspections by the International Atomic Energy Agency (IAEA). In return, the United States, South Korea, Japan, and others would help provide replacement nuclear reactors (that could not be used to produce weapons-grade fuel); in the meantime, North Korea would get large amounts of fuel oil as a substitute source

(Continued)

(Continued)

of energy. While the DPRK was not an easy negotiating partner, to say the least, key actors in the Clinton administration believed that North Korea's nuclear ambitions could be assuaged through negotiations, including through direct U.S.-DPRK talks.

At the outset of the Bush administration it was clear that a different set of actors held a different set of beliefs. Especially following the attacks of 9/11, when North Korea was listed as part of the "Axis of Evil," it was clear that President Bush, Secretary of Defense Rumsfeld, Ambassador to the UN John Bolton, and others, believed that a "crime and punishment" approach was more in order than the negotiation strategy of the Clinton years. The early Bush administration refused to meet one-on-one with North Korea, but would only do so through a six-party framework (including North and South Korea, the United States, Russia, China, and Japan). When the administration got tough on North Korea, cutting off fuel oil, North Korea responded by kicking out inspectors and restarting the fuel reprocessing. North Korea tested a small nuclear weapon in 2006, followed by a larger test in 2009.

Before jumping to the conclusion that "political party" explains the difference in policy approach more so than "beliefs," it is worth noting that later in the Bush administration a different set of Republican policy makers began to pursue a more intensive diplomatic approach with North Korea. Secretary of State Rice and her Deputy, John Negroponte, approved of the diplomatic missions by longtime Foreign Service Officer and then Assistant Secretary of State for East Asian and Pacific Affairs Christopher Hill. And indeed, how to approach relations with North Korea was a hot item in the 2008 U.S. Presidential campaign, with a number of positions being staked out by different candidates. At a minimum, the incident demonstrates that different people can look at the same evidence and come away with different conclusions, in part because they have different beliefs that shape what they see.

There is a long tradition of research on small-group decision making (which cuts across many other fields of inquiry, including the study of juries and marketing and advertising) associated with the concept of **groupthink**. First generated in the 1960s and 1970s by social psychologist Irving Janis (1982), *groupthink* refers to "the Psychological tendency for individuals within organizations to alter their views or perceptions in ways that allow them to conform with other members of a group with which they all identify." In other words, *sometimes* it seems that the individuals who are part of a small decision-making group actually set aside their own sense of what needs to be done in order to conform with the group. Rather than "rocking the boat," or advocating personal positions at odds with the group, they "go along to get along"; they place a higher value on being a member of the group than they do on making a vigilant decision. The italicized modifier, however, suggests that this is not always the case.

Janis came to this study while watching "fiascoes" unfold in American foreign policy: the failed mission at the Bay of Pigs and the Vietnam War, for example. Janis applied his research on small-group dynamics to U.S. foreign policy process, looking to see if he could find evidence that the "best and the brightest" had made critical errors because no one wanted to speak up and say what perhaps others also thought.

Janis hypothesized that if groupthink were occurring, the careful observer should be able to detect certain symptoms of concurrence-seeking behavior. He suggested that the group would, for example, overestimate its power and morality, and share illusions of invulnerability, all of which could lead the group to make riskier decisions than any other they as individuals might otherwise select. There should be evidence of "closed-mindedness" by the group, including stereotypes of enemy leaders and also efforts to discount warning signs. If concurrence-seeking behavior were happening, there would also be pressures toward uniformity in the group, including direct pressure on dissenters to "get in line" and be a loyal member of the group. There might even be self-appointed "mind guards"—members who protect the group from adverse information that might shatter their shared complacency about the effectiveness and morality of the decisions.

According to the groupthink hypothesis, if these dynamics occur in a decision-making group, there would likely be severe consequences for the decision-making process. The basic steps of a sound decision-making process would likely be shut off, leading to a short and biased process that fails to thoroughly scrutinize information, examine risks, or develop contingency plans (why plan for contingencies when you know you are right?).

For Janis, the failed invasion at the Bay of Pigs was the "perfect fiasco." The idea behind the April 1961 operation was for a group of fourteen hundred Cuban exiles to be covertly reinserted into Cuba at the Bay of Pigs, thus triggering the counterrevolution that would drive Fidel Castro from power. What resulted was not just a policy fiasco but also a huge embarrassment for the United States, since American involvement in the plan became apparent. As Janis details, decision makers in this case made several critical mistakes and misjudgments in their assumptions about the operation and in how they handled information. They thought, for example, that no one would find out that the United States was behind the invasion, that Castro's military was too weak to handle this small force, and that news of the invasion would spur popular uprisings against Castro. They should have known better.

A great deal of research has followed Janis's lead. Some of the work in this area has explored what sort of situations might trigger groupthink (for example, does a small, cohesive, homogenous group have more of a tendency toward groupthink than a larger, more diverse one?). Other research has explored what the relationship is between decision-making process errors and policy failure or success. While it is rare that groupthink in its full form occurs, there is strong evidence that the emergence of even some of these dynamics can shut down the decision-making process. Conversely, evidence suggests that to the extent a decision-making process is **vigilant**—

paying close attention to the tasks that are the essential elements of making a decision—the likelihood of a positive outcome is increased. In general terms, the tasks of decision making include the following:

- Surveying the objectives or goals to be fulfilled
- Canvassing alternative courses of action
- Searching for new information relevant to evaluating the alternatives
- Assimilating that new information
- Examining the benefits, costs, and risks of the alternative that is preferred
- Developing, implementing, and monitoring contingency plans

The groupthink hypothesis is widely used to help understand decision making and widely taught in political science, social psychology, organization theory, and even marketing classes and studies of the behavior of juries. Nonetheless, it continues to confound researchers. As mentioned earlier, it is rare to find groupthink occurring in its full form, and it is very common to find some elements of groupthink present without them resulting in the consequences of groupthink. Yetiv has shown, for example, that several symptoms of groupthink can be seen in the decision-making process that led up to the Persian Gulf War in 1990–1991, and yet that process nonetheless remained relatively vigilant and did not result in a fiasco. Needless to say, why groupthink sometimes happens and sometimes does not continues to occupy foreign policy analysts.

Another way that analysts of U.S. foreign policy have studied these dynamics has focused on the management style of presidents: How do presidents structure and manage the groups they form to help make decisions? This approach is highlighted in Chapter Four. Applied to both crises and noncrises, research in this area has tended to focus on how presidents structure advisors along one of three "ideal types." The "Formalistic" model would place the president at the top of a hierarchically organized group where jurisdictions are clearly articulated. The "Competitive" model, however, would place the president on top of a group of advisors who share overlapping responsibilities and who are urged to compete, or debate, for the president's attention. The "Collegial" model is structured more like the spokes on a wheel, with the president at the center of a decision-making group. This model would emphasize teamwork and group responsibility for decision making and problem solving.

A president's selection of one form of organization or another is certainly linked to the president's preferences for how much time he or she wants to spend on foreign policy making, how much control over the process the president wants or needs, and also the president's personal style for dealing with other people. These models are also discussed at more length and with examples in the chapter on the Presidency (Chapter Four). While not all U.S. foreign policy decisions are made by small groups, when they are it makes sense to study the nature of that group and how dynamics within the group may have an impact on the decision-making process and therefore on the choices that are made in the name of the country.

The Bureaucratic Politics Paradigm

A type of explanation that focuses on the impact of organizational structures on the behavior and choices of political leaders has come to be called the **Bureaucratic Politics paradigm.** This scholarly tradition is most associated with the seminal work of Harvard political scientist Graham Allison, who applied different "conceptual lenses" to the record of the Cuban Missile Crisis to show how important bureaucratic and organizational dynamics can be to the foreign policy process. A long tradition of research in this area has followed.

As with the focus on individuals and small groups, the Bureaucratic Politics paradigm begins by setting itself apart from the rational ideal of policy making, noting that there are limits to how close to the ideal human beings in organizations can ever really get. Allison, who has developed his own typology of bureaucratic interaction based on three models, is still one of the most prominent advocates of this approach.

Allison calls the rational model Model 1, or the first set of lenses through which one might try to see the foreign policy process. In this model, the presumption is that foreign policy is the product of rational actions and choices. Foreign policy is arrived at through an exhaustive information search, followed by a rigorous process of assigning the outcomes that are likely to follow from different policies and then weighing the benefits of those outcomes. The action chosen will be the one that corresponds with the policy most likely to lead to the most preferred outcome. As with the use of the rational model in previous forms of explanation, this model often takes on a *prescriptive* function, suggesting that it is the ideal for which policy makers should aim when they make decisions.

Allison calls Model 2 the Organizational Process model. This model sees foreign policy as perhaps nothing more than the "outputs" of large organizations functioning according to standardized patterns of behavior. Policy making, according to this view, is driven by SOPs, divided responsibilities and jurisdictions, and coordination procedures that are established long before a particular foreign policy choice emerges. The search for information in this model is seen as nonexhaustive and problem driven; the effort is to get enough information to be able to make a policy choice and move on. SOPs drive the information search and also the way that participants see the information and evaluate alternatives. Organizational goals can be equated with "the national interest" in this model. This model focuses on the way an organization processes information, which can

Analyst's Conceptual Model	View of What "Policy" Is
Rational	Rational act/choice
Organizational Process	Output of preestablished routines
Bureaucratic Politics	Outcome of bargaining games

FIGURE 3.1
What Does "Policy" Mean?

have an impact on the way it perceives, evaluates, and acts on information and a situation.

The Bureaucratic Politics model, Model 3, sees government behavior as the outcome of bargaining games where power is shared. It sees policy as the outcome of a political process that includes compromise, coalitions, competition, and even confusion among government officials who see different faces of a situation. This model emphasizes "players in position" who promote parochial interests and the way that "where you stand depends on where you sit"; that is, where one stands on an issue will be rooted in where one sits around the cabinet table. In this view, the foreign policy-making process is driven by a limited information search, hidden motives, and "pulling and hauling" among participants who are vying to "win" the policy game. It sees the outcomes of this infighting and political maneuvering as important to explaining foreign policy decisions. In this sense, the Bureaucratic Politics model sees foreign policy as nothing more than the outcome of these bargaining games among participants. It is not necessarily rational or irrational; rather, it reflects the interests of who won the policy game.

INTERSECTIONS

The Domestic Politics of Foreign Policy

There were a number of actions taken by the U.S. government to make the homeland more secure following the terrorist attacks of 9/11, including military action in Afghanistan. Some of the measures were taken in the United States and included bold new measures to monitor communications in order to try to uncover terrorist plots. Part of the reason was that many of the 9/11 hijackers had lived in the United States for years, had travelled frequently, and had regular contact with sponsors abroad. The Bush administration therefore set about trying to unearth any such future plots by, among other means, developing new ways to monitor telephone, email, and web traffic by the National Security Agency—including traffic inside the United States by U.S. citizens. Depending on one's stance toward these measures (only some of which are known to this day), these programs came to be called the "Terrorist Surveillance Program" (TSP for short), "Electronic Eavesdropping," or "Illegal Wiretapping" since the program ran afoul of the law, in the eyes of many. (Will Smith's 1998 movie, *Enemy of the State*, might come to mind.) In this regard, at least, foreign policy and domestic politics run right into one another.

One of the things that made the Bush program so controversial—once word of the program was leaked to the press and the public—was that the Congress had created an avenue for seeking "wiretaps" of American citizens for national security purposes in 1978, following the Watergate scandal. The Foreign Intelligence Surveillance Act (FISA) recognized the need to monitor the communications of some Americans who might be working with foreign agents to undermine national security, and established a process for acquiring warrants for wiretaps from a special court that came to be called

(Continued)

(Continued)

the FISA court. In its history, the FISA court hardly ever turned down a warrant request and did not do so immediately after 9/11 either. However, something about what the Bush administration was doing by 2003 and 2004 started to worry the court, and warrants started to be rejected as illegal, a source of concern in the administration.

Bush and his top advisors decided to circumvent the FISA court, arguing that he had all the authority he needed to run this program based on the Constitution's grant of Executive authority to the President, the President's role as Commander-in-Chief, and the congressional authorization to use military force that was passed after 9/11. Rather than run the program through the FISA court, Bush decided to have the Office of Legal Counsel inside the Justice Department, and the Attorney General, sign off that the program was "legal."

As personnel in these offices changed over time, new actors came to view the program differently and were concerned about its legality. These concerns came to a dramatic crescendo, as detailed in Eric Lichtblau's book, *Bush's Law*, in March 2004, when it was time for the Justice Department to once again certify that the program was legal. The Deputy Attorney General, James Comey, had come to believe that it was not; Attorney General Ashcroft had come to agree with him. Just then, Ashcroft took ill and was rushed to the hospital with a dire case of pancreatitis. In his absence, Comey would thus serve as the Acting Attorney General until Ashcroft was well enough to return to work.

Comey, who would later testify before Congress about these events, met with Bush's top aides on March 10, 2004, the day before the program had to be recertified. He told them that he would not recertify the program. That night Comey got a call that the White House Chief of Staff, Andrew Card, and the White House Counsel, Alberto Gonzales, were on their way to the hospital to see the very ill John Ashcroft, apparently to try to convince him to sign off on the program since Comey would not. A key foreign and national security policy decision was about to play out in a hospital room!

Comey rushed to the hospital in order to be there with Ashcroft when the others arrived. They came carrying an envelope—the documents they wanted signed by Ashcroft. The very ill Ashcroft lifted his head up and in a moment of great clarity rattled off his concerns about the program, making it clear that he agreed with Comey. He then concluded by saying it did not matter what he thought anyway because, "I'm not the attorney general." He pointed at Comey and said, "There is the attorney general."

The scene ended, but not the drama. Comey was summoned to a meeting at the White House the next day. Fearing that the White House would push ahead anyway, Comey and many others (apparently including the FBI Director and several top Justice Department officials) were ready to resign *en masse*. (Such an event would have been reminiscent of the "Saturday Night Massacre" during Watergate, when the Attorney General, his Deputy, and the Special Prosecutor investigating President Nixon were all fired.) Comey met privately with President Bush, and Bush agreed that the program should be brought into compliance with the Justice Department's concerns. The "crisis" was over; the program would be altered somewhat, and thus ended a dramatic example of how complex, political, *and personal*, foreign and national security policy decision making can get.

In order to show the utility of thinking about the foreign policy process from these different perspectives, Allison—joined by coauthor Phil Zelikow for a new edition of the book recently—applies the models to the October 1962 Cuban Missile Crisis. The crisis was precipitated by intelligence information that the Soviet Union was building missile launchers in Cuba that would allow Soviet offensive ballistic nuclear missiles to be placed in Cuba. President John F. Kennedy assembled a team of advisors, which came to be called the ExComm (short for "Executive Committee of the National Security Council"), to help him decide how to respond to the crisis. For two weeks, the world loomed at the brink of nuclear war.

The rational model does an excellent job of showing how the choice of a naval quarantine, or "blockade," of Cuba was the only real (rational) option under the circumstances and requirements of the situation. Given that Kennedy and his advisors wanted to prevent the Soviet missiles from being put in place, and did not want open war with the Soviets to break out, the choice of the quarantine was only option that held out the hope of meeting those goals. Using military force to "remove" the missile sites would have ended the missile threat, but would quite likely have led to war with the Soviets. Diplomacy through the United Nations would allow the Soviets to put the missiles in place while diplomatic processes went on. The quarantine prevented the missiles from arriving in Cuba while allowing time for diplomacy to proceed.

However, the story is not quite that simple. The Organizational Process model helps make sense of the politics of running the quarantine, showing how the actual tactics of the blockade were dictated by existing routines and SOPS that the Navy had previously developed. Knowing that one day it might have to blockade a location, the Navy had developed rules for how to do it. In this instance, however, the Navy's rules clashed with John F. Kennedy's (JFK's) goals. The Navy wanted to be far away from Cuba, so it could not get shot at from the island. Kennedy wanted the Navy close to Cuba so as to buy time for Soviet leader Nikita Khrushchev to decide to stop the ships en route to Cuba. If they ran the blockade line, war could result. Kennedy wanted the blockade line moved closer to the island. This led to a famous exchange between the Secretary of Defense, Robert McNamara, and the Chief of Naval Operations, Admiral George Anderson, where the two loudly squared off over the rules of the blockade. The meeting ended with Admiral Anderson literally throwing the Navy regulations at the Secretary as a way to answer his intrusive questions. While not very rational, it is the kind of thing one would expect to see when SOPs and routines drive behavior.

The Bureaucratic Politics model, when applied to the historical record, shows that even the choice of the blockade was not as rational as it might seem. The model shows that in fact the option of the blockade was chosen as a result of bargaining games in which the president's brother, Attorney General Robert F. Kennedy, figured prominently. A political struggle in which a winning coalition was built led to the blockade option, in which proponents of the blockade tried to plant warnings in the mind of the president, including the fear that war could come about by accident—trying to warn him off of the military option which some argued would be manageable and successful.

Merging Models 2 and 3 together as a single approach to studying decision making forms the Bureaucratic Politics paradigm; it is one of the most used (and often criticized) approaches to studying American foreign policy. The approach holds many interesting insights, including a way to understand the policy process as one where leaders come to situations with "preferences" already formed. Policy making is perhaps less about discovering preferences than it is about trying to convince others about one's preexisting preferences. That was certainly true of many in the George W. Bush administration, who had argued for military force to remove Saddam Hussein from power since the George H.W. Bush administration. It may not always be the case, but the Bureaucratic Politics paradigm can be very useful in helping us make sense of the often very political nature of the foreign policy process.

OTHER APPROACHES

While perhaps the bulk of the work on the study of foreign policy decision making focuses on one level or the other, there are some other approaches to studying the foreign policy process that try to cut across those specific clusters. One is a type of approach that emphasizes how the decision-making process varies depending on "policy type"; another emerges from a school of thought called "constructivism," or "social constructivism." Both of these perspectives on the policy process merit some individual consideration.

Policy Types

One interesting perspective on the policy process is the idea that *foreign policy* is really an umbrella term, and that to understand who actually makes foreign policy decisions, one needs to break up that umbrella term into its subparts. Drawing on the work of Ripley and Franklin, the suggestion is that there are really three policy types, each with different patterns of access and power to the foreign policy-making process.

First, **crisis** policy deals with emergency threats to national interests or values. Emergencies often come as a surprise; typically, they offer limited response time, entail threats to the national interest, and usually include options to the use of force. These are the kinds of situations that people often have in mind when they use the term *foreign policy*. North Korea's invasion of South Korea in 1950 created a "crisis" for the United States; Iraq's invasion of Kuwait in 1990 did as well; and so did the 9/11 terrorist attacks on New York and Washington, D.C.

The political dynamics that drive crisis policy making tend to be dominated by the president and the small group of advisors around the Oval Office. Indeed, since crises often come with great stress and high threat levels associated with them, psychological and social psychological dynamics of crisis can be of heightened importance during these situations.

Congress tends not to be especially engaged in crisis policy making, and often watches with the rest of the public (and the world) as presidents and their advisors decide how to respond during crises. The choice of going to war in Iraq in 2003, for example, was made by President Bush and a small number of key government policy makers around him. Congress voted on a war authorization, and public opinion was an issue, but the locus of decision making was on the president and his war cabinet, with Congress playing a legitimating but not decision-making role.

Second, *strategic* policy lays out the basic stance of the United States toward another country or a particular problem. Containment, for example, as discussed in the previous chapter, was the basic strategy for dealing with the Soviet Union during the Cold War. Free trade is a basic foreign economic policy for promoting U.S. interests in a global trading system.

Strategic policy is normally formulated inside the executive branch, but usually deep in the bureaucracy rather than at the top (presidential) levels. Before grand strategies become public, interest groups and concerned members of Congress have an opportunity to lobby for certain positions they hold. The public usually learns about these policies once the president announces them. Containment, for example, was developed largely in the State Department and then approved by President Truman. The Reagan Doctrine, which announced that the United States would not view communist regimes around the world as permanent but instead would take steps to undermine those governments, especially in Central America, was a strategic policy mostly developed inside the State and Defense departments and the Central Intelligence Agency, and then approved by the president. Free Trade Agreements are worked out between the U.S. Trade Representative and the governments of other countries; the president later signs off on them before they head to Congress for consideration.

Third, *structural defense* policy focuses on the defense budget, or the policies and programs that deal with defense spending and military bases. These policies usually focus on, for example, buying new aircraft for the Air Force and Navy, or deciding what military bases to consolidate or close down. With the defense budget taking up as much as one-fifth of the total federal budget, this is an area of enormous concern and importance.

Structural defense policy usually starts in the executive branch, but is largely crafted in Congress, whose members tend to have their fingers closely on the pulses of their constituents, where monies authorized in support of particular policies will be expended. The Defense Department bureaucracy, interest groups, and defense contractors have much weight in this process as well. Congress regularly votes to spend more money on defense than the president or the secretary of defense asks for, as they see defense spending to some extent as jobs programs for their districts and states.

One of the important contributions of this perspective on the policy process is that it helps orient the analyst with respect to what and who is likely to matter in foreign policy making. If what one wants to understand is who was involved in the decision to use U.S. air power in Libya in 2011 (a crisis situation), for example, this perspective points toward the president and the group of advisors around him in order to find the locus of decision. If one wants to better understand the decision to build the Joint Strike Fighter, the F-35, or the decision whether to build it with two different types of engines as opposed to engines made by one company, however, this perspective points the analyst toward Congress, congressional staffs, DOD staffers, and defense contractors. It allows for a more nuanced approach to understanding the politics of foreign policy making than perhaps some of the single approaches discussed earlier can provide.

Constructivism

There are a variety of approaches to the study of foreign policy that are motivated by what is sometimes called a "critical," or "reflectivist," approach. The idea is that while classic foreign policy studies might do well to explain why a particular policy was selected, they do not get beneath this surface in order to unearth the, as Roxanne Doty puts it, "how possible" questions. This set of approaches has come to be called "constructivism" or "social constructivism" in recent years because of this focus on the structures of power and meaning that identify some actors as "threats" and others not, some actions as acceptable and others not. In other words, the focus is on how actors use power and position to "construct" meaning out of a world where such meaning is not always obvious on the surface. Policy makers define their own world in terms they understand, and constructivism tries to understand how that process happens.

The social world, as Houghton (2007) notes, is very different from the natural world. Everyone agrees that standing in the way of a tornado is a bad idea, but not all agree that, for example, Iran and North Korea pose vital threats to the United States requiring a military response. Lightning exists in the natural world as a threat; defining someone as a threat, however, is a social activity. Constructivism highlights the ways that learning emerges from the interaction, and even socialization, of policy makers.

Trying to understand how that meaning is constructed requires the analyst to study not a single layer but actually multiple layers of analysis at the same time, and to unearth how they interact with one another. The close examination of language, and the symbolic meaning of the words that leaders choose, is common in constructivist approaches. Some would even argue that politics is all about picking the labels that attach to things. Constructivism thus focuses primary attention on how policy makers create and construct realities.

An example of studies of the Cuban Missile Crisis can help show how constructivism differs from traditional levels of analysis. As discussed earlier, Graham Allison's classic study of the missile crisis examined the way that organizational factors (like standard operating procedures) and bureaucratic politics (the "pulling and hauling" among JFK's advisors) helped shape U.S.

policy in the crisis, including the selection of the quarantine option and the way that the blockade was run by the U.S. Navy. Jutta Weldes, however, in a constructivist study of the same episode, is far less interested in option selection than she is in understanding why there was a missile "crisis" at all. Weldes wants to know why U.S. decision makers saw the missiles as an intolerable threat, one that the United States had an obligation to remove. Her study, and others like it, in some sense begin well before the option selection stage of decision making, believing that the real politics lies in the construction of the situation.

Constructivism wants to know where "ideas" come from in the first place, and how they are put into action. The close study of what words (which are symbols of meaning) are used in order to convince others of a position is often called the study of "discourse," and is common in constructivist approaches. The study of "identity" is also central to constructivist approaches, since identity plays such a critical role in seeing and responding to the world. As Houghton notes, the fact that Great Britain and France have nuclear arsenals does not greatly worry U.S. policy makers—or Americans in general; a very small stockpile of weapons held by North Korea, or Iran's potential to build nuclear weapons, concerns them very much. The United States tends to identify itself as friendly with these European "allies," but identifies North Korea and Iran as "enemies." Why? How did that happen? Those are the kinds of questions pursued by a constructivist approach to the study of U.S. foreign policy.

A final example may be helpful. A common theme of American foreign policy over the years has been the "promotion of democracy." Various interventions have had democracy promotion as their aim, ranging from the support of the Contras in Nicaragua to overthrow the leftist Sandinista government in the 1980s, to the invasion of Panama to overthrow Manuel Noriega in 1989, to justifications given for the invasion of Iraq in 2003. William Robinson steps behind the record in his book *Promoting Polyarchy*. Robinson begins with a constructivist tone, noting that different people can mean different things by the term *democracy*. So what does the U.S. government mean when it promotes democracy, especially when it does so via the use of force?

Robinson argues that in case after case, U.S. intervention has been aimed at implementing a distinct form of democracy that he calls "polyarchy," or a type of democracy where a small group of elites actually rule while mass participation is relegated to only one form of political participation: elections. The meaning of *democracy* as constructed by the United States, in his view, is a limited form of democracy that focuses on procedural forms and institutions (elections) more than on meaningful and deep public participation. Robinson calls polyarchy a form of "low intensity democracy," one that is conducive to the political and economic interests of U.S. elites. Obviously a critic, he sees democracy promotion as a façade that enables a narrow slice of elites to have power both in the United States and around the world.

CONCLUSIONS

Analysts of U.S. foreign policy spend a considerable amount of time studying "process." How is foreign policy actually made? Why is a particular course of action taken, rather than a different one? How was it that policy makers came to see a problem in a particular way, and to respond to it in the way that they did? Who decides, and how? This chapter has reviewed some of the main concepts, theories, and approaches to studying the foreign policy process.

Political scientists and political psychologists have identified a variety of factors at the individual level than can affect decision making. Personality, beliefs, the drive to maintain cognitive consistency, the way cognitive filters can lead to misperception, and the use of historical analogies, all shape how policy makers do their work. The stress that comes from operating under crisis conditions can heighten these dynamics and threaten to shut down the decision-making process, leading to poor decisions and bad outcomes.

A variety of small-group and bureaucratic dynamics can also shape policy making. Often foreign policy is made by individuals working in small groups and by actors who are rooted in the bureaucracy. Understanding how these factors can shape foreign policy decisions is a long-standing concern of students of U.S. foreign and national security policy. The impact of increased political polarization and hyperpartisanship, however, is less well understood; it is reasonable to hypothesize that these conditions will make the policy process even more complex and make vigilant decision making an even harder goal. Trying to cope with foreign policy problems in a complex, interdependent, globalized world only makes the tasks of decision making harder.

Several approaches have been developed that try to go beyond studying one layer at a time. The "policy type" approach is rooted in the idea that different types of foreign policy are driven by different dynamics and have different patterns of access and power. Constructivism is a set of approaches that starts from the presumption that politics and political choice exist in a social world, and thus are constructed and perpetuated by leaders. Rather than focusing on the "why" questions that dominate so much of the field, Constructivists are interested in answering the "how possible" questions; how did a situation even come to be defined the way that policy makers saw it, since that construction then drives the policy-making process.

As is evident from this discussion, there is a broad range of potential theories and approaches that try to understand how U.S. leaders make foreign policy. Many of these approaches are complementary and can build on one another; some of them are quite distinct from each other. All, though, are inspired to some extent from the classic perspective from Snyder, Bruck, and Sapin that people make foreign policy decisions, and so to understand the roots of policy means understanding how these people do their work.

The remaining chapters in this section of the book look at various structural aspects and influences on how decisions are made in the foreign policy realm. It begins with the formal and governmental structures by which policy is made and then examines those areas where people not formally a part of the process—societal forces—attempt to influence and shape foreign policy. The approaches discussed in this chapter deal mostly with explaining governmental actors and their role in decision making—the presidency and the network of foreign policy agencies that advise the president, and the Congress. We hope that reference to one or another of the approaches presented here will not only be helpful in understanding how decisions are made in these contexts, but also might be useful in understanding how actors outside the government see and behave in the foreign policy arena.

WHERE DO WE GO FROM HERE?

It is important to remember that presidents and the advisors they surround themselves with to help make foreign policy decisions are human beings, flesh and blood, not that different from the rest of us in most respects. They certainly have better access to more information about foreign policy than do most people, and they have access to power, but they are still people subject to the same human limitations and frailties that plague the rest of us. If human beings generally do not act in ways that maximize rationality but instead settle for lesser outcomes formed by a variety of forces, why would this not also be true of presidents and advisors when making foreign policy decisions?

APPLICATION: WHERE DO YOU STAND? HOW DO YOU "THINK IN TIME"?

One of the insights that emerges from the Bureaucratic Politics paradigm is the idea that "where you stand depends on where you sit," that one's preferences on an issue in part derive from one's position in the bureaucracy. Can you see any evidence of this around you? Examine the policy preferences of people you know; can you see their preferences as in part being grounded in their organizational position? Your professors, for example: How are their policy choices about your courses driven to some extent by their place in the university bureaucracy? Now turn the lens on yourself. What position did you take on the use of air power against Libya (if you didn't form one, go back in time and develop one)? What shaped your preferences here? Did the likelihood of you, or someone you know personally, benefitting from or being harmed by that decision help shape your position?

Another way to bring home some of these concepts is to watch the extent to which you use historical analogies as a shortcut to understanding new and complex events. You can do this with non–foreign policy choices, such as the way you might draw parallels between an assignment given to you in one class and what you see as similar assignments you've received in the past. Jump to foreign policy issues, then. When you think about using force to promote democracy, for example, in your mind do you see Japan after World War II? Iraq? How does that shape your view of U.S. policy toward using air power in Libya? How does it shape your view about using force elsewhere?

STUDY/DISCUSSION QUESTIONS

1. What cognitive dynamics can impinge on foreign policy decision making? How might these be heightened during a crisis?
2. What is *groupthink?* How can the president try to avoid it?
3. If humans, especially under stress, cannot be fully rational, can they at least be more vigilant than not? What barriers to rationality exist in the foreign policy making process?
4. We often think of the president as a "decider," but less often as a "manager." How have presidents tried to manage their advisors in order to help make foreign policy decisions?
5. What is the Bureaucratic Politics paradigm? How does it help us see the "essence of decision"?
6. How does the "type" of policy affect the pattern of who is involved in decision making and how they are involved?
7. What is *constructivism,* and what does it help us understand about the foreign policy process that other approaches likely miss?
8. How can theories of decision making, such as those that are discussed in this chapter, incorporate domestic politics into their explanations? How does the increasingly complex global environment within which U.S. leaders must make decisions shape the foreign policy process?

CORE SUGGESTED READINGS

Allison, Graham T., and Philip Zelikow. *Essence of Decision: Explaining the Cuban Missile Crisis* (2nd ed.). New York: Pearson Longman, 1999. An updated and expanded version of Allison's classic statement about the "bureaucratic politics" approach, this is still the gold standard of group-level explanations of American foreign policy making.

Schafer, Mark, and Crichlow, Scott. *Groupthink Versus High-Quality Decision Making in International Relations*. New York: Columbia University Press, 2010. Excellent new book that applies the latest theories from political psychology and the study of small-group dynamics to a range of American foreign policy cases.

Mann, James. *Rise of the Vulcans: A History of Bush's War Cabinet*. New York: Viking, 2004. An intellectual history, really, of the people close to President George W. Bush who significantly shaped the Bush Doctrine and the wars in Afghanistan and Iraq. A fascinating read.

Snyder, Richard C., H. W. Bruck, Burton Saping, Valerie Hudson, Derek H. Chollet, and James M. Goldgeier. *Foreign Policy Decision Making (Revisited)*. New York: Palgrave Macmillan, 2002. This is a new edition of an old "standard" in the field, which nicely lays out the basics of a "foreign policy decision making" approach, including an emphasis on understanding how policy makers actually see and define the situations they are in when they make policy.

ADDITIONAL READINGS AND REFERENCES

Barber, James David. *The Presidential Character: Predicting Performance in the White House* (4th ed.). Upper Saddle River, NJ: Prentice Hall, 2008.

Burke, John P., and Fred I. Greenstein. *How Presidents Test Reality: Decisions on Vietnam, 1954 and 1965*. New York: Russell Sage Foundation, 1991.

Checkel, Jeffrey T. "Constructivism and Foreign Policy." In Steve Smith (ed.), *Foreign Policy: Theories, Actors, Cases*. New York: Oxford University Press, 2008.

Cohn, Carol. "Sex and Death in the Rational World of Defense Intellectuals." *Signs* 4 (1987): 687–718.

De Rivera, Joseph H. *The Psychological Dimension of Foreign Policy*. Columbus, OH: Charles E. Merrill Publishing, 1968.

Doty, Roxanne Lynn. "Foreign Policy as Social Construction: A Post-Positivist Analysis of U.S. Counterinsurgency Policy in the Philippines." *International Studies Quarterly* 37 (1993): 297–320.

Enloe, Cynthia. *Bananas, Beaches, and Bases: Making Feminist Sense of International Politics*. Berkeley, CA: University of California Press, 2000.

Garrison, Jean A. *Games Advisors Play: Foreign Policy in the Nixon and Carter Administrations*. College Station, TX: Texas A&M Press, 1999.

George, Alexander L. *Presidential Decisionmaking in Foreign Policy: The Effective Use of Information and Advice*. Boulder, CO: Westview Press, 1980.

George, Alexander L. "The 'Operational Code': A Neglected Approach to the Study of Political Leaders and Decision Making." *International Studies Quarterly* 13 (1969): 190–222.

Goldgeier, James M. "Foreign Policy Decision Making." In Robert A. Denemark, ed., *The International Studies Encyclopedia*. Hoboken, NJ: Wiley, 2010.

Goodwin, Doris Kearns. *Lyndon Johnson and the American Dream*. New York: St. Martin's Press, 1991.

Haney, Patrick J. *Organizing for Foreign Policy Crises: Presidents, Advisers, and the Management of Decision-Making*. Ann Arbor, MI: University of Michigan Press, 2002.

Haney, Patrick J. "Soccer Fields and Submarines in Cuba: The Politics of Problem Definition." *Naval War College Review* (Autumn 1997): 67–84.

Herek, Gregory M., Irving L. Janis, and Paul Huth. "Decision Making During International Crisis." *Journal of Conflict Resolution* 31 (1987): 203–226.

Hermann, Charles F., ed. *International Crises*. New York: Free Press, 1972.

Hermann, Margaret G., and Charles F. Hermann. "Who Makes Foreign Policy Decisions and How? An Empirical Inquiry." *International Studies Quarterly* 33 (1989): 361–387.

Holsti, Ole R. "Crisis Decision Making." In Philip E. Tetlock, Charles Tilly, Robert Jervis, Jo L. Husbands, and Paul C. Stern, eds. *Behavior, Society, and Nuclear War*. New York: Oxford University Press, 1989.

Holsti, O. R. "The Operational Code Approach to the Study of Political Leaders: John Foster Dulles' Philosophical and Instrumental Beliefs." *Canadian Journal of Political Science* 3 (1970): 123–157.

Houghton, David Patrick. "Reinvigorating the Study of Foreign Policy Decision Making: Toward a Constructivist Approach." *Foreign Policy Analysis* 3 (2007), 24–45.

Ikenberry, G. John, ed. *American Foreign Policy: Theoretical Essays* (6th ed.). New York: Cengage, 2010.

Janis, Irving L. *Groupthink: Psychological Studies of Policy Decisions and Fiascoes* (2nd ed.). New York: Cengage, 1982.

Janis, Irving L., and Leon Mann. *Decisionmaking*. New York: Free Press, 1977.

Jervis, Robert. *Perception and Misperception in International Politics*. Cambridge, MA: Harvard University Press, 1976.

Khong, Yuen Foong. *Analogies at War*. Princeton, NJ: Princeton University Press, 1992.

Larson, Deborah Welch. *Origins of Containment: A Psychological Explanation*. Princeton, NJ: Princeton University Press, 1985.

Lichtblau, Eric. *Bush's Law: The Remaking of American Justice*. New York: Pantheon Books, 2008.

March, James G., and Johan P. Olsen. *Rediscovering Institutions: The Organizational Basis of Politics*. New York: Free Press, 1989.

McCalla, Robert B. *Uncertain Perceptions: U.S. Cold War Crisis Decision Making*. Ann Arbor, MI: University of Michigan Press, 1992.

Mintz, Alex, and Karl DeRouen Jr. *Understanding Foreign Policy Decision Making*. New York: Cambridge University Press, 2010.

Mitchell, David. *Making Foreign Policy: Presidential Management of the Decision-Making Process*. Burlington, VT: Ashgate, 2005.

Preston, Thomas. *The President and His Inner Circle: Leadership Style and the Advisory Process in Foreign Affairs*. New York: Columbia University Press, 2001.

Ripley, Randall B., and Grace Franklin. *Congress, the Bureaucracy, and Public Policy* (5th ed.). Pacific Grove, CA: Brooks/Cole, 1991.

Robinson, William I. *Promoting Polyarchy: Globalization, U.S. Intervention, and Hegemony*. New York: Cambridge University Press, 1996.

Rosati, Jerel A., and Colleen E. Miller. "Political Psychology, Cognition, and Foreign Policy Analysis." In Robert A. Denemark (ed.), *The International Studies Encyclopedia*. Hoboken, NJ: Wiley, 2010.

Rosati, Jerel A. *The Carter Administration's Quest for Global Community: Beliefs and Their Impact on Behavior*. Columbia: University of South Carolina Press, 1991.

Sigal, Leon V. *Disarming Strangers: Nuclear Diplomacy with North Korea*. Princeton, NJ: Princeton University Press, 1988.

Sprout, Harold, and Margaret Sprout. *The Ecological Perspective on Human Affairs*. Princeton, NJ: Princeton University Press, 1965.

Sylvan, Donald, and James Voss. *Problem Representation in Foreign Policy Decision-Making*. New York: Cambridge University Press, 1998.

't Hart, Paul. *Groupthink in Government: A Study of Small Groups and Policy Failure*. Baltimore, MD: The Johns Hopkins University Press, 1990.

't Hart, Paul, Eric K. Stern, and Bengt Sundelis (eds.). *Beyond Groupthink: Political Group Dynamics and Foreign Policy-Making*. Ann Arbor, MI: University of Michigan Press, 1997.

Walker, Stephen G., and Mark Schafer. "Operational Code Theory: Beliefs and Foreign Policy Decisions." In Robert A. Denemark (ed.), *The International Studies Encyclopedia*. Hoboken, NJ: Wiley, 2010.

Weldes, Jutta. *Constructing National Interests: The United States and the Cuban Missile Crisis*. Minneapolis, MN: University of Minnesota Press, 1999.

Wilson, James Q. *Bureaucracy: What Government Agencies Do and Why They Do It*. New York: Basic Books, 1989.

Yetiv, Steve A. *Explaining Foreign Policy: U.S. Decision-Making in the Gulf Wars* (2nd ed.). Baltimore, MD: The Johns Hopkins University Press, 2011.

Yetiv, Steve A. "Groupthink and the Gulf Crisis." *British Journal of Political Science* 33 (2003): 419–442.

Zegart, Amy B. *Spying Blind: The CIA, the FBI, and the Origins of 9/11*. Princeton, NJ: Princeton University Press, 2007.

Zegart, Amy B. *Flawed by Design: The Evolution of the CIA, JCS, and NSC*. Stanford, CA: Stanford University Press, 1999.

CHAPTER

4

The President

One of the issues on which President Ronald W. Reagan and Soviet communist leader Mikhail Gorbachev agreed was their mutual dread of nuclear weapons, a concern that led them to propose total nuclear disarmament at the 1987 meeting in Reykjavik, Iceland.

PREVIEW

The President of the United States is the most visible symbol of the United States in the making of foreign policy. The bases of presidential power are both constitutional and political, and are mostly balanced by limiting powers either held by Congress or arising from the political process. This chapter begins by analyzing the bases of presidential power, including those powers and limitations placed on the president by the Constitution, and the discussion then moves to politically based sources of presidential advantage and limitation in the foreign policy area. Following these institutional impacts, the chapter examines the human side of the presidential role, specifically, presidential personality and preferred decision-making styles as influences that help explain how different presidents approach the foreign policy aspect of their job and have different experiences and outcomes on foreign policy matters.

KEY CONCEPTS

codetermination
head of government
head of state
commander-in-chief
treaty negotiator
plenipotentiary
executive agreements
presidential singularity
presidential doctrines
limits of policy possibility
START
cognitive style
sense of efficacy and confidence
competitive model
formalistic model
collegial model

The Reykjavik Summit between American President Ronald Reagan and Soviet Prime Minister Mikhail Gorbachev has been called "the most remarkable summit ever held between U.S. and Soviet leaders." In the Icelandic capital on October 11–12, 1986, the U.S. president, who had made political conservatism a major factor in American politics and whose tough stance on the Soviet Union and the Cold War was legendary, and the relatively young and less-known Soviet leader met for the second time in what aides had advertised as an exploratory session with a limited agenda, something less formal than a summit and with lower expectations in terms of likely accomplishments.

In the end, the meeting was nearly momentous: For a brief period, the two very different leaders nearly agreed to total and complete nuclear disarmament within a ten-year period. Aides on both sides were appalled by what they viewed as the rashness of the outcomes of these meetings in which Reagan and Gorbachev had been secreted in a room accompanied only by their translators. Policy aides whose Cold War views of things made such a course seem unthinkable succeeded in pulling the two back from the agreement at the last minute. In the end, they reached no agreement to rid the world of nuclear weapons, but the two leaders came very close to doing exactly that.

The story is remarkable on several levels. While in retrospect it seems clear that the Cold War was beginning to crumble (as discussed in Chapter Two), the evidence of this disintegration was not apparent at the time of the summit, and the Cold War animosities, of which nuclear weapons were the most glaring symbols, remained high. The foreign policy options still looked to most observers, including the closest advisors to both leaders, to be the continuation of Cold War or hot war. They thought they knew how to "wage" cold war with nuclear weapons. The prospects of the competition without them were so fundamentally alien that most analysts could not bring themselves conceptually to contemplate a nuclear-weapons-free world. Among the members of the American delegation, this sentiment was felt so strongly by hard-liners such as Richard Perle (known by his detractors as "Darth Vader" or the "Prince of Darkness") that they worked feverishly to undo what Reagan and Gorbachev tried to do. They succeeded.

What this episode clearly shows is the strength and unpredictability of the human factor in policy making, and especially the degree to which individual leaders such as Reagan and Gorbachev could change things. Although they were the leaders of the two military behemoths that had confronted one another throughout the Cold War, it turned out that they shared a common dislike for nuclear weapons, and a common desire to see them brought under control and even eliminated. In particular, Goodby (2008) argues that "Reagan was unlike any other U.S. president in his revulsion against the immorality of nuclear war, his willingness to do something about it, and his ability to act on his instincts." One of his instincts was that he had found a kindred spirit in Gorbachev, who shared his hatred of nuclear weapons and was in the process of trying to find a way to end the Cold War and bring the Soviet Union into the more normal family of countries. At their first summit at Geneva, Switzerland, in 1985, the two leaders had already publicly declared that "a nuclear war cannot be won and must never be fought." Gorbachev had followed this up by taking out a full-page advertisement in *The New York Times* in January 1986 proposing deep cutbacks in nuclear arsenals. While these statements were greeted with great skepticism in the professional foreign policy community, they struck a responsive chord with Reagan, who was fully committed to the elimination of these awesome and awful weapons.

The initiative, of course, came and went. What acted as the final straw to break the deal's back was a disagreement on the insertion or elimination of a single word in the final protocol at the end of the meeting. The sticking point surrounded Reagan's pet defense project, the Strategic Defense Initiative (SDI), an antimissile defense against a Soviet nuclear attack on the United States. The Soviets opposed the SDI as destabilizing (while holding deep reservations about whether it could ever be made workable) and insisted on language that would restrict continued work on the proposed system. Reagan was equally insistent on continuing work on the system, because he viewed it as a way to bring about nuclear disarmament; in Reagan's view, an effective missile shield would yield offensive nuclear missiles (the heart of the assured destruction threat of the nuclear balance) "impotent and obsolete." If offensive weapons could be made ineffective, Reagan believed, it would greatly aid the process to eliminate them, which was his broader goal.

The problem was how to treat the SDI in the final accord at the end of the Reykjavik meeting. Reagan wanted to allow more or less unrestricted development of SDI to continue, because if the system could be perfected, it would aid disarmament. (Reagan offered to share the technology with the Soviets, an offer of which they were skeptical, to say the least.) Gorbachev, however, insisted that the continuing research during the ten-year period leading to disarmament be restricted. In the final protocol, he therefore insisted that the word *laboratory* be included to cover SDI work, rather than allowing system testing outside the laboratory that would be necessary to ensure the effectiveness of the system. Gorbachev insisted that the single word be included, and Reagan insisted that it not be included. Neither man would back away from his position on the inclusion or exclusion of the word *laboratory*; as a result, no announcement of an agreement to end nuclear weapons was made.

No other American but the president of the United States could possibly have led the country so close to such a momentous decision. It was a particularly dramatic, even enigmatic, initiative for Reagan, an icon of the anticommunist political right in the United States, many of whose supporters would have been very surprised at the proposal; even aides who had heard Reagan talk on the subject previously had not believed he was serious and were nonplussed by the dynamics of the Icelandic summit.

The example also demonstrates the much greater complexity of foreign policy events in the contemporary world than was true in earlier days, notably in the formative period of the American state. The founding fathers of the United States could not have imagined a presidential action of this magnitude either. When the Constitution was drafted in 1787, the framers did not consider foreign affairs to be terribly important, and as a result, they had little to say about them. They did specify a series of presidential powers in the area of foreign affairs, but they carefully counterbalanced them with congressional powers, acting on the basis of a principle of **codetermination** that suggested the coequality of the two branches in the foreign policy area.

The president's power and authority in foreign affairs have expanded greatly over time. Today, the president of the United States is considered by many to be the most powerful political figure in the world. This stature does not arise entirely from the constitutional position of the president in the American political system, where the separation of powers forms the intellectual core of a political system that places the incumbent in a position of relative equality with the legislative branch and thus assures that the two branches "codetermine" policy. Rather, much of this stature arises from the place of the United States in the world: The president is important because he or she is the political leader of the world's most powerful country.

Presidents have varied considerably in how they approach foreign policy and how effective they are in its pursuit. To understand the presidential role in foreign policy and how that role differs among different holders of the office, the rest of the chapter will proceed along two dimensions. The first dimension is presidential powers in the foreign policy area, which will be divided into formal, constitutional powers and limitations and more informal, political sources of presidential authority and limits on presidential behavior. The second dimension will be the human side of the equation, dealing specifically with how individual presidential characteristics such as presidential personality and preferred decision-making styles affect how different presidents conduct foreign policy.

Each of these dimensions is present in the example that began the chapter. When Reagan met Gorbachev in Reykjavik, he was acting as the legal representative of the U.S. government, a position that he is solely empowered to exercise by the Constitution, and had the negotiations been successful, the result would probably have been a treaty, which only the president (or his designated officials) can negotiate. Such a document, however, would have required the positive approval of the Senate, a constitutional limitation on the president. Moreover, it is not clear how public opinion, a political source of support or limitation on presidential action, would have reacted to such a bold and change-producing initiative. In addition, the fact that Ronald Reagan, the staunch anticommunist who had warned darkly of the Soviet Union as an "evil empire" during his first term in office, had come up with such a proposal speaks strongly to the impact that the individual personality of the person in the White House can have on foreign policy matters.

PRESIDENTIAL POWERS AND CONSTRAINTS

The underlying principle of the U.S. Constitution is to divide political power and authority among the various branches of government, the so-called separation of powers, and this principle applies to the area of foreign policy as well as it does to other areas of governance. In the memorable words of the late Edward S. Corwin (1917) almost a century ago, "The Constitution ... is an invitation to struggle for the privilege of directing American foreign policy." Both the executive and legislative branches are given independent sources of authority (the judicial branch, by constitutional provision and tradition, basically limits its role to refereeing differences between the branches rather than exercising an independent role), and the result, as already noted, is the operation of the system on the basis of codetermination in making and executing power.

In contemporary times, the presidency has been the more prominent actor in most foreign policy matters, creating the impression of presidential preeminence in this area of policy. That impression is certainly constitutionally false. The framers of the founding document envisaged a much simpler, less prominent role for foreign affairs and did not elaborate formal powers extensively, but they clearly intended that the legislative and executive branches would both be vital, active participants in the process. Times, however, change. The sheer volume and complexity of foreign affairs in the modern world make it virtually impossible for the Congress to oversee all foreign policy matters to the extent the framers would have preferred, as is seen in controversial areas such as war making and treaty negotiation, both of which are discussed in the following, adding to the perception that the president is the preeminent actor. However, this historical deference to the president on foreign policy matters has eroded in a hyperpartisan environment.

Over time, the pendulum of presidential or congressional primacy has swung back and forth. When foreign affairs were less frequent and less urgent, as they were during the first century and a half or so of the American republic, the Congress was more assertive, sometimes even dominant, as in the Senate's refusal to ratify the Versailles Treaty ending World War I. The Cold War and, more recently, the events surrounding international terrorism have swung the center of activity firmly toward the executive branch, a condition that is unlikely to change in the near term. This is especially unlikely in the current atmosphere in which congressional action on anything is hamstrung by the extreme level of partisanship that ensures the Congress a high level of opposition to whoever may occupy the White House and whatever the incumbent may propose.

These trends certainly mean that the president is not a free agent who can carry on whatever foreign policy he or she may favor. Indeed, the presidency operates within a web of authority and limitations on that authority. To understand the opportunities and constraints that exist, the discussion that follows moves sequentially in three steps. First, it will describe and briefly analyze the constitutional powers and limits on the president. Second, it will move from the formal nexus to the political advantages that the president, as the highest elected politician in the country, has in the foreign policy area. Third, it will conclude with some of the major limitations on presidential authority and autonomy in this area of public policy.

Formal Powers of the President

Because the framers did not view foreign policy as an overwhelming part of the political life of the country from their vantage point in the late eighteenth century, they were reasonably sparse in their enumeration of presidential authorities. Indeed, the Constitution itself describes six specific, and to some extent overlapping, powers and responsibilities for the president. By virtue of office, the president is (1) chief executive (**head of government**); (2) chief (head) of state; and (3) commander-in-chief of the armed forces of the United States. The president's enumerated powers cover (4) treaty negotiations; (5) nomination and appointment of key personnel; and (6) recognition of foreign regimes. Nearly all of these are balanced by sources of congressional limitation to provide codetermination.

Chief Executive (Head of Government) Article II, Section 1 of the Constitution makes the president the country's chief executive. In this role, the president exercises the rights and privileges associated with the executive branch of the government, including supervision and control over the resources of the federal bureaucracy, virtually all of which is part of the executive branch. At the same time, this role also makes the president the head of the government, which means that he or she is the highest elected politician in the country (the only nationally elected politician) and thus the partisan head of one of the two operational political bodies (the executive and the legislature).

The chief executive/head of government role creates two distinct but important aspects of the presidency in foreign policy. As chief executive, the president is the ultimate reporting channel for all the millions of individuals who work within the various executive agencies of the government. In the foreign policy area, this means that the State and Defense departments report to the president, as do the various parts of the intelligence community (the Central Intelligence Agency and the various intelligence agencies attached to the Department of Defense, for instance) and the entire Homeland Security complex of agencies. Although the president does not directly supervise each of these efforts personally in detail (to the occasional embarrassment of the presidency), it does mean that the federal bureaucracy works for the president and is expected—within some limits—to carry out presidential preferences and demands. It also means that the vast majority of federal expertise, which resides in these agencies, is available to the president in the making and execution of whatever foreign policy the president as chief elected politician chooses to pursue, a distinct advantage over a Congress with more limited resources at its avail.

By virtue of being the chief executive, the president is also the country's major political leader—a partisan politician pursuing a partisan agenda who just happens to occupy the country's most powerful single position. As chief executive, the president is responsible for directing federal activities in different policy areas, and there are inevitably differences of opinion about the wisdom of different courses of actions that are politically derived. As the chief executive who defines federal actions within congressional mandates, the president is thus a partisan political figure who is not above partisan disagreements. This aspect of the presidential role—the president as head politician—stands in stark contrast to the office's second role.

Chief (Head) of State The president is also the recognized political face of the United States to foreign governments and the world at large. As such, his position extends beyond the partisan role as the chief politician to being the active symbol of the American government and the rallying point of the American people. In other words, in addition to being the partisan politician president, the president is also the current embodiment of the *presidency* (the constitutionally provided office of president).

This role is particularly prominent in the foreign policy area, although it is an implied role in strictly constitutional terms and reflects international law and practice as well. The president is the sole American official who can initiate and carry on interactions with foreign governments, as detailed below. Part of the reason for this comes from international law and practice connected to the principle of sovereignty. This concept traditionally assigns the sovereign authority of the state to its highest symbolic ruler; at the time the practice took hold in Europe in the seventeenth century, the sovereign was typically a monarch, and the practice has extended in modern times to elected chief executives. Thus, for instance, if the U.S. government seeks to interact politically with France, it is with the office of the president of France, who is the designated sovereign head of state of France.

The head of state function is, in important ways, the symbolic or ceremonial role of the president. Under its guise, presidents meet with and host the heads of government and state of other countries. As the embodiment of the state in much the same way as the flag or national anthem, the presidency (and its occupant) is treated with extraordinary deference, in ways that apparently exceed presidential grants of authority in the constitution itself. As head of state, the president is the recognizable leader whom everybody knows. The president has his or her own personal airplane and helicopter (Air Force One and Marine One), a personal armored limousine transported to wherever the president goes, and he or she also has a personal anthem, "Hail to the Chief." No other political figure is accorded any of these perquisites.

The American system's combination of the roles of head of government and head of state is the source of some confusion and friction within the American political system that is not present elsewhere. Many countries, notably in Europe, assign the roles of head of government and head of state to different institutions and individuals, thereby separating the roles and personages of the head of government and head of state. In the United Kingdom, for instance, the prime minister is the head of government, whereas the monarch is the head of state. This dichotomy allows Britons to engage in active, even acrimonious debate about the political leader of the country (the prime minister) and that person's policies, without simultaneously engaging in actions that may undercut the country, symbolized by Queen Elizabeth II for the past sixty years. Some other European countries have a president with few powers, who is head of state, and a prime minister or equivalent who serves as head of government. In the American system, it is often impossible to separate partisan attacks on the president as chief politician from attacks on the presidency as symbol of the republic, as the *Intersections* box further suggests.

Commander-in-Chief Article II, Section 2 of the Constitution makes the president "Commander in Chief of the Army and Navy of the United States, and of the Militia of the several States, when called into the actual Service of the United States." That language is straightforward enough, but it does not include a definitive statement about what the commander-in-chief is authorized to do with those forces it authorizes him to command. Article I of the Constitution reserves the right to declare war to the Congress (discussed in Chapter Five), and the framers almost certainly presumed that the actual employment of armed forces would occur only after some positive authorization by Congress. In practice, that has not been the case, and the result has been ambivalence and controversy over the extent of the power of the president as commander-in-chief.

In fact, the formal war-making power of the presidency has been used very sparingly during the country's existence. Formal declarations of war have preceded only five American military actions (the War of 1812, the Mexican War, the Spanish-American War, and the two World Wars), whereas American

INTERSECTIONS

The President, the Presidency, Hyperpartisanship, and Foreign Policy

One implication of the principle of sovereignty is that the countries of the world look to a single individual within each state with whom they deal as the authority representing the policies of that country and as the authority to conduct national business. In the United States, the president—as chief executive and symbol of the presidency—fulfills that role.

The fact that the president is both head of government and of state sometimes complicates international dealings, particularly in a hyperpartisan environment. When foreign governments deal with the United States, the presumption is that the president's position is the official position of the country. This has never been entirely the case on controversial matters, and current levels of hyperpartisanship virtually guarantee opposition to the president's position on almost any matter. This situation inevitably has the effect of weakening the authority of the head of the U.S. government with other countries.

This erosion works in various ways. Knowing there is opposition to the president's policies may cause foreign governments to try to enhance that opposition as a way to improve their negotiating position with the United States. That intent is certainly implied in the Netanyahu visit to Washington introduced at the beginning of Chapter One. Another example has been U.S. diversity toward the Libyan revolution's early stages. The position of the Obama administration was originally to offer limited support to the rebels, mainly to ensure that they were not victims of retaliatory atrocities. Some Republicans vocally supported much stronger, more overt support for the rebels; and one of them, Senator and 2008 GOP presidential nominee John McCain, travelled to rebel stronghold Benghazi, where he was greeted enthusiastically as a symbol of support far in excess of official U.S. policy. In this situation, who were the Libyan rebels to believe?

military forces have been employed in warlike situations for literally hundreds of other times, the exact number depending on how one defines an act of war. These other employments of force have sometimes been authorized by some kind of informal congressional resolution (the Vietnam War, the Persian Gulf War of 1990, and the American invasion of Iraq, for instance), but sometimes they have been preceded by no formal action of the Congress at all (the initial deployment of American forces in Afghanistan or American action in Libya, for instance). Over time, there have been congressional attempts to limit the commander-in-chief's ability to employ force without prior congressional authorization (the War Powers Act of 1973 is an example), but none have been particularly effective and all have been challenged by the executive branch as unnecessarily prohibitive of the country's need to be able to respond to national emergencies. Although this debate was dampened by the response to the 9/11 crisis and the apparent need for a decisive military response to it, the exact meaning and parameters of the commander-in-chief's role remains a source of contention between the two branches of government.

Treaty Negotiator The authority to commit the country to legally binding international commitments in Article II, Section 2 of the Constitution is a major source of presidential power. As head of state, the president is the only internationally recognized representative of the U.S. government, and thus the president (or his or her officially designated representatives, known as **plenipotentiaries**) is the only official of the government authorized to negotiate legally binding agreements for the government. This grant of power is, however, tempered by dividing the authority between the president and the Senate in the formal designation that the president "shall have Power, by and with the Advice and Consent of the Senate, to make Treaties, provided two-thirds of the Senators present concur."

Just as the framers presumed that all uses of military force would be preceded by a declaration of war, so too did they presume that all binding agreements between the United States and other countries would be conducted through the formal treaty process. In both cases, if for different reasons, this proved not to be the case. While presidents have employed force without prior authorization for a variety of reasons, the eclipse of the sole utilization of the treaty process can be traced to two factors, one quite specific and concrete and the other more general.

The specific instance was the refusal of the U.S. Senate to ratify the peace treaty ending World War I. This refusal was the result of complex interactions and feuds between President Wilson and the Senate that go beyond present purposes, but it had the effect of meaning the United States did not participate in the major edifice that it helped create and which was supposed to ensure the peace, the League of Nations. This display of Senatorial obstinacy led to reexamination of the possibility of alternatives to formal Senatorial approval of foreign policy commitments.

The momentum to find an alternative was spurred on by the increasing volume of international interactions between the United States and other countries creating legal obligations on the U.S. government. This was an eventuality that the framers did not anticipate, given their beliefs in the relative unimportance and thus infrequency of international events. In the more contemporary world, however, the United States has been increasingly involved in multiple negotiations with many countries, the result of which is to create international obligations for the United States in a volume that the Senate could not possibly process. If the Senate tried to deal with all these obligations, it would have time to do absolutely nothing else, and still would almost certainly not get the job done.

The result was the practice of employing **executive agreements** as an alternative to treaties. These documents are identical to treaties in all important international legal obligations they create for the United States, but they do not require the approval of the Senate. Originally, the use of this tool was limited to fairly routine matters that did not require the active assent of the Senate because of their noncontroversial nature, but they have increased in volume to the point that now the ratio of executive agreements to treaties is over twenty to one, and inevitably, some of these agreements are on matters that contain some controversy.

Since executive agreements are mentioned nowhere in the Constitution, there is no formal guidepost for when such agreements should be used rather than employing the full treaty approval process. Although this would seem to create a *carte blanche* for presidents to simply go around the constitutional restriction by treating all important—and especially partisan and controversial—agreements with foreign governments as executive agreements, this has not been the case. For one thing, most international agreements (treaties or executive agreements) are *non–self-executing*, which means their implementation requires some further governmental action (usually the expenditure of funds) to put them fully into effect. Thus, a president who negotiates an executive agreement the Senate opposes may well find he lacks the resources to implement its provisions, a source of embarrassment with the foreign government with which it was negotiated and a red flag on future negotiations. For another, if a president executes an executive agreement opposed by the Senate, the Congress may retaliate in indirect ways. In 1980, for instance, President Carter faced Senate opposition to the Strategic Arms Limitation Talks (SALT) agreement that was a centerpiece of his foreign policy and threatened to implement it as an executive agreement to bypass that opposition. Congressional negotiators quietly went to the president and informed him that if he did so, his entire legislative agenda for that election year would be dead upon arrival on the Hill. Carter quickly and quietly retreated from his threat.

Nominator of Key Personnel Article II, Section 2 also authorizes the president to nominate "Ambassadors, Other Public Ministers and Counsels" to federal positions, subject to the same advice and consent process assigned to treaties. This means that the president can nominate foreign policy officials who share his or her views to conduct foreign policy, with the rejoinder that the views of those appointees must not be so offensive as to cause more than a third of the Senate to reject them for the office for which they are proposed. In most cases, the nomination process is pro forma, and the Senate has normally provided wide latitude to the president in assembling the ambassadorial and other foreign policy team that he or she prefers.

This process becomes controversial in two instances of presidential nominations. In some cases, candidates may be so obnoxious or objectionable on personal or ideological grounds that they are rejected. In 1989, for instance, George H.W. Bush nominated ex-Senator John Tower of Texas as his secretary of defense. Tower had been a particularly unpopular chair of the Senate Armed Services Committee (which held the hearings on his nomination) and was reputed to be a heavy drinker and womanizer, traits hardly suited to someone who would be entrusted with some of the country's most closely guarded secrets. As a result, the Senate committee rejected his nomination, and Bush was forced to replace Tower with a more acceptable, less controversial candidate, Richard Cheney. Occasionally as well, the appointment process is used for political patronage, such as appointing large political contributors to ambassadorships. President Reagan, for instance, nominated a St. Louis businessman, Theodore Maino, as his ambassador to Botswana. Asked about his credentials for the job in Senate Foreign Relations Committee confirmation hearings, Maino replied that he was qualified by virtue of a "commitment to public service, having a lifetime association with the Boy Scouts of America." In this case, Maino was confirmed.

The appointment power also contains one of the few exceptions to codetermination. Although the president must have senatorial power to appoint high-level officials, he is not limited when he chooses to dismiss those officials. Since presidential appointees serve at the pleasure of the chief executive, they are subject to removal if their service becomes displeasing, and the Senate has no formal recourse to prevent a presidential firing of people it has approved for particular jobs.

Recognizer of Foreign Governments This derived constitutional grant comes from Article II, Section 3, of the Constitution, which declares that the president "shall receive Ambassadors and Other Public Ministers" from foreign governments. This apparently limited grant has been interpreted to extend to enabling presidents either to commence or terminate relations with other countries by appointing or refusing to appoint personnel to other countries or by accepting or rejecting foreign emissaries.

Sometimes this power can have a dramatic effect. From 1949, when the Chinese communists prevailed in the Chinese Civil War, until 1972, the United States had no relations with the People's Republic of China (PRC), maintaining that the legal government of all China was the Nationalist Chinese government located on Taiwan (where they fled after losing the war in 1949). President Nixon, however, felt strongly that this diplomatic anomaly was not in the best foreign policy interests of the country and began a process to open relations between the U.S. government and the mainland Chinese. This process commenced unofficially with the visit of an American table tennis team to China (so-called "ping-pong diplomacy") and reached official status in 1972 when Nixon visited the PRC. President Carter completed the process by extending full recognition to the PRC in 1979. None of these actions required formal congressional assent.

Informal (Political) Powers of the Presidency

The formal, constitutional powers of the president are augmented by an assortment of informal sources of presidential power, some of which derive from the constitutional grants that make the president such a prominent part of the American political landscape. For present purposes, four of these informal sources will be described for illustrative purposes: presidential singularity, the role of public opinion and media access, the president's position as a world leader, and the president's ability to issue formal policy proclamations known as presidential doctrines.

Presidential Singularity One of the greatest presidential advantages over his colleagues and rivals in Congress is that there is one president as opposed to 535 members of Congress. The members of Congress are generally much more faceless and less well known than the president outside their individual states or districts (although cable television is making it easier for some to become recognizable, at least on select matters). Moreover, the president of the United States is unique in that the incumbent is the only American politician who can claim a national constituency, since he or she is elected by the entire American electorate rather than some narrower group of Americans. On policy matters, the president is the only politician who can claim to have a national mandate to act by virtue of his status as the country's leading politician (head of government).

When combined with his symbolic role as head of state, this makes the president of the United States by far the most prominent political figure in the country. In important national moments such as crises, the American people look instinctively to the president for leadership and guidance, whether the occasion is a foreign policy disaster such as 9/11 or a domestic emergency such as Hurricane Katrina or the BP oil spill of 2010. If presidents act appropriately in these moments, the fact that they, rather than their more numerous counterparts in the legislative branch, can take action gives them a distinct leadership advantage. Their visibility, however, also means that their actions are subject to more detailed scrutiny than the advocacies of other politicians, and the fact that they have at their disposal the resources of the federal government means that they bear public responsibility for the success or failure of their actions, whereas others may sit on the sidelines, scrutinize, and criticize.

Public Opinion and Media Access Presidential singularity also makes the president the prime national object of public and media scrutiny. The American people, by and large, are more interested in the activities and thoughts of the president than they are of any other politician (with the possible exception of opposition candidates during presidential election campaigns); what the president does or says is news in a way that is not true for anyone else. It is not, for instance, a coincidence that major news-gathering organizations all have reporters assigned full-time to covering the president (the White House press corps), while a much smaller group of reporters are assigned to covering the 535 members of the House of Representatives and the Senate.

Public opinion and interest and media access are, of course, related to one another. The fact that the public wants to know what the president is doing drives much media attention, and vice versa (media coverage creates public awareness and interest). Presidents use this dynamic relationship to try to rally support for their positions. Their access to the White House press corps, for instance, means they can call formal or informal press conferences simply by announcing their intent to or, more informally, by simply wandering down to the press room in the White House and sitting down for a conversation with journalists. Often these sessions are "off the record" (not for attribution), and electronic or print sources will often quote "unnamed White House sources" who are in fact the president speaking off the record. Increasingly, presidents use the electronic media to reach the public directly, with varying degrees of success depending on the media and oratorical skills of the individual president.

In an age of hyperpartisanship, media access has had a flip side. The proliferation of media outlets such as websites and cable television channels have meant that presidents are scrutinized in more detail than ever before, and this observation is often conducted by people who lack the objectivity of traditional journalists and who have strong political agendas that they layer upon their analysis of presidential activities. In the case of the Obama administration, much of this scrutiny has been directed at undercutting the power and authority of the president, presumably with the intent to lessen the likelihood of his reelection in the 2012 election. This activity has become a part of the struggle for public opinion in which the president has traditionally had the upper hand, and modern presidents (or their surrogates) must spend an increasing amount of their time "fighting" this semiunderground battle through the subterranean media for public opinion.

International Diplomacy and World Leadership Although presidents do not readily admit this is the case, most of them either enter office with or develop an affinity for foreign policy. Part of the reason is that foreign affairs are more glamorous than domestic politics, particularly when the president is acting in his or her ceremonial role as head of state. President George H.W. Bush admitted this attraction during a 1990 domestic budget summit, saying "When you get a problem with the complexities that the Middle East has now ... I enjoy putting the coalition together and ... seeing this aggression does not succeed. I can't say I just rejoice every time I go up and talk to (former congressman) Danny Rostenkowski ... about what he's going to do on taxes." Foreign policy issues, in other words, have an inherent glamour not possessed by many domestic issues.

Foreign policy is, or at least historically has been, an area where the public is more supportive and less critical of presidential actions than in domestic areas. There are several reasons for this, most of which have eroded in recent years. First, the tradition of bipartisanship in foreign affairs (the "water's edge") has made overt criticism of foreign policy largely off-limits. As noted in the example starting Chapter One, this principle has eroded in a more partisan political environment where even the foreign policy successes of the president are viewed as partisan defeats for his or her opponents. Second, the public by and large does not understand foreign affairs and thus has traditionally given the chief executive more deference due to the expertise of the presidency.

This restraint has also been eroded by exploding media coverage of international events (often by reporters of dubious expertise) that makes everyone believe that he or she is an expert. Third, foreign policy has traditionally been more abstract to average Americans, and its impacts have not clearly and obviously had a personal effect on individual Americans, thereby making a detachment from foreign policy issues acceptable. The increasingly intermestic impact of foreign affairs has limited this advantage as well. Finally, the president's role as world leader does afford opportunities for the office holder to travel overseas and be presented as a symbol of the American people (reviewing troops in foreign capitals during state visits, for instance) that put the president in a favorable light. Increasingly, however, presidential visits and the like are to multilateral affairs where organized opposition to the proceedings may diminish the positive impact (for example, the demonstrations at the G-20 summit in Toronto in June 2010).

Presidential Doctrines The fourth informal source of presidential political advantage is the ability of the president to issue unilateral proclamations of U.S. policy that become associated with his or her name as "doctrines." The idea of such pronouncement is rooted in the term *doctrine*, which describes a belief in the best way to accomplish some end (the derivation is military), and presidential foreign policy doctrines are essentially policy statements about how the United States believes its interests are best served in certain situations or in certain physical, geographical areas.

Presidential doctrines have no special legal significance internationally or domestically. A doctrine is a political, not a legal, statement and has no standing in international law. Thus, for instance, the Carter Doctrine of 1980, which declares the maintenance of peaceful conditions that ensure American access to Middle Eastern petroleum, has no legally binding effect on anyone in the region or elsewhere to guarantee that access, although it may politically affect how countries deal with the United States in the area. Similarly, as simple statements of policy preference, their effect on domestic politics is in no way legally binding unless they are accompanied by specific related domestic legislation, which they generally do not possess. Rather, they may serve as frameworks within which the public debates on certain foreign policy issues are conducted. Because they bear the presidential imprimatur, however, there is generally some reluctance to be as critical of these doctrines as might be the case were not the presidential name and the apparently impressive designation as doctrines present.

A number of U.S. presidents have had doctrines associated with them. The earliest was the Monroe Doctrine of 1823, declaring U.S. primacy in the Western Hemisphere—a situation the United States was, at the time, entirely incapable of enforcing. The Truman Doctrine of 1946 set the tone for ideological anticommunism as the Cold War emerged as the central international reality of the time, the Eisenhower Doctrine of 1957 preceded the Carter Doctrine as a statement of U.S. policy in the Middle East, and the Nixon Doctrine established (for a time, at least) the unwillingness of the

United States to become directly involved in Third World internal conflicts with armed force. The Reagan Doctrine of 1986 partially reversed Nixon, by declaring American support for governments under communist rule seeking to free themselves of the communist yoke. More recently, the Bush Doctrine of 2002 asserts an American "right" to take unilateral military action when deemed necessary to protect American interests. There is, to date, no Obama Doctrine.

Presidential Constraints

The constitutional and political advantages of the president are not so overwhelming as to establish whoever is president as such an overarching figure as to be a "free agent" in making foreign policy. In addition to political advantages, there are constraints on the president's capabilities and actions, five of which are worth noting as examples.

Presidents do not propose or implement their policy preferences starting from a tabula rasa (blank slate). Rather, they take office within a context of previous history, and one of the constraints included in that existing reality is a network of *past programs and policies*. When the new president comes from the same party (and possibly even administration) as his or her predecessor, the new office holder may support most, even all, of the existing policies and not find the existing reality too constraining; when, however, the new president is a member of the opposite party, the existing policy network may represent a major obstacle to be overcome. This is especially true in policy areas where the two parties are divided fundamentally along ideological, partisan lines and in which the new president campaigned actively on the basis of repudiating and reversing policies put in place by the preceding incumbent.

The difficulty of overcoming this past pattern of policies and programs had an almost immediate impact on the incoming Obama administration. The most striking examples were the wars in Iraq and Afghanistan that the Obama administration inherited from the outgoing Bush administration. The new president had campaigned vigorously on ending the American military commitment in Iraq, and yet he found it more difficult than he undoubtedly hoped once in office: The last combat troops did not exit Iraq until late summer 2010, and a sizable number (initially fifty thousand) of support troops remained, meaning the American commitment was not ended then. In Afghanistan, the conceptual tying of the effort there to the campaign against international terrorism served as a significant constraint on policy options available to the Obama administration.

This leads to the second, and clearly related constraint, the **limits of policy possibility**. New presidents, and especially outsiders to the White House, typically enter office with a more expansive view of what they can accomplish (and especially what they can change) than is indeed possible. To some degree, this problem arises from the network of policies and programs already in place, but is augmented by the realization that there had to have been considerable support for those policies to have been implemented and kept in place that must be overcome. In the partisan environment currently so prominent in politics, almost any attack on a previous administration's policies will be resisted along party and ideological lines if a new administration comes from the opposite party of its predecessor.

In domestic politics, the limits are primarily related to overcoming the advantages that some groups enjoy from any particular policy that would suffer if those policies were reversed. Partisan opposition to Obama plans to let the Bush tax cuts to wealthy Americans expire at the end of 2010 is an acute case in point. In foreign policy, the limits of possibility may be even more extreme, because policies may be formalized in binding agreements (treaties or executive agreements) between the United States and foreign governments that are difficult to abridge or rescind without considerable diplomatic activity and the possibility of negative impacts on U.S. relations with the country or countries involved. At a more informal level, the post–Cold War world has created expectations of an American leadership role in many areas, and presidents who wish to modify those expectations face considerable international pressure that acts as a constraint. In 2000, for instance, George W. Bush campaigned on the notion that the United States should not be the "world's 911" or global policeman, and that the country should scale back or eliminate its participation in peacekeeping missions in troubled areas such as the Balkans (Bosnia and Kosovo, for instance). Once in office, however, the Bush administration was quietly informed by its European allies that such a change of course would be unacceptable, and this policy change was subsequently dropped from administration rhetoric.

A third constraint on the president is *bureaucratic responsiveness*. While it is true that the entire federal bureaucracy assigned to the executive branch technically works for and is controlled by the chief executive, the actual degree to which the constituent agencies and members of that bureaucracy relate to and enthusiastically support the policies of the occupant of the Oval Office will vary considerably. When any president enters office, it cannot be taken for granted that all its members supported the particular candidate who won or embrace the policy initiatives the new president may favor, and it is indeed part of the limits on policy possibility that particular dissonance within the bureaucracy can make a president less successful than he or she might otherwise be.

Presidents come to understand this problem and try to deal with it. When George W. Bush created the Department of Homeland Security or DHS (discussed in Chapter Five), part of that act required shuffling relevant agencies from their traditional places in the federal hierarchy to the new department, a prospect that was not entirely welcomed. Realizing that some agencies would resent their reassignment and that their employees might react by trying to undercut the president's mission, Bush responded with an initiative to remove civil service protection from all employees, leaving all members of the DHS as political appointees who could be dismissed at will by the White House. This proposal was universally opposed within the federal bureaucracy for its potential precedential value and particularly by those whose job security would have been endangered, and Bush was forced to back down in order to get the new agency approved at all. The episode did, however, leave behind a residue of ill will between the White House and the new antiterrorist agency.

Presidents attempt to ensure the responsiveness of their bureaucracies through the political appointment process. Within the executive branch, several thousand of the top-level jobs are political appointments, people specifically chosen by the administration for positions at the secretarial or subsecretarial levels. In addition to serving as a political reward, these appointees are named because of their devotion to the president's agenda, and it is their job to ensure that presidential wishes are carried out within their agencies. Such officials, however, serve entirely at the pleasure of the president, and as already pointed out, can be removed at presidential whim. The vast majority of officials in these agencies, however, are career professionals, people with considerable expertise in their fields who are protected from removal from office by civil service protection that is intended to ensure that they cannot be forced into actions they view as unconscionable (in theory, this principle is parallel to academic tenure for faculty). The secret for a successful president is either appealing effectively to this vast underbelly of the bureaucracy or finding political appointees who can cajole or coerce the permanent government, as it is sometimes known, into compliance with presidential wishes.

The fourth constraint is *presidential time and time management*. The array of national and international problems that confront any president are clearly excessive to the abilities of any chief executive to perform them all, meaning that much of presidential leadership is an exercise in time management. Presidents can tilt their activity levels toward domestic or foreign policy emphases partially dependent on individual preferences, but they are also constrained by the amount of time they allot to their offices (George W. Bush, for instance, had a very public nine-to-five approach to his job, whereas the Clinton administration was famous for its late-night sessions) and the press of varying policy priorities. Given his academic background (he was an undergraduate major in international relations at Occidental College and Columbia University), for instance, it is almost certain that President Obama would have been much more active in foreign affairs in the early part of his term except for the crush of demands caused by the economic meltdown of 2008, which consumed nearly his entire agenda.

Fifth and finally, there is the recurring matter of *partisanship*. As noted repeatedly, foreign policy is no longer exempt from controversy and disagreement that is almost entirely political in a partisan sense, and this fact can become a limiting factor on the country's conduct of its policy with the world, almost regardless of the impact that partisan interference may have on the country's policy. That partisan politics may interfere with and even negate the bipartisan tradition of dealing with policy beyond the water's edge is exemplified by a July 2010 episode that is the subject of this chapter's *Intersections* box.

INTERSECTIONS

Partisanship and START

One of the major objectives of "New START" is to reduce the size of nuclear arsenals on both sides, as represented by this parade of nuclear-tipped missiles on Red Square in Moscow during the Cold War.

During the early months of 2010, the Obama administration actively sought to improve relations with Russia that had cooled during the latter stages of the Bush administration, and one area that was targeted was nuclear arms control, the same subject that had activated Reagan a quarter-century earlier. A major result of this initiative was a new Strategic Arms Reduction Talks (START) round and a treaty further reducing the size of U.S. and Russian arsenals. The New START Treaty, as it is known, was signed on April 8, 2010, in Prague by President Obama and Russian President Dmitry Medvedev. Because of its gravity, New START was negotiated as a treaty, meaning it required two-thirds assent by the Senate before taking effect. The new agreement was intended as a replacement for the earlier, Bush administration–negotiated treaty, which had expired the previous December.

The agreement seemed innocuous substantively, calling for reductions in the strategic nuclear arsenals of the nuclear superpowers from 2,200 to 1,500 apiece, armament levels about which hardly anyone in either country or on either side of the debate over nuclear weapons in the United States had serious objections. Nevertheless, the treaty was still unsigned in August 2010, because it got caught in the web of partisanship infesting the American political system. To reach the two-thirds majority necessary to achieve positive advice and consent, the

(Continued)

(Continued)

Democratic majority of fifty-nine senators required the support of at least eight Republicans, assuming all Democrats would vote in favor. However, the Republicans almost uniformly (Senator Richard Lugar of Indiana was the vocal exception) voiced their refusal to support the treaty on August 2, meaning its ratification could not occur, a major embarrassment to the administration (and arguably, by extension, the country). The Republicans argued that their assent was tied to assurances of certain guaranteed appropriations for nuclear force modernization (they argued the administration's commitment of $80 billion to this purpose was inadequate by about $20 billion), that the treaty would make deployment of a ballistic missile defense (BMD) system that has been a Republican strategic chestnut for years impossible (a charge denied explicitly by Secretary of Defense Robert Gates, a holdover from the Bush administration), and that the Russians were untrustworthy. Republican presidential aspirant Mitt Romney went so far as to call the accord "Obama's worst foreign policy mistake yet" in a July 2010 op-ed piece in *The Washington Post*.

What motivated this concern from a number of Republican senators? Was it indeed a sincere belief in the inadvisability of the treaty (or aspects of it)? Or was the motivation more blatantly partisan and political, bent on trying to ensure that the president would not be able to claim any form of foreign policy success leading into the 2010 off-year Congressional elections in which Republicans hoped to regain control of one or both houses of Congress?

And what was the international effect both on Obama and the United States if the American president could not negotiate an international agreement that would be approved by the Senate? Certainly, the episode was embarrassing to those charged with Russian–American relations, but was there a wider effect as well? Will this treatment of Obama lead to similar attempts to embarrass and rend impotent the foreign policy actions of future presidents, and notably retaliation against future Republican presidents? Is sacrificing the principle of the water's edge on the altar of partisanship a good idea? New START was finally approved and went into effect in February 2011.

THE HUMAN SIDE: PRESIDENTIAL PERSONALITY AND DECISION STYLE

Formal and informal outside opportunities and constraints create the framework within which individual presidents conduct foreign policy, but knowing these is not enough to understand the manifold differences in how and why different presidents conduct the foreign policies that they do. Presidents are not only, to use the somewhat sterile political science language, "political actors," they are also human beings, and trying to understand the role of the president without also comprehending the human dimension of those who have occupied the office is a sterile, unfulfilling enterprise that results in only a partial picture of what the president does in this area of policy. In order to explore this dimension of the presidency and foreign policy, the discussion will move to two aspects of the human element: presidential personality and preferred decision-making styles of different presidents. While analytically separate, the two are related in the sense that personality will influence preferred ways of organizing decision making in ways that are comfortable and effective for the individual president.

Typologies of Presidential Personality and Management Style

To organize the discussion of how different individuals conduct foreign policy, the analysis will borrow from two frameworks devised by prominent political scientists. The typology for dealing with presidential personality is borrowed from Professor Alexander George of Stanford from his seminal 1980 work, *Presidential Decisionmaking in Foreign Policy.* For dealing with different management style preferences, the analysis leans on distinctions made by Richard T. Johnson in his 1974 classic, *Managing the White House.*

Presidential Personality The taxonomy for differentiating presidential styles on the basis of personality is not inclusive of all the personality traits that collectively comprise who presidents are, but rather on three selected personality traits that are directly relevant to understanding how the individuals in the country's highest office approach foreign policy tasks. For this purpose, the three traits that George argues stand out are **cognitive style**, **sense of efficacy and confidence**, and **orientation toward political conflict**. The first two of these traits are fairly clearly related to another, whereas the third is less closely correlated with the first two.

A president's *cognitive style* refers to how presidents process information, how they define personal needs for information, and how individuals acquire the information that they want. The key influences on these traits include the level of interest a president has in policy material generally and detailed foreign policy information in particular and how much information the president feels comfortable dealing with.

Some presidents have been information minimalists. Ronald Reagan was a prime example: He seldom read serious material, displayed minimal intellectual curiosity about the details of policy issues he was deciding, and had a limited attention span for receiving oral briefings on material (his favored method of receiving information). In fact, his aides made a point of keeping information sessions with him brief because of his tendency to nod off during long presentations. George W. Bush shared this cognitive style.

Other presidents were more information maximalists. John Kennedy immersed himself in the intricacies and details of policy issues, as did Nixon, Carter, and Clinton. All were voracious readers with remarkable memories who felt comfortable with the nuances of policy, which they took great pride in having mastered. In the case of Carter, this attention to detail extended to the point that he insisted on micromanaging some concerns; he was, for instance, the scheduler of time on the White House tennis court.

Cognitive style also is manifested in how presidents like to receive information. Some presidents (Nixon in particular) preferred receiving information in written form, whereas others (both Bushes, for instance) preferred the interaction involved in oral briefings and discussions with senior aides and subject experts. This preference in turn relates to the level of detail a president wants, written materials generally providing much more detail than oral methods of information transfer.

The second key personality trait is a president's *sense of efficacy and confidence,* which refers to what a president feels he understands and is good at doing and, conversely, those areas where the individual may feel less confident and qualified. In the case of foreign policy, this is essentially a measure of how comfortable an individual president feels about making decisions in this complex area of policy, and also how good the incumbent is at convincing others of the merit of the positions and decisions that are reached.

There are really two elements at work here. The first is the degree of mastery of foreign policy issues. Some presidents, by background and experience, enter office with more knowledge than others: Obama and Clinton, for instance, studied international relations as undergraduate students, and George H.W. Bush had considerable foreign policy experience before entering office (as ambassador to the United Nations, head of the liaison office in Beijing prior to full recognition of China in 1979, and as Director of the CIA). Other presidents, such as George W. Bush and Reagan, enter office with virtually no prior experience or obvious interest in foreign affairs. What may be crucial is the degree to which a president assesses his own strengths and weaknesses. Reagan, for instance, recognized his limits as a thinker and hands-on manager and thus delegated authority to those with that knowledge. Bush generally did the same, but occasionally overstepped his expertise, as in his famous initial assessment of Vladimir Putin as a reasonable individual with whom he could "work."

The imprint that a president makes is also related to his or her ability to communicate foreign policy ideas and themes, also a matter of confidence. Reagan, for instance, was the "great communicator" and could galvanize and convert audiences with soaring rhetoric usually based on extrapolations of his own ideas. His entreaty to Gorbachev at the Berlin Wall ("Mr. Gorbachev, tear down this wall" in 1987) stands as a monument to this capability. Presidents who combine great interpersonal and rhetorical skills like Clinton excel in dealing with supporters and opponents alike in convincing them to support ideas. At the other end of the spectrum, Richard Nixon, one of the most reclusive of all presidents, was at his best when dealing with difficult issues in the privacy of the Oval Office, but was chronically uncomfortable in interpersonal settings. He was ill at ease in unstructured settings and had almost no knack for small talk. Standing atop the Great Wall of China in 1972 with China's Deng Xaio-Peng, the only thing Nixon could think to say was, "This sure is a great wall."

The third key personality variable is a president's *orientation toward political conflict.* Differences in political ideas and solutions (political conflict) are, of course, an integral part of the political process, but people differ greatly in how they react to situations of conflict and handle them personally. Some presidents, Franklin Roosevelt being the most prominent example, positively flourished in situations where ideas were being argued and felt that the free-for-all of interchange produced the best policy results. As an extremely self-confident, charismatic individual, he always felt in control of these kinds of situations. At the other extreme, an introverted person like Nixon felt so uncomfortable in situations of disagreement (especially with his own ideas) that he shunned interpersonal settings where even his chief advisors disagreed with one another or with him, a trait he largely hid from the public with a fierce public advocacy of the positions he held. Because he had experienced considerable familial conflict as a child, Bill Clinton also developed a reputation as an interpersonal conflict avoider.

Decision-Making Models The three personality traits, in various combinations and permutations, help predispose different presidents in how they organize the foreign policy apparatus, although there is sufficient difference in individual traits and combinations of traits to make the choice of decision-making model based on personality assessment an imperfect process. As Johnson points, out, however, each president's personality leads the individual, implicitly or explicitly, toward one of three general models of management decision-making style.

The three models can be viewed on a continuum, with one model emphasizing the greatest interaction and creativity (i.e., efficacy) on one end and greater order and formality on the other. In some ways, these extremes reflect a preference for greater effectiveness (emphasis on thorough consideration of all alternatives and choice of the best alternatives, if not in the most orderly and systematic manner) or efficiency (reaching decisions in the most orderly, timely manner). Between these two extremes is a model that tries to achieve a compromise between the two extremes. At the disorderly, effectiveness-oriented end of the spectrum, as suggested in Figure 4.1, is the **competitive model**, while the **formalistic model** stands at the other extreme. In between is the **collegial model**.

The management style of the *competitive model* stresses the free and open expression of diverse advice and analysis within the executive branch. Individuals, departments, and agencies are encouraged to compete with one another openly to influence the president's decisions; in the process, this decision style both tolerates and encourages disagreement on policy

Competitive Model ··················	Collegial Model ··················	Formalistic Model
(Effectiveness)	(Compromise)	(Efficiency)

FIGURE 4.1
Decision Model Continuum

issues between agencies and their leaders. Presidents who employ this style want to ensure that as many options as possible reach the president before any decisions are made rather than having policy discord resolved at lower bureaucratic levels that may constrict the influences the president considers. This model is anything but tidy and lacks efficiency as a basic value, since the percolation of ideas is a more time-consuming process than a more hierarchical approach. It also requires great flexibility and a high sense of self-confidence in the president and his or her ability to ride herd on a process that is disorderly on purpose.

The second extreme style is the *formalistic model.* In important ways, its values are the obverse of those of the competitive model. The formalistic model, as the name implies, places its greatest emphasis on an orderly decision-making process with structured and predictable procedures for making decisions and well-established, hierarchical lines of reporting. In a formalistic system operating optimally, decision options are winnowed upward through the decision process so that a limited number of options reach the president's desk for action, and implementation of decisions is delegated downward through this same system. The effect—and intent—is to isolate the president from many of the details of policy making while allowing the incumbent, should he or she choose, to maintain maximum control over the system.

The third option is the *collegial model.* The purpose of this model is to retain the advantages of the two extreme models while eliminating their disadvantages. As such, it is essentially a compromise between the two extremes where a balance between effectiveness and efficiency is attempted. As an approach, it is not unlike American pragmatism within the ideological orientations discussed in Chapter One, where the end product—a wise foreign policy—is valued more than strict adherence to the process that produces it.

Presidents who employ the collegial model attempt to assemble a team of key advisors, aides, and cabinet officers with generally compatible but not identical views on policy but who are capable of acting as a team. The key notions are an adherence to the concept of "team" and "compatible," but these are not identical ideas. Within this approach, ideally a fairly free and open interchange of ideas takes place between major advisors on policy alternatives, but with the agency heads thinking of themselves more as members of the presidential team than as advocates of their particular agencies. When decisions are reached, however, the members of the team are then expected to fall in line behind the decision and embrace it. Thus, the advantage of the competitive model's emphasis on thorough consideration of policy alternatives is supposed to be accomplished by open discussions, whereas the emphasis on team loyalty adds some of the discipline and order associated with the formalistic model.

Patterns of Presidential Decision Style

Not all presidents have had identical (or even similar) personalities, and due to their personal characteristics and circumstances surrounding their incumbencies, different presidents have chosen different ways to run the foreign policy enterprise. Thus, different presidents since World War II have chosen different basic decision-making models on which to base their conduct of foreign policy, although there has been considerable variation within each model, as there is between models in terms of how presidential foreign policy making actually operates.

Table 4.1 categorizes the twelve presidents who have occupied the office and completed their terms during or since World War II by the basic decision model they utilized. Examining the pattern helps understand better how different administrations have acted and may help organize thinking about future alternatives (the task discussed in the Where Do We Go from Here? section).

Several characteristics about the models and the different presidents who adopted them stand out. The first and most obvious is that the three models have not been equally popular for White House incumbents. Half the presidents since 1945 have chosen the formalistic model, no president has chosen the competitive model in over forty years, and the collegial model has been chosen more often in recent years, a trend that is accentuated if one includes President Obama as a practitioner of that model. Because the Obama presidency is ongoing and in its first term at this writing, it is not included in the table, although, as will be discussed later in the chapter, it has been tentatively categorized as using the collegial model.

There are three other apparent commonalities among those choosing the various models. They are somewhat related to one another, particularly in the context of comparing those who have chosen the formalistic and collegial models

TABLE 4.1

Presidential Decision Styles by Decision-Making Model

Competitive Model	
Franklin D. Roosevelt (1933–1945)	
Lyndon B. Johnson (1963–1969)	Total: 2
Formalistic Model	
Harry S. Truman (1945–1953)	
Dwight D. Eisenhower (1953–1961)	
Richard M. Nixon (1969–1974)	
Gerald R. Ford (1974–1977)	
Ronald W. Reagan (1981–1989)	
George W. Bush (2001–2009)	Total: 6
Collegial Model	
John F. Kennedy (1961–1963)	
James E. Carter (1977–1981)	
George H.W. Bush (1989–1993)	
William J. Clinton (1993–2001)	Total: 4

that are the currently competing means of organization of administration styles. The second characteristic is that the presidents who have chosen the formalistic model were about a decade older (average age of sixty when they entered office) than those who chose the collegial model (average of fifty, if Obama is included; fifty-one if he is not). Third, the formalistic model has been more associated with Republican than Democratic leaders. The only Democrat who adopted the formalistic model was Harry Truman at the end of World War II, and all the adherents to the collegial model except George H.W. Bush have been Democrats. Finally, there is an apparent connection to the Cold War as well. All of the Cold War presidents except Kennedy and Carter chose the formalistic model, whereas the only post–Cold War president who did not choose the collegial model was George W. Bush.

Whether these apparent relationships are meaningful or spurious cannot, of course, be established scientifically because of the small numbers of people involved, but there does seem to be some interconnection. The gravity of managing the Cold War, for instance, may have led to the election of leaders stressing experience (age) that is related to choice of the greater predictability of the formalistic model (John Kennedy, the youngest man elected president at age forty-three during the height of the Cold War, is the glaring exception). At the same time, the more fluid, less-structured international system since the end of the Cold War has produced generally younger presidents for whom the greater flexibility of the collegial model may have appeal (George W. Bush is the obvious exception here). A discussion of how different presidents have employed the various models may shed some additional light on these distinctions, as well as aiding in an assessment of how these characterizations may help understand the likely styles of different presidents or aspirants to the presidency.

The Competitive Model

This has been the least-utilized decision style by presidents, and no president has attempted to employ it in over a generation. The reasons for this are probably multiple, but they have to relate to the fact that this is by far the most demanding decision system for the president to manage, since it places the incumbent squarely in the middle of the rough-and-tumble of policy disagreements (on purpose) and thus maximizes the extent and depth of presidential involvement in the decision process. It requires an incumbent who has an extraordinarily positive self-sense (arguably ego) and who believes he or she can surmount and create order from the chaos inherent in its operation. Only two presidents have tried; arguably only one has succeeded.

Why would a president choose this particular style of managing foreign policy? At the most obvious level and congruent with points already made, it ensures that the maximum number of opinions and options reach the president, rather than being compromised or condensed effectively into footnotes at lower levels of the political process. The result is to maximize personal presidential control over what goes on in the foreign policy area. There is little question that the outcomes of policy disputes by presidents who use this model bear the authentic presidential imprint.

The competitive model is a consummate politician's model. Exposing, debating, and choosing among the largest set of options requires a nimble mind and the political skills to reconcile opposing views and to reach decisions that even those with contrary views can be brought around to support. The political leader who does not possess considerable interpersonal persuasive skills will not only feel intensely uncomfortable in the kinds of debate forums the model encourages, but will likely be drowned in the stridency and even acrimony of the competing advocacy of positions. Because the president will be virtually inundated by information and opinions when employing this model, the danger is informational overload that either paralyzes the ability to decide or that takes up so much time that other important priorities are neglected. It is probably no surprise that, as the demands of the contemporary presidency have proliferated over the last fifty years or so, this model has been rejected by contemporary occupants of the White House.

As noted, only two presidents have attempted this model, Franklin Roosevelt and Lyndon Johnson. They were different men and they adopted the method for different reasons. Because it suited his personality, Roosevelt was successful in employing the model, as his success in managing the largest military coalition in world history while ending the Great Depression attests. Johnson, with a more brittle personality, was less successful. No one has tried since.

The presidency of Franklin Roosevelt was the prototype of the competitive model. The model evolved under Roosevelt and fit his personality and personal style very well. Cognitively, Roosevelt had an almost insatiable appetite for immersion in and command of policy detail that allowed him to operate in the intensely competitive policy environment he had created. He also preferred to sift through options in direct, face-to-face encounters with opposing agency heads, thereby sharpening his own sense of policies. Because he had a commanding personality and brimmed over with personal self-confidence, he felt he was capable of managing the untidy, sometimes acrimonious and fractious operation of this model. His style frustrated those around him (particularly agency heads who were bypassed when the president went to lower-level officials who possessed information or expertise he wanted), and in the hands of a less-skilled politician, the result could have been political chaos. Roosevelt was, however, the consummate politician of his day and arguably in the history of the presidency. Others have recognized the pitfalls of trying to emulate the Roosevelt model.

Lyndon Johnson tried, but in the end could not make the system succeed and eventually abandoned it. The primary reason was that Johnson, who was considered the premier legislative politician of his day, did not possess either the personal sense of expertise and efficacy to impose his views on the advisors he inherited from the Kennedy administration or the enormous skill of Franklin Roosevelt, his personal role model and the principal cause of his attempt to adopt the model. In the end, Johnson simply was not Roosevelt.

Johnson's style contrasted sharply with Roosevelt's. Prior to his service as Kennedy's vice president, his efforts and reputation were based on his skill as the leading congressional figure on domestic policy. As a result, he had spent little time on foreign affairs and lacked confidence in debating or arbitrating foreign policy disputes. He was thus forced to rely on the advice of holdovers from the Kennedy administration who held him in some intellectual disdain as a "country rube" in the midst of the Ivy League "Camelot" that had surrounded the fallen Kennedy. Although Johnson had a legendary ability to "jawbone" members of Congress into accepting his positions (which he largely succeeded in doing in pushing through the Great Society entitlement and civil rights programs after Kennedy's death), this skill did not extend to a foreign policy management system built in the Roosevelt style. Over time, his lack of oratorical skills decreased his ability to explain his positions on Vietnam effectively to the public, and his fragile sense of self-efficacy was further overwhelmed by mounting criticism (antiwar protesters chanting "LBJ, LBJ, how many kids did you kill today?" outside the White House gates, for instance). Gradually, Johnson withdrew from the public. By the election year of 1968, his only major public appearances were on military bases where criticism could be controlled, and he eventually dropped out of the race for reelection. Since his views were overwhelmed by the Kennedy holdovers on the Vietnam War, the competitive model gradually morphed into something more closely resembling the collegial model. Johnson's lack of expertise on foreign policy matters also helped undermine the effective operation of that model as well.

It is difficult to imagine future presidents trying to institute the competitive model. Contemporary politics simply do not produce figures with the political strength and personal confidence of the aristocratic Roosevelt. The Johnson experience with the model demonstrated what happens when a politician with a more fragile personal sense of efficacy and assertiveness tries to employ the Roosevelt model. Given the sheer volume of presidential activity in both foreign and domestic politics, it is hard to imagine how any new incumbent could carve out the time to employ the competitive model effectively.

The Formalistic Model

Over the roughly two-thirds of a century since the end of World War II, the formalistic model has been employed by more presidents than has either of the other two models. This model was especially popular during the Cold War and has been particularly popular among older, Republican presidents. Why has this been the case?

The tie-in to the Cold War may be related to the kind of environment the global competition with communism created. The Cold War did, as already noted, spawn the mentality of the national security state and a sense of grim determination and steadfastness in the face of a visible and menacing enemy. The purpose of the Cold War exercise was explicitly conservative in the true meaning of the term: to preserve Western democracies in the face of the communist onslaught. It was further conservative in that the stakes were very high and the consequences of making a strategic error potentially catastrophic. Going with tried-and-true, conservative solutions seemed more prudent than more innovative, change-oriented approaches. Thus, investing the country's leadership in older, more conservative, and presumably calmer heads had an appeal that would not be so necessarily attractive in a more fluid environment in which adaptation to change was the major value. Virtually all the presidents who adopted the formalistic model fit the mold that would flow from that kind of assessment.

The formalistic model is designed to promote order, structure, and discipline in decision making, all valued characteristics in a highly threatening, militarized environment. The strong emphasis of the model is on highly structured procedures and hierarchical lines of reporting that promote a well-defined set of procedures for considering and winnowing options for decision up the organizational ladder and for implementation once decisions are reached. Open conflict among agencies with different perspectives and solutions is discouraged, with the contrasting value of an orderly process being preferred. This set of preferences led to the development of what is now known as the interagency process (discussed in Chapter Five) by the Eisenhower administration. When it operates effectively, the formalistic model produces maximum efficiency in decision making, but not necessarily the most thorough, effective consideration of all possible outcomes. This trade-off, however, was reasonable in a Cold War atmosphere where the options seemed narrow and "out of the box" thinking could prove potentially calamitous.

Analysts agree that for the formalistic approach to work well, at least one of three conditions must be present. The first is a firm, hands-on management style at the top to achieve policy coherence, and normally this leadership must come personally from the president. If the president chooses not to assume this role, the second condition is to delegate the leadership role to a strong national security advisor or set of advisors—effective delegation of authority. The third alternative is a commonly held worldview among all the major foreign policy actors that allows them to function together on common goals and policies. One or another of these principles applied in each of the cases of adherents of the formalistic model.

Of the six presidents who have adopted the formalistic model, five were Republicans. The single Democrat to employ the model was Harry Truman, whose reasons for doing so were, as will be shown, basically idiosyncratic. The five Republicans, however, adopted the formalistic model for one of two basically contradictory reasons: either to maintain maximum personal control of the foreign policy process, or to allow for the orderly delegation of power to trusted subordinates in situations where the president lacked either the expertise or interest (or both) for heavy personal involvement.

The two Republican presidents who used the formalistic model to impose personal control over the process were Dwight D. Eisenhower and Richard M. Nixon. Although they operated the formalistic system differently and for different reasons, their obvious connection arose from the fact that Nixon was Eisenhower's vice president and thus had eight years of experience operating in this kind of environment before reaching the White House after an eight-year hiatus of Democratic Party rule during most of the 1960s.

The formalistic model was a natural form of organization for someone with Eisenhower's background in the military. Ike, as he was known, had gained considerable experience commanding and coordinating the politico-military effort to overthrow Hitler in Europe, and he believed that the lessons he had learned in the process made him uncommonly well-informed on international affairs and thus gave him the necessary expertise to navigate foreign policy. Moreover, his long and distinguished military career provided him with considerable experience in managing hierarchical decision-making structures, hallmarks of both military organizations and the formalistic model. Eisenhower had a sufficient sense of self-efficacy and confidence that he did not personally feel the need to take the public lead in foreign policy initiatives, a role he assigned to his colorful Secretary of State John Foster Dulles, but there was never any question whether Eisenhower was in firm charge and control of foreign policy.

Richard Nixon's personality caused him to choose the formalistic model for reasons that were quite different from those of Eisenhower. Nixon had, as noted earlier, a very firm command of international relations and felt himself eminently qualified to command and control the country's foreign policy. At the same time, Nixon had a highly complex personality that caused him to shun interpersonal contact except with a small circle of advisors. He preferred to get information on policy from written materials rather than face-to-face meetings with advisors, and his deep-seated discomfort with interpersonal relations caused him to shun any setting that might contain elements of political conflict.

The formalistic model thus put a cocoon around Nixon, allowing him to isolate himself in the White House surrounded only by trusted and self-reinforcing advisors such as Henry Kissinger. Information flowed up the system to Nixon in controlled channels, and the decisions he reached could be funneled downward through the bureaucracy for implementation. Moreover, Nixon's personality was deeply conspiratorial, and he distrusted many of the foreign policy mechanisms of the government, including the State Department, with whom he had a long-standing feud that dated back to his participation in investigations of the State Department's alleged infiltration by communists in the late 1940s and early 1950s. Using the formalistic model to insulate himself from outside influences, Nixon was able to control foreign policy while largely ignoring the State Department—at least until he dispatched Kissinger to the Secretary of State's job in 1973.

If Nixon used the formalistic model to provide himself with the cover to control foreign policy, the other Republicans have used it for the quite opposite purpose of *avoiding* heavy direct involvement in the making of foreign policy. Gerald Ford, Ronald Reagan, and George W. Bush all came to the presidency without demonstrated expertise or special interest in foreign policy, and so each chose to employ the formalistic model as a way in which they could effectively insulate themselves from the foreign policy area by delegating maximum authority to trusted advisors.

Ford's reasons are unique, reflecting the entirely idiosyncratic nature of the tenure of the Ford administration. President Ford has the distinction of being the only chief executive who was never elected to any national office by the American people. The former House minority leader became vice president in 1973 when Nixon's elected second in command, Spiro T. Agnew, resigned his office amidst controversy (the accusation of participation in corruption while he was governor of Maryland), and he was confirmed as vice president by the Senate. He became president according to the constitutional rule of succession when Nixon resigned the presidency in 1974. Thus, Ford became the only wholly unelected president and the only chief executive who could not lay claim to being the only politician chosen by the American people and thus having a mandate from them.

A particularly unassuming, modest person, Ford understood the limitations both of his mandate and of his inexperience in foreign policy, and thus he left the formalistic model that he inherited from Nixon basically in place, relying heavily on Kissinger and the State Department to take the lead in foreign policy. The choice was probably a wise one, as a foreign policy gaffe during his 1976 bid to be elected in which he declared communist Poland to be a free and independent state helped undermine his campaign and lead to the election of President Carter.

The lure of the formalistic model to Reagan and Bush had similar roots in their lack of foreign policy expertise, but it also added a further element of disinterest and information minimalism that represented a conscious choice on each of their parts not to achieve command of the intricacies of foreign policy matters. Reagan had a notoriously short attention span in receiving information, and when he met with foreign leaders, his aides equipped him with three-by-five note cards to guide him through policy discussions. Although he excelled at the ceremonial aspects of the presidency and had some very firm general ideas (such as his aversion to nuclear weapons), he lacked the interest and perseverance to engage in detailed supervision of policy processes. This latter characteristic gave considerable leeway to subordinates operating under general guidance from the Oval Office and led to the most embarrassing foreign policy episode of the Reagan years, the so-called Iran-Contra affair, in which administration officials engaged in illegal and unwise policy acts in the name of the president. Bush largely followed this practice, adopting a hands-off approach to virtually all foreign policy concerns other than those closely associated with his War on Terror.

The non-Republican who adopted the formalistic model, Harry Truman, did so for different reasons, Truman became president in April 1945 on the death of FDR, two weeks before the war in Europe officially ended. Truman was not a foreign policy expert, but in his brief tenure as vice president (a job to which he was first elected in 1944), he had gained confidence in his abilities, which he applied to the struggle in the 1940s that produced the durable strategy of containment. Regarding foreign policy making, however, Truman was mainly motivated by a deep concern for what he considered the dignity of the office of the White House (the presidency), and he felt that the highly disorderly and competitive atmosphere of the FDR years both diminished that dignity and did not fit in with his own personally less-flamboyant style. As a result, the higher degree of order associated with the formalistic model was attractive to him.

The Collegial Model

The collegial and formalistic models are, in some important ways, alternatives to one another. Adherence to the formalistic model dominated the Cold War era but, with the exception of George W. Bush's tenure in office, presidents have chosen the collegial model since. Also as noted, those who have chosen this model have been younger and more Democratic than their formalistic counterparts. One can only speculate why.

The Cold War or its absence is one obvious source of difference. The collegial model has been favored since the end of the Cold War, and one reason may be differences in the foreign policy environment of the Cold War and post–Cold War periods. The Cold War, as noted, was a much tenser and more potentially explosive and apocryphal period, whereas the post–Cold War period has been more fluid, where a major theme has been the search for a successor paradigm to containment. In this setting, a decision process that provides a freer rein to different ideas rather than a more highly disciplined approach to information and idea management may be more appropriate, and presidential aspirants who appear to possess more rigid views (that might be manifested in the adoption of the formalistic model) may seem less attractive than in the more structured, high-conflict times like the Cold War.

The heart of the collegial model is a foreign policy team of key aides, advisors, and cabinet officers with varying perspectives on policy matters but who can act as an effective team of equals, which the term "collegial" describes. It is a team approach, the major purpose of which is to encourage diversity of outlook among policy alternatives through group problem solving among a group of equals. This notion of equality is supposed to foster a collegial, cooperative environment rather than serve as a venue for bureaucratic infighting, and members are encouraged to identify with the foreign policy team above the interests of their particular agencies. The system works best when the president, as the first among equals, has a coherent worldview around which to structure discussions.

For the collegial model to work well, one of two conditions must be met within a given administration trying to employ it. One is a commanding president who articulates a clear vision from which participants in the collegial deliberation of policy specifics can take their bearing and direction. The second is an essential commonality of outlook among the principal actors. When one or the other of these principles has been in place, the collegial model has operated effectively; where they have not been present, the model faltered.

There have been four presidents (not including Obama) who have chosen this model. Two (Kennedy and Carter) came from the Cold War era. The two had different experiences with the model's operation. In the case of JFK, the model evolved from a foreign policy disaster at the beginning of his short tenure; in the case of Carter, he ultimately was less successful because neither condition was fully met.

John Kennedy, at age forty-three, was the youngest man elected president of the United States, and he arrived in office amidst considerable controversy. His youth contrasted greatly with the age and stature of Eisenhower, whom he succeeded; the fact that he was the first Catholic to hold the office created fears in some parts of the population; and his physical defeat of Richard Nixon was razor close, decided in a few controversial precincts in Chicago. Moreover, he brought with him a group of advisors from the academic setting of his native Massachusetts.

Kennedy stumbled out of the blocks, authorizing the disastrously unsuccessful Bay of Pigs Invasion of Cuba in 1961, a decision urged on him by holdovers from Eisenhower's formalistic system. In the wake of that experience, JFK brought together a more congenial group of advisors whom he fashioned into an effective team in time to meet the Cuban Missile Crisis.

Kennedy came from one of the most established and popular political families in the country, and he had the instincts and serene self-confidence of a professional politician. He possessed an unquenchable cognitive appetite for information and immersed himself in the intricacies of policy. He was also a voracious reader and writer, whose book *Profiles in Courage* won him the Pulitzer Prize in 1957. Kennedy's management style also featured a strong personal involvement in the details of policy making, a characteristic shared by other presidents employing the collegial model. By the time of his assassination in November 1963, JFK had devised an effective collegial style of foreign policy management that probably would have served him well in a second administration. James Earl (Jimmy) Carter was the second president to attempt to implement the collegial model, and he was ultimately less successful in doing so. Carter was not as gifted an orator as Kennedy, but he did share some characteristics with him. Carter was also a voracious reader who sought to compensate for his personal inexperience in foreign affairs by immersing himself in books, documents, and reports on the subject, and he engaged himself in the details of policy decisions. He was also comfortable in the give-and-take of policy debates and did not shy away from political conflict (a trait he has retained in his highly public life). As he has demonstrated in his very active postpresidential career, he has a high degree of confidence in his command of complex policy issues.

What undermined the Carter practice of the collegial model was that it could not meet either of the conditions for success. While Carter had a prodigious knowledge of the details of policy, he did not project a strong personal philosophy or paradigm beyond his personal belief that foreign policy should be grounded in American advocacy of human rights, a theme that never achieved traction within the volatile atmosphere of the Cold War. At the same time, the Carter foreign policy team was fractious, marked particularly by the clash between his hawkish national security advisor, Zbigniew Brzezinski, and his more dovish Secretary of State Cyrus Vance. The result was that foreign policy never achieved the coherence or unity that is a hallmark of successful collegial presidents.

The first post–Cold War president to attempt the collegial model was George H.W. Bush, whose term in office oversaw the end of the Cold War. Like Kennedy, Bush came from a patrician New England political family, and he had both a long history of political service and a high sense of his personal expertise in the area based on his experience in Beijing, at the U.N., as director of the CIA, and as vice president under Reagan for eight years. He also possessed excellent interpersonal skills and was especially effective in one-on-one debates over policy. Unlike Kennedy, he was not a particularly polished public figure (his most famous gaffe was being caught during one of his presidential debates with Clinton looking at his watch as if he were bored and wanted the debate over), and he preferred to receive most of his information through verbal briefings.

Bush was ultimately partially successful in operating the collegial model. The heart of his success came from his assemblage of a foreign policy staff that was notably congenial and worked well together. Virtually the entire group were "alumni" of the Ford presidency and shared a commonality of outlook that some critics said bordered on groupthink. The Achilles' Heel for the first Bush presidency, however, was the lack of a strategic vision by the president himself, particularly in the light of fundamental changes in the international environment accompanying the end of the Cold War. By his own admission, Bush always had problems with what he called the "vision thing."

The final former president to employ the collegial model was Bill Clinton. Clinton, quite consciously, had a style very close to his political hero, JFK, whom he admired and sought to emulate. Like JFK, Clinton was an avid reader who considered himself a "quick study" on complex issues and possessed a remarkable memory that made him both an extremely effective orator and debater on complex, extemporaneous subjects. He also possessed an exceptional sense of personal efficacy that manifested itself in great personal skills and a supreme confidence in his ability to "jawbone" political friends and foes alike into agreement on his positions. Unlike Kennedy, however, the "man from Hope (Arkansas)" came from a difficult personal childhood and avoided personal and political conflict whenever possible.

Clinton evolved his collegial approach over time. Clinton was an overwhelming personality who clearly enjoyed and demanded the spotlight, and he initially surrounded himself with a team of advisors who lacked conceptual or personal flair, which meant that Clinton himself could dominate policy proceedings. Like Bush before him, however, he entered office without a clear initial vision about how to manage the post–Cold War world, and his administration foundered conceptually until it hit upon dual emphases on globalization and peacekeeping as tethers for his foreign policy.

What distinguishes the presidents who have adopted the collegial approach is their common overall personality, and particularly their sense of self-efficacy and interest in the foreign affairs area. The president in the collegial model is not unlike a professor guiding a graduate seminar by Socratic method, and his effectiveness is likely to reflect his personal ability to project his own interpretation of events and dynamics while simultaneously encouraging and incorporating the views of others. When presidents have the vision to share and a group of advisors with whom they can work constructively, the collegial model seems to work at its best.

There is one other characteristic of the presidents who have employed the collegial model that may be worth mentioning. Probably because they have distinctly high levels of interest in and knowledge of foreign affairs when they enter office, they have been extraordinarily active in the field after they leave office. Jimmy Carter, for instance, rivals Richard Nixon in his production of books and articles on foreign policy topics, and has been an active monitor of foreign elections and other events internationally. George H.W. Bush has joined Bill Clinton in spearheading relief efforts for the 2006 tsunami in Asia and in response to the 2010 Haiti earthquake, and Clinton's foundation has been very active in promoting the solution to a variety of international problem areas. The only surviving practitioner of the formalistic model, George W. Bush, has demonstrated no equivalent penchant for continuing activity, and neither did most of the other presidents who followed the model, with the possible exception of that most enigmatic of modern presidents, Richard M. Nixon.

The Barack Obama Model?

At this writing, the Obama administration has been in office for less than a term, and the exact nature of how it conducts its foreign policy is not entirely clear. Both in terms of what is known about Obama as a political personality and from the team he has assembled, however, it seems most likely that he will be remembered as an adherent of the collegial model.

Obama raised high domestic and international expectations during the 2008 campaign. Domestic supporters viewed his generally internationalist views as a refreshing alternative to the brooding unilateralism of the Bush years, and Obama's election was viewed very highly by overseas publics and elites as a return of the United States to a more cooperative role in the international system. This enthusiasm was reinforced by the appointment of Hillary Clinton as his Secretary of State and by surrounding himself initially with an able cast of officials, including Secretary Robert Gates, Admiral James Jones, and Vice President Joe Biden, a former senior member and chair of the Senate Foreign Relations Committee.

The collegial style as described fits well with Obama's background and personality. Obama has a clearly scholarly cognitive style and is a highly skilled communicator reminiscent of Clinton. He clearly has a high sense of self-efficacy around foreign policy materials. Running the foreign policy decision process as a kind of graduate seminar fits Obama's background as a law professor about as perfectly as Eisenhower's background predisposed him toward the hierarchical style of the formalistic model.

Obama's early actions have been congruent with a collegial style of management. He is clearly the center of power and ideas within the foreign policy team. As Brzezinski puts it, "Obama himself is the major source of the strategic direction" on foreign policy, and the team of advisors he has assembled seems admirably able to meet the criteria both of providing contrasting perspectives on issues and of being able to unite behind policy decisions once they are reached. One of the innovations that Obama has made is to enlarge the general National Security Council staff group to include members of the National Economic Council (see Chapter Five), where there is somewhat more dissonance than within the traditional national security team.

The major limit on the operation of the Obama collegial model has been the limit of presidential time, a constraint on presidential power already raised in this chapter. As Brzezinski maintains, "He is only able to play this role (as foreign policy leader) on a part-time basis." The reason, of course, has been the need for presidential concentration of effort in dealing with the economic crisis that has gripped the country since 2008, including the enormously partisan political implications and effects of that crisis and disagreements on how to confront it.

CONCLUSIONS

The president is the most visible figure in the arena of American foreign policy. A large part of the reason for this is the dual position of the president as chief executive (head of government) and as the ceremonial leader of the American people (head of state). Both of these constitutionally based positions place the American president in the unique position of being the only politician with international status as the head of the American state and as the only individual who can negotiate with and enter into agreements with foreign governments. He has additional powers (namely, commander-in-chief, appointment of officials) that also have constitutional bases, and in addition, there are political advantages and constraints on the ability of the president to carry out his constitutional role.

The preeminence of the president has been both enhanced and diminished in the contemporary political environment. The complexity and volume of international affairs have meant that the legislative branch of government has less time and ability to watchdog all aspects of foreign policy interactions, and the preponderance of expertise on foreign affairs possessed by the executive branch provides a further source of advantage to the executive. This advantage, however, is circumscribed both by the rise in political partisanship within the political system and increased media coverage of international events. Increased partisanship means anything the president does receives intense scrutiny and criticism along partisan lines, and as the *Intersections* box suggested, foreign affairs is not exempt from this phenomenon. Indeed, it is an arguable aspect of partisanship that any action by the president in either domestic or foreign policy will be opposed simply because the president proposes it. Increased electronic media coverage means that the public is aware, at least at some cursory level, of events in the world that hitherto had escaped them, and they are aided in forming opinions by the army of foreign policy pundits who interpret these events for them.

How effective presidents are in conducting foreign policy is also the result of the kind of people that they are. No one can survive the rigors of becoming president without possessing impressive political skills, but what the individual does once in office is clearly the result of differences in factors such as knowledge and confidence in that knowledge and how the individual deals with political controversy and conflict. The particular configuration of a president's personality characteristics, in turn, helps form the management style that different presidents adopt, and the president's ultimate performance is also inevitably affected by the international political environment and how well the president's personality and management style mesh with the environment that he or she faces. This changing tapestry is addressed in the Applications section of Where Do We Go from Here?

WHERE DO WE GO FROM HERE?

Presidents operate within the framework of constitutionally described and politically determined powers and constraints, but the results achieved by different presidents differ significantly: The formal and informal advantages and disadvantages describe parameters within which foreign policy is carried out, not precise guidelines. How presidents behave and the successes they do or do not enjoy are also the result of their own personalities and management styles and the environments in which they operate. Because those environments themselves are subject to change, the result is an ever-changing tapestry of the presidential role in foreign affairs.

APPLICATION: THE "RIGHT" PRESIDENT AND STYLE FOR THE FUTURE

The discussion in the text suggested that there have been two prototypes for the kind of president and presidential style that has fit the foreign policy environment in the world since the end of World War II. The Cold War period was marked by older, more experienced, Republican presidents whose personalities led them to adopt the formalistic model of management, a system that maximized order in a predictable, if dangerous, foreign policy environment. In the interim between the end of the Cold War and 9/11, the collegial model, favored by younger, more intellectually flexible but engaged presidents, became dominant and seemed to match the more fluid environment of the time.

Since 9/11, there have been two presidents, and each chose a different model for organizing their foreign policy responses to the new environment. Bush chose the formalistic model and Obama has apparently chosen the collegial model as responses to an altered environment that is neither exactly the same as the Cold War nor the immediate post–Cold War period. This new environment is, as the discussion in Chapter Two suggested, something of a hybrid: Its structure is clearly more fluid and ambiguous than the Cold War, but it is has a higher threat level than did the 1990s interim period between the fault lines.

What kind of president and presidential style is most appropriate to this environment? Can, or should, the threat posed by international religious terrorism be met by a fairly rigid policy approach that would probably best be nurtured by a formalistic style, or is the threat fluid and changing enough that a more flexible approach to policy, such as that associated with the collegial approach, might commend?

The kind of presidential candidate that you favor in the upcoming and subsequent presidential elections may be affected by the kind of style you think different contenders might adopt. Particularly when combined with a personal assessment of those leaders (Chapter One) and comparison of the profile of the candidate with your own, the result can be a much clearer portrait of which presidential candidates are more or less compatible with your own beliefs about the foreign policy the country should pursue.

STUDY/DISCUSSION QUESTIONS

1. What was the Reykjavik summit? What momentous event almost happened there? Why is the event important in understanding the presidential role in foreign policy?
2. What is codetermination? What does it mean in terms of the constitutional allocation of powers between the president and the Congress in foreign policy?
3. What are the constitutional powers of the president in foreign policy? Describe each, with special emphasis on the roles of head of state and head of government. How has practice expanded some of these powers?
4. What informal (or political) powers does the president have in addition to the formal powers specified or implied in the Constitution? Describe each. How are these affected by political limits or constraints on presidential powers?
5. What are the three dimensions of presidential personality discussed in the text as they relate to foreign policy? How does each affect how a given president approaches foreign policy?
6. What are the three management models for dealing with foreign policy discussed in the text? Describe each and presidents who have adopted the different models.
7. Apply the personality types and management styles to the conduct of foreign policy by different presidents, using the management models as an organizing device. Are different personal and environmental characteristics attached to different models?
8. The text argues that President Obama employs the collegial style in making foreign policy? Do you agree? Why or why not?

CORE SUGGESTED READINGS

Corwin, Edward Samuel. *The President's Control of Foreign Relations.* Princeton, NJ: Princeton University Press, 1917. Although obviously dated, this classic text lays out the constitutional intent of the framers better than almost any contemporary account.

Crabb, Cecil V. Jr., and Pat Holt. *Invitation to Struggle: Congress, the President, and Foreign Policy* (2nd ed.). Washington, DC: CQ Press, 1984. Coauthored by a veteran foreign policy scholar (Crabb) and a Congressional Research Service professional (Holt), this is the classic statement of the relations between the branches of government in the foreign policy process.

George, Alexander L. *Presidential Decisionmaking in Foreign Policy: The Effective Use of Information and Advice.* Boulder, CO: Westview Press, 1980. In addition to providing the personality variables employed in this chapter, George's work explores the inner workings of how presidents deal with foreign policy questions in great depth.

Hilsman, Roger. *The Politics of Policy Making in Defense and Foreign Affairs: Conceptual Models and Bureaucratic Politics* (2nd ed.). Englewood Cliffs, NJ: Prentice Hall, 1990. Written by a close aide to John Kennedy, this overview of foreign policy decision making offers valuable insights into the operation of the foreign policy process within the executive branch.

Johnson, Richard T. *Managing the White House.* New York: Harper & Row, 1974. Like the George book, this is a classic overview of presidential decision making that also lays out and describes in detail the three management models discussed in the text.

ADDITIONAL READINGS AND REFERENCES

Barilleaux, Ryan J. *The President as World Leader.* New York: St. Martin's Press, 1991.

Brzezinski, Zbigniew. "From Hope to Audacity." *Foreign Affairs* 89, 1 (January/February 2010), 16–29.

Brose, Christian. "The Making of George W. Obama." *Foreign Policy*, January/February 2009, 52–55.

Falkowski, Lawrence S. *Presidents, Secretaries of State, and Crises in U.S. Foreign Relations: A Model and Predictive Analysis.* Boulder, CO: Westview Press, 1978.

Frum, David. "Think Again: Bush's Legacy." *Foreign Policy*, September/October 2008, 32–38.

Gaddis, John Lewis. *Strategies of Containment: A Critical Appraisal of American National Security Policy during the Cold War* (Rev. and exp. ed.). New York: Oxford University Press, 2005.

Goodby, James E. "Looking Back: The 1986 Reykjavik Summit." *Arms Control Today* (online), September 2008.

Kagan, Robert. "The September 12 Paradigm." *Foreign Affairs* 87, 5 (September/October 2008), 25–39.

Mead, Walter Russell. "The Carter Syndrome." *Foreign Policy*, January/February 2010, 58–64.

Mosher, Frederick W., David Clinton, and Daniel G. Lang. *Presidential Transitions and Foreign Affairs.* Baton Rouge, LA: Louisiana State University Press, 1985.

Neustadt, Richard E. *Presidential Power and the Modern Presidents: The Politics of Leadership from Roosevelt to Reagan.* New York: Free Press, 1990.

Oberdorfer, Don. *From Cold War to a New Era: The United States and the Soviet Union, 1983–1991* (Rev. and up. ed.). Baltimore, MD: Poseidon Press, 1991.

Reagan, Ronald W. *An American Life.* New York: Simon & Schuster, 1990.

CHAPTER 5

The Role of Executive Agencies

The founder and president of WikiLeaks, the organization that obtained and publicized classified

PREVIEW

While the executive and legislative branch codetermine what foreign policy decisions are made, most of the actual implementation of that policy falls to relevant federal agencies which are part of the executive branch. These agencies are also the repository of much government knowledge and analysis about foreign policy matters. They are, however, part of the political process, disagreeing and competing with one another and with elements within the legislative branch as part of the partisan deadlock that infects American politics. This chapter will introduce these sources of influence and competition, as well as survey the roles of the major executive branch agencies that form the so-called interagency process: the National Security Council (NSC) and its subsidiary bodies, the Department of State, the Department of Defense, the intelligence community, the Department of Homeland Security, and the various economic agencies involved in foreign affairs.

KEY CONCEPTS

National Security Council
interagency process
National Security Act of 1947
Principals Committee
Deputies Committee
Interagency Policy Committees
State Department
Foreign Service Officers
Defense Department
civilian control of the military
intelligence community
Central Intelligence Agency (CIA)
Director of Central Intelligence
Director of National Intelligence
homeland security
Department of Homeland Security
Federal Emergency Management Agency (FEMA)
economic agencies
National Economic Council
United States Trade Representative

On July 25, 2010, WikiLeaks.org released 76,000 documents detailing American activities in Afghanistan from 2004 to 2010 to the public as the first of what has become a series of disclosures of classified documents to the public. The documents contained in the release covered the day-to-day activities of American forces in the field in Afghanistan during this period, as well as cable traffic among civilian agencies about progress in the War in Afghanistan. Although much of the information released was already common knowledge, some was not, and the net effect of interpretation of the whole set of documents was to raise further questions about progress in the increasingly unpopular war.

The WikiLeaks episode created a minor firestorm of protests from inside and outside government. The reaction from within the government centered on the fact that the documents were indeed "leaks" of classified information, allegedly provided by a young Army enlisted man who disapproved of the conduct of the war. Whoever provided these documents to WikiLeaks violated an agreement he or she had signed promising not to divulge classified information (a requirement for obtaining security clearance in the first place) and was thus prosecutable under the law. The fact that the release put

American efforts in a less favorable light than the administration preferred was also a political violation of the supposed hierarchical relationship between the president and those in federal agencies who nominally work for the chief executive. From both inside and outside the government, there was further concern that the release would lead to the identification of the sources of the confidential information, which in turn might lead to lethal consequences for those so identified. As National Security Advisor General James Jones put it, the release "puts the lives of Americans and our partners at risk."

WikiLeaks.org achieved a heretofore unknown level of notoriety in the process. Founded in 2006 by Julian Assange, an Australian, the website advertises itself as a "forum for the Internet community to generate accuracy, scrutiny, and discussion of sensitive information." The site accepts anonymous submissions of information from sources internationally, maintains operations in Sweden and Iceland, and receives donations from private donors and foundations to remain in business. Although subject to wilting criticism in the United States, it is not clear that there is anything effective that the U.S. government could do to curtail its activities or punish it for the leaks (legal penalties for divulging classified information generally only apply to those who have signed waivers of the right to share such information).

For observers with an historical sense, the WikiLeaks episode immediately conjured an analogy with the release of the Pentagon Papers in 1971. The two events both involved leaks of information the government wanted to keep from the public, and both were directed at unpopular American wars (Afghanistan and Vietnam). They were, however, also quite different in a couple of important ways. One was the substance of what was leaked. The WikiLeaks documents were mostly raw reports back and forth among government sources in Afghanistan and Washington, and most of the information was already public knowledge. By contrast, Daniel Ellsberg's provision of the Pentagon Papers to *The New York Times* involved the leak of an official Department of Defense history of the Vietnam War (the official title was *United States-Vietnam Relations, 1945–1967: A Study Prepared by the Department of Defense*) that revealed a pattern of governmental actions to mislead the American people about the true nature of the war and American efforts there. The WikiLeaks episode, because it involved so much information that was thus difficult for most people to assimilate, had a much shorter "shelf life" as news and controversy; when the *Times* published the Ellsberg-provided history as *The Pentagon Papers* in 1971, the book rose quickly to the top of best-seller list and was one of the factors leading to the American decision to end the Vietnam War.

The WikiLeaks and Pentagon Papers episodes are both illustrations of an underlying mythology about of the operation of the U.S. government, and specifically the executive branch: The myth is that the president as chief executive controls all the actions of those who formally work for him, and the WikiLeaks episode reveals this is not absolutely true. Indeed, while the chief executive wields considerable influence and control over most of the actions that are taken in the name of the United States, the federal bureaucracy is too immense, and its members too diverse in opinion on the issues, for there to be a perfect coincidence between the wishes of the president and those who serve the presidency.

Normally, the disagreements within the government are handled privately within the various forums established by the interagency process, but that concealment is not complete. The voraciousness of the modern news cycle generated by the electronic media means, among other things, that dissidents have easy access to some outlet that will provide them with a forum to express their discontent. Increased partisanship that has infected journalistic endeavors has made it easier for those with contrary views to make them known to wider audiences than has historically been the case. Keeping secrets in the modern political world has become very difficult.

The impact is to make the president's job even more difficult than it would otherwise be. The president's role in foreign policy is overarching, but it is not all encompassing or absolute. Presidential dominance is compromised partially by the kinds of constitutional limits and political constraints discussed in the last chapter, but that is not all. The breach of the water's edge means that almost any presidential initiative in either the domestic or foreign policy area will be the subject of withering criticism and dissection, often along purely partisan lines and in apparent disregard for the international consequences. The President must also remain sensitive and attempt to guide the competing beliefs and influences within the executive branch, and when the president becomes inadequately sensitive to such influences, episodes like WikiLeaks or the Pentagon Papers serve as retribution.

Moreover, no president has the time, knowledge, or expertise to craft and oversee the comprehensive formulation of all foreign policy. The degree to which a president tries to do so varies widely, of course, based on personality traits, notably sense of self-efficacy, and on the competition of other priorities. Given the multiple demands on the president, the best that the individual may be able to do is to set the tone for the actions of any given administration. The president, for instance, may set the agenda for what the military may have to do, but decisions about how to translate those guidelines into numbers of tanks and calibers of bullets fall to others in the decision chain.

To assist in making and implementing policy, the president must rely on a large number of federal agencies that are part of the executive branch of government. It is a diverse group of agencies, including core actors like the State Department (core in the sense of having foreign policy as its central, or core, responsibility and thus always active in the foreign policy area) and more peripheral actors like the Agriculture Department, whose interest is confined largely to matters of international commerce in American grain and other agricultural products. The agencies also vary enormously in size: the State Department, according to 2009 government sources, employs about 36,500 professional personnel, whereas the Department of Defense employs nearly 700,000 *civilian* employees, in addition to the 1.54 million American men and women on active duty and 979,000 reserves.

This chapter focuses on the core actors in the foreign policy process: the most prominent executive branch departments and agencies that serve the president in the general area of foreign policy. Much of the coordination of these agencies has, since the system began to be formalized by President Eisenhower, been focused in the **National Security Council** (**NSC**) system, also known as the **interagency process,** and that complex of interactions is the starting point for the discussion. With that basis formed, the chapter then turns to the primary agencies and departments that form the NSC system: the State Department, Department of Defense, intelligence community, Department of Homeland Security (DHS), and the economic agencies that promote overseas American economic interests.

THE INTERAGENCY PROCESS

What has become known in Washington as the interagency process is an artifact of the **National Security Act of 1947**. That landmark piece of legislation was, as indicated in Chapter Two, a major part of the American political response to the growing Cold War animosity between the United States and the Soviet Union. Its net effect was to create the framework for the national security state that was the foreign policy vehicle for conducting the Cold War policy of containment. To achieve those ends, the Act did several notable things, the most central of which was to create the National Security Council as the primary coordinating device within the executive branch for dealing with foreign and national security matters, and a more extensive series of supportive institutions has evolved to assist the NSC in doing its work. Additionally, the National Security Act created an independent Department of Defense, United States Air Force, and the Central Intelligence Agency (CIA), all of which are discussed in this chapter.

The interagency process developed and matured largely as a response to the evolution of the Cold War. The structure of the contemporary NSC system began to develop during the presidency of Eisenhower, and it reflected both his military sense of hierarchy and structure and preference for a formalistic model for dealing with foreign policy. Subsequent presidents have made greater or lesser use of the interagency process, but by the end of the Cold War, the shape of the organization was basically in place and has survived mostly intact to the present.

The interagency process consists of four hierarchically ordered institutions, each composed of appropriate representatives from the major core foreign policy agencies within the executive branch. At the apex of the system is the NSC itself. Directly below and virtually identical to the NSC is the Principals Committee, and a step below it is the Deputies Committee. At the bottom of the process are a series of Interagency Policy Committees. Acting in concert and dependent upon presidential preference, these four bodies make up the foreign policy decision process within the White House.

The National Security Council

The NSC sits atop the pyramid of working bodies that collectively comprise the interagency process. Unlike the other constituent bodies in the process, the NSC itself is a direct mandate of the National Security Act and thus has statutory standing (meaning it cannot be disbanded without congressional permission). The other bodies within the process were all created by executive order and thus could be repealed without direct congressional approval or disapproval, although no president has formally proposed to do so. The National Security Act both specifies the core composition of the NSC (those members who must be included in its deliberations) and the function of the NSC, which is to assist the president in integrating all aspects of foreign and national security policy as it affects the United States.

Membership in the NSC varies somewhat, depending on the preferences and needs of the individual incumbent president. Certain parts of the membership are specified by the National Security Act of 1947, as amended in 1949, and the composition of the Obama NSC was set forth in an executive order, **Presidential Policy Directive 1 (PPD-1)**, on February 13, 2009. By statute, the council has four members: the president, the vice president, the secretary of state, and the secretary of defense. The chairman of the Joint Chiefs of Staff (CJCS) and the Director of National Intelligence (DNI) are permanent members as the chief advisors to the president on military and intelligence matters. In the current Obama administration, the secretary of the treasury, the attorney general, the secretary of homeland security, and the representative of the United States to the United Nations have been designated as full-time members, as has the assistant for national security affairs (National Security Advisor, or NSA). Within the Obama White House, the president's chief of staff, counsel, and the assistant to the president for economic policy are invited to attend all meetings. When their responsibilities are involved, representatives primarily concerned with international economic issues, homeland security and terrorism and counterterrorism, or science and technology are specified as occasional members of the Council. The president may invite any other officials to attend depending on the matters being discussed at a particular meeting. This pattern varies somewhat between presidents: President Bush, for instance, did not include as many economic advisors on the NSC, whereas Obama largely follows a precedent set by President Clinton.

The NSC operates strictly as an advisory body to help inform the president as he decides on foreign policy issues. By tradition, no votes are taken in the NSC, for fear that the outcomes might constrict the president's perceived options. Rather, the tenor of NSC meetings is to provide a more or less freewheeling exchange of views from the perspectives of the president's closest advisors, and the purpose is to help the president reach ultimate decisions.

The dynamics of NSC meetings varies considerably from president to president, and both its composition and style of operation reflect the president's personality and management style. Presidents who opt for the formalistic model, such as George W. Bush, used the NSC differently than those who preferred the collegial model. Bush, for instance, assembled a very like-minded team of advisors prone to very little internal disagreement among themselves and with the chief executive. In the first Bush term, Secretary of State Colin Powell was somewhat of a dissenter, and it is instructive that he was the only core actor not to stay on for at least a significant part of the second Bush term. Collegial presidents, however, are more likely to choose NSC teams holding compatible but not identical views and to use the NSC forum as a more free-flowing forum wherein differences are aired and eventually reconciled. Within the Obama team, for instance, there is a reasonable range of opinion from fairly liberal Vice President Biden through centrist Secretary of State Hillary Clinton to more conservative Secretary of Defense Robert Gates, who was replaced by Leon Panetta, the former Director of Central Intelligence (DCI), when Gates retired. While they have had significant disagreements on numerous issues, they have managed to present a united front to the public once decisions have been reached. A testimony to the working relationship is that Gates, the lone holdover from the Bush team, remained in office well until mid-2011, despite early predictions that he would only be a short-term transitional figure in 2008.

Principals Committee

When the NSC meets without the physical presence of the president, it is (and has been since 1989) designated as the **Principals Committee** (NSC/PC). Traditionally, the Principals Committee is chaired by the National Security Advisor. During the early years of the first George W. Bush administration, Vice President Richard Cheney attempted to gain greater control of the foreign policy process by trying to wrest the chair from NSA Condoleezza Rice, but was rebuked in the attempt. PPD-1 by the Obama administration confirmed that then-NSA James Jones (now Tom Donilon, who became NSA when Jones resigned in October 2010) would be the chair of the body. The NSA convenes the PC and is responsible for coordinating the agenda and other administrative duties.

The membership of the PC is essentially the same as that of the NSC itself, sans the president. Within the Obama administration, regular members are the vice president, the secretaries of state, treasury, defense, energy, and homeland security, as well as the attorney general, director of the Office of Management and Budget, the UN representative, the president's chief of staff, the director of national intelligence, and the chairman of the Joint Chiefs of Staff. In addition, a series of officials at the next lower level of the hierarchy are invited to all meetings, and officials representing the same functional policy areas that are designated for the NSC (economic issues, homeland security, terrorism and counterterrorism, and science and technology) may be invited as appropriate.

The Principals Committee serves several useful functions, three of which are worth mentioning. First, it can be convened when the president is unavailable for a meeting, thereby facilitating the ability of the government to function in the absence of the chief executive. Second, it can meet whenever the agenda contains items in which the president either lacks personal interest or where his input does not require his or her personal attendance. Third, the president may choose to be absent from some discussions to promote candor in deliberations that might be more restrained in his presence; in other words, in situations where attendees might feel constrained to please the president rather than frankly stating their own beliefs on an issue that might be contrary to the president's beliefs. The most famous instance of this latter usage came during the Cuban Missile Crisis. During this incredibly tense period, the president decided to absent himself from meetings of the Executive Committee (ExComm of the NSC, the predecessor of the PC) to try to ensure that participants would air their true feelings rather than feel the need to tell him what they thought he might want to hear. Reliance on the PC rather than the NSC itself is also a good measure of the level of direct presidential involvement in foreign and national security matters.

Deputies Committee

Directly beneath the Principals Committee is the **Deputies Committee (NSC/DC)**. In many ways, the DC level is the major working level of the entire process, where the members, at a level removed from the actual members of the NSC, roll up their sleeves and formulate the details of policy and its implementation. As the name suggests, this committee is composed of the chief assistants (or deputies) of the members of the Principals Committee. Thus, the Deputies Committee is chaired by the deputy NSA (who is also responsible for convening and coordinating the DC's activities), and its members are the deputy secretaries of state, treasury, defense, energy, and homeland security, as well as the deputy attorney general, deputy director of the office of management and budget, deputy representative to the UN, deputy DNI, deputy to the CJCS, and the deputy NSA. Like the higher committees, representatives from other functional areas can be added when their areas of responsibility are under discussion.

PPD-1 lists five essential tasks of the Deputies Committee, all of which are compatible with prior usage. First, the DC is responsible for reviewing and monitoring the overall interagency process, both above and below its own level. Second, it has the responsibility of properly analyzing and preparing issues for decision at the higher levels, a duty that has greater or lesser importance depending on how much a particular administration wants its options winnowed before reaching the White House itself. Third, the NSC/DC is charged with providing "significant attention on policy implementation" at lower levels once decisions have been reached. Fourth, the DC is charged with "periodic reviews of the Administration's major foreign policy initiatives" as a way to ensure that policy is being implemented as intended, that necessary adjustments are being made reflecting events, and that existing "policy directives should be revamped or rescinded" when appropriate. Fifth and finally, the NSC/DC is responsible for "day-to-day crisis management," on which it reports to the NSC.

Interagency Policy Committees

One of the major changes that the Obama administration announced in its original PPD was in the structure of the third layer of the interagency system. Under previous administrations, this layer had been known as the Policy

Coordinating Committees (PCCs), and their number and structure had been specified across time. The Obama administration ordered a restructuring of this process, visible in three distinctive ways.

The first change was to change the name of the bodies at this level. The PCCs are now called the **Interagency Policy Committees (IPCs)**. While this renaming may or may not have great significance, it does have the symbolic effect of creating a more fluid environment within which to formulate the structure of this layer of the process, which is the second change. The PCCs were divided into two distinct groups of committees, each with specified chairs and memberships, generally a layer down the bureaucracy in the various agencies represented in the NSC, PC, and DC. One set of these committees was geographic in focus, specializing in different geographic regions of the world and chaired by the assistant secretary of state for that region. In addition, there were a series of "functional" PCCs devoted to particular issue areas (for example, defense, economics) chaired by an assistant from the lead agency (the agency with primary responsibility for the particular area of concern).

The designation of Interagency Policy Committees (IPCs) in PPD-1 tears down the old structure and directs the Deputies Committee to develop a successor series of IPCs. The major purpose of these bodies is to provide "day-to-day fora for interagency coordination of national security policy"; in other words, they exist to implement decisions made at the DC level or above, and to provide options to the DC for refinement and transmission upward in the process. Unlike the PCCs that they replaced, the IPCs are chaired either by the NSA or his counterpart for economic policy, the chair of the National Economic Council (NEC), a position created by President Clinton and the subject of discussion later in the chapter.

Adding the assistant for economic policy into the NSC interagency system also signals an intention to broaden the reach of the NSC system more formally to include economic matters of security in the overall interagency process. As noted, President Clinton began this process by creating the NEC by executive order in 1993 and according it a level of prestige similar to that of the NSC. President George W. Bush briefly considered dismantling the NEC because it was a reminder of the Clinton years (since it was created by executive order, a simple countermanding order could dissolve it) but ultimately decided not to do so. Coming to office in the midst of a domestic economic crisis with obvious international economic causes and consequences, the Obama administration opted to elevate the importance of economic concerns within the overall interagency process.

THE EXECUTIVE AGENCIES

While the broad purpose of the interagency process is to compile, reconcile, and reach decisions on the complex matters that compose foreign policy, most of the detailed, day-to-day work in the area of foreign and national security policy is done within the various executive branch agencies that are represented in the interagency process. It is within these agencies that the vast majority of officials and their expertise are housed. The staff of the NSA within the White House under Obama has been expanded to include nearly two hundred staffers (the largest of any president to this point), and it is comprised of very bright and dedicated individuals. At the same time, personnel in the various agencies that help formulate and execute policy number in the hundreds of thousands and provide the expert resource base that is an important part of the informational advantage of the president over other parts of government, as argued in Chapter Four. The various agencies that advise the president have different perspectives and mandates, and they often have very different views about appropriate policy in any given matter, which is part of the reason an interagency process is necessary to determine what U.S. policy will be.

The discussion thus moves to a description and analysis of the principal agencies that advise the president on foreign affairs matters. It begins with the State Department, because that is the agency that has historically been at the center of foreign policy making and which, at least until World War II, was virtually the synonym for the foreign policy establishment. Because of the advent of the Cold War, the concerns of foreign policy were expanded enormously, notably to incorporate a much more prominent role for the idea of national security and the national security state. The National Security Act of 1947 formalized this expansion by creating both a Department of Defense and a Central Intelligence Agency to respond to a new and more overtly threatening international environment, and the discussion thus moves to the DOD and the intelligence area as represented by something called the "intelligence community." The attacks of 9/11 elevated the idea of homeland security, always an implicit part of the charge of the DOD, to greater centrality, and thus resulted in the creation and evolution of the Department of Homeland Security. Finally, the rise of globalization during the 1990s made more prominent the role of international economic concerns in foreign policy, so that the discussion of executive branch agencies concludes with the complex of economic agencies that are active in the foreign policy realm.

The State Department

The most venerable agency in the foreign policy process is the **State Department.** It was the first federal agency authorized under the Constitution in 1789 (its original name was the Department of Foreign Affairs; its name was changed to the Department of State later that same year). Its first secretary was Thomas Jefferson, and it was the lead agency in America's interactions with the world at least until World War II, when the increasing militarization of the international environment led to its partial eclipse by other agencies, notably the Defense Department.

Regardless of this shift in emphasis, it is one of Washington's most predictable rituals for an incoming president to proclaim that he will look to the State Department to play the lead role in foreign policy, and the position of Secretary of State is among the most coveted positions within any administration, attracting some of whom become the most prominent members of any new administration: Colin Powell within the George W. Bush administration and Hillary Clinton in the Obama administration are exemplary of the prestige that still surrounds the secretary's position.

The State Department is physically located at the opposite end of the National Mall from the Capitol in an area known as Foggy Bottom. The area gets its name originally from its proximity to the Potomac River and the resulting fog from that stream which sometimes encompasses the building, but the acronym is also a less charitable way of describing the quality of thinking that allegedly goes on within its walls. The age and venerability of the State Department has been accompanied by a perception in the minds of many that it suffers from some level of intellectual sclerosis, elitism, and unreliability. Some presidents have thought it too unresponsive to presidential preferences (President Carter thought it was too conservative; Presidents Nixon and Reagan thought it too liberal) and not aggressive enough to lead in interagency battles (John Kennedy dismissed the State Department bureaucracy as "a bowl of JELL-O"). Most colorfully, Franklin Roosevelt once disparaged the speed and responsiveness of the agency, saying, "Dealing with the State Department is like watching an elephant become pregnant; everything is done on a very high level, there's a lot of commotion, and it takes twenty-two months for anything to happen."

Despite challenges to its leadership, the State Department remains at the center of perceptions about American foreign policy. The Department of State is the only organization within the U.S. government whose mission is entirely devoted to the foreign affairs of the United States, both in terms of the scope and emphasis of its area of responsibility and in its role as the interface between the American government and other world governments. It accomplishes this mission despite having one of the smallest bureaucracies of any major executive agency.

To understand the place of the State Department within the complex of agencies involved in foreign policy, the discussion will proceed along two tracks. First, the organization of the department will be examined to show both the place of the secretary of state in the scheme of foreign policy and how the department accumulates and organizes the welter of expertise available to it. The discussion will then move to the foreign policy role that different administrations have assigned to it.

Organization The Founding Fathers would not recognize the agency they created in 1789. Thomas Jefferson presided over a "bureaucracy" consisting of five clerks, one translator, two messengers, and two overseas diplomatic missions. By contrast, now the bulk of the U.S.-based employees of the State Department are housed in a ponderous eight-story building on Washington's "C" Street that sprawls across twelve acres of the Foggy Bottom region near the Lincoln Memorial. Despite its growth, however, it is indeed one of the smallest cabinet-level agencies, with a budget and personnel size absolutely dwarfed by foreign policy competitor agencies such as the Department of Defense.

At the head of the State Department is its secretary. As already noted, the position of secretary of state is one of the most coveted positions within the federal bureaucracy, and when a new administration comes to office (or a vacancy occurs for some other reason), there are always multiple high-profile contenders for the job and great speculation about who will fill it. The inevitable debate that surrounds the appointment occurs both in Washington and foreign capitals, where the stature and policy position of the new secretary is viewed as an important indication of the likely direction of U.S. foreign policy. Other than gathering a prior opponent under the new administration's tent, for instance, the appointment of Hillary Rodham Clinton was generally viewed as a positive sign about the importance that new President Obama places both on foreign policy and the role of the secretary.

Different presidents appoint different kinds of secretaries, at least partly on the basis of the management style that they employ in the foreign policy area. One dimension of differentiation among secretaries is whether they are viewed as strong or weak actors in the foreign policy process. Presidents who want to dominate the foreign policy personally tend to appoint less visible and less forceful secretaries, who are generally categorized as weak. Examples include Nixon's 1969 appointment of William P. Rogers, a New York lawyer with little international experience, or Clinton's appointment of the knowledgeable but nonassertive Warren Christopher to the post. At the other extreme, presidents who want to avoid heavy involvement tend to appoint strong secretaries who can dominate the foreign policy area and leave the president free for other parts of the job that he or she finds more interesting. Gerald Ford's retention of Henry Kissinger, Reagan's choice of George Shultz, and George W. Bush's appointment of Colin Powell are notable examples.

A second dimension that differentiates secretaries is whether they consider themselves primarily as advocates of State Department positions or as White House team players. This distinction has particular symbolic importance within Foggy Bottom itself, where the department's highly qualified professionals often feel their advice is underappreciated and underutilized. When a forceful advocate of the department is appointed, their morale is lifted measurably. The appointment of Hillary Clinton, and her early and repeated praise for the department, for instance, was greatly appreciated by department professionals who felt somewhat ignored by Secretary Condoleezza Rice, whose loyalties were much more closely tied to the White House. At the same time, some secretaries view themselves as such strong and qualified people as to be virtually above advice from the department, thereby harming morale. Secretaries stressing a team approach, of course, are more generally associated with the collegial style of management, whereas either very strong and independent or weak individuals are more closely associated with formalistic presidents who either want to dominate or alternately want to be shielded from foreign policy responsibilities.

Secretaries of state thus mirror and give strong indications about the way presidents want to organize their pursuit of foreign policy. Regardless of who the secretary is, however, the incumbent is supported by a professionally expert and organized bureaucracy to help formulate, execute, and coordinate America's face toward the outside world. Below the secretary are two deputy secretaries, as well as reporting officials such as the administrator of the Agency for International Development (USAID) and the U.S. permanent representative to the United Nations (USUN). Most of the department's detailed expertise, however, resides within the functional bureaus and agencies.

At the operational level, the department is divided into six functional areas, each headed by an under secretary. Two of these divisions are basically administrative: the programs administered by the under secretary for diplomacy and public affairs, and those administered by the under secretary for management. The heart of the organization's expertise, however, lies in the four other subdivisions, each charged with a different substantive foreign policy concern.

The heart of departmental expertise falls within the jurisdiction of the under secretary for political affairs, who is listed as the department's "third-ranking official and its senior career diplomat." Under Secretary William J. Burns (the incumbent in 2010) is assisted by a series of assistant secretaries for the various geographical regions and offices under his jurisdiction. The geographical areas include: African Affairs, European and Eurasian Affairs, East Asian and Pacific Affairs, Near Eastern Affairs, South and Central Asian Affairs, and Western Hemisphere affairs. In addition, the under secretary oversees the activities of the assistant secretaries for international narcotics and law enforcement and international organizations.

In addition to those activities reporting to the under secretary of political affairs, substantive expertise is also housed within operations reporting to under secretaries for economics, energy and agricultural affairs, arms control and international security (ACIS) affairs, and democracy and global affairs. Historically, the ACIS function, which includes the bureau of Politico-Military Affairs (PM), has acted as a kind of mirror and watchdog of the activities of the Department of Defense, which has a corresponding office to serve the same function vis-à-vis State. The complex of democracy and global affairs initiatives encompasses a kind of grab bag of functions, some of them arising from changes apparent in the post–Cold War world. Included in its charge are: democracy, human rights, and labor; oceans and international environmental and scientific affairs; population, refugees, and migration; and the office to monitor and combat trafficking in persons.

The core of expertise within the State Department comes from its highly select core of career professionals in the Foreign Service. **Foreign Service Officers (FSOs)** make up merely six thousand of the employees of the State Department (Secretary of Defense Robert Gates was fond of saying, as a sign of misplaced priorities, that there are more members of U.S. military bands than there are members of the Foreign Service). They are a highly select group, chosen on the basis of a highly competitive written and oral testing procedure, passage of rigorous background checks necessary for security clearance, matching of career preference with departmental needs, and the availability of open positions within the Foreign Service. In any given year, thousands of individuals who meet the general qualifications for the service will take the Foreign Service written examination, but by the time the results are filtered through the process, only several hundred or fewer will be selected for the pool of qualified candidates, and many of those people will have to wait extended periods before a slot becomes available for which they are qualified. Successful applicants are typically very highly educated, generally with some graduate degree(s) or practical working experience in the areas for which they are applying, or both.

Even for those admitted as FSOs (sometimes also known as foreign service generalists to emphasize the breadth of their expertise), the process remains competitive, with an "up or out" personnel system that requires that members qualify for successively more responsible positions in order to remain members of the service. Those who succeed through this process come to think of themselves (not irrationally) as members of an elite circle set apart from other parts of the government. The members are surrounded and conditioned by an ingrained set of institutional values and attitudes that strengthen the internal cohesion of the Foreign Service, but at the same time, they erect a psychological distance between FSOs and others within the policy process that many outsiders interpret (once again, not entirely without reason) as a sense of superiority and condescension from the FSOs. One of the stereotypical distinctions within foreign policy circles is depicted by the attitudes that career military officers and FSOs—who often are called upon to work together in diplomatic situations with military implications—have about one another. To FSOs, the military officers are depicted as "knuckle draggers," conjuring an image of lower primates; and to the officers, the FSOs are the "pointy heads," an unkind reference to ivory tower intellectuals. The mutual designations are only partially in jest.

In terms of expertise, however, the FSOs, augmented by the political appointees at the secretarial level and below, form the core of the State Department's expertise and influence base. Generally speaking, those political appointees who are appointed to State share many of the values of the FSOs, including a sense of intellectual prowess (many are drawn from academic and think-tank environments), enhancing the reputation of the department as a more ivory tower organization than the more "practical" level agencies such as the DOD, with which it must compete for influence.

Foreign Policy Role Although there are exceptions, it is fair to say that the influence of the State Department has been in general decline since the end of World War II. Much of the day-to-day affairs of carrying out American business with the world remains firmly within the grasp of the department. The embassies, including the ambassadors who head them, still report through the State Department, Americans overseas rely on offices under the jurisdiction of the State Department for assistance and advice, and the granting or withholding of passports and visas are State Department functions. In simpler times, these kinds of functions largely defined foreign affairs and ensured the dominance of State in the foreign policy decision process. But times have changed.

The role of the embassy is exemplary. Historically, the system of American embassies in foreign countries (and vice versa) was the heart of foreign policy conduct. Particularly before telephonic and other electronic means of communication, these missions were nearly autonomous, since it could take days or even weeks or months for messages to travel back and forth between the embassy in some faraway country and Washington. For the same reason, the government in Washington had to rely largely on information gathered by the embassy on events in target countries. Since news venues were either nonexistent or as slow as normal communications channels, they could not be relied on to provide the government with timely information or expert interpretation. For many practical purposes, the embassies were independent actors in a hostile world environment, and the ambassadors served as the chief advisors to the U.S. government on matters concerning the countries to which they were accredited.

That role stands in sharp contrast to the situation today. With the flow of electronic media coverage of events and information from intelligence sources only nominally related to the embassies, they are no longer the major source of U.S. government knowledge of what is happening in most countries. There is the apocryphal story during the Bush administration of Secretary of State Powell calling the ambassador in a country undergoing upheaval and asking him for the details of some disturbance that was occurring. The ambassador was apparently unaware of the incident and asked Powell if he was sure of what he was asking about. Powell apparently retorted that he knew it was happening, because he was watching it live on CNN in his office.

The same electronic capabilities that allow for information gathering also affect the need for the ambassador to make decisions. Since the embassy can now communicate with its reporting channel at Foggy Bottom via secure communications links instantaneously, the ambassador is no longer a decision maker. Instead, when something arises, the ambassador calls Washington and asks for a resolution, which he or she then relays to the host government. In the process, the role of the embassy is reduced to being largely a messenger service and clerk.

The erosion of State Department centrality and power in decision making can be attributed to several other interconnected factors, three of which can be mentioned here. First, the foreign policy environment has changed dramatically since the middle of the twentieth century. Foreign policy used to be largely about diplomacy, which is the core competence and preferred tool of the State Department, but foreign policy is much more than that now. The great symbol of that expansion has been the increasingly military content of American interaction with the rest of the world captured in the idea of the national security state and embodied in the NSC system of which State is but one of several competing agencies. Since 2001, the foreign policy menu has been further broadened by the emergence of nonstate-based international terrorism, adding yet another dimension to the foreign policy agenda, and one about which the State Department has no special expertise.

Second, this expansion of the foreign policy agenda has spawned rivals to the State Department in the making and execution of policy. The most obvious rival has, of course, been the Department of Defense, the existence of which can be thought of, in one sense, as the admission that the problem of foreign policy has been broadened beyond the expertise of the FSOs at the core of the department. Indeed, the need for something like an interagency process and thus a chapter like this is testimony that foreign policy is now a lot more than the activities of the State Department.

Third, this broadened menu of problems and assortment of actors has provided a challenge to the perception that the State Department is even the most competent agency with which to entrust important problems, and the department has not been particularly adept at reasserting the arguments for its own primacy. An example from the George W. Bush administration illustrates this dilemma particularly well. In the run-up to the American invasion of Iraq in 2003, the White House commissioned the **Defense Department** as the lead planning agency, and Secretary of Defense Donald Rumsfeld interpreted this mandate to allow him essentially to exclude the State Department (which basically opposed the idea of the war) from preinvasion planning. At one point, for instance, the State Department delivered to the Defense Department its analysis of the problems they believed would be encountered if the invasion occurred, projections that proved to be almost completely prescient. When the report was received by the Pentagon, it was sent to a midlevel office in the Defense bureaucracy, where it was effectively buried and its contents ignored. The Defense Department, it might be added, similarly ignored projections of likely barriers to efforts in Afghanistan that have proven equally accurate.

The Department of State remains the historical symbol of American foreign policy and of the American face toward the world, but it is a reputation and power base that has been significantly under assault in a world where militarized threats and more diverse sources of conflict (such as the activities of nonstate actors) have become the more potent symbols of American foreign policy dilemmas. The appointment of Hillary Clinton as a highly visible international figure has resuscitated, at least for a time, some of the prestige of the department and the morale of its staff, but that could change when her successor takes office in 2013. The degree to which the State Department is able to reassert its former preeminence will depend at least as much on whether perceptions of foreign policy remain as highly military and adversarial as they became during the Cold War and have become again since 9/11 (this question is addressed in the Where Do We Go from Here? application). In the meantime, the Department of Defense will be a major competitor to the State Department for that leading role.

Department of Defense

Across the Potomac from Washington in Virginia sits the five-sided building that houses the Department of Defense (DOD). Its headquarters, newly remodeled at a cost of $4.5 billion in 2011, is known as the Pentagon because of its five-sided shape designed for the parcel of land on which it was originally supposed to have been built, a design retained when its location was moved to its current space that does not require the design. To some outsiders, it joins the highly secretive National Security Agency in being called the "puzzle palace" (a term Reagan used for it); to many of those who work in it, it is known simply as "the Building."

Physically, the DOD's most notable characteristic is its size, by virtually any measure. The Pentagon itself claims to be the largest office building in the world (the amount of space it provides was a major reason for keeping the original design even after its location changed). Size, however, is also measured by the number of people who work in the Pentagon and at other DOD entities around the world. In terms of employees, the Department of Defense is the largest employer in the federal government. In addition to the roughly 700,000 civilian employees already mentioned, there are currently over 1.5 million Americans on active duty in the armed forces and an additional 979,000 military reservists. Less directly, there are over 200,000 civilian contractors doing business with the DOD in a variety of roles, from building military equipment to serving in various capacities in or around combat zones.

These commitments have varied across time, reflecting the international environment. Before the Cold War was terminated, for instance, the active duty forces of the United States stood at around 2.15 million, with about another million reservists. During the 1990s, the armed forces were "downsized" to about 1.3 million on active duty, a figure that has risen with the wars in Afghanistan and Iraq. Because of the all-volunteer status of the military itself, an increasing number of defense matters have been shifted to civilian contractors, a practice under some scrutiny that is addressed in Chapter Nine.

Beyond manpower figures, the DOD also is one of the major claimants to monetary resources. Within the federal structure of budgetary categories by function, DOD and service on the national debt compete as the second largest category of budgetary commitments after expenditures on entitlement programs (Social Security, Medicare, and Medicaid, for instance). Before the entitlement programs were expanded in the early 1960s as part of Lyndon Johnson's Great Society programs, expenditures on defense were the largest item in the federal budget, accounting for about half of what the federal government spent in the middle 1950s. The appropriations request for fiscal 2010 was $534 billion, a figure that does not include all expenditures on overseas military activities or much of the cost of military pensions, health benefits, the costs involved in maintaining and building nuclear weapons (which are included in the Department of Energy budget), and the like. The Defense share of the federal budget in recent years has accounted for about 20 percent of total U.S. government spending.

The budgetary claim of the DOD is important for a number of reasons. One is its size relative to spending by the rest of the world. In 2003, the United States achieved the distinction of spending more on defense *than the rest of the countries of the world combined*. While that distinction has not been consistently maintained since, the United States annually spends at or just below half of what the world spends on defense, a status largely justified in terms of American global security dictates arising from the global competition with international religious terrorism. Supporters argue that these levels are necessary to keep the country safe from hostile forces in the world; critics see it as excessive and as a negative symbol of America's supposedly peaceful role in the world. Both perspectives are central to the ongoing debate about budgetary reform.

The Defense budget is symbolically important for at least two other reasons that relate directly to the position that the DOD occupies within the foreign policy arena. The first reason represents a paradox of sorts about defense spending arising from two contrary domestic political forces. On one hand, the defense budget is the largest so-called "controllable" (also called discretionary) element in the federal budget. This designation arises from a budget distinction between *uncontrollable* and *controllable* budget items. On the one hand, an uncontrollable element is a government expenditure authorized by law that is automatically spent unless there is specific legislation that rescinds that expenditure. Almost all entitlement spending is of this nature: The amount of money the United States spends on Medicare and Medicaid, for instance, is automatic unless intervening legislation during any Congress changes it. Controllable spending, on the other hand, refers to expenditures that must be appropriated on an annual basis or the function they support does not receive funding. Within the federal budget, the vast majority (upward of 75–80 percent) is uncontrollable; of the controllable elements, defense accounts for the largest amounts, upward of two-thirds of all the controllable expenditures of the government. From that vantage point alone, defense spending would seem to be the most vulnerable part of the federal budget at times of budgetary scarcity and budget cutting.

The paradox arises because some of those most concerned with deficit reduction argue that the defense budget should be exempt from budget cutting. The basic rationale for exempting the defense budget from other economy measures is the perception of the threat against which defense expenditures provide a shield and the fear that cutting those expenditures would make the United States dangerously vulnerable to attack. As such, critics state that these arguments play upon the fear people hold, a major part of the overall appeal of an emphasis on national defense participation in foreign policy generally. Moreover, as noted directly below, defense spending has additional benefits in that it reaches into virtually all congressional districts and thus provides a source of support both for communities and their representatives.

The other side of the argument is more dispassionate but less emotionally persuasive. The opposition, for instance, argues that there are major sources of waste in defense spending (so-called "waste, fraud, and abuse" as it became known in the 1980s and 1990s), a concern that activated Secretary Gates in August 2010 to announce plans to reduce what he viewed as unnecessary spending (for example, too many senior uniformed and civilian officers within the DOD, redundant military commands). This plan, however, was aimed not so much at budget reduction as it was at allowing the transfer of funds from less to more productive uses. Critics also point to the fact that published defense expenditure figures such as the DOD budget underrepresent the actual amount spent on defense. Many of the expenditures the United States has made in Iraq and Afghanistan have been hidden in "off-the-books" places such as supplemental appropriations or the budgets of other agencies (for example, military retirement costs).

The most fundamental argument that critics make, however, is that meaningful deficit and debt reduction is essentially impossible without including the defense budget in the process. One reason is the simple size of the defense budget: It accounts for one-fifth to one-quarter of all the money the federal government spends, and to take the possibility of defense cuts off the table greatly reduces the overall part of spending eligible for the budgeter's knife. More to the point, in purely budgeting terms, the defense budget is an "easy" place to cut spending, since so much of it is controllable—meaning that economies can be affected simply by not appropriating funds for particular uses that must be funded annually. One cannot, by contrast, make cuts in U.S. debt service (interest on loans) without endangering the creditworthiness of the country, and attempting to cut into noncontrollable elements such as entitlements raises enormous political opposition. The controllable elements of most other budgets have already been pared, and while it makes great political theater to advocate things like cutting earmarks introduced by individual members of Congress, these amount to a basically insignificant contribution to the goal of deficit reduction.

Another important aspect of the defense budget is its domestic impact. The Defense Department is, in a sense, the major source of patronage-based appropriations to individual states and congressional districts, far exceeding the amounts of what some would characterize as "pork" from other sources. Members of Congress battle monumentally to try to ensure that, for instance, defense contracts to build aircraft or naval vessels are allocated to their states or districts, and the impact of opening or closing military bases and other installations in particular locales can have a major economic impact on individual communities. The perverse impact that such competition for federal dollars creates can be seen in phenomena such as federal funding for weapons systems that the military itself does not want, but which is appropriated because building the weapons systems benefits the constituents of powerful members of Congress. This problem is particularly acute for "large ticket" projects such as ships and aircraft that require considerable funding over a long period.

Some revisionists also believe that defense-spending levels have a large impact on the kinds and qualities of military involvements in which the United States has participated. Critics who believe, for instance, that the United States is overcommitted militarily in the world argue that a reduction in defense spending would remove some of the capability to inject itself into situations of questionable importance to the country. As he was leaving office in the summer of 2011, Secretary Gates warned that the implementation of cuts under this rationale could endanger the American status as a superpower.

INTERSECTIONS

Guns, Butter, and Military Activism

The heated domestic debate over continued American military involvement in Afghanistan that arose from President Obama's June 2011 announcement of a troop drawdown combined with political posturing over deficit and debt reduction to produce a volatile mix. A surprisingly large element in this debate was about relative levels of funding for defense and the degree to which defense should participate in greater economies to help reduce deficits. This variant of the old "guns versus butter" debate over spending priorities was given poignancy by the $2 billion a week cost of the war, a conflict and expense increasing numbers of Americans oppose. The ramifications of the debate, however, radiate beyond the immediate context to the warning by Gates against stripping the United States of the ability to take an activist stance in the world of the kind associated with superpower status.

In the immediate heat of the summer 2011 debate that focused on the symbol of raising the authorized federal debt ceiling, it was virtually certain that defense spending would be cut more than the defense budget's defenders in the Pentagon would prefer. One of the things that made the defense budget vulnerable was backlash from the expense and lack of apparent progress in Afghanistan, already the country's longest war at that time. Moreover, champions of reduced defense spending argue that it was excess military capacity that allowed the United States to continue this long and pointless conflict, a luxury no longer affordable with revered programs such as Medicare under fire. Cuts in defense spending thus could both contribute to fiscal responsibility and help mold a more prudent, affordable defense policy. (For a more detailed discussion of the War in Afghanistan, see Snow, *Cases in American Foreign Policy*, Chapter Eight.)

The point of this discussion is that the Department of Defense has great impact and influence within the government, including on its foreign policy. Not only is part of this enhanced impact the result of the sheer size of the Department of Defense in terms of manpower and budget, but also part of it arises from the definition of the environment in national security terms, thereby automatically elevating the importance of DOD among the constellation of foreign policy–related enterprises. Some of the bases of this influence can be seen by examining the organization of the Defense Department and its roles and missions.

Organization The basic operating principle underlying the entire defense establishment is **civilian control of the military**. The genesis of this principle goes back to the American Revolution and even before, and it arises from the fear that an uncontrolled military might pose a threat to the freedom of the civilian population. Since the American colonies were heavily influenced by the British experience, this early concern was associated with the British reaction to the Cromwellian period, as noted in Chapter Two. This attitude was expressed in the Continental Congress during the Revolution itself; an exasperated General Washington once opined that he could understand why the Congress opposed an army during peacetime, but he could not understand why they opposed the Army during wartime. After the American Revolution ended, the regular army was essentially disbanded.

The result of this early history is the tradition that civilian authorities should control the activities of the armed forces. Within the structure of the current defense establishment, this means that all military authorities have civilian counterparts to whom they report and whose permission is necessary for the military to carry out crucial tasks. While there is little if any disagreement in principle within the DOD on this arrangement, it does cause some friction in application, particularly between career military officers with considerable experience in their areas of responsibilities and politically appointed civilian overseers who sometimes get their jobs for reasons other than their expertise.

Any depiction of an organization as vast and complex as the DOD requires some simplification that is potentially distorting. For present purposes, however, the organization can be thought of in four parts. At the pinnacle is the secretary of defense, the cabinet official who reports directly to the president and is responsible for the overall operation of the department. At the second layer, the secretary is assisted by a civilian-dominated series of subcabinet-level functions cutting across the military services and comprising the Office of the Secretary of Defense (OSD). The third part is the military services themselves, each with their separate bureaucracies and sets of interests. Finally, there is the Joint Chiefs of Staff, which has the role of coordinating the military activities of the services and reporting to the president.

The *Secretary of Defense* (or SECDEF, as the individual is known within the acronyms of Washington) is the chief advisor to the president on defense matters, a role designated by the National Security Act. (By contrast, the chair of the Joint Chiefs of Staff is by statute the chief *military* advisor to the president.) The SECDEF advises the president on matters such as the advisability of using force in a particular situation and what kinds of personnel and equipment the military needs to perform its duties. In addition, the SECDEF is responsible for implementing policies mandated by the commander-in-chief and the Congress, as well as managing the internal affairs of the department. The degree to which the SECDEF is a major player in foreign policy formulation varies considerably from secretary to secretary and depends on presidential preference. William Cohen within the Clinton administration was not an overt major contributor to overall foreign policy, for instance, whereas George W. Bush's first

SECDEF, Donald Rumsfeld, was a major architect of the War in Iraq and other foreign policy matters. Secretary Gates kept a low but influential policy profile as part of Obama's team approach to foreign policy, a role Panetta will likely continue.

The *Office of the Secretary of Defense* is the principal civilian bureaucracy within the structure of the DOD. It is specifically organized to provide direct assistance and advice to the SECDEF on all matters of policy that affect the department and its mission as a whole (in other words, functions that cut across service lines) and to ensure that directives and policy decisions from the SECDEF are indeed implemented within the various services. In this sense, the OSD often acts as the principal instrument for assuring civilian control of the military departments, despite the fact that each service department is headed by a civilian secretary. OSD also serves as a counterweight and bureaucratic balance for the wishes and interests of the civilian hierarchy of the department in its interactions with the uniformed services and occasionally as a referee between the services in matters of dispute among them. The exact organization and personnel of DOD varies from administration to administration.

The third layer of the DOD is the *service departments*. Within the Pentagon, each military service has its own department that represents and administers the interests and programs of the individual service. At the top of each bureaucracy is a civilian service secretary (the secretaries of the Army, Air Force, and Navy), and this official is assisted by the highest-ranking military official in each department (the chiefs of staff of the Army and Air Force and the chief of naval operations, whose jurisdiction includes both the Navy and the Marine Corps). Each service chief is responsible for the internal operation of the individual service departments and acts as the service's representative on the Joint Chiefs of Staff.

The service departments stand in juxtaposition to one another and to the civilian OSD. In terms of missions, forces, and the like, there is considerable overlap between the services that each jealously seeks to protect. It has been argued, for instance, that the U.S. military has four air forces (the regular Air Force, Naval and Marine air assets, and Army unarmed airplanes and armed helicopters), at least three armies (the regular Army, the Marine Corps—which is administratively part of the Navy—and the Air Force, which has independent personnel to guard Air Force bases), as well as four sets of special forces (Army, Navy, Marines, and Air Force), all with somewhat different missions, each of which the principal service attempts to protect. The service departments also compete rigorously with one another for budgetary assets (one of the most fervent activities in the Pentagon is the rivalry over what percentage of the overall budget is allocated to each of the services, and especially changes in those percentages). The individual services, individually and collectively, also compete with the civilians in OSD who monitor activities across the services (for example, personnel policy).

The result is an organization of the Department of Defense that appears chaotic and inefficient from the outside, and criticisms of many of the overlaps and redundancies are regularly raised by reformers. It used to be worse.

Before the National Security Act of 1947, the various service departments were entirely independent of one another (for instance, lobbying Congress independently for funding), and bringing them together under one roof was a major purpose of the National Security Act. In addition, the redundancy has often resulted in efforts that lacked coordination and thus effectiveness, leading to further efforts to increase coordination of and control over defense activities. The JCS has been at the heart of such attempts.

The *Joint Chiefs of Staff (JCS)* is the fourth layer of organization within the DOD structure. The JCS consists of the chiefs of staff of the services (Army, Navy/Marines, and Air Force), from whose ranks the administrative head and chief military advisor to the president, the chairman of the Joint Chiefs of Staff (CJCS) is chosen. Created by the National Security Act, the original reason for creating the body was to overcome service rivalries and to facilitate interservice cooperation by creating a small staff of officers drawn from the services to facilitate interchange and coordination. For most of its early existence, however, the loyalty and reward system of the services favored actions demonstrating loyalty to the services and not joint action, meaning service on the JCS (becoming what was known as a "purple suiter," the alleged color one obtains if the colors of the various service uniforms are mixed together) was an absolute hindrance to an officer's career and such service was to be avoided if possible.

In 1986, Congress passed the Goldwater-Nichols Defense Reorganization Act in part to strengthen the CJCS and the Joint Chiefs. The large purpose of the reorganization was to promote and require "jointness" in military affairs: the services acting together rather than in isolation or even competition in military operations. The impetus for this requirement was the negative experience the United States had experienced in military operations intended to free the Iranian hostages in 1980 (the so-called Desert One mission that ended in disaster) and in Grenada in 1983. Among other things, the Act required that all officers achieving flag rank (general or admiral) must have experience on the Joint Staff, thereby elevating service there to a career-making rather than a career-breaking assignment and creating more interservice requirements for the services. The result has been considerable improvement in the services' ability to interact successfully in such places as Iraq and Afghanistan, as well as enhancing the prestige and authority of the JCS.

Foreign Policy Role The role of the defense establishment in the making and implementation of American foreign policy has changed markedly across time and with changing circumstances. Before World War II, there was no formal institution like the Department of Defense around which to organize military views on foreign policy, and such efforts were generally carried out by the individual services and their supporting institutions such as retired veterans' groups. After World War II, of course, this situation greatly changed, as the Cold War confrontation elevated military concerns to a central place in the making and execution of foreign policy. As noted, the National Security Act enshrined this growing importance by making the Secretary of Defense a coequal partner to the Secretary of State in the NSC, and the role continued to flourish through the evolution of the Cold War relationship.

The American military establishment was originally not well suited to an expanded role in foreign policy. The tradition of suspicion of a standing military had historically dictated a small and highly apolitical military officer corps that neither sought nor was provided access to policy-making counsels. The World War II experience of leaders such as Eisenhower, who served as both the military and political leader of the wartime coalition in Europe, began the process by which the American military has become a more sophisticated and influential part of the foreign policy scene. For instance, it is not entirely surprising in the contemporary environment that a military leader such as General David Petraeus also holds a Ph.D. in international affairs from Princeton University.

Increasing sophistication within the officer corps has made it a more sensitive and critical force within the foreign policy process. The historic role of the military has been that of policy implementer, carrying out orders from civilian authorities that they had little influence in formulating in the first place. The role of the military as advisor in the traditional setting was simply to assess how difficult a mission might be, what the requirements were to carry it out, and then to go about that implementation. Because the international environment has become so much more varied and the geopolitical aspects of threatening situations so complex and intertwined, however, a more sophisticated military establishment has had to arise that can go beyond simply implementing policies to advising responsibly about what policies are prudent and attainable.

The Intelligence Community

No other aspect of foreign policy within the U.S. government has been subject to as much recent critical analysis as has the intelligence function. The so-called **intelligence community**, the accumulation of all the various agencies within the federal government that collect and analyze information with foreign and national security implications, has been under close scrutiny since the end of the Cold War, as a series of scandals and revelations raised questions about the competency and skill of American intelligence efforts (the failure to know about the Indian and Pakistani nuclear test plans in 1998 in advance is a prime example), and this criticism was amplified by the inability of the **Central Intelligence Agency (CIA)** and other intelligence agencies to anticipate the 9/11 attacks, a failure that has led to a basic effort to reform how the intelligence community does its business.

The intelligence function is a relatively new phenomenon in the American political experience. Prior to the creation of the CIA by the National Security Act of 1947, the country had never possessed a formal civilian intelligence agency during peacetime, meaning the CIA was built essentially from scratch, using only the wartime Office of Strategic Services (OSS) as a model and source of employees. The whole effort gathered steam during the Cold War, and in important and ultimately controversial ways, it came at least partly to mirror its opponent, the Soviet KGB. Since the end of the Cold War, efforts have been under way, with varying success, to adapt the intelligence community to the contemporary environment.

An intelligence organization can potentially serve all or part of four roles. The first and most basic is *information gathering*, collecting so-called "raw" data about the activities of people, organizations, and countries in which the United States may have an interest. This is the most basic and noncontroversial aspect of the intelligence business, although some disagreements emerge about some clandestine means of learning about events (for example, placing operatives inside foreign organizations, bribing officials to provide information). The second role is *information analysis*, providing interpretations of what raw information means and what its implications might be in terms of likely activities by the entity under scrutiny. This function is slightly more controversial, because raw information is usually susceptible to numerous interpretations, and which one the analyst chooses may reflect the personal views of the subject and policy preferences as well as the "facts." However, the failure to provide some ordering of raw data may lead to confusion and the ability to distort information greatly by some "consumers" (people who use intelligence to help them make decisions). Some critics, for instance, argued that failures of analysis facilitated how some officials in the Bush administration misused raw information about Iraqi weapons of mass destruction (WMD) to "cook the books" and make the case for invading Iraq.

Information gathering and analysis are standard and generally accepted intelligence functions, with the rejoinder that care must be taken to avoid inserting personal prejudices into analysis, and closely parallel the military role of providing advice on the military consequences of different proposed actions. The other two possible roles, however, expand the horizon of intelligence activity in more proactive and potentially controversial ways.

The third potential role is in *policy recommendation*. It involves the collectors of information going a step beyond gathering and analyzing information to advocate policies based on that intelligence. The danger of expanding intelligence to this function is that it might cause the gatherers and analysts selectively to choose information (so-called "cherry picking") that supports particular policy courses, thereby tainting the objectivity of the information provided. For this reason, the intelligence official who is the major statutory advisor to the president (originally the **Director of Central Intelligence** or **DCI**, now the **Director of National Intelligence** or **DNI**) does not have this function as part of his or her role.

The fourth and final role is that of *policy implementer,* or what is known as operations. This function involves carrying out covert or clandestine activities against foreign entities to influence what they do in their relations to the United States. This role is controversial, partly because it is a direct mirror of activities such as those associated with the old KGB that the United States has generally condemned, and because it often involves lawbreaking in the jurisdictions in which it is carried out.

Some argue that operations is not an intelligence function at all, and that if it is to be a part of the American effort in the world, it should be done outside the formal organization of intelligence agencies, as is the case in Great Britain. Supporters of the function argue that clandestine, including illegal, activities are necessary in an anarchical, lawless world, and that since covert actions are usually organized using covertly collected intelligence, the intelligence umbrella is the proper organizational location for operations. Regardless of its formal location within the federal bureaucracy, however, operations perform an often-crucial foreign policy role. The killing of Osama bin Laden in May 2011 is a dramatic example, where the CIA was largely responsible for developing the information and plan that the U.S. Navy SEALs executed in Pakistan. Within the CIA, the major operating directorates are the Directorate of Intelligence (DI), which performs the first two tasks, and the Directorate of Operations (DO), which performs the fourth task.

The United States has now possessed a peacetime intelligence community for nearly two-thirds of a century, but it remains an unsettled, controversial part of the government. A major aspect of the disagreement that surrounds the intelligence community is organizational and is captured in the reform process that has been a major feature of intelligence concern and energy during the 2000s. At the same time, there is also disagreement about the foreign policy role of the intelligence community, particularly in the realm of interagency dealings with the problem of international religious terrorism.

Organization The traditional organization of America's intelligence efforts is the direct descendent of the National Security Act's creation of the CIA in 1947. As the intelligence effort matured, the CIA was viewed as the centerpiece and public face of American intelligence, although the effort was in fact much more than that. At the same time, the DCI was conceived as the focal point of the intelligence community and as the chief advisor to the president on intelligence matters, in much the same way that the CJCS is the chief military advisor to the president.

The public image has an orderliness that has never quite existed in fact. One aspect of the disorder is that the CIA is only one of the intelligence agencies of the government, and although it is the most public, it is not even the largest, employing only about 15 percent of those in the intelligence service of the country. Additional intelligence assets are found in various other sectors of the government, but especially in the Department of Defense. The DOD houses institutions such as the supersecret National Security Agency (NSA), the Defense Intelligence Agency (DIA), and the intelligence units of each of the major uniformed services. These agencies possess the great bulk of the intelligence assets of the U.S. government (exact accounting is impossible, because they have so-called "black"—or secret—budgets). Although the activities of these agencies are nominally coordinated by the DCI, this supervision is imperfect, since the Secretary of Defense is the reporting channel and administrative head of the DOD intelligence units. For these reasons, the SECDEF is normally the greatest opponent of reform efforts aimed at centralizing intelligence functions (see the following).

The other traditional organizational problem surrounds the roles of the DCI. In Washington-speak, the DCI has traditionally been "dual hatted." What this curious phrase means is that the DCI has traditionally been simultaneously the administrative head of the CIA (one hat) *and* the head of the intelligence community (the second hat), the aggregation of the various intelligence units throughout government. Wearing this second hat, the DCI is supposed to coordinate the activities of all agencies, including the parsing of roles and missions among the various agencies. Since those agencies include the CIA, the two hats leave the DCI with a built-in conflict of interest. In addition, the DCI wears a third hat as chief intelligence source for the president, a further drain on his energies.

While imperfect, this organization sufficed during the Cold War, dealing as it did with an essentially monolithic, if very difficult, opponent. As the Cold War dissolved and more diffuse and diverse sources of opposition to American interests emerged, the intelligence community was forced to adapt, and it was not altogether successful in doing so. Prior to 1991, for instance, the CIA had placed great emphasis on analysts and agents with Russian and Eastern European language skills, but had placed very little emphasis on language competencies such as Arabic or Chinese. It has thus had to scramble, with only partial success, to achieve the kinds of competencies necessary to deal with the contemporary environment and its challenges.

The failure to produce actionable and timely intelligence to prevent the 9/11 disasters brought the entire intelligence community, and the CIA as its most visible symbol, to the forefront. An examination of the disaster revealed that there had been significant intelligence failures in the process, and the spotlight was directed by the presidentially appointed 9/11 Commission to recommend reforms of the process. The Commission found two major faults in the existing system. First, it discovered an intelligence system built for a different operational environment than it now faced. Rather than facing what it called a "few very dangerous adversaries" (the Soviet Union and its allies), instead the Commission identified a "number of less visible challenges" (such as Al Qaeda). Second, the Commission argued the intelligence community was so dispersed in terms of allocating authority that it was ill equipped to meet these new challenges.

The Commission made several recommendations that have only been partially implemented. Two major reforms stand out. First, it recommended the establishment of a National Counterterrorism Center (NCTC) with personnel drawn from various agencies to create a central focus on terrorism and to coordinate joint planning and operations among agencies dealing with terrorism. To ensure that the NCTC had sufficient authority to do its job, the Commission recommended it be placed within the White House and headed by a director appointed directly by the president at the level of deputy secretary, thereby giving the incumbent coequal status to the Deputies Committee of the NSC. Further, it recommended that the director be subject to congressional approval and subject to providing testimony to Congress, both of which would raise the public visibility of the director and the NCTC. President Bush rejected the latter suggestions when establishing the center, which operates at a lower level of public awareness, visibility, and political clout.

The other recommendation was the establishment of the DNI as the chief intelligence figure for the United States, above the DCI. Part of the rationale was to remove one of the DCI's hats and thus the built-in conflict of interest, as the DNI would become chair of the intelligence community. The reorganization this entailed also called for having the DCI and various intelligence units housed in other administrative departments placed under the DNI (for instance, the Undersecretary of Defense for Intelligence). To further aid the DNI, formerly black budgets were to be made public, and intelligence budget aspects formerly housed principally in DOD were to be transferred to the control of the DNI.

This latter transfer of power out of traditional departments to the DNI created a bureaucratic firestorm led by SECDEF Rumsfeld, who was entirely opposed to both the control and the budgetary implications of the DNI as it was recommended. President Bush sided with those who opposed fundamental change, creating the position of DNI but not giving the position or its incumbent the important authorities necessary to enact change. As a result, there is a DNI, but it is not a highly sought-after position, because it is one perceived to have very little power within the intelligence community and the government at large. With a weak DNI, the process of organizational change has been sidetracked as well.

Foreign Policy Role Exactly how important reform and a more efficient and orderly intelligence process are to foreign policy depends on the role one envisages for the intelligence community in the contemporary environment. When the competition was largely framed in the politico-military confrontation between the United States and the Soviet Union, a system of loose coordination of the military and political aspects of the competition worked passably well, but that structure of opposition no longer exists (as the 9/11 Commission cited above points out), and so the emphasis on a new and more diverse world environment may require a different policy approach and role as well.

Geographically, it is clear that the old structure no longer matches the problems with which the intelligence community is forced to deal. Rather, the environment has changed in two important ways. On one hand, the emphasis has moved geographically from a European-centered contest (the Cold War confrontation across the Iron Curtain) to a much more fluid emphasis on Third World conflicts, especially centering on the Islamic Middle East. On the other hand, the structure of threats the United States faces is not as clearly defined as it once was. The kind of advice that came from the Cold War structure is not well suited or particularly expert when dealing with the kinds of quasi- and semimilitary threats from nontraditional sources that are associated with the developing world and with international religious terrorism. What exactly does the intelligence community have to contribute to this new structure and content of threat?

Much of the current content of foreign policy for which the intelligence community has relevant expertise and authority is focused on the foreign aspects of the terrorism threat to the United States. Part of that threat is operational, dealing violently with opponents such as Al Qaeda in ways that sometimes mimic military operations (drone attacks against Al Qaeda targets in Yemen controlled and directed by the CIA is an example), but part of it is a cooperative effort with other parts of the government that also have areas of responsibility for dealing with the terrorism problem. The exact nature of interaction and policy contribution of the intelligence community in what is generally described under the rubric of homeland security is still a matter of some development and contention, to which the discussion now turns.

Department of Homeland Security

In addition to spawning an interest in reforming the intelligence community, the major institutional response to 9/11 was the creation of the **Department of Homeland Security (DHS)**. Unlike the more traditional foreign policy agencies, the role and mission of DHS is more explicitly intermestic and diverse than the roles and missions of agencies such as the Department of State. In concept, **homeland security** is more akin to and arguably a major component of national security, one of the major purposes of which (some would argue *the* major purpose) is protecting the country from harm—in other words, homeland security. The two efforts are mostly differentiated by the forces against which each protects the United States: conventional military threats (DOD) or unconventional threats such as terrorism (DHS). These distinctions are easier to make in the abstract than in practice because of the semimilitary nature of terrorism and counterterrorism (see Chapter Ten). The comparison is further clouded by the diverse nature of additional duties assigned to DHS, such as border protection, immigration, and emergency management.

The movement to create the DHS cascaded rapidly through the political process during 2002 after the 9/11, 2001, catastrophe and the failure to capture and destroy Al Qaeda in the last months of 2001 in the Afghan mountains. The bill to create the DHS was introduced in both houses of Congress on May 2, 2002. The legislation was finally passed and signed by President George W. Bush on November 25, 2002, and the DHS formally came into existence on January 24, 2003. Former Pennsylvania governor Tom Ridge, who had served as director of the Office of Homeland Security, was named the first secretary, followed in 2005 by former federal judge Michael Chertoff. Janet Napolitano, former governor of Arizona, was named to the post in 2009 by President Obama.

The new department has been controversial since it was formed. It is not, in a sense, a new agency at all, but rather the shuffling and cobbling together of a diverse and sometimes reluctant group of existing agencies from other parts of the federal bureaucracy. The only truly new unit within DHS is the Transportation Safety Agency (TSA). The agency was hastily formed as a quick and visible response to the terrorist threat, and some of its most important problems have arisen from how quickly it was put together and from the combination of agencies that were and were not included under its umbrella. At the same time, this diversity resulted in its association with problems that arose within the operation of some of its assembled units. The most famous was the response by the **Federal Emergency Management Agency (FEMA)** to the Hurricane Katrina disaster in New Orleans in 2005 and its more recent involvement in the illegal immigrant problem along the Mexican border (the Border Patrol is also a part of the DHS). All have significant political causes and consequences.

Organization The new department was organized into four functional directorates reflecting its organizational rationale: informational analysis and infrastructure protection; science and technology; border and transportation security; and emergency preparedness and response. Appropriate agencies lifted from other government departments are assigned to one or another of these directorates: FEMA as the heart of emergency management and preparation, for instance. In addition, the Homeland Security Act created some anomalous responsibilities, such as monitoring drug trafficking to determine possible connections between that trafficking and terrorism and to coordinate responses.

The DHS has been plagued by organizational problems since its inception, three of which are worth noting. The first and most serious problem was which agencies would and would not be included within the DHS, an essentially political problem that has been the root of most DHS woes, including questions about its effectiveness. The second has been the organizational model for the DHS. The federal government had one previous experience with creating a new agency out of existing agencies (the Department of Energy or DOE), which was less than a great success, but which foreshadowed difficulties for the DHS. The third is funding, a problem that has largely been the result of the difficulty of removing existing agencies from their former homes and moving them to the DHS.

The DHS brought together twenty-two existing federal agencies with over 170,000 employees under the new umbrella. Appropriated from departments and agencies throughout the government, this diverse set of employees had different loyalties, ways of doing things, and cultural perspectives on problems and their solutions, and they all were more or less enthusiastically included in the DHS. The agency thus faced a formidable task in trying to integrate all these groups into a coherent team under the new antiterrorism mandate. Despite all the bureaucratic shuffling that occurred, however, significant candidates escaped inclusion for largely political reasons.

The list of those seeking to and succeeding in avoiding inclusion started at the very pinnacle of the antiterrorism effort. The three agencies with the core responsibility for protecting the country against terrorism (the "golden triangle") were the CIA, the Federal Bureau of Investigation (FBI), and the Immigration and Naturalization Service (INS, rechristened as the now familiar Immigration and Customs Enforcement or ICE). The connection is intuitive. The CIA has responsibility for foreign intelligence, including identifying foreign terrorists and monitoring their attempts to enter the United States, INS/ICE monitors and filters individuals—including terrorists—attempting to cross the border into the United States, and the FBI is assigned primary policing duties against terrorists on American soil. These functions are closely interrelated and seem to require maximum coordination and cooperation, making their inclusion within the new DHS appear a natural thing to do. It did not, however, happen.

Of the three key actors, only INS/ICE ended up as part of the DHS. The FBI, as one of the gemstones of the Department of Justice, did not want to move and represented an asset that the attorney general (who administers the department) would relinquish only very reluctantly. The CIA is an independent agency not part of any cabinet department, covets its independence, and had enough political clout to stay out. Only INS/ICE, an agency with a spotted past that no other agency truly wanted, was included in the new structure. Both the CIA and FBI argued that their organizational missions included antiterrorism but also included other major obligations unrelated to the DHS charter (for instance, FBI responsibility for organized crime, clearly not a part of DHS responsibility). The more basic reason, however, is that neither agency wanted to be included in DHS, and each was able (for political reasons discussed in the *Intersections* box) to avoid inclusion.

These key exclusions arguably reduce the effectiveness of cooperative efforts of golden triangle agencies, since they all report to different cabinet-level officials rather than a single secretary who can mandate their cooperation as a first priority. All three are represented in forums such as the NCTC, but they still remain administratively independent of one another.

Not all relevant agencies were able to avoid the DHS net. Among the twenty-two agencies included were the United States Coast Guard, the Customs Service (although some of its functions, notably revenue collection, remain within the Treasury Department), the Secret Service, the Federal Protective Service, the INS (technically split into two successor parts, a Bureau of Border Security and a Bureau of Citizenship and Immigration Services, of which ICE is the most public symbol), FEMA, the Transportation Safety Administration (TSA), and the FBI's National Infrastructure Protection Center.

The second organizational problem has been the proper organizational model for the DHS. Part of the difficulty is the diverse set of mandates the various parts of the agency has, some of which are almost entirely separate from one another (for example, FEMA's natural disaster relief mandate as contrasted with airport security for TSA). More fundamental, however, is the issue of how to put together a new federal agency from existing components.

The federal precedent for doing so was the Department of Energy (DOE). Like the DHS, the DOE was a response to a foreign policy crisis, the oil shocks of 1973 and 1977 in the oil-rich Middle East. In response, the Carter administration shuffled existing agencies in the federal government to create the DOE in 1977. This reshuffling also created problems of congressional oversight, although less severe than those for the DHS (functions folded into the DOE reported to seventeen congressional committees; DHS functions reported to

INTERSECTIONS

Evading DHS

One of the difficulties facing the Department of Homeland Security has been coordinating the pursuit and capture of terrorist suspects, as depicted in this domestic "bust" by FBI agents.

The prominent success of the FBI and CIA to avoid inclusion in the DHS was largely due to political considerations that spanned the executive and legislative branches of the federal government. The bureaucratic fight within the executive branch was largely a "turf battle," where the parent agency of candidates for inclusion in DHS resisted the loss of a valued part of their organization and, in some cases more poignantly, the loss of budgetary resources that would presumably accompany the transfer of agencies into the DHS. This was particularly a concern of Secretary Rumsfeld, who feared a loss of budget resources to the DHS if intelligence functions assigned to the DOD were transferred to the new agency. In some ways, the loss of monetary resources probably was more important than other causes of reluctance to be included in the DHS.

Agencies seeking to avoid transfer into the DHS were aided and abetted by members of Congress. As discussed more fully in Chapter Six, one of the congressional roles in governance is oversight (or "watchdogging") of the actions of executive agencies, principally through committees assigned to monitor each

(Continued)

(Continued)

agency. This meant that if agencies were taken from their former home and moved to the DHS, the activities of those agencies would be removed from the oversight purview of the committee assigned to the parent agency. Such a move, in turn, implied the loss of jurisdiction over the activities and budgets of those agencies, a loss of power that committees resisted. As it turned out, all members of the Senate and virtually all members of the House served on committees whose jurisdictions would potentially be adversely affected by the new structure, and as a result, were more than willing to aid and abet the attempts by the agencies to avoid being moved. To further avoid the loss of oversight authority, both houses developed weak Homeland Security Committees with very limited jurisdiction or time to impinge on the prerogatives of traditional committees. The Senate committee for this purpose is not even a new and independent committee, instead having the homeland security function grafted onto the Governmental Affairs Committee to form the Senate Committee for Homeland Security and Governmental Affairs.

eighty-eight committees). The DOE remains less than a model of bureaucratic efficiency, and the DHS has followed hard in its tracks.

The third problem has been funding for the DHS and homeland security more generally. The original problem was that the DHS was created "on the cheap," with the Bush administration arguing in 2002 that it would require no additional federal spending, since its operation would be funded by transferring budget resources to the new agency from traditional departments of agencies moved into the DHS. The agencies from which functions were transferred resisted this movement of funds, and with the sympathetic assistance of congressional oversight committees, were largely successful. The result was that DHS efforts were initially underfunded, but accompanied by the mythology that this underfunding was proper given the hoped-for contribution of other agencies to the cause.

There have been two negative legacies of the funding problem. The first is the perception that large-scale funding is unnecessary, despite the very visible, high profile of the antiterrorism mission. Thus, as recently as fiscal year 2010, the budget of the DHS was less than $50 billion, a small part of the federal budget. The other negative legacy is that DHS funds are not well spent. The FEMA response to Katrina is cited as an example of waste in the budget, and there also have been accusations that much DHS money has had a pork barrel impact. In one locale, for instance, federal funds purchased more hazmat (hazardous materials) suits than there are policemen and firemen to wear them.

Foreign Policy Role As already noted, the role and mission of the DHS is classically intermestic, combining foreign policy and domestic priorities. So many of the agencies brought under the DHS umbrella had roles in addition to those that logically flowed from homeland protection from terrorist attack that refinement of the mission is difficult. This problem, of course, was the basis on which the FBI and CIA successfully avoided inclusion, but not all those who tried that ploy succeeded. FEMA, for instance, has as an integral part of its responsibility responding to natural disasters that have no more relationship to terrorism than the sometimes brutal aftermath of terrorist attacks, but its entire mission must somehow be built into the overall organizational role.

Within the foreign policy realm, the obvious DHS role is its position as part of the interagency effort to combat terrorism, which is the principal rationale for the inclusion of its secretary on the NSC. That role, however, is largely domestic, and specifically related to intercepting potential terrorists seeking to enter the United States surreptitiously, a role in which the Coast Guard and Border Patrol have major parts. In addition, the DHS has a major role in mitigating the impact of terrorist attacks that do occur, mainly through its capabilities in the area of emergency management.

The other roles of the DHS intermix with and may serve to dilute the accomplishment of its central mission. In recent years, for instance, the thrust of border protection has moved from guarding against terrorist penetration to assisting in efforts to stem illegal immigration, mostly across the Mexican-American border. This latter effort includes participation in joint endeavors to interfere with the illicit drug trade, and while these efforts do not negate a retained emphasis on protection against terrorist penetration, they certainly do act as a competitor for departmental time and resources. While there is some overlap in these responsibilities (for example, presumably some potential terrorists attempt to enter the United States surreptitiously across the Mexican border) and they all fall broadly under the category of homeland protection, they may nonetheless represent a diversion of attention away from the primary mission.

There is the further question of whether the DHS is a part of the foreign policy formulation as well as the implementation functions of the executive branch. In matters related to border security, officials of the DHS regularly interact with their counterparts in Mexico, thus taking an active part in shaping policy regarding movement across the border (including, presumably, the movement of illicit materials). In terms of the broader question of foreign policy toward terrorism, it is not as clear whether, or to what extent, the DHS plays an active role—or, for that matter, whether it should.

Economic Agencies

The extent to which **economic agencies** of the executive branch of the government have been active in the foreign policy process has changed across time. During the Cold War, they were not prominent at all, since the Cold War competition lacked a significant economic component (other than both sides trying to convince uncommitted states of the superiority of their own economic philosophies and systems). One major consequence of the end of the Cold War was the emergence of Western-style capitalism as the globe's dominant economic system, which in turn helped give rise to the phenomenon of globalization and burnished the reputation of the United States in the international system.

The first contemporary American administration to fully embrace and promote international economic matters as a centerpiece of foreign policy was Bill Clinton's, and many of the institutions and emphases in the current environment came into being during his tenure during the 1990s. The Bush administration of the early 2000s was not so attuned to these concerns and even briefly flirted with the idea of dismantling some of the Clinton artifacts before their attention was diverted to international religious terrorism after 9/11. The Obama administration has revived and sought to build on much of the Clinton initiative, although their efforts have been restrained by the more pressing need to deal with the crisis of the domestic economy.

The role of the economic agencies is a bellwether of where different presidents place economic considerations within the hierarchy of their foreign policy priorities. For the Clinton administration, that role was especially important, reflecting the enormous importance that Clinton placed on globalization as the vehicle for spreading American ideals to the world, or widening the "circle of market democracies," as he put it. The chief instrument for promoting globalization and democratization was the promotion of free trade as a principle and as the cornerstone for economic organizations such as the North American Free Trade Agreement (NAFTA) and the Asia-Pacific Economic Cooperation (APEC), both discussed in Chapter Eleven. George W. Bush shared Clinton's belief in free trade, but placed greater emphasis on using the military instrument of power to promote American policy, especially after the 9/11 events refocused American foreign policy generally. Obama seems to share some of Clinton's emphasis on economic power, but his term has been encumbered by two ongoing wars and the effects of the deep recession of 2008, both of which have consumed much foreign policy energy that might otherwise be directed toward international economic priorities.

What are the economic agencies that are part of the foreign policy process? There are a number of them, but they do not form a tidy or hierarchically arranged set of organizations. That being said, the Obama PPD-1 document of February 2009 establishing the interagency process for the current administration lists five agencies and offices with a role in the heart of policy formulation and implementation, thereby providing a benchmark of relevant entities and a guide to how they are organized as part of foreign policy.

Organization As an organized part of the foreign policy mechanisms of the country, the economic agencies are unlike the other entities discussed in this chapter. They are not organized into a single department like State or Defense, and they do not all have a signature role or mission, such as intelligence collection within the intelligence community. Rather, the function of promoting the economic aspects of foreign policy falls to a number of agencies inside and independent of other cabinet-level departments and brought together in the current administration under the banner of the NSC.

The only economic agency member with full membership on the NSC is the secretary of the treasury, whose portfolio includes the promotion of foreign policy, but he or she is more correctly thought of as the chief advisor to the president on domestic economic concerns that become intermestic, rather than with a primary international economic focus. The other economic agencies involved in the process are NSC part-timers. As PPD-1 puts it, "When international economic issues are on the agenda of the NSC, the NSC's regular attendees will include the Secretary of Commerce, the United States Trade Representative, the Assistant to the President for Economic Policy, and the Chair of Council of Economic Advisors."

This combination of officials has been at the center of much of the controversy regarding Obama economic policy. Part of the reason for this has been the appointment of a series of strong-willed and assertive personalities to key posts, such as Treasury Secretary Timothy Geithner and former assistant to the president for economic affairs Lawrence Summers. Part of the difficulty has also been the result of the extraordinary amount of effort and strain that has surrounded attempts to end the economic impact of the recession.

In terms of foreign policy impact, two of the economic agencies stand out as particularly interesting. The first is the **National Economic Council (NEC)**, of which the assistant to the president for economic affairs is the administrative head. The NEC was created in January 1993 by the executive order of President Clinton. The creation of the Council fulfilled a campaign promise to place greater emphasis on economic growth and prosperity, but it also had the symbolic intent and effect of raising the importance of economic policy to a plane close to the military thrust of the NSC. The name National Economic Council and acronym NEC were purposely chosen to mirror the NSC designations, and Clinton tended to treat them as virtually coequal, if independent, entities. The chief difference between the NSC and the NEC, however, is that the former was created as the result of an act of Congress, which means it can only be disbanded by legislative action, whereas the NEC can be disbanded by simple executive order such as one that created it.

The NEC has always been headed by a director. The first person to hold this position was Robert Rubin, who later became secretary of the treasury, and his first duty was to devise a plan for balancing the federal budget. Under Rubin and successor Laura D'Andrea Tyson, the NEC gradually expanded to take a leading role in promoting free trade. George W. Bush was initially tempted to disband the NEC as an unwelcome artifact of his predecessor but did not do so. Under Bush's auspices, the position was expanded so that the incumbent (at the time Lawrence B. Lindsay) held the dual titles of assistant to the president for economic policy and director of the NEC, roles that Summers played through 2010, but which were assigned to his successor, Gene B. Sperling.

The importance of the NEC depends to a large degree on the president's personal involvement with it. Clinton was personally very interested in economic aspects of foreign policy, saw the NEC as the prime motor of that interest, felt entirely at home dealing with the details of economic policy, and thus placed himself at the center of the NEC, often chairing NEC meetings personally. Bush, by contrast, was not personally heavily invested in the NEC or in economic policy in particular, and found himself more comfortable dealing with traditional national security concerns such as the war on terrorism and the military involvement in Iraq. Obama shares much of Clinton's interest in economics and has thus elevated the economic agencies within, rather than parallel to, the more general national security process. He personally chairs the NEC.

The other position is that of the **United States Trade Representative (USTR)**. This position and the support for it came into being in 1962 with the express purpose of promoting American trade in the world. The position was formalized by the Trade Act of 1974 and was clarified by the Trade Agreement Act of 1988. Originally housed in Washington alone, it has gradually expanded its operations so that the more than two hundred professionals who form its core staff are located in the national capital as well as in Geneva, Switzerland (location of the headquarters of the World Trade Organization) and Brussels, Belgium (headquarters of the European Union). The USTR also has an office in Beijing, China.

Organizationally, the office of the USTR is part of the executive office of the president, rather than being housed in any cabinet-level agency. Its basic roles as they evolved from the 1990s to the present include coordination of U.S. participation in various multilateral trade negotiations, the promotion of American trade, and assistance to other agencies in trade-related matters. The current USTR is Ron Kirk.

CONCLUSIONS

The executive branch of the government houses a large and diverse set of agencies that have as their sole or partial *raison d'etre* assisting in the formulation and execution of foreign policy. Since 1947, the centerpiece of this aggregation has been the National Security Council (NSC) system created by the National Security Act of 1947. The NSC system has gradually expanded and transformed itself into what is now commonly known in Washington as the interagency process, an evolving and constantly changing set of actors and institutions that responds to the preferences of different presidents and changes in the international environment toward which foreign policy is directed.

Within the structure of the executive agencies that assist the president, the National Security Act elevated the role of national security to near coequality with that of traditional diplomatic activity by naming the State and Defense departments as the major statutory partners of the president and vice president as the core members of the NSC. As time and circumstances have changed, other actors have been added to the process and the roles and configurations of various actors have changed. The addition of the DHS to represent the response to the emergence of international religious terrorism represents the kind of organizational innovation that has occurred, and attempts to change the

pattern of relatio
attempts have be
performed.

The juxtaposi
as the Foggy Bott
across the Potoma
and immutability t
be a State Depart
and to advocate th
problems, and ther
to impose some sol
mean, however, th
those with the great
in the future.

WHERE DO WI

The various agencie
the subjects of this
institutional and hun
foreign policy towar ... While core institutions such as the State and Defense departments and the intelligence community will undoubtedly endure as major parts of the system, future participants and roles will certainly be affected by environmental and personal changes as well.

APPLICATION: THE INTERAGENCY PROCESS OF THE FUTURE

As noted in the text, the Obama administration has brought a wider variety of executive branch agencies into the NSC system than has historically been the case. Yet, there are major agencies and functions of government with arguable foreign policy responsibilities that are not part of the system but which may be influential in the future.

Assume for yourself the role of framing the membership of the NSC system for some future point (for instance, 2016 or 2020). Are there any members of the current core or occasional agencies (agencies invited when their area of expertise is discussed) that you would omit from full membership or reduce to part-time status? If so, which ones, and why? How do your changes ripple down through the PC, DC, and IPCs?

If the core purpose of the NSC system is ensuring American security in a hostile environment (the nature of that hostility not specified), are there other government functions and agencies you would add? If global warming is a major priority, should the Environmental Protection Agency be a part of the system? If reducing dependency on petroleum imports is a matter of concern, should the Department of Energy or other related groups be included? Should they be included as core members or as occasional members? Are there any other agencies or functions that should be included or excluded?

...hat do they say about what you ...urity concerns of the United States? ...rs. What do the differences say about

...UESTIONS

... scandal of 2010? What principle or principles of the ...vernment does the incident describe? How does it compare ...rs dispute of the 1970s?

...onal Security Council (NSC)? Describe its formation, role, and ...bership across time.

... interagency process? Describe this system, using the structure of the ...mittees as prime examples of the process in action.

... are the principal executive agencies that assist the president in the formulation ...d execution of foreign policy? Which of these do you consider to be the core actors? Why?

5. Describe each of the following in terms of history, organization, and foreign policy role:
   a. Department of State
   b. Department of Defense
   c. Intelligence community
   d. Department of Homeland Security
   e. Economic agencies
6. How have the comparative roles of the State and Defense departments changed over time? Why have they changed?
7. Why has the intelligence community been a controversial part of the interagency process? What attempts at reform have been made? Why have they not entirely succeeded?
8. Discuss the Department of Homeland Security. What problems have been associated with its formation and subsequent operation?
9. What are the principal economic agencies active in foreign policy? Briefly describe each. How does their changing role reflect presidential preferences in foreign policy?

CORE SUGGESTED READINGS

9/11 Commission. *The 9/11 Commission Report: Final Report of the National Commission on Terrorist Attacks on the United States* (Auth. ed.). New York: W. W. Norton, 2004. This is the full text of the 9/11 Commission's deliberations and recommendations that have been keys to attempts to reform elements of the interagency process since.

Halperin, Morton. *Bureaucratic Politics and Foreign Policy.* Washington, DC: Brookings Institution, 1974. This is a classic formulation of how agencies within the interagency process interact with one another, written by a veteran of the process from the 1960s.

Hilsman, Roger. *The Politics of Policy Making in Defense and Foreign Affairs: Conceptual Models and Bureaucratic Politics* (3rd ed.). Englewood Cliffs, NJ: Prentice Hall,

1993. Written by a veteran of the Kennedy and Johnson administrations, this is a standard source on the politics of the interagency process.
Inderfurth, Karl F., and Loch K. Johnson. *Decisions of the Highest Order: Perspectives on the National Security Council.* Pacific Grove, CA: Brooks/Cole, 1988. This work is a classic overview of how the NSC system has performed historically. For an update, see the same authors' edited volume *Fateful Decisions: Inside the National Security Council.* New York: Oxford University Press, 2004.

ADDITIONAL READINGS AND REFERENCES

Berkowitz, Peter (ed.). *The Future of American Intelligence.* Palo Alto, CA: Stanford University Press, 2006.
Betts, Richard K. "Fixing Intelligence." *Foreign Affairs* 81, 1 (January/February 2002), 43–59.
Boren, David L., and Edward J. Perkins (eds.). *Who Speaks for America? Why Democracy Matters in Foreign Policy.* Ithaca, NY: Cornell University Press, 1998.
Clarke, Richard. *Against All Enemies: Inside America's War on Terror.* New York: Free Press, 2004.
Destler, I. M. *The National Economic Council: A Work in Progress.* Washington, DC: Institute for International Economics, 1996.
Flynn, Stephen. *America the Vulnerable: How Our Government Is Failing to Protect Us from Terrorism.* New York: Harper Perennial, 2005.
Friedman, Benjamin. "Think Again: Homeland Security." *Foreign Policy*, July/August 2005, 22–29.
Hillyard, Michael J. "Organizing for Homeland Security." *Parameters* XXXII, 1 (Spring 2002), 75–85.
Johnson, Loch. *Bombs, Bugs, Drugs, and Thugs: Intelligence and America's Quest for Security.* New York: New York University Press, 2000.
Kettl, Donald L. *System Under Stress: Homeland Security and American Politics.* Washington, DC: CQ Press, 2004.
Lowenthal, Mark M. *Intelligence: From Secrets to Policy.* Washington, DC: CQ Press, 2000.
Maxwell, Bruce (ed.). *Homeland Security: A Documentary History.* Washington, DC: CQ Press, 2004.
Richelson, Jeffrey T. *The U.S. Intelligence Community* (2nd ed.). New York: HarperCollins, 1989.
Sauter, Mark D., and James Carafano. *Homeland Security: A Complete Guide to Understanding, Preventing, and Surviving Terrorism.* New York: McGraw-Hill, 2005.
Snow, Donald M. *National Security for a New Era* (4th ed.). New York: Pearson Longman, 2011.
Trubowitz, Peter. *Defining the National Interest: Conflict and Change in American Foreign Policy.* Chicago: University of Chicago Press, 1998.

CHAPTER 6

Congress and Foreign Policy

Corazon Aquino became the president of the Philippines, in part because of the policy shift in the United States, which Senator Richard Lugar was a central player in organizing.

PREVIEW

Congress was the "first branch" of government, as the Framers spelled out the powers of the legislative branch in Article 1 of the Constitution. Over time, however, Congress has come to take more of a back seat to the president when it comes to foreign policy—especially when it comes to war powers. Congress and the president both have significant foreign policy powers, which can lead to gridlock when the branches are in disagreement. Since the 1960s and 1970s—following Vietnam, the Civil Rights movement, and Watergate—a partisan divide has opened in the area of foreign policy that can also lead to policy stalemate as well as a poor policy-making climate in Washington, D.C. This chapter discusses the powers, advantages and disadvantages, of the Congress in the area of foreign policy. It explores the ebbs and flows of congressional activism that have evolved, even as presidential power in the foreign policy domain has steadily increased.

KEY CONCEPTS

invitation to struggle
polarization
power of the purse
substantive legislation
procedural legislation
confirmation power
congressional oversight
treaty ratification
U.S. v. Curtiss Wright Export Corporation
Youngstown Sheet & Tube v. *Sawyer*
Tonkin Gulf Resolution
War Powers Act
crisis policy
strategic policy
structural defense policy

Richard G. "Dick" Lugar is a Republican U.S. Senator from Indiana. He has represented the Hoosier state since his election in 1976. Born in Indianapolis in 1932, Lugar attended Denison University in Ohio and was a Rhodes Scholar at Oxford before service in the U.S. Navy and ultimately a career in politics. Lugar was on the Indianapolis School Board and served as mayor of the city before running for the U.S. Senate. While Lugar's distinguished career in the Senate has included important efforts to push biofuels, food safety, and school lunch programs, he is particularly known as one of the Senate's key experts on foreign policy.

Lugar was chair of the Senate Foreign Relations Committee in the 1980s and used that position, and his interest and expertise in foreign policy, to push for the comprehensive sanctions bill against the apartheid regime in South Africa as well as to push for democratic change in the Philippines, leading to the ouster of longtime dictator (and U.S. ally) Ferdinand Marcos. It should be noted that the Reagan administration and other fellow Republicans lagged behind Lugar on both policies.

After the Cold War ended, Lugar become instrumental in pushing for the enlargement of the North Atlantic Treaty Organization (NATO) to include former Soviet-bloc countries as a way to promote the democratic stability of a broader Europe. And he teamed with Georgia's Democratic Senator Sam Nunn to start the Cooperative Threat Reduction Program, which sought to find ways to make America safe through the destruction of much of the old

Soviet nuclear arsenal and by keeping former Soviet nuclear scientists gainfully employed, lest they sell their nuclear bomb-making abilities on the open market. Since its inception in 1991, Nunn-Lugar has led to the elimination of over 7,500 nuclear warheads. The United States spends about $400 million per year under Nunn-Lugar, or about $7.7 billion over the life of the program; by contrast, in 2010 the United States spent a little less than that nineteen-year total every month in Afghanistan ($6.7 billion), plus a little less per month in Iraq ($5.5 billion).

In December 2001, Lugar even introduced his own "Lugar Doctrine," outlining what Lugar sees as the central challenge to America's safety. The Lugar Doctrine states that, "the United States will use all of its military, diplomatic and economic power—without question—to ensure that life threatening weapons of mass destruction everywhere are accounted, contained and hopefully destroyed." It also says that, "the U.S. should encourage democratic institutions and decrease dependence on foreign energy sources." Using his position, experience, and staff to help change foreign policy, Lugar has come to be known as one of the foremost foreign policy "entrepreneurs" on Capitol Hill.

Two things are particularly interesting about the case of Senator Lugar for the purposes of this chapter. One is the way that his record shows the kind of policy assertiveness that members of Congress can exhibit. Behind the record, however, is another lesson: It also shows the increasingly partisan and polarized environment in which foreign policy is made. It turns out the people really trying to knock off Senator Lugar in the next election are other Republicans, ones who do not think Lugar is conservative enough.

When the Republicans took back control of the U.S. Senate following the 1994 elections, Lugar was in line to return to the head of the Senator Foreign Relations Committee. Republican Jesse Helms from North Carolina (who would have headed the Agriculture Committee) stepped in, however, and used his seniority to push Lugar aside. Helms wished to use the committee chair position to push a far more aggressive campaign against the Clinton foreign policy and he did. Up for reelection in 2012, Lugar faces a challenge from a "Tea Party" candidate in the Republican primary election. Lugar's record of modern internationalism and bipartisanship has made him, and others like him, a rare breed in Congress—and an endangered species.

Even though the attention of the public and the media tends to be focused on the executive branch when it comes to foreign policy, it was the clear intention of those who wrote the American Constitution that the legislative branch—Congress—would equally share power and responsibility with the executive in all areas of policy, including foreign policy. Throughout American history, the extent of coequality has ebbed and flowed, and most observers agree that the country is currently in a period of presidential dominance (some resurgence of congressional activism notwithstanding). The Constitution has been called an **"invitation to struggle"** because it contains foreign policy powers for both Congress and the President. Conflict between the branches is no accident; indeed, it is at the heart of the American separation-of-powers system.

The United States is one of the few democracies to adopt a separation-of-powers system, and this system has distinct effects on how the American system makes foreign policy. Under this system, the powers of government are constitutionally distributed among the three branches of the federal government. Originally conceived as a means of warding off the potential tyranny that could result if any one leader or group of leaders consolidated the coercive capabilities available to modern governments, the separation-of-powers system has two principal consequences for U.S. foreign policy making today.

First, it creates a legislature with an extraordinary amount of independent policy-making authority. No other legislature in the world plays such a crucial role in determining foreign policy. Some constitutional scholars believe that the Founding Fathers actually intended Congress to be the dominant policy-making organ. Congress, after all, was the first branch treated in the Constitution (in Article I), and considerably more detail is given to enumerating its powers than is given to the executive branch (in Article II). Other scholars doubt that the Founding Fathers necessarily intended to elevate the legislature above the executive. However, no one doubts that they set about to establish a vigorous legislative body that would enjoy comparable status to the president in determining the country's international stance.

Second, that fragmentation of authority between the two elected branches can, and often does, produce the phenomenon known as gridlock, which is the result of policy disagreements between Congress and the president. When the two branches are unable to achieve a working agreement on the country's proper international role and interests, the separation-of-powers system can make governmental stalemate and policy paralysis an ever-present possibility. Gridlock is especially likely to occur when partisan divisions intensify the institutional rivalry inherent in a separation-of-powers structure. The movement toward today's hyperpartisanship and resulting gridlock has been an increasing part of the contemporary environment.

Although Congress is constitutionally empowered to wield vigorous authority in making foreign policy, it has not always done so. American history has witnessed repeated oscillations between periods of executive and congressional dominance of the policy process. As a broad generalization, from the 1930s to the 1970s, Congress often deferred to presidential leadership in dealing with the crises of the Great Depression, World War II, and the Cold War. During the first quarter century of the Cold War, Congress was usually content to follow the foreign policy course set by the president in the belief that the country could not afford to appear divided and irresolute in the face of a protracted global crisis. For instance, it was a member of Congress, Senator J. William Fulbright (D-AR), who wrote in 1961,

> I wonder whether the time has not arrived, or indeed already has passed, when we must give the Executive a measure of power in the conduct of world affairs that we have hitherto jealously withheld.... It is my contention that for the existing requirements of American foreign policy we have hobbled the President (Quoted in Brown, 1985).

Just thirteen years later, however, the same Senator Fulbright voiced a vastly different message:

> I believe that the Presidency has become a dangerously powerful office, more urgently in need of reform than any other institution in American government....Whatever may be said against Congress—that it is slow, obstreperous, inefficient or behind the times—there is one thing to be said for it: It poses no threat to the liberties of the American people (Quoted in Brown, 1985).

What had intervened in those thirteen years was meek congressional acquiescence in the series of decisions surrounding American participation in the Vietnam War.

Fulbright's pronounced change of heart captures, in microcosm, the sea change of opinion that had washed over Congress in the late 1960s and early 1970s. What caused this sudden congressional reassertion of its place in the constitutional order? The decade bounded by Lyndon Johnson's escalation of the war in Vietnam in 1965 and Richard Nixon's resignation in disgrace in 1974 was a time of torment and bitterness for the American people. The protracted agony of Vietnam and the White House criminality of Watergate were back-to-back disasters that eroded the moral legitimacy of the presidency. Long after Johnson and Nixon had left Washington, their legacy of presidential failure lingered, puncturing the myth of superior presidential wisdom. From that bitter decade came a broadly renewed rediscovery of, and respect for, the constitutional design of policy codetermination by the two coequal elected branches. One of the strongest legacies was the desire to limit the president's war-making authority, a subject that is examined later in this chapter. Some of the issues raised in the 1970s are eerily similar to today's concerns surrounding American policy in Afghanistan and Iraq.

In addition to the diminished luster of the presidency were other developments that, taken together, produced a much more assertive Congress in the foreign policy-making process. These developments included a large infusion of young congressional representatives and senators in the mid-1970s, the weakening of party discipline, the erosion of the seniority system, the proliferation and expanded authority of subcommittees, and the growth in congressional staff. All these changes culminated in the reality the United States confronted in the 1990s: a Congress unwilling to submit meekly to the president's lead in defining U.S. foreign policy. Although patriotic responses to September 11th produced a greater deference toward presidential authority, congressional assertiveness has begun to return, especially in the context of the continuing U.S. involvement in Afghanistan and Iraq.

CONGRESS: FOREIGN POLICY PROCESSES AND STRUCTURES

Although there is a tendency to speak of Congress in the singular, it is a bicameral body. It consists of a House of Representatives, comprising 435 members who represent roughly comparably sized districts and who serve two-year terms, and a Senate, consisting of two senators from each of the fifty states who serve six-year terms (with staggered terms so that roughly one-third of the Senate seats are contested in each two-year election cycle). As a result of their size, as well as the wave of internal democratization that swept Congress in the mid-1970s, both chambers are highly decentralized bodies with many committees and subcommittees, each of which offers leadership opportunities.

The fragmentation of authority in Congress expands the opportunities for individual legislators to affect foreign policy issues and opens the body to a wide spectrum of opinion. However, it also creates additional obstacles in forging coalitions large enough to pass legislation. Forty years ago, power in Congress was concentrated in the hands of a small number of powerful committee chairpersons chosen through seniority. By contrast, today's chairs are less able to crack the whip and demand the compliance of their junior colleagues, and these junior colleagues are eager to have leadership power themselves. While this dynamic has been apparent before, it is easy to see today in the form of the new Republican members of Congress elected in 2010 who pose perhaps as many difficulties to their own party leaders such as Speaker John Boehner [R-OH] as they do to President Obama. The resulting opening up of the legislative process means that all views will be heard, but it also indicates that durable majorities may be even harder to forge.

Complicating matters even further are the requirements of the legislative process, which can be extremely unwieldy. In order to enact a law, both the House and the Senate must adopt a measure in identical form. Each house has two parallel sets of committees from which legislation must emerge. First, there are the *authorizing committees*, whose principal job is to review and act on the substance of bills. The most prominent committees in the foreign policy area are the Foreign Relations committees and the Armed Services committees in both the House and Senate. In addition, each body has a committee that deals with the country's intelligence agencies. At the same time, a parallel set of *appropriating subcommittees* exists in each house, responsible for approving funding for authorized programs.

In each house, the actions of the two committees must be reconciled; authorizing and appropriating committees must agree on what programs will be funded at what levels—and they rarely agree entirely. At the same time, the parallel processes in the two houses must agree on programs and budgets between them. If they do not agree (as is regularly the case) on the bills that have been passed, each house must reconcile the bills by a conference committee, the results of whose labor must be approved by each house again. Only once both houses have passed identical bills do the bills go to the president for signature or veto. If the chief executive disagrees with a bill and vetoes it, Congress can override the veto with a supermajority of both chambers; otherwise, either the whole process begins anew or no legislation happens at all in that given area.

Despite their caricature as corrupt and out of touch, most members of Congress are intelligent, hard working, honest, and well informed of the views of their constituents. The very diversity of those constituent views, however, can make legislative agreement elusive. Unsurprisingly, a representative from Pittsburgh will be more likely to seek protectionist relief for the country's (and his or her district's) troubled steel industry, whereas a representative from rural Iowa will argue against trade protectionism, in part because his or her district depends heavily on export markets for its agricultural products. The constant turbulence of competing outlooks is the essence of legislative life. It is not neat, it sometimes leads to deadlock, but it captures the inherent tugging and pushing among diverse points of view that is the essence of democratic life.

Organizing Mechanisms

The organizing mechanisms of political parties and legislative committees impose a measure of order and coherence on these inherently fractious bodies. The majority in each chamber chooses its majority leader and an array of lieutenants to oversee the flow of legislation and attempt to unite party members behind major bills. The minority does the same. Although the formal discipline of U.S. political parties has eroded over the years, each party has become more internally homogeneous and readily identified with certain ideologies and policies. Twenty years ago, both parties were divided between their own liberal and more conservative wings, and there were "moderates" in both parties. Today, the Democratic Party is more consistently the home of political liberals while the Republicans are overwhelmingly conservative; and rarely is there any meeting in the middle. This **polarization** in the parties has increased dramatically over the last thirty years, and has been spurred in part by more moderate members being beaten in their party's primary election by more ideologically extreme challengers (the dynamic that faces Senator Lugar, as discussed at the start of this chapter).

Another organizing mechanism in the House and Senate, the system of committees that is organized by subject matter, ordinarily has the most important influence in determining the fate of legislative proposals. About ten thousand bills and resolutions are submitted to each Congress (a "congress" lasts two years; the 112th Congress was seated in January 2011). Of these, fewer than 10 percent clear all the legislative hurdles to become law. The committee system makes Congress's workload possible. By dividing the vast number of proposals among its standing committees (twenty in both chambers, plus special or "select" committees), bills are given closer attention and members are able to develop a degree of policy expertise that comes with specialization. Since the early 1970s, the proliferating number of subcommittees increasingly handles the work once performed by full committees. This development was necessitated by the growing complexity of policy proposals and the demand of junior members to expand the policy-making opportunities available to them within Congress. Today, about 90 percent of legislative hearings occur before subcommittees. Similarly, subcommittees, by developing expertise on the proposals before them, very nearly hold life-and-death power over bills. An unfavorable vote in a subcommittee makes it unlikely that the bill will even be considered by the full committee, let alone by the full House or Senate.

In the Senate, the most important foreign policy committees are Foreign Relations, Armed Services, Appropriations, and the Select Committee on Intelligence. Given the Senate's special prerogatives in approving presidential appointments and ratifying treaties, its Foreign Relations Committee has long been among the most august in Congress. After possibly reaching the modern peak of its influence under the long-running chairmanship of J. William Fulbright, the committee has seen a gradual erosion of its authority, owing to the diminished status of committees in general, as well as to the succession of less influential leaders who followed Fulbright as committee chair. In recent years, however, the significance of the committee has increased, most observers agree. Under the chairmanship of Jesse Helms (R-NC) between 1995 and 2001, the Foreign Relations Committee certainly became a thorn in President Clinton's side. Joseph Biden (D-DE) chaired the committee intermittently during the George W. Bush administration and oversaw an active committee. Former Democratic nominee for president (2004) John Kerry (D-MA) has chaired the committee since 2009.

The committee structure in the House mirrors that of the Senate. The House's most prominent foreign policy committees are Foreign Affairs, Armed Services, Appropriations, and the Permanent Select Committee on Intelligence. In 2004 both the House and the Senate constructed Homeland Security committees that would help legislate in this area and oversee the Homeland Security Department. Table 6.1 shows a list of the relevant foreign and security policy committees for the 112th Congress (2011–2012).

In addition to congressional committees, congressional caucuses are another set of organizations on the Hill that are important for foreign policy. Caucuses are organizations that help draw attention to issues of interest to members of Congress, and can provide a forum both to learn more about the issues and to be a vehicle for legislative germination. Many caucuses are bipartisan, providing a means for members of the two parties to work together on issues of common interest; some are exclusive to one party or the other. Some examples of foreign policy–relevant congressional caucuses include the India Caucus, the China Caucus, the Taiwan Caucus, the Human Rights Caucus, and the Nuclear Issues Caucus.

The congressional committee and caucus systems are more than just organizing devices. One of the challenges for Congress as an institution and for its members in the area of foreign policy is to be able to "compete" with the president when they have far less expertise and information than does the executive. Committees and caucuses are central ways for members of Congress to gain information on foreign policy issues and thus help them position themselves to be foreign policy players.

TABLE 6.1

Congressional Foreign and Security Policy Committees

House of Representatives	Senate
Armed Services	Armed Services
Foreign Affairs	Foreign Relations
Homeland Security	Homeland Security and Government Affairs
Oversight and Government Reform Committee (Subcommittee on National Security, Homeland Defense, and Foreign Operations)	
Permanent Select Committee on Intelligence	Select Committee on Intelligence
Appropriations Subcommittees on: Defense; Homeland Security; Military Construction, Veterans Affairs, and Related Agencies; State, Foreign Operations, and Related Programs	Appropriations Subcommittees on: Defense; Homeland Security; Military Construction, Veterans Affairs, and Related Agencies; State, Foreign Operations, and Related Programs

CONGRESSIONAL FOREIGN POLICY POWERS

The Founding Fathers were determined to prevent too much power from being concentrated in the hands of the executive, and so they bestowed generous grants of constitutional authority on the Congress—including in the foreign policy domain. The constitutionally grounded foreign policy powers of Congress include its (1) lawmaking power, (2) appropriations power (sometimes called the "power of the purse"), (3) confirmation power, (4) oversight power, (5) war power, and (6) treaty power. All six of these formal powers are either specifically enumerated in the Constitution or are logical derivatives of explicit constitutional grants.

Lawmaking Power

In a sense the preeminent power in any government, the lawmaking power is the capacity to create legal authority for certain actions and to forbid others altogether. The person or agency that possesses the lawmaking power is thus a matter of fundamental importance in the political system. The Founding Fathers settled this crucial issue in the very first section of the first article of the Constitution, which reads in its entirety: "All legislative Powers herein granted shall be vested in a Congress of the United States, which shall consist of a Senate and House of Representatives." Although ordinary legislative enactments are subject to presidential veto, vetoes can be overridden by two-thirds of the House and Senate, thus giving Congress the last word on defining what is legal and what is illegal.

In the field of international affairs, Congress uses its lawmaking power to shape policy in a variety of ways, but these forms tend to fall into one of two categories: substantive or procedural legislation. One way that Congress can act in the foreign policy domain is to adopt **substantive legislation** that directly defines U.S. policy; that is, it can pass legislation that defines the substance of American foreign policy toward a particular issue or country. For example, the 1996 Cuban Liberty and Democratic Solidarity Act, sometimes called the "Helms-Burton Act" after its sponsors (North Carolina Republican Senator Jesse Helms and Indiana Republican Representative Dan Burton), made the embargo of Cuba the law of the land. While the embargo has been around in one form or another since the end of the Eisenhower administration, it had existed solely by presidential order until the Helms-Burton Act. Concerned that President Clinton might try to normalize relations with Cuba, and spurred on by the 1995 shooting down of two airplanes piloted by a Cuban exile group by the Cuban Air Force (killing four), Congress seized the reigns of Cuba policy (or tried to, at least) with this Act.

Another, admittedly older, example is the 1986 South Africa sanctions bill. Since its independence in 1910, the white minority had ruled South Africa. That rule became especially odious in 1948, when the right-wing National Party instituted a thoroughgoing policy of apartheid, or racial separation. The nation's black majority was systematically oppressed through forced segregation, inferior education and jobs, and the denial of basic liberties. By the 1980s, South Africa's twenty-five million blacks increasingly challenged a system that denied them any political voice, while the country's five million whites dominated a three-chambered Parliament that included separate segregated chambers for the nation's three million people of mixed race and one million Indians.

The Reagan administration agreed with Congress that the United States had a moral obligation to help end apartheid but insisted that its policy of "constructive engagement" offered the best hope of a political solution. Constructive engagement assumed that through quiet diplomacy the United States could encourage the South African regime to dismantle apartheid and achieve regional settlements in other parts of southern Africa as well. Thus, the Reagan administration strongly opposed stringent economic sanctions against the white supremacist regime.

By the summer of 1986, however, it was apparent that Reagan's policy on this issue was out of step with many of his fellow Republicans as momentum built in Congress for a tough sanctions bill. In June of that year, the Republican-controlled Senate passed a strong measure that barred new U.S. investments in South Africa (although existing investments were left untouched) and that prohibited imports of crucial South African commodities, such as coal, uranium, steel, iron, agricultural products, and textiles. The measure cleared the Senate by a wide margin of 84 to 14. In September, the House adopted the bill by a similarly lopsided vote of 308 to 77.

On September 26, 1986, President Reagan vetoed the measure, calling economic sanctions "the wrong course to follow." His veto pitted him not only against congressional Democrats but also against some of the leading Republicans in Congress. Indiana Republican Richard Lugar, then chair of the Senate Foreign Relations Committee, announced that he would lead Senate efforts to override Reagan's veto. On September 29, the Democratic-controlled House voted 313 to 83 to override the veto, well over the two-thirds majority required. In the floor debate on the issue, Representative William Gray, a Pennsylvania Democrat, declared, "This bill will send a moral and diplomatic wake-up call to a president who doesn't understand the issue." Two days later, the Senate, by a comfortable margin of 78 to 21, dealt Reagan a decisive defeat by repassing the sanctions bill, thus enacting the measure over determined executive opposition.

The stringent U.S. economic sanctions proved to be instrumental in the decision of South African president F. W. de Klerk to begin dismantling apartheid in 1990. One by one, the symbols and instruments of South Africa's racial oppression fell: The state of emergency that gave Pretoria extraordinary police powers was lifted, the notorious Population Registration Act and Group Areas Act were repealed, democratic political parties were legalized, and negotiations were begun with black leaders to establish a democratic system. Finally, the election of Nelson Mandela began the process toward long-term democratization.

Another form of congressional lawmaking in foreign policy is **procedural legislation**. Procedural legislation can take many forms, but in general it attempts to play a role in foreign policy by laying out the procedures that the executive must follow, including crafting reporting requirements, or creating or changing executive branch agencies. Some examples will help clarify. In terms of agency creation or reform, the 2002 construction of the Department of Homeland Security and the 2004 intelligence community reformulation that created the Director of National Intelligence, as well as the National Counter Terrorism Center (NCTC), are two of the most recent examples of Congress legislating by altering the structure of the executive branch. As sweeping as those reforms are, the National Security Act of 1947 is still the mother of all agency creation in the foreign affairs area, creating the Central Intelligence Agency (CIA), the Secretary of Defense and the Department of Defense, the National Security Council (NSC), the Air Force, and the Joint Chiefs of Staff (JCS).

Another example of procedural legislation is the Goldwater-Nichols Act of 1986, or the Department of Defense Reorganization Act. Frustrated by the lack of coordination across military branches that seemed to be hindering operations, Congress tried to force more "jointness" by centralizing operational control in the hands of the chairman of the JCS and also the joint commanders in the different regions of the globe—the CINCs, or commanders-in-chief (later renamed Regional Combatant Commanders). The Act also created the position of the Vice Chairman of the JCS, whose key mission is to find ways for the separate services to work jointly, perhaps in joint training or even joint acquisitions. In terms of reporting requirements, the War Powers Act of 1973 is a classic example of Congress trying to alter executive behavior by changing the rules by which the president has to play. The War Powers Act is discussed later in this chapter.

Power of the Purse

The **power of the purse** is really two powers in one: legislative control over revenue that is raised by the federal government and congressional control over how that money is spent. On this point, the Constitution is crystal clear: Article I, Section 9, states, "No money shall be drawn from the Treasury, but in Consequences of Appropriations made by Law." Because the lawmaking power belongs to Congress, it follows that the all-important power to determine "appropriations made by Law" is also a congressional prerogative. If, as some have argued, policy is what gets funded, then the power to decide what gets funded is a very great power indeed. The power to resolve perennial issues such as the size and composition of the defense budget and the U.S. contribution to the U.N. budget indicates the kind of policy influence Congress has through its control of the nation's purse strings.

The spending power exists both in the positive form (to fund a program, for example) and the negative form: to prohibit the use of funds. The decision to end funding is both uniquely a congressional function and also an extremely political one. In the 1980s, for example, Congress banned the expenditure of funds to support military or paramilitary operations by the *Contras*, who were carrying out a guerrilla war against the leftist Sandinista government—a favorite of the Reagan administration but not of the U.S. public or the Democrat-controlled Congress. Ultimately the Reagan administration tried to find a way around the Boland Amendment to continue funding of the *Contras*, which led to "Contra" side of the Iran-Contra scandal.

Congress ultimately pulled the financial plug on the Vietnam War in 1973 and 1974. On one hand, this was a momentous decision, cutting off funds for military operations when there were still forces in the theater of operations. On the other hand, however, the American public had already turned against the war; indeed, the decision came as late as three years after the tide had turned against the war. It is worth considering the different dynamics of the Vietnam case as with the Iraq case, where many assumed the Democrats in Congress, having seized control in the 2006 elections, would cut off funding for the Iraq War, given its (and George W. Bush's) increasing unpopularity. Congress never did cut off those funds, however—perhaps indicating that a different political dynamic surrounds the presence of U.S. troops in the field today than in the previous era.

Confirmation Power

Unlike the lawmaking and budgetary powers, only the Senate exercises **confirmation power**. Its constitutional basis is found in Article II, Section 2, which stipulates that the president "shall appoint ambassadors, other public ministers and consuls ... and all other officers of the United States" subject to "the advice and consent of the Senate." Thus, foreign policy makers, such as the secretary of state, the secretary of defense, and many of their associates, must win Senate approval before they can take up their duties. Confirmation applies to most of the four thousand or so executive branch positions designated as "political" and thus serving at the president's pleasure. The need for confirmation assures that the Senate has some voice in these appointments and can block appointees of which it disapproves.

In the normal course of events, presidential nominees win Senate approval; indeed; failure to confirm the president's choice for a position is regarded as a major setback for the White House. Rather than risk the embarrassment of Senate rejection, presidents sometimes choose to withdraw or not nominate their more problematic choices.

Early in his term, for example, George H.W. Bush nominated a number of his more generous campaign contributors for senior executive positions, including ambassadorships. Among the most egregious cases was his selection of Joy A. Silverman to be U.S. Ambassador to Barbados. Silverman had no discernible foreign policy credentials and, for that matter, had had virtually no paid employment in her life. In explaining why she felt she was qualified for the rank of ambassador, Silverman wrote that she had "assisted husband ... by planning and hosting corporate functions." Apparently, her real credential, in the Bush administration's eyes, was the nearly $300,000 she had donated to the Republican Party between 1987 and 1989. Faced with a determined Senate opposition led by Maryland Democrat Paul Sarbanes, the Bush administration quietly withdrew the nomination in favor of a qualified diplomat. Comparable cases, although not common, occur in most administrations.

The confirmation power permits the Senate to influence the policy process. Specifically, confirmation hearings are sometimes used as highly public forums for airing substantive policy controversies and, in the course of doing so, for altering executive positions on important issues. This was the case in 1989, for example, when a number of senators developed serious doubts about the agreement already negotiated with Japan for joint U.S.-Japanese development of an advanced jet fighter, the FSX. The senators seized the opportunity afforded by designated Secretary of State James Baker's confirmation hearings to get Baker to agree to an interagency review of the deal. Baker was confirmed in due course, but the subsequent review of the FSX agreement opened up an interagency brawl between the project's defenders (centered principally in the departments of State and Defense) and its critics (mostly found in the Department of Commerce, the Office of the U.S. Trade Representative, and the Department of Labor).

A more dramatic way the Senate can use its confirmation power to affect the policy process is through outright rejection of presidential appointees to high office. An illustration was the bitter battle over the first President Bush's initial choice for secretary of defense, former Senator John Tower of Texas. A twenty-four-year Senate veteran and former chair of the Armed Services Committee, Tower was by all accounts well versed in the substance of defense policy. His nomination by president-elect Bush in December 1988 to head the Department of Defense, however, quickly ran into trouble among his former colleagues on Capitol Hill. Opposition to Tower came from three fronts. First, some conservative activists, including the lobbying group Americans for the

High Frontier, which was ardently committed to space-based missile defenses, opposed Tower because he did not fully support the "Star Wars" missile shield envisioned by Ronald Reagan. Second, although few would say so publicly, most senators had little personal regard for Tower. His four terms in their midst had won the Texan few friends and earned him instead a reputation for aloofness and arrogance in an institution that prizes smooth collegiality. Finally, and most important, the twice-divorced Tower was dogged by persistent rumors of hard drinking and womanizing that led to questions about whether he exercised sufficient self-control to be entrusted with keeping the country's most important secrets. Although the Senate's eventual vote against confirming Tower closely followed party lines, the first public allegations of the Texan's drunkenness and philandering were made by a conservative Republican activist, Paul M. Weyrich. Despite a thorough FBI investigation of the charges surrounding Tower, the issue of his character remained inconclusive. However, it is no doubt true that the deluge of rumors, created a political climate of doubt that simply could not be dispelled. After Tower's defeat in March 1989, President Bush nominated former Congressman Dick Cheney of Wyoming. Cheney's affable relations with the Hill and unblemished personal record won the future vice president easy confirmation as secretary of defense.

President George W. Bush had several controversial foreign policy confirmation struggles, but perhaps none as well known as the nomination of John Bolton to be the U.S. Ambassador to the United Nations. Bolton, a strong opponent of multilateralism and critic of the United Nations, was nominated in 2005. While Republicans controlled the Senate at that time, strong Democratic opposition and the opposition of Republican Senator George Voinovich (OH) led to a filibuster that could not be broken. Bush then gave Bolton a "recess" appointment, allowing him to serve for about a year and a half. President Obama has also used recess appointments to get around Senate opposition, including giving a recess appointment to a new "chief of mission" to Syria, Robert S. Ford.

Oversight Power

Although not specifically enumerated in the Constitution, the legislative branch's power to review how new laws are implemented and to examine the actual effects of new policies follows logically from the constitutional grant of lawmaking authority. In the course of exercising its **oversight** prerogatives and responsibilities, Congress engages in an ongoing round of studies, hearings, and investigations. Those activities, in turn, require a substantial amount of time and effort from executive branch officials, who are called on to prepare reports ordered by Congress and to provide testimony to congressional committees engaged in oversight activities.

It is useful to distinguish routine congressional oversight from the more dramatic investigations it sometimes undertakes. A good example of routine foreign policy oversight is congressional monitoring of CIA activities. Until its burst of institutional assertiveness in the mid-1970s, Congress had little awareness of U.S. intelligence and covert operations and lacked a systematic means of acquiring information about them. In 1975, however, the Senate established a select committee to investigate allegations of CIA involvement in covert activities such as destabilizing the leftist regime of Chilean President Salvador Allende, orchestrating a secret war in Cambodia, and intervening in factional warfare in Angola. Chaired by Senator Frank Church of Idaho, the committee uncovered evidence of covert operations about which the Congress had virtually no previous knowledge. Determined to make its oversight of intelligence activities more routine, Congress established new intelligence committees in both houses and adopted legislation that required the president to both authorize any covert operations and report those operations to the House and Senate Intelligence committees—examples of reporting requirements that are a hallmark of procedural legislation. The purpose of the legislation was to strengthen democratic accountability over secret CIA operations. By requiring both presidential clearance and congressional notification, the two elected branches of government would be more firmly in control of and responsible for covert operations.

Most of the time, of course, the activities of the Intelligence committees remain subdued, outside the glare of the public spotlight. These committees returned to the fore after the attacks of September 11th because part of the blame for the traumatic events was laid at the CIA's door. The Senate Intelligence Committee Chair, Florida Democrat Bob Graham, and Vice Chair, Republican Richard Shelby of Alabama, led demands for a full accounting of the intelligence community's failures leading up to September 11th and to try to forge a plan to make sure such an attack never happens again. Among the possible reforms emerging from the committee in 2002 was the creation of a cabinet-level intelligence position superior to the DCI, which came to be known as the Director of National Intelligence.

This more dramatic form of congressional oversight occurs when Congress conducts special investigations into especially troubling policy issues, often triggered by a shocking policy failure (such as the 9/11 attacks). In a number of instances, especially during the Vietnam years, the country's foreign policy climate was altered by congressional hearings. Throughout the 1960s, as the war in Southeast Asia escalated in scope, costs, and casualties, so too did doubts about its wisdom. Those doubts were given a prominent and respectable showcase in a series of highly publicized Senate hearings, presided over by the chair of the Senate Foreign Relations Committee, William Fulbright. By 1966, the senator concluded that the war was misguided; thus, he exercised his prerogative as committee chair by conducting a series of televised hearings on the war. The first, held in January and February 1966, created a national sensation. Lavish media coverage served to focus the country's attention on a wide-ranging discussion of U.S. interests in Vietnam, the nature of the threats to those interests, and the best means of countering those threats. Viewers around the country were exposed to the reasoned, articulate criticism of U.S. policy from such men as the diplomat, scholar, and father of "containment" George Kennan and respected U.S. Army Lieutenant General James Gavin, a World War II hero. Their stature, in turn, helped dispel the notion that foreign policy dissent was merely the unpatriotic chanting of a few student radicals. Their cogent analysis and critique of the Johnson administration's policies served to crystallize doubts that many Americans had begun to feel.

The congressional hearings on the Iran-Contra scandal were a particularly dramatic example of congressional oversight (and a media spectacle). As its hyphenated name suggests, the Iran-Contra scandal comprised two separate, but joined, misadventures. The "Iran" half arose from a series of illegal arms sales to the Iranian fundamentalist regime that had overthrown the Shah of Iran and that had held the American embassy staff in Tehran hostage for more than a year beginning in 1979. Reagan, over the strenuous objections of his most senior advisors, authorized the sale of missiles to the Tehran regime in 1985 in the hopes that the grateful Iranians would assist in negotiations to free American hostages in Lebanon and that doing so would lead to better U.S.-Iranian relations. Proceeds from the missile sales were used to finance the "Contra" half of the scandal. This aspect of the scandal referred to clandestine support for an American-sponsored rebellion, by a group known as the Contras, against the Marxist Sandinista regime of Nicaragua, which was in direct violation of congressional bans against such assistance.

When these secret policies were revealed in 1986, a scandal ensued and investigations followed. During the summer of 1987, U.S. television viewers were alternately fascinated and appalled by gripping insider testimony provided by dozens of witnesses, including, most famously, Marine Lieutenant Colonel Oliver ("Ollie") North, the National Security Council staffer who orchestrated much of the ill-conceived policy. By the time the joint House-Senate investigating committee concluded its public inquiry, the American people had received a memorable lesson in the perils of secret, and sometimes illegal, covert actions carried out by amateurs acting in the name of an intellectually disengaged president. The hearings clearly revealed that federal laws had been broken by executive officers, democratic accountability was undermined, and the country suffered a needless international embarrassment.

Examples of applications of the oversight power are a common part of the federal government's operation. They appear most prominently when the executive branch proposes controversial policies or procedures or, more dramatically, actions of dubious legality (Iran-Contra, for example). Sometimes the applications are motivated by partisan concerns, as in the relentless pursuit by Republicans of alleged malfeasance by former President Clinton. At other times, they arise when there are perceptions that the executive has overstepped his boundaries or misled Congress or the American people, as in the case of the Bush administration's justifications for invading Iraq.

War Power

In Article I, Section 8, of the Constitution, the Founding Fathers established that "the congress shall have Power ... to declare War." Records of the Constitutional Convention show broad agreement that the executive must not be enabled to commit the country to a course of war on his own independent authority. While bestowing on the president the role of commander-in-chief of the armed forces and acknowledging that he would have inherent authority to use force to repel sudden attacks, the Constitution's Framers were nonetheless clear in their insistence that the fateful decision to initiate war must await formal declaration by Congress.

The practice of the past two centuries, however, has borne little resemblance to the Founding Fathers' carefully constructed design. As the United States rose from isolation to the leading rank of the world's states and as the technology of modern aircraft and intercontinental missiles created the requirement for rapid response to international crises, the actual power to initiate and carry out wars tilted from the interbranch balance of the Constitution to a pronounced strengthening of the president's role. Of the more than two hundred instances in which U.S. armed forces have been used abroad, only five have been sanctioned by formal declarations of war. The last American military commitment accompanied by a congressional declaration of war was World War II. By the middle of the twentieth century, some authorities believed that the whole concept of declaring war was obsolete. So too, some argued, was the constitutional concept of joint war making by the president and Congress. Instead, the use of broad congressional authorizations has become the norm since Vietnam's Tonkin Gulf Resolution, a blank check to wage war in Southeast Asia. The wars in Afghanistan and Iraq both flow from such authorizations.

The trauma of the protracted, failed, and undeclared war in Vietnam stimulated Congress to set out to recapture its war powers, which had gradually atrophied through disuse. The resulting War Powers Resolution of 1973 represented an historic and controversial effort by Congress to restore the interbranch balance to something more closely approximating the codetermination envisioned by the writers of the Constitution. A controversial document with mixed ongoing effects, this resolution is discussed in detail later in the chapter.

Treaty Power

The treaty power is spelled out in Article II, Section 2, of the Constitution, which states that presidents may make treaties with foreign governments "by and with the Advice and Consent of the Senate ... provided two thirds of the Senators present concur." As with the confirmation power, the congressional treaty power is assigned to the Senate alone. Its possession of these two constitutional prerogatives gives the Senate greater stature than the House of Representatives in the foreign policy process.

The Constitution creates the need for an extraordinary majority to **ratify** treaties. Simple majorities are difficult enough to attain in fractious legislative assemblies: Getting two-thirds of the Senate's members to agree on anything presents a formidable challenge. Why would the Founding Fathers have designed a process that makes treaties so difficult to attain? Deeply isolationist and profoundly suspicious of the monarchies then ruling Europe, the Framers of the Constitution deliberately made it quite difficult for the new country's leaders to enter into formal "entanglements" with foreign governments. George Washington's famous farewell address that warned against the pernicious lure of "permanent alliances" faithfully mirrored the American outlook of his day.

Occasionally, Congress and the president become so deeply opposed on fundamental issues that they are unable to work out their differences and find a compromise formula for a treaty. This difficulty was classically illustrated in the aftermath of World War I, when President Woodrow Wilson was unable to secure Senate approval of the Treaty of Versailles in the form in which he had negotiated it. American membership in the newly created League of Nations was one of the treaty's chief provisions, but the Senate refused to accept it. The fact that the United States did not join the League seriously weakened it as a credible international body, and this emasculated League of Nations was shortly confronted with armed aggression by the fascist regimes of Germany, Italy, and Japan.

Critics of congressional influence in foreign affairs often point to this episode as a cautionary tale against the alleged isolationism and parochialism of Congress in contrast to the progressive internationalism of the executive. In fact, however, the failure of the United States to join the League of Nations was at least as much the fault of President Wilson as it was the Senate. Wilson, a rigid idealist, had refused to include congressional representatives in the U.S. delegation at the Paris Peace Conference and later presented the Treaty of Versailles to the Senate with the demand that it ratify his treaty as is. When the Senate leader, Henry Cabot Lodge (R-MA), persuaded the Senate to adopt a series of rather innocuous reservations to the treaty, Wilson stiffly refused to compromise. In a titanic struggle of wills, Wilson would not budge. In the end, he had so thoroughly alienated enough senators by his rigidity that the Senate dealt him a defeat and rejected the treaty that Wilson had regarded as his crowning achievement.

Mindful of Wilson's historic miscalculation, modern presidents ordinarily attempt to ensure congressional involvement in the treaty-making process in hopes of improving the chances that the negotiated document will be ratified. Sometimes, however, even this strategy is not enough. For example, in the history of strategic arms control agreements, President Carter went to great lengths to keep legislators fully apprised of the progress of negotiations on the second Strategic Arms Limitation Talks (SALT II) Treaty during the 1970s. By the time the draft treaty was ready for Senate consideration in 1980, however, the political climate between the United States and the Soviet Union had markedly worsened. The Soviet invasion of Afghanistan in December 1979 was the final straw. Aware that he did not have the votes to ratify the SALT II Treaty and moving toward a more hard-line position himself, Carter withdrew the treaty from Senate consideration.

While most treaties the president sends to the Senate are ratified, some recent treaties have had interesting journeys. President Clinton, for example, failed to get the Comprehensive Test Ban Treaty ratified. The treaty would ban all nuclear explosions for testing, including tests that are carried out deep underground. Since 1945 the United States has carried out over one thousand nuclear tests. Early tests were carried out in the atmosphere in Nevada and in the South Pacific, for example, but since the 1960s all U.S. tests have been underground. The United States has not tested a nuclear weapon since September 1992, but the Republican-led Senate failed to ratify the treaty when Clinton sent it up in 1999. President Obama has signaled he would like to send the treaty to the Senate again.

Before concluding this section on congressional foreign policy powers, it is important to remember the way that the Congress and the Presidency interact over these checked powers. As the chapter on the Presidency discussed, the executive has many advantages in each of these areas, often able to act first, leaving Congress in a reactive position. The treaty power is a nice example of this tug-and-pull. The Senate certainly looks to be in a powerful position when it comes to treaties, and it is. However, it is also true that the percentage of all international agreements that the United States enters into that take the form of treaties has rapidly decreased. Presidents have increasingly used "executive agreements" as the preferred form of international agreements, rather than treaties. Unlike treaties, the Senate has no real authority over executive agreements and even had to pass a law—the Case-Zablocki Act of 1972—to try to curb their use by the president and to require that the president (through the secretary of state) inform the Senate when executive agreements are made. In recent decades executive agreements have come to be used far more often than are treaties, now making up nearly 95 percent of all international agreements.

Even though the foreign policy powers of Congress play out in an interactive context relative to the president, this section should dispel the myth that the Founding Fathers intended Congress to play second fiddle to the president in charting the nation's international course. Its impressive array of constitutional powers—to pass laws, fund programs, confirm executive appointments, oversee executive conduct, declare war, and ratify treaties—gives Congress a strong repertoire of formal authority to share coequally with presidents in the foreign policy-making process. Interaction between the branches is also a political matter, and it is to this less formal political area of foreign policy making that the discussion now turns.

CONGRESSIONAL ACTIVISM IN FOREIGN POLICY

Just as the president has political advantages and constraints on his conduct of foreign policy, so too does the Congress. The large effect of presidential advantage is to encourage the chief executive to exercise more latitude in making policy with less congressional restraint and criticism. Prominent examples of presidential assertiveness include the presidencies of Richard Nixon and George W. Bush. The political assertiveness of Congress, however, manifests itself in periods of congressional activism in foreign policy. The most recent congressional challenge to a major presidential foreign policy initiative was probably over authorization of the use of force in the Persian Gulf War of 1991, although some Democrats certainly objected to the Bush "surge" policy in Iraq, and some Republicans objected to Obama's use of limited force in Libya. This section looks at both the sources of congressional activism and the constraints on its exercise. This discussion is then applied to the war powers interaction that occurred between the branches in the 1970s and that remains an important topic today.

The contemporary pattern of congressional assertiveness in U.S. foreign policy is nothing if not controversial, and this controversy is particularly striking in the post-September 11th world. With the national disaster and its aftermath, there was an understandable "rally 'round the flag" phenomenon as Americans turned to their leadership, and especially the president, for comfort and direction in suddenly uncertain times. The president quickly became the symbol of American strength and steadfastness in the face of terrorist evil, and the rhetoric of war further reinforced the aura of the commander-in-chief. The president and his office achieved a level of centrality and preeminence in these circumstances that was truly extraordinary; the only real parallel in the lifetime of most Americans being the standing of Franklin Roosevelt after the sneak attack on Pearl Harbor in 1941 (an event to which numerous comparisons were made).

In that atmosphere, President Bush occupied a level of advantage over the Congress that is highly unusual. In the immediate months after September 11th, Congress often appeared little more than an arm of presidential mandates, and it was even deemed unpatriotic in some quarters when critics questioned the president and his administration's policies and responses to the crisis.

The period after 9/11, perhaps until 2006, does not represent the normal condition in the relationship between the president and Congress, and thus it should not be judged as typical in terms of the amount and level of congressional activism in trying to influence foreign policy. The trend in the past half-century or so has been toward more, rather than less, congressional assertiveness in the foreign policy area. A new book on the subject, Carter and Scott's *Choosing to Lead: Understanding Congressional Foreign Policy Entrepreneurs* (2009), nicely documents the increase in foreign policy activism by members of Congress, even at times when the institution itself has not been so active. As time has passed since the terrible attacks of September 11th, Congress has become more active yet again in the area of foreign policy—perhaps not as much as the Framers had in mind, but not as supine as between 2001 and 2006. Indeed, today President Obama confronts an active—and in some cases, hostile—legislature.

Sources of Activism

The congressional activism that marked the period beginning with the reaction to the Vietnam conflict and that continued through the 1990s resulted from several different factors. Different writers compile different lists and place greater emphasis on one factor or another. The list that follows is neither exhaustive nor final, but it is at least representative and should provide the reader with the flavor of the phenomenon and a starting point in developing a more personally satisfying set of factors. This is followed by another list of what are sometimes seen as constraints.

Expanded Role of the United States in World Affairs In the days prior to World War II, the United States and individual Americans could maintain, and plausibly believe, that their role in foreign affairs was very limited: what happened in the world did not much affect them, and what the United States did in the world had little impact on international affairs. The bedrock of "splendid isolationism" between the world wars, after all, had been American aloofness from the corrupt political practices of the European politics that dominated international relations. In that setting, most members of Congress could adopt a casual, nonintrusive view toward foreign affairs, leaving the bulk of foreign relations to the executive branch, and notably the State Department, with the tacit approval of constituents who felt similarly unaffected.

The Cold War and the post–Cold War world have changed all that. As already noted, the United States emerged from World War II as one of the world's two remaining major powers, and the foreign affairs of the Cold War dealt with the potentially life-and-death struggle between Soviet communism and American democracy. In that light, what the United States did in the world directly affected, at least potentially, every American, and members of Congress could no longer afford to be uninformed bystanders to the foreign policy process without incurring the wrath of at least some of their constituents. A post–Cold War world in which the United States is the sole remaining superpower and in which American interests are virtually universal only magnifies the importance of how the United States deals with the world. The ongoing struggle to fashion effective policies to deal with global terrorism provides the most dramatic example of this importance.

At the same time that the United States became a more important component of the world system, government became a more prominent player in the daily lives of Americans. The great growth in government actually dates back to Roosevelt's New Deal as a response to the Great Depression of the 1930s, and it comes forward through the spate of social entitlement legislation that began with Lyndon Johnson's Great Society during the 1960s. The net result is that, in general, Americans look more toward government to deal with their problems than they used to, and this dependence extends to and includes foreign affairs.

Domestic Implications of Foreign Affairs Another major implication of the changing role of foreign affairs has been its politicization. Once again, before World War II, when foreign affairs were less pressing, it was often said that, "politics stops at the water's edge." As discussed earlier, this adage suggested that the realm of partisan politics should remain tethered to domestic concerns and that when conflicts with other countries emerged, Americans should band together and demonstrate a common, solid front against external opponents. This position was easy enough to sustain when there were relatively few domestic consequences of foreign policy actions, but that is clearly no longer the case. In the language and argument used in this text, foreign policy has become intermestic.

Traditionally, Congress has been much more closely attuned to domestic concerns, because domestic (that is, internal) decisions most strongly affect the geographically defined Congressional constituencies within the United States. When there was little measurable impact of foreign policy decisions on those constituencies, members of Congress could defer to the executive without incurring the wrath of those who put them into (and could remove them from) office. A good member did—and does—take care of those who elected that representative. What is different now is that there are significant foreign policy issues that can have an effect on a member's constituents, and members who ignore foreign policy do so at their own peril.

Reactions to Executive Mistakes As the American role in world affairs has become more consequential on the world stage, so too have instances of miscues by American presidents had an increasing impact on both foreign countries and on Americans. When these mistakes become matters of controversy and significant opposition within the United States, it is not uncommon for Congress to rise in indignation and to seek to impose changes on an executive branch that usually tries to avoid such imposition. This motivation appeared most strongly in the 1970s in response to the Vietnam experience and other executive actions. The Vietnam conflict spawned the War Powers Resolution to put limits on the president's ability to deploy troops, but it was not alone as a military action that brought the wisdom of the executive into doubt (rightly or wrongly). In 1975, for instance, American lives were wasted in the feckless *Mayaguez* incident, where U.S. Marines attempted to seize a pirated U.S. commercial vessel that had actually already been released, resulting in the loss of American lives. In 1980, the ill-fated Desert One rescue of the American hostages in Tehran, Iran, resulted in no American hostages being released and nine rescuers dying in the Iranian desert. In the mid-1980s (as noted previously), the attempt by the Reagan administration to defy congressional bans resulted in the Iran-Contra scandal.

The military miscues led to a bipartisan effort in Congress to find ways to improve American military performance. Led by legislators such as Colorado's (D) Senator Gary Hart, Maine's (R) William S. Cohen (later secretary of defense under President Clinton), Georgia's (D) Sam Nunn, and others, this group of about a hundred members undertook a serious examination of the Pentagon with little cooperation—and much resistance—from the defense establishment. The results of their efforts, implemented despite the complaints of the Reagan administration, included the sweeping Goldwater-Nichols Defense Reorganization Act and the Cohen-Nunn Act, both of 1986. As previously noted, Goldwater-Nichols focused on "jointness" across the military and gave greater authority to the JCS chairman. Cohen-Nunn was aimed more specifically at the development and integration of the Special Forces, which at the time were small and lacked coordination across the services. Cohen-Nunn created prominent civilian and military leadership positions in the Special Forces, and began the movement toward the well-developed and coordinated kind of Special Forces that could be seen on display in the operation that killed Osama bin Laden, for example. The Pentagon wanted neither piece of legislation and probably would have gotten neither were it not for the executive branch's poor performance. It is generally agreed that these acts—examples of procedural foreign policy legislation—have had far-reaching positive impacts on military performance.

Internal Changes in Congress The past thirty years or so have also witnessed some clear changes in the nature of Congress. The seniority system, for instance, has been greatly eroded, sapping power from the political parties that manipulated seniority to their advantage. The election of Senator Bill Frist (R-TN), a man with only eight years of Senate service, to majority leader in 2002 is dramatic evidence of this erosion. At the same time, the traditional power and deference accorded to committee chairs has eroded; members no longer feel as obligated to take the lead from chairs or ranking members on committees. Influxes of new members in the 1970s, the 1990s, and in recent elections have resulted in a different kind of Congress, one both more independent and often less predictable for several reasons. For one thing, the members are, in general, younger than they used to be, better educated, and less patient to wait for power. Their willingness to form independent judgments—including those in opposition to executive positions—is further enhanced by the growth in congressional staffs. Most members of Congress, for instance, have a nominal expert on foreign policy on their personal staffs; if they do not, they can turn to staff experts on the committees to which they are assigned. The youth movement has been particularly dramatic in the House of Representatives, which has traditionally been the more quiescent branch of Congress on foreign affairs but which has become increasingly active. The traditional view of quiet, orderly "back benchers" (relatively junior members) deferring to their distinguished, senior colleagues has given way to a much more disorderly, active interchange in both houses. The rise in activism by the Tea Party is particularly symptomatic of this change.

The Impact of Media The modern media, and especially the explosion of television news programming and the ubiquitous presence of the Internet, have greatly changed the policy context for ordinary citizens and policy makers as well. Round-the-clock news available on TV, your computer, and on your smartphone provides an exposure to world events for everyone that was quite impossible to receive as little as fifteen years ago. The result is that people, at least within the informed public (see Chapter Eight), are more aware of what is going on in the world than before, and this fact affects members of Congress.

Prior to the telecommunications revolution, it was quite possible, and usually acceptable, for most members of Congress to be reasonably ignorant of foreign affairs since most of a member's constituents were also ignorant of these matters. At the same time, it was difficult for members to communicate directly with the "folks at home" most of the time. Modern technology has changed that. Local news people can interview senators or representatives live in interactive forums and in real time as foreign crises or events unfold. If a member of Congress is uninformed on an issue or at odds with his or her constituents, there is no way to hide that fact other than ducking interviews, which may send a message in and of itself. The result may not be to force all members of Congress to be experts on foreign affairs, but it does mean they must *appear* to have a working understanding of foreign policy issues to avoid embarrassment. Having to develop opinions rather than simply accepting the views of the leadership inevitably increases the diversity of the opinions that will reach the floors of the two chambers.

Another dynamic that has been facilitated by these technological changes has been the emergence of "candidate-centered campaigns," where the story of the person running in a congressional election trumps the story of the party. While the candidates who win election mostly caucus with the party (Senator Joe Lieberman is an exception, an independent who caucuses with the Democrats), their loyalty to the party can be reduced because of their often-national reputations. These (sort of) free agents can be quite active, including in the area of foreign policy.

Constraints on Activism

The tendency toward activism, of course, is by no means unrestrained. Although Congress may, from time to time, assert itself in foreign policy matters, it also remains constrained from doing so for a variety of reasons.

The Need to Present a United Front Some observers (and some presidents) argue that if Congress does not willingly accept second billing to the president, the United States will present an inconsistent face to the outside world, thus undermining our foreign policy. Politics *must* end at the water's edge, some say. Without clearly accepted presidential leadership, it is argued, other governments will be confused as to who is speaking for the United States and what the country's policy actually is. Whereas the executive branch is headed by a single chief executive and thus can speak with one voice, the decentralized Congress sometimes threatens to act like "535 secretaries of state," the critics say.

The assertion that congressional disagreement with the executive should be muted or suppressed most often occurs, and is probably most convincing, during times of national crisis. During normal times, the attempts to stifle congressional dissonance can be criticized as an infringement on free speech, on legitimate congressional prerogative, and on legitimate political discourse. These distinctions become more blurred when policy is controversial or the country is in the throes of some kind of crisis.

The period after September 11th illustrates the tensions and pressures involved when national crises intrude on the political process. In the immediate wake of the tragedy, the patriotic outpouring and the need to unite against a common foe overwhelmed dissent, including questioning how the government had performed in anticipating the event and why it had failed to prevent or vitiate its occurrence. As time passed public concerns began to be expressed in Congress, but even then, questions of loyalty and the need for a common front remained a major part of the debate. There was still a real absence of critical dissent before the U.S. invasion of Iraq.

There is no permanent resolution to this debate, and it will continue to be a part of the ongoing process as new crises arise and responses to them are fashioned and as long as presidents pursue controversial policies. Whether the common good outweighs individual liberties and whether responsibility lies with maintaining a common front or in expressing dissonance against what are viewed as mistakes or worse are ethical, philosophical, and political questions that cannot be resolved by generalized responses. Rather, they are, and always will be, fashioned to fit particular circumstances in which reasonable people can disagree on proper answers. Indeed, that there is no obvious and permanent answer to these tough questions is at the heart of our democratic experiment.

Lack of Foreign Policy Expertise Few members of Congress are true foreign policy experts; Richard Lugar—the subject of the introduction to this chapter—is the exception, not the rule. Therefore, the argument goes, a policy shaped by Congress is bound to be amateurish and not befitting a great power. It is indeed a fact of legislative life that members of Congress must deal with the whole spectrum of policy issues confronting the country. In any given legislative session, members will have to make more or less informed voting choices on issues ranging from farm price support subsidies to Alaskan wildlife preservation to school voucher programs to health care and the problems of urban decay. For most members, the pressures to be reasonably adept generalists make it difficult, if not impossible, for them to attain the depth of knowledge they need to become true foreign affairs specialists. Exposure to global television can and does reduce the ignorance of individual members regarding foreign affairs, but it does not produce broad expertise.

It does not follow, however, that Congress is inherently incapable of acting wisely on foreign affairs. Not all presidents arrived at the White House already conversant in foreign policy—indeed they rarely do. Presidents, no less than legislators, are faced with similar demands to be more or less conversant with the whole spectrum of policy issues facing the country, no matter how much they might wish to focus on foreign affairs. Yet no one argues that, as a consequence, the president is unable to handle the foreign affairs aspects of the job.

To the extent that Congress is able to act knowledgeably on foreign policy issues, this ability is attributed mainly to the growth in congressional staff and the expertise of the Congressional Research Service. Through the expansion in congressional staff over the past thirty years, as already noted, legislators now have the support of subject-matter experts who do not owe their livelihood to the executive branch and so are not beholden to its policies.

The same critics who want Congress to submit meekly to presidential leadership also berate it for hiring more staffers, but it is that strengthening of its own institutional capability that helps Congress discharge the independent policy-making role envisioned by the Constitution. In addition, the less-noted, but no less important, repository of policy expertise found in the Congressional Research Service gives Congress additional "bench strength" in analyzing international currents and evaluating the pros and cons of alternative foreign policy proposals. Although it may be true that the number of foreign policy experts available to the executive far exceeds the human resources available to Congress, this does not mean that Congress is disabled from taking part in the foreign policy debate in a knowledgeable, responsible manner. It is worth noting that the move to reduce congressional staffs following the 2010 elections can have the unintended consequence of weakening Congress relative to the president in the area of foreign policy.

Structural Aspects of Foreign Affairs As two large deliberative bodies, the strength of Congress is its ability to debate and expose areas of public policy to a thorough analysis and vetting. Congress, at its best, is a magnificent debating society where issues of policy are brought to the public eye and resolved in the public interest. This process is often ponderous and time consuming, and Congress is rarely accused of being overly efficient in its operations. The virtues of Congress, however, can often become impediments in the area of foreign policy in at least three ways.

One is the sheer volume of foreign policy interactions. If the Congress of the United States were forced to review and approve every legally binding interaction with other governments negotiated by the United States, it would simply drown in the responsibility. It would almost certainly not be able to exercise responsible activity for all these concerns, and even if it did, it would have no time to deal with domestic and constituent concerns, which arguably are its primary duty.

The existence of executive agreements to handle most foreign policy obligations is political testimony to this congressional liability, but it also illustrates how Congress can play a role even when it is not centrally involved in a particular matter. Although Congress has no direct power over negotiation of executive agreements, it does constrain the executive in two indirect ways. First, most agreements involve the expenditure of public funds (in the jargon, they are non–self-executing), and the authorization to spend public monies resides with the Congress, which can provide or preclude implementing funding. Second is the principle of retribution. A president who ignores the wishes of Congress and negotiates executive agreements of which the Congress disapproves may find other parts of his legislative agenda in jeopardy in the future. This latter phenomenon occurred in 1980 when Jimmy Carter threatened to treat the SALT II nuclear weapons treaty as an executive agreement. Carter was curtly informed that if he did so, the rest of his legislative agenda for that election year would be stillborn. Carter never repeated the suggestion.

A second problem is the need for speed and flexibility in decision making that accompanies some foreign policy items, especially fast-breaking crises or opportunities. Often foreign policy events unfold rapidly and certainly in a manner that does not permit the kind of full debate and consideration at which Congress excels. In these circumstances, what should the role of Congress be? In practice, the role is often limited to brief consultation with the leadership of Congress as events unfold, and the adequacy and timing of those consultations is almost always a matter of some controversy, usually along partisan lines. These disputes are most frequent when the use of force may be one of the policy options, a circumstance that intrudes directly on the debate over war powers.

A third problem is the need for secrecy. It is not uncommon for some of the information surrounding particular foreign policy events to be sensitive, including substantial cloaking in classified, secret information. Although members of Congress automatically receive access to classified information by virtue of office, the executive branch inevitably voices concern about who should be given access to the country's highest secrets. Occasionally, this concern is voiced about members themselves, but more frequently, it is directed at congressional staffers, who may not feel the same constraints about divulging information—especially information that supports their particular position on an issue. This problem, it should be added, is not unique to Congress. It is a matter of fact that most of the "leaking" of privileged information occurs within the executive branch itself, in the actions of disaffected agencies or individuals who have been rejected in favor of other policy options.

Greater Concern with Domestic Issues A final area of concern is Congress's greater emphasis on domestic rather than international matters. This emphasis arises in large measure from the nature of the responsibilities of members of Congress: Both senators and representatives are elected from specific states and districts, their primary charge is to represent those areas from which they are elected, and the major concerns of most of their constituents, most of the time, are on domestic policies that affect them directly. This dynamic, however, has two direct effects on congressional activity in the foreign policy arena.

The first is that it means many members spend a good deal less of their time worrying about foreign policy than more directly domestic concerns. Historically, levels of interest have varied considerably by region. Representatives from the West Coast and from the Eastern seaboard have been more internationalist and foreign policy oriented, because they are geographically closer to Asia and Europe and because they are thus more affected by international issues such as trade. Conversely, members from the central part of the country, perceiving themselves to be more insulated from foreign affairs, have tended to be more domestically oriented. But this is a general trend that doesn't hold in every case (note Senator Lugar, from the farm state of Indiana or Senator Fulbright from Arkansas). These historic trends have been broken down by the emergence of intermestic policies and globalization.

The second effect is to add a more partisan influence on how Congress views foreign policy matters than would be the case if foreign and domestic issues could be more easily compartmentalized. A member of Congress with the viewpoint that protecting the interests of constituents is his or her first priority will naturally look at foreign policy concerns first from the vantage point of domestic impact, where the partisan nature of the political process is most obvious. Normally, this tendency to extend the partisan debate is most acute in areas outside clear matters of national security, such as September 11th, where the mandate for unity overrides such concerns. On more mundane foreign policy areas, such as those involved in foreign economic policy or environmental affairs, for instance, partisanship reenters the equation. Nonetheless, we have seen strong partisan attacks on the Obama foreign policy response to the 2011 uprisings in Egypt, to name just one example.

CONGRESSIONAL ACTIVISM IN ACTION: THE BATTLE OVER WAR POWERS

The most dramatic instances of the power clash between Congress and the White House happen over war powers—often even while American troops are in combat. In situations where troop deployments are proposed, the president almost invariably seeks maximum discretion under the guise of his role as commander-in-chief and in the name of national unity. Congress normally responds with an appeal to its constitutional war-making authority—triggering a debate over the appropriate balance of power assigned to the branches since, as noted, wars are rarely declared and the congressional war-making power is rarely invoked.

Disagreement between the government's executive and legislative branches has become increasingly frequent since the Vietnam War. Until nearly the end of the U.S. involvement in Vietnam (which was ultimately mandated by Congress), Congress felt it had been excluded from the important decisions that had defined American commitment to the conflict. The time was ripe for a congressional reassertion of power, with the public foreign policy consensus broken by the war and support for the executive shaken by the Watergate scandal.

The conflict in Vietnam set in motion the dynamics, discussed earlier, that tend to stimulate congressional activism in at least three ways. First, when members of Congress perceive that their constituencies are directly and adversely affected by foreign or national security matters, Congress becomes active and will oppose the executive, as it did in this case. A second dynamic involves executive overreach: the so-called imperial presidency, wherein the Nixon administration essentially considered itself so well qualified in the foreign policy arena that it did not need—and thus did not solicit—congressional advice. In other words, the emperor knew best; if the President does it, it must be right (and legal). Third, Congress came to believe the executive was mishandling foreign affairs. In this case, the length of time it took to extricate the country from Vietnam, as well as from other arguably illegal activities such as the Cambodian incursion of 1970 (when American troops violated Cambodian sovereignty in pursuit of the North Vietnamese), only added fuel to the fire.

The result of these factors was a concerted effort by Congress to rein in the executive's discretion in using armed forces. The movement that ultimately led to the War Powers Resolution was the final product of a long-brewing debate among constitutional scholars and policy makers in the two elected branches, over the question "Whose power is the war power?" Why did so many leaders think it was necessary to pass legislation to clarify this most fundamental issue? Why was that controversial legislation politically attainable in the early 1970s? The answers to both questions are found in four factors: inherent constitutional ambiguity, a long-term trend toward executive dominance on matters of war and peace, the bitter legacy of Vietnam, and the shifting political balance of power between a Democratic-controlled Congress and the Republican administration of Richard Nixon.

Constitutional Ambiguity Concerning War Powers

The Constitution's framers wanted to ensure that the new republic they were creating would be free of what they regarded as the ultimate vice of the European monarchies of the day: the easy resort to war by an unaccountable and unresponsive executive. Records of the Constitutional Convention's debates reflect surprisingly little discussion on allocating the power to commit the country to war. This reflects a broad, though not universal, consensus among the convention's delegates that the executive must not have unilateral power to take the country into war. This consensus was mirrored in the Constitution's working draft, which gave Congress sole power to "make war." As Madison's notes make clear, this slight change was intended to give presidents the ability to respond to sudden, unexpected attacks. This change was most definitely not intended to alter the Founding Fathers' determination to assign to the legislative branch the supreme power of determining if and when the country should initiate hostilities against another country. The desire was for checks and balances, but the ultimate power to declare war clearly resided with Congress.

In light of these considerations, why do we so often speak of constitutional ambiguity with regard to the war power? There are two reasons. First, the constitution named the president as commander-in-chief of the armed forces in order to establish the important principle of civilian supremacy over the country's armed forces. However, the role itself contains the seeds of ambiguity. Ambitious presidents eager to maximize their powers have advanced exceedingly expansive interpretations of what it means to be commander-in-chief. Some even insist that it permits the president to commit U.S. armed forces with or without explicit congressional authorization.

Another source of constitutional ambiguity is the later disagreement among the men who wrote the Constitution over the meaning of what they had written some years after the document came into force. By 1793, James

Madison and Alexander Hamilton, both prominent delegates at Philadelphia, were promoting opposite interpretations of the Constitution's war powers provisions. Hamilton argued that the war power was an inherently executive function, subject to a few legislative checks but not thereby denied to U.S. presidents. In contrast, Madison insisted that the Constitution had clearly made the war power a legislative power, leaving the execution of legislative decisions to the president in his capacity as commander-in-chief. The result of this debate is what former Supreme Court Justice Robert Jackson once spoke of as "a zone of twilight" that lay between the powers of the Congress and the President on matters of war and peace. It is in that "twilight zone" that presidents and legislators have found themselves for the past two centuries.

INTERSECTIONS

The Courts and War Powers

The proper way to handle detainees from the War on Terror at Guantanamo Naval base has been a politically charged issue for years.

The political struggle over war powers has from time to time included the U.S. Supreme Court. The courts normally steer clear of foreign policy cases, either because they are not yet "ripe" for decision or because the courts see them as political—as opposed to legal—questions. There have been some key moments in the contemporary era, however, where the courts have weighed in, though their efforts have certainly not ended the debate about the proper distribution of foreign policy and war powers among the branches.

(Continued)

(Continued)

In the landmark case ***U.S. v. Curtiss-Wright Export Corporation*** (1936), the Supreme Court (by an eight-to-one vote) gave a big victory to those who argue the president ought to be dominant in the area of foreign policy. At issue was a ban on arms sales to Bolivia and Paraguay that Curtiss-Wright violated; they argued that the ban was unconstitutional because it emanated from a broad delegation of power from the Congress to the president. Here Congress passed a joint resolution that handed to President Franklin D. Roosevelt the right to decide when and where to apply bans on arms sales. The Court disagreed, however, finding that the president is the sole guardian of foreign policy power by nature of the office. In a concurring opinion, Justice George Sutherland (a Republican who had served one term in the House of Representatives and two terms in the Senate, representing Utah) even argued that the president is the "sole organ" of American foreign policy.

In a subsequent case, however, the Court took a more balanced approach to institutional cooperation in the area of foreign policy, an approach that is often taken to stand in stark contrast to the approach taken in *Curtiss-Wright*. In ***Youngstown Sheet & Tube v. Sawyer*** (1952), at issue was President Harry Truman's order to the secretary of commerce (Charles W. Sawyer) during a steel mill strike to seize the steel mills and keep them operating. The war in Korea necessitated such an extraordinary emergency exercise of presidential power, the Truman administration argued. The Court disagreed, however, with a six to three majority finding no support for Truman's assertion of emergency powers (when war had not even been declared). In his famous concurring opinion, Justice Robert H. Jackson argued that there are three zones of presidential power relative to Congress. The first zone is when the president acts "pursuant to the express or implied authorization of Congress." Here the President enjoys the greatest amount of power—its zenith. A second, and opposite, zone is when the president acts contrary to the "express or implied will of Congress." Here presidential power is at its nadir. The middle zone is perhaps the most interesting area, the zone where the president acts but the Congress remains silent. Congress has not said the president may act, nor has it said that the president may not. The "zone of twilight" is an area of "concurrent authority," and the area from which much of foreign policy and war powers debate emanates.

The Supreme Court mostly dodged other war powers cases through the 1960s and 1970s, which is perhaps hard to believe given that the Vietnam War raged through this period. Time has mostly leaned away from the "zone of twilight" viewpoint, with an eight to one majority of the Court ruling in *Dames & Moore v. Regan* (1982) in a way that cut against Justice Jackson's "twilight zone" rubric. In that case, the majority of the Court argued that really there are only two cases: ones where Congress objects, and everything else. Thus by the mid-1980s the balance seemed to be tilting back in favor of a strong president in the area of foreign policy, both in terms of Reagan's assertive actions and also the Supreme Court's rulings.

The War on Terrorism would bring another set of interesting cases that speak to the balance of power between the branches, especially focusing on the power

(Continued)

(Continued)
of the president to detain and try people captured by U.S. forces and held at the U.S. military installation at Guantanamo Bay, Cuba. In a key rebuke of executive preeminence, a five to three majority of the Court overturned the plan to try enemy combatants at Guantanamo in *Hamdan v. Rumsfeld* (2006). In another loss for the president, the same court later struck down parts of the process that President Bush then developed with Congress in the Military Commissions Act. The Court was standing up for its own prerogatives as much as it was for Congress's, since there had been an effort to limit court oversight of the executive in the War on Terror and in these cases.

These cases, taken together, speak to the political nature of the question of the proper distribution of power among the branches in the area of foreign policy and war powers. Politics in this domain is partisan (with the two parties fighting against one another on the issues), institutional (with the branches vying with one another for power), and a combination thereof, as often one party controls Congress while another controls the White House—leading to an even more vociferous form of politics. This trend has intensified in recent years as the parties have become more polarized, contributing to an increasingly coarse politics in the area of foreign policy.

Executive Dominance on Matters of War and Peace

As noted, U.S. armed forces have been deployed abroad more than two hundred times since the founding of the Republic, but only five times after a formal declaration of war. Although other conflicts, such as Operation Desert Storm in 1991 and the invasion of Iraq in 2003, were authorized by congressional action short of formal declarations of war, the fact remains that 98 percent of these foreign conflicts were undertaken by presidents whose interpretation of their prerogatives as commander-in-chief included committing forces into harm's way without a prior formal authorization by Congress.

Those presidents' broad view of their powers has been buttressed by a long succession of executive branch apologists of presidential supremacy. For example, President Truman dispatched U.S. troops to Korea in the summer of 1950, leading the country into a major conflict that lasted for three years, with neither congressional approval of his actions nor a formal declaration of war against North Korea. He believed that he was empowered to undertake such a step on his own authority, a position buttressed by a State Department memorandum prepared within days of the troop dispatch that asserted that a president's power as commander-in-chief is virtually unlimited and the president can order troops into combat without congressional authorization owing to his inherent foreign affairs powers.

By the late 1960s and early 1970s, this mounting record of presidentially initiated hostilities, coupled with broad dissemination of intellectual rationalizations on behalf of executive dominance, persuaded a growing number of legislators of the need to restore the balance between the two elected branches to a level that more closely approximated the Founding Fathers' intentions.

The Trauma of Vietnam

Reaction to the American experience in Vietnam pushed Congress over the edge into an activist role aimed at curbing the president's ability to use armed force at his discretion. Some of the reaction was the result of self-examination. Before American ground troops were committed to combat, Congress granted the president broad latitude to use force in Vietnam, a grant later regretted. This permission came in the form of the famous **Tonkin Gulf Resolution**, which was adopted in August 1964. Passed after only token debate, the measure was unanimously endorsed by the House of Representatives and met with only two dissenting votes in the Senate.

In its haste to demonstrate a unified U.S. front to the Vietnamese communists, Congress enacted a resolution in support of the president. The exceedingly sweeping language declared, "The Congress approves and supports the determination of the President, as Commander in Chief, to take all necessary measures to repel any armed attack against the forces of the United States and to prevent further aggression." A bit later, in Section 2, it asserted, "The United States is ... prepared, as the President determines, to take all necessary steps, including the use of armed force." Within a week of passing the Tonkin Gulf Resolution, the Johnson administration's justice department argued that the grant of authority was the "functional equivalent" of a declaration of war.

Years later, as the national consensus that spawned the Tonkin Gulf Resolution dissolved in a monsoon of failure in Southeast Asia, members of Congress would look back on their fateful votes of August 1964 with grief and bitterness. By the early 1970s, with the magnitude of the Vietnam disaster clear for all to see, and as questions emerged about the factual circumstances that prompted the 1964 Resolution in the first place, even the most passive lawmakers knew that something had to be done. Never again, they vowed, should the Congress so promiscuously hand over its constitutional prerogatives to the president. Their determination to reclaim legislative war-making powers was strengthened in 1971 when Congress repealed the Tonkin Gulf Resolution, only to have the Nixon administration claim an inherent executive right to prosecute the Vietnam War, with or without explicit congressional authorization.

It was in this context that Congress used the power of the purse to shut down American involvement in the war in Southeast Asia. Starting in 1970, Congress prohibited the use of funds for military operations in Cambodia. In 1973 and 1974 it ended the use of funds for operations in Vietnam itself, as well as in Laos and Cambodia, unless the administration came to Congress to secure a new specific authorization for military force.

Partisanship and Policy Making

By 1973, the Democratic Party had held firm majorities in both houses of Congress for nearly two decades; however, Democrats had captured the White House in only two of the previous six presidential elections. The force of partisanship, then, joined the built-in tensions for political supremacy created by a separation-of-powers system of government. Either force could make political cooperation difficult; together, they produced interbranch gridlock.

In addition to these two political forces, two other closely related factors made legislative-executive relations particularly volatile in the early 1970s: the rising tide of sentiment taking root in Congress in general to reassert its authority and the declining prestige of the presidency caused by the Vietnam fiasco and the Watergate scandal. During most of the Cold War, Congress had frequently deferred to presidential leadership on foreign policy issues. This was due in large part to the belief that U.S. presidents were generally honest and prudent custodians of the national interest. The back-to-back disasters of President Johnson's Vietnam policy and the Nixon administration's dishonesty and criminality, however, combined to rock the foundations of presidential dignity and respect. By 1973, with Nixon evermore grimly impaled on the stake of Watergate, his political opponents—mostly liberal, mostly Democrats, and mostly members of Congress—were only too eager to capitalize on his weakened position to reclaim and reassert legislative foreign policy powers that had atrophied during the Cold War.

The War Powers Act

Given these dynamics, Congress became determined to construct a piece of procedural legislation that would help prevent future wars that drag on forever (Vietnam) as well as secret wars about which Congress is not informed (Cambodia). The resulting **War Powers Act** (WPA) was passed in 1973 over the veto of President Nixon; every president since has opposed the WPA to some degree, seeing it as an unconstitutional infringement on the powers of the Presidency. Compliance with the requirements of the Act has been, at best, imperfect—leading many to see the WPA as a failure; some point to some hidden successes of the Act, however.

The WPA has three key provisions that specify when the president must *consult* with Congress, when he must *report* to Congress, and when he must *terminate* hostilities and withdraw U.S. armed forces. Much of the WPA is relatively noncontroversial, but the components that deal with introducing forces into hostilities are quite contentious. A brief look at each of these provisions should clarify what Congress intended through this legislation and should help the reader appreciate the difficulties of translating general legislative intent into precise, unambiguous statutory language.

The requirement that presidents consult with Congress before committing armed forces to hostilities states, "The President in every possible instance shall consult with Congress before introducing United States Armed Forces into hostilities or into situations where imminent involvement in hostilities is clearly indicated by the circumstances." Although the section's general intent is clear enough, translating that intention into executive conduct presents several problems. It is not entirely clear what presidents would have to do to satisfy the requirement that they "consult with Congress." Do they need to acquire congressional approval before acting? The WPA does not seem to go quite that far, but it does suggest a good bit more than mere presidential notification of impending moves. If the precise meaning of *consultation* is not entirely clear, neither is the precise identity of with whom the president must consult. The WPA does not stipulate who and how many members of Congress must be consulted to fulfill the spirit of the Act. Finally, as the resolution's language concedes, the president must consult with Congress "in every possible instance," implying that in some instances prior consultations are exempted as impractical. For example, at the time of the *Mayaguez* incident in 1975, four key congressional leaders were in Greece, four others were in China, and others were scattered in their states and districts. With whom did President Ford have to consult in that case?

The resolution's second key provision is the reporting requirement, which obligates the president to report to Congress within forty-eight hours anytime U.S. armed forces are dispatched: (1) "into hostilities or into situations where imminent involvement in hostilities is clearly indicated by the circumstances"; (2) into foreign territory while "equipped for combat"; or (3) "in numbers which substantially enlarge United States Armed Forces equipped for combat already located in a foreign nation." Between these two provisions, the WPA should serve to prevent future wars from being kept secret from Congress and help protect Congress's constitutional powers in a new era of undeclared wars.

The third and final key provision of the WPA deals with the termination of hostilities and the withdrawal of U.S. forces. As mentioned above, the drafters of the WPA were determined to prevent prolonged conflicts like Vietnam in the future, so they rewrote the ground rules so that any protracted hostilities involving U.S. forces would require explicit legislative approval. Congress, it was said, would share the controls of foreign policy takeoffs—not just the crash landings.

The WPA spells out two means for achieving this congressional codetermination. First, once the president has reported to Congress that U.S. forces are being introduced into hostilities or into circumstances indicating imminent hostilities, the so-called sixty-day clock begins. Thus, the president will be without legal authority to continue conducting hostilities unless Congress acts within sixty days to: (1) declare war; (2) adopt a specific authorization (such as the Tonkin Gulf Resolution or the resolution that preceded the invasion of Iraq); or (3) extend the president's war-making authority beyond sixty days. Here is the really controversial part: Under the WPA, if the Congress takes no action at all following the president's report, the president is legally bound to terminate hostilities sixty days after that initial report to Congress. (An additional thirty days are authorized if needed for the safe withdrawal of troops, for a total of no more than ninety days maximum, unless Congress specifically provides otherwise.)

The War Powers Act includes another congressional tool for terminating hostilities, although the constitutionality of this mechanism would seem to have been found lacking by the U.S. Supreme Court. This second mechanism that was included in the WPA provides that Congress can order a cessation of

U.S. involvement in hostilities at any point simply by adopting what is called a "concurrent resolution." The crucial point here is that a concurrent resolution is one that is adopted by simple majorities of the House and Senate, and thus does not require the president's signature to take effect and is not subject to presidential veto. In light of a 1983 Supreme Court ruling *(INS* v. *Chadha)* that struck down so-called legislative vetoes, this particular mechanism would appear to be unconstitutional if it were invoked.

Presidents since 1973 have opposed the WPA on the political grounds that it unwisely restricts presidential prerogative in dealing with foreign adversaries and on veiled grounds of constitutionality (the legislative veto). No one has tested the WPA in court. Most argue that Congress has not because it fears the resolution would be ruled unconstitutional, while presidents have not because the mere threat of a test allows them to elude or sidestep its requirements. Auerswald and Cowhey, however, show that there is some evidence that since the passage of the WPA presidents have tended to use force for shorter durations and have been perhaps more sensitive to Congress's concerns about the uses of force than had previously been the case. The use of force in Somalia and the first Persian Gulf War, for example, both had significant "negotiated" elements to them, even though the WPA itself was not invoked.

INTERSECTIONS

Intervention in Libya and the War Powers Act

In February 2011, uprisings in Libya thrust that North African Arab state onto the list of "Arab Spring" countries. In the 1980s the Reagan administration used force against Muammar Gaddafi in response to Libya's support for international terrorism. In recent years, however, even in the midst of the "regime change" agenda of the Bush Doctrine, the United States and Libya had become closer following Libya's renunciation of weapons of mass destruction. Now, once again, the U.S. government was confronted with trouble in Libya as Gaddafi's forces unleashed brutal attacks not just on rebels but also on civilians around the country.

In March, the United Nations Security Council authorized member states to take all steps necessary to protect civilian populations, including a "no-fly zone." NATO began to work together to enforce the no-fly zone and to launch strikes against government forces in what was named "Operation Odyssey Dawn." In July 2011 the administration announced that it would recognize the rebels in Libya as the legitimate government of that state, increasing the pressure on Gaddafi. Over the course of the intervention, U.S. involvement in NATO attacks was mostly reduced to missile strikes from drone aircraft, but nonetheless controversy stirred about whether the Obama administration was pursuing this intervention in ways that violated the War Powers Act.

(Continued)

(Continued)

Unlike the wars in Afghanistan and Iraq, which followed congressional authorizations, the Obama administration did not pursue congressional "approval" of the Libyan intervention. Given that through this operation President Obama had arguably moved troops into hostilities, congressional Republicans especially pushed the point that the President was acting outside the WPA. While Republicans on the Hill have been largely critical of the WPA over the last thirty years, in this case they embraced it as a way to strike back against what they saw as executive encroachment on Congress's war powers.

The Obama administration argued that the WPA does not apply in this case, first because they consulted extensively with Congress on the operation, and second because the nature of the intervention did not meet the standard set by the legislation. The top legal advisor for the State Department, Harold Koh—a fierce critic of executive overreaching on war powers in his academic career—argued that U.S. involvement in the operation fell short of "hostilities" as contemplated in the WPA. Here, Koh argues, U.S. forces were only sometimes faced with peril, given the military capabilities of Gaddafi's forces, and indeed many of the strikes launched by U.S. forces were from drone aircraft—putting no pilots at risk. It has been reported that there was a difference of opinion inside the administration about this legal advice, with some arguing that the WPA did apply, but this was the administration's position throughout the conflict. In the autumn of 2011 the Gaddafi regime collapsed in Libya, although it will take some time before Libya's future becomes clear.

As with many foreign policy cases, this instance raises twin issues. First, it is open for debate whether one sees the role of the United States and NATO as heroic or misguided. Second, the political and hyperpartisan nature of the debate is noteworthy. Interestingly, many who objected to George W. Bush's use of war powers found the Libyan intervention acceptable; conversely, many longtime opponents of the WPA embraced it in this instance to try to tie President Obama's hands. James Madison and Alexander Hamilton could probably not have even imagined a foreign policy setting like the one we now take for granted as "normal."

As a practical matter, compliance with the WPA occurs when it is easy and convenient to do so, and it is ignored or violated (for instance, reporting after the fact or informing rather than consulting) when it is not. A frequent presidential reaction is to ask for a congressional resolution supporting military action in advance of hostilities, as was done in 1990–1991 before the Persian Gulf War and again in 2002 in anticipation of hostilities with Iraq. Presidents generally have dodged the sixty-day clock by reporting to congressional leadership "consistent with but not *pursuant* to" the requirements of the WPA. Critics of the WPA see this record of reporting as indicative of the Act's failures. Some, however, have argued that the WPA has nonetheless accomplished the *spirit* of what it set out to do—to stimulate more partnership between the branches in the area of war powers—if not in the exact form specified in the WPA.

CONGRESSIONAL POWERS AND POLICY TYPES

One thing that should be apparent from the discussion in this chapter is that not all "foreign policy" is alike; indeed, there are different kinds of foreign policy, and Congress tends to play a different role (vis-à-vis the president, for example) in these different policy types. As Ripley and Franklin discuss in *Congress, the Bureaucracy and Public Policy* (and as introduced in Chapter Three of this book) one type of foreign policy that exists—and perhaps the type that most Americans think of when they think of foreign policy—is "crisis policy." **Crisis policy** deals with emergencies and threats to the country. Crises often are a surprise, and they usually include at least the potential for the use of force. These are the kinds of situations in which people tend to rally to the president. Iraq's invasion of Kuwait in 1990 is an example of a crisis, as is 9/11. Crisis policy making tends to be dominated by the president and a small group of advisors that presidents draw on to help make decisions. There is not much congressional activism in this area, since all the dynamics accrue to the advantage of the president. The battle over war powers tends to play out in this context.

Another type of foreign policy is **strategic policy**, which lays out the basic stance of the United States toward another country (U.S. policy toward Cuba, for example) or toward a particular issue or problem (for example, terrorism or climate change). Foreign policy strategy tends to be developed by the executive branch, often through the type of interagency process discussed earlier. Nonetheless, Congress and its members can get access to strategic policy by finding out that a strategy review is under way and making their preferences known, sometimes by holding hearings on the topic.

In 2010 the Obama administration undertook a review of U.S. nuclear posture, seeking to update the answer to the question of why and for what purpose the United States maintains a large arsenal of nuclear weapons. This came to be called the Nuclear Posture Review. It was no secret that the review was under way, and many members of Congress got engaged to try to coax the process along in one way or another. Some also tried to link their vote on the coming START Treaty to the policy that the Obama administration emerged with—some Republican Senators, for example, threatened to vote against the treaty if the administration adopted a "no first use" policy or didn't agree to upgrade U.S. nuclear facilities.

Some dramatic examples of Congress taking the reins of strategic policy were discussed previously, such as the South Africa sanctions bill and the Helms-Burton Act that codified the U.S. embargo of Cuba. While these cases are the exception, not the rule, and Congress is far more likely to legislate procedurally (as in Goldwater-Nichols) than substantively (as with Helms-Burton), the opportunities to set the course of the ship of state certainly exist.

Another interesting example of procedural legislation in the strategic policy domain has to do with treaties in the area of free trade. Sometimes called "Fast Track," Trade Promotion Authority (also discussed in Chapter Eleven) was first constructed in the 1970s to try to make it easier for presidents to negotiate and pass trade agreements. When a president works within Fast Track, which has been authorized several times, most recently during part of the George W. Bush administration, foreign trade treaties go up under a rule that allows no changes to the treaty—making it easier for the president to be able to negotiate, in theory, because there is less concern that Congress will change the terms of the agreement. Such agreements also require only a majority in the Senate, rather than the supermajority specified in the Constitution. However, it also must pass a majority vote in the House of Representatives. The North American Free Trade Act, NAFTA, was passed under these rules, for example.

The third type of foreign policy is called **Structural Defense Policy**, which focuses on the policies and programs that deal with the defense budget and military bases, such as buying new aircraft. Congress has a tendency to actually include more things in the defense budget than the president or the Pentagon even wants, for example, because those projects mean jobs in congressional districts. The struggle over whether the United States will build a second engine for the new F-35 fighter jet, something neither President Obama nor then-Defense Secretary Gates wanted but which many members of Congress would like to see, is a classic example of Congress being very active in this policy type.

If more defense spending is seen by many members of Congress as a good thing, less defense spending is often seen as a bad thing, killing jobs in members' districts. When it comes to closing military bases in the United States—the warning sirens really sound. Starting in the 1990s, as the Cold War came to an end, Congress even constructed a special process for determining base closings, a process designed to protect individual members so that their constituents would not blame them for being ineffective if they lost a military base. The Defense Base Realignment and Closure process (BRAC for short) was established and when utilized would require the Pentagon to issue a study and make recommendations for base closings and consolidations that would be submitted to the BRAC Commission. The members of the commission are appointed by the president but confirmed by the Senate. The commission is meant to be independent and nonpartisan. The commission issues recommendations to Congress about base closings and realignment. Congress then must vote up or down, whole hog or none, on the entire list; no changes or substitutions allowed. Congress is central to the defense budget process; they can't dodge it even when they want to.

CONCLUSIONS

As the combined discussions in Chapters Four through Six have sought to convey, the country's Founding Fathers purposely divided political powers among the two principal political branches of the federal government and created what has famously been called an invitation to struggle between them. The Constitution carefully sought to create a coequality of power between the two branches, although, as noted, opinions differed about the exact nature of that balance at the time. The relationship in the area of foreign policy has been evolving ever since. In order to understand the foreign policy powers of these two branches, it is necessary to see the powers of each body in interactive form (Table 6.2). They are shared powers, which means (among other things) that a political process determines that the "proper" amount of control is to be exercised by either branch.

The political struggle for preeminence is one where the executive has formidable advantages over the less focused legislative branch. For instance, no single member of Congress is the clear focus of national attention in the foreign policy area the way the president is. While Congress can pass legislation, the president can veto it, which can be overridden, but only with a supermajority of both Houses—a steep standard. The Senate must ratify treaties, but presidents have increasingly eluded this power by using executive agreements. Similarly, the Senate must ratify many presidential appointments, but the president can dodge this power in foreign affairs by appointing controversial figures to work at the National Security Council Staff. And while Congress has the power to declare war, the commander-in-chief has sent troops to use force abroad absent such a declaration dozens of times since the end of World War II, and more than twenty times since the passage of the War Powers Act.

At the same time, it is also true that Congress serves a useful monitoring and oversight role, even when it is generally acquiescing to presidential leadership. Individual members of Congress have become increasingly

TABLE 6.2

Sharing Foreign Policy Power

Powers of Congress	Powers of the President	Presidential Advantage
Pass legislation and override vetoes	Veto legislation	Difficult to harness enough votes to override a veto
Spending power		
Senate confirmation power	Nominate and appoint	Can appoint controversial nominees to National Security Council (staff)
Oversight power		Classify information and operations at the CIA or DOD
Declare war	Commander-in-chief	Take initiative to send troops abroad
Senate treaty ratification	Make treaties	Use executive agreements
	Receive foreign ambassadors	

active in the foreign policy arena since Vietnam, with much of that activity being driven both by policy interest and by partisanship. Congress as an institution has become more politically polarized in recent decades, and it tends to be more assertive in the midst of controversial presidential action. Activism is most pronounced when different parties control the two branches, although single-party dominance does not guarantee smooth sailing either.

Times of crisis tend to galvanize the relationship: great crises like September 11th tend to cement support around the executive (the rally around the flag effect), but controversial executive actions (for example, Vietnam) may turn such events into points of contention wherein Congress asserts itself once again. Congress has particular power over the defense budget, and even during periods of acquiescence Congress is at the center of policy making on budgetary matters.

WHERE DO WE GO FROM HERE?

This chapter raises issues that have been debated since the founding of the Republic, issues that can be life-and-death issues, such as decisions to use military force and the role of the Congress in making those decisions. While access to power over foreign policy varies by policy type, at the end of the day the ability to play a significant part in forging American foreign policy is not only about Congress, it is also about us. In our Republic, elected officials make policy, and if congressional access to an entire type of foreign policy is cut off—war powers, for example—then the very health of the Republic potentially suffers.

One of the reasons that Congress may not be as active in foreign policy as some of the Framers had intended is that members of Congress pay attention to voters and what voters care about, and many times the public does not pay much attention to foreign policy issues. So perhaps one way for Congress to get even more involved in foreign policy is if citizens take a more active interest and express that interest to our elected representatives.

APPLICATION: GO TO CAPITOL HILL (VIRTUALLY, AT LEAST)

While the terrorist attacks of September 11th have led to greater security around the Capital, and the January 2011 shooting of Arizona Representative Gabrielle Giffords (and many others who were at her "Congress in Your Corner" event) has caused other steps to be taken to try to ensure the safety of members of Congress, Congress and its members are still incredibly accessible in person and certainly online. When you go to Washington, D.C., you should visit your representative, but why wait until then when you can visit online? Check out the websites of Congress. All members of Congress have websites, and many of them are on Facebook, YouTube, and Twitter too. Their websites usually post information about the work that the member is involved in, including committee work. Congressional committees also have useful websites that announce hearings and post testimony and reports.

Another useful source of information about Congress and foreign policy are the reports of the Congressional Research Service (CRS). The interesting thing about CRS reports is that they are produced for Members of Congress who request a report. CRS reports only get "released" to the public when the Members release them. There are several websites that try to gather as many CRS reports as they can. One of the most useful is OpenCRS.com. Go check it out. Search for "foreign policy report" across a range of policy types and see for yourself what kind of information is provided by this "in-house" research service. You might even find these reports helpful for your classes and term papers.

STUDY/DISCUSSION QUESTIONS

1. What are the main foreign policy powers, both formal and informal, of Congress?
2. Taking into account this chapter and the chapter on the Presidency, how are Congress's powers often at a disadvantage relative to the president?
3. How is Congress constrained from being a major foreign policy player, perhaps especially when it comes to war powers?
4. Congressional activism in the foreign policy domain has been on the rise (though still with ebbs and flows) since Vietnam. Why?
5. Why are War Powers such a complicated question, when the Constitution spells out the powers of each branch?
6. What is the War Powers Act? Has it been a success or a failure?
7. What are "policy types," and how do they help us understand congressional foreign policy power?

CORE SUGGESTED READINGS

Carter, Ralph G., and James M. Scott. *Choosing to Lead: Understanding Congressional Foreign Policy Entrepreneurs*. Durham, NC: Duke University Press, 2009. Excellent study that tracks the rise of congressional entrepreneurialism in foreign policy; includes data collection and case studies.

Fisher, Louis. *Constitutional Abdication on War and Spending*. College Station: Texas A&M University Press, 2000. The gold standard of studies of Congress and war powers in the modern era.

Kelley, Donald R. *Divided Power: The Presidency, Congress, and the Formation of American Foreign Policy*. Little Rock: University of Arkansas Press, 2005. A collection of essays by outstanding scholars, each taking a different angle on the complex relationship between the Presidency and the Congress in the area of foreign policy.

Lindsay, James M. *Congress and the Politics of U.S. Foreign Policy*. Baltimore, MD: The Johns Hopkins University Press, 1994. Still the best explanation of Congress's sometimes hidden role in the foreign policy process.

Mann, Thomas E., and Normal J. Ornstein. *The Broken Branch: How Congress Is Failing America and How to Get It Back on Track*. New York: Oxford University Press, 2008. Focusing on more than just foreign policy, this book is excellent for understanding congressional incentives and behavior.

ADDITIONAL READINGS AND REFERENCES

Auerswald, David P., and Peter F. Cowhey. "Ballotbox Diplomacy: The War Powers Resolution and the Use of Force." *International Studies Quarterly* 41 (1997), 505–528.

Blechman, Barry M. *The Politics of National Security: Congress and U.S. Defense Policy.* New York: Oxford University Press, 1990.

Brown. Eugene. *J. William Fulbright: Advice and Dissent.* Iowa City: University of Iowa Press, 1985.

Brown, Sherrod. *Congress from the Inside.* Kent, OH: Kent University Press, 2000.

Campbell, Colin C., Nicole C. Rae, and John F. Stack Jr. (eds.). *Congress and the Politics of Foreign Policy.* Upper Saddle River, NJ: Prentice Hall, 2003.

Crabb, Cecil V.M. *Invitation to Struggle: Congress, the President, and Foreign Policy* (4th ed.). Washington, DC: CQ Press, 2004.

Fisher, Louis. *The Constitution and 9/11: Recurring Threats to America's Freedom.* Lawrence: University Press of Kansas, 2008.

Frank, Thomas M., and Edward Weisband. *Foreign Policy by Congress.* New York: Oxford University Press, 1979.

Hersman, Rebecca K.C. *Friends and Foes: How Congress and the President Really Make Foreign Policy*. Washington, DC: The Brookings Institution, 2000.

Hinckley, Barbara. *Less than Meets the Eye: Foreign Policy Making and the Myth of the Assertive Congress.* Chicago, IL: University of Chicago Press, 1994.

Howell, William G., and Jon C. Pevehouse. "When Congress Stops Wars." *Foreign Affairs* 86, 5 (2007), 1–7.

Johnson, Robert David. *Congress and the Cold War*. New York: Cambridge University Press, 2005.

Koh, Harold H. *The National Security Constitution.* New Haven, CT: Yale University Press, 1990.

Kriner, Douglas L. *After the Rubicon: Congress, Presidents, and the Politics of Waging War.* Chicago: University of Chicago Press, 2010.

Moss, Kenneth B. *Undeclared War and the Future of U.S. Foreign Policy*. Baltimore, MD: The Johns Hopkins University Press, 2008.

Ripley, Randall B., and Grace A. Franklin. *Congress, the Bureaucracy and Public Policy.* Brooks/Cole, 1987.

Ripley, Randall B., and James M. Lindsay (eds.). *Congress Resurgent: Foreign and Defense Policy on Capitol Hill.* Ann Arbor: University of Michigan Press, 1993.

Stennis, John C. *The Role of Congress in Foreign Policy.* Washington, DC: American Enterprise Institute, 1971.

Wilson, George C. This War Really Matters: Inside the Fight for Defense Dollars. Washington, DC: CQ Press, 1999.

CHAPTER

7

Interest Groups and Think Tanks

The Obama administration had hoped to alter the domestic politics in the United States that surrounds the peace process as a way of moving toward a two-state solution.

PREVIEW

Two sets of actors outside the formal structures of government that try to influence the foreign policy of the United States are interest groups and think tanks. Interest groups are formal organizations with members who share a common interest that try to pool their resources in order to promote policies that are in line with their common interest. The primary way that interest groups try to do this is through lobbying—trying to influence policy makers in Congress and the executive branch—with persuasive information, education, and electoral pressure. Many interest groups also have political action committees (PACs) that raise money for and donate to candidates for office as part of the groups' overall lobbying strategy. The number and complexity of these groups in general, including in the foreign policy realm, has dramatically expanded since the 1970s. Think tanks have traditionally been organizations that pursue knowledge in a scholarly way and try to bring that knowledge to bear on the world of policy making. In recent years, however, many new think tanks have emerged that are not bound by the norms of disinterested social science. Indeed, the think tank world has become far more ideological and partisan as these groups vie for influence using some of the same techniques as interest groups. In practical terms the dividing line between an interest group and a think tank is starting to become blurry.

KEY CONCEPTS

American Israel Public Affairs Committee (AIPAC)
J Street
Council on Foreign Relations (CFR)
Interest Group
Lobbying
Political Action Committee (PAC)
Military-Industrial Complex
Iron Triangle
Subgovernments
Revolving Door
Ethnic Interest Groups
Cuban American National Foundation (CANF)
Think Tank
Heritage Foundation

When scholars and practitioners of U.S. foreign policy think about Jewish American lobbying, they traditionally think about the **American Israel Public Affairs Committee**, or **AIPAC** for short. AIPAC was founded in the 1950s to promote a close relationship between the United States and Israel, in part because many Jewish Americans (and others) were concerned that U.S. policy in the Middle East at that time was tilted toward the Arab states in the region. Over time AIPAC rose to be thought of as not only one of the most powerful ethnic interest groups in Washington, D.C., but as one of the most powerful interest groups of any kind.

AIPAC has its critics, however, including critics within the Jewish American community who see AIPAC as tied too closely to the policy preferences of the Likud, or conservative, party in Israel. Some others are concerned that there is not a strong enough voice for those in the community—as well as Americans of non-Jewish backgrounds—who support a "two-state" solution to the long struggle between Israelis and Palestinians. In Washington, D.C., hardly anything happens fast, but in the domain of ethnic interest groups and their influence, something has happened in the blink of an eye: the emergence of **J Street** as a major new player in the politics of U.S. policy toward the Middle East.

According to its website, J Street (the name is metaphorical, since there is no literal "J Street" in Washington) is a lobbying organization that was formed in 2008 to pressure for continued U.S. involvement in the Middle East peace process toward the goal of a peaceful and enduring settlement including the states of Israel and Palestine. Practically overnight J Street has emerged as a significant player in this policy process. Some of this success, as evidenced by the presence of key Obama administration officials speaking at their annual conferences, has come about because the views of Jewish Americans (and Americans generally) toward the peace process and a two-state solution evolved enough in recent years that there was an opening for a different type of policy advocacy than that of AIPAC. But part of it has emerged because of the efforts of the Obama presidential campaign and administration to try to change the dynamics of the lobbying universe around U.S. policy toward the peace process.

In the 2008 campaign, the Obama team sponsored several Jewish outreach committees in major cities around the United States, hoping to help bring forth some "new leadership" from Jewish Americans (that is, not AIPAC). After winning the election, the Obama transition team met with a much wider variety of Jewish groups than those that the Bush administration regularly consulted, many of which had no or little access to the Bush administration. While these groups would go on to lobby the administration and Congress on a range of issues, they were also the *targets* of lobbying by the new Obama administration. The Obama administration was trying to create room, and a place at the table, for peace-oriented groups such as J Street, as well as for others (in other words, for groups other than AIPAC).

J Street and many other groups (and the Obama administration) have tried to capitalize on surveys that showed that views of Jewish Americans were more balanced toward the Middle East than what AIPAC represented and more balanced than the policy promoted by the Bush administration. For instance, a July 2009 survey found that 60 percent of American Jews opposed further Israeli settlements in the occupied territories, and they supported the proposition that the United States should be actively engaged in the peace process even if that entailed "publicly stating its disagreements with both the Israelis and the Arabs" by large margins.

In spite of high hopes that the Obama administration would be able to move the peace process forward, little progress has been made to date (as discussed at the start of Chapter One). In part this illustrates how difficult it is to craft foreign policy today. The forces of globalization unleashed by the end of the Cold War have made the world more complex in a variety of ways, making it far harder for the United States to control events than it was during the Cold War. And hyperpartisanship at home has made foreign policy proposals far more open to the dynamics of "domestic politics" than was the case in the past. The image of Israeli Prime Minister Netanyahu and President Obama sparring over words not even spoken is an example of this new political environment. The rapid emergence of J Street, and the help it has gotten from the White

House in that rise, is also a sign of the new environment that policy makers must work in, as well as the increasing role of interest groups (and think tanks) in the policy-making process.

So far in the discussion of how U.S. foreign policy is made, primary attention has been focused on the governmental actors who are involved in the policy process, but not everyone who is involved—or wants to be involved—in foreign policy development gets a paycheck from the government. In addition to the elected and appointed officials who compose the federal government, there is a large, diverse, and increasingly complex set of individuals and groups who exist outside the formal realm of government but who nonetheless seek to influence the ship of state. Most of these people and groups can be found in the Washington, D.C., area, and whether or not their offices are actually inside or outside the Interstate 495 beltway that rings the District of Columbia, they are (or aspire to be) "inside the beltway" operators who try to influence foreign policy.

Historically, most of these actors have actually tried to stay out of the public spotlight, lobbying members of Congress or of the executive branch informally at cocktail parties, fundraisers, and at charity and sporting events (Washington Redskins football tickets are still in greater demand than are tickets for the Capitals, Nationals, or the Wizards). This "invisible government," as it is sometimes called, provides a revolving door for individuals to move in and out of government and the organizations that seek to influence government over time. When the Obama administration arrived as the Bush team left, the ritual shuffling of insiders and outsiders also followed.

One of the results of this constant shuffling is an added opaqueness to the public's understanding of what really transpires in government, particularly in the area of foreign policy. In this realm, the general lack of public attention to and awareness of foreign policy matters has meant that not only do most people not understand how foreign policy is made, but those who actually try to influence and make foreign policy do so with relatively little public scrutiny. Foreign policy is perhaps the last preserve of elite groups and individuals with special expertise; these elites are often only too happy to protect the myth that foreign policy is too complicated, too important, or both, for most Americans to be involved in it.

This dynamic is what ensures that individuals and small elite groups can have an impact on foreign policy that is greatly out of proportion with their relative numerical size. As just one example, there are about 310 million people in the United States, but one of the most powerful and respected foreign policy organizations in the United States has only about 4300 members: the **Council on Foreign Relations** (CFR). Perhaps the granddaddy of all foreign policy organizations, the CFR was founded in 1921 and has its headquarters on Park Avenue in New York City and offices in Washington, D.C., just two blocks from the White House. CFR has a large professional staff and publishes the influential *Foreign Affairs* magazine.

The conventional roles of those who seek to influence the government have also bred orthodox ways of categorizing and looking at what those people do. As discussed in this chapter, some of these roles are changing as the post–Cold War and post-9/11 environment evolves. Another important point is that the nature and types of these groups is also changing because of the changing political, electoral, and even legal environment in which these groups operate. So before going any further, it is necessary to start with some basic definitions and distinctions.

TYPES OF GROUPS

The first and historically most important traditional outside influences have been **interest groups**, organizations that represent a group of people or institutions with common interests that they want to see promoted or protected. These organizations have traditionally served as key gatekeepers between the mass public and the formal structures of the government itself. This gatekeeping function entails funneling the public's preferences and positions toward public policy. Interest groups, in a classic sense, gather information about policies their followers want and then represent those preferences to the Congress and the executive branch through a variety of means. The ways that these groups try to promote their interests to the government can be through **lobbying** (trying to convince members of Congress or their staffs or executive agency officials to support their position), education (such as writing articles for newspapers or testifying before Congress), and electoral pressure (trying to convince officials that they will suffer electoral defeat if they defy the will of the group, or by offering electoral support if they support the position of the group). In this sense, interest groups are also classic "linkage" mechanisms that connect the people to the government.

The function performed by interest groups is provided for in the First Amendment to the Constitution, which guarantees the right to "petition the Government for a redress of grievances." The basic idea underlying this right was discussed in the *Federalist Papers* and it finds its modern expression in the idea of pluralism, the notion that multiple competing interests should be freely able to compete for influence in our governmental system.

Largely because these groups seek to exert pressure on the government, their work has always come under some public suspicion and continues to do so—in spite of the fact that interest groups are important, legal, and long-standing members of the American political system. While those who make their careers as lobbyists for pressure groups see their efforts as "Washington representation" for interests that are dispersed across the country, the public—and sometimes aspiring officeholders—can view these groups in a less favorable light. A variety of types of legislation that require groups and individuals who lobby the government to register and to disclose many of their activities reflects the suspicion that many have about these groups (although the rigor with which these regulations are enforced remains a matter of some debate). As discussed below, much of the impetus for campaign finance reform is also aimed at reining in the influence of these pressure groups. Public suspicion of interest groups and their activities also parallels the American people's suspicion of government. The term "Washington insider" has become a pejorative phrase in some circles, encompassing all professional Washington politicians, and is often a phrase used as a rallying cry by candidates who run for office against incumbents, whom they seek to defile by using the term. It doesn't hurt that many Washington representatives are consummate examples of the term.

The aura of favoritism and elitism that surrounds many of the traditional methods of influence—for example, throwing fancy fund-raisers for officials who can help one's cause, contributing campaign funds or funds to a candidate's favorite charity, or hosting trips to lavish vacation and golf spots around the globe under the guise of a "seminar"—offend public sensibilities in an ethics-conscious era, and these images are made more offensive during a time of economic difficulty for many Americans. The conspicuous way, for instance, that large corporations, such as the disgraced Enron, or BP after the oil spill in the Gulf of Mexico, seek to curry political favor sends many politicians scurrying for distance from those who appear to have violated the public trust; and many professional politicians hop on the bandwagon of chastising the very groups with whom they sometimes had a close relationship in the past. Nonetheless, many of the top contributors to political candidates over the last twenty years are key defense industry players, such as Lockheed Martin, General Electric, Boeing, Northrop Grumman, General Dynamics, Honeywell, and Raytheon. Whether or not this pattern of giving is connected to the size or resilience of the U.S. defense budget (which is nearly as large as the total amount of defense spending by the rest of the world combined) is something citizens will have to decide for themselves.

As alluded to above, another source of suspicion about interest groups has to do with the resources that they have at their disposal, resources that some see as leading these groups to have disproportionate power. Many interest groups have as part of their structure **political action committees**, or PACs. The primary purpose of the PACs is to raise money that is then funneled to candidates for office in the form of campaign contributions. The donation strategy of a PAC is obviously linked to the pressure strategy of the group; campaign funds can be directed to officials who have supported a group's interests in the past, or used to try to target an official for defeat if that official has not been supportive in the past. Over the last thirty years, a variety of attempts to limit the amount of this kind of money in political campaigns have been made, both in terms of regulating the amounts of money that can be given and the kinds of contributions that can be made. Like water finding the lowest point, however, money seems to always find a way around these restrictions, making the world of money and politics one of the most complex and fast-changing arenas around. These classic PACs tied to a typical interest group are only one of a variety of types of groups that pump money into politics.

The foreign policy-making process, and the defense budget process in particular, is not immune to these kinds of activities and suspicions. One of the first and most widely publicized critiques of the possible nefarious relationship between interest groups, money, and the policy-making process was made by President Dwight D. Eisenhower in his farewell address to the nation in January 1961. In that address (see the *Intersections* box), Eisenhower warned of the potential power of what he called the **military-industrial complex** and the potentially erosive and corrupting influence it could have on the American system.

INTERSECTIONS

Ike's Farewell Address

As President Dwight D. Eisenhower prepared to leave office in January 1961, he gave a farewell address to the nation that included what has come to be one of the most famous warnings a president has ever given. Noting that the rise of a large standing military in peacetime and a permanent arms industry was a necessity of waging the Cold War against the Soviet Union, Eisenhower warned that these forces

Eisenhower's warning serves to remind us of the close relationship between defense spending and the U.S. economy.

(Continued)

(Continued)

could have serious consequences for the country. "In the councils of government, we must guard against the acquisition of unwarranted influence, whether sought or unsought, by the **military-industrial complex.** The potential for the disastrous rise of misplaced power exists and will persist." Ike went on to issue a second, less noted, warning as well, that policy in an increasingly technological age could become captured by a "scientific-technological elite." (The second warning was going to be about the dangers of "societal breakdown," but that was replaced with the warning that linked better to the first one as the drafting process went forward.)

Political scientists, sociologists, historians, and activists still debate the meaning of Ike's warnings today. It is also interesting to note that Ike's warnings and concern for balance in defense budgeting gave rise to an important interest group that takes Ike's warnings as their starting point, Business Executives for National Security (www.bens.org). For present purposes it is clear that Ike's warnings called attention to the powerful defense policy roles of the three clusters of actors in the iron triangle: the Pentagon, defense contractors, and congressional appropriators. In this area, Ike warns, what might at first look like "foreign" policy is really very much "domestic" policy—what this book calls "intermestic" policy.

The imagery of an "iron" arrangement that locks these three actors into mutual agreement about the need for more defense spending and locks out other actors might not be entirely accurate. In an empirical sense, some have argued that a better way to think about the role of interest groups and think tanks in the policy process is with a term called **subgovernments.** The idea behind this concept is that while a substantial area of mutual interest exists in the agencies, Congress, and lobbying world, and these actors work together regularly on these issues, the relationship can be less "iron" than the iron triangle suggests. Other domestic actors can get into the policy-making mix, and there is not always a perfect concert of interests. Whether in the form of an iron triangle, a subgovernment, or some other formulation, the bottom line is that the process of making foreign policy is very domestic. Former Speaker of the House Thomas P. "Tip" O'Neill famously said, "All politics is local." This is certainly true of foreign policy—increasingly so, and interest groups and think tanks are on the front lines of this intermestic policy process.

The military-industrial complex is only one example, although an important one, of a common concept in the U.S. political system: the **iron triangle** (see Figure 7.1). Iron triangles are formed when agencies of government in a given policy area find common cause with the congressional committee overseeing that policy area and with interest groups or PACs that promote policy in that area. This mutually supportive and reinforcing relationship, where there is very little disagreement among the parties and where other voices are shut out of the policy process, is what makes the triangle an iron one. The iron triangle, as it relates to the military-industrial complex, consists of the defense industry that has big contracts from the Pentagon, the DOD

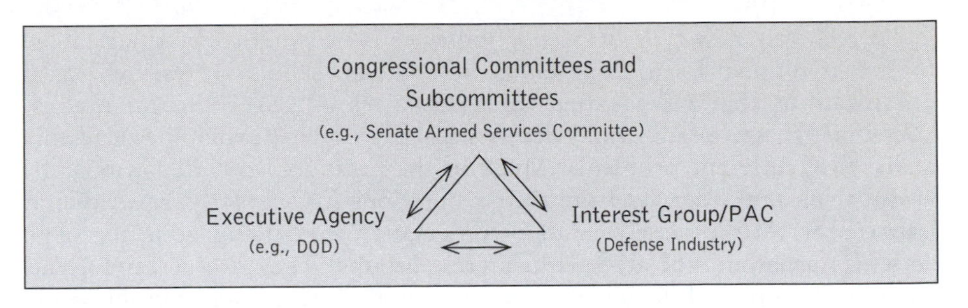

FIGURE 7.1
The Iron Triangle

that works closely with these contractors over time, and the armed services and defense appropriations committees in the House and Senate that oversee these expenditures for various weapons systems. Remember, too, as mentioned previously, that there is often a **revolving door** in the middle of an iron triangle, where the lobbyist for a defense contractor recently worked on the Hill, or where a military officer near retirement who is monitoring a project takes a position with the defense contractor that he or she was just monitoring, as examples of the common movement across roles that happens in Washington, D.C. The highly technical and usually classified nature of defense issues has meant that organizations and companies hire scores of retired military officers.

There is nothing necessarily illegal, unnatural, or even wrong about these relationships; nor are they limited to the defense area. The Air Force, for example, wants the best possible military aircraft and shares with defense manufacturers the desire to produce such aircraft. At the same time, all three sides of the triangle share expertise and common interests in military aircraft. (A member of Congress with no personal or constituency interests in military procurement is unlikely to seek out a seat on committees that deal with these issues.) The relationship develops into a problem when it becomes incestuous and when interests become entrenched and vested. The revolving-door phenomenon is one of the main roots of vested interests. Indeed, you can see the arrows in Figure 7.1 not just as indications of mutual interest and power, but also as a map of personnel movement across and among the actors. Abuses have spawned a variety of laws and guidelines intended to regulate these movements back and forth between government and industry. The Clinton administration, for example, made staff members sign a pledge that they would not go to work for a private enterprise with which they were dealing as part of the administration for at least a year after leaving government to avoid the appearance of impropriety. More recently, the Obama administration has moved to ban registered lobbyists from sitting on government advisory boards and panels. Obama also signed an executive order that bars a registered lobbyist for two years from taking an appointed position in the administration in an area where that person had previously lobbied (if it is deemed really important, however, the person can get a "waiver").

A relatively new type of outside influence is exemplified by think tanks. In their traditional form, think tanks are relatively scholarly, research-based organizations that offer expert advice to various governmental organs. Sometimes these organizations act as scholarly outlets, providing academic analyses of different problems. Much of the prestige associated with individual think tanks derives from their reputations for scholarly integrity and impartiality. At the same time, however, many of them engage in the same activities usually associated with interest groups. They are certainly, and increasingly, a part of the revolving-door phenomenon. If interest groups serve as a kind of gatekeeper between the mass public and the government, then in a way think tanks serve a similar function between the world of expert advice and government. And in an era of hyperpartisanship, the number and types of think tanks, and the dividing line between what is a think tank and what is an interest group, is quickly eroding. Today a range of think tanks is situated around every side of just about every issue, offering "expert" support for practically any policy initiative, including the arena of foreign policy. The information revolution has contributed to this dynamic as well, as these organizations have taken to the WEB as a way to post their "research" and to reach out to the public and policy makers.

SOURCES OF CHANGE

A variety of dynamics are helping to drive change in the roles and influence of interest groups, PACs, and hybrid organizations that blur the lines between these ideal forms. Five factors stand out as potential change agents, things that are altering the playing field and thus giving incentives to organizations to change how they operate in a new era. Note that these factors reflect changes that, in most cases, have already been described in earlier chapters. Almost all of the factors reflect the information explosion directly or indirectly, and the era of hyperpartisanship.

The first factor is the *convergence of foreign and domestic issues*. The old distinctions between a foreign and a domestic issue have largely disappeared into the realm of intermestic policies, especially in the globalized world. Although that confluence affects the way the government itself is organized, it also has an effect on how the public views what government does. Foreign policy had already become increasingly political and partisan, certainly since the Vietnam era. The end of the Cold War made foreign policy more of a domestic issue as well, and it seemed "safer" to debate these issues now that the Soviet bear was gone from the scene. The expansion of foreign trade, especially in the form of the North American Free Trade Agreement (NAFTA) and the emergence of the World Trade Organization (WTO), opened up the American economy to global forces in new ways. The 9/11 attacks brought foreign and national security policy up close and personal to Americans. All of these forces made the issue salience of foreign policy increase.

Public awareness and access is made easier by the *increased transparency of international events*. The global information revolution is at the heart of the public's greater access to foreign affairs at a time when those events are more immediate to them. Moreover, through global television outlets available on cable and satellite, the initial information on breaking international affairs available to the public is often nearly identical to the information available to decision makers. The president and his advisors, as well as members of the public, see the same reportage on CNN, FOX News, and MSNBC (to name a few). Humanitarian and natural disasters seem closer to home thanks to cable and satellite television and the Internet. At a minimum, the government's treatment of the media and its concern for initial public opinion must be greater than in the past. At a maximum, it may mean more detailed scrutiny of public decisions by all those outside government who seek to influence government actions.

This factor relates to a third phenomenon: The greater analytical capability that accompanies global television's ability to cover worldwide news *increasingly makes the global media an actor and influence in that process*. Global television—CNN and the British-based Independent Television Network (ITN), for instance—has clearly been the leader in this regard and is the first source of information to the public and, in many cases, governmental officials. More than that, modern news conglomerates provide considerable interpretation of events to a public that largely lacks the knowledge and perspective to interpret those events for itself. With twenty-four hours a day of airtime to fill and not enough hard news to fill it, it becomes necessary for these stations to augment the bare facts with some notion of what the events may portend and interpretations of those events by "experts," many of whom step just outside the revolving door of think tanks and interest groups in order to be interviewed on TV.

Thus the fourth source of change is the *rise of so-called electronic experts*, or those people who have acknowledged expertise and who are used by all the networks to provide legitimacy to the interpretation of currently breaking events. These individuals, first visibly seen during the Persian Gulf War, are especially important in the defense and foreign policy arena, because much of that material is relatively technical and the public is unfamiliar with it. As a result, these experts augment the expertise of the news organizations and help better inform (or perhaps confuse) the public. In the Persian Gulf War, all the networks featured both military and political experts who were drawn from outside their regular payrolls. They explained everything from the logistics of ground attack to the operation of precision-guided munitions. The same has certainly been true of the wars in Afghanistan and Iraq.

These experts are usually unpaid guests and tend to come from the military, think tanks, and academia. Many are retired military officers (mostly colonels and generals or the equivalent) who have experience, knowledge, and contacts within the Pentagon that give them superior information than that available to regular reporters, who in most cases are distrusted by the military. Another source for experts are the think tanks, especially those located in and around network headquarters in New York and Washington. The wars in Iraq and Afghanistan have given the CFR, as well as other Washington-based think tanks such as the Center for Strategic and International Studies (CSIS), the American Enterprise Institute (AEI), and the Brookings Institution, wide exposure. Finally, experts found in academia, particularly international relations experts from around New York and Washington, frequently appear in the media. The use of all of these experts can become controversial, as they did in 2008, when the news networks do not disclose to their viewers that the experts are not disinterested observers but in some cases have contracts with the very government organizations about whom they are commenting, which could slant their view and interpretation of events.

The fifth and final source of change is *growing public disaffection with the competency of the political leadership*, a phenomenon enhanced by the level of media scrutiny under which officials exist. Running against Washington and its insiders first became a prominent strategy in Jimmy Carter's successful run for the White House. It was a theme in Ronald Reagan's first campaign and became virtually an art form in the H. Ross Perot campaign of 1992. Dissatisfaction with how the system works has become broader than simply being at the level of presidential election politics, however. Witness the number of U.S. representatives and senators who retired in 1992 (although that was also partly because 1992 was the last year that a member of Congress could keep excess campaign contributions beyond campaign expenses) and the number who were defeated for reelection in 1994 when the Republicans took back the House. A similar purging happened in 2006 and 2008, ushering the Democrats back into power in Congress. The elections of 2010 again shifted power in the House back to Republicans, as voters expressed their anger at government and those in power more than they did their fondness of the G.O.P. Part of this dissatisfaction is undoubtedly fueled by the greater access to information that is a legacy of the electronic revolution, and the echo chamber that is created by TV and the Internet.

The discussion that follows provides the basis for examining how interest groups and think tanks operate outside of the government's formal structure and some of the forces that are changing how they operate. The emphasis of the discussion is on how these groups relate specifically to foreign and national security matters.

INTEREST GROUPS

In political terms, an *interest group* can be defined simply as any organized group of people who share common interests distinct from those of others and who attempt to influence public policy in the direction of that interest. As such, interest groups begin with a shared common interest, whether it is maintenance of a strong national defense, the preservation of the environment, or the end of the Cuban embargo. They come together into some formal organization of like-minded individuals to form a group, and that group seeks to represent their common interest to the political system and to influence public policy in the direction of their interest.

Characteristics

Interest groups do not just appear out of nowhere. For instance, not all groups care to lobby the government on behalf of public policy. Further, many people have common interests, but they do not, as a result, organize; political scientists call this the "collective action problem." In order to overcome the collective action problem, someone has to want a group to form around an existing common interest much more than most people who share the common interest—so much more that they are willing to go to the trouble (and often cost) of forming a formal organization. These individuals are sometimes called "political entrepreneurs" because like the entrepreneurs of capitalism who invest their own time and resources in order to gain an economic profit, these political entrepreneurs are willing to invest in order to get a type of political profit: the policy that they want.

Theoretically, the ability to form interest groups and to compete in the arena includes the entire population and is an option available to all Americans. In fact, however, that is usually not the case. Numerous studies have shown that the upper strata of society, as measured by such yardsticks as wealth and education, are overrepresented in interest-group activity. In one sense, this stands to reason, for interest-group activities, like almost everything else, cost money. Hence, those who possess monetary resources will have more access to the system they seek to influence. Similarly, educational attainment and levels of political activity are positively related. Related to this, some interests are much more well-funded to do their work than are others; big business and defense contracts, for example, tend to have access to far greater resources to promote their interests than do many human rights groups.

To understand the role of interest groups requires examining what interest groups do to represent and promote their interests. This forms the basis for looking at the kinds of interest groups that are active in the foreign and defense policy arena.

Interest Group Tactics

Different observers categorize the activities of interest groups differently, and no set of categories will satisfy all observers. For the present purposes, however, the activities are divided into three categories: lobbying, education, and pressure. Each function entails distinct actions, although most interest groups use some combination of them all.

Lobbying Interest groups are most closely associated with *lobbying*. The term itself goes back to the 1870s. Although the First Amendment to the Constitution provides for the right of petition, it prohibits the presentation of petitions on the floors of the houses of Congress. As a result, those seeking influence were forced to make their representations outside the chambers, especially in the corridors and lobbies of the Capitol building. Hence, the term *lobbying* was born.

The purpose of lobbying, like all other interest-group activity, is to persuade those with the ability to make decisions—in the Congress or the executive branch—that their interests should be reflected in public policy. Lobbying connotes the personal representations of positions to individual members of Congress or executive branch agents in the effort to convince them of the virtue of their positions. Although some lobbying occurs within the executive branch, more of it occurs in the interactions between interest groups and members of Congress.

The cornerstones of federal lobbying are the Washington-based offices of the various interest groups and lobbyists. Many of these offices are clustered around K Street in Washington, D.C., leading "K Street" to be a common name for the world of interest groups. The watchdog group Center for Responsive Politics reports on their website (www.opensecrets.org) that there are over twelve thousand lobbyists today in the United States spending about $2.5 billion dollars to do their work. These lobbying firms do work for interest groups as well as companies and even foreign countries.

Today most lobbyists are professionals, usually people with considerable government service within a particular policy area who have developed expertise and extensive contacts that they are willing to share with clients for a price. Professional lobbyists typically work for several clients rather than a single one. Many of these individuals are lawyers who have developed expertise in specific areas of the law, such as food and drug laws; hence, they are attractive representatives for clients such as the pharmaceutical industry. In the foreign policy area, Henry Kissinger Associates is probably the most famous and powerful example of a professional lobbying organization. In 2002, the former secretary of state resigned from the chairmanship of the presidential commission investigating the performance of government agencies prior to the September 11th tragedy in part to protect the integrity of his client list. It is no longer uncommon for former secretaries of state to start a lobby group or a "consulting" firm; Condoleezza Rice began a firm after she left government, along with her former colleague Stephen Hadley (who served as President George W. Bush's national security advisor during his second term).

While most interest groups contract with a lobby firm to do their lobbying, another type of lobbyist is the staff lobbyist. Unlike the professional lobbyist, the staff lobbyist works full-time for the Washington office of an organization that seeks to influence the policy process. In addition to formal lobbying, staff lobbyists typically perform other administrative duties as well. All organizations with large operations in Washington employ some staff lobbyists. The aerospace industries and their typically large Washington operations represent an example in the defense area.

The purpose of all lobbying efforts is to gain access to decision makers and to persuade them of the efficacy of the interest the lobbyist represents. Highly successful lobbyists make themselves so invaluable to people within the process that they virtually become a part of it: for instance, having such great knowledge of a policy area that they are consulted on crafting the language for a piece of legislation. This quality of access is attained in part through the second form of interest group activity, education.

Education Interest groups seek to influence policy by providing expert information in an issue area that can be used to educate both those in power and the public at large of the desirability of their positions. When educational efforts are directed at the general public, they usually take one of several forms. One obvious form is the advertising campaign, which increasingly uses professional television spots to galvanize public opinion on a subject. The ad campaigns on both sides of the abortion issue are a particularly vivid example. Sometimes these campaigns are directed at the general public, and other times at specialized segments of the population. An example of the latter was a series of advertisements in *The New York Times* in June 1992 placed by pro-Serbian groups seeking to convince readers that the situation in Bosnia and Herzegovina was not a Serbian act of aggression and atrocity, but instead the continuation of Serbian resistance to Croatian fascism with roots in World War ll. (Such tactics do not always work, as they did not in this case.) The pro-Israel lobby has also made extensive use of this tactic in support of its struggle with the Palestinians. Another educational effort may be to provide speakers' bureaus to speak to groups or to be available for newspaper and television interviews. At the same time, groups often provide news releases in the hope that they will be printed in local papers.

More commonly, educational efforts are directed toward members of Congress and their staffs. Interest groups collect and make available information about their particular policy area, which, although self-interested, may provide a useful supplement to the members' ability to gain information through their staffs. This information may be provided in the form of position papers, fact books, reference services to which a member has access, or even expert testimony to congressional committees and subcommittees. Often this information is also available to interest-group members and even the general public through the Internet. They also place ads in magazines that professional politicians read; just as ABC places ads in *People* magazine to get you to watch a TV show, for example, if you picked up a copy of *Congressional Quarterly Weekly Reports* or the *National Journal* you would see ads for Boeing, fighter jets, and tanks.

Members and their staffs greatly appreciate this form of activity, if provided honestly rather than as obviously biased propaganda. Despite the expansion of staffs described in Chapter Six, Congress is still at a disadvantage in its competition for information with the executive branch. An interest group that provides honest, valuable information thus extends Congress's capabilities. A few try to mislead Congress, but such a tactic is shortsighted and almost invariably exposed in the long run, thereby compromising the offending interest group in the future. When competing interest groups present conflicting information or interpretations, the member and his or her staff can make a comparative assessment of the various positions.

A good example of an interest group that uses educational programs as a primary tool is the Arms Control Association (ACA). The ACA publishes its own journal, *Arms Control Today,* which it distributes to libraries and interested citizens. The association features a speakers' bureau for places such as college campuses, and its leading staff members are regularly available for interviews. Congressional members also receive the journal, and the ACA provides both expert witnesses for testimony before congressional committees and a resource for information on weapons levels, characteristics, and the like. As a further means of endearment, *Arms Control Today* frequently publishes articles and speeches by sympathetic members of Congress.

Pressure Interest groups also seek to influence policy by exerting political pressure on government officials, a form of influence peddling that represents the most negative and controversial side of interest-group activities. Pressure activities comprise actions designed not so much to persuade officials of the virtue of the group's position as to convince the officials of the negative consequences of opposing the interest or the positive benefits of support. In the past thirty years or so, the negative side of pressure has come to be associated with the emergence of the political action committees introduced earlier. The basic purpose and tactic of PACs is to influence elections by collecting money from their membership and using it to support candidates sympathetic to their causes and to oppose their opponents. Sometimes the PACs accomplish this by making direct contributions to campaigns. Limits on the amount that can be given to any candidate by an organization necessitate a second tactic, which is for the PACs to encourage members of the group to contribute as well, and the group then "bundles" those checks together and presents them to candidates. Following a controversial U.S. Supreme Court decision in 2009 (referred to by the shorthand *Citizens United*), groups, unions, and corporations can spend unlimited amounts of money on political campaigns, including campaigns to elect or to defeat candidates, so long as their efforts are not coordinated with the candidate's campaign that they seek to assist. In the case of groups (sometimes called Super PACs) that have emerged, many times they do not even have to disclose the donors who gave the groups large sums of money.

The cost of modern campaigns, largely inflated by the expense of television advertising, postage, and rent in Washington, D.C., makes the PACs more and more powerful and the increasing target of regulation and campaign finance reform. A variety of attempts to rein in PAC spending have slowed the growth of PACs, but they have had the perhaps unintended consequence of spurring the growth of new "independent expenditure" groups that spend money on campaigns. These groups tend to be organized under various parts of the Internal Revenue Service tax code, such as "527" groups (for example, the notorious Swiftboat Veterans for Truth that targeted John Kerry in the 2004 presidential campaign) and "501C4" groups (such as Crossroads GPS formed by Karl Rove in 2010). Altogether these groups spent nearly $500 million in the 2010 midterm election cycle and will spend far more in the 2012 election cycle. The activities of the PACs and other expenditure groups are more closely associated with domestic than foreign and defense issues, but it is certainly the case that corporate PACs which seek to influence the size and direction of defense procurement are very large and influential; the defense industry is particularly active in this regard.

Pressure can take other forms. Lobbyists, for instance, can offer favors to sympathetic members of Congress. Historically, for instance, interest groups would offer speaking engagements, complete with speakers' fees (honoraria) and expenses, often to exotic locations. Abuses of this practice have resulted in reform legislation that virtually prohibits the practice for any federal employee and eliminates the acceptance of gifts by members of Congress. Making donations to the favorite charities of legislators is another such tactic.

The size of the stakes involved inevitably leads to abuses and, most commonly, bribery, or the offer and acceptance of illegal funds by some official from an interest group. Instances of bribery are rather infrequent, but when they do occur, they are spectacular. One such large-scale bribery case involved banking magnate Charles Keating and his defrauding of the federal government in the savings-and-loan association scandal of the mid-1980s. The corruption touched five U.S. senators, who became known as the Keating Five (Alan Cranston of California, John Glenn of Ohio, Dennis DeConcini of Arizona, John McCain of Arizona, and Donald Riegle of Michigan).

In the foreign and defense area, one of the most famous cases involved a foreign lobbyist, Tong Sun Park of the Republic of Korea. Park, a flashy, well-liked figure, induced support for his government through lavish social occasions for governmental officials, including gifts for congressional members and their spouses during the 1970s and 1980s. The gifts ultimately got him in trouble because they exceeded allowable limits. One person who was forced to resign his position because of this scandal was Ronald Reagan's first national security advisor, Richard V. Allen, who had accepted two watches from Park.

Types of Interest Groups

A huge variety of interest groups exists in the country, and most concentrate on influencing the domestic agenda. However, the reader should recognize that the blurring of domestic and foreign policy means that almost all interests are affected by international events some of the time. With that in mind, the kinds of groups that seek to influence foreign and defense policy can be explored by looking at five overlapping distinctions about the kinds of interest groups that operate today, as well as a special category of groups: ethnic interest groups. All foreign policy interest groups can be characterized by some mix of these markers.

General vs. Specific General interest groups are those whose interests span the spectrum of policy areas, including, but not specifically emphasizing, foreign policy. These groups, such as the American Federation of Labor and Congress of Industrial Organizations (AFL-CIO) and the American Association of Retired Persons (AARP), take an interest in foreign or defense policy when it may directly affect their constituents. If foreign spending proposals were to impinge on retirement entitlements, for instance, AARP would become involved. Similarly, the AFL-CIO is sensitive to any foreign policies that may favor lower-paid foreign workers over American workers who belong to unions. (As you can imagine, trade policy is something that draws the careful attention of the AFL-CIO.) These comprehensive interest groups are often large—with thousands and even tens of thousands of members—and have considerable general influence, but they frequently lack great expertise in the specific area of defense and foreign policy.

Other interest groups exclusively concentrate on foreign and defense policy, or some part thereof. Although it also has some of the characteristics of a think tank, the powerful Council on Foreign Relations (CFR) is an example of an organization that focuses solely on foreign affairs. Its members represent the establishment foreign policy elite and thus bring both great expertise and prestige to the policy process, especially because many members are also former high-ranking officials of government.

One organization that concentrates on a specific aspect of the foreign policy process is Amnesty International (AI). Although it considers itself more of a think tank because of the academic impartiality of its inquiry, AI is dedicated to the protection of human rights globally and investigates and publicizes instances of human rights abuses. It has 2.8 million supports from over 150 countries and was awarded the Nobel Peace Prize in 1977 for its work. AI often comes into direct conflict with the State Department, which has the statutory mandate to produce a list of countries that are human rights abusers. The department's list, partially constructed with geopolitical considerations in mind (how important a country is to the United States regardless of its human rights record), is almost always shorter than the AI list.

Permanent vs. Ad Hoc Permanent groups are groups that have been in existence for a long time and expect to continue to exist for the indefinite future. They must therefore rely on long-term stable relationships, both with their constituencies and with those inside the government whom they seek to influence. This in turn affects the ways in which they operate: Permanent groups are naturally prone to low-key activities that nurture long associations. Examples of permanent interest groups in the foreign and defense area include the various groups that support the armed forces: the Association of the United States Army (AUSA), the Air Force Association (AFA), and the Navy League. In addition to providing some contact with the services for retired personnel, each of these associations seeks to influence the government about their services and general veterans' issues.

Ad hoc interest groups, in contrast, are part of the broader phenomenon of single-interest advocacy organizations that come together simply to affect the outcome of a particular issue but cease to operate when the particular issue is resolved. The original ad hoc foreign policy groups date back to the 1960s, and a prototype of sorts revolved around a national security issue: the Vietnam War. The entire loose, sprawling anti–Vietnam War movement was spawned on American college campuses shortly after U.S. active combat involvement in the war began. (Actually, it began even earlier with teach-ins at major campuses starting in 1964, notably at the University of California at Berkeley.) The movement widened to encompass a broad spectrum, from counterculture youth to the Vietnam Veterans Against the War, that shared a common but single interest in ending the war. Once that purpose was accomplished, the movement splintered and ultimately disappeared.

Continuous Interests vs. Occasional Interests Interest groups with a continuous interest in foreign and defense affairs tend to be comprehensive in their approaches to what interests them and what they seek to influence. The continuity of interest helps create expertise, which makes the group's counsel more sought after than might otherwise be the case. In turn, the reputation for expertise makes the group's recruitment of experts easier. Examples of this kind of group are the Council on Foreign Relations (CFR) and the Foreign Policy Association (FPA).

By definition, groups with an occasional interest in foreign policy are selective in the foreign and defense issues they seek to influence. Normally having a primary focus in some other policy area, these groups intrude into the foreign policy area only when a specific issue directly affects them and only for as long as their interests are engaged. An example is the American Farm Bureau Federation, the primary focus of which is on agricultural policy. When issues such as grain sales overseas arise—which can include the issue of the embargo of Cuba, for example—this group becomes engaged in the foreign policy process. Similarly, the AFL-CIO has a lively interest in NAFTA, and the National Association of Manufacturers has a strong concern about those parts of the Treaty of Maastricht that might exclude U.S. goods from the states that comprise the European Union.

Private vs. Public The largest number of private interest groups are those representing individual corporations that do business with the government (contractors such as the aircraft industries or defense suppliers in general) or are regulated by the government (for instance, the pharmaceutical companies regulated by the Food and Drug Administration), as well as associations of corporate institutions (such as the National Association of Manufacturers or the U.S. Chamber of Commerce). In the foreign and defense policy area, the majority of private interest groups have been attached to defense issues, and particularly defense procurement and budgeting. As international economic issues have became more important in foreign policy since the end of the Cold War, interest groups that have historically focused on domestic economic issues became increasingly engaged in the foreign policy arena. The Chamber of Commerce, for example, and the umbrella group USA Engage, which represents U.S. exporters and opposes trade sanctions, have become increasingly active on foreign trade policy.

Public interest groups, on the other hand, purport to represent the body politic as a whole, especially those citizens whose interests are otherwise underrepresented. Largely a product of the 1960s, these groups typically are financed by large numbers of small donations and maintain an air of impartiality (whether deserved or not). Common Cause is the prototype of this kind of interest group.

National vs. Global People tend to think of American interest groups seeking to influence the U.S. political system as the norm, and most of the time this is the case, but not always. Americans are not the only people interested in influencing U.S. policy, especially its defense and foreign policy. Foreigners, notably foreign governments, also share a lively interest in trying to affect U.S. government actions toward themselves and others, and they do so in a number of ways. Sometimes they use their own citizens, often their ambassador, as an informal lobbyist with the government. Prince Bandar bin Sultan, the longtime Saudi ambassador to the United States, was especially successful in this role, particularly when opposition to selling weapons to the Saudi kingdom arose, as it did during the Persian Gulf War. He was also effective in fending off criticism of Saudi Arabia's alleged support of terrorist organizations such as Al Qaeda by allowing them to operate and raise money in its territory.

Foreign governments also get their interests represented by hiring American lobbyists—often, former government officials—to represent them. People who represent foreign governments must register as foreign agents, and quite often, their value derives from their ability to gain access to officials for their foreign clients. It has been estimated that nearly $100 million per year is spent by foreign governments on U.S.-based lobbyists and lobbying firms, with the United Arab Emirates and the United Kingdom spending the most. Another way for foreign governments to influence U.S. policy is to nurture Americans whose origins are the same as the nation seeking the influence. "Hyphenated Americans" (Italian-Americans, Irish-Americans, and so forth) can be quite-effective if these organizations can plausibly be argued to represent vital segments of the American public. Probably the largest and most successful of these is the Israel lobby and its action arm, notably AIPAC. One of the real explosions in the interest-group world of the last thirty years has been the emergence and proliferation of **ethnic interest groups**. Their rise in activity level and prominence has not been without some controversy, so we discuss them as a distinct type of interest group.

Ethnic Interest Groups Groups that are founded to promote the foreign policy interests of a particular subset of Americans who identify themselves (at least in part) along the lines of ethnicity and national origin are considered "ethnic interest groups." Often these groups pressure the U.S. government to be friendlier toward their previous homeland, including offering more economic or perhaps military assistance for that country of origin. AIPAC is a classic example of this, promoting close ties between the United States and Israel and working to limit policies that AIPAC's leaders and members see as dangerous for Israel (such as arms sales to the Saudis). AIPAC is regularly cited as the most powerful ethnic interest group in America—and one of the most powerful interest groups in general, as well. Conversely, sometimes such groups lobby to limit aid toward, or to place sanctions on, the country of origin when the regime in that country is seen as harsh and dictatorial. The **Cuban American National Foundation** (CANF) is an example of this. CANF was founded in 1980–1981 to promote a rigorous embargo of Cuba, the aim of which has been to try to force the end of the Castro regime on the island. (CANF has evolved a fair amount in recent years, and its power, which was considerable in the 1980s and 1990s, has waned somewhat.) Today, ethnic interest groups—many of which also have PACs—are some of the most active foreign policy lobbies in America, seeking to represent the interests of "hyphenated-Americas" across a broad range of ethnicities.

Political pressure from ethnic interest groups has evoked some controversy beyond the normal discomfort many have with lobbying. Some have raised the concern that these groups are really front operations for foreign governments. Others have argued that the presence of these groups serves to underscore American differences as a nation, rather than seeking common ground and assimilation—the American melting pot. Beyond that, skeptics claim, these groups can have a myopic view of America's "interests" in the world and push policies that the critics see as counterproductive to the United States. Assuming that these organizations are genuinely domestic efforts to promote an interest that is in part rooted in ethnic identity, there is really nothing special about these groups—all interest groups promote their self-interest over the interests of others, claiming that it is in "the national interest." And as discussed at the start of this chapter, sometimes several groups emerge that have different views of what is in the interests of the former homeland, and they compete with each other (as with AIPAC and J Street) as well as against other interest groups. Nonetheless, the proliferation of these groups has raised the eyebrows of some observers.

INTERSECTIONS

Why Can't I Go to Cuba for Spring Break?

The United States has had an embargo policy in place of one sort or another against Cuba since the days of the Eisenhower administration. One of the components of the embargo is a ban on travel to Cuba except under certain specified conditions, such as family travel and academic research; tourist trips are strictly illegal for Americans. The idea is to deprive the Cuban economy of tourism's dollars to try to force political change in Cuba aimed at democracy and capitalism. When the Cold War ended, many argued for dropping the Cuban embargo too. With the fall of the Soviet Union—Cuba's main economic sponsor—the political threat from Cuba seemed to recede, and the sense was that the Cuban economy and political system would collapse like the regimes across Eastern Europe. Some argued for keeping the pressure on Castro's Cuba in order to force change on the island. The embargo stayed, and was even tightened by Congress in 1996, though its rigidity has waxed and waned over time. Presidents Clinton and Obama have tended toward more openings; President George W. Bush did the opposite.

Whatever one might think of the wisdom of economic embargoes as tools of foreign policy, which are discussed in more detail in Chapter Twelve, there is also a

(Continued)

(Continued)

"liberty" argument that some make here. Should the government curtail the rights of citizens to travel to Cuba, when they can travel to many other countries with worse records on democracy and human rights? One of the things that makes the case of the Cuban embargo so fascinating is that it encompasses so many different issues: economic and political, foreign and domestic, presidential and congressional.

Another thing that fascinates observers about the case of Cuba policy is its classic status as an "intermestic" issue. Some have even said that the United States does not really have a Cuba policy, but rather it has a policy toward Cuban American voters in Florida—highlighting the electoral significance of a small but highly motivated voting block in a tightly contested and electorally rich state. Cuba policy is also well permeated by interest groups and PACs, on all sides of the issue. The future of the embargo policy is a hotly contested issue; watch for it in the 2012 election season.

Interest groups and the activities they engage in are a long-standing, integral part of the U.S. political system. In a sense, although they are outside the halls of formal government, they reflect the same kind of system of checks and balances created inside government: Almost all possible interests on most subjects have an organization representing that interest, and they compete with each other over policy. Thus, the right to petition is theoretically available to all citizens and their interests. If there is a shortcoming to this system, it is the link between interests and money. Not all interests are equally well-funded, so often it just is not a "fair fight," and the presence of so much money in politics means that the political process can sometimes look a bit unseemly, if not actually be corrupt.

POLICY ELITES AND THINK TANKS

A sizable community of individuals with expertise on public policy matters has emerged and has increasingly sought to use its knowledge to affect foreign policy. Many of these individuals are aggregated in not-for-profit, nonpartisan research institutes and organizations, including universities, who conduct research on foreign policy matters and seek to share that knowledge with policy makers. In the jargon of Washington, these organizations have come to be known as **think tanks** since the presidency of John F. Kennedy (whose administration witnessed a proliferation of them). Before that metaphor took root, synonyms included "brain banks," "think factories," and "egghead row" (because a number of the early organizations were located in a row on Massachusetts Avenue in Washington, D.C.).

Think tanks and interest groups both operate at the boundary between the government and the public, and like interest groups, think tanks have proliferated in recent years and become more partisan (see Table 7.1). They differ, however, in emphasis, membership, and the range of activities they undertake.

TABLE 7.1

Leading Think Tanks and Political Activity

American Enterprise Institute (conservative)
Brookings Institution (mostly centrist)
Carnegie Endowment for International Peace (centrist)
Cato Institute (conservative-libertarian)
Center for American Progress (liberal)
Center for Defense Information (liberal)
Center for Strategic and International Studies (mostly centrist)
Federation of American Scientists (liberal)
Freedom House (conservative)
Heritage Foundation (conservative)
Hoover Institution (conservative)
Hudson Institute (conservative)
Institute for International Economics (centrist)
Institute for Policy Studies (liberal)
Joint Center for Political and Economic Studies (liberal)
Progressive Policy Institute (liberal)
RAND Corporation (conservative)
Twentieth Century Fund (liberal)
World Policy Institute (liberal)
World Resources Institute (centrist)
Worldwatch Institute (mostly centrist)

One of the basic purposes of both think tanks and interest groups is citizen education, although for different reasons. Interest groups tend to view education instrumentally, as a device to cause conversion to their interest. In contrast, think tanks have traditionally sought knowledge and its educational application more abstractly, as a way to improve government. In recent years, however, a new breed of think tank seems to be edging toward an instrumental purpose. Both types of organizations operate at the boundary between government and the public, although it is a different boundary. For interest groups, the boundary is the line between the formal system and organized citizens with particular interests; for think tanks, the boundary is normally the line between government and the policy-active intellectual community.

The two entities differ in other significant ways. The emphasis of interest groups is overtly political: They usually seek to move policy in self-interested directions. Think tanks, though often ideologically identifiable, in theory at least adopt a more detached, scholarly view of policy. Similarly, most of those associated with think tanks are academics, in one sense or another, or people with experienced-based expertise (such as retired military officers or ex-government officials), whereas traditional politicians are more often associated with interest-group activity.

The two groups are also distinct in their range of activities. Because their heritage is based in academia, think tanks rarely engage in gross advocacy of particular policy issues, whereas lobbying and pressuring in favor of specific legislation are the *raison d'etre* of interest groups. The think-tank phenomenon is not well understood by the general public.

Characteristics

The movement that evolved into the modern think tanks took place around the turn of the twentieth century. Its impetus came from a group of scholars, principally from the social sciences, who believed that public policy and process could be improved by applying social scientific means and research to them.

The first identifiable think tank, the Russell Sage Foundation, was chartered in 1907 and was followed fairly quickly by the Twentieth Century Fund and a handful of others. All of these early efforts viewed themselves as citadels in which disinterested research (research not associated with personal or institutional gain or partisan ends) could be pursued and the results could be dispassionately applied to societal problems. These research interests remained largely peripheral to the foreign policy process until the emergence of the Cold War (the development of nuclear strategy became one of the activities of some think tanks) and the activism in politics associated with the 1960s (especially reaction to the Vietnam conflict). Until that time, relatively few think tanks were in existence, what they did was largely academic, and usually they did not engage in much self-promotion.

How times have changed. According to a major study of the subject, *The Idea Brokers* (1993), about two-thirds of the think tanks operating in the Washington area today have come into existence since 1970. At the same time, and led by the example of the conservative **Heritage Foundation**, many have become more activist and more partisan, openly gearing their research toward promoting particular political ideas and causes. Table 7.1 is adapted (and updated) from *The Idea Brokers* (1993) as a way to highlight the foreign and defense policy activity by some of the most prominent think tanks.

The people who work for them also define the nature of think tanks. Especially among those institutes with a foreign policy emphasis, the employees tend to come from one of three backgrounds: academia, the military, or the government. The academics are usually individuals with doctoral degrees in political science, economics, history, or international relations, who are more interested in applied research (studying and influencing concrete public policy) than in abstract, theoretical, academic research or university-level teaching. As with interest groups, there is a bit of a revolving door between think tanks and the government. Before her appointment as U.N. ambassador and later secretary of state by President Clinton, Madeleine Albright was a college professor (Georgetown) and then served as president of the Center for National Policy. The deputy secretary of defense in the Bush administration, Paul Wolfowitz, was at the Johns Hopkins School of Advanced International Studies before joining the Bush campaign and administration. George W. Bush's National

Security Advisor and later Secretary of State, Condoleeza Rice, was provost at Stanford University, and linked to the Hoover Institution at Stanford (an in-house, conservative think tank). The Director of the Policy Planning Staff at the Department of State (sort of the State Department's own internal think tank) at the outset of the Obama administration, Anne-Marie Slaughter, had served as the dean of the Woodrow Wilson School at Princeton. Scores of former Clinton administration officials went to work in—and even founded new—think tanks when they left office. Many of them came back to government work after Obama's 2008 victory, and some have already left and returned to the academe, think tanks, or lobbying shops.

As one might expect, retired military officers tend to be concentrated in think tanks primarily studying security issues rather than general foreign policy problems. Many who have retired below the rank of flag officer (general or admiral) are located in organizations that do contract work for the government or in institutes run in-house by the services. In addition, a number of the Ph.D.'s who work in think tanks have military backgrounds, probably reflecting a greater action orientation than is normally associated with academic life. Retired flag officers can often be found in very prominent positions at think tanks. One prominent example (of many) of a retired military officer now at a think tank is retired Rear Admiral Gene LaRoque, now the President Emeritus of the Center for Defense Information (CDI). Retired Marine (four star) General Anthony Zinni is now a "military fellow" at the CDI.

Sources of Funding

The research institutes are also defined by the sources of their funding. The think tanks vary tremendously in the size of staff and extensiveness of programs, and thus they vary in the need for and size of external funding. For most organizations, however, funding comes from a combination of six sources: foundations, corporate sponsorship, bequests and large contributions, individual contributions (sometimes including contributions from foreign governments), sales of books and periodicals, and government-sponsored research and contracts.

The first source, large foundations with considerable resources, such as the Ford, John D. and Catherine T. MacArthur, Bill and Melinda Gates foundations, and the Pew Charitable Trust, provide funds to support think-tank research. Foundation support is most likely to be associated with research institutes that do not have an activist political agenda. With regard to corporate sponsorship, as long as the funds are not attached to a political agenda, corporations can and do provide funds for research institutes. Moreover, through bequests and large contributions, some think tanks have endowments that produce revenue to support their activities. The amounts vary. The Brookings Institution, for instance, has an endowment of about $250 million, but most are not that well off and rely heavily on contributions and contracts to cover their activities.

A fourth source of operating funds is individual contributions. Among the major think tanks, The Heritage Foundation probably leads the way, and in the Heritage's case contributors tend to come from the political right in America. Another source is sales of books and journals or magazines. Most research institutes publish their research, for a price, and this feeds into the budget. Finally, some receive funding from government-sponsored research. The leader in this category is the RAND Corporation, which was created in 1948 largely to serve as a think tank for the newly independent U.S. Air Force and which still conducts much of its research for the Air Force and the Army.

Ideological Leanings

Another characteristic sometimes applied to research institutes is their general ideological or political persuasions. A number of institutes created in the 1970s were established out of the conservatives' belief that they needed a formal articulated agenda that could be used to appeal to the public or to provide a program for aspiring conservative candidates. The most prominent case in point of this phenomenon, and one of the most successful, is The Heritage Foundation. Think tanks run a range across the partisan and ideological spectrum. During the latter 1970s and early 1980s, for example, the American Enterprise Institute (AEI) became associated with the moderate wing of the Republican Party; after the Reagan and first Bush administrations, a number of "Reagan Democrats" (conservative, hawkish officials) became affiliated with the institute and later reemerged as the "neoconservatives" under George W. Bush. The Brookings Institution, on the other hand, has always been identified with positions that are more centrist-to-liberal and has sometimes been referred to as the Democratic think tank. The Center for American Progress, which is directed by President Clinton's former Chief of Staff, John Podesta, was formed in 2003 in part as a counterweight for centrists and Democrats to balance against the weight of AEI and Heritage.

Other Forms of Identification

In the foreign and defense policy area, most think tanks are private, freestanding research institutes—the kind of thing most people think about when they hear the term "think tank." But not all work this way. Some institutes are associated with universities—and the number is growing—as universities form "centers" and "institutes"; facing diminishing federal sources of research funding, many universities have adopted more entrepreneurial strategies to attract funding. Among the most prestigious and best-established entities are the Center for Science and International Affairs (a cooperative enterprise of the Massachusetts Institute of Technology and Harvard University); the Foreign Policy Research Institute (affiliated with the University of Pennsylvania); the Institute for Foreign Policy Analysis (associated with the Fletcher School of Law and Diplomacy at Tufts University); and the Hoover Institution (formally private but with a working relationship with Stanford University).

Another form of affiliation is with a governmental organization. Each of the military services, for instance, maintains its own in-house think tank. These organizations are usually associated with the war colleges. Thus, the Army maintains its Strategic Studies Institute (SSI) at the U.S. Army War College in Carlisle Barracks, Pennsylvania; the Navy, its Center for Naval Warfare Studies (CNWS) at the U.S. Naval War College in Newport, Rhode Island; the Marine Corps has the Center for Emerging Threats and Opportunities (CETO) in Quantico, Virginia; and the Air Force has multiple research operations at the Air University in Montgomery, Alabama. The State Department also maintains the same kind of capability in its Center for the Study of Foreign Affairs in its Foreign Service Institute.

Thus, the evolution of the think-tank phenomenon has been an eclectic affair. There are just about as many different kinds of think tanks as there are ways to categorize them. The pattern is continuing to evolve, particularly because as government funding became tougher to come by, think tanks were forced to compete with one another and with other institutions, such as universities, for dwindling resources. Think tanks came to rely more on individual donors for funding; many donors or their personal foundations gave more than $1 million dollars to Brookings in 2009; the same is true (from a different part of the ideological spectrum) for Heritage. Thus, the activities of many think tanks have come to mirror the political preferences of their donors, contributing to the hyperpartisan nature of the environment within which foreign policy is made today.

Patterns of Function and Activity

The research institutes and the policy intellectuals that staff them engage in a variety of different activities. Some organizations, of course, place greater emphasis on certain functions than on others, and the pattern is evolving, as are the organizations themselves. Some of these activities are shared with interest groups; some are distinct. The activities and functions can be divided into six types: research, publications, expert advice, talent banks, serving as a focal point for like-minded individuals, and making connections to the media.

The first and most fundamental category, naturally, is *research*. Much of the prestige and early influence of the original research institutes was the result of their adherence to an objective, scholarly pursuit of knowledge based in social scientific methods of inquiry. The research emphasis, which produces and disseminates knowledge applicable to dealing with societal problems, distinguishes the think tanks, giving them their character and identity. Moreover, the analyses they perform are the basic product they have to sell to the system; this is how they help set the political agenda and influence the public debate. In the absence of providing a research base, think tanks would be little more than interest groups representing the policy-intellectual community of scholars and activists with interests and expertise in the area.

The concern about the purity of research efforts also comes from another angle, notably the emergence of activist, openly political, think tanks—of which The Heritage Foundation is the prototype. That organization openly admits that it engages in inquiry for promoting the conservative agenda, and it publicizes only those research findings that support its point of view. The fear is that this emphasis—especially as newer organizations follow this type of lead—will undercut the reputation for scientific integrity that has been important to think-tank influence in the past.

The research institutes promote their research through *publications*, which may take several forms. One is the commissioning and publishing of books on topics of public interest. A common pattern is for the think tank to employ a visiting scholar for a period of time (a year or two) on a contract with the express purpose of producing a book. Ideally, these books attract broad public readership, or at least the attention of policy makers. The results can be added prestige for the think tank, influence on the policy process, and not least important, revenue to support the institute. The Brookings Institution has always supported a vigorous book list, as has CSIS and the Council on Foreign Relations.

Another form of publication is technical reports. The RAND Corporation disseminates short technical reports that are available to policy makers and the public. Staff members also write articles for the opinion and editorial pages of leading national newspapers, such as *The New York Times*, *The Washington Post*, and *The Christian Science Monitor*. In addition, a number of think tanks produce journals that are used as research sources by scholars and others conducting policy-relevant research. A few examples of these journals for foreign and defense policy include the *Brookings Review* (Brookings Institution), *Cato Journal* (Cato Institute), *Foreign Affairs* (Council on Foreign Relations), *Foreign Policy* (Carnegie Endowment), *Defense Monitor* (Center for Defense Information), *Washington Quarterly* (Center for Strategic and International Studies), *Policy Review* (Heritage Foundation), *World Policy Journal* (World Policy Institute), and *World Watch* (Worldwatch Institute).

Many research institutes provide *expert advice* to the government in a number of ways. Some organizations, for instance, contract with the government to provide specific expertise on technical matters. This activity is more often associated with consultants (sometimes known as "beltway bandits" because of their locations along the Washington beltway and the alleged quality of their work) but is occasionally done by think tanks as well. More commonly, however, the research institutes act in more subtle ways. A staff member who has just completed a major study may be asked to provide expert testimony to a congressional committee or to serve on a presidential commission investigating an area in which the organization has expertise. At the same time, that expertise can also be applied to "watchdogging" governmental activities. The Center for Defense Information, as well as many other groups such as the Project on Defense Alternatives, critically analyzes the defense budget proposal produced by the Defense Department and circulates that critique throughout the government as well as to the public.

In addition, think tanks provide a *talent bank* (the term used by the Nixon administration) for the government. This process works in two directions. In one direction, when an administration leaves office and is replaced by another (especially when another political party wins the White House), some personnel dislocation occurs among the several thousand officials who hold political appointments and who find their services are no longer required as the new president forms his own distinct team. Many officials so removed do not want to leave the Washington scene altogether and even have aspirations of returning to senior government service in the future. For such people, appointment to a position in one of the research institutes can provide an attractive option that serves both the individual and the organization. From the individual's viewpoint, a think-tank appointment can serve as a safe haven, a sanctuary between periods of government service wherein the person can remain abreast of what is happening in Washington and available for recall. From the organizational vantage point, the association of important former governmental officials can enhance both the prestige and expertise of the organization. This movement is, of course, much the same as the revolving-door phenomenon already noted about interest groups.

In the other direction, the staffs of the research institutes provide a ready talent pool for filling governmental positions. It has been argued, for instance, that the Brookings Institution, as well as the John F. Kennedy School of Government at Harvard University, provides a kind of "government in waiting" for any new Democratic president, just as The Heritage Foundation and AEI provide a source of policy inspiration and personnel for Republican administrations.

Think tanks also are a *focal point for like-minded individuals*. This function formed one of the major purposes of formalizing the conservative movement through Heritage and other organizations following Barry Goldwater's crushing defeat by Lyndon Johnson in the 1964 election. The feeling was that conservatives had failed to develop and articulate a politically attractive agenda because they had no mechanism around which those of like persuasion could rally. A research institute with an active research and publication program filled this bill. Research leading to the articulation of policy positions can help clarify the policy agenda for any group. A publications program utilizing books, technical reports, talking papers, or articles in a house-sponsored journal can help circulate ideas and establish networks of like-minded scholars and policy analysts. These organizations often operate largely outside the public view but can become quite powerful, as in the case of the Jewish Institute for National Security Affairs (JINSA). JINSA is perhaps best thought of as a hybrid model: part interest group (it has members), part think tank (it does studies and tries to disseminate its expertise). JINSA, though, like an increasing number of such hybrid organizations, is anything but dispassionate in its analysis.

A newly emerging function of think tanks is the *media connection*, and more specifically, the role of the *electronic expert* mentioned earlier in the chapter. This phenomenon is the result of the media's burgeoning need for information and expertise, combined with the opportunities for organizational and self-promotion that the electronic expert's role provides for the think tanks. The media's needs date back to the Vietnam period. Events, and especially their analysis and understanding, often went beyond the expertise of the television networks and print media who, for instance, did not possess staff experts on Southeast Asian history and politics or the principles of mobile-guerrilla warfare (the style of war employed by the North Vietnamese and their Viet Cong allies). Those media, with headquarters and major bureaus in the same locales as the major think tanks (which did have staff with expertise in those very areas), created an obvious marriage of convenience. The media's need was for experts who exuded authority, whereas the think tanks sought the exposure that having members of their staffs appearing on the evening news could provide.

This role has been expanding because of trends in electronic mediation. CNN was the trendsetter, followed by other full-time news organizations such as CNBC, MSNBC, and Fox News, for example. By necessity, these channels engage in a great deal of news analysis in addition to reporting (there is, after all, lots of time to fill in twenty-four hours!). To analyze the news requires expert authorities, and the think tanks are a fertile ground. In addition, CNN changed the extent and depth by which breaking news events, and especially foreign events, are covered. Knowing that CNN and others will produce very detailed coverage of an international crisis forces the other news organizations (wire services, leading papers, and television networks) to cover events in more detail than ever before. The alternative is to concede news coverage supremacy to CNN. Unwilling to do that, the need for experts proliferates.

This phenomenon reached new heights during the Persian Gulf War and more recently during the response to 9/11 and the wars in Iraq and Afghanistan. Each television network recruited its own complement of experts to appear daily to explain what had happened, supplemented by periodic appearances by others. One can expect this trend to continue and expand in the future as the public is "always on" with tools such as smartphones and iPads, social networking sites (which the media also use to push news to the public) such as Facebook and Twitter, and other means of constant contact.

CONCLUSIONS

Both think tanks and interest groups can be seen in the context of the system of informal checks and balances on which the political system operates. Nearly every interest has a group to represent it and to make sure its voice is heard; the think tanks span the range of intellectual points of view. In the overall context of the U.S. government, interest groups are a more important phenomenon than think tanks. The former are larger, more numerous, more visible, richer, can bring electoral pressure to bear, and hence are more powerful. Think tanks, however, are probably more represented and effective in influencing foreign and defense policy than in other areas because international relations is an important area of social science inquiry.

The two kinds of institutions share similarities and differences. Both, for instance, seek to influence policy rather than to govern directly (although some think-tank staffers and interest-group lobbyists move in and out of government), but they do so differently and for different reasons. Interest groups act self-interestedly: They attempt to move public policy so it will favor those they represent. The early think tanks in particular sought to improve government not from self-interest but out of an academically driven sense of improving the government. As discussed, however, this norm is becoming more ambiguous as advocacy think tanks bring a political and often partisan agenda into their work.

The purposes of the two groups are reflected in the means they use. Although both institutions seek to educate the public and those who govern, their methods differ. The tools of interest groups are persuasion (lobbying), education, and pressure. The extreme form of their actions is found in the activities of PACs and other campaign expenditure organizations. The use of pressure by PACs is the natural result of acting out of self-interest: Specific outcomes are highly personalized. Because they presumably act disinterestedly, the think tanks use persuasion based in expertise and objective knowledge as their major tool.

Some of these distinctions are vanishing, as some think tanks begin to operate more and more like interest groups, and vice versa; hybrids seem to be on the rise, groups that are part think tank, part interest group, such as JINSA. The politically activist, and especially conservative, movement within the research institute community during the 1980s produced a hybrid think tank with a specific political agenda. The tools may remain educational in the broad sense, but they result from directed research. This research is aimed not at increasing the general pool of knowledge but at providing knowledge that reinforces political predilections.

Finally, the two institutions form a bridge between government and the broader society that is the subject of Chapter Eight. In broad terms, interest groups aggregate, articulate, and seek to influence the public at large as well as the direction of foreign policy. At the same time, the media are the object of some educational elements by both groups, and the growing phenomenon of the electronic expert provides a new link between the media and the think tanks.

WHERE DO WE GO FROM HERE?

The text has discussed the basic character of interest groups and think tanks in America, particularly those that focus their efforts on foreign policy. It has also seen how these groups have become increasingly active and ideological or partisan in recent years, thus lending their contribution to the hyperpartisan environment within which foreign policy must be made today. The "always on" nature of modern technology has helped speed this process, but it has also made these groups more accessible to you than was perhaps the case twenty years ago. Back then, as a college student one might have subscribed to *Foreign Affairs* magazine (with a nice low rate for students), for example, but this world was otherwise rather invisible outside of the Washington beltway. Not so, today. It is worth thinking about how you are connected to these organizations, or could be, before we bring this chapter to a close.

APPLICATION: JOIN A GROUP, OR USE A THINK TANK

Are you a member of an interest group that tracks a foreign policy issue, or one that lobbies in the foreign policy area? You might be without even really knowing it. Unions, for example, get active in the foreign policy area, especially in the area of foreign economic policy (a topic examined later in the book). Perhaps you joined Amnesty International in the past. Assess your "memberships," and find out what kinds of educational and lobbying efforts interest groups are doing while they claim to "represent" you to policy makers.

Another way to think about it is, are there interest groups out there that purport to represent you and you never even noticed? For example, ethnic interest groups like to argue that they represent the views of all Americans who share a particular ethnic identity. Do you have an ethnic background in your ancestry, recent or distant, that a group claims to represent? Go to the web and find out! Are there a lot of groups out there claiming to represent the interests of (fill in the blank)-Americans, or just one or two? Do they promote policies with which you agree or disagree? Join one that you like, if you're not already a member. Use this as a way to get more engaged in foreign policy issues, and perhaps even in the foreign policy process.

If you are taking this political science class, chances are good that you are also taking others, or will in the future. Another way to consider a connection to think tanks is to go to their websites and use their research for the papers you are writing (appropriately citing that research of course!). As discussed, many think tanks make their research accessible through the Internet for free (some will charge you for certain things). Hunt around and find research on a topic that you are pursuing. Remember that think tanks increasingly come at a problem or question from a particular perspective, so you will want to draw on research from several think tanks, not rely on only one and thus introduce their biases into your work. Maybe you will find that there is a think tank, or interest group, out there that you agree with so much you will want to try to get an internship there in the future.

STUDY/DISCUSSION QUESTIONS

1. What are the purposes of foreign policy interest groups? How do they serve a gatekeeping function between the government and the public?
2. How do interest groups go about trying to influence foreign policy?
3. What are ethnic interest groups, and why do some find their emergence to be controversial?
4. What is the iron triangle? How is Eisenhower's warning about the "military-industrial complex" a precursor of this political science concept?
5. What purpose have think tanks traditionally served? How is that changing?
6. In what ways is the distinction between an interest group and a think tank starting to break down?
7. What role do political action committees (PACs) play? What other kinds of groups like PACs have emerged recently that also might try to influence foreign policy?
8. In terms of normative conceptions of democracy, is it fair that interest groups and think tanks have emerged as such important players in policy making? In what ways is it fair and reasonable? In what ways is it unfair and undemocratic?

CORE SUGGESTED READINGS

Mearsheimer, John J., and Stephen M. Walt. *The Israel Lobby and U.S. Foreign Policy*. New York: Farrar, Straus and Giroux, 2007. A must-read for anyone interested in foreign policy lobbying, this is also one of the most controversial books in recent years by political scientists. The authors try to sketch out the broad influence of what they call the "Israel lobby" (with only mixed success, we think).

Smith, Tony. *Foreign Attachments*. Cambridge, MA: Harvard University Press, 2000. This is an excellent discussion of the rise and role of ethnic interest groups in America, and engages in the controversy over whether the emergence of ethnic identity groups is good or bad for the country.

Torres, Maria de los Angeles. *In the Land of Mirrors: Cuban Exile Politics in the United States*. Ann Arbor: University of Michigan, 2002. Torres provides one of the best treatments available on the rise of Cuban "exile" politics in America.

Wiarda, Howard. *Think Tanks and Foreign Policy: The Foreign Policy Research Institute and Presidential Politics*. Lanham, MD: Lexington Books, 2010. The author tracks the emergence of foreign policy think tanks as they have become major players in the foreign policy process.

ADDITIONAL READINGS AND REFERENCES

Abelson, Donald E. *Do Think Tanks Matter? Assessing the Impact of Public Policy Institutes* (2nd ed.). Montreal: McGill-Queens University Press, 2009.

Ainsworth, Scott H. *Analyzing Interest Groups: Group Influence on People and Policies*. New York: W. W. Norton, 2002.

Browne, William P. *Groups, Interests, and U.S. Public Policy*. Washington, DC: Georgetown University Press, 1998.

Cigler, Allan J., and Burdett Loomis (eds.). *Interest Group Politics* (6th ed.). Washington, DC: CQ Press, 2002.

Delgado, Richard, Jean Stefancic, and Mark Tushnet. *No Mercy: How Conservative Think Tanks and Foundations Changed America's Social Agenda*. Philadelphia, PA: Temple University Press, 1996.

Grossman, Gene M., and Elhanan Helpman. *Special Interest Groups*. Cambridge, MA: MIT Press, 2001.

Hrebenar, Ronald J. *Interest Group Politics in America* (3rd ed.). Armonk, NY: M. E. Sharpe, 1997.

Mahood, H. R. *Interest Groups in American National Politics: An Overview*. Upper Saddle River, NJ: Prentice Hall, 2000.

Marrar, Khalil. *The Arab Lobby and U.S. Foreign Policy*. New York: Routledge, 2009.

McGann, James G., and Richard Sabatini. *Global Think Tanks: Policy Networks and Governance*. New York: Routledge, 2011.

Miller, Stephen. *Special Interest Groups in American Politics*. New Brunswick, NJ: Transaction Books, 1983.

Nownes, Anthony J. *Pressure and Power: Organized Interests in American Politics*. Boston: Houghton-Mifflin, 2001.

Ricci, David M. *The Transformation of American Politics: The New Washington and the Rise of Think Tanks*. New Haven, CT: Yale University Press, 1994.

Rich, Andrew. *Think Tanks, Public Policy, and the Politics of Expertise*. New York: Cambridge University Press, 2005.

Smith, James Allen. *The Idea Brokers: Think Tanks and the Rise of the New Policy Elite*. New York: Free Press, 1993.

Weiss, Carol H. *Organizations for Policy Analysis: Helping Government Think*. Newbury Park, CA: Sage, 1992.

CHAPTER
8

The Public and the Media

Cameras, smartphones, and social networking sites are revolutionizing the way revolutions

PREVIEW

The Public and the Media both play important, though complicated, roles in U.S. foreign policy. The public (or at least those who vote) picks winners in elections, and those winners go on to make foreign policy and, in the case of the president, to appoint others who help make foreign policy. The public can both push for certain foreign policies and serve as a restraint against unpopular foreign policy initiatives. In general, however, the mass public pays little attention to foreign policy except during major crises (such as the attacks of September 11th). Some members of the public, however, pay particularly close attention to foreign policy issues and try to play a more direct role in promoting their foreign policy preferences to government policy makers. Much of how the public, especially the mass public, "sees" foreign policy issues comes through the media. Print and electronic journalism and increasingly bloggers and Twitter entries—and even "fake" news—try to inform the public and help hold government officials accountable to the public; and perhaps they also try to convince the public to see things a certain way. As this chapter discusses, the relationship between the people, the press, and the government is complex and symbiotic, not always in ways that are conducive to democratic accountability.

KEY CONCEPTS

Nightline
fourth estate
Tet Offensive
leaks
Operation Desert Storm
Almond-Lippmann consensus
mass public
rally
informed public
effective public
opinion leaders
halo effect
Diversionary Theory of War
prior restraint
Pentagon Papers
watchdogging
media diplomacy
CNN effect
soft news

In June 2009 voters went to the polls across Iran in a presidential election. When the official count was released showing that President Mahmoud Ahmadinejad easily won reelection over a number of candidates including "moderate" Mir Hossein Mousavi, protests erupted. Iran's religious leader, Ayatollah Ali Khamenei, sanctioned the result, leading Mousavi to protest to Iran's governing council that the vote should be set aside due to fraud. The "Green Revolution" followed; mass protests in the streets against the ruling regime were met with a brutal crackdown by the police (including the secret police and government-run militias).

One of the striking things about the Green Revolution is that to the extent that it was "televised," it was on Twitter. With the government controlling the media in Iran, and with the ability of foreign journalists to work curtailed in such a dangerous environment, news organizations around the world turned to Twitter and other social networking sites such as Facebook and YouTube to follow the flow of events in Iran. The protesters used Twitter and other sites to send the word out about where a protest would be, where the police were, and news about friends who had been hurt, arrested, or killed. Pictures and video (such as the notorious footage of the death of the young Iranian woman Neda Agha-Soltan) were taken by participants and uploaded to the web. An international ad hoc coalition of supporters forwarded the messages and video footage on to Western news outlets such as the BBC and redirected protesters to "safe" and open web proxy servers around the world when the Iranian government tried to and ultimately did shut down the activity.

While many have joined the bandwagon that these technologies have fundamentally altered the flow of world politics, it is also worth remembering that the Green Revolution failed (at least for now) and that Ahmadinejad is still in power (although some suggest that the military seized much power from civilian and religious leaders during this period). It is also true that just as Americans could follow the action on Twitter, so too could the Iranian government and police (and they could use "fake" Twitter accounts and posts to deceive the protesters, who warned each other to send Tweets only to those people they already knew). As Clay Shirky discusses in the January/February issue of *Foreign Affairs* magazine, the political power of social networking media is promising, perhaps, but not necessarily determinative. The Save Darfur Coalition Facebook page has more than 28,000 friends, but perhaps to little effect. Malcolm Gladwell calls this "slacktivism," trading social networking for the hard work of affecting real political change.

Even with those critiques in mind, it is striking to note the changed way that the American public engages with news about global events and foreign policy. In the 1979 Revolution in Iran, when Americans were held hostage inside the American embassy in Tehran for 444 days, a nightly show appeared on ABC to update viewers on the hostage crisis, *America Held Hostage*. Over time, as it became clear that the hostage crisis was going to continue on, the show started to give quick updates on the situation and then go on to focus on other news. In 1980 the show was renamed **Nightline**. In a sense, then, the media environment followed and was driven by the flow of events; thirty years later the media environment would be an essential vehicle for the events.

If you think that policy makers in the United States do not pay attention to such things, you had better think again. The White House has an elaborate web page (www.whitehouse.gov), it has a Facebook page, it blogs, it is on Flickr and YouTube, and it Tweets! The same is true of an increasing number of members of Congress, as well as the executive branch. Only the Supreme Court seems out of the loop on such changes.

These technological changes intersect with the public and foreign policy in a number of ways. At a time when events around the world affect Americans more quickly and directly than ever before, and when news about these events is perhaps easier to get than ever before, that news may lead to even less understanding than in previous times. News on the Internet, blogs, and Tweets all have in common that they are short and to the point; understanding international affairs requires more depth and focus. So at a time when it is more important than ever that Americans—and their leaders—understand global affairs so as to craft wise policies, it may be tougher than ever. Beyond that, the hyperpartisan nature of our politics has leaked into foreign policy, meaning that there is a lot of screaming about foreign policy, but less understanding.

Central to the philosophical underpinning of the American political system is the notion that sovereignty ultimately resides with individual citizens, who in turn delegate part of that sovereignty to government to carry out the duties of state. Governmental authority, including the authority to conduct foreign policy, flows from and is limited by the sovereignty that has been ceded by the people. Those who govern pay a price for their authority in the form of the principle of accountability. According to this principle, the people reserve the right to inspect what their government does in carrying out the public trust and hence to decide whether the job is being done correctly. In terms of public assessment, those who govern can be deemed adequate and retained or inadequate and removed from office. Elections are thus important accountability moments (see the first *Intersections* feature for more on elections and foreign policy). This need for accountability ensures that the public's opinion cannot be ignored in the conduct of foreign policy.

The role of the media, as provided for and protected by the First Amendment guarantee of a free and unrestrained press, assists the public in rendering its judgments by investigating and publicizing the performance of those who govern. Because a large part of the media's job is to act as watchdogs against incompetent or corrupt governmental action, a natural adversarial relationship exists between what is often called the "**fourth estate**" (a term for the press that was first used in the nineteenth century to contrast it with the three classes of citizens of England) and those in government.

Our lives today are permeated by electronic information: from social networking sites such as Facebook to Twitter feeds to constant flows of twenty-four-hour news and opinion easily available by cable, satellite, iPads, and smartphones. For many Americans, part of that content is foreign policy news and information. The evolution of the electronic information revolution has facilitated the rise of increasingly niche media that cater to a particular audience and that promote seeing the "facts" in a certain way. Just as Congress, and the political struggle between the White House and Capitol Hill, has become increasingly partisan and divisive, the media environment within which these actors work and conduct their public lives has also become more divisive. This certainly contributes to the hyperpartisan nature of foreign policy making today, making it even more challenging to build consensus in the area of foreign policy. Since it is almost impossible to talk about public opinion without also talking about the role of the media (as the place from which people get the information to help them form their opinions), this chapter considers the role of these two forces in the foreign policy process together in one place.

BETWEEN THEORY AND PRACTICE

The relationship among the public, the media, and the government is not as simple and straightforward as it sounds. Although the people have the theoretical ability to monitor, critique, and demand alterations in policy, in fact their ability is compromised in the area of foreign policy by a number of factors that make accountability more difficult. Before turning to an examination of the effects of the public and the media on the foreign policy process and on individual foreign policies, it is useful to look at some prominent examples of practical impediments to applying notions of authority and accountability between the government and the people and between the media and the government. This is not meant to be an exhaustive list, but is meant to provide some examples of the influences on the process. Three sources of difficulty are control of the foreign policy agenda, secrecy, and public ignorance of foreign policy. Each is illustrated by contemporary examples.

Control of the Agenda

In the realm of foreign policy, unlike in many domestic policy areas, Americans in or out of government do not always have the ability to determine the kinds of problems with which they will deal. Instead, in much of foreign policy, the agenda setters are foreign governments or elements within foreign countries that create situations to which the United States must respond. The President and other government officials can try to control the foreign policy agenda, but their control is certainly less than absolute. The terrorist attacks of September 11th clearly show how foreign elements can seize the foreign policy agenda. Before the attacks, only a few experts in the terrorism field knew of the existence and intentions of Osama bin Laden and Al Qaeda, and international terrorism was hardly at the top of the public foreign policy agenda of the United States (whether it should have been is a different question). After the attacks, however, responding to terrorism became the central fixation of foreign policy makers whether they wanted it to be or not. Control of the agenda had moved.

The inability to control the agenda makes applying the principle of accountability more complicated. Foreign governments—or foreign nongovernmental groups—do, at times, act to make the U.S. government look better or worse, depending on whether a particular government likes or dislikes the administration in office or a policy being pursued. Officials in the former Soviet Union, for instance, regularly acted during presidential election years to paint the incumbent in a better or worse light, depending on whether those officials felt reelection was in their best interest. Similarly, the activities of bin Laden and his followers have clearly been aimed at swaying American public opinion away from the continued U.S. presence in Saudi Arabia, Iraq, and Afghanistan, and support for Israel. Dramatic violence and mayhem guarantee maximum media coverage and hence public impact.

Secrecy

Foreign policy is often conducted in an adversarial context; this is especially true of national security policy. The ability to hide information from adversaries and to conceal what one knows about them and how one knows it can provide some advantage in dealing with other actors. All this secrecy, though, can be a disadvantage for democracy. The inability to know everything the policy maker knows can hamper the ability of the public to hold policy makers accountable for their actions, especially in the area of foreign and national security policy. There is some trade-off between accountability and security; a natural tension exists between secrecy and democracy. The debate, especially in a post–Cold War world, is how much compromise of democratic ideals remains necessary.

The need to conceal has both legitimate and illegitimate bases. On the positive side, it is sometimes necessary to conceal information that provides the basis for making a decision because to reveal that basis would compromise the source from which it came or the method that was used to acquire the information. This is known as *source sensitivity* and provides much of the rationale for classifying (restricting access to) information within the intelligence community and the government in general, to protect "sources and methods."

The conduct of diplomacy provides another legitimate example. When negotiating with another country, the negotiator is trying to obtain concessions that will move a situation as close to the national interest as possible. The nature of negotiation is give-and-take, with each side willing to compromise to get what it wants. One never, however, admits in advance how much one is willing to give away, because once that is revealed, there is nothing left to bargain about. Furthermore, often the private positions revealed in diplomacy are at odds with the public positions one takes. The November 2010 revelations on the WikiLeaks website of a range of State Department cables detailing private conversations with foreign dignitaries provides one glimpse into this world of (what was supposed to be) private diplomacy. (See the WikiLeaks discussion in Chapter Four.)

Secrecy means that public assessment of performance begins with only a partial record of what happened and what influenced policy decisions. How can we know if a source has to be protected from exposure or recrimination if we are denied information or sources? For that matter, do we know if secret information exists or is accurate? If we do not know the bargaining position our negotiators bargained from, how can we know if the deal they got was the best one possible? The answer, of course, is that accountability is left imperfect.

The negative side of secrecy is that it may be imposed for the wrong reasons, such as to obscure the government's incompetent or illegal actions or, directly or indirectly, to influence public support for a policy. In the Iran-Contra scandal of the 1980s, for instance, the facts of selling arms to Iran in exchange for assistance in gaining the release of hostages held in Lebanon and the diversion of arms-derived funds to the Nicaraguan Contras were kept secret from the American people and Congress. At least part of the reason for keeping that information secret was that the public would not have approved of the actions, both because it was an ill-considered policy and because it violated stated policy and even law.

The existence, or absence, of information about whether Iraq possessed weapons of mass destruction (WMD) that underpinned the crisis of 2002–2004 is also illustrative. The Bush administration repeatedly asserted Iraqi possession of WMD but never produced positive information supporting its claims, citing the need for secrecy when it bothered to provide any support for its assertions.

The cloak of secrecy left Americans unable to render judgment that would have clarified policy options, leaving partisans on both sides to bicker without any real authoritative information. When it turned out that there were no WMD in Iraq, and that much of the information that was used to claim that they did exist was unreliable, it was too late. One cannot unring a bell, after all. The only remaining question was whether George W. Bush would be reelected in 2004 (he was, following a close election).

General Public's Lack of Foreign Policy Knowledge

Most analyses of what the public can and should do to affect and judge foreign policy have concluded that the role has been and continues to be very limited, mostly in the form of passive reaction to initiatives taken by the president. The reason traditionally cited for the public's historical ineffectiveness in influencing the foreign policy process is its legendary ignorance of international affairs. A very small percentage of the population keeps abreast of foreign events, has traveled abroad, carries a passport, speaks a foreign language, or has taken formal courses at any level dealing with foreign cultures, history, or international relations. This lack of knowledge, combined with widespread perceptions that foreign affairs are so intricate and involved as to be beyond the comprehension of the average citizen, reinforces the people's general ineffectiveness in influencing how government conducts foreign and national security affairs.

One of the central roles of the media is to try to increase citizen awareness. As a foreign policy actor, the media's relationship to the process contains several aspects. One of these is whether the media are agenda setters, forcing policy attention on the events they cover, or whether they reflect the agenda presented by events and policy makers. This question is of mounting importance because of global television's and the Internet's increasing reach and proficiency at graphically covering events and disasters live and in real time. In other words, would the international system have been forced to take any action in Bosnia and Herzegovina had the slaughter of civilians in Sarajevo not been an undeniable and unavoidable fixture of the nightly news? Television brought Somali starvation into American living rooms; however, similar privation in such places as neighboring Sudan went unreported and hence unnoticed by the public or policy makers for a long time. The 2011 referendum on the secession of Southern Sudan from the rest of the country was partially a response to that neglect. Journalists—of both the professional and the amateur variety—post stories and pictures to Internet sites, on blogs, on Facebook, on Twitter, often as they are happening (as has been the case throughout the "Arab Spring"). Does television and the Internet make a difference?

The relationship between the media and those in authority is also relevant. Ideally the relationship between these two actors is and should be partly an adversarial one, because part of the press's role is to expose governmental misdeeds, the attempts of officials to gain excessive power (the real concern of the Constitution's Framers), and instances of incompetence. The problem has become greater in recent years. On one hand, Americans now have more media coverage of everything, including foreign policy. On the other hand, the Vietnam and Watergate episodes greatly worsened relations between government and the media. In Vietnam, for instance, the media believed they had been duped into falsely reporting progress by the military before the **Tet Offensive** of 1968 (an attack by the North Vietnamese that, if casualty figures dutifully reported by the media from U.S. government sources had been truthful, the North Vietnamese would not have had adequate personnel to stage). After watching the events of the Tet Offensive on television, including fighting inside the U.S. Embassy compound in Saigon, the American public started turning against both the war and Lyndon Johnson's presidency. (Johnson would later announce that he would neither seek nor accept the nomination of his party to run for another term.)

The adversarial relationship receded somewhat after September 11th. The media accepted and reported government activities in the War on Terrorism dutifully and virtually uncritically, a phenomenon that caused some critics to question the media's objectivity and diligence in investigation and to draw unfavorable comparisons between that coverage and the uniformly proadministration coverage of Vietnam prior to Tet. The tensions between the normal of "professional" journalism and patriotism seemed to be building. As the postinvasion period of the Iraq War failed to unearth evidence of Iraqi weapons of mass destruction or ties to September 11th, however, some of the adversarial tone did start to creep back into reportage. It was hard for much of the press to be too tough on the government in this story, as (with the exception of some reporters for Knight Ridder news service and a few others) they were mostly on the same train that the Bush administration was riding. As an example, *The New York Times* had to distance itself from the work of one of its "star" reporters, Judith Miller, when it became apparent that much of her reporting on Iraq's WMD programs in the lead-up to the invasion and on the search for WMD in Iraq, turned out to be less than reliable.

There are really three relationships at work here between the public, the government, and the media. The first relationship is the one between the public and the media. The main pressures in that relationship include the degree to which the media provide the public with adequate and accurate foreign and defense policy information and interpretation, the degree to which the public takes advantage of the information provided, and whether the media serve to lead or reflect public opinion (or both). The key new variables in the public-media relationship are (1) the emergence in the past decade of the global electronic media and how this changes both the public's access to and awareness of foreign policy events and issues, and (2) the rise of media conglomeration (several electronic or print media—or their combination—owned by a single large corporation) that may adversely affect the breadth of reporting and opinion despite increases in media volume. Along with conglomeration has come an impressive cutting back on the foreign news bureaus of American newspapers and television networks. We may, in other words, be hearing the same slant on the news in multiple apparently independent sources.

The second relationship is the one between the media and the government. This relationship has been especially strained in the foreign policy area because of the information advantages the government enjoys here. The media is trying to get information from the government, which means they are in a sense captive to what the government will give to them. One way to restrict access to information and to keep things secret is the use (and overuse) of classification procedures. From the media's vantage point, very little information should be restricted, and entirely too much information is classified. The media have the further suspicion that information is classified not based on legitimate need but instead is used to cover up misdeeds or to influence policy in directions that full disclosure would not support.

The only people legally bound to maintain the secrecy of classified information are those who have voluntarily done so as a term of employment with the government. Members of the media do not fall under that restriction, which is a source of discomfort to those charged with maintaining the confidentiality of information. The media can try to get people who have access to classified information to **"leak"** it to the press, but one needs to exercise caution about **leaks**. Sometimes a leak is not really a leak at all, but more of a "trial balloon" where the government releases information as a test of sorts, to see how people will react to a piece of information or a potential policy change. When a release of information really is a "leak" from the inside, often the person leaking the information has an agenda behind the leak: perhaps to try to embarrass someone, or to try to shift the terms of a policy debate that the person is losing inside the government. In 2003, for example, members of the Bush administration attempted to discredit a prominent critic of the case they made for the invasion of Iraq (former Ambassador Joseph Wilson) by leaking to the press that his wife (Valerie Plame) was an undercover CIA agent. The contorted logic for this leak was either to punish the Wilson family for his dissent or to make it look as if his information emerged from some malfeasance by his wife. Either way, this odd episode helps show that while leaked information might be helpful and useful to the public, the public needs to be critical evaluators of these leaks since there is usually some kind of motive behind them.

The third relationship is the one between the government and the people. The media serve as a conduit in this regard, because most of what people know about international affairs and the government's reaction to those events comes from the media. The major question is how well and how thoroughly the media dispatch this role. With the information revolution the government has increasingly tried to talk directly ("unmediated") to the people. Presidential press conferences and speeches, for example, are one way for the president to talk directly to the public. The White House website and its iPhone and iPad apps are also examples of how the president tries to communicate and build a relationship (on the president's terms, of course) directly with the people, going around the press in the process. The White House also has a blog, a Twitter feed, and is on Facebook. Many other government agencies (such as the Defense Department and State Department) use similar strategies for connecting with the public directly, as do many members of Congress.

This brief introduction forms the basis of an inspection of both the public's and the media's role in the policy process. As stated at the outset, there is a conventional view of both, especially of the public. Although the discussion that follows reiterates the basic elements of the conventional wisdom about each, it also explains how roles may be changing and evolving as the world and technology evolves.

THE PUBLIC

For most of U.S. history, and certainly before World War II, the public played a minor role in making and implementing the country's foreign policy. This was largely due to the fact that the public was only rarely affected by foreign policy events, had little information about them, and, hence, had very little need or desire to be involved.

The permanent ascendance of the United States to a position of global leadership after World War II began the process of changing that situation. As the leader of the Western coalition facing an apparently implacable Soviet enemy with whom nuclear war could come at any time, the government needed to convince the public that what the United States did in the world was morally right and necessary.

With the need for public participation established, the question became the level and quality of public participation. At one extremity in the debate were the foreign policy professionals, who wanted the public's role to be as minimal as possible. Their most articulate spokesperson at the time was George F. Kennan. He and others, known as elitists, argued that the public's role should simply be to accept and ratify the wisdom of the professionals. At the other extreme were more egalitarian voices, maintaining that because it was the public that had to bear the burden of foreign policy decisions, the public must be involved. The debate has never been resolved (and perhaps never will be) in a way that is entirely acceptable to everyone.

One way to look at the traditional role of the public is as a parameter setter. Because the public does not possess detailed expertise in foreign affairs, it cannot set the agenda, nor is it likely to provide detailed guidance to policy makers on foreign policies. What the public can and does do, however, is set the broad outer boundaries, or parameters, of policy that it will accept. Within those boundaries, policy makers have reasonable discretion to act. When government exceeds those limits, however, its policy can be in trouble. Government officials must therefore determine whether support will be forthcoming before it acts, especially if its actions will have a direct bearing on the citizenry. The U.S. government learned this lesson the hard way in the Vietnam War, where government actions exceeded public tolerance and public opposition ultimately forced the United States to abandon the effort.

Interestingly enough, this relationship was stated perhaps most articulately by a Prussian general staff officer more than 175 years ago. In his seminal work *On War* (1831), Carl von Clausewitz identified a "holy trinity" without whose support a government's foreign policy effort (in his case, the conduct of war) could not be successfully sustained. The elements of the trinity are the people, the army, and the government. Clausewitz maintained that the active support of each segment was critical to a war's success.

In retrospect, many observers—especially in the military—think the flaw in the Vietnam debacle was in ignoring the trinity. More specifically, the failure to activate public support (or opposition) before American intervention eventually led the public to turn on the war and caused the effort, as Clausewitz would have predicted, to collapse. Currying popular support of a proposed military action in advance of possible hostilities has become the norm since Vietnam, reflecting lessons learned from that conflict and at least implicitly paying homage to the Clausewitzian trinity. In the contemporary era, however, the role of the media as a key player—a "mediating" force—in the relationship between the public and the government must also be taken into account, and perhaps cultivated by the government.

Operation Desert Storm was the first application of this new understanding about the relationship between the public and the government. A first act in forming the force that would be dispatched to the Persian Gulf was a large-scale activation of reserve units. This was the first time the reserves had been called to overseas duty since the Korean War forty years before. Activating the reserves was an implicit way of testing public opinion: Would Americans endorse sending friends, neighbors, and loved ones to war? The reserves and the public responded, thus giving the military the kind of assurance it sought. This form of soliciting support was reinforced by requesting not a declaration of war but rather a congressional resolution supporting troop commitment, a sequence repeated by George W. Bush in 2001 and 2002 before the military operation in Afghanistan and the invasion of Iraq (and one loosely similar in terms of the dynamics to Johnson's Gulf of Tonkin Resolution, if not Theodore Roosevelt's Great White Fleet). The Bush administration also built a system for the media so that they could cover the war, should it occur, but not as freely as they did in Vietnam; they would not be censored, per se, but they would certainly be led.

Is the relationship between the government and the people on important foreign and defense policy concerns established in Desert Storm a precedent for the future or an aberration? To assess that question, we must first look at the traditional view of the public's role and then show how that role may be changing and also how our understanding of that role is evolving as well.

The Traditional View: Multiple "Publics"

Much of the literature on the public and foreign policy has stressed not what the public can and should do but the limitations on that role. The conventional view of the literature is that the source of this limitation is the historically high degree of general citizen disinterest in and ignorance of foreign affairs, which some argue makes meaningful public participation impossible. Early research in the area even emphasized that the public not only knew little about foreign policy, but what beliefs they did have were unorganized, unpredictable, wrong, and perhaps even irrational. This view came to be called the **Almond-Lippmann consensus**, after the work of prominent political scientist Gabriel Almond and writer and commentator Walter Lippmann.

The first step toward unpacking the limitations of the Almond-Lippmann consensus is to divide the public into a series of segments of increasing knowledge about foreign affairs, beginning with the **mass public,** the majority of people who have very little knowledge of or interest in foreign policy, and culminating with the small body of core decision makers who actually make and influence policy. This begins to give us a richer sense of the way the "public" engages with and is engaged by foreign policy.

The Mass Public At the outer limits of influence is the mass public, sometimes also called the uninformed, or inattentive, public. It is by far the largest portion of the population, encompassing 75 to 80 percent of the total. The mass public is defined as that portion of the population that does not regularly seek out information about international affairs. Operationally, the mass public does not read stories about foreign affairs in newspapers or newsmagazines, does not read books on the subject, and perhaps even avoids those parts of news broadcasts dealing with foreign policy. As a result the mass public not only tends not to know much about foreign affairs (which creates a democratic accountability problem), but they also tend not to have well-developed "belief systems" about foreign policy either, or frameworks that help create a coherent view of world events and the role of the United States in the world. So their knowledge in the area is spotty, and their reactions to foreign policy (when they become aware of it) can be inconsistent.

Because of all this, the mass public tends to become aware of or involved in foreign policy issues in three circumstances. The first occurs when a foreign policy event has a direct and personal bearing on people. Forty years ago, the draft for the Vietnam War was of this nature, as was the boycott of the 1980 Summer Olympics in Moscow; more recently, the mobilization of reserves for Operation Desert Storm, the War on Terrorism, and the Iraq War are examples of the kinds of things that get the mass public's attention on foreign policy (at least temporarily).

A second circumstance occurs when broad publicity is given to international events. Publicizing the plight of Kurdish refugees fleeing Saddam Hussein's forces in the wake of Desert Storm created a public awareness that otherwise would have been lost on all but the most dedicated student of foreign policy. The attacks of September 11th and the widespread publicity about Al Qaeda and terrorism is a further example, as was the relentless (if largely off the mark) reporting of alleged Iraqi violations of WMD stockpiling in 2002 and 2003.

There is a tendency for the mass public to "rally around the flag" at a time of national crisis or danger, whether it comes from natural (for instance, floods) or human (for example, terrorism) causes. One of the natural advantages of the presidency, as discussed in Chapter Four, is the singularity of office: There is only one president at a time. In these times of crisis, the public tends to rally around the president, giving a spike of support or approval that, while temporary, the president can use to support some policy action or response to the crisis. Figure 8.1 shows such a rally event for President George W. Bush; a dramatic spike in the approval ratings of the president followed the terrorist attacks of 9/11.

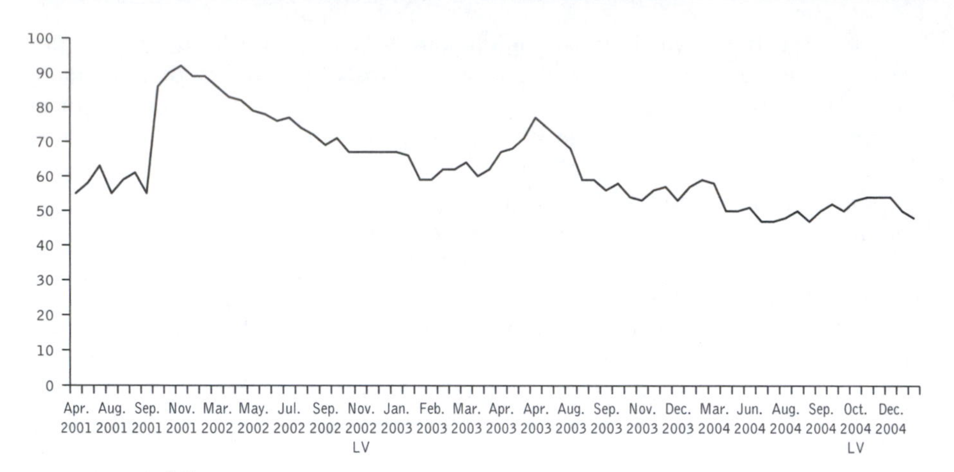

FIGURE 8.1
Rally Around the Flag (and President)

Do you approve of the way George W. Bush has handled his job as president?

Source: The Washington Post–ABC News poll, http://www.washingtonpost.com/wp-srv/politics/documents/post-poll_011709.html, accessed on August 10, 2011.

The tendency for the mass public to rally around the flag, and thus the president, in times of crisis can also make it tempting for presidents to take advantage of crises to divert the public's attention from something else. Richard Nixon's trip to Egypt in 1974 to divert attention from the Watergate scandal, which would shortly force his resignation from the presidency, is a particularly strong example. (Nixon's approval ratings in the polls temporarily rose more than twenty points during the visit.) President George W. Bush's dogged focus on Iraq served, purposely or not, to divert public attention from a sluggish American economy in 2002 and 2003, although this returned as a major campaign issue in 2004.

In the third circumstance, the president, others in the government, or outside groups (such as interest groups and think tanks) might make conscious efforts to mobilize public opinion. It is usually true that the public is less critical of foreign policy actions than domestic actions and will generally "**rally**" behind the president in foreign policy matters. As a result, the president can often build a consensus behind his position that would be more difficult to build around a domestic policy. Think of President George W. Bush's effort to convince Americans of the need to remove Saddam Hussein from power in Iraq as an example of this dynamic. If the mass public had more knowledge of and experience in foreign affairs, they might have been more skeptical of the case for invasion that was made.

The attention of the mass public can thus be difficult to capture and tends to emerge only over large, highly visible events. For the most part, the attention provided by this group is sporadic, short term, and somewhat malleable. On the majority of foreign policy issues, members of this group simply have no coherent, elaborated opinions and are much more likely to have their opinions shaped by others. Moreover, this group tends to be demographically distinct: lower educational and occupational attainment, geographic isolation from the major policy centers, and the like.

The Informed Public The second segment of Americans is the **informed (or attentive) public**, including 10 to 20 percent of the population. As the title suggests, the definition of the informed public is virtually the opposite of that of the mass, or uninformed, public. Members of the informed public regularly seek out information on international affairs and foreign policy. They read foreign policy stories in newspapers and magazines (either online or in the old-fashioned print edition) and watch television coverage of international events. They also may seek out foreign news on satellite radio (such as the BBC), and subscribe to podcasts about international events.

Several groups of people typically fall into the ranks of the informed public. Local civic leaders who influence the opinions of their communities are one group, as are local journalists, clergy, and others to whom the public at large turns to help them form opinions. For most members of the informed public, their contact with foreign policy events is still rather indirect rather than direct. In general, they have relatively few, if any, direct contacts with the foreign policy process, although that is perhaps changing as more and more localities have direct relationships with foreign investors, establish "sister city" arrangements, or do business with defense installations or government contractors. With some exceptions, however, this means that informed public members achieve their understanding of foreign and defense policy issues secondhand and vicariously rather than through direct personal experience.

The relationship to foreign and defense policy affects the informed public's quality and depth of understanding on these issues. With the exception of a foreign or defense policy that directly affects their lives (for example, a foreign automobile manufacturer building a plant in their vicinity or a military base closure), members of the attentive public are likely to have general rather than detailed knowledge about foreign affairs. A civic leader, for example, may know that there are ethic divisions in Iraq that have posed challenges to the unification of Iraqis around a new democratic government, but he or she may not know much at all about Sunnis, Shiites, and Kurds, their history together (and apart), their connections to ethnic brothers and sisters in neighboring countries, and the complexities of religion and ethnicity in Iraq in particular and the Middle East more generally.

The informed public does play a role in the foreign policy process. It does not set the agenda but instead tends to be reactive: It learns about issues when they emerge and expresses a general reaction that helps form the parameters within which policy can be crafted. At the same time, the status of members of the attentive public within their communities means that they inform other members of their community who have less interest in issues. As such, the role of the informed public is to convey information and opinion, and perhaps help the mass public form their own opinion about issues.

The Effective Public The third group is the **effective public**, sometimes also called "**opinion leaders**" or foreign policy elites. Defined as that part of the public that actively seeks to influence the foreign and defense policy process, this group consists of a relatively small number, usually considered as less than 5 percent of the overall population.

Frequently associated with the elite public are current and former policy makers, national opinion leaders, and foreign policy experts. Policy makers, actual members of government at the national and, to a somewhat lesser degree, state levels, are active in foreign policy matters but are not primarily foreign and defense policy experts (see the discussion of core decision makers that follows). Thus, for instance, a member of Congress from the upper Midwest will not necessarily be an expert on foreign and defense matters, but he or she probably does have a lively concern about the long-standing U.S. embargo of Cuba, which effectively bans American exports of agriculture to Cuba except under certain circumstances. Similarly, the governor of a Sun Belt state has a multitude of domestic concerns that consume most of his or her energies, but the location of a Honda assembly plant in the state does create a foreign policy interest.

National opinion leaders are people whose positions and expertise make them molders of opinion and agenda setters. Examples include members of the national media whose jobs bring them into direct contact with foreign and defense issues or former government officials with recognized expertise—people such as Henry Kissinger and Zbigniew Brzezinski.

Finally, the foreign policy expert community is made up of people who, by training and experience, have detailed knowledge but who do not happen to be in government. This group consists of scholars in relevant disciplines (international relations or economics, foreign or defense policy, contemporary diplomatic history), leaders of large interest groups with a direct foreign or defense interest, and experts in research organizations or think tanks.

What distinguishes the effective public from the informed public is the former's depth of knowledge and the centrality of foreign and defense matters to their personal and professional lives. Members of the elite public not only read one or more national newspapers (for example, *The New York Times, The Washington Post,* or *The Wall Street Journal)* and newsmagazines (for example, *Newsweek, Time,* or *The Economist),* but they also read (and write) articles in specialized journals (for example, *Foreign Affairs, Foreign Policy, The Bulletin of the Atomic Scientists,* or *Survival*) and books on relevant subjects. They may also be prominent bloggers on foreign policy.

In addition, the professions in which the elite public involves itself lead to a certain level of activism and policy advocacy, for example, criticism of government policy and advocacy of alternative policies. This activity is often associated with being part of the "shadow government in waiting," those Democrats who are not in governmental positions during Republican administrations and vice versa. As such, individuals in this group can be the elite public part of the time and core decision makers at other times.

Core Decision Makers The final group consists of the core decision makers. This group encompasses individuals responsible for actually formulating and executing foreign and defense policy. This group is also the smallest, numbering several hundred people within the government who are actually involved in formulating policy. Those who actually make policy occupy key roles in both the executive and legislative branches. Within the executive branch, the most numerous are found at the levels of assistant secretary and above in the State and Defense departments, the international divisions of other cabinet-level agencies, and the NSC staff. Within the legislative branch, the most prominent examples are the chairs and ranking minority members of the most important congressional committees and their senior staffs. Thus, the chairs and ranking opposition members of the Foreign Relations (Foreign Affairs in the House) Committee, Armed Services Committees Select Committees on Intelligence, and the chairs of the appropriations subcommittees on defense and foreign policy matters are obvious examples.

The distinctions between core decision makers and the elite public are imprecise. Some individuals move back and forth between the two designations as their status changes, and some are not clearly and unambiguously in one group or the other. The assistant secretary of defense for policy, the assistant secretary of state for East Asian and Pacific Affairs, or the chairs of the Foreign Relations or Armed Services committees clearly are part of the core by virtue of their positions. However, individuals with an interest and some expertise in the area are more difficult to locate. Before they became president, Bill Clinton and George W. Bush (with experience as state governors) were probably on the boundary between the elite and the informed public on foreign and defense matters; Barack Obama was somewhere around the boundary between the elite public and the core decision makers, since he was new to the U.S. Senate but was a member of the powerful Senate Foreign Relations Committee.

This conventional analysis of the public's role is pessimistic and negative. It essentially argues that the vast majority of the population knows and cares little about foreign and defense policy issues to the point that their opinions can be largely ignored or easily molded to fit the policy maker's agenda. In this view, only those in the two inner circles—the elite public and the core—have the experience and expertise to make intelligent decisions on these issues. The view thus supports the elitist school of thought about the public's role. This raises a number of questions, including whether this situation is acceptable in the world of the future, and what changes to this traditional view of the public have emerged in the study of public opinion and U.S. foreign policy.

TOWARD A NEW VIEW OF THE PUBLIC AND FOREIGN POLICY

A number of relatively recent findings by U.S. foreign policy scholars have challenged the traditional view of the mass public, suggesting that even they may be more orderly and predictable in how they respond to foreign policy issues than the conventional view would suggest. Indeed, since the Vietnam era, a vast amount of research has focused on these issues and tends to find that the mass public's attitudes about foreign policy are far less volatile and far more structured than the old view suggests. Research also tends to highlight the potential potency of public opinion about foreign policy endeavors, especially the extent to which presidents and members of Congress feel public pressure and fear public retaliation at the polls. Three such findings are worthy of some further discussion: the importance of the president's view of the public, the "rally" trend mentioned above, and public responses to different kinds of use of force.

How Presidents See the Public's Role

One thing that probably makes a difference, in terms of how and whether the public plays a role when it comes to American foreign policy, is what the President thinks about that role. As Foyle (1999) details, presidents who believe that the incorporation of the public's views into the foreign policy process is important will look for ways to do that; presidents who do not think it is important are less likely even to pay attention. The former view of leadership in a democracy is often called the "delegate" view (such as Bill Clinton), and the latter the "trustee" role (such as George W. Bush).

Foyle goes a step further to point out that presidents may not only differ in the extent to which they take public opinion into account when crafting foreign policy, they may also differ in whether they think public support is necessary to a policy's success. If a president thinks that the support of the public is important (regardless of whether or not the president wanted to take public opinion into account when crafting the policy), then the president will be far more active in trying to build public support for a policy than would a president who does not think public support matters to a policy's success.

There is no one answer to the role of the public in the area of foreign policy, then, but rather, as Foyle points out, the answer is "mediated" to a large extent by the president's beliefs about what that role should be. Such an understanding helps provide a more nuanced view of the public and foreign policy than the conventional view might provide.

Rallies and Haloes

As discussed previously (and in Figure 8.1), there is a general tendency for the mass public to rally around the president in times of national crisis. Whether in the aftermath of a terrorist attack, such as the attacks of 9/11 or the 1995 bombing at the Alfred P. Murrah Federal Building in Oklahoma City, or while

Americans are being held hostage, as occurred in Tehran, Iran, during the Carter administration, the mass public tends to rally to support the president in times of emergency. Some would argue that these foreign policy crises set off an innate "us versus them" mechanism, helping people set aside the differences they may have had with the president for at least a limited amount of time.

The flip side of the coin can be called a "halo" effect. The idea behind a **halo effect** is that the public tends to support the president at higher levels following a military strike that the public sees as quick and successful. Following the invasion of Panama in 1989, for example, or of Grenada in 1983, public support for the president spiked temporarily. The dynamic here is different from a rally event, because in the rally someone (or something) else does something to you; in a halo effect, you initiate the action, but the public views it as quick and successful. Together these trends suggest an underlying order and predictability to the mass public that might not be accounted for in the conventional view.

It is worth pointing out that if political scientists can spot these trends, so too can presidents and their pollsters—and they have access to far more resources to poll the public than social scientists and polling operations do. Some have argued that a president might be tempted to try to take advantage of these trends, especially if their public support is slipping, and execute some limited use of force abroad hoping to trigger the halo effect. The fancy name for this (admittedly cynical) view is the **Diversionary Theory of War,** suggesting that presidents might initiate conflict in order to divert the public's attention (which was otherwise turning negatively against the president). A couple of interesting movies are even based on this premise: *Wag the Dog* (1997) and *Canadian Bacon* (1995).

There is a significant and complicated debate in the political science literature about the Diversionary Theory of War. The October 26, 1983, invasion of Grenada (Operation Urgent Fury), for example, happened so close in time to the October 23 bombing of the Marine barracks in Lebanon (that killed 241) that many point to the Grenada operation as a diversion. Republican critics of President Bill Clinton assailed the cruise missile strikes on Afghanistan and Sudan that he ordered against Al Qaeda following two 1998 U.S. Embassy bombings in Africa because, they said, he was really trying to divert the public's attention from the Monica Lewinsky scandal that had just broken into the press.

Counterexamples also abound that emphasize how risk-averse American presidents are when it comes to risking casualties. They are, after all, politicians who have to stand for reelection; even if they are lame ducks, they care about whether their party holds the White House in future elections. In the summer of 1992, for instance, Saddam Hussein's challenges to the inspection regime agreed to at the end of the Persian Gulf War led many to suggest that President George H.W. Bush should order a bombing campaign against the Iraqi leader. Bush's standing in the polls leading into the 1992 election was so low, however, that some in the media suggested that Bush might use force to divert the public and trigger a halo. Bush did not order an attack, even though one might have been justified, at least in part because of a risk aversion to losing American lives (especially so close to an election). Whether or not one subscribes to the diversionary perspective, these trends are so reliable and well documented that they suggest an underlying order to the mass public's view of foreign policy.

Types of Interventions

There is a common saying about art, "I don't know much about art, but I know what I like." Well it turns out that this saying might explain a lot about the mass public and the use of force in American foreign policy, at least since Vietnam. They may not know much about foreign policy, but they know what they like; and it turns out there is a surprising amount of order to their evaluations of foreign military interventions—far more than the Almond-Lippmann consensus would expect. Building on previous examinations of how the mass public responded to growing casualty figures in Vietnam (especially the research by John Mueller), Bruce Jentleson's work has led the way here.

It is possible to think about using force abroad as serving one of two political purposes: to overthrow the regime in place in a foreign country (regime change), or to force a change in the foreign policy behavior of a foreign country (likely to impose some restraint on their behavior). The mass public is generally wary of using force abroad, seeing it as the last option, but has certainly supported the use of force both after the end of the Cold War and after 9/11. Its support for foreign military interventions appears to be tempered by the political objective of the operation.

In general terms, there is more public support for the use of force when that use is aimed at forcing foreign policy restraint on an opponent rather than if it supports military operations aimed at regime change. Now, of course some military operations can have a dose of both objectives; the strike on Libya in 1986, for example, was both an effort to punish Libya for its support for international terrorism and also an effort to kill or perhaps trigger the overthrow of Libya's leader Muammar Gaddafi. Targets of the strike included, for example, military and intelligence sites thought to support and train terrorists (which sounds like trying to force foreign policy restraint on Libya) as well as on sites where Gaddafi was thought to be sleeping (regime change). In this case, as in others, it is possible to see the pattern of public support based on how different poll questions were asked of the mass public.

When people were asked if they supported the strike on Libya as a way to send a message about terrorism, the support scores were very high; when polls asked if they supported following up the strike with U.S. troops to overthrow Gaddafi, the support scores were relatively lower. In case after case, Jentleson's work shows how the mass public supported uses of force aimed at imposing restraint on an opponent at a generally higher level than they did efforts at overt regime change. That structure—which Jentleson argues is an underlying "prudence" of the mass public—is far greater than the conventional view would suggest exists.

A couple of caveats are in order. One of the other objectives of U.S. military interventions since the end of the Cold War has been in the context of humanitarian crises. Here the public's reactions have been quite mixed;

INTERSECTIONS

Foreign Policy Presidential Campaign Commercials

1988 Democratic Party Nominee Michael Dukakis rides in a tank and hands a campaign commercial to George H.W. Bush.

The classic statement about American presidential elections is that they are all about "pocketbook" issues; the famous sign in the campaign headquarters of the 1992 Clinton presidential campaign was—in case anyone was tempted to forget—"It's the economy, stupid." Nevertheless, there have been key times when foreign policy issues loomed large in presidential elections. Elections are classic intermestic events because of the way they are both domestic and foreign policy issues at the same time.

In one sense, elections are always important events for the nation's foreign policy: Elections pick winners, and winners make policy and also select other people who will enter the government to make policy (such as foreign policy advisors and assistant secretaries of state and defense). In a second sense, though, foreign policy issues have sometimes become very important to the dynamics of the race for the White House itself. The website of the American Museum of the Moving Image has an ongoing display called "The Living Room Candidate" that catalogs the campaign commercials of the major party candidates for president in the TV age (http://livingroomcandidate.org). Many of these, and others, can be found by searching on YouTube and also on the C-SPAN website.

While there are many great commercials worth watching, two warrant attention here. The first is an ad that brings home the close connection between foreign

(Continued)

(Continued)

and domestic policy, and how foreign policy can be a major issue in a presidential election: the 1988 "tank" ad that Vice President George H.W. Bush (the Republican candidate) ran against Massachusetts Governor Michael Dukakis. The genesis of this commercial was a September 1988 photo shoot that the Dukakis campaign staged to try to show that Dukakis could be tough in the area of foreign and defense policy; the campaign brought the press to a spot where Dukakis approached from the distance riding atop a tank, smiling at the cameras. The imagery was so bad that the Bush campaign produced a commercial using those images, scrolling accusations on the screen as the tank—and Dukakis—approached. An event that was meant to make Dukakis look strong on defense turned into a Bush campaign commercial that did just the opposite. However misleading the ad might have been in some respects, its imagery struck a chord and helped seal the fate of that election: a win for George H.W. Bush.

The 2004 election featured some classic ads, but one is especially noteworthy. Harkening back to an image that Ronald Reagan used once, depicting the threat from the Soviet Union as a "bear in the woods," President George W. Bush ran a sequel of sorts, updated for the new "threat environment." If the danger of the Soviet Union during the height of the Cold War could be likened to a bear, George W. Bush's 2004 reelection campaign put forth that the danger from terrorism after 9/11 was more like the danger of being attacked by a pack of "wolves." With the camera focusing on wolves in the forest, the narrator accuses the Democrat challenger, Massachusetts Senator John Kerry, of taking positions on defense that would have weakened America's defenses: "And weakness attracts those who are waiting to do America harm."

The 2004 election was very close, and was ultimately decided by fewer than two hundred thousand votes in Ohio. No one knew for sure how the terrorism issue would play in the election. Would voters want to stay with President Bush during this time of "war," or would they want to make a change, since the head of Al Qaeda—the organization that carried out the attacks of 9/11—Osama bin Laden, was still at large? The Wolves ad was the Bush campaign's way of making its case that Bush was the more reliable choice.

Another point worth considering here concerns the links between foreign and domestic politics and how presidential elections can be intermestic events. One of the differences in the 2004 ad compared with previous election cycles is that the ad ends by showing President Bush and featuring his voice saying, "I'm George W. Bush, and I approve this message." This kind of end to commercials came about as a result of the Bipartisan Campaign Reform Act of 2002, sometimes called "BCRA" for short, or the "McCain–Feingold Act" after the bill's sponsors in the Senate John McCain (R-AZ) and Russ Feingold (D-WI). The purpose of this particular addition was to try to make ads more reliable; if the candidate stands in the ad and says he or she approved it, only a very risk-acceptant candidate would put forth an ad

(Continued)

(Continued)

that featured statements that were untrue. That was the idea, in theory. In practice, however, many would say that it has not quite worked out that way. Political ads may be even less reliable today, with hyperpartisanism more prevalent and ads fueled by the dynamic that the viewer is an even less critical evaluator of the claims made in ads because of the candidate's stamp of approval. This may actually give more license to play loose with the facts.

the early excitement about the possibility of using the American military to help relieve suffering has been tempered by the experiences in Somalia and the long haul in Bosnia. The tragic genocide in Rwanda, however, also reminds the American public of the necessity for some level of activity around these aims.

Finally, the public's support for the invasion of Iraq in 2003 perhaps complicates this picture. A majority of Americans supported that invasion, although it turns out the main case for the war was undermined by later events: There were no weapons of mass destruction; Saddam did not work with Al Qaeda and had nothing to do with the 9/11 attacks; and of course the transition to democracy in Iraq has been a slow and arduous process that could still unravel and that has cost the lives of 4430 American service members. Today, according to Gallup polls, a majority of Americans think it was a mistake to send troops into Iraq, but support for the invasion ran high until mid-2004.

Other Sources of Change

The mass public may be in a catch-22 of sorts when it comes to their relation to foreign policy: People do not learn about foreign affairs because of its seeming unimportance to them, and they do not know enough about foreign relations to realize its salience. What can change these traditional attitudes? Is it possible for more uninformed Americans to become part of the informed public, and for the informed public to move on to higher levels of involvement and understanding? Although this matter is admittedly speculative, at least four forces could be making a dent in the ignorance/disinterest syndrome that has limited the public's effectiveness in the foreign policy arena. They are greater access to information, educational reform, increased public awareness of the relevance of foreign policy, and attempts to mobilize public opinion.

Greater Access to Information This factor is largely the product of the information revolution that is intertwining the global economy and politics and producing a cascade of greater information about foreign affairs problems. The key element here is global television, especially television operations such as CNN, BBC, ITN, and the other global news operations that both collect and disseminate the news worldwide, and the Internet as a way to transmit news and information in real time all around the world. Moreover, a variety of related technologies, including video camcorders, smartphones, satellite linkages, and fiber optics, give television networks as well as individuals the ability to provide instantaneous coverage and transmission of events as they happen, thereby adding to the drama of breaking events.

The impact of all these changes on how Americans and citizens of other countries are affected in terms of their attitudes to foreign affairs remains mostly speculative, but it is clearly growing as access to global news becomes more pervasive to these citizens. The prototype of this phenomenon, CNN, for instance, started in 1980, and the ability to provide instantaneous coverage over thousands of miles is even newer than that. Many derided CNN during its infancy; now competitors are everywhere. When dramatic events occur around the globe, people turn in large numbers to CNN, as they did during the Persian Gulf War, and other cable news networks. As a result, many citizens have become more aware of events they had previously ignored.

Without Bernard Shaw's unrelenting coverage, for instance, would we have learned very much about the Chinese government's suppression of the "democracy movement" in Tiananmen Square in 1989? Or would we have seen the Persian Gulf War beginning live, before our eyes, through CNN's cameras in their Baghdad hotel room? Would we have learned of Serbian barbarity against the citizens of Bosnia and Herzegovina in 1992? At the same time, how much does selectivity of coverage (the slaughter in Mozambique over several decades, for instance, was not covered by the media and was ignored by governments) affect the foreign policy agenda? Although global television cannot give the citizenry a sophisticated understanding of problems and policy, it can whet people's appetites for knowledge and make ignorance less sustainable. To move greater numbers outside the ranks of the uninformed requires a second force: educational reform with an emphasis on international affairs.

Educational Reform The need for educational reform became a popular shibboleth of the 1990s, with President Clinton as a leading standard-bearer. Spurred on by the dismal rankings of American children in science and mathematics compared with children in other countries, there was a clear mandate, if not funding base, to improve the educational system, a theme Presidents Bush and Obama have continued to champion.

One area in which education has failed most emphatically is in giving the school-age population wide exposure to global cultures and issues. The litany is disturbingly familiar: Unlike advanced industrial democracies in Europe and Asia, not to mention China, in the United States less than one-third of elementary schools offer any foreign language instruction, and only about half of the students in middle school and high school take foreign language classes (and far fewer become proficient); most of them take Spanish or French. Most students lack even basic geographical knowledge, and even among college students, less than 10 percent take foreign language courses and even fewer ever take a course in foreign affairs, international relations, or foreign culture.

That picture is changing, albeit slowly. At the collegiate level, increasing numbers of colleges and universities are adding an international education requirement to basic graduation requirements. Student enrollment in foreign language courses has been increasing in recent years, as have study abroad programs (although the economic crash slowed some of that progress). For these efforts to be maximized, however, increased funding for education is needed. Funding has proven a major barrier as education competes for scarce resources with other policy areas in numerous states. Unfortunately, if anything, education funding is likely to be cut in an increasingly tight budgetary environment.

Increased Relevance of Foreign Policy The changing nature of the national security environment caused and stimulated by the collapse of communism and reemphasized by the events of September 11th has more than an abstract importance to U.S. citizens. In the absence of a Soviet enemy to confront, the United States needed fewer military personnel and hence less military equipment and support services, all of which had provided many jobs for Americans in the past. During the 1990s, the armed forces shrank by more than one-third. Responses to international terrorism, however, including military actions in Afghanistan and Iraq, have placed foreign affairs problems squarely and unavoidably before the public. This has led to an increase in attention to international affairs by the mass public, as they see foreign events as closer to home than they perhaps did in the past. Still, even this can be fleeting; attention skyrocketed immediately after September 11th, but has settled down significantly in recent years.

INTERSECTIONS

The Public and the War in Afghanistan

Support for the war in Afghanistan by the mass public has evolved in interesting ways over the course of ten years of war. While the public was extremely positive about the war in the early months following the attacks of 9/11, support for the war started to become more complicated in 2005, and since 2009 it has become a very controversial subject with many crosscutting dynamics. In the early months of war, with the quick rout of the Taliban, large majorities of the U.S. public supported the war. As the war dragged on as an extended counterinsurgency operation, however, an increasing number of Americans began questioning whether the effort and cost—both in lives and dollars—was worth it. By September 2009, for example, only about half of those polled thought troops should stay in Afghanistan. By 2011, a slim majority of Americans preferred that U.S. troops be removed from Afghanistan quickly.

At first this trend looks like what one might expect: high levels of support after 9/11 (a rally event), followed by declining support as the costs of war mount.

(Continued)

(Continued)
Looking more deeply, however, two curious subplots emerge in the story, subplots that highlight the role of partisanship in foreign policy opinions. First, the war's strongest supporters identify themselves as Republicans and conservatives—making the War in Afghanistan one of the rare policy areas where President Obama receives high levels of support from the opposition party. Those who identify themselves as "independents" are about evenly divided on the war. Second, a majority of Republicans and a large majority of independents support President Obama's plan to significantly draw down U.S. forces in Afghanistan by 2012. Democrats are more likely to prefer a faster removal of troops. How partisanship and the Afghan War will interact for the 2012 election perhaps will be less significant than economic issues, but it will be an important issue driving the 2012 presidential election cycle.

Second, the killing of Osama bin Laden led to an increase in the evaluation of the U.S. public of how the war was going in Afghanistan. A slim majority, according to a Gallup poll, said that the war was going well following bin Laden's death—only the second time since 2006 that a majority evaluated the situation as such. This halo effect has dissipated, but it reminds us that events shape public opinion, as does how those events are portrayed. Following events in Afghanistan, and the portrayal of those events by different media outlets, will make for excellent viewing as we enter the presidential election season.

Mobilizing Public Opinion In the past, national leaders made overt appeals for mass public support only when the most dramatic and personal events occurred, such as those involving peace and war. That situation has certainly changed. Not only are international events more directly relevant and more visible to Americans than before, but also the blurring of domestic and foreign policy—the emergence of intermestic politics—means that more support will have to be generated to back those policies that could affect domestic priorities. The domestic impact of international terrorism in terms of heightened security measures (have you flown on a commercial airliner recently?) and efforts to mobilize public support for those measures is a good example of this dynamic in action.

The case of assistance to rebuild Afghanistan and Iraq provides an example in the other direction. Historically, a foreign state's request for aid would have been a routine matter and would not have generated much controversy. In a period of fiscal stringency and growing deficits juxtaposed by an obvious mandate to rebuild and stabilize situations to which we have contributed, how much aid should the United States supply? As some critics asked loudly and publicly, should the United States be underwriting change in those countries when it cannot feed and house the homeless in this country or fund basic services? Hardly anyone could argue that assisting Iraq or Afghanistan is a bad idea or not in the national interest or even that we do not have some obligation to assist. The level of that assistance, and how much we should solicit foreign assistance (at what political costs), is a more debatable, problematic proposition given the competing domestic demands. Because the public is, in general, more focused on domestic political matters that have a more obviously direct impact on them, refocusing their attention on foreign affairs requires a considerable amount of mobilization that will necessarily involve the media. Indeed, it is nearly impossible to talk about the public without also talking about the place from which the public gets its news (and often its opinions): the media.

THE MEDIA

Media is a shorthand term used to describe those individuals and organizations that collect and disseminate information (news) and interpretations about what is happening in the world. The media are divided historically into the print media, consisting of newspapers and newsmagazines, and the electronic or broadcast media, consisting of radio and television. This distinction, however, has become quite blurred in practice with the emergence of hybrids such as the electronic transmission of newspapers over the Internet and the expansion of Internet-based sources of information with pedigrees difficult to categorize in traditional terms, thus creating a new genre. With the emergence of blogs, independent websites, and Facebook pages, to name a few, it is increasingly difficult to draw easy textbook distinctions among the media. Moreover, cross-ownership of various media from different categories may blur the distinctiveness of content in the various forms.

Print Media

Of course, the print media are older than the purely electronic broadcast media. Their independence in observing and reporting on the operation of government is included in the First Amendment to the Constitution and was justified as a way to prevent the undue accumulation of power by individuals or governmental institutions. Their independence is assured because all the print media are independently owned by individuals outside government and are unregulated by governmental agencies. Although no one doubts the value of private ownership, it probably does influence the content of news. Privately owned media must make a profit to remain in business, after all (or have an owner with really deep pockets who is willing to take the economic losses), and are thus prone to report what readers and viewers will consume, which is usually late-breaking, spectacular events rather than more reflective matters.

The operative principle to ensure continued independence is the doctrine of "**prior restraint**" on publication. This doctrine, first articulated in a 1931 Supreme Court case *(Near* v. *Minnesota)*, states that there can be no prior censorship by government of reportage. (A practical exception is reportage of ongoing military campaigns that might provide information to the enemy.) This position was reinforced in the famous "**Pentagon Papers**" case, *New York Times* v. *United States*, when the Nixon administration tried to prevent the *Times* from publishing a secret history of American involvement in Vietnam that had been assembled by the government and leaked to the press. In June

1971 the U.S. Supreme Court found that the government could not prevent publication, or exercise prior restraint (although the government could take legal action after publication if some illegality had occurred). Some would argue that the dynamics that surround the disclosures by WikiLeaks bear some resemblance to this historic episode.

The print media cover foreign policy through the flagship newspapers, newsmagazines, and wire services. Probably the most influential are the key national newspapers, such as *The New York Times* and *The Washington Post,* which have the time and resources to assign reporters and bureaus full-time to coverage of foreign and international events, and the national newspapers or publications that do not have a specific geographical locale (for example, *USA Today, The Wall Street Journal,* and *The Christian Science Monitor*). People in the policy process, the elite public, and members of the informed public read the flagship and national papers. The function of the major newsmagazines is to provide depth and interpretation to events initially reported on by the newspapers. These sources have become available to increasing parts of the public through printed national editions of major newspapers and electronic versions made available on the Internet. Finally, wire services, such as the Associated Press, provide foreign and defense policy news to local newspapers that do not have the ability to collect and report on foreign affairs on their own.

Electronic Media

The electronic broadcast media, unlike the print media, are subject to at least cursory regulation through the licensing process of the Federal Communications Commission (FCC). Basically, FCC regulations ensure that radio and television stations do not use transmission bands that interfere with one another's signals; less formally, FCC regulations mandate that in their reportage, the electronic media are expected to honor the principles of equal time to political candidates, the right of rebuttal, and the fairness doctrine in reporting.

The electronic media cover foreign policy issues through the major television and, to a lesser extent radio, networks and report the news to their affiliates. In addition, the emergence of international news–based outlets such as CNN and ITN and others have created more or less the equivalent of the national newspapers in the form of a television station devoted solely to the news. Local television and radio stations rely on sources, such as the newspaper wire services and television feeds, to report foreign policy news, often covering a local "angle" on foreign policy and international affairs.

The Internet is a constantly evolving and growing source of information, including information about foreign policy and global affairs. It is impossible to count the number of sites covering foreign policy news—some solely, others at least in part—that have emerged in recent years. Some of these are web-based news sources not unlike traditional media; some are sites run by interest groups or think tanks; some are "blogs" that professional or amateur journalists maintain; some are merely websites that someone around the world has assembled about a certain topic. Unlike the more traditional media, there are few, if any, legal and certainly professional standards regarding the accuracy of what is transmitted over the web. As a result, the consumer of web "news" needs to be more critical about what he or she reads. As increasing numbers of Americans report that the web is their primary source of news, the issue of reliability is likely to become increasingly important.

As a new source, the Internet has advantages and disadvantages flowing from those distinctions. Positively, the Internet provides generally free access to an almost endless amount of information, limited only by the ability of the purveyor to link into the "Net" and the ingenuity of "surfers" in accessing those links. Negatively, universality of access means there is little or no filtering of Internet information for accuracy or general content. As a result, the Internet user has little basis for knowing if information obtained from nontraditional Internet sources is correct, and guidelines for assisting in assessing the cogency of Internet information are in their infancy. The explosion of Internet users worldwide, however, means access to those users is of increasing vitality to those with information to share; as long as that access remains unregulated, however, there will continue to be nefarious uses that only the discerning can distinguish.

One factor about the web as a source of information is that there is a huge range of types of sites out there, representing many different perspectives on global events and foreign policy. Thus news through the web is decentralized and increasingly addresses "niche" audiences. Conversely, an additional factor is the partial merger between the Internet and television news and the corporate consolidation that is occurring in the media industry. It is not uncommon for television reporters to have their own websites, to which they direct viewers seeking more in-depth information or background on stories they report; nor is it uncommon for news to be reported by one entity about international affairs when it turns out the news source is materially connected to the news that is being reported. Finding neutral observers is increasingly difficult in the modern media age.

Traditional View of the Media

The media's function in the area of foreign policy, although evolving, has been controversial. To understand how the media stand between the people and the government, we first look at the traditional functions the media perform, noting how they are influenced by the nature of international affairs. The discussion then moves to how technological innovation is changing and expanding those functions.

The media's basic job is to observe and report the activities of government and the actions and thoughts of individual political figures. In this role, the media are sometimes actively sympathetic and cooperative with those about whom they report, and sometimes they are not. The media also serve as watchdogs of the public interest, particularly in areas where they perceive the possibility of breaches of the public trust. In this role, the government and the media are almost always adversaries.

In general reportage, but especially in the area of foreign policy, the media do not communicate comprehensively with the entire public nor do they even really attempt to do so. This is largely the result of the general public's lack of interest and the kinds of media that cover the area. Readership of the flagship newspapers, for instance, is demographically defined in terms of educational level, wealth, and means of livelihood, as is viewership of outlets such as CNN, Fox News, or msnbc. In other words, the foreign policy–reporting mechanism is directed at the relatively well educated and affluent, and it is transmitted through those channels that the educated and affluent read and watch.

Any attempt to harness the media to the task of broadening citizen awareness and participation in the foreign policy process must begin with this recognition. Either broader segments of the public must be drawn to the national media, or foreign reportage must be expanded in those channels from which the masses receive their information: local newspapers, local television, and local radio. Media activity in the foreign policy area can be thought of in terms of the following five functions.

Collection and Reportage of the News In this function, the media observe what the government (and the broader world) is doing and inform the public of those actions. Collection and reportage of the news is also presumably the most objective and least controversial activity in which the media engages, but the nature of foreign policy occurrences complicates the straightforward reportage in several ways.

First, too many events happen around the world for the media to cover all of them simultaneously and with equal depth. Thus, the media are necessarily selective in what they cover and report, and some people inevitably conclude that not all the worthiest items are being covered. A common complaint about the American media in particular is that they only cover news from the developing world in times of wars, natural disasters, and other cataclysmic events. In this sense, the mainstream media might serve an "indexing" function, where news producers decide what stories from a multitude of possibilities are worthy of the public's attention.

Second, the sheer scale and scope of events that occur worldwide stretches the resources of any news-gathering outlet to cover everything. Corporate buyouts and downsizing of network news divisions (especially foreign news and the closures of foreign news "bureaus") and the failure or buyout of many newspapers—all products of media conglomeration—mean that fewer reporters are available to cover foreign news stories, leaving the American media increasingly reliant on foreign news organizations. Moreover, foreign events are often unpredictable, making orderly planning problematic.

Third, the media often tailors its coverage to what the media sees as the audience's interests. From 2002 to 2003, for instance, CNN foreign policy coverage that was beamed to American audiences concentrated on Iraq and terrorism to the virtual exclusion of other world events. CNN-International (the version available to non-American audiences) presented a far different, more comprehensive variety of story subjects.

Finally, as Daniel Hallin argues, the media will "report" a story differently depending on the circumstances of the story. When a sphere of consensus exists among opinion leaders, the media is likely to reflect that consensus in its reporting (such as in the early years of the Vietnam War). When it becomes clear, however, that there is no consensus, the media is likely to report on this sphere as a "legitimate controversy." The fractured and increasingly partisan media environment might well even prey on such a circumstance.

Investigating or Watchdogging At the simple level of reportage, print or electronic journalists may do little more than reiterate what public officials tell them (an allegation made about early coverage of the Iraq crisis and war). By self-appointment, however, reporters feel the need to determine the veracity of public pronouncements and to report instances in which they believe the public trust has not been well served (**watchdogging**). This function, which has increased dramatically in the past quarter-century, often places government officials and the media at loggerheads.

The event that more than any other triggered an adversarial and untrusting relationship between government and the media was the Vietnam War. In the early stages of the war (roughly 1965 through 1967), reportage of the war was largely favorable to the military; the press corps dutifully reported progress in the war based on briefings at Military Assistance Command Vietnam (MACV) in Saigon known as the "five o'clock follies." According to the progress reported to the media and transmitted to the American people, the enemy's forces were being rapidly depleted to the point that when U.S. Commanding General William Westmoreland reported to Congress late in 1967 that he saw "the light at the end of the tunnel," the assertion was not widely disputed. When Lyndon Johnson subsequently reported there was no light at the end of the tunnel, the public was unprepared for the news—news that was brought home vividly on television during the Tet Offensive.

The Tet Offensive of January 1968 broke that bond between the media and the government. When CBS anchor Walter Cronkite saw the first film footage of the Viet Cong in the American Embassy compound, he is reported to have said, "What the hell is going on here?" What was going on was the end of media trust in the government's conduct of this particular instance of foreign policy. That relationship, and the media's consequent perceived need not to take the government at its word, was reinforced by events such as the Watergate scandal, the Iran-Contra scandal, and the exclusion of the press from the U.S. Invasion of Grenada in 1983 (the first reports of which were received in the United States over Radio Havana).

The debate about to what extent the American media should be "patriotic" in their reporting, especially reporting about military conflicts, did not begin with Vietnam and it did not end there. In tranquil times few take issue with the media's "watchdog" role; but in times of crisis, media scrutiny is often taken as unpatriotic, and governments in power rarely like prying questions—especially during crises. Nevertheless, perhaps it is worth remembering that a supine and compliant media does no service to democracy.

Interpretation Because of the general public's lack of knowledge of international affairs, explaining the flow of events is a particularly important function. Many people simply do not have the knowledge base to put foreign policy questions in focus and perspective. In the absence of media interpretation, they would have only government officials, whose explanations are often motivated by self-interest and thus may be self-serving, to provide context.

This function, although valuable, is also controversial because of the media's alleged ignorance of the subtleties and nuances of many foreign issues. Most print and electronic journalists are not trained in foreign affairs any more than the average citizen is. The problem is even more severe in the defense policy area.

Since the draft was suspended at the end of 1972, most young Americans—including the vast majority of reporters—have had no military experience on which to base observation. The media at least partially understand this deficiency, which helps explain why, for instance, so many of the electronic experts used to help cover military interventions and wars are retired military officers, but it also means few reporters truly understand or empathize with these concerns.

The national press, both print and electronic, is also alleged to have a liberal bias. Part of the basis for this claim is geographical: The national press is concentrated in New York City and Washington, D.C., which are generally more liberal than much of the rest of the country. It also partly results from the fact that more liberal, reform-minded young men and women tend to be drawn to journalism. Many members of the defense establishment believe this liberal bias is also antimilitary, thereby adding to the strained relationship between the media and the military.

This perception has been counterbalanced by an alleged conservative bias in reporting after September 11th. Rather than providing critical reportage of the conservative Bush administration's foreign and domestic policies, the counterargument is that the media were cowed into accepting and uncritically reporting the administration's "line" out of a fear of political retribution or criticism. CBS senior correspondent Dan Rather, in an interview with the London-based *Guardian* on May 17, 2002, expressed this concern in terms of the analogy of a former South African practice of assassinating dissidents by placing burning automobile tires over their heads. "In some ways the fear is that you will be necklaced here, that you will have a flaming tire of lack of patriotism placed around your neck. Now it is that fear that keeps journalists from asking the toughest of the tough questions."

Another consideration is that foreign policy interpretation must occur largely in close proximity to events, when their full meaning cannot be known and when some or all of the parties involved may be directed to keep certain facts secret. The danger of the media's "instant analysis" is that when false interpretations of events are offered and accepted, they may continue to affect perceptions even after corrections have been made.

Influencing Public Opinion on Issues As with all the other functions, influencing public opinion is tinged with controversy. Whether the media do in fact influence or lead opinion or whether they simply reflect the opinions that they believe the public already holds is a matter for some debate. The overt expression of opinions occurs primarily on the editorial pages of newspapers. But how many people read or are influenced by editorial positions? Journalists claim that the influence is minimal or even nonexistent, but people in government believe that the editorial power of the national flagship newspapers or the television networks is very great.

There is also the question of how the media seek to influence opinion. In the traditional sense, the editorial page of the newspaper, or clearly identified electronic media editorials, has been considered legitimate, provided that fairness and access by those holding other opinions are available. The controversy emerges when editorial bias sneaks into the objective "news hole" in the form of biased selection of stories and reportage and the like. The question that then arises is whether the media are serving the function of informing or whether they are propagandizing. This same criticism is also directed at television news analysis shows such as *60 Minutes, Dateline,* and *20/20,* and it is particularly potentially troubling as media giants (Fox's Rupert Murdoch, for instance) gain greater editorial control of the media through conglomeration and restrict the available editorial range on issues.

Agenda Setting Do the media try to influence what important issues become parts of the public agenda, how the public should perceive these agenda items, and what policy outcomes are desirable? This is a controversial question that becomes a problem when the media appear to attempt to frame issues that collide with government efforts to frame the agenda. Instances of this collision in the foreign policy arena are legend and are often the most heartfelt. The modern prototype was Vietnam, especially after the Tet Offensive. Beyond the simple disillusionment with the military's truthfulness on that occasion, many members of the media came to believe that the war was not winnable and U.S. withdrawal was the proper course. This conclusion was openly expressed and was reflected in the kind of stories chosen and in the way those stories were presented.

The media can also change their minds quickly, altering their projected images of events. Despite coverage that bordered on cheerleading in support of intervention in Somalia, within days of authorization of that action, leading columnists, as well as the editorial page of *The New York Times,* were already questioning the attainability of the political objective of stabilizing the situation. When eighteen Americans were killed in an ambush in Mogadishu, much of the media jumped on the bandwagon of those demanding an American withdrawal.

This problem, which often manifests itself in the media's alleged distortions of complex realities, is especially serious for television, particularly at the national level. Foreign policy issues are normally complex and controversial, requiring considerable sharing of information with a public that is unequipped to make its own judgments. Television, however, is the medium of the short, pithy explanation; the thirty-second sound bite with a vivid optical imprint, the specialty of television, is quite unlike the leisurely analysis provided by a

New York Times or *Newsweek* feature. Network news stories are rarely more than a minute-and-a-half long, which may not be long enough to form other than cursory impressions.

Although brief, the impressions created by the visual media can be very strong and influential, especially when violence and suffering are depicted. A thirty-second film clip of Bosnians being attacked on the streets of Sarajevo created an enormously strong anti-Serbian reaction that may or may not have been justified. It can also impel governments into action and lead to strong public appeals to force government actions, as occurred when CNN showed pictures of the Kurds in Southern Turkey as Saddam Hussein's forces reacted to their uprising following the end of the Persian Gulf War.

These examples of media activity and its impact are traditional, the stuff of journalism textbooks. The fruits of the high-technology revolution manifested in the telecommunications revolution are creating a whole new area of possible activity.

Impact of the Telecommunications Revolution

As noted earlier, a series of technologies associated with the enormous growth in knowledge generation, dissemination, and assorted derivative technologies is transforming the modern world of production, economics, and communications. This high-tech revolution is being aided by advances in telecommunications and is substantially enhancing the ability to acquire and disseminate information, which is the heart of the media's role. The electronic media, including the Internet, are the major beneficiaries of this process. In subtle ways that neither practitioners nor theoreticians fully understand, these advances are changing the international affairs that are the substance of foreign policy reporting as well as the way policy is made.

Because there is currently no satisfactory theoretical understanding of this phenomenon, it can only be viewed impressionistically, using examples. To that end, this chapter now explores how the telecommunications revolution is transforming foreign policy by strengthening the role of the media and the Internet and downgrading the importance of more traditional policy mechanisms.

Increased Ability to Influence Events Global television, and increasingly social networking sites such as Facebook and Twitter, is a prime factor in this increased influence. Telecommunications advances have made the world increasingly transparent to media coverage and reportage. When we combine with this the ability to reach out almost everywhere with technologies such as the smartphone, there is very little that happens in the world that the media—and any regular person with a smartphone and an Internet connection—cannot observe and report if it chooses to do so. That fact in and of itself affects what and how governments do their business.

One of the most dramatic instances of this transparency and its consequences occurred in the summer of 1991 in Moscow, where a group of conspirators launched a temporarily successful coup against then–Soviet

President Gorbachev. In earlier days, when the media could be and were excluded from the inner workings of the former Soviet government, this event might have proceeded quietly, and countercoup activities, such as Russian President Boris Yeltsin's very public resistance, might have been brutally suppressed, hidden from the public glare.

In this instance, however, worldwide television was already there, and the coup leaders did not know how to keep them away from the events. Reporters covered and transmitted live visual images everywhere, and the coup leaders flinched. The day after the coup took place, the collective leadership felt obliged to hold a televised live news conference explaining that there really had not been a coup and promising to restore Gorbachev after he recovered from his supposed illness, an absolutely unprecedented event in Soviet history. At that point, the coup was doomed. The hapless coup conspirators in Moscow experienced the power of media exposure to its fullest extent. In 1989, when television cameras recorded the brutal suppression of prodemocracy students in Beijing's Tiananmen Square, the veil of violent suppression was lifted to the light of public inspection. The coverage of the attempted revolution in Iran in 2009, discussed at the beginning of this chapter, is another dramatic example.

Impact on the Policy Process One impact of this development on the policy process is sometimes called "**media diplomacy**," whereby governments conduct some of their relationships with other governments by sending information about positions and the like back and forth through interviews with news outlets. The media also intrude through the extensive coverage of diplomatic negotiations that until very recently were always held in heavily guarded secrecy.

Relations between the United States and the former Soviet Union illustrate the use of the media as a conduit for information between governments. For example, in 1991, on the eve of Gorbachev's visit to the United States to conclude negotiations on strategic arms reductions (START), the Soviet government apparently had a last-minute change of position on one of the important issues to be discussed. The problem the Soviets faced was how to relay this change to the highest levels of the U.S. government in the most efficient way possible. The traditional method would have been to call in the U.S. ambassador and ask him to transmit the message back to Washington. Feeling this method would be too slow, the Soviets instead called the CNN Moscow bureau chief, who reported the story quickly on the network. The Soviets doubtless sought out CNN because they knew President George H.W. Bush was an avid CNN watcher. In a similar vein, the same President Bush used global television to voice his displeasure with the attempted coup against Gorbachev and to issue warnings to Saddam Hussein during the Persian Gulf War of 1990–1991.

Another example that shows how technology has evolved in recent years is China's unveiling of a new military stealth jet on the Internet in January 2011. While there had been much speculation about a new generation of Chinese jet fighters being built, the brief appearance of a prototype of the new J-20 on an unofficial military news website was taken by many as a way for the Chinese government to use the modern media to signal its advances in this area.

The extensive coverage of diplomatic events also represents change. One of classical diplomacy's canons is that it should be as quiet and confidential as possible, thereby creating an atmosphere of candor and flexibility in which compromises can be reached. (If positions are publicly known, compromise becomes more difficult because then it becomes necessary to back away from original positions, thus giving the appearance of losing ground.) Massive media coverage has changed that. It is not unusual for negotiators to end their sessions with a press conference to discuss what happened in the meeting, a heretofore unthinkable idea. The extensive discussions between the Clinton administration and the Israelis and Palestinians during the 1990s illustrate this use of the media especially well.

Public figures are still in the learning stages of being television actors. In 1990 when Saddam Hussein held British children—his effective hostages—on his lap during the early stages of Desert Shield, he probably thought he was being reassuring, but it did not come off that way. By contrast, following the attacks of 9/11 when Defense Secretary Donald Rumsfeld gained much popularity in part due to his skillful appearances on television, President George W. Bush used the media-savvy Rumsfeld as an effective media salesman for the Bush administration's Middle East policies.

The Media as Part of the Process At one level, the way the media cover events influences public perceptions and thus helps structure the responses that the government can make. At the same time, media figures such as ABC's Ted Koppel, through the *Nightline* program, can actually become active parts of the process. Koppel held teleconferences with participants in disputes on late-night television that earned him the nickname of "television's secretary of state."

The impact of such activity is not well established, but it is undoubtedly substantial. Certainly, media coverage of natural or human-made disasters creates a vividness of perception, as well as a common view of events, that would not be possible in the absence of those images. Our picture of the Balkan disaster in Bosnia and Herzegovina, for instance, would have been much more clouded had it occurred thirty years ago, or especially nearly eighty-five years ago, when the result of a similar situation was World War I.

The Media as Publicist, Interpreter, and Agenda Setter As a result of the global reach of the electronic media, the volume of material to which the public and policy makers are potentially exposed will continue to expand exponentially. Through their choices of what to publicize among a volume of events and issues beyond their ability to broadcast and the public's capacity to absorb, the media will help define the public agenda. This same increased volume and diversity of coverage means that the public will be exposed to more and more unfamiliar situations for which they will require interpretation. The media are logical candidates for at least part of that role.

The emergence of twenty-four-hour-a-day news broadcasting organizations has created a much larger news hole for the media to fill. Thus, coverage has to be expanded to areas that have not heretofore received very much coverage.

On a global level, the ripe candidates are Asia, Africa, and Latin America, which demand greater exposure of their problems and will almost certainly get it. Once again, the problem lies in the shortage of expertise in the public that requires the media to explain what they are covering.

A beneficiary of this factor is almost certainly going to be the electronic experts, those academics from the universities and think tanks, former government officials, and retired military officers who possess the knowledge of global issues that the media staffs frequently do not have. This factor is almost sure to become more prominent as the media expand their coverage to ever more distant corners of the globe.

There has been much speculation about a "**CNN effect**," or the idea that there is an impact of the twenty-four-hour news cycle and omnipresent Internet reality on the foreign policy process; however, there are few clear answers. The idea that the media can single-handedly set the foreign policy agenda by its decisions about what to show and what not to show, while tempting, misses the reliance of the mainstream media on the government itself for news about the world. With the closures of most foreign bureaus around the globe, the American press mostly collects its foreign news from briefings and leaks from the White House, the Defense Department, and the State Department. The influence road between the media and the government can run in both directions.

One effect that participants in the policy process seem to agree on is that the modern media age forces the policy process to speed up. The days when a president could sit on news for a week or more, as President Kennedy did in the Cuban Missile Crisis, are gone; private satellite companies, such as the ones that produce the images for Google Earth, would have found those missile launchers. The policy process probably has to go faster today than in the past and be more mindful of how events and policy can be susceptible to "spin" as well.

One obvious negative effect of this dynamic is that it is most likely the case that events are happening faster and are more interconnected than in the past; in a global village, we are all much more closely linked than in the past. And yet just at the time when things are more complicated and interconnected, policy makers have to make decisions faster and with more partial information; and they do so in a far more politically polarized public opinion environment. This is, in fact, one of the central challenges of making foreign policy in this new era.

Soft News and Fake News Two other relatively recent developments in the media-public-government relationship are worthy of mention. One is the emergence of "**soft news**" about foreign policy, meaning news that takes more of a "human interest" angle on the news. A "hard news" program about the War in Afghanistan, for example, would cover up-to-date statistics about casualties, troop deployments, and counterterrorism and counterinsurgency strategies. Soft news, on the other hand, might focus on the story of a wounded Marine and his life before and after Afghanistan. Soft news is more focused on entertaining rather than fully informing the viewer. We have seen an increase in soft news through newsmagazine shows such as *Dateline* and *20/20*. These types of shows have tried to capitalize on the success of harder news shows such as *60 Minutes* and *Nightline*, and also take advantage of the way these shows are often far cheaper to produce than are scripted television shows and thus can have a higher profit margin.

While members of the informed public and elites may not find much value in soft news, there is some reason to believe that these shows have the potential to alter the relationship between the mass public and foreign policy. In *Soft News Goes to War* (2003), for example, Matthew Baum finds some evidence that being exposed to an issue through a soft news program can lead viewers at least some of the time to want to learn more about that issue, and they then turn to "harder" news. This might be a pathway to help move people from the ranks of the mass, disinterested public into the ranks of the interested public—or beyond.

A more pernicious force is the emergence of "fake news," things that are meant to look like they are "real" news and the products of professional journalism but which are, in fact, only masquerading as such. Fake news is really an attempt to trick or convince the public of something that may not be true. Governments use this tactic regularly and increasingly, as do interest groups and other nongovernmental actors. Trying to make what is really an ad in the newspaper look like it is a real newspaper story is one example of this. Actually planting fake stories in the press is another tactic. In December 2010 it was reported that newspapers in Pakistan reported on leaks from WikiLeaks that served to bolster the Pakistan government and deride India; but the "cables" were not real—the stories were made up. Who planted these stories is perhaps unclear, but who benefits from them is more obvious.

Foreign governments are not the only ones who use fake news as a tool to try to shape public opinion. In the 1980s the Reagan administration's effort at "public diplomacy" included such tactics and led to some fake stories that found their way out of newspapers in Central America and into the U.S. press. In the aftermath of the U.S. invasion of Iraq, the U.S. government paid private American contractors to plant stories—not all true—in Iraqi newspapers.

These are only a few suggestions on how the media will become more important in the future. How its role will evolve is difficult to predict: The pace of technological, economic, and political change is so rapid that establishing a sense of direction is almost impossible; and precise prediction is fool's work. For example, if someone had predicted five years before the event that a coup against a democratizing government in the Soviet Union would be foiled at least in part because of the Western news media's live coverage of the event, who would have believed it?

CONCLUSIONS

The roles of both the public and the media in the foreign policy-making process are changing. In the past, the traditional roles of both were relatively modest. The general public was basically compliant and reactive, allowing the elite to craft policy unless it went beyond public tolerance written in the most general terms. As for the media, they always focused more on the domestic agenda because they lacked the physical and technological ability to report extensively and in a timely fashion on all but a thin slice of international reality.

Both circumstances have changed. As the boundary between domestic and foreign policy has blurred and the direct, personal impact of foreign policy has increased, so has the public interest. In the days of the Cold War, the content of what the public was exposed to was more heavily oriented toward national security. With the Cold War over, international economic foreign policy factors became more important for a time, as were glaring abuses of the human condition. These issues are less abstract and more personal: They affect jobs and livelihoods and hence have greater salience than, say, the deterrent effect of a particular ballistic missile. The events of September 11th swung public and media attention back to national security and patriotic furor over how to deal with these newly identified enemies.

From this change may come greater public interest in foreign policy, gradually widening the population that forms the interested public. Academics and others have been calling for such interest in the past with little effect; direct personal self-interest may provide a more effective lever. However, access to reliable and unbiased information about these complicated events is increasingly hard to come by. Our hyperpartisan politics have come to the foreign policy domain, and many are concerned that the modern media realities that surround the public and the policy-making process serve to pull us farther apart.

The telecommunications revolution has been more important in expanding the media's role in the foreign policy area than in domestic politics. All advances of this revolution are enhancing the media's ability to cover the domestic scene, although that ability was already present in abundance. The capacity to cover and interpret foreign policy events was always more circumspect, bounded by the speed with which oral descriptions and pictures could be transmitted from the far-flung corners of the globe. Technology has now made it as physically possible for news organizations based in New York City or Washington to air news about events in Africa as it is to cover occurrences in Ohio.

The media's coverage of the 1992 election marked the beginning of a new relationship between politicians and the media. The extensive use of guest appearances on shows such as *Larry King Live* by then-presidential candidates Bill Clinton and H. Ross Perot showed that politicians had attained a new awareness of how to co-opt the media, a phenomenon that was even more prominent in the campaigns that would follow. In effect, the media turned a campaign into entertainment. This evolving landscape continues to unfold as candidates for 2012 craft their media personae.

The public and the media share more than an individually enhanced role in the foreign policy-making process. Their roles are also intertwined. In the past, a basic limitation on the public's ability to receive and interpret information was timely access to information. A decade or two ago, for instance, it was not technologically possible to buy today's *New York Times* in many communities, and CNN was a struggling infant considered primarily an oddity. Currently, today's *Times* is available nearly everywhere, and most

American homes receive CNN and many other news channels on cable or dish networks. The omnipresence of the Internet only adds to this virtual glut. In other words, the availability of timely information has exploded. Neither the public nor the media will likely dominate the foreign and defense policy-making process anytime soon, if ever. Although the greater public knowledge of issues provided by the media is not a threat to the roles of formal governmental institutions and experts, the government must be more aware and sensitive than before, which is what democratic government is about.

WHERE DO WE GO FROM HERE?

This chapter raises several, interrelated issues. The trends and dynamics of the different publics and foreign policy are made and remade by the media trends that are discussed. Democracy depends on an active and educated citizenry, but we know that—especially when it comes to foreign policy—the vast majority of Americans have little interest in or knowledge of foreign affairs. This creates a large accountability problem, since it also means the people have little way to know whether the government is pursuing wise policies or not. The evolution of the world system since the end of the Cold War and since 9/11 has created a world that is more complex and more interconnected—making the challenge of citizenship in this area even tougher.

However, the modern media environment—including the emergence and proliferation of social networking—offers more opportunities for members of the American public to learn more about international affairs, at a lower cost, than ever before. Beyond that, the ease of foreign travel and the nature of American society with its family relations to and immigration from all parts of the globe mean that the United States is perhaps distinctly positioned to be connected, people-to-people, to the rest of the globe.

Anne-Marie Slaughter, a Princeton political scientist and director of the State Department's Policy Planning Staff in the first two years of the Obama administration, has argued that today's college students can be thought of as our first truly "global" generation. Coming of age after the end of the Cold War, taking advantage of foreign travel and study abroad, and having access to technologies that allow people to stay in touch regularly and cheaply (by email, text messaging, Facebook, Twitter, and Skype, for example), young people in America are uniquely positioned to see themselves as connected to people and events around the globe. Thus, moving forward perhaps more people will move from the mass disinterested public and into the interested public and beyond.

APPLICATION: LOCAL COUNCILS ON WORLD AFFAIRS

One great way to get connected to foreign policy issues close to home is to find the closest World Affairs Council. Most of America's larger cities have such an organization that is professionally run, but many smaller towns also have World Affairs Councils that are managed by volunteers, so there is likely to be one nearby. These local Councils put on programming about international events and American foreign policy, bring in speakers, and generally provide an easy way for people to become more educated about foreign affairs. Many of the Councils use the "Great Decisions" discussion program that is assembled by the Foreign Policy Association as a vehicle for learning and activities. While the modern media environment means there is a lot of bad information out there, it has also never been easier to learn more about international affairs than it is today.

STUDY/DISCUSSION QUESTIONS

1. In what ways does democracy depend on the public and the press for its health? Why does the foreign policy domain make that relationship more complicated?
2. What is the conventional view of the role of the American public in the foreign policy process? In what ways is that view at least incomplete?
3. What is a "rally?" What is a "halo?" How might leaders try to take advantage of these trends?
4. What kinds of media bias are relevant for our understanding of the role of the media in the foreign policy process?
5. What is "soft news," and how is it related to the uninformed public?
6. How has twenty-four-hour cable news and the increasing reach of the Internet altered the relationship between the U.S. government and the media?
7. What advantages over the media does the U.S. government still enjoy?
8. How has the modern media environment both made it easier and also harder for citizens to learn about foreign policy? How has it made it easier and harder for decision makers?

CORE SUGGESTED READINGS

Baum, Matthew A. *Soft News Goes to War: Public Opinion and American Foreign Policy in the New Media Age*. Princeton, NJ: Princeton University Press, 2003. A very interesting study that examines how the information revolution and "soft news" might actually help capture more Americans' interest in foreign affairs.

Foyle, Douglas C. *Counting the Public In: Presidents, Public Opinion, and Foreign Policy*. New York: Columbia University Press, 1999. An excellent extension of the literature on the public and foreign policy, this book presents a study of how modern presidents see the role of the public vis-à-vis the policy process and shows different ways that presidents and the public interact in this domain.

Fried, Amy. *Muffled Echoes: Oliver North and the Politics of Public Opinion*. New York: Columbia University Press, 1997. Focused on the Iran-Contra scandal, this book examines the dynamics of the modern media, the "echo chamber," and foreign policy.

Mueller, John E. *War, Presidents and Public Opinion*. New York: Wiley, 1973. This book is a classic, the modern starting place for studying public opinion and foreign policy. Mueller pays particular attention to tracking the relationship between casualties and support for the wars in Vietnam and Korea.

Strobel, Warren P. *Late-Breaking Foreign Policy: The News Media's Influence on Peace Operations*. Washington, DC: U.S. Institute of Peace Press, 1997. This is an outstanding analysis of the role of the media since the end of the Cold War.

ADDITIONAL READINGS AND REFERENCES

Alterman, Eric. Who *Speaks for America? Why Democracy Matters in Foreign Policy.* Ithaca, NY: Cornell University Press, 1998.

Bishop, Bill, with Robert G. Cushing. *The Big Sort: Why the Clustering of Like-Minded America Is Tearing Us Apart.* New York: Houghton Mifflin, 208.

Brace, Paul, and Barbara Hinckley. *Follow the Leader: Opinion Polls and the Modern Presidents.* New York: Basic Books, 1992.

Brody, Richard A. *Assessing the President: The Media, Elite Opinion, and Public Support.* Stanford, CA: Stanford University Press, 1991.

Cohen, Bernard C. *The Public's Impact on Foreign Policy.* Boston: Little, Brown, 1973.

Everts, Philip, and Pierangelo Isernia (eds.). *Public Opinion and the International Uses of Force.* New York: Routledge, 2001.

Farnsworth, Stephen J., and S. Robert Lichter. *The Mediated Presidency: Television News and Presidential Governance.* Lanham, MD: Rowman & Littlefield, 2006.

Fiorina, Morris P., with Samuel J. Abrams and Jeremy C. Pope. *Culture War? The Myth of a Polarized America* (3rd ed.). New York: Longman, 2010.

Hallin, Daniel C. *The Uncensored War: The Media and Vietnam.* New York: Oxford University Press, 1986.

Hallin, Daniel C. *We Keep America on Top of the World: Television Journalism and the Public Sphere.* New York: Routledge, 1994.

Holsti, Ole R. *Public Opinion and American Foreign Policy.* Ann Arbor: University of Michigan Press, 1997.

Jacobs, Lawrence R., and Robert Y. Shapiro. *Politicians Don't Pander: Political Manipulation and the Loss of Democratic Responsiveness.* Chicago: University of Chicago Press, 2000.

Jentleson, Bruce. "The Pretty Prudent Public: Post Post-Vietnam American Opinion on the Use of Military Force." *International Studies Quarterly* 36 (1992): 49–74.

Jentleson, Bruce, and Rebecca L. Britton. "Still Pretty Prudent: Post-Cold War American Public Opinion on the Use of Military Force." *Journal of Conflict Resolution*, 42 (1998): 395–417.

Kull, Steven, and I. M. Destler. *Misreading the Public: The Myth of a New Isolationism.* Washington, DC: Brookings Institution Press, 1999.

Mueller, John. *Policy and Opinion in the Gulf War.* Chicago: University of Chicago Press, 1994.

Nacos, Brigitte L., Robert Y. Shapiro, and Pierangelo Isernia (eds.). *Decisionmaking in a Glass House: Mass Media, Public Opinion, and American and European Foreign Policy in the 21st Century.* Lanham, MD: Rowman and Littlefield, 2000.

Robinson, Piers. *The CNN Effect: The Myth of News Media, Foreign Policy and Intervention.* New York: Taylor & Francis, 2002.

Smith, Perry M. *How* CNN *Fought the* War: *A View from the Inside.* New York: Carol, 1991.

Sobel, Richard. *The Impact of Public Opinion on U.S. Foreign Policy Since Vietnam.* New York: Oxford University Press, 2001.

Spragens, William C. *The Presidency and the Mass Media in the Age of Television.* Washington, DC: University Press of America, 1979.

Sunstein, Cass R. *Republic.com 2.0.* Princeton, NJ: Princeton University Press, 2007.

Von Clausewitz, Carl. *On War.* Princeton, NJ: Princeton University Press, 1984.

Wittkopf, Eugene R. *Faces of Internationalism: Public Opinion and American Foreign Policy.* Durham, NC: Duke University Press, 1990.

PART II

Foreign Policy Outcomes

CHAPTER

9

Traditional Issues in National Security

Force modernization, symbolized by the controversy over the F-22 fighter pictured, is a major issue concerning future national security spending in a resource-constrained environment.

PREVIEW

National security and foreign policy concerns are very similar and overlapping. In recent decades, concerns about national security have been seen as synonymous with or even of a higher priority than traditional foreign policy, and the proper balance is under scrutiny today. This chapter begins by looking at the relationship between the two concepts, and then examines in more detail the perspective of national security in foreign policy. With these bases established, it then turns to national security concerns that, like the brunt of the F-22 case that begins the chapter, transcend the Cold War to the present. The discussion first looks at the problem of conventional forces and war, with emphasis on the contemporary problems of the kinds of war for which the United States should prepare and the related question of military manpower. It then moves to the question of strategic nuclear weapons, with a major emphasis on contemporary nuclear problems, notably proliferation and arms control.

KEY CONCEPTS

F-22 Raptor
national interests
instruments of power
national security
realism
threats
vital interests
less-than-vital (LTV) interests
interest-threat mismatch
risk
mission-force mismatch
all-volunteer force (AVF)
strategic nuclear weapons
deterrence
nuclear proliferation
N + 1 problem
ballistic missile defense (BMD)

In 1981, the United States Air Force (USAF) decided it needed to begin developing a fifth generation of fighter aircraft in anticipation of the development of a similar breed of aircraft by the Soviet Union and the People's Republic of China as part of the Cold War military competition. The program to develop this new fighter aircraft was launched in 1986 and continued for over twenty years, despite the collapse of the confrontation in which it was supposed to compete, the utter disintegration of one of the opponents that the new plane was designed to counter (the Soviet Union), and the transformation of the other opponent from military adversary to economic partner and competitor (China). Neither the Russians nor the Chinese have produced a fifth-generation fighter to date, although outgoing U.S. Defense Secretary Robert Gates warned as he was leaving office in 2011 that both countries were now pursuing this goal.

The outcome of this 1980s program was the **F-22 Raptor** aircraft, one of the most expensive and controversial aircraft ever devised by the United States. The most sophisticated and superior aircraft in the world today, the F-22 is a supersonic fighter jet that incorporates stealth technology to obscure itself from enemy defenses, and it has been modified over time to incorporate additional missions such as air support for ground operations. In 2004, Angus Houston, chief of the Australian Defence Force, opined that the "F-22 will be the most outstanding fighter plane ever built."

Despite this enthusiasm, the F-22 has had a long and checkered history that at least temporarily came to an end when the fiscal year (FY) 2010 defense budget was passed with no additional funding for F-22 production. That history began when the Air Force determined the need for a fighter with the kinds of capability developed for the Raptor, continued through the research and development stage despite the end of the Cold War (the first prototype of what the F-22 would become was initially flown in 1990, and what essentially became the actual aircraft was first tested in 1997), and the first units entered the operational inventory in 2005, all at an estimated program cost of $65 billion.

The number of Advanced Tactical Fighters or ATFs (the original designation of the F-22) has steadily declined as costs have escalated and questions about the need for the aircraft have multiplied. The U.S. Air Force originally projected a fleet of 750 of the aircraft, a number pared down to 648 by then-Secretary of Defense Richard Cheney in 1990. The number was reduced to 442 F-22s in 1994, and in 1997 the number again shrank to 339. A Congressional cost cap further reduced the projected size of the fleet to 277 in 2003, and by 2006, the DOD had settled on a total purchase of 183 of the planes. At that time, the accumulated cost of the program was estimated at $62 billion, and the General Accountability Office (GAO) said that the cost per aircraft was $361 million. In April 2009, Congress, at the rigorous insistence of Secretary of Defense Gates and President Obama, voted to end F-22 production at 187 aircraft.

While continuing to be the gemstone of the U.S. Air Force, the F-22 program has had a rocky existence quite unaccustomed for that service. During the Cold War, the Air Force was the most favored of the military services, flashing its technological miracles before bedazzled lawmakers and generally coming away with whatever resources it desired, and those who proposed the ATF in 1981 envisaged the same happy fate for what became the F-22. But that is not what happened. Why?

The derailment of the fifth-generation stealth fighter is complicated, but its demise can largely be attributed to four general factors that cumulatively raised enough questions and objections to bring about the program's conclusion short of its advocates' dreams. Each of these factors, individually and collectively, reflects an idea conceived in the Cold War but reaching fruition in a very different environment. All have relevance as the United States looks toward the defense future.

The first and most overwhelming problem has been cost. The F-22 may be the most capable fighter aircraft ever produced, but it is also the most expensive. Within the context of a life-or-death struggle with a global communist movement bent on producing a similar or superior capability, the cost was successfully justified, but a changing international environment largely undercut that rationale. The argument that the benefits justified the costs was progressively difficult to sustain in the post–Cold War world.

Second, the need for the expensive capability the F-22 possesses has largely evaporated. An original stimulus was that the Soviets and Chinese were pursuing a fifth-generation aircraft, but as noted, such programs were either cancelled or delayed indefinitely when the Cold War ended, and it is not clear that in the present environment either country can be considered enough of an adversary to revive the prospects, despite Gates's warning. At the same time, such an expensive addition to U.S. military capabilities can be questioned in terms of relevance and obsolescence. The United States has not engaged in significant aerial combat with fighter aircraft since the Korean War of the 1950s and already possesses the world's most capable fighter aircraft. Does it really need a yet more capable fighter aircraft? At the same time, many analysts believe the days of *manned* fighters are numbered and that the future belongs to unmanned drone fighter combatants. If true, the F-22 is a very costly interim solution for the transition period to unmanned aircraft.

Third, the Congress has attached a ban on overseas sales of the F-22. The rationale is that the United States should not equip other countries that might be competitors with the same capability built into its own most sophisticated aircraft. At the same time, the surest way to amortize the considerable "sunk" costs (research and development costs already expended) is by building and selling more of the aircraft (thereby driving down unit costs), and foreign sales (notably to the Japanese, who have expressed an interest) are prime candidates. The sales ban, ironically, means the F-22 is a solution to a threat that no one else can mount without sharing the capability that justified the F-22 in the first place. In other words, the only fighter that can challenge an F-22 is another F-22, and if no one else has them, there is no challenge for U.S. F-22s to meet.

Fourth and finally, a cheaper and more versatile alternative, the F-35 Joint Strike Fighter, exists as an alternative. The F-35 does not possess as sophisticated air-to-air capabilities as the F-22 (a point made forcefully by USAF defenders of the F-22), but the aircraft can be modified to serve the needs of the air arms of the various military services. The combination of versatility and lower costs weighed heavily on a budget-conscious Secretary Gates in 2009. The F-22 lost that competition to the F-35.

The story and fate of the F-22 is a parable of sorts for how the role and nature of national security has changed. The Cold War elevated national security concerns largely defined in military terms to the center stage. In that foreign policy environment, the F-22 was certainly not an unusual proposal, and had the Cold War persisted, the F-22 would probably have entered the inventory in something like the numbers originally requested without major controversy. Times have changed dramatically, however, leading to the conclusion that the Raptor was too expensive a program for an environment in which it was hardly needed.

The F-22 saga is instructive because it illustrates the consequences of change and the ongoing problem of defining threats and equipping forces in the current foreign and national security environment. The mind-set that gave birth to and nurtured the F-22 still exists and at least subconsciously influences how many observers and policy makers frame national security concerns. Many of the national security structures and approaches that are grouped into the category of "traditional issues"—the subject of this chapter—bear at least some conceptual resemblance to the F-22.

Many of the ways in which Americans view their place in the world and the nature of the foreign policy challenges the United States faces are artifacts of the Cold War experience, where the overwhelming foreign policy problem for the United States was the containment of communist expansion. That problem was multifaceted, including significant political and economic elements, but it was primarily a very serious national security, military concern. The twin foci of the relationship were a potential conventional World War III in Europe and a strategic nuclear war between the superpowers that could have destroyed them both—a truly existential threat to national existence. Each contingency confronted planners with different, very costly requirements, and the two problems were linked by the very real possibility that a nonnuclear—conventional—confrontation could somehow spin out of control into the central nuclear conflagration that could destroy both of them.

The rest of this chapter attempts to assess the role of national security in foreign policy and to examine those traditional but ongoing areas of foreign policy that are legacies of the Cold War experience. It begins by introducing the concepts of foreign and national security policy and the relationship between them. It then moves to the language and logic of foreign policy in national security terms—interests, threats, and risks—and how that language frames the foreign policy dialogue. The chapter then looks at the structure of traditional concerns with large-scale conventional weapons and war and nuclear balance with an emphasis on proliferation and arms control.

NATIONAL SECURITY AND FOREIGN POLICY

The basic purpose of a country's foreign policy is to protect and promote that country's **national interests**, those conditions and circumstances that are compatible with and necessary for the realization of the values of that particular country. A major thrust of national security is directed at deflecting or otherwise negating conditions that interfere with the country's realization of its interests. Since conditions that can or could impede realizing those interests can take on different faces—economic, political, and military in the most basic formulation that is usually attached to such discussions—the state has and can employ various means to overcome impediments to its interests. These means are generally known as the **instruments of power**, and like the problems they seek to overcome, are generally divided into categories matching the threats they seek to deflect or negate—for instance, the economic, political, and military instruments of power. Many analysts create additional categories of these instruments such as information or intelligence, and while such additions are entirely reasonable, the three basic instruments will be used here for illustrative purposes.

Traditionally, matters of **national security** have been associated with the use of the military instrument of power, economic differences with the economic instrument, and diplomacy with the political instrument, in which case national security is a subset of the more general concern of foreign policy.

The heart of national security, like foreign policy more generally, is keeping the country safe (or secure) from threats from foreign opponents, a description very close to that of foreign policy. What has traditionally differentiated the two concepts is the military emphasis of national security policy—what kinds of threats exist that would do *physical* harm to Americans or the United States, and what can be done to prevent or minimize such threats or acts. That neat distinction has, however, been muddied in the past half century or more by two basic factors.

The first blurring influence has been the rise in the prominence of military threats within the concerns surrounding the promotion and protection of national interests. The military competition with the Soviet-led communist world was so overwhelming that it virtually eclipsed other concerns historically associated with foreign policy on the assumption that if the Soviet threat could not be deterred militarily, no other value mattered. The first purpose of state, after all, is to preserve itself and its people, and Soviet military force threatened that value. To some extent, the threat of terrorism has replaced the containment of communism as the first objective of post-9/11 foreign policy, although there is a growing body of thought that suggests that terrorism does not pose as fundamental a threat as communism did and thus may not deserve the same status as did the Soviet threat.

The second source of blurring has been a gradual expansion in the concept of what constitutes national security. Russia still retains the capability to destroy or gravely injure the United States with its remaining nuclear arsenal (subject to reductions discussed later in the chapter), but traditional military threats to national security have receded since the early 1990s, allowing an expansion of what makes the country safe or feel safe (a dictionary definition of security) from harm. Terrorism, for instance, does not pose a conventional military threat to the United States (see the discussion in Chapter Ten), the growing vulnerability of the American economy is now generally conceded to be a national security concern, and it is not uncommon to hear people talk about things such as energy or environmental security in the same kinds of terms. National security, in other words, has come to be more than simply military security.

The result is that the relationship between foreign policy and national security is no longer clear and distinct, if it ever was in fact. Rather, it is possible to think of that relationship in a number of different ways, of which four will be examined here briefly.

1. *National security policy is a part, or subset, of foreign policy.* This is the traditional view, and the view most associated with the traditional foreign policy bureaucracy—for example, the Department of State. Such a view at least implicitly assumes that diplomacy, the preferred instrument of power of those holding this view, is supreme, as is dealing with other problems such as environment and energy that are amenable to solution by diplomatic means. The use of the military instrument is seen as a background factor to help induce recalcitrant opponents to negotiate or as the instrument to be considered and occasionally used when diplomacy fails.

2. *National security policy is equal to or virtually synonymous with foreign policy.* This formulation is the view that took hold during the Cold War and is reflected in structures such as the National Security Council, as discussed in Chapter Five. It represents an elevation of national security concerns largely defined in military terms to a much more prominent place at the foreign policy table than was true before the Cold War, and has been institutionalized in terms of the enormous commitments of American resources to the military enterprise. Additionally, if one defines a large portion of the foreign difficulties the United States encounters in the world in national security terms, the elevation of the concept to coequality becomes true tautologically.

3. *National security policy is the prime driver of foreign policy.* This position is a subtle combination of the first two positions. It suggests that while foreign policy is conceptually broader than national security policy, the structure of problems the country faces is so overwhelmingly militarily threatening that national security policy effectively overrides and even trumps more traditional foreign policy concerns and methods, at least for a large part of the time. This position represents a small but subtle retreat from the position associated with the Cold War in that it suggests that traditional national security concerns may not be *quite* as pressing as they were earlier, but that they remain extremely important.

4. *National security policy serves to distort foreign policy more generally considered.* This is a position that is not broadly discussed in the general debate over foreign policy, but it is a perspective that has become germane in the last decade or so, when military force has been used in situations where it arguably was inappropriate and inadvisable. The case of the invasion, conquest, and occupation of Iraq is a case in point of what Bacevich (2010) has called in a scathing critique of U.S. policy "the sacred trinity": "U.S. military power, the Pentagon's global footprint, and an American penchant for intervention." The decision to attack Iraq was almost entirely confined to the White House and the Pentagon, generally over the muted objections of other foreign policy actors (notably the State Department and the intelligence community, both of which objected on different grounds). The American action in Iraq was condemned virtually universally outside the United States and almost certainly made the pursuit of other American priorities more difficult than they would have been otherwise. At the same time, there are some foreign policy problems, such as terrorism and internal wars, that can be conceptualized in traditional national security terms but which are not amenable to traditional military solutions. When a national security viewpoint dominates decision making in such instances, the result can be to distort the problem and how to approach it.

While there may be disagreement about how foreign and national security policy are related to one another, there is no doubt that an important part of the American interface with the world is framed and dealt with through the lens of national security. Even if that relationship is changing with time, much of the foreign policy agenda remains largely defined in national security terms and with national security solutions suggested as major means to deal with problems. Thus, understanding foreign policy requires familiarity with the framework of terms and concepts that underlies a national security approach to foreign policy.

INTERESTS, THREATS, AND RISKS

National security views of the world have traditionally been dominated by a worldview known as **realism,** a concept introduced in Chapter One. The vantage point of realism is that the world as it exists (the "real" world from which the approach takes its name) is dominated by the concept of national sovereignty that atomizes the member countries of the system and leaves them in a competitive relationship where their interactions are dominated by the interplay of their conflicting interests in a competitive, hostile, even anarchical environment. The basic concepts associated with a national security approach to foreign policy start from that base.

As in foreign policy more generally, national security policy begins from the basic question of what conditions exist in the international environment, and the answers are framed in terms of national interests. These interests are implicitly arranged in hierarchical terms of both their importance to the United States and to Americans, and in traditional conceptions of national security. A further distinction arising from these concerns is whether or to what extent military force may be relevant and appropriate to their realization, since military power is the most clearly distinguishing characteristic of national security approaches to foreign policy. With national values and priorities established, the concern of national security analysis then turns to what impedes realizing those interests and thus what problems must be addressed and neutralized if American interests are to be achieved. These impediments are generally conceptualized as **threats** that have military content and that potentially require military remediation. Since the volume of potential threats nearly always exceeds the capacity of the state to neutralize them entirely, national security analysis must also address **risk**, the gap between threats and the capacity to negate them.

National Interests

In formal terms, a national interest is a situation or condition that is important to the state (a condition in which it has an interest). The state is not, of course, equally interested in all conditions that affect it—the United States has interests both in its physical survival and in seeing American values accepted in foreign countries, but one is clearly more important than the other—and thus those conditions valued are normally arranged in order of priority to distinguish between more and less important concerns.

Over twenty years ago, Donald Nuechterlein (1991) provided a durable two-axis framework for organizing the differences between various kinds of interests. It is produced here as Figure 9.1.

	Intensity of Interest			
Content of Interest	Survival	Vital	Major	Peripheral
Defense of homeland				
Economic well-Being				
Promotion of national values				
Favorable world order				

Source: Donald E. Nuechterlein, *America Recommitted: United States Interests in a Reconstructed World.* Lexington, KY: University of Kentucky Press, 1991, 27.

FIGURE 9.1
National Security Interest Matrix

The distinctions are both intuitive and hierarchical in descending order of importance on both axes. On the vertical axis of interest content, *defense of homeland* refers to protecting national territory from outside attack (this concept is sometimes extended, not without controversy, to American overseas territories or assets), *economic well-being* refers the ability to protect or promote the national economic good, and so on. From a national security vantage point, the horizontal axis is more fundamental. However, the distinctions on this axis are somewhat less intuitively obvious and more controversial, and they help define the debate over national security.

The clearest of these distinctions is *physical survival*, the ability to guarantee that the state persists as an independent entity. When combined with defense of homeland, it is the clearest and consequentially most agreed domain of national security concern defined in traditional military terms—no one disagrees that the prime legitimate role of military force is to ensure that the United States is neither conquered nor physically destroyed.

The second category is **vital interests.** This concept forms the most basic distinction between traditional national security and nonsecurity concerns, because it forms the traditional boundary between when force is and is not appropriate as an instrument of power. The term itself is used somewhat loosely in general discussions, to justify actions that might be considered dubiously appropriate for military applications. Its meaning, however, is precise: A vital interest is a situation or condition that is so important that a state will not willingly compromise on it and will take all necessary actions, up to and including military force, to realize it. Thus the boundary between vital and **less-than-vital (LTV) interests** marks the line separating when force will and will not be contemplated, at least in traditional interpretations (those based in the philosophy of realism) of national security.

Interpreting and applying the concept of vital interests to concrete situations is complicated by at least three factors. The first is a qualification in the definition itself: the use of the word *willingly* as a conditioner. The word is included in the definition because there may be situations in which a state lacks the relevant ability to defend an interest it deems vital and thus may be forced to accept a negative outcome. The distinction surrounding the boundary for using force does not apply neatly in these circumstances.

A second complication arises from the essentially circular definition that some analysts have employed to the vital interest concept, in essence arguing that a vital interest is a condition or situation worth going to war over. This definition is circular and insidious because it means that anytime a country uses military force, very important (that is, vital) interests must have been at stake. Such an assertion is questionable in the case of some applications of force and highly debatable in others. This distinction, for instance, allowed some apologists to justify the U.S. war effort in Iraq in the face of the realist objection that no truly vital interests were engaged or threatened.

The third problem is the ambiguity of the term in application. Simply put, there is no universal agreement on all the situations and conditions that constitute vital interests for the United States or any other country. On some matters such as those surrounding physical survival, a consensus exists, but in many instances, the determination of importance is subjective: What seems vital to one individual or group may seem less-than-vital to another. This subjectivity is why the boundary between vital and less-than-vital categories of intensity (major and peripheral) is often depicted as a band or confidence interval rather than as a sharp, discrete boundary. One of the major recurring ways of depicting the entire debate over national security is where the line is both in general and in specific cases.

The other intensities of interest fall outside the parameters of traditional national security interest and can be dealt with more succinctly. Situations of *major intensity* are conditions in which if the interests are not realized, the result would be harmful but not intolerable. The election of a Mexican president not dedicated to the aggressive suppression of drug trafficking through Mexico to the United States would violate the American interest in eliminating the illicit movement of illegal narcotics across the border, but it would not be intolerable enough to cause the United States to use military force against Mexico to produce a more compliant Mexican executive (although the use of force is occasionally raised in discussions about the border problem). A *peripheral interest* is a situation or condition that would inconvenience Americans but little more. An Iranian ban on exporting beluga caviar to the United States would fall into this category.

The matrix depicted in Figure 9.1 allows one to differentiate the interests defined in national security terms from those that are not. As just discussed, situations of survival or vital intensity fall within the clear domain of national security concerns, although there is disagreement about where the boundary between vital and major interests resides in different applications. In terms of the content of interests, defense of homeland, which is largely defined in military and homeland security terms in the contemporary United States, clearly falls within the domain of national security, as do at least some matters of economic well-being (for example, secure access to Middle Eastern petroleum resources necessary to power the economic system). The upper-left quadrant of Figure 9.1 is intended to reflect those interests within the general preserve of national security. Conversely, the promotion of national values and favorable world order generally do not involve survival or vital interests, and major and peripheral interests, regardless of content, are rarely thought of in national security terms, leaving the other three quadrants outside the realm of national security. Policy concerns in those quadrants are covered in Chapters Eleven through Thirteen.

Threats

Challenges to national interests are normally conceptualized as threats in national security terms. Formally, a *threat* is a promise to do something harmful to the threatened party if it fails to comply with some demand(s) made by the threatening party. In international relations terms, threats normally arise over incompatibilities in the interests of two countries (or groups) coupled with the demand by one party that the other conform to its preferred condition or situation represented by its interest or face a negative consequence. Thus, being threatened means being subjected to demands to act in a way that violates one's interests or to be subjected to potential harm.

These abstract ideas may become clearer by example. The question of border control has become a major issue for the United States in its relations with Mexico, representing an escalating intensity of interest somewhere in the nether region between major and vital interest, and the United States demands of Mexico that it share the U.S. sense of urgency and diligence on its side of the border. Historically, Mexico has not had preventing its people from immigrating northward as a major priority, because migration relieves some population pressures in the country and the inflow of money from immigrants back to families in Mexico aids the economy. Thus, American demands and Mexican interests do not coincide in this area.

How does a country respond when it is threatened by another country? The somewhat ambiguous answer is that it depends on two factors and their assessment in any given situation. The first factor is the *credibility* of the threat: Is it believable? Determining credibility in turn requires two determinations. One is whether the threatening party physically *can* carry out the threat (*capability*). Someone can threaten to shoot you, but if that person does not have a firearm, the threat lacks capability and thus credibility. If the threatening person does have a gun, the second determination is whether the person has the *will* to carry out the threat. Shooting someone is, after all, a criminal act, and if one breaks the law, that person runs the risk of apprehension, trial, and punishment: Thus, is carrying out the threat worth the possible consequences? Unfortunately, in real situations, a threatening party will likely seek to obscure his or her capability and will, thereby making both determinations more difficult.

The second factor in responding to a threat is its *importance* (or intensity) to both parties. Clearly, the willingness to carry out or to challenge a threat depends in some measure on how important a favorable outcome is and thus how strenuously one will act in the particular situation. Indeed, putting the question in these terms is another way to phrase it: Is the outcome worth going to war over?

The Mexican border issue helps clarify these distinctions. If Mexico refuses to exercise due diligence on its side of the border, what can the United States threaten to do to get Mexico to comply with U.S. demands? One possibility is to threaten military force; for instance, the United States could threaten to invade northern Mexico, occupy the border region, and thus seal the border to illegal crossing. The threat is credible in that the United States certainly has the capability for such an operation (at least after it ends its occupations in Iraq and Afghanistan), but does it have the will to enforce the threat, knowing it would be condemned internationally as an act of aggression? The answer depends on how important the situation—and thus its alleviation—is to the United States. Mexico, of course, would have to engage in its own analysis of such an American threat and how important the status quo is as opposed to complying with American demands.

This discussion highlights the uncertainty and subjectivity of threat analysis and assessment. Both qualifications arise from the very nature of security. Security has both physical ("safety") and psychological ("sense of safety") elements. The psychological sense of security derives from what people *think* makes them safe, and people differ on what makes them feel secure. For instance, those who advocated invading Iraq essentially argued that Saddam Hussein's regime made them feel insecure, whereas opponents of the war disagreed on that point. If Saddam Hussein posed a threat to U.S. interests, then it was a problem with which the national security mechanisms needed to deal; if he posed no particular threat to American security, then his continuation in power fell outside the realm of American national security.

There is an additional complication in the logic of interests and threat that also further helps to distinguish the differences between the Cold War period and the present: the **interest-threat mismatch**. This concept refers to the misalignment of important interests and major challenges (or threats) to the interests of the United States. In the classic rendering of the mismatch proposed by one of the authors over two decades ago, it refers to the situation where major U.S. interests (survival and vital) are hardly threatened (there are no significant threats against them) and where the threats that do exist are hardly interesting (they are threats against lesser—major and peripheral—interests in terms of Figure 9.1). The concept is meaningful in national security terms because the important interests are those that most unambiguously fall within the jurisdiction of traditional national security concern.

The mismatch did not exist during the Cold War, where important interests and threats were closely aligned—or matched. Soviet nuclear missiles threatened America's premier interest in its survival, and vital interests such as a free Western Europe and Eastern Asia (for example, Japan and South Korea) were imperiled by communist conventional forces. Interests and threats were thus aligned and provided clear, unambiguous directions about what threats needed to be countered and even how to deal with them.

This clarity evaporated with the end of the Cold War. While Russia can still largely vaporize the United State physically with nuclear weapons, it lacks the plausible motivation to do so, and neither Western Europe nor Japan is particularly threatened by anyone (with the partial exception of North Korea, discussed later in this chapter). Thus, there are few interesting threats to significant interests. The world remains an unstable and threatening place, of course, but the locations of those threats—and especially the violent challenges traditionally associated with national security—are in places and over issues of generally lower interest intensity to the United States than before. The closest thing to an alignment between contemporary threats and interests is in the Middle East. Even there, significant disagreement exists about whether U.S. interests are vital or major and hence of the salience of the threats that exist.

Risk

The third sequential concept underlying distinctive national security approaches to foreign policy is risk. The concept refers generally to the potential dangers or consequences of threats that are not countered, each of which poses the possibility of harm the country *risks* by inattention. Even in an environment where the objective physical threats to security may not exceed the ability to neutralize threats, the list of psychologically generated threats (conditions that are perceived as threatening by some but not all) is virtually infinitely expandable, limited only by the human imagination. Thus, some estimates of threat will always exceed the capacity to confront them all. Reconciling the discrepancy between problems and the ability to resolve them all is the province of *risk management*.

Risk varies. A simple way to think about the problem of risk is to express it in terms of an heuristic (that is, suggestive but not precise or literal) formula:

$$\text{Risk} = \text{Threat} - \text{Capability}\ (R = T - C)$$

Put in verbal form, this depiction suggests that the risk a country incurs is the difference between the cumulative threats it faces and its capability to negate those threats. More precisely, risk is the result of accumulating each individual threat the country encounters (e.g., the threat posed by Al Qaeda plus the threat posed by a nuclear-armed North Korea, and so on) and applying the resources the country possesses against those threats. When resources fall short of negating all sources of threat (which is normally the case), the result is risk.

Risk varies because each element determining it can assume different values. As already suggested, the major variable in the amount of threat derives from the psychological realm: what makes people feel threatened. Both the actions of adversaries posing threats and the perceptions of threatened parties can vary, often as the result of direct and purposeful manipulation. An adversary can increase threat by acting (or speaking) in a more threatening manner or decrease threat by more conciliatory words or deeds. North Korea's changing posture toward the United States offers examples of both directions. Similarly, threatened parties can make the threat increase or decrease by how they interpret the adversary's intentions, either through frightening the public with negative interpretations or by lowering that fright with less ominous views. How much of a threat terrorists pose to the United States or the argued consequences of different outcomes of the Afghanistan War are cases in point of how threat levels can vary—or even be manipulated—for political purposes.

Capability also varies, depending on the amount of national resources the country devotes to the alleviation of foreign-based threats. In some ways, the debate over how much national wealth should be expended on national security can be thought of as an argument over how much risk the country is willing to bear as opposed to how many resources should be devoted to domestic priorities. Since capabilities are largely concrete and physical, they are not as malleable (or elastic) as threats.

Much of the purpose of risk management and national security is risk reduction: How does the country make itself less at risk—or safer? The classic means of doing so involve manipulation of the determinants of risk—threats and capability. Threats can be made less problematical either by reducing threatening conditions—defeating or winning over adversaries, for instance—or by redefining what is threatening and what is not. Similarly, increasing the physical capability to negate threat—making the U.S. borders impenetrable to terrorists, for instance—is also a classic mechanism of threat reduction. Increasing capability, of course, is limited by the physical extent of relevant national resources and the willingness to devote those resources to national security risk reduction rather than for some other uses (of which there are always many). This latter concern has become particularly poignant in the ongoing debate over deficit reduction.

These concepts help provide the conceptual framework for analyzing the traditional issues examined in the rest of this chapter and the more contemporary problems examined in Chapter Ten. The traditional issues—conventional (nonnuclear) war with a powerful adversary and strategic nuclear war—both have their origins in the Cold War, when calculations of risk were formulated on very different threat and capability estimates than are contemporary risks. Part of the current national security debate arises at least implicitly from how much the Cold War calculus must be adjusted in the contemporary environment. The major manifestations of these traditional issues examined in this chapter—the roles for conventional forces and manpower and nuclear weapons proliferation—can be analyzed within this framework of ideas.

This framework is particularly appropriate to the discussion of foreign policy more generally, because it is the forces available to the country that define the military instrument of power and the credible actions and threats that can be issued regarding military force. In terms of the actual threat of employing military force in the defense of national interests, conventional forces have traditionally had the more prominent role, since the role of nuclear forces beyond deterrence is questionable.

NONNUCLEAR (CONVENTIONAL) FORCES AND MISSIONS

National security determinations during the Cold War were simpler than they are today. The United States faced a very robust military threat from the Soviet Union that was potentially so dangerous and deadly that there was little disagreement about whether it had to be combated by a very robust risk-negating capability. It was also conceptually easier to deal with, since the Soviet opponent's military capability was well-known and concrete, providing reasonably clear guidance about what threats needed neutralizing and how to neutralize them. Moreover, since both sides were organized conventionally along classic European lines, the potential military event for which they prepared was essentially a reprise of World War II on a grander and much more lethal scale.

Nuclear weapons confounded that extrapolation, since a conventional clash between the two adversaries could escalate to a nuclear war that might destroy them through escalatory processes neither could fully anticipate because the situation would be truly unprecedented. The resulting uncertainty gradually changed the purpose of the military element to risk reduction for both sides where each confronted the other with such a formidable force that each would be dissuaded from starting a war that could spiral somehow to Armageddon. Nuclear weapons were part of this calculus, and at the conventional level of nonnuclear war, dissuasion was accomplished with a large, modernized version of the forces that contested World War II, undergirded by a conscript-based personnel system. The utility, cost, and relevance of both elements—conventional forces and conscription—are major parts of the contemporary national security debate about how military forces contribute to foreign policy.

Traditional Forces

The Cold War model of military organization remains at the heart of contemporary American military forces and their usage. In order to understand these forces and the uses for which they can and cannot be used for contemporary purposes requires proceeding sequentially through two concerns. The first is the structure of U.S. military forces, and particularly the comparison of U.S. conventional capabilities with those of friends and adversaries. That discussion will allow for an examination of U.S. forces in contemporary situations. The second emphasis will be on the method the United States uses to procure and retain military personnel—military manpower—and the consequences of how that method produces a force that can support U.S. foreign policy goals. In a resource-constrained environment, both are central variables in the expense of defense.

Force Composition The United States spends roughly as much as the rest of the world combined on defense, and the bulk of these expenditures is on conventional forces patterned on the European, Cold War model. The result of this expenditure has been to produce the world's most formidable conventional forces. Some of this capability, and particularly its modernization to levels other countries cannot possibly match, is controversial, as the F-22 study at the beginning of the chapter sought to illustrate.

The contemporary organization of the U.S. military has its roots in World War II and in concepts with which military thinkers from the early state system in the seventeenth century would have been comfortable (with the exception of airpower). This structure was developed over time so that the major European powers that dominated the world mirrored one another closely. The major contemporary problem surrounding these forces is their relevance in a world where the only countries that possess similarly structured forces are either American allies or "friendly" countries (not allied with the United States but not considered likely future opponents, such as India), whereas the countries and movements posing military challenges to the United States eschew this structural model and the methods of fighting associated with it.

There are several ways that can be used to describe American conventional forces, two of which will be employed here. The first is in terms of so-called heavy forces versus light forces. In some circles, the terms "heavy" and "conventional" (or "legacy," in current military parlance) are used interchangeably and describe forces designed to engage in large-unit, concentrated firepower combat. The symbols of these kinds of forces include tanks and heavy artillery on land, large payload bombers and drone aircraft in the atmosphere, and large capital ships on (for example, battleships) or under (namely, submarines) the sea. These forces are configured to fight against similarly configured forces (for example, tanks fighting other tanks) in brutal warfare. The last time the United States fought using classic applications of heavy forces was in World War II during the 1940s and the Korean War between 1950 and 1953. The United States has employed such forces in some cases since, but not against opponents with similar capabilities.

The alternative form of force configuration is "light" forces. As the name implies, forces with this designation are generally more lightly armed (hence the name) and mobile than their heavy counterparts. Special forces, guerrillas, and light infantry are prime examples of light forces applied to ground warfare, where most light force is used. Light forces are particularly well suited to missions that do not require (or seek to avoid) direct confrontations with larger forces and are particularly effective in harassing other forces. When light forces confront heavy forces on terms dictated by heavy forces, they are at a disadvantage and generally fare poorly (for example, soldiers with rifles confronting tanks), and so light forces avoid such situations whenever possible. At the same time, heavy forces are at a disadvantage when light forces operate in places of their preference (for example, tanks trying to pursue guerrillas in mountainous jungles or swamps where there are no roads).

American military forces combine heavy and light elements, although the emphasis and level of resource expenditures has traditionally favored heavy forms. This historically based prejudice adds enormously to the costliness of the American military, since heavy forces are generally much more expensive than light forces. Heavy forces also created a much more multifaceted array of military capabilities, although their relevance may be circumscribed in contemporary conflicts.

The question of relevance has been raised in contemporary applications of U.S. force in places such as Iraq and Afghanistan. Of course, these countries are both located in the developing world, where the kind of infrastructure that best supports heavy forces (and in which they were developed) is missing or deficient or where such forces are unaffordable by local governments. Indeed, it is arguable that the heavy model is particularly inappropriate in very underdeveloped countries such as Afghanistan. For the developing world, the light model is more appropriate, particularly since one of the ways that opponents in the developing world practice so-called asymmetrical warfare (see Chapter Ten) is by adopting the light model as an antidote to the enormous lethality of heavy forces. Because they are more lightly equipped, these forces are also cheaper than heavy forces.

The second way to describe American forces employed here is by configuration. The United States deploys a range of light and heavy forces for all potential fighting media that is unmatched anywhere else in the world. The U.S. Army, for instance, is organized on a model in which infantry supported by armor (tanks) and heavy artillery is the most basic element, although that service also contains light elements, such as Rangers and Special Forces. It is not the only heavy army in the world, but it is the premier example of such a force, both in terms of the quality and quantity of its equipment and, by most estimates, the quality of its members.

The disparity between American and other armed forces is much greater in the areas of naval and air forces. The U.S. Navy is by far the largest, most diverse, and most powerful blue-water navy (one capable of operating in all the world's oceans) in the world, and has at its service the most advanced nuclear-powered vessels, especially in submarines and aircraft carriers, the backbones of underwater and surface combat. No other country in the world can, or even tries, to match the capabilities of the U.S. Navy, which has not had to engage in meaningful combat on or under the seas since World War II.

The conventional airspace is also essentially an American preserve. As the F-22 example illustrated, the United States has the largest force of the world's most capable fighter aircraft, and the same is true of its fleet of bomber aircraft, unmanned aerial vehicles (UAVs or drones); and American satellite and related technologies dominate the militarization of space. No other country challenges either the combat or power-projection capabilities enjoyed by the United States, and the fleet of American aircraft carriers provide a flexibility of airpower projection unmatched anywhere else in the world. The last time the United States faced significant aerial combat from another air force was in Korea.

This impressive array of conventional power helps define the conventional superiority of the United States and why any realistic opponent would find a challenge to the United States on conventional grounds foolhardy, thereby contributing to the obsolescence of this kind of warfare. It is arguable that the U.S. Armed Forces have become essentially muscle-bound, so strong that no one will take them on, meaning that opponents must and have switched to alternative strategies in which those American muscles are less relevant. American naval power means little in Afghanistan.

One can postulate that the result is a **mission-force mismatch** that accompanies the interest-threat mismatch in the contemporary world. In this particular permutation, the problem is that the problems (or potential missions) of the United States are not particularly appropriate for the kinds of forces the United States possesses, and the kind of forces that are available have few missions (that is, other conventionally based threats) to which to respond. This problem is, of course, largely of the Americans' own making, since it was American conventional dominance that has caused potential foes to alter the military playing field on which to contest the Americans so that they have at least some chance of success.

American possession of both substantial heavy and light military capability may define the United States as a military superpower because of the flexibility and amount of military capability it produces, but it does so at a considerable cost. Heavy forces in particular are subject to perpetual modernization and are very expensive. Light forces are cheaper, but when the two capabilities are added together, the sum is very large. This combination may allow maximum risk reduction by being applicable to a broad range of potential threats, but whether the attendant cost is sustainable in the current economic and reduced threat environment is questionable. America's current military manpower system adds to that cost.

Military Manpower

Regardless of the military balance among warring or potentially warring parties and the cleverness (or lack thereof) of those planning the optimal uses of that weaponry, military force—and war—is ultimately about the people who must be armed and conduct war. To cite an old military aphorism, "war is people." Thus, a discussion of military issues must include a significant emphasis on the most basic part of the military equation, manpower.

The discussion of military manpower in a contemporary American sense is enigmatic. In 1972, as the Vietnam War was beginning to wind down and the war had reached the pinnacle of its unpopularity, the U.S. government decided to suspend the lightning rod of public discontent with the war—its conduct largely by young men involuntarily called into military service through conscription. As of January 1, 1972, the "selective service system" by which eighteen- to twenty-six-year-old American men were conscripted (drafted) into service was suspended, replaced by a totally voluntary means of military manpower procurement, the **all-volunteer force (AVF)**. Although selective service could be reinstituted, no American has been compelled to military service since—a period now spanning four decades.

The overwhelmingly positive outcome of the movement from a conscript-based to a volunteer-based military force has been to assist the United States in achieving the overwhelming conventional superiority, because the AVF system produces a superior force comprised entirely of military members who want to be in uniform and who have developed a sense of professionalism that makes them among the most envied military personnel in the world. The enigma is that there have been costs—largely hidden until recently—to this outcome. The first is that the force is limited in size yet very costly, and both characteristics limit the ways in which it can be employed and the extent and effectiveness of the military instrument of power to preserve and promote American interests. The second cost is that this force is also less a citizen force than its predecessor. Secretary Gates in an October 2010 address at Duke University lamented on this latter point that military service has "become something for other people to do."

The Current Situation The U.S. military has been in a state of constant deployment in war for over a decade, the longest period that this has occurred in American history. This period has included playing the lead role in two foreign wars (Iraq and Afghanistan) while maintaining a presence in other countries around the world. For most military members, the consequence of this situation has been multiple assignments in combat and other remote areas and roles at levels and paces of engagement far beyond those recommended by the military itself.

The problem of force size (the current size of U.S. active duty forces is about two-thirds what it was at the end of the Cold War) arises from a much higher level of usage of the forces than was envisaged when they were designed. Because it costs more to maintain (pay salaries and benefits, for instance) professional than conscript forces, fewer forces can be recruited without greatly increasing manpower costs. Americans like the release from the cloud of involuntary service that the absence of a draft produces, but they are reluctant to pay the much greater costs that such a large force would create.

The result is the constrained size of the military. Using September 30, 2009, figures provided by the Department of Defense, the active duty manpower of the United States stood at 1.445 million military members spread across the armed forces, with a force in the various service reserves of 880,000. While these numbers may seem formidable, they are down considerably from Cold War numbers (in 1989, for instance, active duty manpower stood at 2.15 million and reserves at over 1 million). The largest numbers of those forces are assigned to support rather than combat roles, leaving a much smaller effective American fighting force.

The consequence is an effective armed force that is limited in its capabilities and particularly simultaneous uses. When there were 150,000 American forces in Iraq and another 40 to 50,000 in Afghanistan, the effect was to strain the deployment of those forces to the limit. The result is that the

United States possesses a badly overworked armed force in considerable need of being rested and replenished after the Iraq and Afghanistan missions are completed. The only alternatives to this overused force are to make it larger or use it less.

Operationally, there are three possible ways to enhance the force. One is to increase the effectiveness of existing forces—force multiplication—and this was indeed the grand design of Secretary of Defense Donald Rumsfeld during the George W. Bush administration. Most of these enhancements are technological and add to costs. A second form of enhancement has been to "privatize" aspects of the military endeavor by turning over some traditional functions (for example, food service, security for embassies and other U.S. facilities) to private contractors. These efforts have been criticized on the grounds that private contractors are very expensive (more expensive than added military manpower) and in some cases unreliable, as isolated cases of abuse by individual contractors in war zones has demonstrated. The third alternative is a larger volunteer force, but that option is constrained both by cost and the willingness of additional Americans to volunteer. A volunteer military is necessarily bounded by how many qualified men and women are *willing to join the military*, and there are upward limits to how many will join in the absence of compulsion.

The real constraint, especially in a resource-constrained environment, is cost. The major source of expense is compensation: Extrapolating from current manpower levels and personnel costs included in the DOD budget, the average cost of a military member is about $115,000 apiece for salary and fringe benefits. For fiscal year 2010, the official defense budget of the United States was about $534 billion, of which $244 billion was devoted to personnel. These figures are low: Overall figures do not include items that are defense-related but not included under DOD for the overall budget (for example, nuclear weapons costs included in the Department of Energy budget) or personnel (such as medical costs found in the Veterans' Affairs budget); when these are added, the overall cost of defense is over $900 billion, and according to Akedis (2009), the personnel cost is over $300 billion and climbing as things such as the long-term health care expenses of returning veterans mount. Even if potential qualified recruits were available, the result of force enlargement would simply be to bloat these figures proportionately.

These factors create real questions as the United States faces the future. The early period after 9/11 was arguably one in which the pursuit of foreign policy goals with armed force was basically unconstrained by considerations such as manpower size and cost, but will that situation continue into a future in which the shadow of that horrendous event is more distant and faded and in which the specter of federal budget deficits has become such a prominent concern?

Manpower Questions To a large part of the American population, the need for premier military power is so compelling and continuing American dominance is so vital to American national security that it must be borne regardless of the consequences. From this vantage point, the problem of national security is so much more vital than other woes the country faces—such as the health of the economy—that military spending and its results must be exempted from any belt-tightening that is applied to other government activity. A growing number of Americans believe that military spending is the most obvious place within federal expenditures where enough savings can be realized to make a meaningful dent on budgetary concerns, and that meaningful reform is impossible if defense is exempted. Manpower represents one-third of defense spending, and it is the vital underbelly of both sides of any national debate: Robust manpower is necessary for the country to assume an assertive national security posture, and it is an obvious place within which to make budgetary cuts.

If one assumes that deficit reduction is or will become an overwhelming national priority in the next few years that cannot be negated entirely by economic growth from economic recovery, what are the military manpower implications of various solutions?

There is great inertial pressure to continue the AVF concept without significant alteration. Although this option does nothing to address the overall budgetary crisis, it does have its supporters. The military clearly likes the AVF concept and would be most reluctant to abandon or seriously modify it. Their reasons center on the quality of force the AVF produces and on the lack of problems it creates compared to a force with reluctant conscripts, who are a constant morale and discipline problem. Moreover, it has been forty years since the military has had to deal with personnel other than volunteers, and all those (for example, drill sergeants) who could manage unruly, unenthusiastic members have long since retired.

Politicians also like the AVF, because it does not leave them in the uncomfortable position of bearing responsibility for forcing the involuntary service of the offspring of constituents who might retaliate against seeing their sons and daughters (a revived conscription system would almost certainly have to draft women as well as men on constitutional grounds) forced into military service and, in the extreme, combat. For this reason, supporting a movement away from the AVF toward a system with a conscription component would be politically suicidal.

Aside from not addressing whatever military problems the current manpower regimen creates, continuation also raises a more subtle difficulty: the separation of the military from society. It is a problem flowing from Gates's lament that military service is not a consideration for most Americans. Rather, military matters are handled by the voluntarily recruited professionals, thereby freeing the average citizen of any feeling of participation in the violent affairs of the state. Some argue that this means the public lacks a stake in military involvements and that the result may be that it is easier for political authorities to commit military forces into harm's way than it might be if those officials had to answer directly to voters who were subject to involuntary participation in those affairs via some form of conscription. This problem is explored in the *Intersections* box, "Politics and Manpower."

INTERSECTIONS

Politics and Manpower

Before the end of conscription in 1972, all American males were subject to being drafted, including Elvis Presley, seen being inducted into the Army in 1958.

There is a growing sentiment within portions of the American public (notably older Americans who themselves were subject to involuntary military service) that the AVF manpower system has a pernicious effect on American policy regarding the use of military force. Put simply, it is argued that if the decision to employ force was more personalized for Americans in the form of potential service and sacrifice, the American public would not allow the frivolous use of such force. A common variant of this argument is the rhetorically intended question, "Would the United States have been able to invade and conquer Iraq if political authorities had been forced to consult with an American public that would have had to bear directly the consequences of that decision?" The answer, of course, is that it might well not have approved, meaning the military would not have been engaged in what those who raise the question argue was a frivolous (and very expensive) use of American force.

Does this argument have merit? The proposition it posits suggests something about the responsibility of political authorities to their constituents and the degree

(Continued)

(Continued)

to which citizen views constrain the actions political authorities take. If the knowledge that the decision to invade Iraq (or Afghanistan, for that matter) would have meant conscripting young Americans to fight that conflict, the decision to do so would have had the effect of proposing a referendum to the American people with the effective options being (1) that we accept the conscription consequences of a decision to go to war and are willing to serve (or have our loved ones serve), or (2) that we reject the proposition that going to war with Iraq is worth drafting and potentially sacrificing our young men and women. The "vote" on this measure would be cast the next time those voting for the war had to stand for reelection. Those who argue that conscription would serve as a useful brake on what they view as the promiscuous use of military force possible under the AVF concept, in effect are saying that the possible alienation of the voting public would yield a more cautious use of force than is currently the case.

Do you agree or disagree with this proposition? If you agree, would you be willing to take the chance of personal conscription to provide this inhibition to overuse of the military?

Military Manpower as Metaphor The picture that has been painted of the contemporary manpower situation is more pessimistic than is typically portrayed, but it is a necessary perspective to consider as the United States removes itself from the wars in Iraq and Afghanistan and considers what national interests it will contemplate supporting with military force in the future. The manpower situation indeed represents a metaphor for this entire discussion.

This discussion begins with several arguable (in the sense that not everyone will accept them) observations about manpower and its use in support of national security objectives. The first is that manpower is the most important factor in military capability, and it is a factor that can only be attenuated marginally by efforts at force multiplication. The insufficiency of American forces in both Iraq and Afghanistan speaks to this point: There have simply not been enough Americans on the ground to occupy those countries effectively enough to suppress or contain opponents of the occupation. General Eric Shinseki warned of this in 2003 when, as Chief of Staff of the Army, he argued that the United States would need 330,000 troops in Iraq for an effective occupation. Secretary Rumsfeld rejected this figure, both because he believed in force multiplication and because there were not adequate ground forces available for the task Shinseki laid out. The lesson, however, is clear: If the United States wants to invade and occupy countries in the future, it needs larger forces than it currently has.

The second observation is that the AVF currently produces about as large a force as can reasonably be expected utilizing the all-volunteer methodology.

This is true for at least two reasons. One is that there are limits on how many Americans can be recruited to the call of arms: Military service is a special occupation, and it is not universally attractive. The other reason is that, at over $100,000 per military member, there are finite limits to how large a force the country can—or is willing to—support.

The third observation is that the pattern of utilizing the current manpower cannot be sustained for much longer without failures in the system becoming more apparent than they already are. The current spate of wounded veterans who will require extensive physical therapy and care, and especially the emerging levels of veterans with psychological problems, will only continue to grow as long as the current, highly stressful pattern of deployment continues. Something must be done for the forces themselves, or their effectiveness will be compromised.

This leads to the fourth and final observation, which is that something must give. The military establishment that the United States possesses is arguably the finest in the world, but as the manpower situation symbolizes, it is a system under strain, for which there are only two solutions that offer the real possibility of solving the current dilemma. Each relates to the need to realign military resources and the purposes they serve: the force-threat mismatch.

One solution is to increase the forces the United States has so that the military instrument of power can be available for a wider range of uses: a force structure capable of dealing effectively with the Iraq and Afghanistan contingencies as well as some other military problem such as that posed by Iran, for instance. This solution argues for increasing capability as a way to reduce risk, but it is bounded by the political realities about resource (capability) expansion. Expanding capabilities would mean additional spending at a time when the political trends are for smaller, rather than larger, expenditures. It would also mean expanding the size of forces, which could only be accomplished through some form of involuntary service. Neither option is politically viable.

The other possibility is to redefine the threat by reducing the number and quality of circumstances that are perceived as threatening, thereby reducing risk by manipulating the threat element in the risk formula. The alternative to needing additional forces to confront threats worldwide is to downgrade the problems the country faces to a less-threatening level that does not potentially require the application of American military force. Those who see threat levels as very high and dangerous, of course, would resist such a reformulation.

Manpower serves as a symbol for the entire conventional military set of problems. The United States retains large conventional forces and manpower levels because of its perception of a hostile national security environment, but the country would like to solve its problems through the contradictory means of reducing government spending while maintaining a robust national security capability. Manpower symbolizes this combination of attempted frugality and robust capability: Americans want the finest, most capable forces they can have, as long as American citizens are not required to participate in or sacrifice to keep those forces and they do not create intolerable costs.

NUCLEAR FORCES AND MISSIONS

The other traditional military inheritance from the Cold War is **strategic nuclear weapons**. In some important ways, nuclear weapons were the defining characteristic of the Cold War. The first nuclear bombs were fabricated and used against Japan in the final days of World War II, nuclear weapons became a major component of major power arsenals during the Cold War, and indeed, one working definition of a superpower during this period was the possession of a large stockpile of nuclear weapons. As nuclear weapons arsenals grew to dimensions that meant their unrestrained use could signal the end of human civilization, the avoidance of nuclear war—nuclear deterrence—came to dominate thinking about the military dimension of the confrontation. Ultimately, fear of nuclear war helped reduce the superpower confrontation to an unaffordable symbolic competition, the realization of which helped lead to the end of the Cold War.

Nuclear weapons do not possess the centrality in national security calculations they once did, but that does not mean that they have become irrelevant to national security thinking. A major, system-threatening nuclear war is still a physical possibility, if at somewhat lower levels of destruction than at the height of the Cold War. What is principally different is that the motivation to conduct such a war has essentially disappeared: There are no hostile nuclear-armed, ideologically distinct superpowers facing one another any longer. While the major countries no longer feel the necessity to take the elaborate steps they once did to contain the likelihood that such a war could begin, concerns about other aspects of nuclear weapons have not disappeared and remain, notably in the areas of nuclear proliferation and arms control.

Existential Deterrence and Necessary Peace

These two imposing terms help describe the nuclear relationship as it evolved during the Cold War, and thus serve as a starting point for understanding the role of nuclear weapons in national security considerations. The term "existential deterrence" is often associated with the political scientist Robert Jervis and describes the threat that large arsenals of strategic nuclear weapons (weapons aimed at the homelands of the superpowers) posed to the Cold War rivals and the world at large: Because nuclear weapons could destroy humankind if used in an all-out war (threaten existence), human existence depended upon convincing all parties who could start such a war not to do so (deterrence). The result was the absence of war (peace) not from good feelings or relations between nuclear possessors, but borne of a survival necessity—*necessary peace* (a term coined by one of the present authors in a 1987 book).

How did the national security environment reach this condition? World War II was effectively concluded when the United States used two nuclear bombs against Japanese cities (Hiroshima and Nagasaki) on August 6 and 9, 1945, to convince the Japanese leadership of the futility of continuing the war and thus hasten their surrender. At the time, the Japanese had no equivalent weapons (the United States was the only country at that point to have successfully developed a nuclear weapon), and thus could not protect themselves or threaten credible retaliation. These attacks were the only time nuclear weapons have been used in war, and that occasion was one where only one side possessed them. Nuclear weapons have never been employed in anger when both sides in a conflict possessed these awesome instruments of destruction.

The nuclear balance and thinking about how to regulate the use of nuclear weapons evolved after the end of World War II. The United States enjoyed a nuclear monopoly until 1949, when the Soviet Union exploded its first nuclear bomb. During the 1950s, superpower arsenals grew and weapons innovations were added to their array of weaponry. The deadliness of nuclear arsenals was qualitatively increased as weapons based on nuclear fusion replaced early fission-based weapons, creating the situation where it became essentially impossible to calculate the survivability of the superpowers after an all-out exchange between them. In the latter 1950s, intercontinental ballistic missile (ICBM) means of delivery were added, ending the illusion that there was any effective defense against a nuclear attack (the technology for intercepting and destroying ballistic missiles was not then—and arguably still is not—available). Nuclear arsenals thus grew in deadliness to the point that by the middle 1970s and beyond, the superpowers faced one another with strategic nuclear arsenals of well over ten thousand warheads (bombs) apiece. A war between the two incorporating any sizable exchange would almost certainly destroy them both, and possibly the rest of humankind, in the process. Other states—in order, Britain, France, China, and Israel—also developed their own capabilities by the 1960s, making the world an increasingly deadly place.

At first, the gravity of this situation was not fully understood, and the implicit assumption of many in the 1950s, when much of the robust technological innovation in the nuclear weapons field was unfolding, was that a nuclear war was inevitable: The question was not so much if such a war would occur as when it would break out. The world arguably came to the brink of such a conflict during the Cuban Missile Crisis of 1962. In that tense, thirteen-day confrontation, the United States and the Soviet Union faced off against one another over Soviet attempts to place nuclear weapons in Cuba with which to menace U.S. territory. Ultimately, the Soviets backed down from this effort, thereby averting an escalation to a shooting conflict that could have become nuclear.

The aftermath of the Cuban crisis was the joint realization that both superpowers had a mutual interest in avoiding a civilization-threatening nuclear war. At the conceptual level, the result was an increasing emphasis on the deterrent value of nuclear weapons and in reinforcing the condition of nuclear deterrence as a way to lower the likelihood of a nuclear war the consequences of which were unknown. At the more concrete level, the major thread was the beginnings of arms control efforts to contain both the number of nuclear powers and the size of the arsenals of those who did have weapons. Both threads remain lively in the contemporary context.

The concept of **deterrence** became prominent in the 1960s. The heart of the concept of deterrence is to persuade an opponent not to do something you do not want him or her to do: dissuasion. Normally, the action being deterred is military in nature, and the deterrent threat in return is either to deny the threatening party accomplishment of its goal or to punish him in retaliation at levels beyond any possible gain from an initial act.

Put this abstraction in nuclear weapons terms. The nuclear threat posed by the Soviet Union to the United States (and vice versa) was that the Soviets could attack and destroy the United States with nuclear weapons. The problem for the United States was how to keep the Soviets from carrying out that threat: deterrence or dissuasion. After nuclear warheads and ballistic missiles were wedded, the United States could not deny the Soviets the ability to carry out their threat and destroy the American homeland if they chose to launch such an attack. What the United States could do, however, was to maintain enough nuclear weapons after such an attack to counterattack and destroy the Soviet Union in retaliation, thereby denying them any semblance of "victory" from the initial attack and convincing them not to launch it.

This grisly calculation became known as *assured destruction*—the certain knowledge that launching a nuclear attack would be suicidal, since it would be returned in kind. Since both sides had this capability, the relationship was mutual, and thus a critic of the dynamic labeled it mutually assured destruction, or MAD. This dynamic was always uncomfortable: It threatened genocide, for one thing, and should the threat fail, the result could be the incineration of humankind.

It did, however, work, in the sense that nuclear war has been averted. Whether this condition was the result of extremely good sense on the part of the nuclear superpowers or of their more minimal ability to avoid committing the single most stupid—and probably last—act in human history is an interesting question. In addition, the longer the relationship persisted, the more apparent it became to both contestants that nuclear war between them must be avoided at all costs, and that since a conventional war could escalate through processes impossible to anticipate and predict precisely in advance (since nothing like it had ever happened before), *any* war between them was unacceptable.

This realization is at the heart of the necessary peace concept in which peace is the result of a cold calculation about the unacceptability of its alternative rather than because of some inherent desire for peace, and it bore directly on the eventual breakdown of the Cold War itself. The heart of the Cold War was the politico-military confrontation between the two superpowers, and the unacceptability of war reduced that prospect to a hollow, ritual status in which both sides spent enormous amounts of resources preparing for a war they sought to avoid at virtually any cost. As the Soviet economy deteriorated in the 1970s and 1980s, this charade became increasingly less sustainable and played a part in the decision by Gorbachev and his associates to bring the Cold War to an end.

While the central dynamics of nuclear weapons may have receded from the international center stage, nuclear weapons have not disappeared altogether from the scene. Both threads that emerged from the Cuban crisis remain lively, if more subdued than during the Cold War. The question of who will have nuclear weapons—**nuclear proliferation**—remains a concern as new states decide whether to obtain the weapons. At the same time, controlling the number and quality of nuclear weapons—arms control—remains an ongoing process, one of the major aspects of which is the question of ballistic missile defense.

Nuclear Proliferation

The question about who will and who will not possess nuclear weapons and what can be done to prevent additional membership in the nuclear "club" (those countries that have the weapons) goes back to the introduction of nuclear weapons to military arsenals, and the dynamics of the concern have not changed much since the beginning. In the latter 1940s, the United States was the only country to possess these weapons, and they worried about the deleterious effects of the Soviet Union getting them. When the Soviets joined the club, the concern shifted to what negative effects British possession would have, and the British joined the Russians in decrying the membership of the next nuclear power, the French, and so on. The nuclear weapons club currently has nine members (the five permanent members of the UN Security Council plus Israel, India, Pakistan, and North Korea), and Iran stands on the threshold as a potential new initiate whose membership is basically opposed by the current members.

The nuclear proliferation problem historically has had two distinct foci: so-called *vertical* and *horizontal* proliferation. Vertical proliferation refers generically to efforts to control the size arsenals that current members possess and is the subject of the next section on arms control. When proliferation is raised in most contemporary discussions, the reference is normally to horizontal proliferation: the spread of nuclear weapons to states that currently do not possess them. In general terms, this proliferation is opposed by most states (both nuclear possessors and those who do not have nuclear plans or aspirations) except those who wish to build or retain the option to build them.

The dynamics of horizontal proliferation are captured in something known as the **N + 1 problem**. In this formulation, "N" refers to the current number of countries that possess nuclear weapons, and "+ 1" refers to the problems created for the nuclear system by each additional potential member. As suggested, the current "N" consists of the nine states already enumerated, although Israel officially neither confirms nor denies possession. South Africa briefly obtained these weapons, but disarmed in the 1990s as part of its transition to majority rule. The most frequently cited "+ 1" state is Iran, as discussed in the *Intersections* box.

INTERSECTIONS

Iran, N + 1, and U.S. Options

Iran is the current N + 1 state in international concerns, and negative reactions to its possible admission to the nuclear club have followed predictable lines. Iran's membership, it is argued, can only destabilize the current, stable balance, and thus is to be opposed. The reasons for fearing that Iranian possession will be so destabilizing when the admission of other states was not is difficult to sustain without the implicitly condescending assumption that Iran is somehow negatively different from the others. Israel has been particularly vocal on this point, creating a more urgent environment in which the United States weighs its policy options.

The dynamics of N + 1 begin with an anomaly. Older members may have opposed—and in many cases did—some of the current members' attempts to join before they succeeded, but since their addition has not created nuclear conflicts, they have accommodated themselves to the current members. The membership of "N" thus almost always opposes expansion of the membership to other ("+ 1") states on the grounds that such accretion might destabilize the current balance. Partly this is because the consequences of such additions cannot be known specifically in advance; they represent an unknown source of risk, and given the disastrous potential of nuclear conflict, one best contained by avoidance. Potential new members do not accept the logic or substance of these arguments: Why, they ask, should current members expect the aspirants to act more rashly with nuclear weapons than current possessors? The responses are either condescending or racist or both. They are condescending because they assert that new members are less rational than current members (some of whom, of course, were considered irrational themselves before moving from "+ 1" to "N" status). They can be racist because most of the countries in the potential queue for new membership are from the developing world.

The Iranian case illustrates this dynamic. The addition of a nuclear-armed Iran would be different because of the strong, unorthodox views of its theocratic leadership, whom it is alleged would be more willing to use these weapons against their opponents despite the likelihood of an international response that would destroy Iran. The strongest purveyors of this view are the Israelis, because some Israelis are convinced that a nuclear Iran would attack and seek to destroy Israel. This belief causes some Israelis to advocate taking the most extreme measures to avoid a nuclear Iran.

Were it not for Israeli fears, it is probable that the United States would adopt the normal posture for "N" states toward Iran: condemnation of the Iranian effort and sanctions to make the effort less appealing, but grudging acceptance if it occurs anyway. Israeli fears and the possibly dire consequences of a desperate Israeli military action to delay or destroy the Iranian weapons program make this passive U.S. response less acceptable. The problem is that beyond what has already been done to dissuade the Iranians—basically increasingly severe economic sanctions against the regime—it has not been at all clear what other options the United States has other than a military strike of the very nature they are trying to convince the Israelis not to undertake.

Why are nonpossessing states such as Iran tempted to acquire nuclear weapons? The answers undoubtedly vary from aspiring state to aspiring state, but at least three motivations, in some combination in individual cases, can be generally attributed to the decision.

The first motivation may be *prestige*. Nuclear weapons possession was, after all, the distinguishing attribute of the Cold War superpowers, and there is a continuing belief that a country can only achieve great power status if it has nuclear weapons. This argument apparently has some traction in Iran, which retains some of its Shah-era pretensions of great power status, particularly within the Arab world of which it is not a blood member. Foreign actions seeking to dissuade or punish the regime for moving forward in this area contribute to Iranian xenophobia toward the outside world.

A second motivation may be *deterrence*, the major motivation of the current members for maintaining their forces. It is an undeniable fact that no state with nuclear weapons has ever been attacked in a concerted way by another (a partial exception is India and Pakistan, which fought briefly in 2001 before they realized the implications of war with nuclear weapons and backed away), but otherwise, nuclear weapons seem to act as a deterrent to outside aggression. The Iranian nuclear program is at least partly fueled by a fear of American or even Israeli nuclear weapons, and many Iranians, among others, believe the United States would not have invaded Iraq had Saddam Hussein not abandoned his nuclear program. Indeed (and somewhat ironically from an American vantage point), deterring the United States is a motivation for some potential proliferators.

The third reason relates to *special problems* that nuclear aspirants may perceive. Iran, for instance, is the largest Middle Eastern state, but because its population majority is not Arab, it is considered an outsider and even an adversary by the majority of Islamic Arab states in the region. Nuclear weapons would add to its stock in the region, although some argue it could set off a nuclear arms race in which the Arabs seek to deter the Persian bomb and there is a possible Israeli preemptive strike to disarm the Iranians.

The primary tool for trying to prevent horizontal proliferation has been the Non-Proliferation Treaty (NPT), which was negotiated in 1968 and entered into force in 1970. Almost all the world's major powers are members of this accord. The major nonmembers are India, Pakistan, and Israel, and North Korea removed itself from membership in 2003. Although it has talked of rejoining the regime, its membership remains in abeyance, especially since 2006, when it declared itself a nuclear-weapons state. Despite these exceptions, the NPT remains the major international regime effort to forestall further proliferation of nuclear weapons.

The structure and dynamics of the NPT mirror the N + 1 formulation. The treaty creates two categories of members, each with different obligations. The first group are the current nuclear states ("N"), who are not required to divest themselves of nuclear weapons, but who promise to engage in efforts to reduce their arsenal sizes with the ultimate goal of disarmament (vertical proliferation) and who agree not to share nuclear weapons technology with other states which may seek that knowledge or the materials necessary to build weapons. The other category of NPT member states are the nonpossessors. By signing the NPT, they agree to forfeit the right to build nuclear weapons in the future, a pledge they can negate only by removing themselves from the treaty by giving six months' notification of intention (a provision only North Korea has exercised).

The NPT thus creates a nuclear caste system of possessors and nonpossessors. States that have the weapons are technically obligated to engage in efforts to divest themselves of their arsenals, but until the post–Cold War period, none seriously did. Nonpossessors vow not to try to break into the club, which is an acceptable sacrifice for countries that are uninterested in obtaining them (for example, Sweden or Switzerland) and states that cannot do so for lack of technical wherewithal or funds (for instance, most African countries) or because of the international repercussions of their possession (for example, Germany and Japan due to the legacy of World War II).

That leaves the states that may want to acquire nuclear weapons in the future or who at least desire to reserve that option. These are the most problematical states in terms of the treaty. The major states in that category were Israel, India, and Pakistan, all of which have remained nonmembers but have joined the nuclear club. Recognizing their status as nuclear states in NPT terms is objectionable to members of the accord, since it apparently rewards behavior the treaty is supposed to discourage, yet their participation in NPT processes would help make the regime more universal and would bring all the countries important in nuclear terms under its umbrella.

Just how large a problem is proliferation? In some ways, it has been overinflated since the problem was first raised in the 1960s, when the greatest spate of proliferation occurred as Britain, France, China, and Israel all became nuclear powers. At the time, there was widespread fear that nuclear weapons possession would expand exponentially, and treatises on the subject written during the 1960s and early 1970s routinely predicted as many as twenty or thirty nuclear states by the end of the millennium. That number, of course, has proved to be wildly excessive, as only three countries (India, Pakistan, and North Korea) have been added since. Whether the current prospect of a nuclear Iran will result in another spurt of nuclear participation is a matter of conjecture. There have certainly been predictions that Iranian possession could produce a Middle East nuclear arms race to produce an "Arab bomb," and there have been similar suggestions that the North Korean program, if not reversed, could force countries such as South Korea and even Japan to go down the nuclear road. Such predictions, however, must be tempered by the historical excess of proliferation predictions in the past.

Arms Control

The two aspects of proliferation, vertical and horizontal, come together over the issue of arms control. As the name implies, arms control efforts are attempts to reduce or eliminate different kinds or quantities, or both, of particular weapons or to restrict who can have particular weapons. Certainly, the NPT addresses both concerns. Its mission is to reduce nuclear weapons possession by controlling how many countries possess the weapons, and also reduce the sizes of arsenals in its calls for nuclear disarmament by nuclear possessors.

Nuclear arms control efforts also played a major role in gaining control of and eventually ending the Cold War. One important result of the Cuban crisis was to convince the two superpowers that they had a mutual interest in self-preservation. That realization first manifested itself in the area of attempting to place limits on the size of the nuclear arsenals with which they faced one another—an exercise in vertical proliferation limitation. The first major treaty between the Cold War rivals was the Limited Test Ban Treaty (LTBT) of 1963, which banned atmospheric testing of nuclear weapons, and it was followed by a whole string of other treaties—of which the NPT is one—with the common goals of limiting both horizontal and vertical nuclear proliferation.

The arms control process remains a central part of national security relations between the United States and Russia and thus of the American national security agenda. Immediately after the Cold War ended and the old Soviet Union splintered into fifteen new states, part of the effort involved negotiating arrangements whereby all of nuclear weapons held by the Soviet Union came under the control of the Russian Federation, an objective reached primarily through agreements with the Ukraine and Kazakhstan, where most of the Soviet nuclear weapons not housed in Russia resided. Since that point, the negotiations have followed two separate tracks.

The first regarded the American withdrawal from the Anti-Ballistic Missile (ABM) Treaty in December 2001. The purpose of the 1972 ABM Treaty was to limit the deployment of **ballistic missile defenses** (**BMD**) by the two superpowers. The principal idea was that BMD systems were probably unworkable and that even if they could be made operational, the protection they could provide against the kinds of massive nuclear attacks the superpowers could launch would be ineffective and possibly delusional, making the possessor believe it could survive a nuclear war when in fact it could not. The Bush administration, following the tradition of prior Republican administrations, wished to pursue the BMD option, which could only be done by abrogating the agreement, a move reluctantly accepted by the Russians.

The other, and more enduring, strand of post–Cold War arms control has been aimed at the vertical proliferation issue: efforts to reduce the arsenal sizes of the two major nuclear powers. This process had been ongoing since the 1970s, symbolized by negotiated agreements with colorful acronyms: the Strategic Arms Limitation Talks (SALT), that produced two agreements, SALT I in 1972 and SALT II in 1979; the Strategic Arms Reduction Talks (START), which produced follow-on agreements in 1991 and in 1993 (the latter not completely implemented until 2000); and the Strategic Offensive Reductions Treaty (SORT), negotiated in 2002. The purpose of all these arrangements has been to shrink the strategic inventories of the two countries. A follow-on agreement known as "New START" was signed by the two sides in 2010, reducing the legal arsenal sizes to about 1,550 for both sides and restricting the kinds and numbers of delivery vehicles for those weapons. The gross numbers and diversity of the arsenals represents a vastly different array from the 12–15,000 weapons the Cold War adversaries had aimed at one another's homelands during the height of hostilities in the 1970s.

Arms control has receded as a national priority as the perceived danger of nuclear war has diminished. Trying to cap and reverse a truly assured-destruction world was clearly more of a priority then than it is now, when neither country seriously believes the other harbors any intentions to attack it with these weapons. In terms developed earlier in the chapter, the area of strategic nuclear weapons and their control has become an example of risk reduction accomplished by the reduction of threat, thereby allowing for a concomitant reduction in physical capability.

CONCLUSIONS

The Cold War that emerged in the shadow of World War II and which dominated American foreign policy for over forty years provided the seedbed for many of the traditional national security issues that continue to provide the context for the contemporary world. As discussed in this chapter, that influence is evident in two distinctive ways.

The first way is conceptual. Prior to World War II, national security was a comparatively minor consideration for most of American history, and there was little consideration and development of anything resembling a coherent, comprehensive American national security outlook on the world. The Cold War changed that. It created a condition of constant and pressing threat to American survival quite unprecedented in the American experience. In the process, it led to the development of notions of a national security state and the articulation and elaboration of an entire framework of ideas around which to view America's national security condition and place in a hostile world environment, concepts discussed in the first major section of the chapter.

The second influence was in the structure and purposes of American military development and forces. Here again, the World War II experience was instructive, as the two principal Cold War opponents were allies in the effort to overturn fascism; and when they turned against one another, they did so with the force structure and understanding of military actions honed in the second worldwide military conflagration of the twentieth century. The result was to perpetuate, in modernized terms that added greatly to their lethality, the kinds of forces they inherited. This extension was most evident in so-called conventional, nonnuclear forces, but it was extended to the strategic nuclear relationship as well.

Those forces, and how they were thought of, survived the Cold War, albeit in reduced quantities in most countries. The force structure and methods of threat management that continue to dominate the contemporary national security scene are comfortable and familiar to the world's leaders, including those in Washington. There have been notable cuts in the effort (and expense) associated with strategic nuclear force, but those changes have not been fundamentally reflected in the conventional forces that absorb the majority of American resources to maintain and employ.

The military environment of the twenty-first century is arguably quite different from that of the century it succeeds. The United States has fought two major conflicts, in Iraq and Afghanistan, that resemble neither World War II nor the Cold War, and it is at least open to question whether the forces and concepts inherited from the past century no longer have the total relevance they had then. An examination of the contemporary environment and responses to it form the basis of Chapter Ten.

WHERE DO WE GO FROM HERE?

This chapter has focused on the calculations underlying national security (interests, threats, and risks) and how these concepts can be applied to the traditional problems of conventional, European-style military preparation and warfare and strategic nuclear war. These were the dominant military considerations of the Cold War, and much of the planning and force structure that drives current military capabilities and thinking is a legacy of that period, as noted. Much of this carryover is currently manifested in questions about the propriety and expense of conventional forces and manpower and the proliferation of nuclear weapons to places such as Iran and North Korea. The major questions raised about all these concerns include their salience and affordability in today's environment.

APPLICATION: ASSESSING CONTEMPORARY NATIONAL SECURITY THREATS AND RESPONSES

President Dwight D. ("Ike") Eisenhower, the country's thirty-fourth chief executive and the general who commanded the Allied forces in Europe during World War II, argued that the key factor in national security was the economic health of the country, a condition he equated with a balanced federal budget. As the leader of the United States during the height of the Cold War competition during the 1950s, Eisenhower presided over a national security environment replete with a high degree of perceived threat, yet he insisted on constraint in defense spending to provide the capability to neutralize the resulting risk. His basic presumption was that the "cure" of large, unrestrained defense spending would be worse than the "disease" represented by the communist challenge to the West. Defense spending during Ike's two terms in office (1953–1961) was not immodest, reaching roughly one-half of government expenditures in 1955, a period before entitlements were a major budgetary component. Yet that spending could have been much higher and was within bounds where government expenditures did not exceed revenues.

Contrast that environment and assessment with the contemporary situation. The threat level (and perception) is high today, although the physical dimension of threat was probably higher then than it is now. The United States maintains a substantially larger and more expensive conventional force than it did after the conscript-based force that fought the Korean War was demobilized. Defense spending—creating the opposite effect of Eisenhower's balanced budget—is rampant and has generated concerted cries for budgetary constraint, in effect arguing Ike's point about the relationship between national security and government expenditures.

There is one great difference in the dynamics of the two environments separated by a half-century. To a military professional such as Eisenhower, defense spending could not and should not be exempt from austerity measures that would provide the possibility of a balanced budget. These exemptions to the largest repository of controllable, discretionary funding effectively ensure that a contemporary balanced budget is unachievable. The implicit argument underlying this approach abnegates Eisenhower's assumption, in effect arguing that defense expenditures are more important to national security than a balanced budget. While almost everyone has come to accept the notion that defense spending is "on the table," there is disagreement about whether cuts large enough to have a real impact on the deficit are desirable.

On which side of this argument do you place yourself? The last time the United States had a balanced budget was over a decade ago at the end of the Clinton administration, and it was a time of general prosperity and relatively low perceived levels of threat. Reaction to or justified by the attacks of 9/11 (that is, the Iraq War) and the Bush tax cuts of 2001 turned Clinton budget surpluses into deficits, and these deficits were greatly increased by Obama's efforts to deal with the economic crisis that emerged in 2008. The off-year elections of 2010 raised a concern with the fiscal situation and renewed demands for deficit reduction and elimination.

But how can these goals be reached? The discussion of manpower alternatives raised some of these concerns, which can serve as the basis for examining how the federal budget can be brought closer toward alignment with Eisenhower's ideal. Do you agree that budgetary balancing is such a vital element in a strong national security environment that budget cuts should include traditional defense spending? If so, what size general budget cuts would you recommend, and what risks would you be willing to incur as a result?

STUDY/DISCUSSION QUESTIONS

1. What is the F-22 fighter issue? How does it symbolize the current debate over traditional military spending and effort?
2. What are the possible relationships between national security and foreign policy more generally? How was the thinking about this relationship shaped by the Cold War experience?
3. What is a national interest? What kinds of national interests are there? What is a vital interest, and why is the boundary between vital and less-than-vital interests contentious but critical to questions of national security?
4. What is a threat? Why is the concept of threat so central to national security? Relate threat to risk and the threat-risk relationship to understanding national security.
5. Define conventional forces. How and why are they a major part of the contemporary debate about national security? Include "heavy" and "light" forces in your discussion.
6. How is the military manpower question a metaphor for traditional forces, missions, and emphases? Elaborate.
7. Discuss the role of strategic nuclear weapons in the Cold War. How has that role changed? How are these changes demonstrated in the nuclear proliferation and arms control areas?
8. What priority should traditional missions and forces have in the current, budget-constrained environment?

CORE SUGGESTED READINGS

Brodie, Bernard. *Strategy in the Missile Age*. Princeton, NJ: Princeton University Press, 1959. Although the so-called "golden age" of thinking about deterrence and nuclear war produced a whole series of thoughtful and incisive analyses, this groundbreaking volume by the author of one of the first examinations of the subject (see below) remains one of the most authoritative and readable discussions of the subject.

Clausewitz, Carl von. *On War.* (Rev. ed., trans. and ed. by Michael Howard and Peter Paret.) Princeton, NJ: Princeton University Press, 1984. There has probably been no more authoritative source of the Western formulation of war and the purposes for which it is fought than this treatise by the Prussian strategist writing about his experiences in the Napoleonic Wars, and it remains required reading for those who seek to understand war in its political context.

Schelling, Thomas C. *The Strategy of Conflict*. Cambridge, MA: Harvard University Press, 1960. Much of the formulation of objectives, interests, threats, and risk presented in this chapter owes its direct lineage to the thoughts of Schelling in this important work written at the height of the Cold War.

Wiegley, Russell F. *The American Way of War.* New York: Macmillan, 1973. Over time the United States developed a distinctive way of looking at conventional military force, and Wiegley's careful history of that development from the beginnings of the republic to the Cold War remains one of the best analyses on the subject.

ADDITIONAL READINGS AND REFERENCES

Akedis, Jim. "The Pentagon's Most Expensive Weapon." *PPI Policy Memo* (online), November 30, 2009.

Allison, Graham T. Jr., and Gregory F. Treverton (eds.). *Rethinking America's National Security: Beyond Cold War to a New World Order.* New York: W. W. Norton, 1992.

Bacevich, A. J. *Washington Rules: America's Path to Permanent War.* New York: Henry Holt and Company, 2010.

Borden, William Liscum. *There Will Be No Time: The Revolution in Strategy.* New York: Macmillan, 1946.

Brodie, Bernard. *The Absolute Weapon: Atomic Power and World Order.* New York: Harcourt Brace, 1946.

_____. *War and Politics*. New York: Macmillan, 1973.

Clark, Ronald W. *The Greatest Power on Earth: The International Race for Nuclear Supremacy from Earliest Theory to Three-Mile Island*. New York: Harper & Row, 1980.

Collins, John M. *Grand Strategy: Principles and Practices*. Annapolis, MD: Naval Institute Press, 1973.

Drew, Dennis M., and Donald M. Snow. *Making Strategy for the Twenty-First Century: An Introduction to National Security Processes and Problems*. Montgomery, AL: Air University Press, 2006.

Gates, Robert M. "A Balanced Strategy." *Foreign Affairs* 88, 1 (January/February 2009), 28–40.

Jervis, Robert. *The Illogic of American Nuclear Strategy.* Ithaca, NY: Cornell University Press, 1984.

Lieber, Kier A., and Daryl G. Press. "The Rise of U.S. Nuclear Superiority." *Foreign Affairs* 85, 2 (March/April 2006), 42–54.

MaCaffrey, Barry R. "Looking Beyond Iraqi Freedom: Future Enemies Won't Roll Over So Easily." *Armed Forces Journal* 140 (July 2003), 8–9.

Nuechterlein, Donald E. *America Recommitted: United States National Interests in a Reconstructed World*. Lexington: University of Kentucky Press, 1991.

_______. *A Cold War Odyssey*. Lexington: University of Kentucky Press, 1997.

Office of the President of the United States. *Quadrennial Defense Review*. Washington, DC: U.S. Department of Defense, 1997, 2001, 2006, and 2010.

Rhodes, Richard. *The Making of the Atomic Bomb*. New York: Touchstone Books. 1998.

Snow, Donald M. *Nuclear Strategy in a Dynamic World: Policy for the 1980s*. Tuscaloosa: University of Alabama Press, 1981.

_______. *The Necessary Peace: Nuclear Weapons and Superpower Relations*. Lexington, MA: Lexington Books, 1987.

_______, and Dennis M. Drew. *From Lexington to Baghdad and Beyond: War and Politics in the American Experience* (3rd ed.). Armonk, NY: M. E. Sharpe, 2010.

Stoessinger, John G. *Why Nations Go to War* (11th ed.). Belmont, CA: Wadsworth Publishing, 2010.

CHAPTER 10

Contemporary Security Problems in an Asymmetrical World

Much of the debate over the new nature of war arose from the U.S. experience in Vietnam, including the first major encounter in 1965 in the Ia Drang Valley.

PREVIEW

Since the end of the Cold War, the structure of national security challenges facing the United States has changed. The threat of nuclear war has abated, and American conventional military dominance has meant that traditional military challenges have greatly diminished. In their place, national security threats have increasingly been defined in nontraditional, unconventional ways, including a linkage to nation building.

This chapter surveys this changing structure and its broader foreign policy implications. It begins by raising and examining the question of how new forms of violence relate differently to American foreign policy than did the challenges of the Cold War period. It then examines the two major contemporary forms that such challenges take: asymmetrical warfare and international religious terrorism. Both phenomena are examined in terms of their salient characteristics and how they pose different threats and challenges to American foreign policy.

KEY CONCEPTS

asymmetrical warfare
symmetrical warfare
cost tolerance
nonstate actors
insurgents
protracted conflict
nation Building
martyr/suicide terrorism
commander-cadre model
virtual network model
protean model
homeland security
Ia Drang
antiterrorism
counterterrorism

The Battle of the **Ia Drang** Valley was the first major military clash of the Vietnam War, the first time American and North Vietnamese troops faced one another in major combat. Technically, the "battle" was a thirty-four day campaign that occurred mostly in November 1965. Moore and Galloway (1992), the campaign's major chroniclers in a book that became one of the most significant films about the Vietnam War (*We Were Soldiers Once ... and Young*) describe it as "one month of maneuver, attack, retreat, bait, trap, ambush, and bloody butchery" that was "the Vietnam War's true dawn—a time when opposing armies took the measure of one another." The campaign culminated in a pitched battle from November 14 to 17, 1965; when the fighting was over, 305 American and 3,561 North Vietnamese soldiers had perished. It was the first bloody punctuation mark in a conflict that would drag on for a decade before the fall of Saigon to North Vietnamese communists and their South Vietnamese allies in 1975. Among the war's other effects was the demonstration of the looming obsolescence of the traditional American way of war.

The battle in the Ia Drang (the word *ia* is a Montagnard term meaning "river") is important on several levels relevant to the present and future. The first is that the battle is symbolic of the transformation of modern warfare from its traditional methods to the contemporary pattern of internally based wars fought in unconventional ways. Both styles of warfare were present in the Ia Drang, and the two visions of war influenced both what happened and how it was viewed.

Second, and based on this collision of visions of war, both sides thought they learned lessons from the encounter that Moore and Galloway (both of whom were participants—Moore as a lieutenant colonel, Galloway as a correspondent) described as "dangerously deceptive." General William Westmoreland, the American commander of all forces in South Vietnam, surveyed the outcome in conventional military terms, saw a favorable twelve to one "kill ratio" of North Vietnamese to Americans, and along with his aides concluded the battle showed the war could be won: that the Americans "could bleed the enemy to death over the long haul, with a strategy of attrition." American obsession with the so-called weekly "body count" (the number of enemy versus American dead) throughout the war reflected this belief. In Hanoi, Ho Chi Minh and his advisors also viewed the battle as evidence they could win the war. They had fought the Americans to a draw despite the overwhelming firepower advantages the Americans possessed, and as Moore and Galloway summarize, "In time, they were certain, the patience and perseverance that had worn down the French colonialists would also wear down the Americans."

It is this fundamental asymmetry of calculations and expectations that is so important about the Ia Drang experience. The initial American appraisal was entirely traditional, a calculation based on the outcome of two conventional national armed forces grinding against one another until one is triumphant and the other gives up and surrenders. Had the North Vietnamese chosen to fight a conventional, symmetrical war in the Western fashion, the American assessment might have proven correct. The North Vietnamese, however, did not think or fight conventionally; instead, their calculation was based on an unconventional, asymmetrical analysis of what it took to win. Ultimately, their assessment proved more prescient to the situation at hand.

There were other lessons to be learned. The United States entered the war with major innovations that were designed to act as force multipliers making the American soldier more effective and combat losses lower. The most notable of these introduced in the Ia Drang was the Air Cavalry, transporting soldiers to the battlefield on helicopters to enlarge the number of places where combat could occur. The results were colorful and dramatic, and pictures of the "Air Cav" are among the most vivid images of the war, but they were rarely decisive (for one thing, an individual helicopter could only deliver a small number of men to a battle area, thereby limiting their impact). The war, with Ia Drang as its starting point, was also the first time the United States sought to apply its World War II–style heavy forces to what amounted to a civil war in the developing world, and it turned out to be a poor fit that was not recognized at first. In time, American forces would adopt ways of fighting appropriate to the military and political situation at hand, but a long period of adjustment was necessary. One of these adjustments, with which policy makers are still struggling, is the intensely political nature of these kinds of wars. Lyndon Johnson captured the spirit of this difference when he declared that Vietnam was about winning the "hearts and minds" of the Vietnamese people. This contest for political loyalty is commonly phrased today in terms of nation building.

The Battle of the Ia Drang was a microcosm of what the war in Vietnam would be, and the Vietnam War was a harbinger for the kinds of situations the United States has encountered since and with which it is still struggling. While the subsequent experiences in places such as Iraq and Afghanistan have not been precise, isomorphic mirrors of Vietnam, they share similarities, notably facing a determined adversary in a hostile Third World environment where the United States is less than a welcomed "guest" and where conventional ways of thinking and fighting do not directly apply.

Not everyone agrees with or accepts the analogy of what began in the Ia Drang with the contemporary environment. At one level, this is easy to do, because there are significant physical differences between Vietnam and a place such as Afghanistan, and because of the opponents in the two cases. These "atmospherics"—details of setting—do not obscure the underlying dynamics of the comparison between what started in the Ia Drang and what confronts contemporary Americans. Vietnam was—or became—the first modern American asymmetrical war, and it is a pattern that has come to dominate the landscape of actual and potential opportunities the United States has to employ armed force.

The purpose of this chapter is to explore the two most prominent forms of what is commonly called **asymmetrical warfare**, which are direct legacies of the American experience that began in the Ia Drang: asymmetrical war and terrorism. Both preceded Vietnam as international phenomena, but both were also part of the Vietnam experience for the United States and part of the environment that dominates the current world in which American foreign policy operates.

The analysis will proceed in three sequential steps. The first will be to introduce the ideas of asymmetrical war and terrorism *as foreign policy problems*: How is each related to the more general topic of foreign policy, and how does each contribute to the conduct of foreign policy? The analysis then moves to a look at the dynamics of asymmetrical warfare, with a particular eye to the Afghanistan and Iraq situations and the prospects for the future. Finally, the chapter turns to the problem of terrorism, with an emphasis on its foreign policy aspects.

ASYMMETRICAL WARFARE, TERRORISM, AND FOREIGN POLICY

If foreign policy's major thrust is in how the United States deals with problems that confront it in the world at large, then asymmetrical war and terrorism are clearly items on the foreign policy agenda. Because both are violent in nature, they are normally thought of as problems for which the national security mechanisms of the United States have relevance, making them national security questions.

What makes these contemporary forms of national security challenges different is that the direct line between foreign policy goals and national security is by no means as straightforward as it was during the conceptually simpler Cold War days that form the backdrop of current problems. Indeed, there are two principal points of difference between situations where one may confront asymmetrical war or terrorism and past national security concerns, and both of these serve as points of influence in the relationship between these phenomena and foreign policy.

The first problem is that neither asymmetrical warfare nor terrorism can be neatly categorized as traditional, military national security problems. Both certainly have military aspects: Asymmetrical warfare is a variant method of conducting military hostilities, for instance, and terrorists employ some of the same weapons of war as do more conventional warriors. At the same time, both variants employ techniques to negate the overwhelming use of force against them by better-armed, better-equipped opponents such as the United States. In traditional warfare, the military instrument of policy is a direct and appropriate response to a military threat from a similar adversary. When the challenge comes from an asymmetrical warrior or a terrorist, that direct linkage is not so obvious, and as a result, it is not so clear whether or how the military instrument can be applied to solving the foreign policy problem that either presents.

Indeed, it is even arguable that confronting either the asymmetrical warrior or terrorist is a sufficiently different task from traditional military problems that traditional solutions and thinking may be misleading for these kinds of situations. In that case, the effect can be to prescribe solutions that are inappropriate to the situation and that end up frustrating foreign policy makers and military advocates alike when they are applied with inconclusive or even counterproductive results. Thus, the United States adopted a traditional approach to the irritant represented by Iraq before the invasion by applying traditional military force that was initially quite effective, but which resulted in an effective asymmetrical opposition that bogged down the United States for over seven years of frustrating occupation of that country. Shortly after September 11, 2001, the United States declared a "global war on terror" (GWOT) against international religious terrorism that, more than a decade later, has not noticeably succeeded in ending the terrorist threat.

The second problem is where the situations occur that may manifest themselves as either asymmetrical warfare or terrorism. Generally speaking, both phenomena are related to and occur in similar places and situations. One way to look at terrorism, for instance, is as a particularly extreme tactic of the asymmetrical warrior, since it clearly is a method that violates accepted ways of conducting "politics by other means" (the Clausewitzian dictum). Both asymmetrical warfare generically and terrorism more specifically are the tactics of the militarily weak when confronting a stronger opponent that they cannot defeat or influence by more traditional means but with which they are locked in a dispute. It is where these conflicts are likely to occur that raises the major foreign policy questions that must be addressed.

Most of the time, the seedbeds of both asymmetrical warfare and terrorism situations are in fairly underdeveloped, Third World locales where the question of U.S. levels of interest in various outcomes is debatable. These situations lack the clarity of the Cold War and its nearly perfect overlap of interests and threats to those interests. Instead, the situations tend to occur in places where arguable interest-threat mismatches exist and where it is not clear that the United States has sufficient foreign policy interests to justify actions that would put it into either asymmetrical warfare or terrorism situations, testing where the boundary between vital and less-than-vital interests lies.

Where the vitality of interests is questionable, other factors enter into the calculus of involvement. One major dynamic of asymmetrical wars is that they tend to be long, drawn-out affairs, since protraction is, as suggested in the North Vietnamese assessment of the Ia Drang experience, the only way that the weaker force has a reasonable prospect of success against a vastly militarily superior opponent. A strategy of attrition designed to wear down and overcome the patience of the superior force may be the only way to have a chance to succeed. Protraction is particularly effective against an impatient foe who desires quick and decisive outcomes. The Vietnam experience suggests that it is an approach that can work against Americans.

If these kinds of potential or actual experiences occurred in places where undeniably vital American interests were involved, long commitments might be tolerable, but that is generally not the case. Rather, most of the venues are in places where American interests are ambiguous and their vitality debatable. In such situations, becoming involved and entrapped in one of these kinds of frustrating conflicts is likely to stimulate opposition to continuation on the grounds that such an effort is unlikely to succeed and not in the national interest. The debate over continued American activity in Afghanistan can certainly be analyzed within these parameters.

The result is a conundrum of sorts. When troubling instability occurs in a Third World country and the United States contemplates an appropriate foreign policy response, it must now consider the possible ramifications in terms of the likelihood that different responses will place the United States in an asymmetrical war or elicit a terrorist response. The analysis is never easy, because the easy answers are unlikely to be applicable. One easy answer is the traditional application of overwhelming conventional force to crush whatever impedes realization of American interests in a quick and decisive application. In such a case, U.S. interests are achieved with minimal costs, and the question of how important the interests were will likely not be raised seriously. This was, however, the approach taken in the American invasion of Iraq, and things did not work out that way.

The other easy answer is to look at a situation, conclude that anything the United States does militarily will have a negative impact in terms of asymmetrical warfare or terrorism, conclude that such an outcome is not worth the effort, and thus demure from any response. This approach may mean simply ignoring a festering problem that will only worsen with inattention, a prospect political opponents will surely herald. Unfortunately, the ability to predict that actions will have untoward consequences is not well developed enough to confidently predict such an outcome in advance and thus to commit or abstain as a result.

Virtually no one, for instance, envisaged that the United States would still be fighting an open-ended war in Afghanistan ten years after it began. Had such an outcome been clear, there is a very real prospect the involvement would have been avoided—or at least channeled into a lesser response.

Real situations are likely to be more ambiguous. Not all U.S. actions result in asymmetrical quagmires, meaning one cannot rule out the future use of traditional instruments of power in all developing-world situations. What it does suggest, however, is that the direct applicability of military force to the solution of foreign policy problems must be qualified and conditioned in contemporary situations.

As this introductory discussion suggests, the application of national security solutions to foreign policy questions has become more complex in the contemporary international system than it was before, as the questions of asymmetrical warfare and terrorism both as causes and consequences of different foreign policy dilemmas have become more prominent aspects of the national security calculation. A more exact assessment of that impact requires looking at each phenomenon independently.

ASYMMETRICAL WARFARE

Involvement in **asymmetrical warfare** is a response to a foreign policy problem. The nature of the problem is how to deal with countries and groups within countries who adopt unconventional military means to face superior opponents that include the United States. This kind of situation has, since the end of the Cold War, been descriptive of an increasing proportion of the developing-world crises in which the United States has contemplated military intervention; Afghanistan is the latest example. Because these situations are sufficiently novel and unlike the kinds of conventional conflicts described in the last chapter, they require separate examination here.

What exactly is asymmetrical warfare? In the broadest, most generic sense, a war is asymmetrical when those contesting it do not fight in the same manner: organizing differently, employing different sets of rules of engagement, equipping themselves differently, and the like. In practice, when one adversary looks at the military situation and concludes that it will be impossible to prevail by fighting in whatever the prescribed manner of fighting is, the question is what to do. That combatant is faced with a set of choices. One possibility is simply not to engage in a contest at all, in effect surrendering to the superiority of the adversary. A second possibility is to fight on the opponent's ground and hope for the best in a very unfavorable situation. Both of these outcomes entail the high likelihood of losing. Faced with defeat when playing by the acceptable rules, the alternative is somehow to change the rules and conduct of the contest to remove that disadvantage. If this is the decision that is made, the side making it has decided to fight asymmetrically.

Stated in this manner, the name *asymmetrical warfare* is much newer than the phenomenon it seeks to describe. What is now called asymmetrical warfare is the adjustment in war which a contestant that cannot compete successfully within the accepted rules of warfare makes to give itself the possibility of overcoming an obviously superior opponent that will certainly defeat it unless it successfully adapts. This approach to warfare has known many names and had many champions throughout history. The legendary Chinese strategist Sun Tzu, in *The Art of War* (1963), may have articulated the first version of asymmetrical war when he called for unconventional, indirect means to subdue adversaries. These ideas have matured and mutated through time, and twentieth-century guerrilla warfare as practiced by the Chinese communists in their civil war or the Vietnamese in their campaigns first against the French and later against the Americans were what is now called asymmetrical war. The current variants in places such as Afghanistan are merely the most contemporary modification of this approach to warfare.

The last point is important and worth elaboration, because it helps frame the difficulty of confronting and subduing the asymmetrical warrior. Asymmetrical warfare should be thought of as an approach to war, not as a set of specific methods (for example, battlefield or campaign strategies and tactics) that particular asymmetrical warriors employ. Rather, it is a methodology, a way to look at a particular situation in which one is at a disadvantage and to guide adaptation to level the playing field or to tilt it to one's own advantage. How that end can be accomplished will build on the successes of past asymmetrical warriors and reject their failures, but each asymmetrical war will be different from those that went before, because each adapts past experience to the special circumstances of individual applications of the methodology. The result is to complicate assessing any particular asymmetrical situation and preparing to counter it: The lessons of the Vietnam War, in other words, have only limited instructive value for combating asymmetrical warfare in Afghanistan.

Asymmetrical warriors understand the problems that their approach to war presents to major powers such as the United States, which neither likes nor is particularly adept at this form of warfare. For the major powers with a European background, the accepted way of fighting has been the traditional model of European warfare by which the major contests of the twentieth century were fought and at which the United States is overwhelmingly proficient. If two opponents clash when both agree to fight in this manner, the result is **symmetrical warfare**, the situation in which both sides agree to fight in the same way, especially fighting under the same rules of engagement. This is the way that the United States has fought in the past; is the way it prefers to organize, equip, and train itself to fight; and is a form of warfare at which it is most likely to prevail for the reasons detailed in Chapter Nine.

This situation presents a dilemma for the United States and a tempting model for its potential adversaries. Any country or group that may find itself opposed by the United States knows the American preference and the futility of fighting the Americans on their own terms. As a result, they are drawn to the asymmetrical war methodology, since its successful adaptation to their circumstances may provide them with an effective way to confront and stave off the world's "remaining superpower." The track record of the United States when confronted by an asymmetrical opponent is not so overwhelmingly positive as to discourage asymmetrical thinking by that opponent, and the prospect of facing an asymmetrical foe does, or should, give the United States pause when faced with such an opponent. Understanding these difficult dynamics requires looking first at the characteristics of contemporary asymmetrical warfare, and then assessing the particular problems this form of warfare presents to the United States in terms of using military and other forms of power to achieve its foreign policy goals.

Characteristics of Asymmetrical Warfare

Because asymmetrical warfare lays out approaches rather than dictates for its conduct, any description of its characteristics will be bound by the particular circumstances in which they are articulated. The characteristics of asymmetrical warfare are not the same today as those with which the Huns faced the Roman Empire or that the twentieth-century Vietnamese presented to the returning French colonialists after World War II, and current characteristics may not apply exactly or at all in 2050. Having said that, the discussion can be organized and channeled around five salient characteristics: the politico-military context and dynamics of asymmetrical war; the prevalence of so-called "nonstate" actors in contemporary asymmetrical war; the protracted nature of this kind of war; its prevalence as the form of warfare in unstable developing countries for which some form of developmental assistance may seem to be needed; and the certainty that it will change in the future.

Politico-Military Context The Clausewitzian dictum states that "war is the continuation of politics by other means." What the great Prussian strategist meant by this is that war is a political act undertaken for the purpose of gaining compliance with policies on which the contending sides disagree. In traditional parlance, the purpose of war is to force an opponent to accept one's policies, and the means of doing so is to defeat the opponent's armed forces as preface to being able to assert one's will on the other.

In the traditional, Clausewitzian formulation, the relationship between war and its underlying political purposes is intimate but separated. The intimacy arises because the political goals (or foreign policy goals, when wars are between states) guide what the military must accomplish by military action. The total defeat of the Axis powers was necessary in World War II, for instance, to force the extinction of fascist rule in Germany and Japan, whereas the goal of restoring two sovereign Korean states in the Korean War required only defeating the North Koreans sufficiently to discourage their future attempts to annex South Korea.

Contemporary asymmetrical war challenges and even rejects these distinctions. In terms of conduct, the asymmetrical warrior cannot adopt destroying enemy forces as his goal, because he lacks the wherewithal to do so. Lacking the ability to *impose* his will by sheer force, he must instead convince the opponent of the futility of continuing the struggle and the impossibility of achieving his goals within the bounds of the costs of war he is willing to bear. This limitation in turn affects the way the asymmetrical warrior must intermix the political and military dimensions of warfare.

While warfare remains an act intended to produce a desired political end, the asymmetrical warrior does not recognize any distinction between the political and military dimensions of war. For one thing, he rejects the distinction between military and civilian objects in war, arguing that war is a societal clash in which everything is militarily fair game. Thus, it is not a violation of the asymmetrical warrior's code of behavior to embed its presence in and hide behind the civilian population, because every place is a battlefield and no one and no place is exempt. Moreover, the purposes of fighting are enlarged as well. The asymmetrical warrior cannot defeat and cause the surrender of the opponent, so his military motives are likely to be more directly political: attacking civilian targets to demonstrate that the enemy cannot provide them protection and thus does not deserve their loyalty, for instance. With regard to the opponent (and especially the symmetrical warrior), this may mean attacking the enemy simply to create casualties that raise the cost of war and demonstrate the futility of continued prosecution of the war effort. In either case, the underlying rationale of the military action is the opponent's will to continue, and the direct objective is not so much traditional military defeat as converting the enemy to the belief that his efforts are not worth the effort and sacrifice. Military actions thus have a much more direct and intimate relationship to the political goals they seek to achieve in traditional war between states.

The political dimension is one of the major ways in which internal wars differ from traditional conflicts and complicate the politico-military mix. Internal wars are, at base, contests for the political loyalty of the population in and over which they are conducted—Johnson's battle for the hearts and minds of men. Ultimately, these conflicts are won by the side that captures popular support, and that means that military actions must be calculated and carried out with an explicit concentration on the political impact on peoples' loyalties. This is not a problem in conventional interstate wars. American bombers did not have to concern themselves with whether the German population was alienated by bombs raining on their heads, since the purpose was not to win their loyalty, but to break their will and ability to continue. In a contest of hearts and minds, however, that calculation is very different, and the combatants must weigh whether a particular act, regardless of its purely military impact, has a positive or negative impact on the loyalty structure of the affected population. Bombing a village where there is a suspected Taliban or Al Qaeda presence may make sense from the narrow vantage point of reducing enemy capability, but the resultant collateral damage to the village and its inhabitants may outweigh the purely military benefits.

Nonstate Actor Base A second confounding way in which contemporary asymmetrical wars are distinguished from conventional wars is the nature and affiliation of the opponent. In conventional wars, of course, the opponents are the armed forces of sovereign states, and they make no efforts to portray themselves as anything else. The actions that those armed forces take can be directly attributed to the governments that sponsor them, and the state is responsible and accountable for the actions that those armed forces commit.

These easy distinctions are obscured in contemporary conflicts, where the opposition is likely to consist of **nonstate actors**, groups that do not clearly represent a state, a definable group of people, and especially a piece of territory that claims the combatants as their own. There are two basic subcategories that these nonstate actors can be broken down into, insurgents and terrorists. Each group poses some similar and dissimilar problems for those who confront them.

Insurgents are the more familiar, less unconventional form of opposition. Insurgents are normally citizens of the country in which they operate, and their purpose is generally to overcome and replace the government with a regime they will dominate. They may well have a territorial base within the country, but it is likely to be contested and contain both its supporters and adherents of the government it seeks to replace. In some cases, the insurgents may operate out of neighboring states as well as their own, and in many developing countries, they may be associated with a particular ethnic or tribal group. In the case of insurgents, it may be possible to identify generally who they are and where they reside (their operating bases), but it is often difficult to attack those bases without also attacking friendly elements within the locations they dominate.

The Taliban in Afghanistan illustrate this phenomenon. The Taliban movement has its base in the predominantly Pashtun ethnic regions of Afghanistan (the southern and eastern areas) along the border with Pakistan. There are large Pashtun communities within each country (Pashtuns are the largest tribal group in Afghanistan and the second largest ethnic group in Pakistan), and the Pashtuns are the recruitment base for the Taliban. Not all Pashtuns are Taliban, but almost all Taliban are Pashtuns, meaning the heart of attacking and subduing the Taliban insurgency is found in the Pashtun territories. It is difficult to distinguish which Pashtuns are Taliban and which are not, making the attempt to convert more Pashtuns away from the insurgents and to support for the government difficult. Moreover, Afghan and Pakistani Pashtuns are highly sympathetic toward one another, so members of the Afghanistan insurgency have no difficulty moving back and forth from Pakistan to avoid or initiate attacks.

The other prominent form of nonstate actor in the contemporary environment is the international terrorist group. The prototype of this kind of organization, of course, is the Islamist terrorist group Al Qaeda. Such an organization is constitutionally different from an insurgent group, as its name implies. By virtue of being *international,* the membership and locations of these organizations cross interstate boundaries, with members recruited from different countries (none of which acknowledge its members as their own) and located in different countries. Members of these organizations do not claim to represent particular governments or places, and it is not clear, unlike insurgencies, that they seek to replace governments or claim territorial sovereignty. These groups may have formal or informal safe-haven arrangements in some states, although no state has formally claimed sponsorship for such an organization since the Afghan Taliban were overthrown in 2001. Insurgents may act from sectarian motives (establishing an Islamic state, for instance), but their goal of overthrowing and replacing governments is secular; *religious* terrorists, on the other hand, have some sectarian motivation—often an extreme, fringe interpretation of the religion they purport to serve, as in the case of Al Qaeda—as their *raison d'etre.* They often have no acknowledged secular purpose such as gaining and exercising political authority in specific territories. The fact that they are *terrorists* generally means that they are relatively small and weak and thus generally do not pose a direct threat to the existence of regimes.

Al Qaeda is the prototype for this form of nonstate actor. The membership of the organization is not recognizably national: The core of its membership is Saudi and Egyptian, apparently, but it also recruits members from anywhere in the world (including the United States) where recruits share its peculiar fundamentalist Islamic ideology. It has affiliated groups (for example, Al Qaeda on the Arabian Peninsula) in various countries, none of which it officially claims as its base. It has not had a formal state sponsor since the Taliban were overthrown in Afghanistan, but it operates from de facto sanctuaries in a number of states such as Pakistan and Yemen. In all cases, its location is in relatively inaccessible "badlands" areas of fairly underdeveloped countries.

These two subcategories present some similar problems to those seeking to suppress them. The major similar problem is that they lack a territorial "center of gravity" (a place or condition which is vital to the group and which, if destroyed, would impair or destroy the group's ability to continue) that can be targeted and exorcised without consequences that are unacceptable. The United States, for instance, tracked bin Laden for over a decade before locating and killing him. It is thus difficult to find targets against which to retaliate.

How to attack these nonstate actors is also conceptually and physically challenging. One can retaliate against the territory or people of an opposing state, but when neither of those objects can be discretely identified, it is difficult to find acceptable and effective targets for retaliatory vengeance. The use of drone aircraft to deliver aerial bombs in Pakistan, for instance, reveals the dilemma. In attacking hoped-for insurgent or terrorist targets, the actions taken may also inadvertently cause damage to innocent civilians who may become enraged by this "collateral" (unintended) damage to the point that they become recruits for the insurgent or terrorist cause, the exact opposite of the intended result.

Protracted Conflict Because asymmetrical warriors lack the conventional punch to overcome and defeat the hostile ability of a symmetrical opponent, their only possible strategy against such an opponent is attacking that opponent's hostile will to continue the fight. Unlike conventional conflicts between symmetrical foes, asymmetrical wars are rarely ended by one side or the other being decisively defeated on the battlefield and surrendering to the opposition. Asymmetrical warfare is a contest of wills as much as it is a contest of arms.

Cost tolerance (the will to continue resistance) is exceeded when one side or the other concludes that quitting the contest is preferable to its continuation.

In rational terms, this is a cost-gain calculation that weighs the benefits and prospects of continuing against the costs of doing so. If the goals are important enough and the prospects are adequately encouraging, then continuation is the rational choice. However, if either the prognosis for success or the importance of its achievement are questionable, then continuing the struggle may not be the rational choice, in which case cost tolerance may be exceeded and quitting the field may appear to offer the best (or least poor) outcome.

To the militarily inferior practitioner of asymmetrical warfare, the result is a strategy of protracted warfare, with two major prongs intended to convince the opponent that its continuation is not worth it. One prong of this strategy is *attrition*, inflicting enough casualties on the symmetrical opponent so that he questions the worth of the sacrifice such casualties present to him. Interestingly, both the North Vietnamese and the Americans, after Ia Drang, adopted this essential strategy, believing that the more sacrifices the opponent endured, the more likely its cost tolerance would be overcome. For the Americans, the problem was that a favorable outcome to the contest was more important to the North Vietnamese than it was to them. Thus North Vietnam was willing to incur far more casualties; its cost tolerance was much higher than that of its American adversaries.

The second major emphasis is *protraction,* making the conflict so long and indeterminate that the opponent tires of it and interprets its inconclusiveness as evidence that it cannot prevail. This element of strategy works particularly well when confronting a democratic opponent; it is one of the few established verities of international politics that political democracies do not like and will eventually come to oppose long wars. The condition of public disaffection is moderated if people believe the purpose of the enterprise is sufficiently important to justify perseverance and the prospects of success are at least arguable. Part of the strategy of dragging the war out is to convince the opponent that neither prospect is very great, thereby reinforcing the tendency toward overcoming cost tolerance. This part of the asymmetrical warrior's task is aided by the kinds of countries in which the asymmetrical approach is likely to be adopted.

Occurrence in Unstable Developing World Locales The conflicts in which asymmetrical warfare is most often encountered are in the parts of the world that are, and have been for a half-century or more, the most unstable and violence-prone: the countries of the developing world. Instability in these areas is the distinguishing characteristic that precipitates violence of one sort or another. The underlying causes vary, but the theme remains: Violence occurs in the least-stable parts of the world politically, and it is usually domestic in origin or at least has strong local roots and solutions. The result is to insert a nonmilitary element into these situations: Their full resolution may require efforts to ameliorate the conditions that cause violence, a concern with so-called **nation building.**

This dynamic is important because it affects both the forms of violence and the prospects of successful involvement in these kinds of situations by outside forces. Since most of these conflicts begin as civil contests over who will rule in a country, they tend to be particularly desperate. They tend to be total conflicts, where neither side will easily abandon its position, and as a result, conflict is likely to be protracted. Control of one's own homeland is sufficiently important to the contestants that their cost tolerance is likely to be very high. This tenacity is a problem for outside parties contemplating possible interference, since the outcome will almost inevitably be less important to the outsider than it is to the indigenous participants. The United States learned this lesson the hard way in Vietnam, and it may be relearning it again in Afghanistan.

The second relevant implication is the question of the importance of the situation and its outcome to outsiders. In terms of the United States, this dimension is explored more fully in the next section, but it is worth raising here. Developing-world situations generally do not engage the most important interests of the major powers (violence in a former colony may be an exception), meaning that the interest-threat mismatch becomes part of the dynamic of examining and determining whether to do something in any particular case. Regardless of the situation before the outsider decides to act, the simple fact of outside intervention by a great military power such as the United States is likely to transform or highlight the asymmetrical dynamics of the contest, adding the problem of protraction to the calculation of possible importance and thus cost tolerance.

Third, a favorable resolution to the internal conflict usually entails improving the physical circumstances of the population as a way to win their loyalty. Because these countries are normally very poor and underdeveloped, this may suggest that a long-term, even massive commitment of resources to underwrite raising living standards may be dictated to win the peace. Such a commitment may be very expensive and its success uncertain. This effort, known as nation building, has become intensely controversial, as the *Intersections* box suggests.

INTERSECTIONS

The Debate Over Nation Building

The idea of providing developmental assistance to help stabilize and pacify underdeveloped countries and regions is a subpart of the development and modernization debate that has raged in academic and policy circles for over a half-century. The original academic interest developed during the 1950s and 1960s, as a loose group of political scientists and others developed views of how best to bring those parts of the world emerging from colonialism up to the standards of the most advanced countries. Their loosely theoretical writings generally advocated massive intervention by the advanced countries in terms of investments in developing societies, and many of these prescriptions were adopted in part or in whole, especially during the 1960s and 1970s.

(Continued)

(Continued)

The solutions often did not have the desired effects for a variety of reasons, and the result was a backlash in the 1970s and 1980s, particularly among conservative analysts who advocated less government intrusion as part of their neoliberal approach to the world. Finding particular voice in the George W. Bush administration, the neoliberals argued that the developmental efforts advocated by earlier theorists were not only wrong in terms of effects but philosophically objectionable as well.

The concept of "nation building" has been the whipping boy in the ensuing debate. The disagreement would be ignorable if it remained strictly within academic bounds, but it has not. While a truly effective way to engage in the kind of stabilization and modernization the nation builders desire has not emerged, the problem remains part of the context over what to do about the kinds of countries where asymmetrical wars occur. If nation building is impossible, then the military effort may be quixotic, since it will not result in stability. If nation building is possible but more difficult, lengthy, and uncertain in terms of outcomes than the early advocates projected, then the question is whether the effort is worth it. Negative answers would suggest that the willingness to engage in asymmetrical warfare needs to be reevaluated. (For a detailed discussion of this debate and its evolution, see Latham, 2011.)

Asymmetrical Warfare as Methodology This point has already been made, but deserves reiteration as a characteristic of asymmetrical warfare. Contemporary experience that has evolved in the current period is that no two asymmetrical wars are entirely alike, but instead each instance represents an at least partially new and unique phenomenon. This dynamic flows from the fact that asymmetry is a methodology—a way to organize and think about the problem—not a set of solutions (a method). Knowing about the last asymmetrical conflict is, as a result, only a partial guide to how the next one will occur and how or if one can successfully affect the outcome.

The dynamic nature of asymmetrical war makes it very difficult for those who must confront it to master. The United States, for instance, produced a new counterinsurgency manual in 2006, the purpose of which was to prepare American forces for the kinds of conflicts that have been described here as asymmetrical. The problem with the manual is that it quite understandably examines the subject in an historical context that may or may not be adequate for the future (the manual is listed as a Core Reading at the end of the chapter) and thus may not prove to be adequate guidance about future involvements in these kinds of conflicts.

Asymmetrical War, Nation Building, and Foreign Policy

At the end of the United States' first major asymmetrical war in Vietnam, there was a national soul searching about what had gone wrong and, possibly more important, how the same mistakes could be avoided in the future. A chastened American military reexamined its approach to developing world conflicts and fashioned its first approaches to unconventional warfare. Its heart was not truly in the enterprise, however, and the emphasis was downgraded, particularly after 9/11. The heart of the 1970s self-examination was a conclusion that was captured in a somewhat amorphous, ambiguous catchphrase: "No more Vietnams." On the surface, this was a lesson with which hardly anyone could argue, given the military and political disaster that Vietnam had become. But what exactly did it mean?

At the time there were two explanations of the meaning of "No more Vietnams." The immediately more popular interpretation was that the United States should in the future avoid direct participation in developing world conflicts, and especially internal wars in the Third World. Where American Cold War interests were at stake (for example, conflicts where one side was supported by the Soviet Union or China), the United States should be willing to supply assistance in the possible forms of financing, equipping, and even training indigenous forces to withstand communist blandishments, but this commitment would not extend to the direct commitment of American armed forces to these kinds of conflicts (that is, Vietnam-style wars). This position was first articulated in July 1969 by then-President Richard M. Nixon and became known as the Nixon Doctrine.

As the Vietnam experience receded in the national memory during the 1980s and 1990s, these restrictions came to be seen as too inhibiting, and so a second, modifying interpretation was put forward. The argument was that the Nixon Doctrine effectively prohibited the application of American forces almost anywhere in the world where they might be requested, since Vietnam-analogous situations represented most of the opportunities to employ American force, especially after the end of the Cold War. Supporters of the Nixon Doctrine's restrictive interpretation saw this limitation as a virtue and as a barrier to what they viewed as the gratuitous use of American force in situations where it was unneeded and was likely to be unsuccessful. Champions of modification, however, argued that the original interpretation unduly tied the hands of the world's remaining superpower and left the United States as a paper tiger—an impotent power unwilling to use its military might.

No one, of course, was willing to renounce the cautionary lesson of Vietnam altogether, and so they mounted a two-pronged attack on "No more Vietnams," parts of which are still in the public dialogue. One prong of this revisionism was to reinterpret the Vietnam experience. Some argued the problem was that the military was unduly shackled in conducting the war, and had crippling restrictions not been in place, the United States would have prevailed. Vietnam, in other words, did not have to have been a lost cause. Others added to this critique that Vietnam was a unique experience, and that its uniqueness meant any generalization about its impact was fallacious. Other apparently analogous situations are not really analogies at all. Both of these forms of revisionism remain in defenses of ongoing American commitments.

The other prong was to reinterpret what "No more Vietnams" truly meant. Rather than being a blanket admonition against developing world interventionism, it argued a more restricted interpretation. Proponents of this view maintained that the lesson of Vietnam was that the United States should avoid involvement in strictly internal wars in the developing world where its intervention could not prove critical, but that not all Third World conflicts were of this nature and that conflict situations needed to be examined individually on their merits, keeping in mind the admonitions from Vietnam but not being paralyzed by them. Intervention in non-Vietnam-like developing-world conflicts could be justified under the right circumstances.

The reason for this discursion is that the United States is facing an arguably analogous, if less intense, experience as it moves toward disengagement from Afghanistan. In physical terms, of course, the involvement of the United States in Afghanistan has not been of the scale and hence the trauma of Vietnam; nonetheless it has become a part of the ongoing role of the United States in the world, a part of which is how activist American foreign policy should be. In the early 1970s, the motor that drove the national debate was the outcome of Vietnam and the enormous political impact of the sacrifice in blood and treasure the United States had paid for a dubious outcome. The cost in American blood is not so great this time, but the costs in American treasure have been significant. The major emphasis of the debate this time may center on whether the United States can *afford* another Afghanistan.

Afghanistan is a wraith hanging over this debate because many of the future situations where the United States may contemplate the use of military force to achieve foreign policy goals will be akin to Afghanistan, in the sense of presenting the likelihood of being or—with American intervention in and thus the transformation of—becoming asymmetrical wars. If the question of dispatching American forces to a place like Yemen is contemplated, it must be held up against the characteristics of Afghanistan and given a realistic assessment of whether those characteristics hold and if their negative aspects can be overcome. The uncertainty of such analysis is, of course, increased by the fifth characteristic, which asserts that asymmetrical warfare is an adaptive methodology: The next asymmetrical war will not be the same as the last one.

The dilemma of nation building is part of the debate. One of the reasons for pessimism is not only that it is costly, but also that the investments will tend to be bad ones. A postwar Afghanistan will still be desperately poor and underdeveloped, and it is not at all clear that any nation-building efforts in which the United States and its allies can engage will change that situation much. If nation building is futile in this case, then the whole enterprise may have been as well.

This process of assessment provides a bridge to the question of dealing with terrorism in three ways. First, terrorist organizations tend to be born and to find solace in the form of safe havens in the same kinds of countries (unstable, developing states) where the United States is likely to be tempted. The terrorist or the asymmetrical warfare problem may be there first, but they are likely to be colocated. Second, in some important ways terrorism is a form or tactic of asymmetrical warfare: an asymmetrical method employed when one is particularly weak and cannot even confront the symmetrical warrior using unconventional military means. Terrorism and asymmetrical warfare are conceptually related. Third, the September 11th experience remains a vivid motivator for the United States and a reason that has been and will continue to be invoked as justification for national security operations. A response to terrorism can lead to involvement in an asymmetrical warfare experience (as it did in Afghanistan).

TERRORISM

The memory and images of that fateful Tuesday—airplanes flying into the World Trade Center twin towers and the side of the Pentagon in Washington, a fourth plane on its way to the capital crashing in the Pennsylvania countryside—hover over Americans and U.S. national security like ever-present ghosts, a reminder of the terrorist horror of September 11, 2001, and a terrifying harbinger of things possibly to come. While the death of Osama bin Laden removes some of the anxiety from our consciousness, threats of what may yet be remain part of daily life. Over a decade after those terrible events, American national security policy, and foreign policy more generally, remain fixed on the problem and threat of terrorism in ways reminiscent of the danger of communism during the Cold War.

The Cold War threats are both similar and different. The primary comparison is their ubiquity: The challenge of Soviet-led communism was never far from the forefront of American concerns, and all foreign and national security policy was evaluated in at least some measure by its contribution to "triumphing" in the anticommunist crusade. Terrorism has occupied a similar place in our consciousness. The two are different in that they reversed the evaluation of the relationship between deadliness and dangerousness to Americans and the country. Due to nuclear weapons, the Cold War was potentially a terribly deadly confrontation, since its deterioration to "hot" war could have become a fiery Armageddon; that very prospect caused the two competitors to mute the competition away from the brink of war, gradually making war much less likely and the situation less dangerous. The age of terrorism has reversed that dynamic: Terrorists cannot now—and arguably never will—pose the prospect of a civilization-threatening inferno of death (the competition is less deadly), but at the same time, they refuse to moderate their reign of violence, leaving the competition more dangerous (a greater likelihood of violence occurring at any time).

The mechanisms for dealing with the phenomenon differ as well. The primary dynamic of regulating the Cold War (keeping it cold) was deterrence, persuading one another not to launch a nuclear attack, and the resulting stalemate eventually contributed to the realization of the futility of the competition and its cessation. Deterrence, however, clearly does not work regarding the dissuasion of Al Qaeda and its affiliates, who continue to plot and carry out attacks despite a robust campaign to make such a campaign personally costly to them. Deterrence is either inapplicable or ineffectual in the face of modern international terrorism, and those charged with American national security policy have struggled—and continue to struggle—for some effective way to manage and defuse the terrorism problem.

These efforts remain a work in progress, and the purpose of this section to try to describe and assess the arguable "war" on terrorism announced swiftly by the Bush administration in the immediate wake of the September 11th disaster. To do so, the discussion will proceed in a way parallel to the examination of asymmetrical warfare, beginning with a discussion of the characteristics of terrorism. Just as the more generic asymmetrical warfare is constantly changing, so is the terrorist challenge, which will conclude the analysis of terrorism and terrorist characteristics. The narrative will then move on to terrorism as a foreign policy consideration.

Terrorism Characteristics

Like asymmetrical warfare, terrorism is a very old practice, and one that has been adapted by disaffected groups which generally have little chance of successfully pursuing their interests (normally described in terms of grievances) by other, more conventional means. Historians of terrorism generally trace what is now considered terrorism back to biblical times, notably the resistance of the Jewish population of Palestine to the Roman occupation (particularly the Zealots in the first century A.D.). As an historical phenomenon, terrorism has ebbed and flowed as a part of the international scene, but it has never disappeared altogether, even if the groups and grievances come and go. Individual terrorists and their causes have historically been transitory; terrorism persists.

Modern terrorism is conventionally dated back to the French Revolution and Robespierre's Reign of Terror against recalcitrant opponents of the revolution; indeed, the modern term *terrorism* gained currency at that time as a result of such events. The modern terrorist epoch is distinguished by its explicitly political agenda and proposed outcomes. The current spate of international terrorism is only the latest wave in a series of reasons for terrorism that include the anarchists of the late nineteenth century, anticolonial movements in the middle twentieth century, and the so-called New Left of the Vietnam era. Like these manifestations, Al Qaeda–based terrorism is having its day on the world's center stage, but like the others, most dispassionate analysts agree that it will gradually fade into the historical backdrop as well. The problem is that, like the movements that preceded it, contemporary terrorism can wreak considerable havoc until it plays itself out, and no one is able (or bold enough) to predict how long it will be until this spark is extinguished.

It is important to distinguish between terrorism as a phenomenon and particular manifestations of terrorism. Like asymmetrical warfare, terrorism is a methodology—a set of ideas and attitudes about how to organize to combat a particular situation. Part of the task of dealing with terrorism involves anticipating the application of the method regardless of who is conducting it or why. Dealing with terrorism also involves confronting and defeating its current practitioners, in this case mostly radical Islamists with a fundamentalist worldview antithetical to that of the West and to most Muslims. This aspect of the problem requires defeating these particular adversaries, discrediting their ideas, or both.

This distinction is important because, as with asymmetrical warfare, defeating the method and the practitioners is not the same thing. Terrorism is an enduring phenomenon in international life, and no one has yet devised a countermethod that makes it universally unappealing. Until a counterstrategy occurs (if it ever does), some groups will continue to adopt terrorism in the future. Despite its endurance, however, terrorism is rarely successful in achieving its major goals, indicating that it is possible—if difficult in many cases—to defeat individual causes that practice terrorism.

The discussion of terrorism will proceed with that basic distinction in mind. It will begin by defining terrorism, including terrorist acts and the objects of their attacks. It will then move to modern terrorists and the groups they form, followed by a look at their purposes. The section will conclude with the methods that have been devised for trying to contain and defeat the current spate of terrorism.

Defining and Specifying Terrorism Despite the ubiquity of terrorism as a topic of foreign policy concern, there is disagreement about what exactly it *is*. Most definitions include three basic elements: terrorist acts, terrorist targets, and terrorist purposes. Some definitions (including that of the U.S. government) add the fourth element of who commits these acts. Contemporary definitions including a specification of actors normally distinguish the use of terrorist methods by nonstate actors or governments, arbitrarily maintaining that true terrorism is committed only by those entities. This may be true of most modern terrorism, but historically states have used terror against their government (the French during the Reign of Terror or the National Socialists in Germany, for instance), and so the specification included in these definitions is a characteristic of modern terrorism, not a part of the definition.

For the present purposes, terrorism is defined as *the commission of atrocious acts against a target population normally to gain compliance with some demands on which the terrorists insist*. The definition thus incorporates the three major elements of other definitions (acts, targets, and purposes) while omitting the fourth (actors).

Terrorist acts are violent displays that have several salient characteristics. For one thing, they are uniformly illegal actions intended to kill people or destroy things; in all cases, they involve acts that break laws. From one perspective this means that those who commit these acts are no more than common criminals and should be treated as such. The implication of this view is that terrorists should be subject to the criminal code in the countries where they break laws and thus be subject to the justice system. Terrorists, however, reject this interpretation, maintaining that they commit these acts for political purposes and that terrorist acts are acts of war. Thus, their perpetrators are warriors, not criminals. The old saw that "one man's terrorist is another man's freedom fighter" captures this distinction.

The purpose of committing terrorist acts is to frighten the groups against which they are committed; indeed, the root of the word *terrorism* is the Latin word *terrere*, which means to frighten. Terrorist acts are intended to send a message to target groups: You may not have been harmed by a particular act, but the next attack may maim or kill you. The certain way to avoid a similar fate is to conform to terrorist demands, because attacks will continue until their targets accede to those demands. Particular terrorist acts may serve a number of other, more subsidiary purposes. Jenkins, writing in 2004, suggests six others, including gaining special concessions (the release of fellow terrorists from jail, for instance), generating publicity for the cause, creating demoralizing publicity in the target society, provoking government overreaction that discredits the government, forcing compliance from the target population, or punishing the target for disobedient behavior. Stern (2003) adds a seventh motive, improving morale within the movement itself. In all cases, the overarching purpose is to induce fear in the target population.

How well terrorist acts accomplish their goals depends on the targets they choose to attack, and two distinctions can be made about those terrorist targets. Borrowing from the language of nuclear deterrence, one category of physical target is *countervalue*, or attacking the things that people most value, notably their lives and the things that make life commodious—from schools to power plants to airliners or bridges. Maximum fear is presumably achieved by killing people—from a terrorist perspective, preferably in sizable numbers—but the danger that something like the Golden Gate Bridge might be the object of an attack regularly brings California National Guardsmen scurrying to San Francisco to protect the iconic structure from harm. The alternative set of targets is *counterforce*, attacks against military targets, and particularly military capabilities that could be brought to bear against terrorists. The *U.S.S. Cole*, attacked in 2000 in a Yemeni harbor, was such a target. In some cases, the two kinds of targets are indistinguishable, as in the November 5, 2009, killing of thirteen personnel and wounding of twenty-nine more, mostly military members, in Fort Hood, Texas, by Major Nidal Hasan.

The final element in the definition of terrorism is terrorist objectives. This refers to the "why" of terrorism: what motivates terrorists and what do they hope to accomplish. Almost all terrorism is motivated by achieving political goals. These goals can be negative, as in removing a regime from power that acts in ways of which they disapprove (for example, the assassination of Egyptian President Anwar Sadat in 1981 by fanatics who disapproved of his secularization of that country), or they can be what the terrorists view as positive (for example, the institution of societal values such as *sharia* law in a target society).

Terrorists are generally not successful in achieving their objectives, and their failure increases with the grandiosity of the objective and the size and resistance of the unit at which the goal is aimed. Terrorism is, after all, a method of the weak, which means that the terrorists' goals normally represent a minority position in the target society, and one which cannot be overcome in standard, prescribed ways (for example, electing a majority to a legislative body that can enact what they want).

The ability of terrorists to achieve their objectives depends to a large degree on how foreign what they propose is and the amount of leverage they have to bring it about, and this varies greatly depending on the target society they seek to influence. Osama bin Laden, for instance, argued in the 1990s that the reason he was making what he viewed as war on the United States was because of the continuing military presence of the Americans on the Arabian Peninsula—notably Saudi Arabia—after the 1990–1991 Gulf War. His argument was that this presence "desecrated" the holy places of Islam and was intolerable. The United States, of course, remained in the Saudi Kingdom at the explicit invitation of the government, carefully kept a low profile, and initially did not take bin Laden's demands to evacuate terribly seriously. The terrorist leader's demands seemed ridiculous to most Americans who knew about them (most Americans did not) and were hence ignored. As a result, bin Laden had little ability to affect American policy directly and chose the 2001 attacks and subsequent activities as ways to achieve his goals.

A major reason that terrorist objectives are so ineffective is because rather than lowering the will to resist, instead attacks often make the resolution to resist greater, as clearly the September 11th attacks did. In any direct sense, Al Qaeda has failed to move the U.S. government, but the results of September 11th and Al Qaeda's subsequent campaigns against the United States are nonetheless intriguing. The United States has, in fact, basically removed most of its forces from Saudi Arabia, although no American official would admit that the terrorist attacks had anything to do with that withdrawal. At the same time, Al Qaeda has argued grandiosely that its long-term objective is to bring the Americans to their knees.

Terrorists and Their Organizations Who are the terrorists? If one is to mount a successful campaign to contain or eradicate particular terrorists—in the present environment, mostly Al Qaeda and its affiliates—it is helpful to "know the enemy." Additionally, only a small number of terrorists act entirely on their own (so-called lone wolves, discussed below), so that an assault on the practitioners of terrorism also requires knowing how terrorists aggregate themselves with like-minded others to pursue terrorist objectives.

Any individual or group with what it views as a sufficient grievance against a political authority and no chance to redress it through conventional means may contemplate and adopt terrorism. The terrorist method means being willing to commit sometimes horrendous violence against other human beings, a traumatic decision for most people. In addition, terrorists put themselves in a position of considerable personal risk, since the fate of many terrorists is the forfeiture of their lives—especially if the individual agrees to an act of martyr (suicide) terrorism. All of these are serious personal factors; the decision to become a terrorist may strike most people as aberrant, but it is not light or fanciful.

The actions that terrorists carry out mean they are sociopathic. Terrorist acts are crimes in all organized societies, indicating that these actions violate norms that are successfully inculcated in most societal members. The ultimate form of the terrorist act involves the taking of human life, which is universally condemned and only gains sanction when justified by some greater good, such as the wars of states or religious *jihad*. The potential terrorist must engage in an act of conscious rejection of social norms against what he or she vows to do in the name of the terrorist cause.

The consequences of becoming a terrorist are dire, further marking the terrorist as different. The terrorist shares with the soldier the knowledge that his participation may result in his own personal demise, and this potential sacrifice requires some greater justification, such as recourse to a higher principle. Traditional soldiers, of course, deeply resent such a comparison, because their code of conduct prohibits the commission of acts of violence against noncombatants, but the similarity of possible consequence is part of why terrorists like to fashion themselves as soldiers.

The case of **martyr/suicide terrorists** particularly illustrates this point about the "specialness" of those who choose to become terrorists. This category is distinguished by the person's willingness to and advance knowledge that he or she will engage in acts of self-immolation in service to the terrorist cause. Most of the contemporary practitioners of this form of terrorism have been Islamic terrorists who insist that they martyr themselves rather than commit suicide, because personal acts of suicide are mortal sins within Islam punishable by exclusion from Paradise after death. Regardless, they join other suicide terrorists (such as some Japanese suicide resisters to the American occupation of Okinawa and *kamikaze* pilots) in their willingness to sacrifice their lives for their particular causes.

If it is hard to pigeonhole exactly who becomes terrorists and why, it is somewhat easier to describe the ways in which they aggregate themselves. In terms of affiliation, terrorists can be members of more or less formal terrorist organizations, or they can act autonomously. Each form of organization has advantages and disadvantages that can be described in terms of *capacity* (the amount of damage or effect their actions have) and *resiliency* (their ability to avoid detection and suppression). These categories are developed by Stern (2003), among others, and are useful in describing various organizational alternatives.

There has been a post-9/11 evolution of terrorist organizations. The earliest forms, including the early years of Al Qaeda, tended to follow the **commander-cadre model**. This form of organization is conventional, not unlike the ways in which more traditional, legitimate organizations operate. Commander-cadre organizations are hierarchical, with leaders (commanders) formulating policies (terrorist attacks) and passing them down to their followers/employees (cadres) as orders. The advantage of such organizations is that they can develop into large, complex forms that allow the development and execution of complex, extensive operations, such as the 9/11 attacks. In other words, this form maximizes terrorist capacity.

Commander-cadre organizations have an Achilles' Heel in an electronic world. Like other large, complex organizations, these kinds of terrorist operations rely on communicating decisions and recommendations up and down the organization. Large corporations, for instance, do so fairly openly, but since they are criminal enterprises, terrorist organizations must communicate clandestinely. The problem is that modern communication is almost entirely electronic, and it is subject to surveillance and interception by sophisticated monitors such as the American National Security Agency (NSA). Intercepts of communications after 9/11 allowed the United States to locate and target numerous members of the Al Qaeda network (including bin Laden) after 9/11, making resiliency the Achilles' Heel of such organizations.

The increasing vulnerability of commander-cadre organizations led to the adoption of a second organizational form, the so-called **virtual network model**. The prototype of this variant was the American hate group Aryan Nation, whose communications were constantly being intercepted by the FBI, resulting in the harassment and prosecution of its leaders. Their response was to cease all direct communications with members and followers, instead using communications methods such as the Internet to broadcast general appeals (short of prosecutable calls to commit terrorist crimes) to followers to carry out acts from which the leadership could disassociate itself and thus avoid complicity. These organizations thus ceased to exist in any literal sense, and the result was an increase in resiliency. The negative side of this arrangement is the lack of control in organizing and executing large and complex attacks (a reduction in capacity). Well-publicized actions carried out as the result of virtual network entreaties include the murderous attacks against a Birmingham abortion clinic and in Atlanta by Eric Rudolph and the Ft. Hood, Texas, rampage by Major Hasan.

The trade-off between capacity and resiliency created by the two traditional models has resulted in a third, more contemporary variant that Stern (2003) describes as the **protean model**. Named after the Greek god Proteus, who could assume different identities, this model is a hybrid of the other two, composed of relatively small, geographically diverse affiliates (or "franchises") of the parent organization (in this case Al Qaeda) who act semiautonomously, receiving mostly hortatory direction from the central terrorist organization but limiting communication internally and with the parent organization, called Al Qaeda Central by Hoffman (2006).

The protean model, like the asymmetrical warfare model, is a methodology as much as it is a set of instructions. Its central direction is how to adapt and evade destruction in an increasingly hostile environment equipped with advanced tools to hunt it down. In its current iteration, it apparently resolves the dilemma of maximizing capacity and resilience by compromising both: communicating enough to mount regular attacks but not so much as to invite its destruction. Some of this is accomplished by locating the affiliate wings of the organization in remote sections of dysfunctional countries that can neither suppress them personally or are not in a position to aid suppression by outsiders. Al Qaeda in the Arabian Peninsula's Yemeni base is an example, as are Al Qaeda operations sometimes attributed to a Somali base.

Dealing with Terrorism

Finding a way to deal with terrorist organizations such as Al Qaeda has been the most prominent item on the American national security agenda since 2001. In the first shocked response to September 11th, the problem was largely framed in national security, rather than more broadly conceived foreign policy, terms: The first reaction was to declare "war on terrorism." This general orientation has basically endured, even if the explicit war analogy is less frequently voiced as time has passed. The problem, however, has been institutionally defined as **homeland security**, a variant of national security more generally, and responses to it have been classified both in terms of methods and approaches (antiterrorism and counterterror) and in the locus of appropriate response (national or international). The latter distinction creates a bridge toward thinking about terrorism as a foreign policy concern.

The Homeland Security Response The first problem that had to be confronted in attacking the terrorism threat was how to conceptualize and organize the response to it. Terrorism is only partially a military problem (as argued in the next section), and so an entirely military response housed somewhere within the traditional national security and defense establishment was not clearly appropriate. At the same time, terrorism did not fit neatly into any of the more political activities or jurisdictions within the government; instead, it was (and is) a hybrid problem that cuts across jurisdictional lines. As a result, it required an independent conceptualization and response.

The response was the idea of homeland security. In one sense, homeland security is the ultimate national security concern, since it deals literally with keeping the territory of the United States safe from harm. This depiction is captured in the interest matrix of Chapter Nine; the core of homeland security is found in the cell where survival and defense of homeland intersect. The September 11th attacks certainly represented an assault on the homeland, and preventing a reprise was at the heart of the required response to the problem. However, maintaining the sanctity of the homeland had fallen to a variety of agencies located in different parts of the federal bureaucracy and with distinct administrative homes, cultures, and loyalties. Bringing these various agencies together to form a seamless, effective defense of the homeland became the major problem of the effort against terrorism.

While there was little disagreement about the underlying principle of unifying government around the homeland security mandate, the devil turned out to be in the details of its implementation. In 2002, the Congress passed the Homeland Security Act at President George W. Bush's request, a piece of legislation he compared in importance to the National Security Act of 1947. The major thrust was to create the Department of Homeland Security (DHS) as the exclamation point of the terrorism suppression effort. However, implementation became difficult both because of the size of the effort and the reluctance of some agencies to come under its umbrella.

The administrative task of unifying federal assets with homeland security responsibilities was unprecedented. The idea was not to create an entirely new agency from scratch, but instead to amalgamate existing assets under the new DHS banner. This effort entailed trying to mesh 170,000 personnel from 21 sometimes-reluctant agencies into a single DHS effort. In addition to the logistics of such an amalgamation, there was significant resistance from some of the most important additions, which feared losing power and influence in the process.

The heart of the homeland security effort fell upon three different government functions housed in different federal agencies, none of which was anxious to become part of the new DHS. The first function was overseas operations, notably intelligence efforts to identify potential terrorist threats to the United States and, in some cases, to initiate and carry out actions to negate those efforts. The Central Intelligence Agency (CIA), an independent agency with cabinet status, had lead responsibility in this area. The second effort was protection of the physical border of the United States, with principal responsibility at the time assigned to the Immigration and Naturalization Service (INS), part of the Department of Justice. The third effort was surveillance and apprehension of terrorists within American borders, the primary responsibility for which fell to the Federal Bureau of Investigation (FBI), which was the crown jewel of the Justice Department.

Cooperation among and coordination of these three agencies was clearly optimal for the homeland security effort: The CIA would identify threats from the outside and pass along the information to the INS, who would then try to stop terrorists at the border; those who made it into the United States would be dealt with by the FBI. There were several problems with this relationship, including an historical rivalry between its parts (notably the FBI and the CIA) and the fact that they all reported to different cabinet secretaries or directors. The obvious way to solve this problem was to place them under one master (the Secretary of DHS), who could enforce cooperation among them.

The problem was that none of them wanted to become part of the DHS. The CIA and the FBI in particular argued against their inclusion on the grounds that their mandates included terrorism but also encompassed many other activities. This was true, but it was also true of many agencies that were folded into the DHS. In the end, powerful patrons in both the executive branch and

Congress successfully kept the FBI and CIA out of the new agency, whereas the less powerful INS, refashioned as Immigration and Customs Enforcement (ICE), was included. In the intervening years, the DHS has struggled both to fashion itself as a single agency with a single loyalty and focus, and to reconcile and adapt itself to the fact that it does not have sole jurisdiction over all the government assets necessary to carry out its mandate. That effort remains a work in progress.

Homeland Security Focuses The question of how to implement the terrorism suppression effort has largely been along two lines of consideration. One of these is functional, and includes efforts that can be classified as **antiterrorism** and **counterterrorism**. The other consideration, which helps bring the discussion back toward its foreign policy moorings, is the relative emphasis on national or international efforts to achieve the goal.

The terms *antiterrorism* and *counterterrorism* are often used interchangeably, although they have distinctive meanings and methods. Antiterrorism refers to defensive efforts to reduce the vulnerability of targets to terrorist attacks and to reduce the effects of such attacks that do occur. The chief venue for engaging in antiterrorist activities is domestic, with the purpose of frustrating the terrorist who is attempting to harm Americans or American assets (unless those assets are overseas). It consists of two related kinds of activities. One of these activities is reducing vulnerability by making it harder for terrorists to gain access to points where they can attack; airport security conducted by the Transportation Safety Agency (TSA), a part of DHS, is an example. The other involves mitigating the effects of attacks, either by reducing the damage that can be done (for instance, closing streets such as Pennsylvania Avenue in Washington, D.C., in front of the White House to vehicular traffic) or by mitigating the postattack environment after an attack (such as efforts by the Federal Emergency Management Agency in disaster areas). Counterterrorism, however, consists of offensive, including military, measures against terrorists or sponsoring agencies to prevent, deter, or respond to terrorist attacks. The counterterrorist, in other words, seeks to preempt terrorist acts, and if an attack occurs, to retaliate and punish the attacker and render the source incapable of future action. Counterterrorist actions include clandestine actions by military or quasi-military forces.

How can antiterrorist and counterterrorist missions most effectively be accomplished? One way to look at that question is in terms of national versus international efforts. Most of the early homeland security efforts of the Bush administration focused on things the United States could do on its own (national emphases) to address the continuing terrorist threat. Reorganization of government to form the DHS is an obvious example, and legislation such as the USA PATRIOT Act to permit federal law enforcement agencies more leeway in dealing with suspected terrorists is another. When the efforts move to overseas operations, however, then a more international orientation seems appropriate. The intelligence area is exemplary: The United States regularly cooperates with its European allies in the collection and sharing of information about terrorist activities directed against them, and that sharing presumably increases the capability of all of them to confront and contain the threat. When efforts are directed at the sources of terrorist activities, however, they move into countries such as Pakistan, where national sensitivities must be considered, and some of these may be delicate matters that can appear to compromise unilateral, national efforts. The effort to kill bin Laden illustrates these difficulties.

As is well known now, bin Laden was hiding "in plain sight" in the Pakistani city of Abbottabad, home of Pakistan's equivalent of West Point and the residence of many retired Pakistani military officers. Despite official cooperation between the two countries to identify and nullify terrorists in Pakistan, the United States carried out the operation against bin Laden entirely on its own, apparently out of fear that it would be compromised if the Pakistanis learned about it. Thus, cooperation has practical limits. But why?

Cooperation Is Not Unconditional The government of Pakistan is sensitive to domestic criticism of its participation in the American counterterrorist program, on two grounds. One is that the attacks are undertaken on Pakistan territory and in violation of Pakistani sovereignty, a major symbolic sticking point. The other is that these attacks often include collateral damage in the form of the killing of civilians who happen to be in the attack zones. To deflect the resulting criticism, the Pakistani government formally maintains that it has no part in the American initiative, thereby allowing it to condemn both the violation of Pakistani sovereignty and civilian casualties. At the same time, that government performs a critical, if necessarily secret, role in that program. They provide that service, such as sharing information on terrorist locations, secretly so that they can condemn the United States when civilians are killed as collateral damage. While privately pleased by the elimination of bin Laden, the Pakistanis felt the need to condemn it publicly as a violation of Pakistani sovereignty.

Terrorism as a Foreign Policy Consideration

Since September 11, 2001, terrorism and its suppression have been all-encompassing concerns of the United States and its relations with the world. Given the calamity and outrage of those attacks, this emphasis, even fixation, is understandable, but it has also colored—and even arguably distorted—the analysis of the terrorism phenomenon and its place as a part of foreign policy. The possible distortion comes from the tendency to look at one end of the terrorism phenomenon, its effects, and to respond to it with policies primarily designed to counteract those effects. Given the very real threat that terrorists pose, this emphasis is also understandable, but it also tends to frame the problem instrumentally and in the process possibly to overmilitarize dealing with it. One effect is to de-emphasize the other end of the phenomenon, which is the causes of terrorism and, more specifically, what has caused a particular terrorist threat against the United States. A foreign policy that seeks to contain or eliminate terrorism should, one can argue, better balance the two ends of the terrorism equation.

If, as argued earlier, particular terrorist threats are transitory (even if the practice of terrorism is not), then it would seem that a foreign policy that seeks to identify and erase the reasons particular terrorists act in general and against Americans in particular would be a good place from which to start fashioning policy. In the current environment, the first question might be, "What is it about the United States and what it does in the world that has caused terrorists to target the United States?" As victims of an outrage such as 9/11, it is somewhat difficult to phrase this question, because it suggests some culpability in the sense of having done things that have started or contributed to the chain of events of which terrorist acts are the ultimate outcome. Still, the terrorist threat can only be ended in one (or both) of two ways: by defeating and physically eliminating the threat, or by eliminating the reasons the actions are being taken. Most of the efforts since 9/11 have been directed at how to eradicate the terrorist threat. The question is whether that is an adequate approach.

The answer depends to some degree on the nature of the problem. If terrorism is essentially a military problem, then a military response to it (for example, declaring war on terror) and a military or semimilitary campaign against Al Qaeda may be the appropriate response to the problem. That approach has made progress in reducing the capacity of Al Qaeda Central, for instance, but it has certainly not solved the problem of terrorism overall. Is a policy aimed at one end of the problem enough?

Officials within the U.S. and allied governments are not unmindful of the need to try to determine why terrorism is being directed at the United States and elsewhere, but their efforts have been shackled in at least two ways. First, the effort to determine what motivates terrorists runs the risk of sounding empathetic (even if it is not) and thus "soft" on terrorism, a politically suicidal position. Second, the effort may appear to produce sympathetic responses such as changing policies that have offended the terrorists and thus appear to be "giving in" to the enemy, another politically unpalatable position. It is intellectually easier simply to demonize the terrorists and assert, as President Bush did, that their motivation was that they "hated our freedom."

Having said this, is it possible to approach policies that might assuage those who act as terrorists against the United States, or at least act in ways that minimize the appeal of violent anti-Americanism to potential new terrorists? Bin Laden's followers may simply hate American freedom, but they may also have other motives. If so, what are they? And what can be done to blunt those motives as an appeal to end the current spate of terrorism? The *Intersections* box, "Occupation and Terrorism," offers one way in which such an approach might be framed.

INTERSECTIONS

Occupations and Terrorism

The military problem of dealing with terrorists such as the Al Qaeda recruits seen in training here includes that foreign occupations may stimulate recruitment of new members.

The current campaign of terrorism directed against the United States by Al Qaeda is a product of the early 1990s. Al Qaeda was born sometime around 1988 among foreign *mujahidin* fighters from the resistance to the Soviet occupation of Afghanistan. The group articulated its first demands against the United States in the form of bin Laden's "Epistles" (see Additional Readings) in the mid-1990s, at which time the terrorist group arose prominently on the radars of American counterterrorist analysts. The first active attack directed at American soil was the 1993 assault on the World Trade Center's twin towers in New York, and it was followed by a series of overseas attacks against American assets abroad (namely, the embassies in Uganda and Kenya) in the latter 1990s. The fury of Al Qaeda was, of course, punctuated on September 11th.

Why was the United States singled out for this treatment? Bin Laden's initial grievance was about the continued American presence in his native Saudi Arabia after the Gulf War of 1990–1991, in which bin Laden had volunteered his *mujahidin* and Al Qaeda assets to defend the kingdom and had them rejected. American "presence" in the holy lands of Saudi Arabia was unacceptable because it included a permanent American military presence in the area that had not existed previously. The United States only redoubled this phenomenon when it invaded and conquered Iraq and occupied Afghanistan.

(Continued)

(Continued)

Is the American military occupation of parts of the Middle East the irritant that "gives legs" to current terrorist efforts against the United States? Certainly, there has always been some relationship between occupiers and the formation of terrorist movements; foreign occupation clearly represents the kind of grievance that can give rise to a terrorist response. As already noted, the first terrorists were Jewish resisters to the Roman occupation of Palestine, and occupations routinely evince unhappiness that sometimes becomes violent and even terrorist. Whether it is labeled terrorist or not depends to a large degree on who is doing the designating. For instance, were members of the French Resistance during World War II terrorists or "freedom fighters"?

Not all occupations produce terrorist responses, but some do. Occupation is, at least hypothetically, a sufficient condition for a terrorist response, and some terrorism undoubtedly comes into being without an occupation as its inspiration. In formal terms, occupations may be one sufficient cause of terrorism among others, and its absence in some cases suggests it is not a necessary condition, either. Nonetheless, there may be some link worth exploring and thus some consideration given to the assertion that the American occupation of Afghanistan, for instance, may actually be creating as much or more terrorism against the United States as it is destroying. It is a controversial and hypothetical possibility, but not one that is so implausible as to be dismissed out of hand.

A foreign policy approach to terrorism policy may produce a different assessment and different policy outcomes than an approach that is grounded solely or even principally in national security concerns. It is certainly easy to place terrorism within the range of U.S. interests, threats to those interests, and the risks that inattention to the problem entails. This analytical perspective leads to the classification of the problem in national security terms, but it may be that a broader, foreign policy perspective is more beneficial.

What kind of a problem is terrorism, after all? It is partially a military problem, since terrorists practice a form of asymmetrical warfare, employ military means in carrying out their nefarious activities, and consider themselves warriors in some sense. Terrorist activities are, like foreign policy problems more generally, greater than their military elements and orientation. Like most forms of asymmetrical warfare, what terrorists do has a much more directly political content—purpose and method—than conventional warfare such as warfare between states. As with modern asymmetrical war, terrorism is really about the battle for the "hearts and minds" of both its target audience (although it generally attempts to create fear rather than inspire loyalty) and in the population that forms its recruitment and support base (by convincing them that what they are doing is in their best interest). The competition for people's loyalties is a political, not a military, struggle wherein force may provide a preconditioning or facilitating influence on the political outcome but cannot determine it. Terrorism is indeed politics by other, very extreme means, and combating it on an international level is an exercise in the interplay of policy, in this case foreign policy.

CONCLUSIONS

The period since the Cold War has witnessed a movement away from the traditional base of American foreign and national security policy concern. Europe remains a central interest of the United States, of course, and the United States retains much of the national security, notably military, structure with which it carried out the Cold War competition. What is different is that Europe is no longer threatened in the same way it once was.

The contemporary structure of the national security problem has shifted away from Europe toward the developing world, with a particular emphasis on the Middle East. The movement toward the developing world brought with it the problem of asymmetrical warfare, since countries in these parts of the world cannot afford the kinds of costly conventional capabilities that marked the Euro-centered international system. Moreover, when the United States became the principal opponent of some developing states, their only viable option was to adopt an asymmetrical warfare position, a decision aided by their observation of the American experience in Vietnam. The more specific emphasis on the Middle East added the problem of terrorism.

The result was the threat-force mismatch with which the United States continues to grapple and adapt. American forces were built for one threat but confront another for which the existing forces and strategies for their use are arguably poorly suited, and the country has been attempting to make the necessary adjustments to these changes ever since. Its inability to overcome the challenges presented by Al Qaeda-based terrorism and the ongoing, inconclusive War in Afghanistan suggest that it has not entirely surmounted these difficulties.

A further contrast between the two periods is in the relative roles of national security and foreign policy in dealing with threats to the national interest. The two were effectively merged in the Cold War competition, and much of that way of looking at the world has survived into the contemporary setting. As suggested in this chapter, however, asymmetrical warfare and its close conceptual cousin terrorism represent a different kind of politico-military challenge to the country, and one where foreign policy interests and national security means of risk reduction are not so neatly aligned.

One of the cogent ways in which the current period is different from the Cold War era is in the realignment of interests and threats, both matters of foreign as well as national security concern. Many of the nontraditional problems associated with asymmetrical warfare or terrorism arise in parts of the world where vital American interests are not as clearly engaged as they were in Europe. In the case of terrorism, important interests are engaged mainly *because* of the existence of terrorism in places otherwise low on an

American interest scale. Afghanistan is the primary example: Absent a terrorist problem, does anyone seriously believe the United States would have intruded on that country's instability with armed forces?

WHERE DO WE GO FROM HERE?

Two major questions come out of the analysis in this chapter. One concerns the nature of asymmetrical warfare and terrorism as problems and how (or whether) the United States can adapt its national security efforts more adequately to negate these forces when it confronts them. The other question, of more central importance in a text on foreign policy, is the extent to which the United States should involve itself in situations in those parts of the world where one encounters these problems. This second question gains particular cogency in a resource-constrained world where how much the United States expends on national security efforts may have a direct impact on its economic health and threaten the very foundations of American security, as President Eisenhower suggested in his concerns about budget balancing discussed in Chapter Nine. Balancing traditional national concerns with prevailing realities remains a major foreign policy area of needed adaptation.

APPLICATION: OLD ASSUMPTIONS IN A CONTEMPORARY ENVIRONMENT

Historian Robert Dallek, in a 2010 article in the journal *Foreign Policy*, argues that American national security policy has been premised on three questionable assumptions for "the last 100 years of American thinking about foreign policy," and the continuation of this line of reasoning has particularly pernicious effects in the contemporary environment, because in Dallek's own words, these assumptions "have made it nearly impossible for Americans to think afresh about more productive ways to address their foreign problems." Each of these influences is clearly evident in contemporary national security policy and in its applications in places such as Afghanistan and Iraq.

The first assumption is *universalism*, which he describes as a belief in "America's power to transform the world from a community of hostile, lawless nations into enlightened states devoted to peaceful cooperation." This evangelical desire and belief in uplifting the world certainly goes back to Woodrow Wilson's attempts to transform the world order and comes forward to George Bush's attempt to democratize Iraq. The problem with this assumption is that it is premised on the questionable assertions that all states want to be transformed in the American image and that the United States is capable of creating that change. The second assumption is *nonappeasement*, "a need to shun appeasement of all adversaries or to condemn suggestions of conciliatory talks with them as misguided weakness." This assumption was particularly strongly held by the neoconservatives who surrounded George W. Bush. Finally, there is *military containment,* "a belief in the surefire effectiveness of military strength in containing opponents, whatever their ability to threaten the United States."

The effects of adherence to these assumptions are to make American policy toward the world activist and to promote national security and military solutions to world problems. Activist expansionism is built into the evangelical desire to uplift the human condition, and national security solutions are promoted both by adopting a *macho* rejection of appeasement and a favorable attitude toward the efficacy of American force.

What would be the effect on American foreign policy if these assumptions are confronted and either rejected or substantially diluted, as Dallek suggests in his article? One result would almost certainly be a reduced military role for the United States that could, at least theoretically, lead to decreased spending on defense. Hardly anyone would argue about the change as an abstract principle, but what would its consequences be? Would a less-assertive United States be more at risk to opponents emboldened by a more inward-turning America? Or would those countries who have either been subject to or might become objects of American activism be relieved and cause the United States less problems? More specifically, what would be the effect on the asymmetrical warfare situation confronting the United States? Or for that matter, would a United States that eschewed these principles be less of a terrorist-producing threat than it is now? All the simple answers to these questions are almost certainly inadequate, but that does not mean the questions should not be raised anyway.

STUDY/DISCUSSION QUESTIONS

1. How was the Vietnam War, and especially the Battle of the Ia Drang, a harbinger of the future of U.S. national security policy? Explain.
2. How do asymmetrical warfare and terrorism create new problems for thinking about and conducting foreign policy? Describe the differences from more traditional problems, using Yemen as an example.
3. What is asymmetrical warfare? Why do people adopt it? Why is it particularly attractive to someone confronting the United States?
4. What are the major characteristics of asymmetrical warfare? How do they create particular problems for the United States?
5. Discuss the foreign policy implications of U.S. potential involvement in situations that may become asymmetrical warfare problems. Include the impact of nation building and "No more Vietnams" in your answer.
6. What is terrorism? What are its major characteristics following from the definition? Describe each.
7. What forms do terrorist organizations take? What are the advantages and disadvantages of each form? What is the current pattern? Why?
8. Discuss the nature of efforts to suppress terrorism. What are the major problems of dealing with terrorists? What have been the special problems of creating a homeland security mechanism for the United States?
9. Does treating terrorism as a foreign policy rather than a national security problem change one's approach to the subject? How? Which emphasis is superior, in your opinion?

CORE SUGGESTED READINGS

Haass, Richard N. *Wars of Necessity, Wars of Choice: A Memoir of Two Iraq Wars.* New York: Simon & Schuster, 2009. Using the Iraq War experience as a backdrop, this contemporary account thoroughly examines the question of whether the United States should actively involve itself in the kinds of conflicts examined in the body of the chapter.

Hoffman, *Inside Terrorism* (2nd ed.). New York: Columbia University Press, 2006. Although there is no established "primary source" on modern terrorism, Hoffman's effort is as good a summary of the problem as is available.

Stern, Jessica. *Terrorism in the Name of God: Why Religious Militants Kill.* New York: ECCO, 2003. Focused on the actions of international religious terrorists, this is a very readable account both of terrorist activity and terrorist organization that helps lead to a more sophisticated understanding of the phenomenon.

The United States Army and Marine Corps Counterinsurgency Manual: U.S. Army Field Manual 3–24, Marine Corps Warfighting Publication No. 3–33.5. Chicago, IL: University of Chicago Press, 2006. With forewords by General David Petraeus, Lt. General James F. Amos, and Lt. Colonel John A. Nagl and an introduction by Sarah Sewell, this document is the "bible" of current American efforts to deal with the problems of counterinsurgency (COIN) that arise from the problem of asymmetrical war.

Van Creveld, Martin. *The Transformation of War.* New York: Free Press, 1991. Written by a noted Israeli analyst, this fine book was an early warning about the patterns that have since emerged as asymmetrical warfare.

ADDITIONAL READINGS AND REFERENCES

Berkowitz, Bruce. *The New Face of War: How War Will Be Fought in the 21st Century.* New York: Free Press, 2003.

bin Laden, Osama. (Online.) "Jihad Against Jews and Crusaders: World Islamic Front Statement." February 23, 1998. (http://www.fas.org/irp/world/para/docs/980223-fatwa.htm).

_______. (Online.) "MSANEWS: The Ladenese Epistle: Declaration of War, I–III." October 12–14, 1996. (http://msanews.net/MSANEWS/199610/19961012.3.htm).

Bynam, Daniel. "Talking with Insurgents: A Guide for the Perplexed." *Washington Quarterly* 32, 2 (April 2009), 125–138.

Christia, Fotini, and Michael Semple. "Flipping the Taliban." *Foreign Affairs* 88, 4 (July/August 2009), 34–45.

Clark, Wesley. *Winning Modern Wars: Iraq, Terrorism, and the American Empire.* New York: Public Affairs, 2003.

Clausewitz, Carl von. *On War.* Princeton, NJ: Princeton University Press, 1976.

Cronin, Audrey Kurth, and James M. Ludes (eds.). *Modern Terrorism: Elements of a Grand Strategy.* Washington, DC: Georgetown University Press, 2004.

Dallek, Robert. "The Tyranny of Metaphor." *Foreign Policy*, November 2010, 78–85.

Dershowitz, Alan M. *Why Terrorism Works: Understanding the Threat, Responding to the Challenge.* New Haven, CT: Yale University Press, 2002.

Ewans, Martin. *Afghanistan: A Short History of Its People and Politics.* New York: HarperCollins Perennial, 2002.

Hilsman, Roger. *American Guerrilla: My War Behind Japanese Lines.* Washington, DC: Brassey's (U.S.), 1991.

Jenkins, Brian. "International Terrorism." In Robert J. Art and Kenneth N. Waltz (eds.), *The Use of Force: Military Power and International Relations* (6th ed.). New York: Rowman & Littlefield Publishers, 2004.

Jones, Seth G. *In the Graveyard of Empires: America's War in Afghanistan.* New York: W. W. Norton, 2009.

Latham, Michael E. *The Right Kind of Revolution: Modernization, Development, and U.S. Foreign Policy from the Cold War to the Present*. Ithaca, NY: Cornell University Press, 2011.

Lowther, Adam B. *Americans and Asymmetrical Warfare: Lebanon, Somalia, and Afghanistan*. Westport, CT: Praeger Security International, 2007.

Moore, Lt. Gen. Harold G. (Ret.), and Joseph L. Galloway. *We Were Soldiers Once … and Young: Ia Drang—The Battle That Changed the War in Vietnam*. New York: Harper Perennial, 1992.

Nacos, Brigette. *Terrorism and Counterterrorism: Understanding Threats and Responses in the Post-9/11 World*. New York: Penguin Academics, 2006.

Pillar, Paul D. "Counterterrorism after Al Qaeda." *Washington Quarterly* 27, 3 (Summer 2004), 101–113.

Price, David G. "Global Democracy Promotion: Seven Lessons for the New Administration." *Washington Quarterly* 32, 1 (January 2009), 159–170.

Sloan, Stephen. *Beating International Terrorism: An Action Strategy for Preemption and Punishment*. Montgomery, AL: Air University Press, 2000.

Snow, Donald M. *National Security for a New Era* (4th ed.). New York: Longman, 2011.

_______. *September 11, 2001: The New Face of War?* New York: Longman, 2002.

_______. *When America Fights: The Uses of U.S. Military Force*. Washington, DC: CQ Press, 2000.

Stern, Jessica. "Mind over Martyr: How to Deradicalize Islamic Extremists." *Foreign Affairs* 89, 1 (January/February 2010), 95–108.

_______. "The Protean Enemy." *Foreign Affairs* 82, 4 (July/August 2003), 27–40.

Tzu, Sun. *The Art of War*. (Trans. by Samuel P. Griffith.) Oxford, UK: Oxford University Books, 1963.

Economics and Foreign Policy

One of the major goals of the Doha Development Agenda is to stimulate increasing world trade

PREVIEW

The international economy has become an increasingly important part of the environment in which foreign policy is made. Much of the current economic order is based on reactions to the negative assessments of the role that international commerce played in the events leading to World War II, and at the Bretton Woods Conference of 1944, a series of ideas about how to reconstruct that order were institutionalized in what became known as the Bretton Woods system.

Among the ideas that were not included in the Bretton Woods institutions was one promoting free trade, an idea that formally entered into the equation in the middle 1990s as one aspect of the process of economic interactions known as *globalization*. The idea of free trade has been an integral part of the emergence of the globalizing world order, implemented through a series of global, regional, and bilateral organizations that have made the promotion of globalization and free trade central to American foreign economic policy. However, this thrust remains politically controversial on both theoretical and applied grounds.

KEY CONCEPTS

World Trade Organization (WTO)
Doha Development Agenda
globalization
protectionism
free trade
micro level effects
macro level effects
tariffs
comparative advantage
Bretton Woods
International Monetary Fund (IMF)
International Bank for Reconstruction and Development (IBRD)
International Trade Organization (ITO)
General Agreement on Tariffs and Trade (GATT)
hard currency
high-technology
privatization
deregulation
Washington consensus
multinational corporations (MNCs)
Free Trade Area of the Americas (FTAA)
fair trade

Since 2001, the members of the **World Trade Organization (WTO)** have been engaged in discussion among themselves and with nonmembers about how to expand the role of free trade more generally through the international system. The United States, as the world's largest and most powerful state economically, is a member of the WTO and has been a lea ding participant in these discussions, which have now continued for over a decade without producing notable positive results. The United States has been both a promoter of the proceedings and, in some cases, a major roadblock to the very progress that it seeks to promote. The reasons for this apparent anomaly are complex and are significantly wrapped up in the intermestic politics of international economics.

The ongoing talks are known within international economic circles as the **Doha Development Agenda,** named after the capital of Qatar where they were first convened in late 2001; the terms *Doha Round* or simply *Doha* are used more or less interchangeably to describe these gatherings, which subsequently have occurred in Cancun, Mexico (2003), Geneva, Switzerland (2004),

Hong Kong (2005), and again in the home of the WTO headquarters, Geneva, in 2006 and 2008. The lack of progress on fundamental issues dividing the participants has precluded subsequent major conclaves. At the top of the list of policy disagreements has been how to deal with global agriculture, an area where the United States has major interests and contentious positions.

The United States is both a major agricultural producer and exporter, giving it a major interest in any negotiations that can affect the sale and flow of agricultural products (in the case of the United States, especially grains and corn) across international boundaries. The issue has both domestic and international economic aspects. Domestically, American agricultural output has increasingly been concentrated in the hands of large agricultural interests (the so-called agribusinesses), and much of their profitability is derived from the sales of their products in foreign markets. Agribusiness is a big and also highly profitable industry, meaning that organized agribusiness has large amounts of capital available to represent its interests effectively in framing American policy positions on that production (e.g., subsidies to farmers) and conditions of foreign sales (e.g., tariff levels).

Internationally, there are conflicting interests in agricultural trade practices and policies as well. Major producing areas such as the United States generally favor trade liberalization that reduces barriers to the free movement of their goods into world markets, but this movement is often resisted by others. Opponents tend to include those areas where agricultural production is either protected by government policies or where agricultural production is economically inefficient.

To try to deal with this problem, the Doha negotiators have devised three "pillars" of agricultural policy that they believe should underpin trade liberalizing agricultural policy. The details of those bases of policy go beyond present purposes, but they do illustrate both the dynamics of international trade policy and its intermestic nature.

The first pillar consists of *rules of export subsidies.* In some countries (including the United States), governments encourage exports by offering financial incentives for production of goods specifically for export that are not available to producers for domestic markets. The purpose of these subsidies is to give producers an advantage by effectively cutting their costs of production through paybacks by the government. In the area of general consumer goods, China has been accused of using these incentives to help it build up its enormous trade surplus with the rest of the world. The second pillar consists of *rules on domestic support* for some producers at the expense of others. These differ from export subsidies in the sense that they are not targeted specifically toward goods for exports, but apply instead across the board in the affected area. U.S. farm subsidies for grain farmers are an example. The third pillar consists of *tariff cuts,* lowering the barriers on the entrance of foreign goods into a country.

General free-trade policy, steeped in the international application of the Ricardian theory of comparative advantage (discussed later in the chapter), suggests positive actions on all three of these pillars as the basis of trade liberalization: reduction or elimination of export subsidies, domestic economic supports for particular economic activities, and the reduction or elimination of tariff barriers. Those who support economic globalization and its primary goal, free trade, argue for all three sets of actions. The problem is that all three have different effects on the various economic sectors in different countries, creating resistance to these pillars in particular national circumstances. These differences are often incompatible among countries being expected to help draft and enforce standards (including standards against themselves), and the result in the Doha Round has been gridlock and lack of progress toward goals of global free trade that are the holy grail of globalization advocates.

The U.S. position in the agricultural area is illustrative and helps form a bridge to the more general topic of the chapter. As an agricultural exporter, the United States clearly favors promotion of the third pillar of tariff reduction, both for its beneficial impact on the cost of American grains in foreign markets and as a general principle regarding its overall support for globalization. The United States also generally opposes the use of export subsidies, because of the accusations it makes against others for using these devices to gain unfair advantage in the American market (automobile imports have often been singled out in this regard). On the question of domestic supports, however, the United States becomes less vocal and supportive. The reason for this silence, even opposition, is domestic politics. Farm subsidies are a staple element in agribusiness profits, and they are important to the prosperity of states that produce American grains and corn for exporting. Attacking such subsidies is politically dangerous. As an example of the political power of prosubsidy interests in the United States, they have successfully eliminated major reductions in agricultural subsidies in budget reduction negotiations since the 2010 election.

The example of Doha agricultural initiatives is only a microcosm of the complexities and convolutions of international economic dynamics, policies, and utilities as part of American foreign policy. The large point is that policies in this realm are both complicated and contentious. In some ways, foreign economic policy is the epitome of intermestic politics, since it is normally almost impossible to separate entirely the domestic and international elements and ramifications of these decisions. In a world environment where economic considerations challenge more traditional national security concerns as contributors to national power, they are basic to a full understanding of American foreign policy.

The purpose of this chapter is to begin the quest to understand the role of economics in foreign policy, and it begins by looking at the question historically, emphasizing the generally feckless attempt to separate the international economic relations with other countries from political and military relations.

The crafting of a new and hopefully improved international economic environment has been the goal of this effort and has occurred within the context of an ongoing internal and international debate about the particulars of the international economic order. Internally within the United States, this debate has included disagreements about the desirability of American activism in the economic order versus older views preferring greater aloofness and isolation, the individual versus the national benefits of greater involvement in the economic order, and the appropriate role of the government in promoting and supporting different economic policies and emphases. Internationally, all of these same questions abound, and the Doha example illustrated at least the tip of some of these.

All of these questions have become especially lively in the last quarter-century. The catalyst has been the emergence of a new international emphasis on greater interaction economically among states. It has been represented by the concept of **globalization**, the movement to draw the world closer together in economic terms that has been largely fueled and activated by the high-technology revolution of the late twentieth century and supporting economic rationales in leading developed states, especially the United States. The result has been an increased international emphasis on globalization, with free trade as its most prominent shibboleth. In turn, the globalization phenomenon has been less than constant in its effects, helping to activate historically based and other objections. In the contemporary setting, all of these factors come together as the world economy attempts to rebound from the global economic recession that first emerged in 2008. In turn, that reaction helps define some of the parameters that surround the utility and limits on international economics as a tool of foreign policy.

INTERNATIONAL ECONOMICS IN THE AMERICAN EXPERIENCE

It has been a long and enduring part of the American foreign policy tradition to try to separate more general foreign policy—those interactions with foreign governments that are primarily political or military in nature—from economic relations with other states. This tradition goes back to the founding days of the American Republic. In his famous Farewell Address, George Washington sounded the theme when he applied his cardinal principle of nonentanglement (which he expressed as the desire for "no permanent alliances" with other countries) to the commercial realm. "The great rule of conduct for us in regard to foreign nations is in extending our commercial relations, to have with them as little political connection as possible," he said, adding, "Harmony, liberal intercourse with all nations, are recommended.... Even our commercial policy should hold an equal and impartial basis."

From the beginning, the myth emerged that the economic and political realm in foreign policy could be separated, and while it is a proposition that was and remains dubiously true, it has been enduring. The penultimate expression of this belief was expressed in American foreign policy during the period between the World Wars in the early twentieth century. "Splendid isolationism," as its champions described it, applied in the political realm, but it did not mean the United States would not and should not engage in commercial relations with all countries; indeed, one of the purposes of nonalignment and noninvolvement in

Europe's political affairs was to facilitate American commerce to all emerging sides in World War II.

World War II upset, but did not entirely displace or discredit, the notion that the economic and political realms of foreign policy are distinct, even independent, of one another. As the Allies, led by the United States and Great Britain, assayed the causes of the war and began trying to craft postwar policies and conditions to avoid its repetition, they could not avoid the realization that the Great Depression and the economic forces it unleashed had played a role in the downslide toward the bloodiest conflict in world history. As countries were swept into the maelstrom of depression, most inadvertently made matters worse by erecting stifling barriers to trade among them as a way to try to protect disappearing jobs, and in the process only accelerated the descent they were trying to reverse. No country in the world was harder hit by these dynamics than interwar Germany, and the enormous deprivations of the German people provided fallow ground in which Hitler and his supporters planted the seeds of Nazism. The economic element could not be avoided as part of the cause of war, and as a result, the post–World War II had to include provisions to reduce the likelihood that economic disturbances could once again grease the slippery slope to war in their calculations. The fruits of their deliberations, which are discussed in the next section, have helped to form the institutional framework within which international economic foreign policy is currently conducted.

As the Allied planners were negotiating their plans, the world, of course, plunged into a new conflict, the Cold War. The heart of that conflict was political and military, expressed in the contest of which political system, the authoritarian communists or the anticommunist democracies, would prevail on a global scale. At the same time, this competition had an economic distinction underlying it: the contest between the socialist economic models associated with communism and the free-market capitalism of the West. One of the decisive elements in the victory of the United States and its allies in the Cold War was that Western economics proved decisively more productive than the Soviet-encumbered socialist model.

Since the end of the Cold War, there has been no fundamental international economic division with a philosophical basis other than the minor challenges issued by places such as Castro's Cuba or Chavez's Venezuela. Essentially all economies are wedded to some form of the Western capitalist model as it evolved during the latter half of the twentieth century, and as influenced by the electronic, high-technology revolution that began in the 1970s and 1980s, and continues to evolve. The shibboleth of international economics has become globalization, and while there are disagreements about its applications in some situations—for instance, parts of the world in which its applications produce different and sometimes less positive results, and impacts on some groups within countries—no one seriously questions the overall principle as part of the foreign policy environment.

However, this does not mean that the economic environment is devoid of political content or disagreement. Foreign economic policy is, after all, *policy,* which means it involves choices between options that inevitably hold advantages for some and disadvantages for others. The result is that a debate remains about economic foreign policy, and two aspects of that debate are worth mentioning by way of introducing the more detailed discussion of the topic. Both significantly speak to the intermestic nature of the subject area.

The first of these is a disagreement over the extent of involvement in the international realm, and it has been expressed most fully in the debate over **protectionism** versus **free trade**. They are the extreme ends of the spectrum regarding the extent to which international commerce should be interfered with and regulated by governments. Protectionism, as the name implies, is the practice of placing barriers on the entry of goods and foreign services from abroad in the form of **tariffs**, quotas, or outright prohibitions on importation. The purpose of such barriers is to "protect" indigenous industries from outsiders who can produce similar goods and services at a lower cost (what is known as **comparative advantage**) and thus would sell at lower prices than indigenous products, thereby undercutting their sale. Tariffs, which are essentially taxes or levies on affected goods, raise the cost of otherwise cheaper foreign goods to higher prices than indigenous goods, thereby protecting them by making them cheaper to consumers. Protectionism is a practice historically associated with any country undergoing the development process whose "infant industries" (as less-efficient, new internal concerns are often called) cannot compete freely against foreign intruders. Much of the resistance to the Doha development process surrounds concerns that developing countries have over lowering trade barriers and exposing their products to competition in which they cannot compete successfully.

Free trade is the other end of the spectrum. In its purest form, free trade entails the removal of all nationally imposed barriers to trade, so that commerce can flow "freely" across state boundaries. Free trade is at the heart of globalization and argues that opening the international system to the greatest possible competition enhances overall global economic development and thus the greater good of everyone. As might be suspected, countries who are the most vociferous proponents of free trade are those who have a comparative advantage in the largest numbers of industries and are the most enthusiastic supporters of the Doha process.

The other debate surrounds the differential impact that economic decisions have on individuals and societies and can be expressed in terms of **micro-** versus **macro level effects**. The basic distinction is easy to state: Micro level effects are the direct consequences of economic actions on the lowest levels of economic analysis, ultimately on individual people. Macro level effects refer to the overall systemic effects that particular economic actions have; in the current debate, this distinction is usually reserved for the impacts on national economies, or even on the entire international economic system.

While in principle these two levels of effects are not necessarily incompatible and contradictory, in application they often are, particularly within national debates over appropriate policies defined along the continuum of policy involvement expressed in protectionist versus free-trade terms. To presage a later more detailed discussion, microlevel concerns and protectionism are more often associated with one another, because economic decisions that may affect overall national economies favorably can—and usually do—have adverse effects on particular individuals, who often seek protectionist responses to their individual fates. However, free-trade advocacy is more generally couched and defended in macroeconomic terms suggesting, for instance, that opening the economy will cause greater efficiencies and thus higher productivity for the society as a whole and thus eventually for individuals. Support for and justification of policy in terms of either pair of determinations has ebbed and flowed in the American policy debate.

The debate begins with the immediate post–World War II period, in which the major victorious allies laid out their blueprint for a new economic order, known as the **Bretton Woods** process, that would discourage or make impossible a reprise of the conditions that had contributed to the spiral to that war. That process produced a series of international organizational responses to define international economic interchanges. It was originally premised on the continuing global dominance of the U.S. economy, and when that economy faltered relatively compared with other world economies, the result was a transitional period of almost two decades spanning the 1970s and 1980s, which in turn laid the foundation for the international system of globalization.

The Road to Bretton Woods

As wartime leaders assayed what had led to the descent into World War II, one factor they identified as underlying that process was the international economic system and, more specifically, economic protectionism as it had exploded during the 1930s, driving countries further apart and thereby inflaming hatreds both within and across national boundaries. That conclusion led to the determination to re-create the mechanisms of that economic system in ways that would prevent a replay of those conditions and dynamics after the war.

The root cause of the problem was the impact of the Great Depression. As the stock market crash of 1929 spread around the world, and especially in Europe and North America, one of its most obvious manifestations was spreading and increasing unemployment. In order to soften the political blows that accompanied unemployment rates that climbed to one-quarter of the workforce in some countries and industries, governments responded by attempting to protect national jobs. They did so by shielding industries from outside competition, raising tariffs and other barriers to imports from the outside to save indigenous jobs. These actions, in turn, cost more jobs in the countries whose products had traditionally been sold in the countries that now excluded those goods, and in retaliation, similar restrictions were placed on the countries imposing barriers on them. These actions and counteractions did not improve the job situation anywhere, but instead created increased economic isolation and animosities.

The ensuing angry mood helped fuel the political momentum toward war. Countries blamed one another for their economic miseries, a form of scapegoating to try to assuage their internal populations from the grim realities in which they found themselves. Of all the European countries, conditions were worst in Germany, whose economy had already been weakened by having to pay large reparations as punishment for "starting" World War I, and those burdens made the impacts of the depression even worse for the proud Germans. In the atmosphere of despair and recrimination that surrounded the fledgling Weimar Republic, radical voices arose in the political dialogue, blaming weakness on the part of elected leaders for the misery all were experiencing and promising to solve those problems. Among the most vocal of the leaders was Adolf Hitler. His xenophobic message had been decisively rejected in a more prosperous Germany in the 1920s but resonated in the desperation of the early 1930s. In January 1933, Hitler became chancellor of Germany through normal, open political election.

Many planners entrusted to reconstruct the postwar order viewed these interwar, Depression-created dynamics as critical to allowing the most destructive war in human history to occur, and thus those dynamics were high on the list of conditions to be reformed. They were particularly struck by three characteristics of the prewar situation. One was the absolute chaos that prevailed during this period: The League of Nations, the political predecessor of the United Nations, was unable or unwilling to arrest the political deterioration of international affairs, even after hostile, expansionist regimes began the process of aggression and violence. This chaos was reflected in the economic realm as well. The second and related characteristic was that no institutional framework was available to deal with and ameliorate deteriorating economic conditions within and between the principal states of the world. There were neither effective mechanisms to aid individual states when their economies began to unravel (e.g., bank failures), nor were there international means available to check the erection of national barriers to commerce that were stifling international trade. This led to the third characteristic, which was to blame protectionism for the economic causation of the war and to vow that a reconstructed international order would be founded on some other, firmer foundation.

The United States played a special role in the process. The Americans were arguably among those most responsible for the processes that caused the trouble in the first place. The Wall Street Crash of October 1929 was the signal event of the Great Depression in a United States that was, on the eve of the crash, the largest economic power in the world, and its effects quickly spread to Europe and helped create and fuel the downslide there. At the same time, America withdrew from international politics after World War I into a period of isolationism, during which the country deluded itself into thinking it could remain active in world commerce but aloof from the international politics that was the environment for that commercial activity. The United States turned even further inward as the Depression gripped Europe, adding to the atmosphere of isolation.

By becoming the "arsenal of democracy," the war pulled the U.S. economy out of the Depression. As a result, the United States was virtually the only country in the world to escape the war with a strong, vibrant economy. Only the Americans possessed the economic wherewithal—the American dollar and American products—to underwrite postwar recovery and the construction of a new international economic order. Under these circumstances, the world had little choice but to accept American leadership in reconstructing the economic order.

The planning for the postwar economic system began during World War II itself, largely through the joint efforts of Americans and Britons (as well as the French). These efforts had two basic tracks. One was political and security oriented, and the result was the drafting of a United Nations charter that was adopted in 1945 in San Francisco and formed the basis of the UN system. The other planning track was economic, and the role of the United States was parallel to its role in the reconstruction of the international political order. For the same kind of symbolic reason that underlay holding the much higher-profile talks to draft the UN charter in California, the United States hosted the first conference to discuss the postwar economic order at the small New Hampshire resort town of Bretton Woods, at the foot of Mt. Washington in July 1944, to begin to institutionalize the process. The meeting was formally known as the International Monetary Conference, and forty-four countries sent representatives. However, that meeting is remembered more succinctly as Bretton Woods, and its outcome created the Bretton Woods institutions.

The Bretton Woods Institutions

The setting of Bretton Woods was symbolic on several levels. Held when the outcome of the war was still in doubt, the meeting indicated the resolve and optimism of the participants. The location of the meeting at the picturesque Hotel Washington isolated the participants from the public glare that holding the three-week meeting in a more visible location might cause, and the location at a town served only by a single road meant that the participants would not be distracted by outside influences.

The conferees began their deliberations by agreeing that interwar protectionism had contributed significantly to the war and thus had to be attacked if economic stability were to be reinstated and stabilized. Specifically, they were concerned about international financial and economic practices leading up to the war: large fluctuations in the exchange rates of currencies (largely the result of inflationary volatility), chronic balance-of-payments problems experienced by some countries, and the high tariffs that had come to dominate the 1930s. All of these conditions restricted the flow of international commerce, and there was a clearly understood underlying belief that moving toward a system of considerably freer trade was a desirable postwar goal. The conference produced agreements that would lead to the creation of two institutions in the latter 1940s to help underpin economic revitalization and the proposal for a third institution which, for largely political reasons, would have its implementation deferred for nearly half of a century.

Two international organizations were created to address different aspects of the prewar problems from which they sought to insulate the future. The first of these was the **International Monetary Fund (IMF)**. The original purpose of the IMF was to deal with currency stabilization and balance-of-payments difficulties that had exacerbated relations between countries during the 1930s. It would do so by authorizing what amounted to lines of credit to countries suffering difficulties in this area. Countries seeking IMF relief were subject to investigation and criticism of national practices that had created their problems and to promises to rectify poor practices as a condition of IMF help. This function continues to be an important part of IMF activity in the contemporary environment: What is effectively the IMF "seal of approval" of the soundness of economic practices has become a virtual sine qua non for getting private foreign investment in developing countries.

The other organization created at Bretton Woods was the **International Bank for Reconstruction and Development (IBRD or World Bank).** The World Bank was established as a source of lending to countries, with its capital based on subscriptions (deposits) made by its various member states. The first priority of the IBRD's existence was to provide financing to help the war-torn countries of Europe and Asia recover from the war's effects by reconstructing assets destroyed during the war. In the 1950s, the emphasis shifted to the second charge, development, providing monetary resources to aid in the development of the less-developed countries. This latter mission remains the vital center of the World Bank's activity.

The IMF and IBRD were both created without major international or domestic controversy. Because the United States was the only major country in the world with a fully functioning, vibrant economy, American participation was a sine qua non for the prosperity of each organization, and this was assured by locating the headquarters of the two economic institutions in adjacent buildings in downtown Washington, D.C., only blocks away from the White House. To assuage potential American opposition to the involvement in these ongoing international obligations, the United States was also given a premier position in each organization. Voting, for instance, was allocated proportionately based on the percentage of initial contributions to each organization. In the case of the IBRD, for instance, the United States provided approximately one-third of the initial capital to the organization, and in return was given roughly one-third of the votes, a condition that continues. At the same time, it was agreed that the president of the Bank would always be an American, and a series of Americans from either the American private or public sectors has always been the chief executive officer of the IBRD. The president of the IMF, by a similar convention, is always European.

The conferees also attempted to attack what they saw as the third element of international economic activity in need of reform, international commerce or trade. This effort, however, was unsuccessful. The new Truman administration that emerged after the death of President Franklin D. Roosevelt in April 1945 enthusiastically supported the formation of an international organization devoted to the promotion of trade parallel to the IMF and IBRD, but its advocacy and enthusiasm were thwarted by political opposition, mostly within the United

States itself—which is instructive as an example of the impact of domestic politics on international affairs generally and the debate over free trade more specifically.

The goal of the Truman administration was to reduce barriers to trade across the board, and it had both a domestic political and an international component. The domestic thrust was to pursue bilateral and multilateral reductions in tariffs and quotas (numerical limitations on how much of a good or service can be imported). The mechanism for doing so was already in place under the provisions of the 1934 Reciprocal Trade Agreements Act (RTAA), a trade liberalization action passed in reaction to the highly protectionist Smoot-Hawley Tariff Act of 1930 and as a hoped-for stimulus to American business by increasing the export of American goods and services into foreign markets. The RTAA itself authorized the administration to reduce barriers on specific items by up to 50 percent with other countries, but only if those restrictions were reciprocal. It did not authorize the elimination of any trade barriers and thus was only a modest first step in the process, and its limiting requirement left it largely ineffective as other countries raced to raise barriers to trade during the 1930s. However, the bill did form the precursor to the so-called "fast-track" approaches to trade (what the Bush administration called "trade promotion authority"). Fast-track items could not be amended by Congress, whose options were either total approval or disapproval. Fearful that the fast-track provisions gave the president too much authority to push for freeing trade, Congress suspended these provisions during the Clinton administration, and then reinstated them under George W. Bush. This authority was limited by a Congressional requirement for periodic renewal and lapsed in 2007. There has been no serious movement to reinstate it.

The international thrust came in the form of the proposal for a new international organization parallel to the other Bretton Woods institutions, the **International Trade Organization** (ITO). The new ITO was to have two sequential purposes: to promote free trade among its member states, and to create an enforcement mechanism with the authority to investigate and punish those who violated trade agreements into which they had entered. Both of these emphases—promotion and enforcement—were controversial within the United States. Promoting free trade confronted the American tradition of isolationism and aloofness from international affairs, and enforcement appeared to threaten the sovereign authority of the United States over its own affairs, historically a volatile principle. Overcoming objections on either count was no simple matter, and surmounting them both proved impossible.

Rejection came in steps. A preliminary meeting formally proposing the ITO was held in Geneva, Switzerland, in early 1947 to lay out the basic underlying principles of trade that would be incorporated in the charter of the new ITO. These principles were called the **General Agreement on Tariffs and Trade** (GATT) and spoke to the first purpose, the promotion of free trade, but not to the second goal of providing an enforcement mechanism to guarantee that countries lived up to their obligations. At the time, the GATT was conceived of as a temporary framework that would evaporate

INTERSECTIONS

Shifting Opponents to Free Trade

Free trade is not a universally embraced idea, as suggested by this protest outside a meeting of the World Trade Organization.

While opposition to free-trade arrangements has echoed familiar themes across time, the American groups who have voiced opposition or support have changed. Support for free trade has always had its strongest institutional support within the executive branch of government and its strongest opposition in the Congress. This institutional difference reflects the different constituencies of the two branches of government. On the one hand, the executive branch, symbolized by the presidency, is inherently national in constituency and outlook and tends to view policy areas in macrolevel terms of what is "good for the country," and most of the arguments for free trade are macrolevel in emphasis. Members of Congress, on the other hand, represent narrower constituencies within their states or Congressional districts, and thus are more sensitive to microlevel influences, such as the deleterious impact a free-trade arrangement may have on uncompetitive industries in their districts that cannot compete with foreign corporations and whose exposure to those competitors costs constituents jobs.

Although the dynamics may be institutionally similar, the supporters and detractors have changed politically. In the 1940s, the opponents to the ITO tended to be Republicans who favored protectionism because their supporters, notably manufacturing and agricultural producers, had been traditional opponents of trade promotion on the grounds that it promoted greater entanglement in world affairs (isolationism) and because it exposed the American economy to potentially damaging competition (protectionism). Thus, big business elements formed the core of the

(Continued)

(Continued)

opposition, and proponents of the ITO were largely liberal Democrats, including trade unionists, who either believed in free trade on principle or felt it would benefit the American economy and thus promote American jobs. Opponents were joined by an odd coalition of very liberal Democrats who believed the ITO was making too timid an approach to free trade and conservative Republicans who opposed the international organization because it represented what they viewed as an assault on American sovereignty.

In the current debate (including the debate surrounding the formation of the WTO in 1995), this coalition had shifted. Political party roles had been reversed. Republicans, representing big business and more prone to viewing the macrolevel effects of trade liberalization on large American and multinational corporations, supported the free-trade initiative on the grounds that it would benefit the overall American economy (and thus Republican supporters, such as investors). The opposition was headed by Democrats, particularly those representing trade unionists in areas of production where the United States no longer held an obvious competitive advantage. Within the executive branch, there was the partial anomaly of a Democratic president, Bill Clinton, in seeming opposition to his party's position but viewing the matter from the macrolevel view of the executive branch.

The supporting cast remained largely the same as in the 1940s, but with a somewhat different focus in one instance. Very liberal Democrats again opposed the new organization, but their opposition came because of different deficiencies, such as the inadequacy of environmental requirements as part of guaranteeing that free trade occurs within fair boundaries—reflecting the same concern with the timidity of the proposal for a slightly different reason than in the 1940s. This group has also tended to argue that the interests of developing countries are underrepresented in the WTO, one of the concerns underlying the Doha Round. At the same time, the same concern of very conservative Republicans with the question of the infringement of sovereignty is again present in the opposition coalition. In the 1940s context, the opposition coalition defeated American acquiescence in the ITO; it would fail to defeat the WTO in 1995.

into the new Bretton Woods institution. When the ITO proposal ultimately failed, however, all that was left was the GATT, which endured as the core of international efforts in the area of trade promotion until the WTO came into force in 1995.

The ITO was formally proposed in Havana, Cuba, in November 1947. By the time the meeting was convened, domestic and foreign opposition to the principle of free trade had been organized sufficiently to dilute the outcome. These early "rejectionists" argued against both the domestic and international impacts of an ITO on a variety of grounds that are summarized in the *Intersections* box directly above. Domestically, it was argued, the impacts would include leaving uncompetitive industries and their workers at the mercy of foreign competition (a microlevel argument) and that the organization would compromise American sovereignty by allowing ITO bureaucrats to impose sanctions on American actions (a macrolevel objection). The British argued that the arrangement would damage special relationships it had with members of the British Imperial Preference System (an arrangement that created special trading privileges between Great Britain and members of the British Commonwealth). In an explicit break from the precedent set with the other two Bretton Woods institutions, the ITO proposal also rejected the principle of weighted voting by which the United States gained disproportionate influence in the IMF and IBRD: Within the ITO, the voting principle would be one state, one vote.

Although the Havana conference produced a draft charter for the ITO, it was doomed because the United States, one of its most enthusiastic early supporters, became instead the primary barrier to its implementation. Given the international economic climate of the time, any economic initiative that was not supported by the United States was stillborn, and the ITO Charter was dead on arrival in the United States.

American politics, geopolitics, and the globalizing impact of the ITO clashed, and the ITO was the victim. President Truman refused to submit the ITO Charter to the Senate in 1948 because it was an election year. Considered the underdog in the race for an elected term in office (as vice president, he became president in 1945 after Roosevelt's death) after sixteen years of Democratic control of the White House, Truman feared that promotion of the treaty would make free trade a divisive issue that might cost him crucial votes in what was projected to be a very close election. In 1949, geopolitics entered the picture. In that year, there were two major treaty initiatives that could be sent to the Senate for its advice and consent: the ITO Charter and the North Atlantic Treaty, the purpose of which was to create the first peacetime military alliance in U.S. history, the North Atlantic Treaty Organization (NATO). The looming Cold War made the North Atlantic Treaty seem the primary priority for the United States; reasoning that he could gain Senate concurrence on one but probably not both treaties, Truman chose to submit NATO instead. In April 1950, the president finally did send the ITO Charter to the Hill for ratification, but before the Senate acted on it, North Korea invaded South Korea, and the ITO was swamped by the Korean War. In November 1950, Truman withdrew the ITO Charter from Senatorial consideration. Formalized free trade went into abeyance.

What was left in the wreckage of the ITO was that supposedly temporary interim device, the GATT. Protectionists did not like this agreement much more than they did the ITO, since it remained a forum for the promotion of the principle of free trade, which they opposed. Other opposition, however, was not so great, because of the nature of the GATT as opposed to the ITO.

The great advantage of the GATT for those less than enthused with free trade was that the GATT was not a formal organization like the ITO. Rather, the GATT had two advantages that made it less unpalatable to other opponents of free trade. The first was that the GATT was a series of negotiating sessions (known as rounds) between sovereign states, where individual states were free to propose, accept, or reject all outcomes of the process if they so desired. Thus, it was less of a threat to those concerned with the dilution of sovereignty that membership in the ITO might entail. Second, since the GATT was not a formal organization, it did not have a large permanent staff or the mandate to engage in investigation and prosecution of violators of proposals passed in various GATT rounds. Thus states were only bound by what they specifically agreed to, and no entity could bring them to "justice" for noncompliance with the norms.

These institutional weaknesses displeased proponents of free trade, but they were the best they could do under the circumstances of a Cold War environment where much more attention was focused on security concerns than on economic promotion. The movement toward realizing the third pillar of the Bretton Woods trilogy of concerns remained submerged within a series of GATT rounds until 1993, when the Uruguay Round (GATT negotiating sessions were generally named after the country in which the particular set of discussions—or rounds—began) produced a proposal for a World Trade Organization (WTO). The WTO contained the same basic thrusts as the ITO—trade promotion *and* mechanisms to enforce trade agreements—that had undermined the ITO, but conditions were sufficiently different by the 1990s so that when President Clinton submitted the WTO statute for ratification, he succeeded, and the WTO, with American membership, came into being in 1995.

THE CHANGING INTERNATIONAL ECONOMY AND THE BRETTON WOODS SYSTEM

The postwar international economic system and the dominance of its most visible structures, the Bretton Woods institutions, have undergone a two-step evolution that reflects the changing position of its most dominant member, the United States. To understand how that system has evolved to its present condition, it is necessary to view these two periods, the decline of Bretton Woods and the transitional period.

The Decline of Bretton Woods

The institutions and system created at Bretton Woods dominated international economics for over two decades. During this period, the United States was the bedrock of this arrangement, holding sway over international economic activity and development because the United States was the dominant economic force in the world. Because other countries desperately needed American goods and resources, the U.S. dollar was the only **hard currency** in the world (the only currency universally accepted in international trade).

Since world commerce depended on the dollar as its primary lifeblood, the United States had enormous, usable economic power. These factors reinforced American preeminence and gave the United States an immense amount of influence in and control over how the international economic system evolved and America's role in it.

Since the strength of the Bretton Woods system—and American support for it—was predicated on the continued preeminence of the American economic system and its currency, the system, and American unconditional support for it, was bound to founder somewhat as the position of the United States in world economics changed. This change occurred in terms of the relative position of the United States atop the international economic pyramid, and as a consequence, when that position inevitably eroded, so too did some level of American enchantment with the system.

In the late 1940s, the American economy was producing two-fifths of all the goods and services in the world, a testimony to both the vibrancy of the American productive system and the paucity of competitors to American output. This was, of course, an artificially high proportion, and one that was bound to shrink as other countries recovered from the war and reasserted themselves. However, conscious American policy contributed substantially to stimulating challenges to American dominance.

The stimulus for this American action was the Cold War. Faced with the geopolitical Soviet menace, American policy during the 1940s was to assist in the recovery of European and Japanese economies through assistance programs such as the Marshall Plan. The motivation was largely geopolitical: to increase the stability of these countries as continuing bastions against communist encroachment. The initiatives worked, arguably too well. Pumped up by the infusion of American dollars, the economies of the Western European states (further stimulated after 1957 by the creation of the European Common Market, now the European Union or EU) and Japan did recover, as the United States intended that they should. In the process, however, the United States had to concede some of the loftiness of its world position. By the beginning of the 1970s, the share of global gross national product of the United States shrank to about 20 percent. In 2011 it is about 17 percent. The effect, however, was to change the dynamic of the American place in the international economic order. The United States did not cede its position as the world's most powerful economy; it instead became a first among relative equals.

The dominance of the U.S. dollar reflected this change. Because goods and services purchased in international trade are usually made in the currency of the producing country, the rise of economic productivity elsewhere also meant a demand for products from those countries and a demand for currencies other than the dollar with which to make those purchases. The U.S. dollar remained acceptable universally, but international dealings could now also be conducted using, for instance, the German *mark* or the Japanese *yen*. In other words, more currencies became "hard," at least for some purposes, leading to a reassessment of the dollar.

The value of the dollar was also based on its convertibility. What this meant was that the dollar was based on the gold standard, which meant the U.S. government guaranteed its value in gold. Theoretically, every dollar in circulation was backed by gold, with one ounce of gold valued at $35. At least in theory, this meant that anyone with $35 could exchange that amount for an ounce of gold, thereby establishing a permanent, concrete base for the American currency. This basis was always something of a fiction (the United States never possessed enough gold to redeem more than a small percentage of the dollars in gold had there been such a demand), but the guarantee was a useful fiction that created an aura of confidence around the value of the dollar that helped stabilize the entire global financial system.

Several domestic political events and trends in the 1960s in the United States helped undermine continuing adherence to the gold standard. In the mid-1960s, President Lyndon B. Johnson made the fateful decision (with Congressional acquiescence) simultaneously to finance the Vietnam War and the complex of entitlement programs known collectively as the Great Society without raising taxes to pay for them (a harbinger of sorts for the contemporary environment). The result was the first sizable budgetary deficits and the first consequent accumulation of national debt since World War II. Among the associated effects was a decline in confidence in the American economy, accompanied by rising domestic inflation and competition from foreign goods and services. These factors were interactive—inflation made American goods more expensive and thus less competitive with foreign equivalents—and called into question American global dominance for the first time.

These trends coalesced in 1971, when it became apparent to decision makers in the Nixon administration that continued adherence to the gold standard was an increasingly unsustainable millstone around the neck of the American economy. The inflationary spiral of the 1960s had resulted in such a flood of dollars into circulation at home and abroad that the fiction of redemption of dollars for gold was becoming increasingly hollow. Moreover, pegging the value of the dollar to gold resulted in overvaluation of the dollar against other currencies, making it more difficult for American producers to compete with their foreign counterparts (it took many units of a foreign currency to buy enough American dollars to purchase U.S. goods compared with the amount of the currency necessary to buy goods from other countries).

Faced with a growing economic crisis, the U.S. government renounced the gold standard in 1971. Rather than guaranteeing to redeem dollars with gold, the dollar's value would be allowed to "float," its value determined by market calculations of how much it was worth measured in terms of other currencies instead of pegging its value to precious metal. The dollar would become a commodity like any other commodity, and it would be worth whatever those desiring it were willing to pay. In the process, monetary units became a trading commodity like grains or petroleum, and the dollar had to compete in global terms. Instead of being the aloof arbiter of international economic dealings, the United States was "reduced" to being another, if the biggest and most prominent, player in international economics.

The Transition Period

American renunciation of the gold standard set in motion a two-decade period of change in the international economic system and the American role in it. During the 1970s, the United States seemed to enter a period of decline and lack of self-confidence with both political and economic causes and consequences. Because of other influences, this condition changed in the 1980s, as economically driven events and policies produced a renaissance that helped create the underpinning for the current economic system of globalization.

Decline The 1970s was a difficult political and economic period for the United States. Internal political difficulties within the country centered on two events, each of which served to undermine American confidence and support for the political system. In the international realm, the eight-year American involvement in the Vietnam War ended inconclusively with the removal of the last American combat troops in 1973, and was punctuated in 1975 as Saigon fell to the communist North Vietnamese. Domestically, the reelection of Richard M. Nixon in 1972 was quickly followed by revelations that his campaign had engineered a break-in of the Democratic Party headquarters in the Watergate complex in Washington, which ended with Nixon's resignation from office in 1975. The cumulative result of these events was a loss of confidence in and support for government that has arguably never completely disappeared.

Economic signs of decreasing dominance were amplified and economic turbulence assured by the oil shocks of 1973 and 1977. Led by its Middle Eastern members, the Organization of Petroleum Exporting Countries (OPEC) took a series of joint actions that greatly raised the cost of oil to consuming countries and in the process changed the nature and quality of international commerce. Because most developed countries were highly dependent on oil as an energy source, the result was an increasing level of international competition to gain funds to pay for oil, as all consuming countries ran up a large balance-of-trade deficits with the oil producers that would have to be compensated by balance-of-trade surpluses with other parts of the world. This competition, in turn, contributed to and even accelerated the erosion of American competitiveness and fueled the appearance of American decline in the world. Decline became the operating noun to describe the American position in the world, and the question in the minds of many Americans was not whether the country was in decline but how pervasive and permanent that decline was.

The evidence of American decline seemed to cut across the board. American industries appeared to have become soft, no longer innovative and competitive with European and Japanese rivals. The automobile industry was an often-cited example. American industries were losing market share across a wide variety of products from consumer electronics to heavy machinery and hospital equipment. Some dark projections hinted that this condition might worsen to the point that the United States would fall into second-class status.

Revival Driven by advances in technology and changing policies and attitudes within the business and policy communities, this decline was arrested and reversed in the 1980s. It was a quiet, virtually subterranean revolution driven by small entrepreneurs and scientists and reform-minded government officials. The entrepreneurs were heavily involved in the so-called **high-technology** revolution, a phenomenon that featured great advances in electronic capabilities manifested primarily in information-producing technologies associated with computing and communications. The most visible outcome of this process has been the information revolution signified by the Internet and its various, rapidly evolving permutations. Because American entrepreneurs and academic and research institutions were the worldwide leaders in this rapidly developing phenomenon, they helped restore confidence in and leadership by the United States as the economic leader of the world.

The policy arena of the 1980s was heavily influenced by the efforts of Republican President Ronald W. Reagan and Conservative British Prime Minister Margaret Thatcher, whose shared economic philosophy led to changes in how government and the economic sphere operated together. Both advocated a reduced role for government in the economic sector and what they viewed as a much more pure form of economic capitalism. Aspects of the Reagan program were controversial (he pushed through the Congress a significant series of tax cuts that, like those of George W. Bush in the early 2000s, raised government deficit spending significantly, for instance). His legacy is best remembered by his exhortation to "get government off the people's back" as implemented under two principles that, when wedded to the Ricardian principle of comparative advantage during the 1990s, formed much of the base for the current globalizing economy.

The two major shibboleths to the Reagan–Thatcher view of the relationship between government and the economy were aimed at reducing the government's role. The first of these was **privatization**, the process of getting government out of operating businesses and turning over previously government-operated business functions to private hands. The idea was that privatization would result in greater efficiency and thus greater value for consumers and greater profits for the businesses themselves. In the United States, the breakup of government-controlled monopolies such as long-distance telephone services was a prime example of privatization in action.

The second shibboleth was **deregulation**, reducing or eliminating the extent to which governments regulated the activities of private-sector enterprises. The idea here was that government regulations placed often undue and unwise restrictions on what private enterprises could do, thereby stultifying the ability of the private sector to be innovative and thus competitive in both domestic and international markets. The result of removing strictures, the argument went, would allow more efficient operation of enterprises and thus improve their profitability and competitiveness. A major positive example of this phenomenon often cited is the deregulation of the airlines; a more dubious example was the deregulation of the banking industry during the 1990s and early 2000s, for which much of the economic crisis of 2008 has been blamed.

THE GLOBALIZING ECONOMY

The cardinal guiding value of the international economic system since the early 1990s has been globalization, a blanket concept that encompasses the growing together of world economies into what is emerging as at least the outline of a truly global, overarching set of economic relations. It is a revolution that has both domestic and international roots and manifestations that derive from the American experience as the American economy revived in the 1980s. The Reagan–Thatcher model, for instance, suggested a view of how domestic economies should organize their relationships with government to produce the optimal economic results, and this model became known as the **Washington consensus**, by which the United States has sought to persuade or cajole other countries to emulate as a kind of admissions fee for joining the greater world prosperity represented by the globalizing economy. With downturns and embarrassments such as the economic crashes of 1998 and 2008, some of the burnish has worn off this "pure" model, but it nonetheless remains a basic building block for conceptualizing the international system. Since the model is quintessentially American, it has also been the vehicle for reasserting American dominance and influence despite signs of weakness and erosion in the American system.

The Reagan–Thatcher "revolution," as its more enthusiastic supporters like to describe it, formed the basis of the developing globalization system but not its entirety. The less-regulated capitalist system that became the model of the 1980s applied in its purest form to the organization of economies *within* countries and principally provided guidance about how to make those economies more efficient and competitive by removing physical and psychological barriers to free-enterprise ventures. This model became the new "gold standard" for making a country's economic system competitive in the globalizing system as it has evolved in the 1990s and 2000s, and emulation of the Reagan–Thatcher–based reforms has become both a major component in the economic policies the United States has exported and a major criterion by which private investors judge the worthiness of different countries for foreign direct investment (FDI).

As such, the model has become a cornerstone of American economic foreign policy, but one that is not universally embraced or necessarily appreciated. American advocates extol the economic virtues of this system in programs of developmental assistance through the U.S. Department of Commerce and elsewhere. From an economic viewpoint, the requirements that accompany the advocacy may make sense, but they often come into conflict with cultural and political barriers that make them less than acceptable in some places. Culturally, the adoption of Western-based capitalism contains, for instance, an implicit embrace of secular society, which is objectionable in some parts of the world. Politically, one of the universal requirements is economic austerity programs that are painful (generally because they require politically difficult enforced savings that require deferred spending and thus the postponement of improvements in living conditions) and often appear hypocritical when imposed by a United States notably reluctant to apply the same kinds of standards to itself (e.g., a frequent item on the agenda is putting policies in place that will result in balanced governmental budgets). Moreover, there are countries that are not developmentally far enough along to perceive that they will benefit from these kinds of policies, a problem underlying the difficulties of forging a successful Doha process.

Within the current debate, particularly in the United States, one element of the model that was created in the 1980s and to some extent refined in the 1990s should be mentioned, because it is relevant to current concerns partially, but not exclusively, related to the American economy that forms the base of American participation in global economics. While the Reagan–Thatcher model called for a reduction in government participation in the economy, it did not argue for the complete absence of a government role. National governments were useful in creating favorable policy environments for economic growth. One way this contribution could occur was in supporting areas the private sector was uninterested in or unequipped to fill, such as social security for longtime employees. At the same time, the promotion of balanced budgets (a notable failing during the 1980s) was favored because they meant the government placed less demand on resources that might otherwise be available for investors. Moreover, the regulation of questionable practices that might lead to economic turmoil was a residual responsibility left to government. In other words, the responsible Reagan–Thatcher apostles did not support what has subsequently become known as, among other things, "cowboy capitalism."

While the contribution of the 1980s was to create a model for national economic activity that could result in a world of increasingly strong economies, in and of itself it was not enough to create the globalizing economy and what Friedman calls the "system of globalization." To do this, two additional steps were necessary prerequisites. The first was the physical ability to integrate world economies, a possibility enabled by the high-technology revolution. The second was the philosophical adoption of the standard of free trade. Both were products of the 1980s (and in some ways, before) that reached maturity during the 1990s and continue into the present period.

The Impact of High Technology

The ubiquity of the high-technology revolution is, from the vantage point of the early 2010s, so obvious as not to appear to require mention, but its pervasiveness is in fact a very recent occurrence. The Internet itself, for instance, was the result of computer science research in the 1970s and 1980s (initially as a means to allow defense-related scientists at American universities to communicate their research findings and data to one another), and its application as a universal means of communication was first explored in the 1980s and initially applied in the 1990s. Its effects are, as noted throughout the text in various contexts, enormous and affect nearly all aspects of daily life. Its contributions to enabling the possibility of a universal global economy—the ultimate expression of globalization—can be summarized in terms of two basic effects.

The first of these has been the acceleration of scientific research, largely the product of advances in computing that allow the more rapid analysis of information and thus basic scientific knowledge. The half-life of knowledge has been steadily compressing as a result, and new discoveries are being made at what is historically a dizzying pace. The same quantum increases in computer-generated knowledge are also applied to applications of that knowledge to more practical, commercial purposes.

The second and related area is the information revolution, which is both a cause and effect of the revolution in knowledge. The root of this phenomenon, born during the development of the Internet as a scientific tool, was the application of computing power to communications. Prior to the 1980s, the computer was thought of primarily as a way to facilitate the accumulation and analysis of information by speeding up its processing and analysis. The commissioning of the Internet to facilitate the sharing of this computer-generated knowledge was followed by the realization that more information and knowledge than simply scientific data could be disseminated by computers, which in turn led to two aspects of the contemporary environment: global communication and global access to knowledge.

Global communication was a major enabling factor in creating and sustaining a globalizing world economy because it allowed producers across large distances to communicate with one another rapidly, thereby allowing the coordination and transmission of activities heretofore impossible. The implications of this capability are enormous and ubiquitous, but a couple of examples may serve to clarify them.

One outcome has been the further development of so-called **multinational corporations (MNCs)**. Before the computer age, the term *international corporations* generally referred to companies headquartered in one country but doing business (i.e., selling goods and services) in other countries. These companies were primarily national companies (companies owned, managed by, and producing goods in one country) with multinational activities, because the technology of the situation allowed little more. By contrast, the high-technology revolution has allowed the emergence of truly multinational corporations. Companies can now be owned by nationals in many countries, be managed by international teams with headquarters in various countries, and produce products or services with contributions of parts or ideas from sources in several different countries. What has enabled all this is telecommunications: Management can coordinate decisions, for instance, by global conference calls and can develop products that can be produced in different countries and shipped to other locations for assembly because far-flung sources can be effectively managed across space in real time by global communications technologies.

Another internationalizing example is the creation of global financial markets. Before the telecommunications revolution, investors were largely limited to the stock exchanges in their own countries because of limits in information availability and market access. For instance, opportunities for Americans to invest in Asian ventures were limited by the speed at which those opportunities and supporting evidence could be obtained, and often it could not be accessed in a timely manner. Moreover, access to markets in, say, Tokyo was restricted in time and technology. In 1990, the idea of being able to buy stock instantly in real time in Asian markets halfway around the world was inconceivable; today, it is a mouse click away.

The telecommunications revolution has also changed fundamentally the way knowledge is transferred and thus access to technology and its applications. While the private sector is generally reluctant to share technological innovations for proprietary reasons, the value of science is in broad sharing and dissemination of knowledge, and this means that anyone who has access to a computer can be the recipient of new knowledge that can be applied to technological applications or form the basis of further scientific applications. The result has been to enlarge greatly the global scientific and technological base to places and people who previously lacked access to such knowledge, and consequently there has been both an acceleration of the pace of knowledge production, absorption, and dissemination and the creation of alternative centers of science and technology. Possibly the primary example of this "flattening" of world access to information (to use Friedman's analogy in *The World Is Flat*) is the emergence of a competitive Indian economy centered around such places as Bangalore.

The Return of Free Trade

The technology revolution created a physical framework within which the world's economy could expand, but a conceptual basis was needed to organize thinking and policy making to realize it. The needed conceptual element was the renewed attention to the principle of free trade. In other words, the concept that had been the deferred aspect of the Bretton Woods discussions was revived, now with a different and more compelling physical setting that made its potential benefits more obvious and less objectionable.

The basic underpinning of free trade has been the application of the Ricardian principle of comparative advantage to the international level. The comparative advantage principle, as articulated by the economist David Ricardo in the late nineteenth century, is that within any economic unit, those who produce a good or service at the lowest possible cost with the greatest quality (or, in other words, those who have an advantage compared to others in producing the commodity) should be encouraged to produce enough of that good to meet the market demand, whereas those who produce that same commodity less efficiently should be discouraged from continuing to do so, and should pursue an area of production where they do possess or can develop comparative advantage. Theoretically, at least, the market's "unseen hand" will result in all producers making things and rendering services at the lowest possible cost with the highest quality to consumers, who will benefit as a result. Also theoretically, everyone can find an area in which they can achieve comparative advantage, so that no one is punished by applying the principle. Market integrity is guaranteed because there will likely be more than one producer of any commodity who can achieve rough comparative advantage, thereby avoiding monopoly creation and the distortions that a monopoly capitalist can exercise in the marketplace.

The beneficial operation of the theory of comparative advantage is not universally accepted, and two objections that become prominent in objections to globalization are often cited. One of these is market distortions, in which producers may seek to manipulate the marketplace to give an advantage to their own goods and undercut competitors. At the international level, national trade barriers that artificially place added costs onto imported goods, thus removing their natural comparative advantage, are an example that free trade seeks to surmount. Another objection is the assumption that all entities within the economic unit can in fact find something at which they have or can develop comparative advantage. In the contemporary international economic situation, for instance, a major problem that underlies the proceedings in the Doha Round is the fact that some developing countries cannot compete in any area, which means that the removal of barriers protecting their products and services in the domestic market would allow cheaper, better goods from the outside in, thereby undercutting their indigenous enterprises but leaving them no alternative pursuits at which they could compete effectively.

That said, the principle of comparative advantage applied at the international economic level is free trade. The world is the economic unit in which the principle is applied, and the removal of trade barriers allows goods and services with comparative advantage to flow freely across international borders from which the barriers to that movement have been removed. The effect is that the most efficient global producers will gain advantage, whereas less efficient producers will be put out of business and will have to adapt by establishing a market presence elsewhere, where they can gain advantage. In theory, the opportunities are diverse enough that all parties can find a niche in which they have the advantage, so that no countries or sectors within countries are excluded from the resulting prosperity. Given the size and scale of the adjustments that are involved in the world, this process is long and its interim steps and effects are problematical. If, however, the principle is sound, in the long run the result should be the maximum economic benefit to everyone. As might be expected, those countries that are already at a comparative advantage in the most areas are more enthusiastic about this process and are least deterred by what should, according to the principle, be temporary dislocations; whereas those countries with the least advantage are most reluctant to shed the forms of protection that allow their indigenous productive means to operate.

The promotion of free trade has been the official U.S. international economic policy for over two decades, the economic preference of the last four U.S. presidents (George H.W. Bush, Bill Clinton, George W. Bush, and Barack Obama). This policy has been a more or less prominently displayed and advocated part of American foreign policy more generally depending on various factors such as the condition of the world economy and thus international enthusiasm or tepidness on the subject and the American perception that economic promotion was central to achieving American foreign policy goals.

Whether loudly proclaimed as it was during most of the 1990s or not so loudly advocated as in the past several years, it remains central to American foreign economic policy.

IMPLEMENTING GLOBALIZATION AND FREE TRADE

The American commitment to the concept and implementation of an international economic system increasingly marked by free trade among the member countries is an idea that is accepted in principle by most elements within the political spectrum of the United States. As noted, the last four presidents of the United States have all extolled the idea of moving toward the goal of a world economic system based on this principle, and there is a noticeable absence of organized widespread opposition to this position, although groups that are particularly negatively affected by it still rally against the total idea. Oppositionists, as identified in the *Intersections* box earlier in the chapter, cover the range of reasons for opposition and find homes in each of the major parties. Environmentalists, for instance, find many of the international arrangements and institutions promoting free trade to be inadequate in terms of insisting on environmental concerns as part of creating a level playing field on which the international battle over comparative advantage is fought, and they are joined by trade unionists expressing similar concerns. Members of both groups tend to be Democrats. At the other extreme, some businessmen and other conservatives worry about the overreach of free-trade bureaucracies and their negative impingement on conditions of business and even limits on sovereignty, and these groups tend to be Republican. Anti–free traders do not, however, pose a major political threat to the pro-free-trade positions of either major political party in the United States.

What has limited the ability of recent administrations to promote particular aspects and manifestations of free trade, however, is the generally high level of partisanship within the American political system and the resultant distrust that it breeds. The clearest example of this problem has been the negative fate of so-called fast-track (or trade-promotion) authority for the president. The purposes of these provisions historically have been to give presidents more flexibility to deal with foreign economic matters and to reach timely accords that promote underlying ideas such as free trade. To do so, the fast-track provisions placed limits on the ability of Congress to meddle in and tinker with trade agreements reached by the administration, essentially saying that Congress had to accept or reject such agreements in total, abrogating the ability to amend and placing strictures on debates. The result was increased leverage for the executive branch and decreased power for Congress in this area of policy. When there was not enormous underlying institutional and interpersonal distrust and animosity between the president and Congress, this trade-off was acceptable. In an atmosphere of universal distrust and its partisan expressions, fast track was a victim, a power taken first from Clinton and later from Bush. Its reinstatement is problematic but unlikely as long as hyperpartisanship remains.

Despite these kinds of limits, the promotion of free trade remains central to the United States. The principal mechanism by which this goal is carried on is through the pursuit of universal or regionally based multilateral agreements such as the Doha Round of the WTO or the Central American Free Trade Agreement (CAFTA) or bilateral arrangements such as the recently completed free-trade treaties with Colombia, Panama, and South Korea. At the same time, residual philosophical differences still remain about the direction that policy should take, expressed in advocacy or opposition to all or part of the movement for free trade and founded on basic divisions about America's role in the world.

Free-Trade Mechanisms

Because international trade is conducted across sovereign borders by entities that include both governments and private enterprises, the development and institutionalization of the idea of free trade is a matter of international agreements between states that seek either to impose or remove barriers against trade between them. The movement toward the World Trade Organization begun conceptually at Bretton Woods is the most visible symbol of that institutionalization, but it is by no means the only intergovernmental effort in which the United States and other countries are engaged to alter the rules affecting goods and services flowing across national boundaries. Other efforts include regional multilateral arrangements of various levels of formality, as well as bilateral agreements. All have the common goal of facilitating free trade. Much of the American leadership in this area occurred during the 1990s, when globalization seemed an inexorable and overwhelmingly positive phenomenon, and the momentum has slowed since the turn of the millennium.

Despite continuing minority opposition to the concept, the United States has been and continues to be the prime proponent of the free-trade movement. As in many areas that involve the internationalization and regulation of activities, the United States has not always been an entirely constant and unwavering force. Because the creation of international regimes to regulate national behavior in any arena contains the possibility of sovereignty-infringing restriction, there is always some political reluctance to commit the country to a future in the affected area that is not entirely in American hands, even when Americans may have been crucial in opening the area for discussion. Early American enthusiasm followed by opposition and non-membership in the International Criminal Court (ICC) is one obvious case in point, and the movement toward free trade has encountered similar, but not as decisive, opposition as well.

The fate of the WTO is exemplary. As will be recalled, the Truman administration was one of the earliest champions of its predecessor, the ITO, but cooled in its enthusiasm for political reasons (the 1948 election and the rise of the Cold War) that caused the proposal to lie fallow for four and a half decades while the weaker but less politically threatening GATT served as the major forum for free-trade promotion. With the Cold War over and the United States reassuming a dominant role in the international economic system in the early 1990s, the United States was a major champion of the WTO, which came into formal existence with American leadership and membership in 1995.

The WTO is the current pinnacle of international organizational focus of the movement for free trade, but it is neither the penultimate step toward global free trade, nor is it the only formal manifestation of the movement. Although virtually all the world's most important countries are part of its 153 current members (Russia, with observer status, is the major exception), it still has not been able to incorporate parts of the least-developed world, which, as noted earlier, lack comparative advantage and fear being swamped by membership. The Doha Round is an attempt to find avenues to incorporate these states into the fold. At the same time, it has not achieved—nor is it likely to in the near or intermediate future—its penultimate goal of universal free trade.

In the absence of an overarching commitment to free trade, a number of narrower options have been pursued by the United States and others. These fall into two broad categories, regional and bilateral agreements. Of these, the regional solutions have been the more prominent, largely because their "reach" is greater.

Regional arrangements have been of two kinds. The first are formal intergovernmental agreements that include mechanisms both to promote and enforce free trade. By far the most extensive and intensive of these is the European Union (EU). Born as the European Common Market in 1957 with six member states, it has gradually expanded to include twenty-seven member states in Europe, the economies of which are virtually entirely integrated and among whom no economic barriers to trade exist. The EU as a unit is a major actor on the international economic scene and has served as a model toward which other regional arrangements can aspire but that none have come close to approximating. The United States is not a member.

Beneath the EU are a number of other formal arrangements. Those in which the United States is member include the North American Free Trade Agreement (NAFTA), which is essentially a trilateral agreement between the three major North American countries, the United States, Canada, and Mexico, which came into existence in 1994 for the purpose of removing barriers to trade among the three neighboring countries. Because the United States is by far the largest economy of the three, it has tended to dominate an effort that has occasionally been marred by controversies such as the movement of undocumented, illegal migrants across the Mexican-American border into the United States. At a somewhat lower level of priority are organizations such as the Central American Free Trade Agreement (CAFTA), an arrangement between the United States and several Central American and Caribbean states (currently El Salvador, Honduras, Nicaragua, Guatemala, the Dominican Republic, and Costa Rica) that has been implemented by the gradual ratification of the agreement by member states since 2006. The size and lack of diversity of the member economies limits the reach such an agreement can have.

Not all these efforts have succeeded, and some have not reached the status of full formal organizations. In 1994, for instance, the United States proposed a comprehensive free-trade agreement, the **Free Trade Area of the Americas**

(FTAA), among all the political democracies in the Western Hemisphere (all countries except Cuba), but despite periodic efforts, it has not been translated into a formal commitment, largely because many Latin American countries, and especially South American giants such as Brazil, have viewed it as an indirect way in which the "colossus of the north" could overtake and undermine their economies. Although the idea has not disappeared altogether, its website now describes its purpose more modestly as a "collaboration" to "ensure the prosperity, democracy, and free markets" of its thirty-four member states.

A more ambitious, and partially successful, attempt toward regional economic integration has been the Asia-Pacific Economic Cooperation (APEC), an effort begun in 1989 by the Australians and co-opted and championed by the Clinton administration in the 1990s through the president's personal attendance at its annual meetings. The APEC has as its basic vision the integration of the economies of the countries of the Pacific Rim through the removal of various barriers to trade among them. The twenty-one member states of the APEC are an impressive list that includes, in addition to the United States and its fellow NAFTA members, China, Japan, South Korea, Russia, Indonesia, Australia, New Zealand, and Thailand, as well as Chile and a number of smaller states. The original idea of APEC was to move toward complete free trade by 2011 among the members, but that goal has not been attained and may never be. In the meantime, the organization's website refers to it as a "forum" for promoting free trade among its diverse membership.

Short of multilateral involvements, the United States has also entered into a series of bilateral arrangements with other countries to reduce or remove barriers to trade with them. The list of countries included in such arrangements, as provided by the International Trade Administration of the U.S. Department of Commerce, includes Bahrain, Morocco, South Korea, Panama, Chile, Israel, Peru, Singapore, and Colombia. With the possible exception of the arrangement with South Korea, most of these agreements have more political and symbolic significance than economic benefits.

The institutionalization of free trade remains a work in progress. At the level of the WTO, it remains limited by the lack of universality of membership and the reluctance of all the members to embrace widespread reductions at the international level. Institutionalization has been more successful at the regional and bilateral levels such as NAFTA and especially the EU, but these arrangements lack universal reach and applicability. Part of the reason for this is the continuing reluctance of states to cede sovereign control over national commerce to international control, but part of it is also the result of continuing disagreement, certainly within the United States, over the desirability of free trade.

The Free-Trade Debate

Advocates of globalization and its handmaiden free trade like to use an analogy to justify their support: "A rising tide lifts all boats." The idea behind this representation is that free trade leads to the expansion of the global economy (the rising tide), and that as a result, all countries (all boats) benefit (are raised).

It is a very positive and appealing analogy, and it is true at one level, but it contains and implies its limiting factors. The counterargument to the analogy is that while free trade may, at one level of analysis, provide a positive impact, that effect is not uniform. Rather, its detractors assert, the rising tide "lifts some boats more than others" (not everyone is affected equally beneficially) and it "swamps" some other boats (not all individuals and entities benefit, and some are actually injured by the phenomenon). Thus, the analogy and the values that underlay it are more debatable than its admirers would admit.

The counteranalogy to the rising-boats analogy contains a hint at the objections. The notion that free trade or globalization raises all boats but some more than others is based on different perspectives and effects that the process creates. The basic analogy of raising *all* boats suggests a systemic or macro impact that appears to be true and the basis of arguments for greater free trade: Freeing trade stimulates economic growth in the economy *as a whole* where it is applied. The qualification that some boats are raised more than others, however, implies that the effects are differential: that within the overall (macro) units, some individuals and groups benefit more than others (a microlevel perspective). The negative impact is most obvious in sectors that do not enjoy comparative advantage and thus suffer from exposure to outside sources for whatever it is they produce, whereas the systemic effects are more indicative of the overall strength of an economic system that, on balance, benefits from free trade.

The counterargument also includes the objection of those whose countries do not benefit at all and derives from the analogy that some economies are "swamped" by globalization. Some countries are uncompetitive virtually across the board (which is why they are the subject of courtship in the Doha Round). These countries derive essentially no benefits while incurring penalties from inclusion in any free-trade arrangement, since their uncompetitive means of production are undercut by cheaper, better imports that destroy indigenous producers while offering the country no compensation, because they produce nothing at comparative advantage. Countries in this category, which Friedman refers to as the "turtles" (because they are too underdeveloped to adapt rapidly) are among the poorest countries in the world and are outside both the globalization process and thus the beneficial effects that the movement toward free trade provides. For these kinds of countries, to continue the analogy, the question is how to make them impervious to capsizing or swamping, which is a matter of improving their seaworthiness (building stronger boats through development).

Within the domestic political debate in the United States (and elsewhere), the debate about the advocacy of free trade tends to center on the question of differential impacts of free trade or globalization on different groups within society and the society as a whole. To examine this argument, it is useful to frame it in terms of a matrix that contains two different sets of concepts already introduced, with one element added to one of the concepts. The basic concepts are the levels of analysis at which the discussion is conducted and the underlying approaches to the free-trade/globalization question. It is depicted in Figure 11.1.

		Level of Analysis	
		Macro	Micro
	Free Trade		
Approach	Fair Trade		
	Protection		

FIGURE 11.1
Levels of Analysis and Approaches to Free Trade

The basic distinctions are by now clear. The macrolevel of analysis centers on the national or international level and the effects that globalization-spreading free trade has on those units of analysis. At the national level, this focuses on increases in measures of overall economic performance (e.g., gross domestic product, volume of trade), which have usually been positive whenever barrier-removing actions have been taken, and most support for free trade has been based at this level. At the international level, the focus is on overall worldwide (or at least affected systemwide) growth economically, and at positive political spin-offs, such as greater cooperation and friendship between the countries that participate in these schemes. Indeed, one of the important political arguments in favor of globalization is that it is likely to diminish the amount of international violence by reducing animosities and intertwining countries in webs of economic interdependence that make war between them difficult or even impossible. (The first step in European economic integration was to combine the coal and steel capabilities of France and Germany in such a way as to make it impossible for either to independently to produce the steel necessary to build war machines they could use against one another as they had in the past.)

The microlevel of analysis centers on the impacts that free trade has on individuals and groups within national economic units. Since the process emphasizes adjusting economies away from products and services in which they lack comparative advantage to areas where they do, inevitably in practice an adjustment must occur that will have a negative impact on those displaced—at least temporarily—and this is the level at which most objections are raised. Indeed, it is the question and process of how to deal with and make temporary and minimally painful the microlevel suffering that forms the most basic and difficult question of approaches to implementing globalization-generating change.

Approaches to free trade encompass two familiar concepts and one new concept: **fair trade**. The first two concepts have already been discussed and require minimal reiteration. A free-trade approach to international economic conditions begins with the premise that removing barriers to trade is economically efficient and beneficial in promoting economic growth and thus, particularly within a capitalist worldview, maximum profits. Within Western views of economics, the opposite view, protectionism, is also an answer to the question of maintaining national economic strength and thus profitability, but one that reaches an opposite conclusion about what nurtures that outcome: exposure of one's economy to competition with others or protection of the economy from that competition. The advocacy of one position or the other reflects, at least implicitly, an assessment of the comparative advantage that the overall economy or selected parts of it possess.

Advocates of one pure position or the other can center on the total economy or parts of it as the unit of analysis. It may be philosophically inconsistent to make a distinction between various parts of an economy regarding its adherence to the free-trade principle, but that does not mean it is not advocated or practiced in fact. The United States, for instance, generally favors free trade, but is selectively diligent about promoting the principle depending on what is being deregulated. The United States is especially committed to the removal of all restrictions on the flow of agricultural products across national boundaries, because American agribusiness is very efficient and generally has a comparative advantage over agricultural goods produced in other countries. As NAFTA demonstrated with regard to corn exports to Mexico, the results of removing barriers can be devastating to indigenous producers—notably Mexican peasant farmers undercut by American imports—that create a real conflict between the United States and other producers (this is a primary source of contention in the Doha Round). With pressure from domestic producers, however, the United States is far less enthusiastic about removing barriers on a variety of industrial and consumer goods on which the United States does not possess comparative advantage.

The fair-trade position (also sometimes called "freer" trade) sits between these two extremes. Fair traders tend to focus on the equity of free-trade arrangements, both for domestic interests and internationally. The concerns of the fair traders have often appeared to be obstructionist and even protectionist, but they also have within them the seeds of reconciliation of the two positions.

The fair-trade argument with regard to the removal of barriers to foreign sources of goods and services seeks to ensure that foreign producers operate under the same basic rules as do American producers, thus producing fairness or equity in the competition. One example of this insistence surrounds environmental standards in different countries, a source of general concern among opponents of free trade. The problem is that some foreign producers gain or enhance their comparative advantage over their American counterparts by adopting minimal environmental standards in their production practices, normally with the assent of their governments. In the United States, meeting environmental standards, notably cleaning up toxic waste by-products of production, is borne by the producers and entails additional costs that add to the price of goods produced.

By avoiding the imposition and costs of such cleanup, foreign producers can lower their production costs and thus the prices of their goods. The asymmetry of environmental requirements imbalances the terms of competition by making it cheaper for noncompliers to do business, in addition to creating ecological problems. The result is an advocacy for strict environmental requirements in free-trade arrangements. Other examples include requirements to honor proprietary intellectual property rights on patented ideas (e.g., pirating and selling books, movies, or music) and manipulation of currencies to create an artificially lower cost of indigenous goods offered in international trade. This latter charge is often made by the Americans against Chinese monetary policy regarding the value of the *renminbi*.

With regard to the domestic economy, fair traders often seek fairer treatment of victims of free-trade arrangements, especially industries whose lack of comparative advantage undermines them when free trade is institutionalized. The problem arises because, although the Ricardian principle suggests that when free trade is instituted the dispossessed will move to new areas where they can become competitive, it does not say much about *how* this adjustment occurs. The *laissez-faire* answer is that those dispossessed will have to fend for themselves and devise solutions to their own situations. This process can be unsuccessful, and even if ultimately successful, it is likely to be protracted, painful, and politically difficult. Fair traders insist that provisions be included in free-trade arrangements to anticipate and compensate those who will be losers in this process, through the provision of education and training programs for those whose jobs in uncompetitive industries are lost, the recruitment of alternative industries and jobs into affected areas, and the like. The impact of growing free trade on the labor-intensive textile industry in the Carolinas is often cited as a prime example of the devastating effects that free trade without assistance for those adversely affected can have.

The distinctions between these approaches gain additional meaning organized around the macro- and microlevels of analysis of the economy. Macroanalyses, as already noted, tend to concentrate on the overall systemic effects at the national level (or sometimes, sectors of the national economy), and it has become virtually a matter of economic dogma that free trade is the best way to promote overall economic growth (the tide that lifts all boats). As a result, macrolevel analyses tend to be pro-free trade and associated with those political units most concerned with the overall economy—in the federal structure, the executive branch of government. Microlevel analysis, however, hones in on the effects of free trade or protection on individual industries and ultimately on individual people, who may be affected favorably or unfavorably by such impacts. This analysis thus contains an element of criticism of free trade largely missing from macrolevel analyses and has, in the contemporary debate, been more associated with protectionism, although the criticisms are rarely put explicitly in those terms because they appear parochial.

The fair-trade position offers a compromise of sorts on the macro–micro dimension. Fair traders tend not to be hostile to free trade in general, accepting the overall logic of the free-trade argument. They are, however, more sensitive to the negative effects on particular sectors or industries, and seek inclusion of provisions in free-trade arrangements to soften or eliminate negative impacts. Their efforts can be focused either internationally (trying to ensure that foreign competitors compete "fairly") or domestically (trying to compensate adversely affected sectors and individuals), but they are concentrated more on the question of equity than are the free traders. Their promotion of what they sometimes call "freer" trade puts them at some philosophical odds with the pure free traders, who are more doctrinally committed to free trade as a pure capitalist market solution to international economics in which government intervention is undesirable and in opposition to compensatory efforts as adding costs to the terms of production.

INTERSECTIONS

Making Free Trade Fair in a Hyperpartisan World

The American debate over free trade has been overshadowed by the acrimonious hyperpartisan fight over the economic crisis and how to overcome it. However, the two subjects are intertwined, and when the current crisis subsides, the debate over free trade is likely to return with now-familiar alignments on one side or the other.

The free-trade, macro argument has become the haven of political conservatives who also seek to restrict the reach of government through smaller government (e.g., lower taxes and fewer federal programs). This "marriage" has both philosophical and practical aspects. Philosophically, free trade contains the underpinnings of unfettered (or minimally influenced) market capitalism with minimum government involvement. Practically, macro benefits go to large investors who prosper when overall economic health translates into manifestations such as a robust stock market from which those investors benefit and others benefit indirectly if at all.

The fair-trade argument is more clearly a Democratic position. While it accepts the proposition that greater trade is desirable, it also argues that benefits are differential and that those who are disadvantaged should have recourse and be compensated for their losses. Programs aimed at retraining workers, for instance, fall to government, because private enterprise will not provide them, expecting the "market" to make such adjustments. Moreover, Democrats are more inclined to push for international regulations in areas such as environmental standards to make trade fair.

Each group rejects the other's position. To conservatives, governmental activism to produce fairness is philosophically obnoxious as evidence of government intrusion. To liberals, unfettered free trade guarantees inequities and is equally unacceptable. Familiar partisan battle lines thus emerge over what is "free" and what is "fair."

CONCLUSIONS

The purpose of this chapter has been to create the context within which international economics acts as a factor in and subject of foreign policy. It began by tracing the roots of, debate about, and evolving structure of international economics from its origins in the reaction to the perceived economic causes of World War II. That debate resulted in the establishment of norms for international economic interaction and institutions to help guide that pattern of interplay, the Bretton Woods system. Although it took longer to incorporate, these ideas included the idea of free trade, which is now the most prominent characteristic and point of contention about international economics and thus to foreign economic policy.

As argued, the whole area of international economics, and particularly free trade, is classically intermestic in content, with both domestic and international ramifications. Indeed, international economic policy has much more direct domestic impact than almost any other area of foreign policy, since its impacts are ultimately felt by American consumers and workers, a relationship that is explored in the Applications section that follows.

The result is that international economic policy is more controversial than it might otherwise be. Moreover, since the end of the Cold War it has been a virtual mantra that in the international environment which has succeeded that confrontation, economics will play a larger role in the international arena than it has played heretofore. While the international obsession with terrorism has ensured that security and military concerns are not excluded from contemporary considerations, there is no question that the so-called "economic instrument of power" is now a more prominent part of foreign policy than it has been in the past. Within the parameters of the ongoing debate about the nature and future of the globalization system in which free trade is a central component, the discussion turns in Chapter Twelve to the applications of economic instruments in making and executing more general foreign policy.

WHERE DO WE GO FROM HERE?

There is broad general agreement within the American policy community about the overall virtue of globalization and free trade built on the assessment that, for the most part, the country and its citizens benefit from the economic interaction with other countries. There is little overtly protectionist sentiment in the debate, and such disagreement as does exist is over the specific impact of particular manifestations of globalization on specific groups or segments of the U.S. population, a concern related to the fair-trade position. One of the areas where this latter concern is particularly evident is in the unease that the United States has in its primarily economic foreign policy interaction with the People's Republic of China.

APPLICATION: THE U.S.–CHINA TRADING RELATIONSHIP

Between 1949, when the communists succeeded in the Chinese Civil War, and 1972, the United States and China treated one another officially as if the other did not exist. Following their clash during the Korean War in the early 1950s (in which Chinese "volunteers" officially unsanctioned by the government fought the Americans), the world's current first and third most populous countries had no formal relations whatsoever. The United States recognized the government of Taiwan (officially the Republic of China) as the legitimate government of both that island and the mainland, despite the reality that the People's Republic of China (PRC) governed and controlled the world's fourth largest landmass among sovereign states. The Chinese responded with equal disdain for the United States, and what little interaction occurred between them was vague saber rattling.

All that began to change in 1972, when President Richard Nixon visited China and established informal linkages with the PRC (a process begun a year earlier with an invitation by China for a U.S. table tennis team to visit to China in a gesture that become known as "ping-pong diplomacy"). President Jimmy Carter established full formal diplomatic relations with China in 1979, the same year that Chinese leader Deng Xiaoping opened the Chinese economy to private enterprise as part of his program of the "four modernizations." The Chinese economy has exploded since, currently ranked as the world's second largest (in terms of gross domestic product) and projected to overtake the size of the U.S. economy in upcoming years.

A major component in Chinese growth has been trade between the two former enemies, and particularly the emergence of China as a major source of consumer goods for the U.S. market. "Made in China" has become ubiquitous in American stores across a wide range of products. This trend has been generally accepted by Americans because these goods are normally less expensive than counterparts made in the United States, but they have also become controversial on at least two counts.

First, there is the question of whether the competitiveness of Chinese products is the result of comparative advantage or Chinese unfair economic practices. Most of the goods China creates for the U.S. market are comparatively labor-intensive, and because wages are much lower in China than they are in the United States, they gain advantage from that source. Critics contend that the Chinese government artificially keeps wages low to ensure their advantage, an unfair practice. Moreover, critics such as Donald Trump maintain that the Chinese artificially keep the value of their currency, the *renminbi*, lower than its true value, thereby increasing their advantage, and that if the Chinese currency were allowed to establish its true value, that value would rise, leaving Chinese goods more expensive because the *renminbi* to buy them would cost more. This issue is a classic free-trade–fair-trade issue with macro–micro implications. The overall U.S. economy (through its consumers) benefits from cheaper goods, but industries undercut by allegedly unfair Chinese practices are unfairly punished by the Chinese.

Second, the result of the flood of Chinese imports into the United States has been a huge and growing trade imbalance between the two countries. Simply put, Americans buy much more from China than vice versa, and the result is that China has accumulated great profits in American dollars, many of which it has reinvested in the United States in things such as U.S. Treasury bonds and other instruments by which the U.S. government borrows money. In fiscal year (FY) 2011, the U.S. government took in revenues (i.e., taxes) that only covered about 60 percent of its expenditures, and the other 40 percent was borrowed. China was the largest lender to the U.S. government, and it currently holds about $3 trillion in American currency.

This imbalance is troubling to many who argue that it gives the Chinese potential leverage over the U.S. government. What, critics argue, would the American government do if the Chinese either decided they would no longer fund U.S. obligations or demanded that the United States repay existing debts? Others say this is extremely unlikely, because doing so would so upset the American economy that all the accumulated dollar reserves and U.S. loan obligations would lose most of their value, thereby hurting the Chinese as much or more than the Americans. Clearly, this problem would not exist were it not for the lowering of trade barriers between the two countries that have allowed the Chinese to flood American markets.

In this case, the effects of free trade on the United States and Americans are ambivalent. At the level of foreign policy interactions, the United States probably treats China more deferentially than it might otherwise because we owe them so much money and, unless effective measures to reduce federal deficits are instituted, that dependence will continue. At the other end of the scale, the sudden absence of Chinese-made goods on American shelves would sharply reduce the availability and raise the price of many of the categories of items Americans routinely consume.

What do you think of this situation? As things now stand, most of us benefit from being able to buy cheaper clothes and other consumer goods from the Chinese, and reversing that situation would make it more expensive to exist, thereby lowering our standard of living somewhat. At the same time, every time we buy a shirt made in China, in some small way we are contributing to indebtedness to the Chinese that either we or our children will have to pay for. Moreover, there is the lingering shadow of that indebtedness on the overall reality of U.S.-Chinese relations. Should we do something about all of this? If so, what do you suggest?

STUDY/DISCUSSION QUESTIONS

1. What is the Doha Development Round? How does its approach to world agriculture illustrate the difficulties of moving toward free trade? Use the "three pillars" of agricultural policy to organize your discussion.
2. What is the theory of comparative advantage? How is it critical to thinking about an international economic system based on free trade and globalization?
3. Why was World War II critical in the evolution of American thinking about international economics? Discuss the changes that it helped to bring about.
4. What was Bretton Woods? Discuss the proposals for and successes of the Bretton Woods Conference in building international economic institutions. What was the U.S. role in this process?
5. Why was an organization promoting free trade not part of the Bretton Woods outcomes? Trace the path of free trade from the 1940s to the creation of the World Trade Organization.
6. What factors entered into the transition period in the international economy and the U.S. place in it between 1971 and the 1990s? Elaborate.
7. Discuss the nature of and factors contributing to the globalizing economy.
8. What have been the principal means by which the United States has attempted to promote free trade? Elaborate, using examples.
9. Summarize the continuing debate over free and fair trade, including the notions of levels of analysis and approaches to the subject in your answer.

CORE SUGGESTED READINGS

Friedman, Thomas L. *The World Is Flat: A Brief History of the Twenty-first Century.* New York: Farrar, Straus and Giroux, 2005.This volume is one of Friedman's most complete defenses of globalization, the virtues of which he has advocated consistently for years. He also explains in some detail how technological factors are creating conditions wherein the global competition is spreading, a phenomenon for which the "flatness" of the world is the symbol. India in particular is featured.

Spero, Joan Edelman, and Jeffrey A. Hart. *The Politics of International Economics* (7th ed.). Belmont, CA: Wadsworth, 2009. Coauthored by an active participant in American economics efforts (Spero), this book remains one of the best available overviews of the nature, structure, and dynamics of the international economic environments.

Steger, Manfred B. *Globalization: A Very Short Introduction.* New York: Oxford University Press, 2009. As the title suggests, this slender volume is a first reader for the layman unfamiliar with the sometimes arcane language and dynamics of international economics, globalization, and free trade.

Stiglitz, Joseph E. *Globalization and Its Discontents.* New York: W. W. Norton, 2003. Although slightly dated, this primer by a recipient of the Nobel Prize for Economics presents an understandable overview of the very complex dynamics of the pros and cons of the globalization and free-trade system.

ADDITIONAL READINGS AND REFERENCES

Abdedal, Rawi, and Adam Segal. "Has Globalization Reached Its Peak?" *Foreign Affairs* 86, 1 (January/February 2007), 103–114.

Altman, Robert, "The Great Crash." *Foreign Affairs* 88, 1 (January/February 2009), 2–14.

Barshevsky, Charlotte. "Trade Policy in a Networked World." *Foreign Affairs* 80, 2 (March/April 2001), 134–146.

Bauman, Zygmunt. *Globalization: The Human Consequences.* New York: Columbia University Press, 1998.

Brown, D. Clayton. *Globalization and America Since 1945.* Wilmington, DE: Scholarly Resources, 2003.

Dierks, Rosa Gomez. *Introduction to Globalization: Political and Economic Perspectives for a New Era.* Chicago, IL: Burnham, 2001.

Drezner, Daniel W. *U.S. Trade Policy: Free versus Fair.* New York: Council on Foreign Relations Press, 2006.

Eichengreen, Barry J. *Globalizing Capital: A History of the International Monetary System* (2nd ed.). Princeton, NJ: Princeton University Press, 2008.

Fergusson, Ian F. *World Trade Organization Negotiations: The Doha Development Agenda.* Washington, DC: Congressional Research Service, January 2008.

Friedman, Thomas L. *The Lexus and the Olive Tree: Understanding Globalization.* New York: Farrar, Straus and Giroux, 1999.

Kirshner, Orin, Edward M. Bernstein, and Institute for Agriculture and Trade Policy (eds.). *The Bretton Woods-GATT System: Retrospect and Prospect After Fifty Years.* Armonk, NY: M.E. Sharpe, 1995.

Landau, Alice. *Redrawing the Global Economy: Elements of Integration and Fragmentation*. New York: Palgrave, 2001.

McBride, Stephen, and John Wiseman (eds.). *Globalization and Its Discontents*. New York: St. Martin's Press, 2000.

Mattoo, Aaditya, and Arvind Subramanian. "From Doha to the Next Bretton Woods." *Foreign Affairs* 88, 1 (January/February 2009), 15–26.

Naim, Moises. "Think Again: Globalization." *Foreign Policy*, March/April 2009, 28–34.

Panagariya, Arvind. "Think Again: International Trade." *Foreign Policy*, November/December 2003, 20–29.

Park, Jacob. "Globalization After Seattle." *Washington Quarterly* 23, 2 (Spring 2000), 13–16.

Schaeffer, Robert K. *Understanding Globalization: The Social Consequences of Political, Economic, and Environmental Change*. Lanham, MD: Rowman & Littlefield, 2003.

Shah, Anup. "Free Trade and Globalization." *Global Issues* (online), November 28, 2010.

Snow, Donald M. *Cases in International Relations* (3rd ed.). New York: Pearson Longman, 2008.

Stiglitz, Joseph E. *Free Fall: America, Free Markets, and the Winking World Economy*. New York: W. W. Norton, 2009.

World Trade Organization. *The Geneva Briefing Book*. Lausanne, Switzerland: World Trade Organization, 2004.

CHAPTER 12

Economic and Political Instruments of Foreign Policy

Protectionist measures such as tariffs are a tempting way to try to prevent domestic industries like this steel factory from shutting down.

PREVIEW

The purpose of this chapter is to examine the instruments of foreign economic policy. Although international economics is a somewhat different subject matter than traditional security policy, it is still a domain within which U.S. leaders try to craft policy in order to promote what they see as U.S. security interests and values. As the chapter discusses, policy making in this area is as inherently political as in other domains, and perhaps increasingly so. The president and the executive branch mostly control foreign economic policy (although with the help of the different agencies that the book has previously discussed), but there are strong avenues for congressional involvement in this area as well. In recent years the activity levels of trade groups and the public in lobbying about trade policy and foreign aid have become increasingly intense and divisive. The chapter discusses some ways that analysts and practitioners think about using economic instruments to promote state power, and provides some examples of how these instruments have been used in the past and are being used today.

KEY CONCEPTS

power
two-level game
economic liberalism
tariffs
nontariff barriers
economic nationalism
Office of the U.S. Trade Representative
Trade Promotion Authority ("Fast Track")
coercive diplomacy
public diplomacy
foreign aid
USAID
Millennium Challenge
military assistance
sanctions
embargo
"smart" sanctions
Helms-Burton Act

While the 2000 election is famous (or infamous) for a variety of reasons, a link between it and foreign economic policy may not immediately jump to mind. The drama of the Florida recount unfortunately dominates most people's memories of that election, leading us to forget about many other curiosities. While George W. Bush led the Florida count by a few hundred votes, Gore won New Mexico by a thin margin, and a reversal of the Florida drama played out there. George Bush won New Hampshire by a margin of votes that was smaller than the number of votes garnered by consumer-protection hero and progressive crusader Ralph Nader. In each of these states, economic issues played a part, but economic concerns were particularly strong in West Virginia. Bill Clinton had won the Mountain state in the two previous elections, and it was seen as a modern Democratic Party stronghold, having voted (up until 2000) for the Democratic candidate every election since 1976, except for Ronald Reagan's landslide 1984 reelection. In a surprise to some, and certainly a disappointment for Al Gore, George W. Bush won West Virginia—but narrowly. Forty thousand votes, out of nearly 650,000 that were cast, could have switched West Virginia's electoral votes to Al Gore and with it, the election.

On the campaign trail in steel country (West Virginia, Michigan, Ohio, and Pennsylvania), an area whose economies were badly suffering, George W. Bush promised to address concerns about unfair trade practices by foreign competitors to the domestic steel industry. A lifelong free trader, Bush suggested that once in office he would use the instruments of foreign economic policy to "protect" domestic industries, a decidedly anti–free-trade position. No doubt then-Governor Bush thought that foreign competitors were dumping steel on the American market, driving U.S. steel manufacturers out of business; few doubt that he also had political motives in mind: winning West Virginia and Ohio, and maybe even Pennsylvania. Bush indeed won Ohio and West Virginia, and would win them again in the 2004 election.

Once in office, Bush followed through on his promise, slapping tariffs on steel imports from allies South Korea, Japan, the EU, and others, in March 2002. Reports in the media suggested that Bush's advisors were split over the decision, with Treasury Secretary Paul O'Neill against the move and Bush's political advisor Karl Rove in favor of it. Protectionist and political impulses won out over the belief in *laissez-faire* economics. However, in 2003 the tariffs were lifted when the World Trade Organization ruled that they were illegal and the EU threatened to retaliate against American goods and services.

The most interesting part of the story is not so much that politicians might from time to time set aside their economic or other beliefs to curry favor with voters, but the way the incident highlights that foreign economic policy is inherently political. Politics is about picking winners in democracies, and foreign economic policy is most certainly political in the sense of being harnessed to electoral ends. Indeed, this is not a unique case, but rather a typical case of American policy makers trying to use foreign economic policy as a tool to promote state (and maybe even personal political) interests.

SOURCES OF POWER: HARD, SOFT, STICKY, AND SMART

The Prussian general and military expert Carl von Clausewitz famously observed that war is a continuation of politics waged with different means. It is useful to think about foreign economic policy as a continuation of politics by economic means, rather than thinking of it as something inherently different from the other foreign policy contexts that are discussed in this text. For centuries countries have tried to accrue power in order to increase their sense of "security." Economic power is a key part of any security equation; how one gets it, retains it, and grows it is a matter of statecraft as old as any other.

What is perhaps different about the way that the United States has approached foreign economic policy as a matter of statecraft is the general predisposition toward capitalism, markets, and free trade that has been a hallmark of the American political culture. These ideals may have set the United States apart from other states over time; other states pursued, for example, colonialism and imperialism as their approach to foreign economic policy (namely, the British Empire) or communism (such as the Soviet Union), but all have in common a link between ideals and interests. The U.S. preference for markets and free trade may be an ideal (although some debate that point), but it also reflects a sense that these arrangements are in the interests of the United States and the U.S. economy. The example that started the chapter of selectively using tariff barriers highlights how interests often trump ideals. It is thus often better to think about how the United States uses economic and other nonmilitary levers to pursue what leaders see as in the country's interest rather than abstract principles when the two come into conflict.

The concept of ***power*** is one of the most often-used and yet ill-defined concepts in the study of politics. For some, "power" means having certain resources; for others, it means the ability to get the outcomes that you want; other times it means the ability to influence others. In the study of foreign policy and international relations, though, there have been some efforts to be clearer about what "power" means and how states try to get and use it.

Hard power often refers to resources that exist and can be "counted." In a sense, they are the "stuff" of power. Military assets, for example, are hard power. The size and vitality of a nation's economy is a form of hard power. These are all resources that can be offered to others in a positive or negative form. Military power can be used as a "carrot," or an inducement, in the form of military aid or assistance; it can also be used as a "stick," a punishment used to take away resources, or land, from others. Economic resources can also be used in carrot or stick form, in order to try to persuade others to help attain national objectives. The chapter will discuss each of these in more detail, but the discussion starts here with trying to build a framework for thinking about these tools.

In recent years the term *soft power* has been used frequently, especially in reference to the United States. As first described by Joseph S. Nye Jr., the term *soft power* is meant to capture the importance of resources that are less tangible (or able to be counted) than hard power. Soft power normally refers to such things as culture, beliefs, and attitudes—things that draw others to you. An important base of American power, it is argued, is American ideas such as freedom, democracy, and self-government, and also American music, culture, movies, and even fast-food restaurants. There used to be a Gatorade commercial campaign with the tagline "Be Like Mike," asserting that everyone wanted to be like basketball great Michael Jordan. A great base of American soft power, many argue, is the extent to which people around the world want to be like the United States. Power like this eludes attempts at counting, or quantification, but many argue it is an essential component of American power in the global system, or an emerging weakness that must be strengthened through things such as better use of foreign aid and public diplomacy campaigns, as will be discussed shortly.

Another conception of power that is often used, again with reference to the United States in particular, is "sticky" power. Walter Russell Mead, in particular, has used this conception to try to get at the way that part of America's power in the world is based on how others come into contact with the United States through things such as trade and travel, and then they are "stuck" to the United States, drawn into a web of relations that has benefits from which other states would not want to be extricated. Central to this conception of power is international economics and economic institutions, led by the United States. A key form of America's "sticky power," then, is global capitalism and the institutions that keep it running, led by the United States. Some of these institutions—the Bretton Woods international organizations, for example—were discussed at length in the previous chapter.

With this in mind it is interesting to note that the top trading partners of the United States are (in descending order) Canada, China, Mexico, Japan, Germany, the United Kingdom, South Korea, France, Taiwan, and Brazil. Many of these are obviously neighbors and longtime allies, but they also constitute trade relationships that are fulsome and extend to other areas as well (evidence of the "sticky" nature of trade). It is also important to note that our second-largest trading partner is the People's Republic of China, a power relationship that is complex, to say the least.

A final way to think about power that bears on this discussion is *smart power,* a term that has been used frequently recently. The idea underlying smart power is that an essential component of statecraft is the ability for the United States to successfully blend soft, hard, and sticky power together in a coherent approach to foreign policy. The United States may have dominated the global economy in the past, for example, but will not do so in the future. Proponents of smart power assert that U.S. leadership going forward will be based on the capacity of the U.S. government to blend hard- and soft-power resources, diplomacy, public diplomacy, foreign-aid programs, and the like, in order to promote a global system that favors the United States. The United States will not have the power to "command" the global system to behave in a certain way (certainly not like after World War II), but will have to use a range of economic and political tools to lead and coax in order to create a system conducive to the interests that leaders set forth.

Two-Level Games and Foreign Economic Policy

Before moving forward, it might be useful to consider an analytic device that many use to help understand the dynamics of international bargaining and negotiations. The metaphor of a "two-level game" tries to capture the twin pressures that U.S. leaders face when crafting foreign economic policy—either in the form of positive agreements or in the form of punishments. The idea of a **two-level game**, as developed by Robert D. Putnam, is that national leaders must simultaneously "negotiate" both at an international level (with leaders of other countries or organizations) and at a domestic level (finding a policy that is acceptable to other powerful actors in the political system). Indeed, as the text has laid out in previous chapters, at the domestic level the president must think about Congress but also about a range of societal-level forces, such as public opinion and interest groups. Foreign-trade deals, for example, must not only be acceptable to U.S. leaders and the leader abroad with whom the United States is negotiating, but they also must be acceptable at the domestic level. So when crafting foreign economic policy with the tools discussed below, the two-level-game concept helps remind us that U.S. leaders are constantly "playing" at both levels.

There are competing visions of how the national government should (or should not) approach foreign economic policy. One, the free-trade view introduced in Chapter Eleven, emerges from the overarching perspective of classic **economic liberalism**. The U.S. dedication to free trade, or *laissez-faire* economics, is as long-standing as the Republic. In short, this view holds that markets are the best mechanism for wealth creation and that government intervention in the economy harms the generation of wealth. This view derives from a belief in the mutual benefits of exchange, that different countries will take advantage of their comparative advantage in the global economy, and that economic relations can be a positive sum, or win-win game. This view holds that tools such as **tariffs** (a form of taxation), **nontariff barriers** (such as import quotas), and other barriers to trade only get in the way of wealth generation in the long run. This vision of global economics finds its clearest expression in the idea of free trade developed in the last chapter.

A second view introduced in Chapter Eleven, protectionism, or **economic nationalism**, also has a long tradition in U.S. history and emerges from the realist perspective on politics that sees international economics not as separate from politics but indeed as a part of the struggle for states to get and maintain power and security. The idea here is that economic power is a key component of national power, that power resources are not distributed evenly around the globe, and that part of the responsibility of national leaders is to cultivate and protect the national economy from the influence attempts of others—that indeed, doing so is a key component of one's "security." The economic nationalism perspective, also sometimes called *mercantilism* or *neomercantilism* (to denote the modern versions of it) was laid out forcefully in 1791 by Founding Father Alexander Hamilton in his Secretary of the Treasury Report on Manufactures: "Not only wealth but the independence and security of a country appear to be materially connected with the prosperity of manufacturers. Every nation, with a view to these objectives, ought to endeavor to possess all the essentials of national supply within it."

Although it is common to treat free trade and protectionism as polar opposites as they may have appeared in the last chapter, in practice this is probably overstated—a false dichotomy. Indeed, on the ground in policy making, leaders are constantly using blends of these two ideal types in order to pursue what they see as in the economic and political interest of the United States. With this in mind, it might be helpful to go back to the story with which this chapter begins: the steel tariffs adopted by President Bush in 2002. President Bush was certainly a proponent of free trade and in general a proponent of capitalism and free market. Nonetheless, when faced with an opportunity to use an economic lever in order to try to protect parts of the U.S. economy, he took it. Leaving aside that the move probably backfired both politically and economically, it is a classic example of how national leaders approach foreign economic policy: free trade when it is in what they see as U.S. interests; protectionist efforts when they see them as in U.S. interests. Foreign economic policy is about blending tools in order to try to promote the goals that national leaders have established.

Coordination Mechanisms

As in the area of security policy, presidents do not make decisions about foreign economic policy alone. They do, however, increasingly draw on the help and expertise of some different Executive branch agencies than are consulted in other policy domains. While the State Department is a key player in crafting and implementing foreign economic policy, a range of other agencies play a central role here. In terms of advising the president, the president draws on the advice of both the Council of Economic Advisers (CEA) and the National Economic Council (NEC), both introduced in Chapter Five.

The CEA was established in 1947 as an economic advisory body to the president; they primarily advise the president about the domestic economy (such as the budget, taxes, and unemployment). The NEC, however, is far newer and is meant to advise the president on global economic policy. As noted earlier, it was established by then-President Clinton in 1993. The NEC was meant to be an economic version of the more long-standing National Security Council (NSC). Like the NSC (which was also discussed in Chapter Five), the NEC is meant to be the hub of an interagency process, with a director who tries to coordinate the range of agencies that play a role in international economics, such as Treasury, State, Energy, Commerce, Agriculture, Labor, and the U.S. Trade Representative.

Three other Executive agencies warrant special mention. With the increased emphasis on trade agreements that has been a hallmark of U.S. foreign economic policy—particularly since the end of the Cold War—the Commerce Department has become a much more central figure in foreign policy than perhaps used to be the case. Commerce is a lead agency when it comes to promoting trade and especially with respect to promoting U.S. exports abroad. The "commercial services" function at Commerce in many ways mirrors the types of services that U.S. Embassies and the State Department provide for U.S. citizens abroad, in this case trying to support U.S. businesses that seek access to foreign markets.

The Treasury Department is a key figure in foreign economic policy as well. The International Affairs Office has responsibility for promoting U.S. economic interests around the globe, and it works closely with the international economic institutions discussed in the previous chapter, such as the World Bank, IMF, and WTO. Another wing of the Treasury Department, the Terrorism and Financial Intelligence Office, houses a number of units relevant to foreign policy, including serving as the point agency for pursuing the financial backers of terrorists and terrorist organizations. Also inside this part of Treasury and particularly important for foreign economic policy is the Office of Foreign Assets Control (OFAC). OFAC enforces economic and trade sanctions that are imposed by the United States on other countries and on terrorist organizations. While the United States has used trade sanctions since early in the Republic, managed by an office inside Treasury, today's OFAC dates to the Korean War era, when President Truman blocked access to all Chinese and North Korean assets that the U.S. government could control.

Finally, the **Office of the U.S. Trade Representative** takes the lead in negotiating trade agreements with other countries. Starting in the 1960s and following both congressional and presidential initiatives, today the U.S.T.R. holds Cabinet-level rank and is responsible for coordinating U.S. trade policy, negotiating trade agreements, and advising the president on trade matters. The U.S.T.R. answers to both the President and the Congress. The United States has Free Trade Agreements in place with seventeen countries (see Table 12.1), and others pending before Congress, as well as many other trade initiatives that are managed by the U.S.T.R.

TABLE 12.1

Free Trade Agreements

Bilateral agreements in force:	Australia, Bahrain, Chile, Colombia, Israel, Jordan, Morocco, Oman, Panama, Peru, Republic of Korea, Singapore
Multilateral agreements in force:	North American Free Trade Agreement **NAFTA:** Canada, Mexico, United States Dominican Republic, Central American Free Trade Agreement **CAFTA-DR:** Costa Rica, Dominican Republic, El Salvador, Guatemala, Honduras, Nicaragua
Agreements being negotiated:	Trans-Pacific Partnership Agreement

Source: U.S. Trade Representative, "Free Trade Agreements," April 2011. www.ustr.gov/trade-agreements/free-trade-agreements (modified by the October 2011 passage of an agreement with Colombia, Panama, and South Korea).

Congress and Foreign Economic Policy

It is important to note that Congress has important and constitutionally guaranteed powers with respect to foreign economic policy. Article 1, Section 8, of the Constitution specifically gives Congress the power to "regulate foreign commerce," thus designating Congress as a central player in this domain. Congress has helped structure the foreign economic policy components of the Executive branch, such as in ordering the creation of the U.S.T.R.; and many trade agreements are treaties, which must be ratified by a two-thirds supermajority of the U.S. Senate. As the chapter on Congress discusses, the Legislature has also from time to time approved the use of a different mechanism for negotiating and ratifying trade agreements—the **Trade Promotion Authority** (the so-called **"Fast Track"**), by which trade agreements come before both the House and the Senate for a simple majority vote, during which no amendments are allowed. The Trade Promotion Authority lapsed in 2007 and has not been reinstated, as noted in Chapter Eleven, so new trade deals must be ratified by two-thirds of the Senate through normal Treaty procedures.

Not every piece of foreign economic policy is passed by Congress, of course. Presidents regularly use their initiative to offer foreign economic rewards and levy punishments, and for example, via executive order direct OFAC to implement sanctions against a target state. This chapter discusses some examples of both policy forms. Before turning to that, however, and a discussion of the economic instruments that are used as part of foreign policy, some discussion of the strategies that drive the use of these tools is in order.

NONMILITARY STRATEGIES FOR INFLUENCE

Because economic instruments of power can, and often do, supplement or even replace traditional uses of military power for achieving national ends, it is useful to examine two ways in which this occurs. One way is through the use of what is known as coercive diplomacy. The other is through so-called public diplomacy. Each augments other foreign policy instruments and has at least some economic content.

Coercive Diplomacy

The politics of two-level games, when played with friends, can be complex to navigate. The gradual removal of trade barriers with a long-standing ally, such as South Korea, can be difficult to achieve because of domestic opposition driven by fear of job losses in some sectors. Businesses that fear the loss of "protection," labor unions, and others often make their voices heard in Congress when it comes time to put trade agreements in place. More difficult still, however, is how to manage the use of economic and other instruments as part of a strategy to punish one's enemies.

Not every attempt to use economic levers to influence the behavior of other states (and nonstate actors) is part of a cohesive approach called **coercive**

diplomacy, but some are, and it makes sense to gain an appreciation of the strategy before thinking about how U.S. leaders have used it, and how they have used elements of it, in the past.

Coercive diplomacy, as best explicated by Alexander George (1991), is a "defensive strategy that attempts to persuade an opponent to stop or undo an aggressive action." Coercive diplomacy may involve the threat of the use of force or even a limited exemplary use of force as a means of restoring the peace, but the purpose of coercive diplomacy is for "diplomacy" to carry the day. Coercive diplomacy might be used to try to induce an opponent to undo an action they have taken, to stop short of completing an action they are in the midst of taking, and in its more assertive form to try to force the change of another government.

There is not a single way to assemble a comprehensive description of all attempts at coercive diplomacy. U.S. leaders who wish to pursue one, however, need to decide what to demand, whether to create a sense of urgency, and what mix of potential punishments and inducements to include in the effort. Economic tools are often central to these attempts. As George describes it, the central task of a coercive strategy is to create in the opponent the expectation of costs of sufficient magnitude to erode his motivation to continue what he is doing.

Two brief examples may be helpful. The United States pursued a form of coercive diplomacy against Imperial Japan before the start of World War II. In order to try to force Japan to remove its troops from China and give up its aspirations of dominating Asia, the United States pursued an oil embargo of the islands that comprise Japan. This economic instrument may have seemed like a low-risk initiative to U.S. policy makers, but it was not seen as such by Japan. Rather, the threat of a lack of access to oil was seen as a blow to the island country's very existence. The attack on Pearl Harbor followed. This failed effort at coercive diplomacy was heavy on "sticks," or punishments, and failed to achieve in the mind of the opponent what U.S. leaders had hoped, which was to reduce, rather than stimulate, Japanese aggression.

A second failed attempt to use a form of coercive diplomacy occurred after Iraq invaded Kuwait in 1990. President George H.W. Bush quickly announced that the invasion "will not stand," and an effort at coercive diplomacy began. The United States led an effort to put broad international economic sanctions in place to coerce Saddam Hussein to remove his forces from Kuwait. Coordinated through the United Nations and progressively imposing penalties prescribed in the UN Charter, this effort was then bolstered by a broad military coalition arrayed around Kuwait that threatened to eject Iraq's military by force. Ultimately this effort failed, and the military option was required to remove Iraq's forces from Kuwait. The total effort, however, clearly involved both economic and more traditional security efforts to try to bring about the desired reversal of Iraq's conquest of Kuwait.

Even though these two examples both failed, the idea of using economic and other instruments to try to induce different behavior in an opponent can be very appealing. It is a flexible strategy, allowing the use of both carrots and sticks, and it is a lower-cost strategy, when it succeeds below the threshold of employing force, than using military force to try to solve problems. Still, the examples of failure point out that this approach can be difficult to employ successfully and demonstrate that a country must have multiple ways to try to bring about compliance with its demands.

Public Diplomacy

Another influence strategy that has received renewed attention in recent years is **public diplomacy**. Traditional diplomacy refers to the formal interactions between representatives of governments, such as the contact that the U.S. Ambassador in Germany would have with representatives of the German government. Public diplomacy refers to efforts by the government to speak directly to members of the public in foreign countries. It represents an organized effort to put forward an American view of situations and foreign policy problems and to use information to try to persuade foreign publics. It is perhaps a kindler, gentler way to refer to "propaganda."

Since the end of the Cold War, public diplomacy campaigns have often been compared to commercial campaigns that companies use to develop a brand name for a product—to cultivate the image that comes to mind when someone thinks about Lexus vehicles, or Uncle Ben's rice. Recognizing that the image of the United States abroad has suffered in recent years, there has been renewed attention in both the Bush and Obama administrations to trying to "brand" American foreign policy. For example, in the Bush administration, Karen Hughes, a communications guru and longtime aide to George W. Bush, served as the Under Secretary of State for Public Diplomacy and Public Affairs from 2005 to 2007. Before her, New York advertising executive Charlotte Beers held the post, promoting the "Shared Values" campaign as a way to combat the negative view toward the United States that was growing around the world, especially in the Arab world.

Public diplomacy campaigns today incorporate many mechanisms. The U.S. Information Agency (USIA), which had been an independent agency during the Cold War, was folded into the State Department during the Clinton administration at the insistence of Senator Jesse Helms. Its functions now reside within the Bureau of International Information Programs. It produces radio and TV programs, publications, websites, and blogs and sends speakers abroad, all aimed at putting forward a persuasive "American" view. It does this in English and in foreign languages, all aimed at populations abroad. Another mechanism is the use of "people-to-people" exchanges that are officially organized by the State Department. A 2011 exchange, for example, brought officials and citizens from China to the United States to meet with U.S. citizens.

During the Cold War, public diplomacy campaigns mostly took the form of Radio Free Europe and the Voice of America—radio broadcasts into the "closed" societies of the Soviet Union and Eastern Europe. A similar effort was constructed to send radio programming into Castro's Cuba in the 1980s,

Radio Marti, followed by TV Marti as well. Many such efforts continue to this day, including Radio Sawa, broadcasting music as well as news in Arabic around the world twenty-four hours a day, seven days a week.

The communications and technology revolution, to which this book has referred many times, has spurred interest in public diplomacy as a tool of foreign policy. The ability of the U.S. government to reach out directly to people living around the world, without a "filter," has dramatically increased, and U.S. policy makers have been eager to try to leverage these new technologies. They have not always done so successfully, or without controversy, however. Indeed, polling populations around the world about their view of the United States has not shown much return on the hundreds of millions of dollars' worth of investment every year.

The case of Alan Gross is an example of how controversial these efforts can become. Gross is an American citizen who was working as a contractor for the U.S. government in Cuba. According to the Cuban government, he was arrested there in 2009 for conspiring to overthrow the government. It appears that Gross was delivering phones and communications equipment to dissidents in Cuba. Gross went on trial in 2011, and this case reminds us of the thin line between public diplomacy or information campaigns and covertly (or overtly) trying to overthrow a government.

TOOLS OF INFLUENCE

A wide range of tools beyond the use of force is available to U.S. policy makers in order to try to influence others and to address foreign policy problems. While military force can be used to punish an enemy or assist an ally, economic instruments can also be used as carrots and sticks in order to wield influence. Most often policy makers will use several of these tools at once in order to try to influence other actors and address foreign policy problems. Military assistance might be partnered with other forms of foreign assistance and increased trade flows, for example, as a way to reward or try to induce behavior that U.S. leaders see as in American interests. Sanctions, an end to foreign assistance, and even the use of force might be packaged together as a way to put pressure on a regime—steps that were taken by the United States against Libya in 2011, for example. As the chapter has discussed, selecting which tools to use, and how to use them, is a question of statecraft. The discussion now turns to the tools themselves.

Foreign Aid

Foreign aid, or "foreign assistance," refers to a complex set of programs designed to promote U.S. interests around the world. The U.S. government currently spends funds abroad within seven specific categories: democracy, human rights, and governance; education and social services; economic development; environment (the smallest program); health; humanitarian assistance; and peace and security (the largest in terms of dollars spent). For

MILITARY:	Punishment	Reward
	Destroy targets	Protect an ally
	Take away land	Defend an ally
	Occupy	Military assistance or withdrawal of forces
ECONOMIC:	**Punishment**	**Reward**
	Sanctions	Aid
	Boycott	Spur investment
	Embargo	Trade agreement
	Freeze assets	Give credits

FIGURE 12.1
Carrots and Sticks

2012, the Obama administration requested from Congress approximately $35 billion in foreign assistance spending; almost $12 billion of that would go to peace and security programs, while about $800 million would go to programs aimed at the environment.

Four budgetary points deserve notice. First, it is important to remember that these are extremely small amounts in the context of a multitrillion-dollar federal budget. Second, even these small budgetary figures are a large increase over recent years. When the Cold War ended, the American government's enthusiasm (and especially that of congressional Republicans) for foreign aid dropped dramatically, hitting a low mark in the late 1990s. President Bush increased the foreign assistance budget, and the budgets of the Obama administration are nearly double the size that they were under President Bush. Third, and related to this, much of the increase in funding has been targeted at the growing global HIV/AIDS epidemic, and more recently, combating terrorism. Finally, while the United States is one of the world's largest foreign-assistance donors in terms of absolute dollars, when the size of a country's economy is taken into account, the United States lags behind all other advanced industrial democracies on foreign aid by the resulting ratio of assistance to total GDP.

The organizational centerpiece of U.S. foreign-assistance programs is the U.S. Agency for International Development (**USAID**). Like the USIA, the USAID had been an independent Executive branch agency until the 1990s, when it was folded into the Department of State. Some foreign-aid spending comes through other elements of the State Department, but USAID is the frontrunner in this area. The spending on foreign-aid programs goes to foreign governments but also to contractors, nongovernmental actors, and international organizations.

Foreign assistance can take a variety of forms. Loans, debt forgiveness, equipment, training, and commodities (such as goods and medicine) are common types of assistance. While government agencies such as USAID oversee the use of particular assistance programs, most often the assistance is actually carried out by nongovernmental organizations (NGOs), charitable groups, and private contractors.

Foreign aid has its critics. Many argue that, especially in a time of economic hardship at home, even such a small part of the federal budget ought to be used to address domestic problems (or not spent at all). Some have also urged bureaucratic changes in the U.S. government to streamline the aid process; indeed, there have been many such reforms in recent years. Others point out that often the money that goes to foreign regimes ends up being wasted, or worse yet, funneled into the private bank accounts of corrupt officials. Aid might even spur more corruption, with some pointing to evidence that as aid levels increased, economic development decreased over the last several decades.

There are many reasons to support foreign-assistance programs as well. One set of arguments in favor of foreign aid hinges on the link between foreign aid and strategic U.S. interests. Foreign aid is not all about altruism, after all. A large portion of U.S. assistance goes to key allies such as Egypt and Israel, in order to support broader U.S. foreign policy goals such as promoting stability in the Middle East. Other assistance, such as spending on HIV/AIDS, is in part motivated by self-interest in addition to altruism—to stop the spread of infectious disease that might eventually affect Americans if it is not controlled overseas. In other words, these programs are aimed at helping create the kind of world in which the United States can thrive.

The post–World War II Marshall Plan is a good example of this combination of motives. The 1947 European Recovery Program was an economic recovery act for Western Europe. It was altruistic in the sense that the United States invested some $13 billion dollars in the economies of Europe to help them recover after the war. The Marshall Plan also pursued the strategic interests of the United States, however, by helping show the strength of capitalism, building up America's allies against the Soviet bloc, and helping spur the growth of markets that would become larger consumers in the American economy. The motives clearly demonstrate both altruism and self-interest.

Another point that highlights the dual nature of foreign aid, which is often not well-appreciated by Americans, is that most of what goes "out" as foreign aid ends up finding its way back into the American economy. Large portions of U.S. food aid, and credits that can be used to buy products and services, is tied to spending on American goods and services (what is known as procurement tying). Thus, food aid is good for broad U.S. goals (it can make the United States look good in the eyes of starving and malnourished people around the world), it is altruistic (feeding hungry people is a good thing to do), and it benefits American farmers, who get paid to produce the food. This same logic also applies to much military assistance. Military-aid programs often emphasize selling military equipment (such as aircraft) to foreign governments; the money never leaves the United States, but is instead used to pay American manufacturers of the equipment. Indeed, the U.S. government is quite open about the fact that it sees foreign-assistance programs as aimed not only at providing a helping hand to others but also at promoting American political, economic, and strategic interests.

Millennium Challenge

At the turn of the new millennium in 2000, the United Nations issued a declaration of "Millennium Development Goals," aimed at reducing poverty and increasing health, education, and development by 2015. As part of their effort to respond to these goals and to change how foreign aid works, the Bush administration began the **Millennium Challenge** by founding the Millennium Challenge Corporation (MCC) in 2004. This new agency would administer the Millennium Challenge Account, a new component of the U.S. foreign-assistance portfolio. The MCC functions somewhat differently from the rest of the federal bureaucracy that deals with foreign assistance. It is a government corporation that has a chief executive officer and a board of directors (which is chaired by the Secretary of State). It has a staff of about three hundred and an annual budget of approximately $1.2 billion (far less than what was originally envisioned for the MCC).

The goal of the MCC is to promote economic development, good governance, and market solutions with low- and middle-income countries struggling with development. The kinds of programs that are funded, usually in the form of five-year "compacts" with the countries, include anticorruption programs, agricultural projects, clean water projects, programs to address HIV/AIDS, and irrigation and transportation construction. As an example of one of the MCC compacts, in February 2008, a five-year, $698 million compact was initiated with Tanzania. The funds are aimed at projects that will reduce poverty and stimulate economic growth through targeted investments in transportation (roads), energy (reliable electrical power), and clean potable water.

The MCC is a small part of the fabric of foreign assistance, but it is a new approach and one that many foreign-assistance advocates hope will grow over time. As is discussed in the following section, much of U.S. foreign assistance is actually in the form of military assistance and aid to address drugs and terrorism. The MCC could become a more primary vehicle for supporting programs aimed at the other foreign-assistance priorities, which are traditionally more the domain of USAID. Needless to say, there are some bureaucratic struggles over this issue, both between the agencies involved and their supporters in Congress.

Military Assistance

Providing **military assistance** in one form or another to friends and allies is a common form of "foreign aid," although it may not be what Americans commonly think of when they consider the nature of foreign-assistance programs. Military-assistance programs often take the form of providing equipment or training to other countries, often as a reward for their pursuit of foreign and security policy aims that the United States shares. Peacekeeping funds for non-UN operations also are a form of military assistance. Military-assistance programs are overseen by the State Department but implemented by the Department of Defense.

During the Cold War, military assistance was a key way to aid—and lure—allies. From the 1970s through 2011, for example, a large proportion of foreign military-assistance spending went to the Middle East as a way to promote a range of policy goals in the region; most of it has gone to Israel and Egypt, with far smaller amounts going to Jordan and others in the region. Since the 1970s Israel has been the largest single recipient of foreign aid, much of it in the form of military assistance. In recent years Iraq and Afghanistan have also received large portions of this budget.

The use of foreign assistance of all types—but especially military assistance—as a lever or "carrot" to induce and reward assistance with the War on Terrorism has become a central theme since 2001. The other side of the coin, cutting or withdrawing aid as punishment for the lack of support, has also been utilized as a "stick." Aid to countries such as Yemen, Libya, Pakistan, and many of the states in Central Asia, for example, has been linked to counterterrorism, as well as aid to Colombia for assistance with "narcoterrorism." When all of the components of the foreign-assistance budget are combined, they make up approximately $50 billion, with military assistance composing roughly $15 billion of that total.

Sanctions

The use of economic **sanctions** is another instrument of statecraft that is often used against target states or groups in order to influence their behavior. It is important to remember that sanctions can be used in either positive (carrot) or negative (stick) form, because once imposed, the removal or easing of sanctions can be used to try to coax or reward changed behavior. Sanctions can be put in place either by legislation or by executive order. Sanctions are a common tool of U.S. foreign policy and one that many see as occupying a sort of middle ground between diplomatic communications on the one hand and the use of military force on the other. In practice, however, sanctions are rarely used on their own but as part of a package of initiatives (such as foreign assistance or the threat of force) aimed at target states or groups.

The term *sanctions* is actually an umbrella term meant to identify a range of economic levers that policy makers may use. One extreme form of sanctions is an **embargo**, or a total ban on trade, travel, and investment, with another country. This is a rare form of sanctions; as discussed in the section that follows, even the famous "Cuban embargo" is not really a full embargo of Cuba, since it allows limited economic interactions such as Cuban Americans sending money to relatives in Cuba. A less extreme, though still severe, form of sanctions is a *boycott*. A boycott is a restriction on the import of all or some particular goods or services from another country. The term tends to connote a total ban—such as the one in place against "conflict" or "blood" diamonds from Sierra Leone—but could also take the form of limits (or quotas) that

INTERSECTIONS

The Curious Case of the Cuban Embargo

Cubans taking to the Florida Straits to escape Cuba underscores the danger, and the proximity, of this foreign policy challenge.

The United States has had an embargo of Cuba, in one form or another, since the days that Dwight Eisenhower, who left the presidency in 1961, was in the White House. The purpose of the embargo, which was put in place by presidential order, was to hurt the Cuban economy so that perhaps the Cuban people would rise up to overthrow Fidel Castro; a secondary goal was to punish Cuba for some of its foreign policy behavior. A Soviet ally just ninety miles off the Florida coast deserved some kind of harsh American response, many thought. Since Cuba was a communist state, sanctions against it as part of the policy of containment made sense. But what to do with the embargo policy once the Soviet Union ceased to exist and the Cold War collapsed? When the Cold War came to an end between 1989 and 1991, some argued that the embargo should be made even tighter, since now without Soviet assistance to prop it up, the Cuban economy could finally collapse under the pressure of the embargo. Others argued that the end of the Cold War should also mean the end of the embargo; it was now time to "normalize" relations between the United States and the island.

In this context, embargo proponents in Congress put together a bill to tighten the embargo, the Cuban Democracy Act (CDA). The bill aimed to toughen the embargo on the Cuban economy and the Castro government (the so-called "Track I" of

(Continued)

(Continued)

the policy) by extending the trade prohibition to foreign subsidiaries of U.S. corporations. At the same time it tried to reach out to the Cuban populace ("Track II") by fostering more "people-to-people" contacts between the United States and Cuba. President George H.W. Bush opposed the bill on the grounds that it would tie the hands of the president on a key foreign policy matter by having Congress dictate what U.S. foreign policy would be toward Cuba (rather than the President deciding what it would be—a potentially troubling precedent to have set, if you work in the White House). Institutional prerogatives would trump policy preferences. In a surprise move, however, Bush's 1992 presidential campaign competitor, Democrat Bill Clinton, made a grab for Cuban American voters in Florida and New Jersey, promising to sign the CDA. At a campaign stop in Little Havana, Clinton declared that he had read the bill and liked it. Clinton raised some money, helped put Florida "in play," and outflanked a Republican president on his political right in one fell swoop.

Ultimately President Bush tried to minimize his losses, promising to sign the bill. Clinton, however, succeeded in winning four times as many Cuban American voters as had the previous Democratic candidate for president, Michael Dukakis. Clinton did not win Florida in 1992, but he won the election; and he did win Florida in 1996, carrying almost twice as many Cuban American votes as he garnered in 1992.

This was not the first time that U.S. foreign economic policy toward Cuba—the embargo—was caught up in electoral politics, but it set the stage for several very high-profile showdowns in the future over the embargo that just happened to coincide with elections. Election politics is only one political dynamic worth pointing out in embargo politics. Indeed, the embargo has led to strange political bedfellows. For the past ten to fifteen years, those who oppose part or all of the embargo policy include much of the political Left (which has been antiembargo for a long time), but increasingly it includes traditional Republican audiences such as Libertarians, and also trade groups, big business, big agriculture, the Chamber of Commerce, and many governors from states across the country.

President Obama's electoral victory included Florida and a large portion of Cuban Americans even though he argued he would like to loosen but not end the embargo. Since he entered the White House Obama has used his "licensing authority" to loosen the embargo a bit, but most elements of the embargo are now codified in law through the 1996 Helms-Burton Act (another election-year event). A slim majority in Congress still wishes to retain the embargo, and so it lives on. Whether you agree with the embargo or not as a part of American foreign policy, it is hard to look at it and not recognize that the Cuban embargo is as much about U.S. domestic *politics* as it is about foreign *policy*.

are put in place on imports from another country (such as the restrictions on the number of cars per year that could be imported from Japan that were in place in the 1980s). It should be evident that there is a strong link between these instruments and both trade policy and efforts at coercive diplomacy, as discussed earlier.

Another form of sanctions is to freeze the financial assets of a country's leadership that are held in your country. For example, during the Iranian Revolution in 1979 when Americans at the U.S. Embassy were held hostage, President Carter froze billions of dollars worth of Iranian assets held in the United States. (He also severed diplomatic relations with Iran and put a boycott in place on oil from Iran.) More recently, the United States government froze assets of the Libyan government with an estimated value of nearly $33 billion, and in July 2011 announced that it would make those assets available to the anti-Gaddafi rebel coalition, the Interim National Transitional Council, when it recognized that group as the legal government of the country.

A final form of sanctions is called *divestment*. If a positive form of foreign economic policy is to promote investment in a country, the opposite is also true in the case where the United States orders American individuals and commercial enterprises to divest their activities in another country. A form of divestment was part of the sanctions ordered against South Africa in the 1980s that many argue helped move the apartheid regime toward its end.

Two other points are worth noting about sanctions. First, they are tempting tools for policy makers to use as a way to protest behavior with which the U.S. government disagrees. They became so common in the 1990s that some agued there was a sanctions epidemic breaking out in American foreign policy. Note, too, that these sanctions are often bundled together with other tools as part of an influence attempt. Second, they rarely work, at least to the degree or end for which they were imposed. To some extent this is because the global economy is such that pressure from the United States can often be compensated for by the economic activities of others, and cases of comprehensive, multilateral sanctions are very rare. Even when they do "work," as with the fall of apartheid in South Africa, it is hard to know for sure that the sanctions per se are the cause of the change.

"Smart" Sanctions

Another aspect or type of sanctions that has received increased attention in recent years is so-called **"smart" sanctions**. Smart sanctions are meant to be more targeted types of sanctions, aimed at a country's rulers rather than blanket sanctions that indiscriminately harm a country's population. If traditional sanctions are the economic equivalent of a military "carpet bombing" campaign, smart sanctions are designed to be more like a "surgical" air strike that targets the regime but tries not to punish the innocent. They can include mechanisms like freezing the personal assets of a foreign leader or reducing a leader's (and even that person's family's) ability to travel abroad by not allowing visas to be issued. Whatever the tool, the idea is to use targeted economic mechanisms to build pressure on the leadership of a country rather than make the population suffer.

The interest in developing more targeted sanctions, rather than using blanket sanctions against a country, emerged from at least two impulses. First, there was a growing sense that sanctions as they had been used rarely accomplished their goals. Comprehensive sanctions may have played an important part in bringing down the apartheid regime in South Africa, but that is perhaps the exception that proves the rule. In that case, there was near-universal adoption of sanctions around the globe; rarely has a similar coordinated effort been possible against any other country. So if these kinds of sanctions policies do not work very well, perhaps it is time to try something else.

Second, there is a strong strain of concern in the United States and around the world about the ethical, humanitarian, and moral implications of broad sanctions policies. This dynamic rose to prominence in the 1970s and has certainly accelerated since the end of the Cold War. Sanctions may or may not work to change the behavior of a regime (or change the regime), but one thing about them is sure: They will harm the population, especially those who are weakest and most at risk in a population, including children, women, the sick, and the elderly. Already unable to force change, making the population sicker and weaker likely undermines U.S. policy goals rather than promoting them. Thus the interest in crafting more targeted, "smart" sanctions that do not, as the old saying goes, "punish the innocent."

Unfortunately, "smart" sanctions also have difficulties in application. To date, they appear not to have been any more successful when employed than their broader cousins. Their reputation was also badly damaged by the very public scandal that surrounded the UN's Oil-for-Food Programme in Iraq. This program, which ran from 1993 until 2003, was the kind of initiative that was meant to allow a more targeted approach to sanctions. Under it, Iraqi oil would be sold on the global market and the money earned would be used to buy food for the Iraqi population. The Iraqi people had been suffering tremendously under a very broad set of sanctions that dated back to the end of the Persian Gulf War in 1991. The sanctions showed little promise of changing the behavior of Saddam Hussein's regime (or changing the regime). However, what had changed was the status of Iraq's people. Iraq had become transformed from one of the most economically and educationally advanced countries in the region to one of the poorest.

Pressure at the UN built to change the way the sanctions policy worked. Some wanted to give up altogether on sanctions, but others put forward the Oil-for-Food Programme as a way to lessen the impact of the sanctions on the population while preventing Saddam's regime from reaping the profits of selling oil again. In a tragic case of good intentions gone bad, it turns out that the program led to billions of dollars in kickbacks from the oil industry to Iraqi and UN officials involved in administering the program, as well as substantial oil smuggling. Rulers got rich, and many of the program's managers did too, but relatively little relief was brought to the Iraqi people. One of the program's directors quit in frustration, noting that sanctions (however well-meaning) only harmed innocent civilians. The scandal underscores the difficulty of using the sanctions lever to try to influence others.

According to the Treasury Department's Office of Foreign Assets Control, in 2011 the United States had some form of sanctions in place against twenty targets. Many of these are classic cases of sanctions levied against states, such as those against Cuba, Iran, Syria, Burma (Myanmar), and North Korea. Some others are more targeted. Sanctions with respect to Cote d'Ivoire, for example, are actually prohibitions against any individuals having transactions with a list of people who have been identified as upsetting the peace in that West African country. There are also a variety of sanctions in place meant to block the economic activity of those involved in terrorism and the drug trade.

Examples of Sanctions

Three examples of the use of sanctions by the United States should help illustrate the points made earlier, beginning with the most long-standing set of sanctions: the Cuban embargo. The embargo of Cuba began in the Eisenhower administration in October 1960, following the Cuban Revolution and the turn toward the Soviet Union by Castro's government. The embargo was set in place by executive order and banned all trade with Cuba, except food and medicine. Ike cut diplomatic relations with Cuba just before he left office in January 1961. An effort to overthrow Castro—the fiasco of the Bay of Pigs Invasion—failed in April 1961. President Kennedy then tightened the embargo and ordered a ban on all travel by U.S. citizens to Cuba.

In the 1970s, however, during the period of *détente,* presidents of both parties made efforts to ease the embargo and make relations with Cuba more normal. For example, President Ford eased some trade restrictions in 1975, and President Carter lifted the travel ban in 1977. That year Cuba and the United States opened "interests sections" inside the Swiss Embassy in each country as well, as a step toward more normal relations. This thawing in the relationship would be short-lived, however, as the embargo was tightened during the Reagan years. It should be noted that while the United States and Cuba were extensive trading partners before the embargo was put in place, in many ways the Soviet Union kept the Cuban economy afloat during the Cold War, thus reducing the impact of the sanctions.

When the Cold War ended many argued that the embargo should die with it. With no Soviet Union, and thus no real "communist threat" from Cuba, many argued it was time to normalize relations with the island once again. In 1995, President Clinton ended the embargo of Vietnam and normalized relations with that onetime foe; would Cuba be next? Embargo proponents argued that the sanctions could never really "work" so long as the Soviets propped up Cuba; however, now the embargo could really harm the Cuban economy and perhaps force political change on the island. How could Castro survive the wave of democracy that had swept through so many communist states? This side won the debate, with steps taken by the administrations of both George H.W. Bush and Bill Clinton to tighten the embargo and to try to get U.S. allies to join in as well.

One of the interesting developments of the 1990s was that Congress started to take the lead on the Cuba policy, codifying it into law rather than having it exist by executive order. The 1996 **Helms-Burton Act** (the Cuban Liberty and Democratic Solidarity Act) explicitly codified all components of the embargo that had been in place as law, leaving presidents some limited "licensing" authority with respect to travel to the island and "remittances," or money that can be sent to people on the island. To end the embargo now would mean having Congress change it. Clinton had few options other than to sign this bill, since it followed the shooting down of two private aircraft with Cuban Americans aboard over the Florida Straits by the Cuban Air Force, killing four.

Beyond tightening restrictions on trade with Cuba and codifying the embargo, Helms-Burton included three other measures that are worth pointing out as examples of types of sanctions. One part of the law (Title IV) requires the administration to develop a list of foreign companies which do business with Cuba involving property that had been expropriated after the Cuban Revolution. (Many people fled Cuba during and after the Revolution and came to the United States; companies that do business with or on the former property of these people are said to be "trafficking" in stolen property.) The administration is then to identify the leaders of those companies so that they—and their families—can be denied visas should they wish entry to the United States. That means no business meetings in the United States, no shopping in New York City, no American colleges for their kids. It is an interesting effort to put pressure on companies based in Canada and Europe, in particular, from doing business in Cuba. It is also a provision that is sharply condemned by those against whom it is aimed—who are, by and large, close American allies.

A second element of the law worth pointing out, and another example of the "extraterritorial" nature of the law (a fancy way of saying the effort to extend American law to people outside of the United States) is its requirement (in Title III) that people in the United States who had property in Cuba seized after the Revolution that is now being used by foreign companies can sue those companies in U.S. courts for trafficking in stolen property. The company that owns Bacardi Rum had pushed this idea for years before it was made into law. Again, this was an effort to build more multilateral pressure behind the embargo.

In the negotiations between Congress and the Clinton administration over the bill, the president was able to have a waiver put into this section of the bill that would allow him to prevent these suits from going forward. President Clinton then used the waiver provision every six months as specified by the law to prevent any of these potential lawsuits from proceeding. During the 2000 election, then-candidate George W. Bush would often say, when asked about his view of Helms-Burton, that he would "fully enforce" it, hinting that perhaps he would not use the waiver and thus allow the suits to go forward. However, when the time came, Bush used the waiver provision too, keeping the suits on ice. President Obama has done so as well.

Finally, the law stipulates that one of the conditions that must be met for the embargo to be lifted is the holding of free and fair multiparty elections in Cuba that result in the election of someone *other than* Fidel or Raul Castro (itself an interesting interpretation of what counts as a free and fair election). As should be evident, there are several components of the Cuban embargo, many of which are now law, and nearly all of which have been tightened and loosened over time. The embargo is not, therefore, a single policy but better thought of as a package of sanctions, each of which can be altered, designed to coerce political change in the island.

Individual elements of the embargo have indeed been altered in recent years. In 2000, for example, Congress passed a law that allows limited sales of food and medicine to the island, an effort inspired both by the "smart" sanctions movement and also by the interest in helping American farmers. Over $2 billion worth of sales have occurred since then. President Clinton used his licensing power to make it relatively easier for people to travel to and send money to their families in Cuba. President Bush severely tightened those restrictions in 2004. President Obama—the eleventh U.S. President since the start of the embargo, has loosened them again during his time in office. Meantime, Fidel Castro has stepped away from power, with his brother Raul assuming his place.

Another interesting (and shorter) example is Iran. Between the end of World War II and the 1970s, the United States and Iran were close allies. Successive U.S. presidents saw the Shah of Iran as a close friend and power balancer in the region who both helped assure the flow of cheap oil from the Middle East and acted as a restraint on Soviet influence in the region. During this period Iran was a key trading partner with the United States and a major recipient of foreign assistance, including large amounts of military assistance. When the Shah fell in the 1979 Iranian Revolution, however, the backlash against the United States was severe—including the 444-day hostage crisis that started when the Iranians seized the Americans at the U.S. Embassy. Then President Carter imposed sanctions on Iran and ended diplomatic relations with that country.

In recent years, U.S. sanctions on Iran have followed concern about Iran's potential nuclear weapons program. The United States has led an international effort to tighten economic pressure on the Iranian regime in order to get them to open their program up to international inspection and walk away from the potential to build nuclear weapons. Congress has passed several sets of sanctions against Iran, most recently in 2010 when new restrictions were passed, which seek to punish companies that work in the Iranian oil and natural gas industry by not allowing them access to the U.S. banking system. One thing that has hindered the ability of American-led sanctions on Iran to hurt Iran is that other major powers, especially Russia and China, have been far more reluctant to join in the effort. As discussed previously, these sanctions are imposed as a kind of "stick," but could be eased or lifted as a "carrot" to reward a policy change in Iran.

A final note about both Cuba and Iran is that both countries are on the official list assembled by the U.S. State Department of states that sponsor terrorism. This list is required by law, and restrictions on trade, arms sales, foreign assistance, and other transactions automatically go in place when a country is put on the list. Sudan and Syria were the other two countries on the list as of 2011. Cuba's presence on the list is curious to many, since a 1997 Defense Intelligence Agency report specifically stated that Cuba poses no significant military threat to the United States. The inclusion does, however,

INTERSECTIONS

U.S.-India Nuclear Pact

In 2005, India's Prime Minister Manmohan Singh and U.S. President George W. Bush announced that they had negotiated a landmark nuclear agreement—an example of the "carrot" side of diplomacy. Highlights of the agreement include that India promises to ban further testing of nuclear weapons and to allow more intrusive inspections of its civilian nuclear power facilities, and the United States will allow American companies to build nuclear reactors in India and to provide fuel for those plants. This agreement is significant on many counts. First, it essentially recognizes India as a nuclear weapons state outside of the long-standing Nuclear Non-Proliferation Treaty (NPT), which forbids states from acquiring nuclear weapons beyond the original nuclear powers (United States, Russia, Great Britain, China, and France) and places sanctions on those—such as India—that stray beyond the NPT.

Second, the agreement, which was passed by the U.S. Congress in 2006, marks a new stage for a U.S.-India partnership. Relations between the United States and the world's largest democracy had fluctuated during the Cold War. However, starting in the Clinton administration and accelerating in the Bush administration, the United States and India have pursued a much closer and broader relationship, one that includes trade, concerns about terrorism, and an eye on China's economic and military rise in Asia.

Finally, as Kirk (2008) discusses in detail, the domestic politics in the United States about this agreement are also noteworthy. There was resistance to the agreement in many quarters, especially by those concerned with nuclear proliferation; some worried about China's and Pakistan's reactions (both short- and long-term) to the deal. Nonetheless the deal moved through Congress, in part thanks to the lobbying efforts of not just the business community but also the work of Indian Americans and of a relatively new ethnic interest group: the U.S.-India Political Action Committee. In other words, this deal is a classic example of how pervasive intermestic foreign policy has become; the changing domestic politics of U.S.-India relations was a key factor in the ability to bring this agreement to fruition.

reinforce the rationale for sanctions in the first place, and since there is no organized political opposition to some form of penalty against Cuba, there has been no organized objection to this curious designation.

Finally, Libya is an interesting example of U.S. sanctions policy. In the 1980s the Reagan administration imposed a variety of sanctions on Libya for its support to international terrorism, including a travel ban and a boycott of Libyan-imported oil. Those sanctions were widened following the 1986 terrorist bombing of a Berlin disco. Military action also was taken against the Gaddafi regime, and Libya was on the State Department's list of terrorism-supporting states. The UN joined in the sanctions regime against Libya following the terrorist bombing of Pan Am Flight 103, which exploded over Lockerbie, Scotland, in 1988. In 1996 the Libya sanctions were joined with others in a law passed by Congress called the Iran-Libya Sanctions Act (ILSA).

Starting in the late 1990s, the Gaddafi regime and Great Britain had some secret contacts about how Libya could become reintegrated into the global economy. These discussions started to come to fruition in 1999 when Libya surrendered the Lockerbie bombing suspects for trial. Further progress was made in 2003 when Libya agreed to pay compensation to the families of the bombing's victims. In 2004 President Bush ended the full range of U.S. sanctions on Libya following these steps and Libya's turning over its weapons of mass destruction program to the United States.

In 2011, however, the sanctions would return, as already noted. As the political protests of the Arab Spring spread to Libya, the Gaddafi regime turned the full force of its military on the protesters, and horrendous violence well chronicled by the electronic media followed. The United States, the EU, and the UN reemployed sanctions and imposed a no-fly zone on Libyan aircraft. NATO air power was also put use against targets of the Gaddafi regime. This effort to use sanctions and limited military force to drive the Gaddafi regime from power is one of the most recent examples of these dynamics.

CONCLUSIONS

The acquisition and use of power in order to promote foreign policy aims is perhaps more art than science. As this chapter has discussed, there is a broad range of instruments that U.S. policy makers have at their disposal short of using military power against a target in order to try to influence others. Trying to find the right mix of hard and soft power, the right levers to pull and buttons to push, the right mix of carrots and sticks, is the essence of statecraft. In recent years much greater attention has been paid to the importance of public diplomacy efforts as part of these overall efforts as well.

The use of foreign assistance is a common tactic in efforts to reward allies and punish enemies. The American public may not understand "foreign aid" very well, with recent surveys showing that most Americans think the foreign-aid budget is far larger than it is, but policy makers realize that foreign-assistance programs offer several avenues for promoting U.S. interests abroad and addressing common problems. Still an extremely small part of the federal budget, foreign-assistance efforts have increased in recent years. Terrorism and security concerns drive much of the foreign-assistance agenda, but the efforts to address humanitarian problems, hunger, and disease are also important components of U.S. foreign-assistance policies.

Economic sanctions are a widely used instrument of power, if not a widely effective one. Sanctions are attractive as a way to punish enemies that is fairly low-risk to Americans and U.S. military forces. As discussed previously, they also exist in a variety of forms and so can be added to and tightened—or subtracted from or loosened—as part of an ongoing effort to influence the behavior of others. These are not "on" or "off" mechanisms, but normally complex combinations of particular components. Both the appeal and, perhaps, the weakness of sanctions as policy instruments exist in this complexity.

WHERE DO WE GO FROM HERE?

One of the interesting things about the issues and actors discussed in this chapter is how domestic they are. Unlike other chapters that stress the National Security Council, the Department of Defense, or the CIA, this chapter features the foreign policy significance of the Treasury Department, the U.S. Trade Representative, and the economic advisors around the president. Congress also looms large in foreign economic policy as well, both on trade agreements and with economic sanctions. Given the way that trade policy affects the domestic economy, foreign economic policy can enter the domestic body politic rather easily, and can also easily become enmeshed in our increasingly hyperpartisan politics.

APPLICATION: JESSE HELMS, BONO, AND THE POPE

If issues of foreign economic policy can become political and partisan (such as the debate over NAFTA or the struggle to develop "smart" sanctions), then how is it that people with such different political views as archconservative Republican Jesse Helms (former Senator from North Carolina), progressive rock star and U2 front man Bono, and the Pope find common cause on some of these issues? In recent years these three leaders, and others, have found ways to work together to draw attention to the plight of the world's poorest and sickest people and helped pressure governments to do more to alleviate this unnecessary suffering.

There are other notable examples as well. Recall that Bill Clinton won the 1992 election by beating George H.W. Bush. Since they both left office, they have travelled together extensively to raise awareness—and money—on behalf of disaster relief, most notably after the 2005 Asian Tsunami. Clinton and George W. Bush joined forces for Haiti in 2010 after the devastating earthquake there.

One thing worth taking some time to consider is taking an inventory of where you stand on these issues. To what extent should moral concerns drive U.S. foreign policy? How much effort should the United States expend on humanitarian concerns around the world? What role should the U.S. military play in these efforts? If sanctions tend to harm a society's more fragile members, are they appropriate steps to take? And ultimately, what role will you play in these efforts? There is a wide range of nongovernmental organizations that work with this bundle of issues; will you join in any of these efforts and become a foreign policy actor of your own?

STUDY/DISCUSSION QUESTIONS

1. What is the difference between "hard" power and "soft" power? How does foreign economic policy fit into these conceptions of power and others?
2. Describe the idea of trade policy as a "two-level game." What actors are relevant at each level?

3. How are "free trade" and "protectionism" not so much opposing concepts as they are tools that are used by foreign economic policy makers?
4. How do "coercive diplomacy" strategies use economic levers to try to influence target states?
5. What is "public diplomacy" and why has attention to it increased so much in recent years?
6. What specific mechanisms are parts of the umbrella term "foreign assistance"? What changes to the foreign-aid framework were initiated by the Bush administration?
7. What specific types of actions count as forms of "sanctions"? Why are they so attractive as policy instruments?
8. Discuss the outlines of the Cuban embargo and the comprehensive sanctions against the Apartheid regime in South Africa. Why did one work while the other seems not to have? Can you generalize from these two cases about how sanctions work?
9. In a normative sense, do you think that economic instruments are more ethical or moral to use than military force? What about sanctions in particular?

CORE SUGGESTED READINGS

Armitage, Richard, and Joseph S. Nye Jr. *CSIS Commission on Smart Power: A Smarter, More Secure America*. Washington, DC: Center for Strategic and International Studies, 2007. The report—generated by a bipartisan commission—is an excellent view of how policy makers think about combining military power, economic power, and public diplomacy better for the future.

Brown, Sherrod. *Myths of Free Trade: Why America's Trade Policy Has Failed*. New York: The New Press, 2006. Brown, a U.S. Senator from Ohio, presents the case against "free" trade, pointing out what he sees as the "myths" such as free trade and job creation, as well as giving the reader a bird's-eye view of the politics behind trade agreements.

Erikson, Daniel P. *The Cuba Wars: Fidel Castro, the United States, and the Next Revolution*. New York: Bloomsbury Press, 2008. Erikson, who joined the Obama administration's State Department in 2010, presents an excellent perspective on the history of the U.S. embargo of Cuba and the challenges of U.S.-Cuban relations for the future.

Kunz, Diane B. *The Economic Diplomacy of the Suez Crisis*. Chapel Hill: University of North Carolina Press, 2009. An outstanding study of how the Eisenhower administration used economic leverage to stop the 1956 joint invasion of Egypt's Sinai Peninsula and the Suez Canal by Britain, France, and Israel.

ADDITIONAL READINGS AND REFERENCES

Art, Robert J., and Patrick M. Cronin (eds.). *The United States and Coercive Diplomacy*. Washington, DC: U.S. Institute of Peace Press, 2003.

Baldwin, David A. *Economic Statecraft*. Princeton, NJ: Princeton University Press, 1985.

Bergsten, C. Fred. *The United States and the World Economy: Foreign Economic Policy for the Next Decade*. Washington, DC: Institute for International Economics, 2005.

Cortright, David, George A. Lopez, and Joseph Stephanides (eds.). *Smart Sanctions: Targeting Economic Statecraft*. Lanham, MD: Rowman & Littlefield, 2002.

Destler, I. M. *American Trade Politics* (4th ed.). Washington, DC: Institute for International Economics, 2005.

Drury, A. Cooper. *Economic Sanctions and Presidential Decisions*. New York: Palgrave Macmillan, 2005.

Evans, Peter B., Harold K. Jacobson, and Robert D. Putnam (eds.). *Double-Edged Diplomacy: International Bargaining and Domestic Politics*. Berkeley: University of California Press, 1993.

Friedman, Thomas L. *Hot, Flat, and Crowded*. New York: Penguin Books, 2009.

George, Alexander L. *Forceful Persuasion: Coercive Diplomacy as an Alternative to War*. Washington, DC: U.S. Institute of Peace Press, 1991.

George, Alexander L., and William E. Simons (eds.). *The Limits of Coercive Diplomacy* (2nd ed.). Boulder, CO: Westview Press, 1994.

Haass, Richard N., and Meghan L. O'Sullivan. *Honey and Vinegar: Incentives, Sanctions and Foreign Policy*. Washington DC: The Brookings Institution Press, 2000.

Haney, Patrick J., and Walt Vanderbush. *The Cuban Embargo: The Domestic Politics of an American Foreign Policy*. Pittsburgh, PA: University of Pittsburgh Press, 2005.

Hogan, Michael J. *The Marshall Plan: America, Britain, and the Reconstruction of Western Europe, 1947–1952*. New York: Cambridge University Press, 1987.

Ikenberry, G. John, David A. Lake, and Micheal Mastanduno (eds.). *The State and American Foreign Economic Policy*. Ithaca, NY: Cornell University Press, 1988.

Irwin, Douglas A. *Free Trade Under Fire* (3rd ed.). Princeton, NJ: Princeton University Press, 2009.

Kennedy, Paul G. *The Rise and Fall of the Great Powers*. New York: Random House, 1987.

Kirk, Jason A. "Indian-Americans and the U.S.-India Nuclear Agreement: Consolidation of an Ethnic Lobby?" *Foreign Policy Analysis* 4 (2008): 275–300.

Lancaster, Carol, and Ann Van Dusen. *Organizing U.S. Foreign Aid: Confronting the Challenges of the 21st Century*. Washington, DC: The Brookings Institution, 2005.

Lord, Carnes. *Losing Hearts and Minds? Public Diplomacy and Strategic Influence in an Age of Terror*. New York: Praeger, 2006.

Mandelbaum, Michael. *The Frugal Superpower: America's Global Leadership in a Cash-Strapped Era*. New York: Public Affairs Press, 2010.

Mead, Walter Russell. "America's Sticky Power." *Foreign Policy* 141, March 2004.

Morley, Morris H., and Christopher McGillion. *Unfinished Business: America and Cuba After the Cold War, 1989–2001*. New York: Cambridge University Press, 2002.

Nye, Joseph S. Jr. *Soft Power: The Means to Success in World Politics*. New York: Public Affairs Press, 2005.

Picard, Louis, and Terry Buss. *A Fragile Balance: Re-examining the History of Foreign Aid, Security, and Diplomacy*. Sterling, VA: Kumarian Press, 2009.

Seib, Philip (ed.). *Toward a New Public Diplomacy: Redirecting U.S. Foreign Policy*. New York: Palgrave Macmillan, 2009.

Snow, Nancy, and Philip M. Taylor (eds.). *Routledge Handbook of Public Diplomacy*. New York: Taylor & Francis, 2008.

Tarnoff, Curt, and Marian Leonardo Lawson. *Foreign Aid: An Introduction to U.S. Programs and Policy*. Congressional Research Service Report R40213, April 9, 2009.

CHAPTER 13

Trans-State Issues and American Foreign Policy

U.S. President Barack Obama received the Nobel Peace Prize in 2009.

PREVIEW

Trans-state issues are challenges that cut across state boundaries and require some level of collective action to solve. Many of these problems are such that even a few dissenters from collective agreements (sometimes called "defectors") can easily ruin any global effort to address the problem. Therefore, the very nature of these problems makes them very difficult to solve. U.S. power alone cannot fix them, and without U.S. leadership (or at least participation), little progress is likely to be made. Making matters worse, the domestic politics in the United States that surround these types of problems have become particularly partisan, making concerted U.S. effort on them even less likely. Furthermore, these issues also tend to involve the participation of intergovernmental organizations (such as the UN) and a host of nongovernmental organizations, making the coordination process even more complicated. If there is any set of issues that brings the dynamics of this new era to the fore—where it is perhaps harder than ever for the United States to craft a coherent policy approach given the domestic politics of the issues, and where the issues themselves are harder to solve because of their globalized nature—it is these issues. This chapter examines human rights and democracy, and environmental degradation and change, as examples of this broad range of issues.

KEY CONCEPTS

interdependence
sovereignty
intergovernmental organizations (IGOs)
nongovernmental organizations (NGOs)
chlorofluorocarbons (CFCs)
negative human rights
positive human rights
Beijing summits (1995)
"third wave" of democratization
International Criminal Court (ICC)
genocide
Universal Declaration on Human Rights
fossil fuels
greenhouse effect
global climate change
Copenhagen Accord
Kyoto Protocol

Barack Obama was sworn in as President of the United States on January 20, 2009. Lawyer, law professor, and community organizer, Obama served in the Illinois state legislature and four years in the U.S. Senate before his election. In October 2009, the Nobel Peace Prize Committee announced that Obama had won the prize for that year, noting "his extraordinary efforts to strengthen international diplomacy and cooperation between peoples." They also gave special notice to Obama's hope to reduce the world's nuclear arsenals and to how Obama had already helped create a "new climate in international politics." The official press release noted,

> Multilateral diplomacy has regained a central position, with emphasis on the role that the United Nations and other international institutions can play. Dialogue and negotiations are preferred as instruments for resolving even the most difficult international conflicts. The vision of a world free from nuclear arms has powerfully stimulated disarmament and arms control negotiations. Thanks to Obama's initiative, the USA is now playing

a more constructive role in meeting the great climatic challenges the world is confronting. Democracy and human rights are to be strengthened.

The committee concluded by emphasizing its agreement with Obama's assertion in a September 2009 speech to the United Nations General Assembly that, "Now is the time for all of us to take our share of responsibility for a global response to global challenges." For his part, Obama responded to the announcement by saying he was "surprised and deeply humbled," and that he considered the award to be less about his accomplishments in his short time in the White House and more a call for action to address these global problems.

Now fast forward: While Obama was able to sign and get the Senate to ratify a nuclear arms deal with the Russians, many of his other global initiatives have not gained significant traction. The Middle East peace process has been stalled. The hopes to build a new global response to climate change were dashed when several key actors backed away, including the United States when it became clear that the Senate would not ratify any such agreement. The global move toward democracy that started happening after the end of the Cold War was actually backsliding (although popular uprisings in the Arab world may lead to greater democracy in the Middle East and North Africa in the years to come). In short, progress in addressing the world's global challenges has been slow.

In many ways this should come as no surprise. The very nature of trans-state issues is that they have an impact on several (if not all) countries, but no single country can "solve" the problem without collective action. By this nature alone, these are perhaps the most difficult and intractable problems the world faces. Another factor that makes these problems so tough to solve is their diffuse nature; getting the kind of broad bipartisan agreement that is necessary for the United States to try to lead on these issues is harder than ever. Extreme controversy seems to surround proposed solutions to trans-state problems. The hyperpartisan nature of the issues and their global nature combine to make them the hardest to solve. When Alfred Nobel died in 1896, leaving part of his fortune that was gained from the explosives industry (dynamite was one of his inventions) to fund the Nobel Peace Prize, could he even have imagined the dynamics that surrounded Barack Obama's acceptance of the award given in Nobel's name?

Trans-state issues are also particularly difficult to address (let alone solve) today because they are inherently intermestic issues, and often what one needs to achieve at the international level does not correspond to achievability at the domestic level. This is especially true in the United States, which is a consistent leader in promoting international responses to trans-state issues, but then ends up opposing them once the global response is crafted because of the hurdles of domestic politics.

In a world where **interdependence** among actors in the system is rapidly increasing, the dynamics of the new era have either created or accentuated a growing set of other concerns. Modern advances in technology, transportation, communication, production, and political and economic liberalization facilitated by the fall of the Soviet Union and the end of the Cold War have made it easier for people, goods, information, and ideas to flow across state borders in ways that states cannot easily control, restrict, or even track and monitor. The result is that a series of concerns which were either absent or seemed less important during the Cold War have risen in importance—and urgency—today.

These problems are often referred to as *trans-state issues,* defined as problems caused by the actions of states or other actors that transcend state boundaries in ways over which states have little control and which cannot be solved by the actions of individual states or other actors within states alone. The term, however, is far from a perfect name for this class of issues. One of the sets of issues discussed below is human rights and democracy, but this set of problems only meets part of the criteria in the definition. Violations of human rights can be solved by the actions of individual states; the problem is that all states, for different reasons, do not enforce the same standards. There is a viewpoint, discussed later, which argues that when human rights are curtailed anywhere, they are curtailed everywhere: that the fabric of human rights and freedom is a seamless cloth and so our rights are all interconnected.

Moreover, not all trans-state problems or their solutions result from state action; nongovernmental organizations such as crime cartels and terrorist groups may cause global problems, whereas **intergovernmental organizations (IGOs)**, groups that have states as members (such as the UN), and **nongovernmental organizations (NGOs)**, groups that transcend state boundaries and have individuals as members, such as Doctors Without Borders/Médecins Sans Frontières, may contribute to solutions. As a result, this chapter concentrates on examples of major emerging trans-state issues that have achieved and are likely to retain prominence on the foreign policy agenda for some time.

RANGE OF CONCERNS

The roster of these global problems covers a broad array of both physical and social conditions on the globe. The list is depressingly long and includes environmental problems such as ozone depletion and global climate change, depletion of ocean fisheries, human rights believed to be universal to humankind but irregularly enforced by different state governments, the spread of democracy, the increasing problem of refugee flows (often caused by internal wars and failed states), food supply, desertification, access to clean water, and infectious disease and the threat of pandemics.

There are multiple causes of this emerging set of problems. Possibly the most prominent are those technological developments that have contributed to an increasingly interdependent world among those countries sharing in the general prosperity (the global economy). Acceleration of these technologically based trends has been aided by the virtual collapse of ideological opposition to the values of Western-style democracy and market-based economics. In some cases such as environmental degradation, the problems are the result of direct human actions in some countries that affect others, such as the use of **chlorofluorocarbons (CFCs)** that attack the ozone layer and expose increasing parts of the world to the harmful effects of ultraviolet radiation. Drug smuggling is an instance where the actions of individuals and groups within countries create a problem that individual states cannot control. This points to yet another source: the rise of organized private groups within and among states that contribute both to the growth of problems and their solutions. The emergence of a new Russian mafia as part of privatization in that country has affected places such as Brighton Beach, Brooklyn (where many Russian immigrants live). Private NGOs are especially prominent in identifying problems and the need for solutions, especially in the human rights area.

Also contributing to the rise of many of these emerging global issues is the lifting of the ideological competition of the Cold War. Many of the human rights issues, for instance, could not be frankly addressed in international forums because the Cold War competitors would (often correctly) maintain that the issue was being raised to embarrass them. Although one can overstate the degree to which the veil has been lifted, the end of the ideological competition has facilitated more frank and honest consideration of human rights than was the case previously. Before the 1975 Helsinki Accords were signed, discussions of human rights violations in the Soviet Union and Eastern Europe (as well as China) were viewed by some as merely propaganda. The accords, which among other stipulations required all participants—and specifically communist and noncommunist Europe—to honor basic rights, began the opening of the communist world and may have contributed to the process resulting in the fall of communism. Similarly, some of the world's worst industrial pollution has occurred in the formerly communist world, and the fall of communism facilitated a more honest definition of the problems of environmental cleanup, especially in Europe.

In many ways, the trans-state and other emerging issues represent the downside, or at least the challenge, to what are otherwise thought of as good, progressive international trends: the rise of democracies and capitalist-based economies and freer trade and other phenomena stimulated by the technological, communications, and transportation revolutions to which we have referred in discussing change more generally. That is, the good sides of the end of the Cold War and deepening of globalization are all around us. The dark side of these trends has also risen, and the fruits of these advances are not universally enjoyed.

These issues are also intensely political in at least three ways. First, many are classically intermestic, with both domestic and international dimensions and repercussions. The environment is such an issue; in international forums the United States urges that rain forests in other countries be preserved to aid in controlling carbon dioxide levels, but at the same time the country has not reached anything like a consensus on logging and the use of public lands in the American West. Similarly, differential environmental regulations (such as the disposal of toxic waste) between Mexico and the United States have been a continuing point of contention in passing and implementing NAFTA.

Second, in a more directly international context, many trans-state and other emerging issues have become major parts of the dialogue between the advanced industrialized world and the developing world. The structure of a number of the transnational issues brings these worlds into at least partial conflict. In areas such as environmental pollution, economically developing states such as China and India are often asked to forgo certain activities (for example, rain forest degradation) for the greater good of environmental protection while advanced industrial states remain major pollution producers. The promotion of human rights initiatives, as another example, often emanate from the West and can be seen by some in the developing world as a new form of Western cultural imperialism.

The third way that these issues can be intensely political has to do with the junction between global efforts to address these problems and the principle of **sovereignty**, the idea that all states are equal and there is no higher authority that can compel the behavior of states. While it is technically true that all states are sovereign and thus encounter no higher authority in the global system, in practice some states are more sovereign (that is, more powerful) than others, and no state can really stand apart from the rest of the system. The presence of so many IGOs—such as NATO or the EU—and NGOs (both of which are in some sense competitors to the nation-state as a form of organization in world politics) also underscores that sovereignty is far from absolute. Many countries are very sensitive to this point, but the United States has been particularly so. The George W. Bush administration, for example, took a particularly hard line against international efforts that might infringe on American sovereignty or security, whether it was an effort to address the environment (Kyoto Protocol), crimes against humanity (the International Criminal Court), or (perhaps as surprisingly) a stronger treaty against biological weapons. The idea that international agreements might force the United States to engage in actions it would not otherwise undertake was anathema to the Bush administration and often put the United States at odds with much of the rest of the international community. The Obama administration has been less strident about U.S. involvement in these efforts, but only by degree.

The United States has an important role in the evolution of these problems and their solutions. The human rights movement is, in many important ways, an extension of the dialogue within the United States on matters such as civil and women's rights; it should have been no surprise that women's rights champions Bella Abzug and First Lady Hillary Rodham Clinton were prominent figures at the women's rights conferences held in Beijing in August 1995, for instance. At the same time, problems plaguing the United States, such as the flood of illegal narcotics entering the country and the destabilizing effects of the drug trade on neighboring countries, especially Mexico, are trans-state issues at their core. Controversy on these issues seems to follow the United States because American ambivalence often leads to U.S. policy changes on them. The Clinton administration, for example, was much more in favor of vigorous American participation in a range of global efforts at problem solving; the Bush administration reversed much of that effort, and the Obama administration has returned to the table.

What is central and common to these issues is that they defy solutions by single states. In the case of a trans-state issue such as stopping the flow of drugs, the United States is only in partial control of its fate. Despite efforts to

INTERSECTIONS

Fill Up Much?

Gas prices go sky high in the United States, harming an already weak economy; at the same time the burning of fossil fuels contributes to global climate change.

If you've filled up your gas (or diesel) tank lately, you know full well the high price of gasoline. For an economy that is really premised on cheap oil, $100 per barrel (more or less) oil and the gas prices that follow are a choke on macroeconomic growth as well as on individuals' pocketbooks. Gas costs twice what it cost not long ago, without pay raises to make up the difference. Coincidentally, doing something about getting "off" oil could also be great for attacking global climate change, since carbon emissions dropped dramatically in the United States as the economy slowed. Could this be a harbinger of things to come?

According to estimates from the U.S. Department of Energy, gas prices in the United States are determined by a variety of factors, including the price of oil, the cost of refining the oil into gasoline, the distribution costs, state and federal taxes applied at the pump, and some speculation activities on global "futures" markets. While tax rates vary by state, the national average is that about 14 percent of the price at the pump is made up of taxes: a little less than 50 cents a gallon. (The federal tax on gas is currently 18.4 cents per gallon.) While gas prices are high now, they are extremely low in the United States compared with many other countries, especially the advanced industrial democracies in Europe where people pay far more than in the United States. The main reason for the price difference is that these other countries tend to have much higher tax rates on gas, with the taxes going to pay for public transportation and infrastructure repair (neither of which tends to get much attention in the United States).

For years those who have advocated taking stronger steps to get the United States off its addiction to oil have urged higher fuel taxes. The thinking is that with fuel prices so low, the market gives little incentive to other technologies (such as wind or solar or hybrid engines) since they are so much more expensive by comparison. But as the price of fuel rises, some of these options become more attractive. A car with a hybrid engine in it, for example, may be $5000 more expensive than the same car with a regular engine in it, but if the hybrid engine gets twice the miles per gallon and the price of gas is high, in the long run it can cost less to buy the car with the hybrid engine in it. Higher gas taxes can help spur the development of better hybrid and all-electric cars and, advocates say, get the United States off oil consumption—the burning of which contributes to the world's greenhouse gas problem and global climate change. Indeed, the fall of emissions in 2009 would seem to indicate the soundness of the argument.

But at what cost? Increasing taxes is anathema to most U.S. politicians these days, especially taxes that are so clearly linked to the health of the economy—such as gas taxes. Indeed, some have argued for *lowering* the gas taxes as a way to stimulate the economy. Must the steps that are taken to address the underlying causes of global climate change also harm the U.S. economy?

When George W. Bush entered the White House in January 2001, his administration seemed to think so. One of the first things they did was to make it clear that the United States would not participate in the Kyoto Protocol, the global effort to curb carbon emissions, because of the concern that the U.S. economy would be harmed by the mandated reductions—while other economies such as India and China were protected from such steps. Even if Bush had wanted the Senate to ratify the treaty, it's not at all clear the votes were there anyway.

(Continued)

(Continued)

Barack Obama became president in 2009 after promising to do more to curb carbon emissions. He had hoped to go to the December 2009 global climate meetings in Copenhagen ready to have the United States lead a renewed effort to collectively address climate change. But a bill in the Senate that would address carbon emissions, and be the backdrop of the U.S. position in Copenhagen, was dead—the victim of Republicans and Democrats worried about the economy and the potential impact of new restrictions on emissions. Not only that, but public skepticism of "global climate change" had been rising, and fewer and fewer Americans see it as a major problem. Even though there is a strong scientific consensus about the issue, more and more Americans do not accept it, and so have no interest in policies aimed at doing something about it—especially steps that might harm the economy or cost jobs.

The key thing to keep in mind here is that the United States is not unique in this regard. The U.S. intermestic politics of climate change have clearly hampered the ability of the United States to lead on this issue; but without the United States, little can be done to address this trans-state issue. And every country in the world has some variation on these dynamics (some more than others). The pain you feel at the pump is a nice reminder of how complex this issue is—and this is but one of many key trans-state issues with which the U.S. foreign policy-making system tries to cope.

educate the citizenry about the deleterious effects of drug use and attempts to intercept incoming supplies of illicit materials, the campaign only stands a chance of being successful if there is widespread international cooperation to shut down the sources of drugs and to make their transshipment more difficult. Stopping international terrorism faces similar issues. At least some degree of coordinated effort is required to make progress on these issues.

As parts of the foreign policy agenda, these issues are often enigmatic. Most are issues on which Americans generally agree in principle, but often not in practice—especially when they are adversely affected by the "solution." No one, for instance, is *for* pollution, but proposals to subject sports utility vehicles (SUVs) to the same emission standards as automobiles are opposed by many SUV owners, because doing so would raise vehicle costs. Americans lament the lack of public transportation in many parts of the country, but resist tax increases which would pay for improvements that would both help the economy and help lower greenhouse gas emissions. At the same time, many of these issues seem abstract and thus easily ignored because their effects are neither obvious nor immediate. How am I adversely affected *today* if a few more acres of rain forest are destroyed?

The rest of the chapter focuses on two clusters of these emerging trans-state issues, clusters selected because of their visibility and importance in the American dialogue, and because they are nice examples of this broader class of issues. They are abuses of human rights and the promotion of democracy, and protection of the environment in the face of its degradation. Of these, human rights receives the most attention because it is high on the policy agenda and demonstrates many of the trends that have emerged from the technological revolution and shrinking of the globe due to associated advances. It is not strictly a trans-state issue because theoretically state action could solve it. It is an emerging issue because some states reject or resist universal definitions. Environmental degradation is a classic trans-state issue. Each issue has received a great deal of exposure and discussion both within the United States and in international forums and is likely to continue to do so.

Each discussion begins by describing the problem and why it is an important issue. It then looks at the status of the problem, including progress and barriers to progress. Each discussion concludes with an assessment of U.S. interests and the position—or positions—that the United States has adopted in recent years.

HUMAN RIGHTS AND DEMOCRACY

The central proposition dominating the human rights movement is the idea that all humans have certain basic, inalienable rights and there is a universal obligation to enforce and protect those rights; prominent among those human rights is political freedom and self-determination: democracy. The concern is not strictly a trans-state issue because individual states could, through their own individual actions, enforce a uniform code. All states, of course, do not do this; there are widespread differences in the quality of the human condition and even disagreement—sometimes honest and heartfelt, sometimes cynically political—about what composes the conditions to which humans are entitled. Moreover, the expressions and concerns are often gender based, since women in many societies have historically enjoyed far fewer rights than men. The treatment of children has also become a prominent part of the dialogue.

Describing the Problem

Human rights and democracy are an important part of the international agenda because they are tied to ongoing world change. Interdependence and the growing world economy have created greater economic prosperity. As the process of globalization has intensified, so too have calls for increased human rights and political freedom. Economic and political democracy, in other words, are the economic and political expressions of freedom, and their connection helps produce what Singer and Wildavsky (1996) call a "quality economy," where free people are highly motivated and thus more productive and innovative than those who are not free.

Demands for uniform human rights tend to come in two varieties, one discussed here, the other touched on later. In the first category are basic civil and political rights (such as the freedoms of speech, assembly, and religion contained in the U.S. Bill of Rights). This category also includes social rights as fought for in the civil rights and antidiscrimination movements in the United States, such as freedom from discrimination in hiring or in public places. These are sometimes referred to as **negative human rights** because they state actions that cannot be taken *against* people.

In the second category are basic human economic and social rights—the right, for example, to an adequate diet or a certain level of education. These are sometimes referred to as **positive human rights**, or minimum quality-of-life standards, because they entail positive conditions to which their advocates maintain people are entitled.

The assertion of a set of human rights is a relatively recent phenomenon in the history of the global system. Historically, the superiority of the sovereign authority of the state has meant that rulers routinely have been able to do to their citizens whatever they were physically capable of doing. The classic, absolute assertion of sovereignty maintains that, within the sovereign domain of the state, the ruler has the right to do whatever he or she wants, and there is no right that allows outsiders to challenge such action, even when it entails the suppression and even slaughter of parts of the population. Although there have been periodic expressions of the notion of human rights, they have been comparatively infrequent. Originally, U.S. democracy provided rights for male citizens, for instance, but did not provide political rights for women, and early U.S. citizens kept slaves.

The philosophical birthplace of the human rights and democracy movement arguably is in the seventeenth-century work of John Locke, the British philosopher from whom many of the ideas that underlay the American republic were derived. Among his contributions, which can be seen in contemporary discussions, are notions of popular sovereignty (the idea that individuals, not the state, are the primary repository of sovereignty) implicit in advocacies of intrusions against governments engaged in human rights violations.

Contemporary advocates of human rights and democracy (for example, NGOs such as Amnesty International and Freedom House) can be thought of as grounded in two related foci. Where human rights, including the political freedom that defines democracy, are not present in particular countries, advocates aim to provide democratization for all citizens. Since the end of the Cold War, the late political scientist Samuel P. Huntington argued we have entered a **"third wave" of democratization** (the first two waves came immediately after the world wars) that is spreading democracy to regions where it was previously not present or certainly not universal (the former Soviet Union and Central and South America, in particular).

The other focus is less universal, involving the forceful advocacy of human rights for categories of citizens within countries who have been denied rights. The most visible and forceful advocacies have been for *women's rights*, the extension of political and economic rights to women in societies that have treated women as inferiors. These cover a wide range of physical concerns, from basic political rights of participation and equal standing under the law to more social concerns such as the right to enter into and out of marriage freely, reproductive rights, and even matters such as genital mutilation (female circumcision). This category of rights was the subject of the **Beijing summits** in August and September 1995. The first to convene was the NGO Forum on Women, sponsored by the United Nations, with roughly 25,000 delegates in attendance. Prominent attendees included then-Pakistani Prime Minister Benazir Bhutto, who publicly deplored the Asian preference for male children, which she said led to widespread abortions of female fetuses. Then-First Lady Hillary Rodham Clinton also appeared, stating, "It is a violation of human rights when women are denied the right to plan their own families, and that includes being forced to have abortions or being sterilized against their wills." She also condemned female genital mutilation, domestic violence against women, and the rape of women during war.

The second meeting was the UN Fourth World Conference on Women, whose 4,000 delegates representing 185 countries convened at the Great Hall of the People on September 4th. The conference was able to reach agreement on the basic platform by adopting two resolutions, the Platform for Action and the Beijing Declaration. The Beijing Declaration provided the outline of a "Bill of Rights for Women," containing provisions calling for equal inheritance rights, equal access to education and medical services, and the right of all women to decide freely concerning matters of sexuality (namely, childbearing), to cite a few of the more prominent rights. The Platform for Action provided a framework for implementing the provisions in the Declaration. In recent years countries have made an increased effort to extend these rights to the treatment of children as well.

Status of Human Rights and Democracy Issues

Now that the Cold War competition no longer dominates the foreign policy agenda, the issue of human rights has emerged as a major foreign policy concern for many governments, including that of the United States. Indeed, the promotion of democracy—even in the form of military action to force regime change—was a key component of the Bush Doctrine that emerged after 9/11. In the absence of a major ideological opponent to Western-style democracy, it is not surprising that the issue has largely been framed in Western terms.

The following discussion focuses on two matters. The first is contemporary forces that have pushed human rights issues into such prominence. Although the advocacy of human rights goes back to the founding days of the United Nations after World War II, it has gained considerable momentum since the end of the Cold War. The other emphasis is on the status of the human rights and democratization movement, particularly in terms of the formalization of ideas of universal human rights.

The human rights movement has clearly benefited from the end of the Cold War and the emergence of the Western system of political democracy and market-based economics as the nearly universally accepted form of political and economic organization. This wave of democratization has been aided by at least three other forces that have acted as proponents and publicists: the modern electronic media, the influence of outstanding individuals, and the activities of NGOs.

State brutality has long been reported by the traditional print media, but the advent of the electronic global village, to borrow Marshall McLuhan's famous term, has made such reporting much more accessible and vivid. Burgeoning telecommunications capabilities have produced truly global news organizations that can transmit information from any point on the globe to another in real time, virtually as events are happening. The nature of visual reporting creates an evocative atmosphere not possible with the written word: We can see atrocities, for instance, with a shock value the printed word could hardly evoke.

The result is coverage and publicity of events that more than likely would have been neglected only a few years ago. Practically no place on the globe is too remote to be physically inaccessible anymore. Although the savage genocidal war in Sudan has provided stark evidence that it is not impossible to keep out the media and hence suppress direct coverage of atrocities, it is becoming increasingly difficult to hide inhumanity even in authoritarian states.

Individual leaders have also done much to spur the world's awareness of human rights violations, sometimes running against other foreign policy priorities. During much of the Cold War, for instance, the human-rights records of countries took a backseat to their levels of anticommunism. Thus, the United States sometimes found itself supporting brutal dictatorships in which human rights were regularly suppressed because the regimes were strongly anticommunist. Former American President Jimmy Carter, however, won the admiration of oppressed people throughout the world for his elevation of human rights to the top of the foreign policy agenda during his single term. Carter stated his position forcefully in his memoir, *Keeping Faith* (1982): "Whenever I met with a leader of a government which had been accused of wronging its own people, the subject of human rights was near the top of my agenda." Carter won the Nobel Peace Prize in 2002 for his work. Another example is Pope John Paul II. In visits to his native Poland in 1979 and 1983, he rallied the people behind his call for religious freedom. His advocacy became a rallying cry for the popular movement that overthrew communist rule in Poland in 1989.

Nongovernmental organizations have also become prominent in the human rights movement. Some serve as monitors of the human rights records of states. Amnesty International (AI), for example, annually produces a list of countries where it alleges human rights abuses occur. Its list is often compared to a similar one prepared by law by the State Department (AI's list is invariably longer), and Congress often requires the State Department to explain the discrepancies. A newer and more aggressive counterpart is Human Rights Watch, which burst into the public spotlight when it accused the Chinese government of an orphanage scandal in 1995. The organization clandestinely videotaped alleged neglect and mistreatment of Chinese children in a supposed model orphanage and then released the tapes, to the embarrassment of the Chinese government. Freedom House also tracks political openness and freedom around the globe.

In addition to the monitors, a growing number of NGOs also seek actively to mediate and assist in situations where human rights are abused: for instance, to tend to refugees in war zones. These organizations provide a variety of services, from the provision of food (CARE) and medical care (French-based Doctors Without Borders/Médecins Sans Frontières). Their work also serves to publicize the suffering they seek to alleviate.

The human rights movement did not begin with the end of the Cold War, even though that event has certainly accelerated activism on the human rights front. The banner was first raised in the twentieth century by President Woodrow Wilson in his Fourteen Points at the end of World War I, and the issue resurfaced in World War II, where the victorious Allies were not only fighting for their physical survival, but also "in the name of freedom." This phrase was coined jointly by American President Franklin Roosevelt and British Prime Minister Winston Churchill in the Atlantic Charter of 1941, which laid out the Allied goals for the war. A postwar emphasis on human rights was further stimulated by revelations about Hitler's Holocaust, which intensified the broad desire to create a more humane world.

This postwar emphasis was formalized in 1945 when representatives of fifty-one countries gathered in San Francisco to sign the charter that formed the United Nations. The UN charter called for the original signatories, and the nearly 140 other states that have since become signatories, to "pledge themselves to observe and to respect human rights."

The United Nations has been the focal point for the global human rights movement since the organization's inception. In addition to sponsoring international conferences such as one of the 1995 Beijing conferences on women's rights, the United Nations has also produced a series of five treaties by which signatories bind themselves to specific observations of human rights. The first two of these were passed in 1948; the other three are products of the 1960s.

The first important document was the Convention on the Prevention and Punishment of the Crime of Genocide. It was adopted by the UN General Assembly in 1948 as the direct result of international revulsion toward Germany's systematic extermination of the European Jewish population (the Holocaust). The most important legal mechanism contained within the convention creates standards for punishing those guilty of acts "committed with intent to destroy in whole or part a national, ethnic, racial, or religious group." The convention provided the legal precedent for establishing war crimes tribunals for both Bosnia and Rwanda and is embedded in definitions of crimes against humanity adjudicated by the **International Criminal Court (ICC)**. The United States did not ratify the convention until 1988, a clear sign of American ambivalence about the issue, and the United States has not ratified the treaty that would make it a part of the ICC—even though the United States was central to its creation.

The UN General Assembly also adopted the **Universal Declaration on Human Rights** in 1948. This document provided the most sweeping set of international norms protecting the rights of individuals from their governments (the negative, or political, rights noted earlier) and creating standards of living to which people are entitled (the positive, or social, rights). The rights declared to be inherent for all individuals are very broad. They include (1) the right to life, to due process of law, and to freedom of thought and worship;

(2) the right not to be tortured or enslaved; and (3) "the right to a standard of living adequate for the health and well-being of self and family." Critics argued, sometimes disingenuously, that the declaration was too broad and vague for universal application (often because they did not want to enforce its principles); defenders hailed it as constituting new standards for evaluating the performance of states.

Three human rights documents approved as a series of treaties by the General Assembly during the 1960s sought to give additional substance to these early initiatives: the International Convention on the Elimination of All Forms of Racial Discrimination; the International Covenant on Economic, Social, and Cultural Rights; and the International Covenant of Civil and Political Rights. Of these, the International Covenant of Economic, Social, and Cultural Rights, which was passed in 1966, is considered the most basic.

The United States and Human Rights

The attitude of the U.S. government, which did not sign the 1966 covenant until 1977 and did not ratify it until 1992, exemplifies the ambivalence Americans have had about these international standards. The United States has been a major player in drafting almost all the accords; the political rights in the Universal Declaration and subsequent political statements closely parallel the American Bill of Rights. The United States is a party to most of the major human rights accords that exist. At the same time, there has been considerable opposition to adopting these treaties in the United States, and the United States is not a party to several of them even today (see Table 13.1).

TABLE 13.1

Key Human Rights Covenants Without the United States

- Convention Concerning Forced or Compulsory Labor of June 28, 1930
- Convention Concerning Freedom of Association and Protection of the Right to Organize of July 9, 1948
- Convention Concerning the Application of the Principles of the Right to Organize and Bargain Collectively of July 1, 1949
- Convention for the Suppression of the Traffic in Persons and of the Exploitation of the Prostitution of Others of March 21, 1950
- European Convention for the Protection of Human Rights and Fundamental Freedoms of November 4, 1950
- Convention Relating to the Status of Refugees of July 28, 1951
- Convention Concerning Minimum Age for Admission to Employment of June 26, 1973

Source: U.S. Department of State, Bureau on Democracy, Human Rights, and Labor, *2010 Human Rights Report: Appendix C—Description of International Human Rights Conventions,* Washington, DC: 2011. http://www.state.gov/g/drl/rls/hrrpt/2010/appendices/154529.htm (accessed on August 10, 2011).

There are philosophical and political objections. One is the dilution of sovereignty; if the United States signs an international treaty, that document's provisions become part of U.S. law enforceable in U.S. courts. If a treaty's provisions contradict U.S. law, the treaty's dictates *supersede* the existing statute and take precedent over it. It is because of this feature that the opposition to these treaties on the basis of diluting sovereignty is often argued; it is also why treaties require senatorial action.

This leads to a more practical, political concern, particularly as these treaties assert the positive or social rights of people. The debate over the status of women, minorities, or children, and especially to what conditions they are entitled, has both a domestic and an international aspect. The international assertion of a right to an adequate standard of living for all people, for example, has an obvious parallel in the domestic debate over welfare, health care, and a whole host of other entitlements. If one is politically opposed to the provision of certain entitlements to groups of American citizens, then one will be wary of promoting the same rights internationally, especially if international agreements might pose standards that would have to be enforced within the United States to which some Americans are opposed.

Clearly, the issue of human rights has not been satisfactorily resolved, either domestically or internationally. A significant gap remains between the language of international proclamations and the everyday experiences of millions, even billions, of people worldwide. The result is a continuing human rights agenda over which the United States, as the remaining superpower, has little choice but to preside or, more modestly, actively to try to influence. Without U.S. support, solutions to these problems are likely to be fleeting.

Part of the ambivalence of the United States toward human rights as an issue was reduced by the end of the Cold War. The Cold War produced a geopolitical tension between evaluating regimes primarily on their adherence to democratic values or their professed anticommunist ideology, a wrenching situation when regimes were both anticommunist and antidemocratic. In those circumstances, the communist-anticommunist dimension often prevailed, and the United States was occasionally forced to favor democracy at some points while siding with opponents of democracy at others. President Carter was the first to try to move to primary concern with democracy, but the Cold War sometimes overwhelmed his emphasis.

The elimination of the communist-anticommunist concern has removed that barrier. The United States feels far less ambivalence about supporting democracy and opposing its opponents, although the strength with which that opposition is voiced may be influenced by other factors such as economics, as in the case of China. Some ambivalence continues, however, especially as antiterrorism has come to take on a central role in U.S. foreign policy. States with strong leaders and oppressed people who nonetheless cooperate with the United States against Al Qaeda pose a similar conundrum to that of the Cold War with respect to anticommunism.

The "third wave" of democracy was enthusiastically embraced by the Clinton administration as a centerpiece of its policy of "engagement and enlargement," which replaced the "containment" strategy of the Cold War. Enlarging the sphere of market-oriented democracies was the rallying call. The George W. Bush administration also gave democracy promotion a central place in the foreign—and military—policy of the United States, and clearly the Obama administration also wishes to support the democratic aspirations of people around the world. There is little resistance to this, for at least four reasons (largely framed in traditional geopolitical terms).

First, there is a widely shared belief that the spread of democracy enhances national security. Democratic states historically have not gone to war with one another except where democracy is not well established and disputes predate democratization. The U.S. invasion of Iraq should show that democracies are not necessarily inherently peaceful, but the argument is that they tend not go to war with each other. Second, democratic states are the most reliable bulwark for protecting human rights. Although violations of individual rights occur from time to time even in democratic societies, systematic violations of basic political rights are less likely because they are antithetical to the very concept of democratic self-government. Democratic governance and human rights are two sides of the same coin.

Third, for the most part, democratic regimes are more responsible and law-abiding members of the international community than are dictatorships. After all, political democracies are grounded in the rule of law and the accountability of the governors to the citizenry. However, democracies are also subject to changes in public opinion that may make today's policy untenable tomorrow. Finally, the growth of the global economy is closely related to the combined effects of political democratization and free and open market-based economies. Many argue that the two are related because they represent the political and economic manifestations of the same basic principle, freedom of action.

Many of these concerns were jolted by September 11th and the subsequent reorientation of American foreign policy toward geopolitics and antiterrorism. The performance of countries as partners against terrorism often seemed to overwhelm their human rights record, and the presence of democracy and political freedom around the world has actually started to shrink a bit in recent years. The United States went from being a critic of Russian handling of the separatist movement in Chechnya to siding with the Russian government as they label Chechen fighters "terrorists." The United States made agreements with openly undemocratic governments in central Asia who were willing to be helpful in the war on terrorism and the invasion of Iraq.

Two other issues in the human rights and democratization agenda warrant discussion, though perhaps they receive less public attention than the issues discussed above. The first is the absence of reliable enforcement mechanisms, a problem that human-rights standards share with other evolving international norms. This issue arises largely from the struggle over the meaning of sovereignty and is exemplified in the birth of the ICC and the eventual U.S. opposition to it. The second issue is a disagreement over whether there is a single, universal standard of human rights. The two problems overlap in that where there are states that disagree with presumptive universal rights, they will be reluctant to allow them to be enforced. Indeed, some would argue that democracy and human rights are different concerns altogether.

The problem of enforcement has bedeviled many international efforts. It is a fundamental characteristic of the international system, deriving from the principle of sovereignty, that no force is superior to that of the state; in other words, no international body has jurisdiction over the territory, including the population, of another country. In the human-rights field, this becomes a problem when governments abuse their citizens—especially to the extremity of the systematic slaughter of population segments (**genocide**). In this case, there may be (and are) appeals to a higher authority in order to right wrongs. However, even some nonoffending states, including the United States, sometimes resist such demands, fearing the precedent they set: If someone else's sovereignty can be violated, then who is to say mine might not be sometime in the future? This point became highly emotional in the United States concerning the ICC.

The absence of legitimate supranational (above the state) mechanisms means that international efforts must be more indirect. For example, when faced with evidence of human-rights violations, states or combinations of states may threaten to cut off foreign aid until the abuses cease, which may be effective if the target relies on such assistance. If the violator does not depend on foreign aid, of course, such a threat is ineffective. Economic sanctions offer another possibility, but the result may be that the population target one seeks to help will bear the burden of the suffering (Haiti is an example). Asylum for political dissidents is another possibility; during the Cold War the United States offered asylum to Cubans fleeing communism (but not to people fleeing anticommunist dictatorships such as Haiti, the inconsistency of which became a political issue in the 1992 presidential election).

The problem of universality compounds the difficulty. The simple fact is that there is substantial disagreement among different parts of the world on what constitutes human rights. Many of the most serious differences are gender related; in much of the world, the rights of women (including female children) are considerably more circumscribed than they are for men. In most cases, these differences are encased in long-held practices and traditions creating advantages for men that they do not want to forfeit.

Both disagreements came to the forefront during the two-week World Conference on Human Rights in Vienna in 1993—the first global meeting on the subject in twenty-five years. In preparation for the June event, preliminary regional meetings were held in Thailand, Tunisia, and Costa Rica. These meetings produced declarations arguing that the Universal Declaration of Human Rights was a mere cultural expression of Western values that did not apply to non-Western societies, most of which were under colonial bondage in 1948 when the declaration was written.

The most strident expression of this objection was set forth in the Bangkok Declaration signed by forty Asian governments. The declaration argued that notions of freedom and justice are contingent on "regional peculiarities and various historical, cultural, and religious backgrounds." The assertion of universal standards was, according to the Bangkok signatories, no more than another expression of Western imperialism. At the African meeting, the delegates argued for a focus on the economic and social (positive rights) agenda because many of the poorest people in the world were represented at that conference. This logically led to a reemphasis on the development agenda, a frequent point of controversy between the advanced industrialized North and the global South on trans-state issues.

Despite these sources of objection, the Vienna conference was able to adopt a declaration that, if implemented by UN bodies, will strengthen human rights. Three provisions of the Vienna conference stand out. First, the conference backed an American proposal for stronger UN efforts in rectifying human rights abuses, including a call for establishing a high commissioner on human rights. Second, the conference expanded the definition of human rights by calling for special efforts on behalf of women, children, and minorities. The 1994 Cairo conference on children and the 1995 Beijing summits on women were called to further elaborate on these issues. Finally, the conference strongly endorsed the obligation of all states to protect human rights "regardless of their political, economic, and cultural systems," a provision passed over the noisy objections of a handful of states that had dominated the regional conferences. The UN endorsed the conference and established the position of the UN High Commissioner on Human Rights to raise more attention for these issues.

These issues have gained even more prominence following the 2011 revolutions and uprisings in the Middle East and North Africa. Calls for political change and openness spread through Iran, Tunisia, Egypt, Yemen, Bahrain, Jordan, Syria, Libya, and elsewhere. The United States has once again been in the odd position of sometimes promoting change and sometimes backing strong-arm governments against the protestors. The certainty and stability of the policies of an authoritarian government can be tough to give up when faced with the unpredictability of what might follow, especially given some degree of anti-American sentiment in the region.

THE ENVIRONMENT

Environmental degradation has proved to be a classic trans-state problem, created by the actions of many states and affecting even those who are not "guilty" parties; the efforts of individual states are simply inadequate to solve it. Progress can only be made as a result of a significant amount of global cooperation and coordination. The dynamics of environmental issues share many of the characteristics of the human rights and democracy issue. It often pits the advanced industrialized world against the developing world, with the question of development never far from the surface. It is also an area on which the United States is in substantial internal disagreement. Many of the issues of environmental degradation, global climate change, resource usages, and the like, have their equivalents in the internal American partisan political debate.

This internal debate has been highlighted by the transitions from President Clinton, who took a leading role in global efforts to address climate change—to President Bush, who was far more skeptical of international efforts to address these issues through regulations and who refused to submit the Kyoto Protocol for Senate ratification—to President Obama, who hoped to take on more of a leadership role for the United States on environmental issues.

Describing the Problem

Environmental degradation covers a broad range of more specific issues. In many respects, human mastery of nature has created rising affluence, breakthroughs in the treatment of diseases, and previously unimagined opportunities for personal fulfillment to those who are the beneficiaries of scientific progress around the globe. But these benefits have been selectively enjoyed and have had costs in terms of the global ecology that has become the focus of environmental efforts.

The range of specific issues on the environmental agenda is long, complex, and often interrelated. Air quality, water pollution, desertification, nuclear waste, energy policy, the global ecosystem, and global warming—all are part of this broad agenda. Each issue is trans-state in that none can be solved unilaterally by individual states. They are classic problems of the "commons," where actions by one actor affect the other actors in the system and where perhaps "defectors" can easily hide their misdeeds because of the scale of the commons. At the same time, each exists as an internal policy issue within the United States that divides Americans and makes it more difficult to develop a uniform posture across time in international forums.

Status of Environmental Challenges

It is not possible to provide a comprehensive overview of all aspects of the environmental agenda in this book. For present purposes, the discussion will focus on two related policy areas that are broadly representative of the problem of environmental degradation and that are linked to some extent: global warming and deforestation. Global warming is largely the result of the excessive burning of **fossil fuels**, which produce carbon dioxide (CO_2) that accumulates and has harmful effects in the atmosphere. Other than reduced emissions, the chief natural means of dealing with carbon dioxide is through natural photosynthesis by trees—especially those in the green belt that surrounds the earth's equator—which are rapidly being depleted.

Global warming, which is the direct consequence of CO_2 emissions, has been a vexing global and domestic policy problem. The physical problem is relatively easy to describe. When fossil fuels, notably oil and coal, are burned to produce energy they also produce carbon dioxide (CO_2), most of which enters the atmosphere. When there is too much CO_2 to be absorbed by green plants and transformed into water and sugar (as well as oxygen), it accumulates in the upper atmosphere, where it joins other gases such as methane to trap solar radiation and other heat sources. The result is the **greenhouse effect**, where heat cannot escape into space and thus continues to warm the earth's surface, much as a greenhouse traps heat and moisture. Other gases add to this problem as well.

There is general scientific agreement that global warming is happening and about its effects. Since 1900 the amount of CO_2 in the earth's atmosphere has increased significantly, with a consequent average temperature rise of 2 to 3 degrees Fahrenheit. Continued accumulation at present rates would result in an increase of between 2 and 9 degrees by the middle of the twenty-first century. And CO_2 rates continue to climb, with growth rates in 2008 at double the rate of growth just in the 1990s. This range, in turn, leads to more or less apocalyptic estimates of the consequences in terms of ice cap melting and the like. As leading glaciologist Lonnie Thompson, who studies ice cores from around the world, recently concluded, "There is now a very clear pattern in the scientific evidence documenting that the earth is warming, that warming is due largely to human activity, that warming is causing important changes in climate, and that rapid and perhaps catastrophic changes in the near future are very possible." (see Figure 13.1)

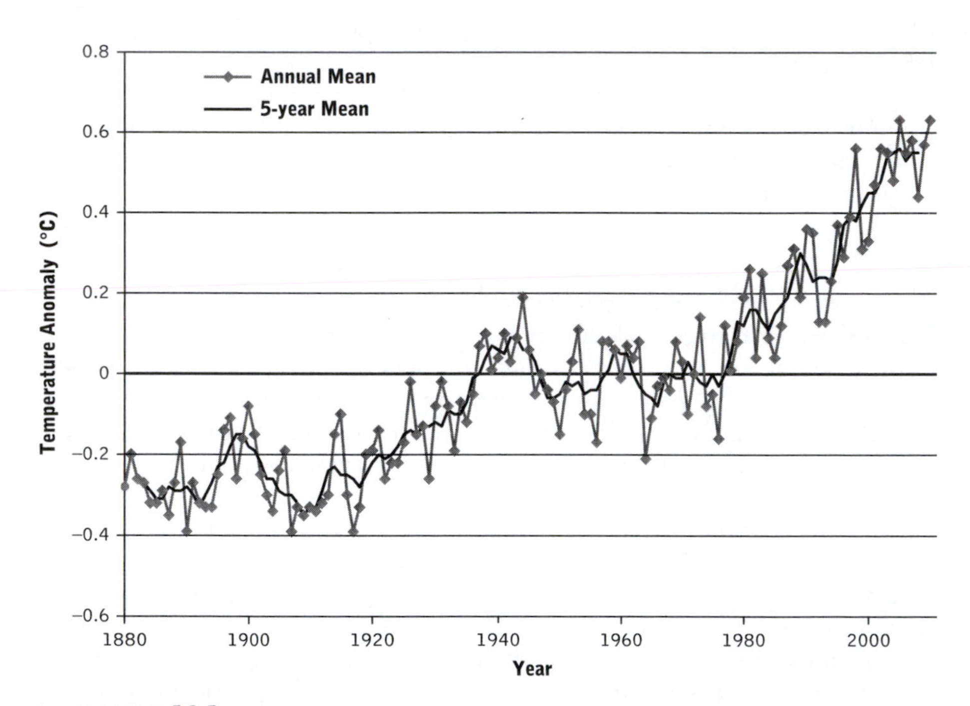

FIGURE 13.1
Warming the Planet

Source: NASA Goddard Institute for Space Studies, Surface Temperature Analysis, 2010. http://data.giss.nasa.gov/gistemp, (accessed on August 10, 2011).

There is also scientific agreement on the actions needed to stop or reverse the process. One, and possibly the major, solution is to reduce CO_2 production by curtailing the burning of fossil fuels. This will happen eventually because supplies of petroleum are finite and dwindling. In the meantime, it is also true that the vast majority of the world's energy comes from this source, and that energy usage is the best indicator of economic productivity. Moreover, no cheap, short-term alternative energy sources are readily available that are capable of substituting for fossil fuel burning at the current rates of energy production. A number of alternative sources such as biofuels (derived in part from sugarcane) are possible, but all cost more to produce (and drive the price of food up too). The reduction in CO_2 emissions may come at the expense of economic prosperity, and the volatile policy question is at whose expense will it come? Whereas developing states typically have less-stringent antipollution laws in an attempt to attract foreign business and industry, many advanced industrial nations (such as the United States) are the world's biggest consumers of fossil fuels.

The **Kyoto Protocol** to the Climate Change Convention was an attempt to deal with the carbon emissions side of the problem. The Protocol would require developed countries to cut their emission levels of greenhouse gases, while developing countries would get more leeway on their emissions rates (including China). The Bush administration found this scheme objectionable and withdrew from the Protocol in 2001.

In December 2009 the countries of the world, and dozens of NGOs, met in Copenhagen to try to create a follow-on agreement, the **Copenhagen Accord**, to the Kyoto Protocol, which expires in 2012. President Obama hoped that the United States would take on a leadership role at the conference. In the midst of hyperpartisanship, however, it became clear that the United States would not be able to ratify any agreement coming out of Copenhagen. While some nations have signed on to this agreement to try to reduce carbon emissions and restrict temperature increases, there is no consensus in the United States about how to address the issue—and even a surprising level of disagreement over the very nature of the problem.

The other solution is an increased ability to absorb and convert CO_2 through photosynthesis, which leads us to our second issue: deforestation. Although deforestation intensifies global warming, there are many other causes of global warming. As a cause, however, deforestation arises from the supposed economic benefits that states gain from cutting down their trees (and especially their rain forests): profits from timber and alternate land use for industrialization (which will, by the way, lead to the emission of more CO_2).

Approximately 6 percent of the world's land area is rain forest, with the largest and most important forests found in Brazil, Indonesia, and Malaysia. These forests contain half the world's species of flora and fauna and are the sole locus of many of those species. As a result, their retention is vital for the biological diversity of the globe. In addition to providing natural habitat for a number of species whose existence would be endangered in their absence, the rain forests are essential for producing oxygen through photosynthesis and as natural disposals for greenhouse gases, especially carbon dioxide.

The rapid clearing of these forests causes many environmental problems. Not only does deforestation contribute to the greenhouse effect and to endangering many species, but without trees to stabilize and enrich topsoil, many deforested areas are not suitable for farming within a short period of time. Rich topsoil is washed away, denuding the land and clogging streams and water tables, which reduces the water supply and further restricts agricultural output. Thus, the irony is that while clear-cutting is often done to increase the availability of farmland, clear-cut land does not remain productive for long, thus leading to pressure to clear-cut more land for farming.

In industrialized countries in the West, 90 percent of forests have already been cleared. In the developing countries of South America and Southeast Asia, it is estimated that as many as 40 million acres of forest (an area about the size of the state of Washington) are being cut down each year. At one point, the world's rain forests covered an estimated 6 million square miles. Due to inadequate fire control, unsustainable commercial logging, overgrazing, and airborne pollutants, deforestation has already claimed up to one-third of the original forests, and the rates of deforestation are rising.

From a global perspective, the arrest or reversal of the deforestation of the rain forests is clearly desirable. However, the problem is that these forests are located within the sovereign territory of individual states whose perceived interests clash with the broader global perception. Sovereign authority and planetary preservation and prosperity thus come into conflict, and the absence of any global organization to deal with these issues means there is no institutional mechanism to highlight or mediate the problem.

International efforts to deal with the affected countries have had varied results. In Brazil, some progress has been made in slowing deforestation of the Amazon Basin through debt-for-nature swaps, where large amounts of Brazil's huge economic debt is canceled in return for assurances that the forests will be preserved. However, there is little accumulated indebtedness in Indonesia and Malaysia, making this form of incentive ineffective. The Malaysians, in particular, have resisted international appeals, insisting on the principle that all natural resources lying inside their state boundaries are to be regarded as under the sole prerogative of the Malaysian government, for which the exploitation of its natural resources are a major part of its developmental strategy.

U.S. Policy and the Environment

Like human-rights advocacy and population control, environmental degradation is also a domestic issue. As a major industrial power, the United States is the world's second-largest contributor to the production of carbon dioxide gases (by far the largest when you control for population size). Although the United States has no major rain forests to deplete, the use of public lands, including national forests, is an ongoing source of heated discussion. The tension between domestic and international concerns creates great domestic ambivalence and disagreement on environmental issues. It also can be a deeply emotional issue for many. The country's position at international forums depends on which group has the ear of the White House at any point in time.

Nothing exemplified this ambivalence better than American performance at the Earth Summit in Rio de Janeiro in June 1992. Sponsored by the United Nations under the formal title of the United Nations Conference on Environment and Development (note that the term *development* finds its way into the title), the meeting drew together over 35,000 participants, including representatives from 172 countries, 110 heads of state, and 15,000 representatives from hundreds of NGOs around the world.

The conference's key product was a one-thousand-page document known as Agenda 21, the purpose of which was to lay out actions that would result in "sustainable development," meaning that in the future development efforts must be done in ways that do not further pollute an already polluted environment.

The agenda for the meeting was extensive and hence well beyond this book's present concern. However, it did touch in major ways on the issues raised here. For instance, a number of advanced industrialized states made a concerted effort to develop strong restrictive provisions on the use of rain forests. They were motivated by concerns about carbon dioxide and, to a lesser extent, biological diversity. Certain Asian states, including India but especially Malaysia, objected strenuously to the conference proceedings. The Malaysians argued with special vehemence that the provisions represented a direct assault on national sovereignty. Their position gradually was adopted by so many other countries that the conference was unable to pass anything stronger than a nonbinding resolution calling on states to refrain from deforestation.

The U.S. stance on the biodiversity treaty, a major product of the conference, exemplifies the ambivalence and political impact of domestic politics on U.S. environmental policy. The biodiversity treaty attempted to ensure the protection of a maximum number of species of flora and fauna through international agreement. Similar to an EPA environmental impact statement, the treaty puts the onus on governments to protect species when engaging in environment-altering activity. The treaty was supported by almost all states in the world, and the American EPA Director William K. Reilly, who was the chief U.S. delegate to the conference, was a principal backer as well (since the effect was to do what his agency did anyway).

The problem was that many American interest groups, including many Western cattle and logging interests whose support was deemed important to President George H.W. Bush's 1992 reelection campaign, vehemently opposed the treaty as an extension of the authority of the hated EPA. When President Bush made an eleventh-hour appearance before the Rio conferees, his speech included a specific denunciation of the biodiversity treaty, thereby reversing the position the American delegation had defended. Subjected to uniform criticism of his speech, Bush was reduced to arguing that "I'm President of the U.S., not president of the world.... I can't do what everybody else does."

INTERSECTIONS

Collapse at Copenhagen

There were high hopes that a true global climate change treaty with binding restrictions on greenhouse gas emissions would emerge from the December 2009 Copenhagen conference. While there are many reasons that such a treaty did not emerge from Copenhagen, including several beyond the United States, the collapse at Copenhagen does serve to highlight the hyperpartisan and intermestic nature of foreign policy making in the United States today. President Obama rather clearly preferred a meaningful treaty with binding restrictions, but it was even clearer that the U.S. Senate would never ratify such a treaty. The domestic politics of global climate change and the party balance in the Senate—where, remember, the treaty would require the votes of two-thirds of the Senate, not just a simple majority (which the Democrats could have delivered), doomed any such treaty.

A similar episode helps elucidate this predicament. On a separate but related track, Congress had been working on an "energy bill" that would address greenhouse gas emissions. At the time the Democrats controlled the House of Representatives and could probably have passed such a bill, but the Senate was more of a question mark. As Lizza reports in *The New Yorker*, a small, bipartisan group of senators had been working for months on such a bill, with key roles being played by Senate Majority Leader Harry Reid (D-NV) and influential South Carolina Republican Lindsay Graham.

The energy bill was only one of many issues confronting these two senators, however, and Reid was locked in a tight reelection battle coming in 2010 in his home state. In Reid's case, strong turnout from the growing Hispanic community in Nevada would be essential for reelection. One step Reid took was to announce that he wanted to proceed with comprehensive immigration reform—a bill that was already dead in the Senate. By standing up as a champion for immigration reform that would include a path to citizenship, Reid was clearly hoping to remind Hispanic voters in the Silver State why they should turn out at the polls for him.

Graham also faced electoral pressure, though further in the future (2014). In Graham's case, however, the pressure came from conservative members of his own party—and a possible challenge in the Republican primary from a candidate who would attack Graham from the Right on his position on climate change, torture, and some other issues (even though Graham is hardly a liberal or even moderate). Graham had also been working on the immigration bill, and Reid's raising of that issue—while good for Reid—was seen by Graham's team as deadly, handing another issue to those who may challenge him in a future election. That the immigration bill was already dead did not matter; what mattered was that the bill would again link Graham to an issue that could be used against him by rambunctious Republicans in his home state. Already on life support, this led Graham to pull the plug on the energy bill, and with it any hope for tough greenhouse gas restrictions in the United States. It is a classic case of how partisan and intermestic foreign policy making now is in the United States.

After winning the 1992 election, President Clinton reversed this position and submitted the treaty for senatorial approval, which was granted.

This political dynamics was reprised over the Kyoto Protocol. The agreement, part of the UN Framework Convention on Climate Change, was adopted in 1997 with the enthusiastic participation of the Clinton administration. However, Republican presidential candidate George W. Bush, backed by many of the same constituents that his father was listening to at Rio, vehemently opposed Kyoto and rejected American participation when he entered the White House. Bush saw the Protocol as an intrusion into American sovereignty and filled with double standards that were unfair and would hurt the U.S. economy. With these same domestic political winds swirling, President Obama—though willing—was unable to lead at the Copenhagen meetings to create a follow-on to the Kyoto Protocol.

CONCLUSIONS

This chapter examines the dynamics of trans-state issues by discussing two critical ones: the interrelated concerns of human rights and democracy, and environmental change. There is no shortage of additional issues that could have been explored: traditional concerns such as population growth or fisheries and the depletion of the world's oceans due to overfishing or dealing with worldwide medical crises (the emergence of new viruses completely resistant to antibiotics joins AIDS at the top of the list) to nontraditional problems such as international crime syndicates. What do these problems share in common, and how do they enter the American foreign policy dialogue? All are political challenges that require the actions of states working in concert to solve or at least to contain them. Unfortunately, the commitment of different states varies considerably.

The Brazilian government plans, allows, and sometimes executes the clear-cutting of the rain forest. The Mexican government owns the oil industry, one of the largest polluters in Mexico. The Panamanian government repealed all of its antipollution laws in an attempt to attract foreign industries. These government actions all directly cause pollution. West African governments have pocketed funds intended for water treatment plants and water and sewer systems. The U.S. government is one of the largest polluters in the country at the millions of acres of military bases. The list goes on.

Most of these issues share the further political commonality of having both an international and a domestic side where the two aspects further complicate the formation and implementation of effective policy. At the international level, trans-state issues transcend boundaries in ways over which states have little control and that they cannot solve unilaterally. Canada, for instance, cannot solve the problem of acid rain caused by sulfur dioxide emissions from the smokestacks of U.S. industries.

The domestic component of these trans-state problems often receives less attention than it deserves. There almost always is a domestic counterpart to the debate over the trans-state issues that makes formulating coherent international positions more difficult than would otherwise be the case. In the United States, for instance, there are or have been domestic equivalents to each of the issues examined in this chapter. The American equivalent of the human rights issue has been the civil rights movement, and until the United States began the process of creating legal equality for all its citizens (an ongoing phenomenon), it was necessarily more reluctant to complain about the human rights abuses of others. The question of responsible use of the environment has its American equivalent in the debate over the uses of federal land, and there is considerable debate about global warming's causes and solutions (often in opposition to scientific agreement) in the United States.

The confluence of international and domestic elements complicates the formation of coherent policy. How can the United States, for instance, simultaneously favor human entitlements and not provide for the homeless? How can the United States simultaneously demand greater environmental responsibility around the world ("sustainable development" was, after all, an American idea) and call for the relaxation of environmental regulations at home?

This interaction of international and domestic aspects of these emerging issues provides further evidence of the convergence of foreign and domestic policy that has been a recurrent theme of this volume. In the context where one party occupies the White House and the other controls the Congress, as has been true for most of the period since 1968, and where the two parties have very different positions on these issues (and in some cases real disagreements inside the parties too), the result can be the impossibility of forming a negotiating position that can be sustained at international meetings and also on the home front. This is especially the case where funding is involved to support the outcomes of international conferences.

The final note to make about the trans-state issues is that they are unlikely to go away. As the world's population continues to grow, the pressures behind both of the sets of issues discussed here will, if anything, increase in intensity. Moreover, the wordwide reach of the global media makes their impact all the more visible and the potential effects of problems generated elsewhere on Americans more easily recognizable. Disease, for instance, knows no frontiers (the motto of the World Health Organization), and stemming the global ravages of a disease in a small African village—the outbreak of the deadly Ebola virus in Zaire in May 1995, for example—may require highly international efforts. Trans-state issues, like foreign policy more generally, do not end at the water's edge.

WHERE DO WE GO FROM HERE?

This chapter focused on the dynamics that surround two key trans-state issues: human rights and democratization, and environmental degradation. While the details of each of these issues are complex and different from one another, they fall into a class of events that have some dynamics in common. These are problems that extend beyond the borders of any one state, so in that sense they are "trans-state." Perhaps more important, however, they are challenges that to solve require the coordinated actions of many states (maybe all?) and the participation of international and nongovernmental organizations. They also tend to be issues around which great domestic and partisan controversy swirls in the United States. As the chapter discusses, crafting a common and accepted U.S. position on any of these issues is hard enough; gaining broad international agreement around that position can be even harder.

APPLICATION: WHERE DO YOU STAND?

Taking the time to think through your own position on any of these difficult and complex issues is an important task; why not start with the democracy issue? What do you do to promote democracy, and what are some of the trade-offs involved in the answer to that? It is hard to be against "democracy." Are you willing to support the movement to promote democracy everywhere? What if taking a stronger stand on democratic reform leads to a worse relationship with the government in China and that leads to a trade war, are you still ready to do it? Or in another case, what if a democracy in a country would be less friendly to the United States and U.S. interests in fighting terrorism than the undemocratic authoritarian government that is there now? You won't have to look far to see how that risk plays out, since those dynamics will be evolving in Egypt for years to come following the 2011 "revolution" there and in other parts of North Africa and the Middle East.

Another element of this worth considering is the role of U.S. military force. In the aftermath of the experience in Iraq and Afghanistan, do you support using military power to promote democracy? The United States used air power in Libya in 2011 to help enforce a UN sanctioned no-fly zone, and thus to try to prevent the continued attacks of Qaddafi's forces against the uprising there; did you support that? What if the UN had not voted for this, would you have supported it without the UN seal of approval? If the use of air power is "okay," what about employing ground troops? How far are you willing to go to promote democracy and human rights? These are complex issues with no easy answers; taking the time to consider your position will be time well spent.

STUDY/DISCUSSION QUESTIONS

1. Why are trans-state issues so difficult to solve? Why are they so political and partisan in the United States?
2. What might some of the trade-offs be between trying to solve these issues and trying to retain the concept of sovereignty?
3. What kinds of rights fall into the rubric of human rights? Is democracy a human right?
4. What is the difference between positive and negative human rights? Is one more controversial than the other?
5. Why has the United States not always been on the forefront of the human rights and democracy promotion movement?
6. What is global climate change, and why is it so controversial?

7. What did the Kyoto Protocol try to do? Given its failings, why did the world not act more strongly at Copenhagen?
8. How does making policy with respect to trans-state issues such as those covered here differ from, for example, policy making with respect to more classic security issues?

CORE SUGGESTED READINGS

Diamond, Larry. *In Search of Democracy*. London: Routledge, 2011. In this new book by one of the most respected scholars of democratization, Diamond examines cases where democracy has taken root and when it hasn't, with the Bush Doctrine in the rearview mirror.

Gore, Al. *Earth in the Balance*. Emmaus, PA: Rodale Press, 2007. There are better books on the science of global climate change, but this is the book that helped bring the issue to the forefront in the United States.

Mertus, Julie. *Bait and Switch: Human Rights and U.S. Foreign Policy* (2nd ed.). New York: Taylor & Francis, 2008. An award-winning book that details how the United States perhaps talks more about promoting democracy than it really promotes on the ground.

Power, Samantha. *A Problem from Hell: America in the Age of Genocide*. New York: HarperCollins, 2002. The journalist, scholar, Pulitzer Prize winner, and member of the Obama administration came to public prominence with this book. Power here examines the lack of political will that the United States has often had concerning taking action to stop genocide.

ADDITIONAL READINGS AND REFERENCES

Apodaca, Claire. *The Paradoxes of U.S. Human Rights Policy*. New York: Taylor & Francis, 2006.

Betsill, Michele M., and Elisabeth Corell (eds.). *NGO Diplomacy: The Influence of Nongovernmental Organizations in International Environmental Negotiations*. Cambridge, MA: MIT Press, 2007.

Brysk, Allison (ed.). *Globalization and Human Rights*. Berkeley: University of California Press, 2002.

Caldwell, Lynton K., and Robert V. Bartlett (eds.). *Environmental Policy*. Westport, CT: Greenwood Press, 2000.

Cline, William R. *The Economics of Global Warming*. Washington, DC: Institute for International Economics, 1992.

Deihl, Paul F., and Nils Petter Gleditsch (eds.). *Environmental Conflict*. Boulder, CO: Westview Press, 2001.

Diamond, Larry, and Marc F. Plattner (eds.). *The Global Resurgence of Democracy*. Baltimore, MD: Johns Hopkins University Press, 1993.

Donnelly, Jack. *International Human Rights*. Boulder, CO: Westview Press, 2006.

Dunn, Tim, and Nicholas J. Wheeler (eds.). *Human Rights in Global Politics*. New York: Cambridge University Press, 2008.

Feinstein, Lee, and Todd Lindberg. *Means to an End: U.S. Interest in the International Criminal Court*. Washington, DC: Brookings Institution, 2009.

Firor, John, and Judith E. Jacobsen. *The Crowded Greenhouse: Populations, Climate Change, and Creating a Sustainable World*. New Haven, CT: Yale University Press, 2002.

Haas, Peter M., Robert O. Keohane, and Marc A. Levy (eds.). *Institutions for the Earth: Sources of Effective International Environmental Protection*. Cambridge, MA: MIT Press, 2000.

Harris, Paul G. (ed.). *Climate Change and American Foreign Policy*. New York: Palgrave Macmillan, 2000.

Hopgood, Stephen. *American Foreign Economic Policy and the Power of the State*. New York: Oxford University Press, 1998.

Hunter, Lori M. *The Environmental Implications of Population Dynamics*. Santa Monica, CA: RAND Corporation, 2000.

Huntington, Samuel P. *The Third Wave: Democratization in the Late Twentieth Century*. Norman: University of Oklahoma Press, 1991.

Korey, William. *The Promises We Keep: Human Rights, the Helsinki Process and American Foreign Policy*. New York: St. Martin's Press, 1993.

Lizza, Ryan. "As the World Burns: How the Senate and the White House Missed their Best Chance to Deal with Climate Change." *The New Yorker*, October 11, 2010. http://www.newyorker.com/reporting/2010/10/11/101011fa_fact_lizza.

Pollack, Henry. *A World Without Ice*. New York: Penguin, 2009.

Power, Samantha. *Chasing the Flame: Sergio Vieira de Mello and the Fight to Save the World*. New York: Penguin, 2008.

Shapiro, Robert J. *Futurecast: How Superpowers, Populations, and Globalization Will Change Your World by the Year 2020*. New York: St. Martin's Press, 2003.

Singer, Max, and Aaron Wildavsky. *The Real World Order: Zones of Peace / Zones of Turmoil* (Rev. ed.). Washington, DC: CQ Press, 1996.

Thompson, Lonnie. "Climate Change: The Evidence and Our Options." *The Behavior Analyst* 33 (Fall 2010), pp. 153–170.

CREDITS

Chapter 1: p. 1, MAGNUS JOHANSSON/Reuters /Landov; p. 25, AFP/Getty Images.

Chapter 2: p. 31, Korotayev Artyom/ITAR-TASS Photo/Corbis; p. 61, Henning Langenheim/akg-images/Newscom.

Chapter 3: p. 68, Everett Collection Inc/Alamy; p. 76, AFP/Getty Images.

Chapter 4: p. 93, PhotoEdit; p. 111, NATALIA KOLESNIKOVA/AFP/Getty Images/Newscom.

Chapter 5: p. 132, CARL COURT/AFP/Getty Images/Newscom; p. 163, CHRIS SCHNEIDER/epa/Corbis.

Chapter 6: p. 172, ROMEO GACAD/AFP/Getty Images/Newscom; p. 201, t14/ZUMA Press/Newscom.

Chapter 7: p. 215, Chip Somodevilla/Staff/Getty Images; p. 221, GEORGE WIDMAN/Associated Press.

Chapter 8: p. 248, Ben Curtis/Associated Press; p. 267, Michael E. Samojeden/Associated Press.

Chapter 9: p. 290, Gustavo Gonzalez - DoD via CNP/Newscom; p. 311, c51/ZUMA Press/Newscom.

Chapter 10: p. 327, Scripps Howard Photo Service/Newscom; p. 356, MASSOUD HOSSAINI/AFP/Getty Images/Newscom.

Chapter 11: p. 363, Sascha Burkard/Shutterstock; p. 375, UPPA/Photoshot.

Chapter 12: p. 402, Jerry Bernard/Alamy; p. 418, LYNNE SLADKY/Associated Press.

Chapter 13: p. 430, OLIVIER MORIN/AFP/Getty Images/Newscom; p. 436, Lindsay Douglas/Shutterstock.

INDEX